NATURAL RESOURCE CONFLICTS

NATURAL RESOURCE CONFLICTS

From Blood Diamonds to Rainforest Destruction

Volume 1:
International Conflicts, Africa,
the Middle East, Asia, and the Pacific

M. Troy Burnett, Editor

An Imprint of ABC-CLIO, LLC
Santa Barbara, California • Denver, Colorado

Copyright © 2016 by ABC-CLIO, LLC

All rights reserved. No part of this publication may be reproduced, stored in a retrieval system, or transmitted, in any form or by any means, electronic, mechanical, photocopying, recording, or otherwise, except for the inclusion of brief quotations in a review, without prior permission in writing from the publisher.

Library of Congress Cataloging-in-Publication Data

Names: Burnett, M. Troy (Mark Troy), 1971- editor.
Title: Natural resource conflicts : from blood diamonds to rainforest
  destruction / M. Troy Burnett, editor.
Description: Santa Barbara, California : ABC-CLIO, [2016] | Includes
  bibliographical references and index. Contents: Volume 1.
  International Conflicts, Africa, the Middle East, Asia, and the
  Pacific — Volume 2. The Americas, Europe, and Key Concepts.
Identifiers: LCCN 2016033350| ISBN 9781610694643 (hardcopy) | ISBN 9781610694650 (ebook) |
  ISBN 9781440845550 (volume 1) | ISBN 9781440845567 (volume 2)
Subjects: LCSH: Natural resources—Environmental aspects. | Natural
  resources—Political aspects. | Natural resources—International
  cooperation. | Environmental degradation. | Conservation of natural
  resources.
Classification: LCC HC85 .N3533 2016 | DDC 333.7—dc23
LC record available at https://lccn.loc.gov/2016033350

Set ISBN: 978-1-61069-464-3
Volume 1 ISBN: 978-1-4408-4555-0
Volume 2 ISBN: 978-1-4408-4556-7
EISBN: 978-1-61069-465-0

20 19 18 17 16   1 2 3 4 5

This book is also available as an eBook.

ABC-CLIO
An Imprint of ABC-CLIO, LLC

ABC-CLIO, LLC
130 Cremona Drive, P.O. Box 1911
Santa Barbara, California 93116-1911
www.abc-clio.com

This book is printed on acid-free paper ∞
Manufactured in the United States of America

Contents

Volume 1.
International Conflicts, Africa, the Middle East, Asia, and the Pacific

Preface	xxv
Introduction	xxix
Volume 1 List of Entries by Region	xxxix
Volume 1 List of Entries by Topic	xliii

Part I. International Conflicts

1. Is the World's Increasing Population Stressing the Earth's Resources and Becoming a Major Source of Conflict? — 3
   Overview — 3
   M. Troy Burnett and Max Lu
   The Earth's "Population Problem" Is Overstated and Wrong — 6
   Jeffery Gentry
   Overpopulation Stresses Resources, Which in Turn Stresses People — 10
   Max Lu

2. How Have Natural Resource Conflicts Led to the Demise of Past Civilizations? — 14
   Overview — 14
   Mia Bennett

The Collapse of Easter Island—A Valuable Lesson for
Our Modern World 17
   M. Troy Burnett
Soil and the Collapse of the Mighty Roman Empire 20
   Mark Hecht

3. As the World's Population Becomes More Urbanized, How Are
Cities Being Designed to Avoid Conflicts? 24
   Overview 24
     Robin Morris Collin and Robert William Collin
   Copenhagen, Bogotá, and Singapore: Three Inspiring Examples
of Sustainable Cities 27
     Roman Adrian Cybriwsky
   Making Sustainable Cities—The Need to Focus on
Transportation 32
     Roman Adrian Cybriwsky

4. How Have Global Warming and Climate Change Promoted
Conflict in Pastoral Communities? 35
   Overview 35
     Troy Sternberg
   Mongolian Pastoralism, Climate Change, and Conflict 38
     Ariell Ahearn and Troy Sternberg
   Conflict in Syria—Pastoral Communities and Global Warming 40
     Troy Sternberg

5. Will Air Quality Be a Source of Regional Conflict? 44
   Overview 44
     Mia Bennett
   Conflicts and Air Pollution—The Future Is Here 47
     Mia Bennett
   Air Quality: Hardly Ever a Source of Regional Conflict 51
     Bryan Comer

6. What Role Does Ecotourism Play in Natural Resource Conflicts? 56
   Overview 56
     Barbara McNicol
   Ecotourism: Cooperation or Bust? 58
     Edward Jackiewicz and Olga Govdyak
   Successful Ecotourism: Inauthentic Tourism Experience
versus Integrating Environmental Management and
Conservation 63
     Barbara McNicol

7. How Do Global Warming and Climate Change Influence a
   Nation's Security Policy? 67
   Overview 67
       Bruce E. Johansen
   Climate Change: An Emerging Concern of National Security 70
       M. Troy Burnett
   War Is Environmentally Obsolete 73
       Bruce E. Johansen

8. Is Nuclear the Right Option to Avoid Future Energy Conflicts? 76
   Overview 76
       Robert Goble and M. Troy Burnett
   How to Avoid Future Energy Conflicts? Promote Nuclear! 79
       Duane Bratt
   Nuclear Energy Is a Conflict Multiplier 83
       M. Troy Burnett

9. Could Conflicts over Water Actually Promote Peace and Stability? 88
   Overview 88
       J. C. Veilleux and M. Troy Burnett
   Countries Do Not Go to War over Water 92
       J. C. Veilleux
   Transboundary Water Management—Some Success Stories 95
       Mia Bennett

10. What Steps Should Be Taken to Help Provide Access to Clean
    Water for More People in the World? 99
    Overview 99
        Dennis Moran and M. Troy Burnett
    Infrastructure First, Then Better Management 103
        Nathan Eidem
    Infrastructure Is Fine, But We Need to Focus on Regulation,
    Management, and International Cooperation 105
        Coralie Noël

11. To Mitigate Conflicts over Water, Is It Better to Treat Water as a
    Commodity or a Human Right? 108
    Overview 108
        M. Troy Burnett and William Osei
    Water Is, and Always Has Been, a Commodity 112
        Mark Hecht
    Water Should Be a Human Right! 115
        John Agnew

12. Which Water Basins Are Presently Sites of the Highest
    Potential for Conflict?   119
      Overview   119
        Mia Bennett
      From Aral Sea to Aral Desert   122
        Mia Bennett
      Moving People, Moving Earth: The Yangtze River and the Three
      Gorges Dam   125
        Mia Bennett

13. Will the International Trade in Hazardous Waste Promote
    Stability or Conflict?   130
      Overview   130
        M. Troy Burnett
      Controversy and Conflict with the Trade in Hazardous Waste   133
        Tera Trujillo
      International Trade of Hazardous Waste Causes Stability   136
        Nicole Lomba

14. With Future Conflicts Seemingly Guaranteed, Is a Technological
    Breakthrough Needed to Avert the Climate Crisis?   139
      Overview   139
        M. Troy Burnett
      Necessity Will Compel Technological Innovation   142
        Bruce E. Johansen
      How Can Society Respond to the Climate Crisis? By Changing Our
      Own Behavior   146
        Benjamin K. Sovacool

15. To Mitigate Conflicts over Natural Resources, Is It Better to Promote
    Preservation or Conservation?   149
      Overview   149
        M. Troy Burnett
      Preservation or Conservation, the Government Must Play
      the Key Role   152
        Jacqueline Vaughn
      Preservation First!   153
        Peter Jacques

16. How Does the Illicit Trade in Endangered Species Promote
    Regional Conflict?   156
      Overview   156
        Ariana Tran and M. Troy Burnett

The Link between Illicit Trade in Endangered Species and
Regional Conflict   159
    Ariana Tran and M. Troy Burnett
The Need for Cooperation in the Illicit Wildlife Trade   162
    Cynthia Tafoya and M. Troy Burnett

17. Should Cultural Exceptions Be Made in Whaling Laws?   165
    Overview   165
      Mia Bennett
    No! A Dead Whale Is Still a Dead Whale   168
      M. Troy Burnett
    In Defense of Cultural Exceptions for Whaling   171
      Mia Bennett

18. How Are Issues and Conflicts over Invasive Species
Being Addressed?   176
    Overview   176
      Susan L. Woodward and Joyce A. Quinn
    Invasive Species—A Complex Issue with No Simple Solutions   180
      Joyce A. Quinn
    Prevention, Eradication, and Education   187
      Susan L. Woodward

19. How Does the Loss of Biodiversity Promote Conflict?   195
    Overview   195
      M. Troy Burnett
    Biodiversity and Conflict: Issues and Resolutions   197
      Jason Macleod
    Conflict in Kenya—The Unintended Consequences of Biodiversity
Conservation   200
      M. Troy Burnett

20. Are Debt-for-Nature Swaps a Viable Means to Promote
Stability in the Developing World?   204
    Overview   204
      M. Troy Burnett
    A Critical View of Debt-for-Nature Swaps   207
      Mia Bennett
    Though Far from Ideal, Debt-for-Nature Swaps Provide
One Creative Solution to the Debt-Habitat
Destruction Problem   210
      M. Troy Burnett

Part II. Africa

21. Was the Rwandan Genocide of 1994 a Result of Conflict over
    Natural Resources? 217
        Overview 217
            William von Lopik
        The Rwandan Genocide: A Complex Confluence of Causal Factors 219
            M. Troy Burnett
        The Role of Environmental Factors in the Rwandan Genocide 222
            William Van Lopik

22. What Role Have Natural Resources Played in the Sudanese
    Civil War? 225
        Overview 225
            M. Troy Burnett
        Oil in the Sudan: A Conflict Multiplier, Not the Sole Cause 228
            Meredith DeBoom
        Conflict in Darfur—The Resource Perspective 231
            M. Troy Burnett

23. Do Diamonds Have a Negative Influence on Development in Africa? 236
        Overview 236
            Laura Kerrigan and Jacob C. Brenner
        Diamond Mining and Violence on the African Continent 239
            Laura Kerrigan and Jacob C. Brenner
        Diamond Mining: A Positive View 243
            M. Troy Burnett

24. Will the Mining of Coltan in the Congo Further Destabilize the Region? .. 246
        Overview 246
            M. Troy Burnett
        The Mining of Coltan in the DRC: The Same Sad Story of
        Exploitation and Conflict 249
            Joseph Oppong and M. Troy Burnett
        With Attention and Guidance Coltan Mining Can Benefit the DRC ... 252
            Olga Govdyak and Edward Jackiewicz

25. How Will the Grand Ethiopian Renaissance Dam Affect Peace in the
    Region? 254
        Overview 254
            Jennifer C. Veilleux and M. Troy Burnett
        The Contentious GERD: A Thorn in the Side of Nile Basin Politics 257
            M. Troy Burnett

The Renaissance Dam—A Platform for Peace *Jennifer C. Veilleux*	261
26. Does the Kimberley Process Work?	264
Overview	264
M. Troy Burnett	
The Kimberley Process Is Broken	266
Meredith DeBoom	
In Defense of the Kimberley Process	270
M. Troy Burnett	
27. How Does China's Increasing Demand for Natural Resources Affect Stability in Africa?	273
Overview	273
Mia Bennett	
China's Appetite for Resources Promotes Instability in Africa	276
Mia Bennett	
The Chinese in Africa—Altruistic, No! But Benign and Potentially Stabilizing	279
M. Troy Burnett	
28. How Have Large-Scale Conservation Efforts Promoted Conflict in Sub-Saharan Africa?	282
Overview	282
M. Troy Burnett and Gregory Maddox	
Conservation Development Has Destabilized Africa	285
Gregory Maddux	
The Promise and the Potential of Conservation in Africa	288
Gregory Maddux	

Part III. Asia and the Pacific

29. Can It Be Argued That the Wealth Generated from Oil Is a Primary Cause of the Disempowerment of Women in the Middle East?	295
Overview	295
M. Troy Burnett	
Oil, Religion, Islamic Kinship, and the Disempowerment of Middle Eastern Women	297
Kirsten Von Meter	
Oil Wealth Expands Opportunities for Women in the Middle East	299
Natalie Koch	

30. Is the Jordan River a Source of Regional Conflict or Stability? 303
    Overview 303
        M. Troy Burnett
    The Jordan River: A Source of Conflict 305
        Amy Hackney Blackwell
    The Jordan River as a Nexus for Peaceful Cooperation 308
        Chris Hrynkow

31. What Impact Does Control of Valuable Resources Have on Politics in the Middle East? 312
    Overview 312
        Larry Simpson and M. Troy Burnett
    It's Not Just about Religion, But Economics as Well 315
        Spencer Tucker
    Oil and Water—The Resource Disputes That Contribute to Conflicts in the Middle East 318
        Larry Simpson

32. Is China's Green Great Wall an Adequate Solution to Desertification? 321
    Overview 321
        Bruce E. Johansen
    The Great Green Wall and Its Many Cracks 324
        Bruce E. Johansen
    The Great Green Wall—A Herculean Effort 326
        M. Troy Burnett

33. What Conflicts Have Arisen as a Result of China's Building of the Three Gorges Dam? 331
    Overview 331
        Allen Raichelle
    The Environmental Conflict over the Three Gorges 334
        Elizabeth J. Leppman
    Though Controversial and the Source of External and Internal Conflicts, Building the Dam Was Necessary! 337
        Charles Fuller

34. How Can Conflicts Be Avoided with Japan's Fishing Industry? 341
    Overview 341
        Tracy Dobson and M. Troy Burnett
    Thinking Outside the Sea: How to Reduce Conflict with Japanese Seafood 343
        Lynn Galvin

Better Management Is Needed to Sustain Japanese Fisheries 346
    Riley Walters

35. Is the Crisis in Australia's Murray-Darling Basin the Result of Climate
    Change or the Decisions and Actions of Humans? 348
    Overview 348
        Bruce E. Johansen
    Australia's Drought and Changing Atmospheric Circulation Patterns 351
        Bruce E. Johansen
    Human Actions are the Root of the Crisis in the Murray-Darling Basin 353
        Mia Bennett

36. Is Sustainable Development and Conservation or Further Resource
    Exploitation and Conflict the Future in Borneo? 357
    Overview 357
        M. Troy Burnett
    Tensions Mount as Destruction of Borneo Continues 359
        Bruce E. Johansen
    Development, Stability, and Conservation Are Possible in Borneo 361
        Donald Rallis

37. Was the Conflict in East Timor, Indonesia, the Direct Result of
    Natural Resources? 364
    Overview 364
        M. Troy Burnett
    East Timor: A Conflict Rooted in Natural Resources 366
        Micah Fisher
    Nationalism, Geopolitics, and the Bleeding of East Timor 369
        Keith Bettinger

38. Is the Resource of the Mekong River Basin a Potential for
    Regional Conflict? 374
    Overview 374
        Jennifer C. Veilleux
    The Potential for Conflict in the Mekong River Basin 377
        Aaron Williams and M. Troy Burnett
    Cooperation and Coordination in the Mekong River Basin 380
        Jennifer C. Veilleux

39. Will the Ganges River Be a Source of Regional Conflict between India
    and Bangladesh? 383
    Overview 383
        Mark Hecht

Ganges River as the Source of Regional Conflict between India and Bangladesh	386
Edward Jackiewicz	
For Now, Peace and Stability	390
Mia Bennett	
40. How Have Natural Resources Caused Political Instability in Post-Communist Central Asia?	394
Overview	394
M. Troy Burnett	
Tensions in Post-Communist Central Asia—The Case of the Ferghana Valley	397
Mia Bennett	
A Fragile Stability in Central Asia	400
Natalie Koch	
Glossary	405
Volume 1 Bibliography	427
About the Editor and Contributors	457

Volume 2.
The Americas, Europe, and Key Concepts

Preface	xxv
Introduction	xxix
Volume 2 List of Entries by Region	xxxix
Volume 2 List of Entries by Topic	xli

Part I. North America and Europe

1. Can Future Energy Conflicts Be Avoided by the U.S. Government's Support and Promotion of Green Technologies?	473
Overview	473
Harry Henderson and M. Troy Burnett	
Governments Must Take the Lead to Promote Green Technologies	476
Dan L. McNally	
Let Markets Determine the Future of Energy	479
William T. Bogart	

2. Was the Canadian-Spanish Turbot Fish Conflict an Anomaly or a
   Harbinger of Things to Come? 483
   Overview 483
   Mark Hecht
   Canadian Turbot War as a Sign of Things to Come 486
   Mark Hecht
   The Turbot War—The Conflict That Has Served to Minimize Conflict 488
   M. Troy Burnett

3. How Have National Park Systems Fomented Conflict with
   Aboriginal Peoples? 491
   Overview 491
   Barbara McNicol
   National Parks and the Displacement of Aboriginal Peoples 493
   Kelly Kay
   Changing Relationships: Joint Management in National Parks 497
   Barbara McNicol

4. Has Montana Mismanaged Its Resources? 500
   Overview 500
   Mark Hecht
   Not-So-Pristine Montana—Environmental Destruction and the
   Mismanagement of Natural Resources 503
   Mark Hecht
   Mismanagement in Montana—A Fault with Mining in the
   United States 506
   Gary Goreham and M. Troy Burnett

5. How Has Environmental Justice and Toxic Racism Been a Source of
   Social Conflict in the United States? 510
   Overview 510
   Jason D. MacLeod
   Environmental Justice: Shaking Up the Modern Environmental
   Movement 512
   Kelly Kay
   Pollution's Racist Gaze: Environmental Justice and Toxic Racism 517
   Gerardo Del Guercio

6. To Minimize Conflict in the Circumpolar North, Should the
   Northwest Passage Be Considered Canadian Sovereign Territory or
   an International Strait? 519
   Overview 519
   M. Troy Burnett

Pragmatic Cooperation to Minimize Conflict over the Passage 522
Elizabeth Elliot-Meisel
You Want to Minimize Conflict . . . Confirm Canada's Claim to the
Northwest Passage 524
M. Troy Burnett

7. What Social Conflicts Have Resulted from the United States'
Enactment of the Endangered Species Act? 528
Overview 528
M. Troy Burnett
The Endangered Species Act and Social Conflict 531
Jason Macleod
The ESA—A Hotbed of Conflict 535
Kelly Kay

8. What Is the Best Way to Minimize Conflict over
New England Fisheries? 538
Overview 538
M. Troy Burnett
New Strategies for Minimizing Conflict and Restoring
New England Fisheries 541
Peter Baker
The Fisherperson's Solution: Sector Management 543
Eric Brazer Jr.

9. What Role Have International Peace Parks/Transboundary
Protected Areas Played in Lessening International Conflicts? 547
Overview 547
Jake Brenner
International Peace Parks—Good for the Environment and People 550
Chris Hrynkow
Transboundary Protected Areas—The United States–Mexico Case 553
Jake Brenner

10. How Has the Proposed Keystone Pipeline Been a Source of Conflict
between the United States and Canada? 557
Overview 557
Mia Bennett
Harsh Resistance to the Keystone Pipeline 560
Bruce E. Johansen
How Keystone Has Unnecessarily Soured Relations between
Canada and the United States 564
Mia Bennett

11. Do the Benefits of Exploiting Alberta's Oil Sands Outweigh the
    Adverse Environmental Effects and Political Controversy? ... 568
    Overview ... 568
        Mia Bennett
    Not Worth the Headache! ... 571
        Bruce E. Johansen
    The Environmental Impacts Are High, but the Social and Economic
    Benefits Are Worth It ... 575
        M. Troy Burnett

12. What Is the Primary Cause of Conflict in the Klamath Basin? ... 579
    Overview ... 579
        Brian Chaffin
    Conflict in the Klamath Basin: Farmers vs. Conservationists vs.
    First Nations ... 582
        Kelly Kay
    Restoring Ecosystem Function and Repairing Communities ... 584
        Brian Chaffin

13. How Should the Colorado River Basin Be Managed to Mitigate
    Interstate Conflict? ... 587
    Overview ... 587
        Leann Sullivan
    The Difficult Task of Managing a Basin with Multiple Stakeholders ... 589
        M. Troy Burnett
    Colorado Basin Management—A Simmering Conflict ... 592
        Leann Sullivan

14. Is the Exploitation of Greenland's Rare Earth Elements Worth the
    Environmental Costs? ... 596
    Overview ... 596
        Mia Bennett
    The Mining of Greenland's Rare Earths—Worth the Cost ... 600
        Mark Hecht
    Nunarput utoqqarsuanngoravit (You, Our Ancient Land) ... 603
        M. Troy Burnett

15. Do the Economic Benefits of Hydraulic Fracturing
    Outweigh the Risks? ... 606
    Overview ... 606
        David E. Newton
    The Benefits of Fracking ... 609
        Bruce Everett

The High Cost of Fracking *John Rumpler*	611
16. Will Global Warming and the Thawing of the Arctic Promote Conflict or Cooperation?	614
Overview	614
Bruce E. Johansen and M. Troy Burnett	
The Potential for Conflict in the Arctic	616
Betsy Baker	
Warming and the Circumpolar North—An Optimistic Perspective	619
Barry Zellen	
17. To Avoid Conflicts, How Should California Manage Its Water Resources?	622
Overview	622
M. Troy Burnett	
California's Water Crisis—The Need to Share the Burden	625
Zachary Smith and Jane Whitmire	
To Avoid Conflict the Environmental Issues Must Be Addressed	627
Grenetta Thomassey	
18. Will the Drilling of Oil in the Gulf of Mexico Be a Source of Regional Conflict between Domestic Stakeholders in the United States?	631
Overview	631
Mia Bennett	
Environmental Devastation as the Source of Conflict in the Gulf of Mexico	635
Albert C. Hine	
The Simmering Conflict in the Gulf of Mexico	638
Mia Bennett	

Part II. Central/South America and the Caribbean

19. Sitting atop a Large Oil Reserve, How Should Ecuador's Yasuní National Park Be Managed?	645
Overview	645
M. Troy Burnett	
Ecuador Has Little Choice: Develop the Resource!	648
Ariana Tran and M. Troy Burnett	
Yasuní Park, Its Biodiversity and People Need to Be Preserved	650
Cynthia Tafoya and M. Troy Burnett	

20. Is the Conflict in Chiapas, Mexico, between the Zapatistas
    and the Mexican Government Primarily a Conflict over
    Natural Resources? 654
    Overview 654
        M. Troy Burnett
    The Chiapas Conflict: A Battle for Indigenous Recognition and Rights 657
        Lindsay Naylor
    The Conflict in Chiapas: The Role of Natural Resources 660
        William Van Lopik

21. How Do Environmental Conditions and Resource Management
    Explain the Differing Levels of Conflict/Crisis in Haiti and the
    Dominican Republic? 664
    Overview 664
        Mia Bennett
    Hispaniola: An Island Divided 667
        Cynthia Tafoya and Edward Jackiewicz
    One Island, Two Separate Worlds 670
        M. Troy Burnett and Paul Bartel

22. Is Oil the Main Source of the Conflict over the Falkland Islands? 673
    Overview 673
        M. Troy Burnett
    There Is No Single Cause for the Ongoing Conflict over the Falklands 675
        Camille Gaskin-Reyes
    Oil in the Falklands: A Major Part of the Problem 677
        M. Troy Burnett

23. Was the Mayan Civilization Brought Down by a Natural
    Resource Crisis? 681
    Overview 681
        Peter Matthews and M. Troy Burnett
    The Mayan Collapse—A Constellation of Social and
    Environmental Factors 685
        Anabel Ford
    War, Disease, Famine, Natural Resources—The Usual Suspects
    in the Collapse of the Mayan Civilization 687
        Joel Palka

24. How Did Water Rights Become a Source of Conflict between the
    Quechua People and the Government in Peru's Colca Valley? 691
    Overview 691
        Paul H. Gelles

Conflict in the Colca—The Story of the Eleven Heroes *Paul H. Gelles*	695
Compromise and Recovery in the Colca Valley *Paul H. Gelles*	697

25. **How Have Plans to Build Hydroelectric Dams in the Patagonia Region Been a Source of Conflict?** — 700

Overview *M. Troy Burnett*	700
Controversies Aside, Chile and the Region Need Power *Dawn M. Drake*	702
Dams in Patagonia—Controversial and Unsustainable! *Leann Sullivan*	704

26. **How Should the Natural Resources of the Amazon Rainforest Be Managed to Avoid Conflict?** — 707

Overview *M. Troy Burnett*	707
Ending the Destruction, Conserving the Forest, and Promoting Cooperation *Rhett A. Butler*	710
Awareness of the True Value of the Rainforest Will Promote Conservation and Cooperation *Margaret Lowman*	714

Key Concepts

Afforestation	717
Agenda 21	719
Amazon Conservation Team	720
Amazon Rainforest	720
Amazon River	721
Amnesty International	721
Amu Darya	722
Antienvironmental Movement	722
Arctic Council	723
Arctic Ocean	724
Association for the Conservation of Amazonian Wildlife	724
Association of Southeast Asian Nations	725
Augusto Pinochet	726
Bedouins	726
Biomes	727
Borneo	727

Bureau of Land Management	730
Cap and Trade	730
Carbon Sequestration	732
Carbon Taxes	733
Carrying Capacity	735
Carson, Rachel	736
Chernobyl Disaster	736
Chukchi	737
Climate Change	738
Coal	738
Cold War	739
Comparative Advantage	740
Conflict Diamonds	740
Conservation International	743
Convention on Biological Diversity	744
Convention on International Trade in Endangered Species	745
Correa, Rafael	745
Dams: Environmental Impacts	745
Darfur	746
Dead Sea	748
Deepwater Horizon Oil Spill (2010)	748
Defenders of Wildlife	749
Deforestation	749
Demographic Transition Model	751
Desertification	753
Drought	754
Earth Summit	754
East Timor	755
Easter Island	755
Ecofeminism	756
Ecosystem Services	756
Ecosystems	757
Ecotourism	757
El Niño	758
Endangered Species	758
Endangered Species Act (1973)	759
Environmental Determinism	759
Environmental Ethics	760
Environmental Impact Statements	764
Environmental Justice	766
Environmental Protection Agency	767

Environmental Refugees	767
Ethiopian Wildlife Conservation Organization	768
Exclusive Economic Zone	769
Extinction	769
Fertile Crescent	770
Fish and Wildlife Service	771
Forest Conservation	772
Forest Stewardship Council	773
Fossil Fuels	774
Fossil Fuels and Climate Change	774
Freshwater	776
Ganges River Valley	778
Glacier National Park	780
Global Environmental Monitoring System	781
Global Warming	781
Globalization	782
Greenhouse Effect	782
Greenhouse Gases	783
Greenland	783
Greenpeace	784
Gross Domestic Product	784
Groundwater	785
Gulf Hypoxia	788
Harappan Civilization	789
Hutu	789
Hydraulic Fracturing ("Fracking")	789
Indigenous	790
Indigenous Peoples and Premodern Claims	791
Intergovernmental Panel on Climate Change	792
International Union for Conservation of Nature	793
International Whaling Commission	793
Intifada	794
Inuit	794
Inuit Brotherhood (Inuit Ataqatigiit)	795
Invasive Species	795
Irredentism	796
Janjaweed	796
Japan: Environment	797
Jordan River	798
Kagame, Paul	799
Kyoto Protocol	799

Los Angeles River	800
Lost Boys	800
Malthusian Theory	801
Marcos, Subcomandante	804
Marine Life, Fisheries, and Global Warming	804
Marine Pollution	805
Montreal Protocol	807
Mugabe, Robert	807
National Center for Atmospheric Research	808
National Coalition for Marine Conservation	808
Natural Gas	809
Natural Resources Defense Council	810
Nature Conservancy	810
Neocolonialism	811
Neoliberalism	811
Nile River Basin Cooperative Framework Agreement	812
Nongovernmental Organizations	812
Organisation for Economic Co-operation and Development	813
Organization of Petroleum Exporting Countries	814
Overfishing	814
Overpopulation	815
Palm Oil	817
Pastoralism	818
Petroleum (Oil)	819
Population Geography	819
Rainforest Action Network	820
Rainforests	821
Renewable Energy	821
Republics of the Former Soviet Union	822
Resource Curse	823
Revolutionary United Front	823
Rwandan Patriotic Front	824
Sharia	824
Sierra Club	824
Silent Spring (1962)	825
Slash-and-Burn Agriculture	825
Southern African Development Community	826
Sovereignty	826
Sudan Liberation Army	827
Suharto	827
Superfund	828

Sustainable Development	828
Sustainable Forestry	830
Syr Darya River	831
Tar Sands	831
Tutsi	832
United Nations Convention on the Law of the Sea	832
United Nations Educational, Scientific, and Cultural Organization	833
United Nations Environment Programme	833
United Nations Framework Convention on Climate Change	834
U.S. Bureau of Reclamation	834
Wildlife and Environment Society of Southern Africa	835
World Wildlife Fund	836
Zapatista National Liberation Army	836
Zimbabwe African National Union-Patriotic Front	837
Glossary	839
Volume 2 Bibliography	861
About the Editor and Contributors	879
Index	893

Preface

M. Troy Burnett

The inspiration for this project emerged from an observation in the 1987 report from the United Nation's World Commission on Environment and Development. The title of the landmark report was *Our Common Future*, and the authors noted that: "Nations have often fought to assert or resist control over war materials, energy, supplies, land, river basins, sea passages and other key natural resources" (Brundtland, 1987). Ever since, scholars of conflict have focused on natural resources as both a reason for controversy and violence as well as a potential source of compromise, negotiation, and peace. The 2004 report of the UN Secretary-General's High-Level Panel on Threats, Challenges and Changes further stressed the connection between the environment, natural resources, security, and development and highlighted the pressing need for effective institutions and programs to ameliorate emerging conflicts (UN Secretary General, 2004).

Indeed, as the Earth's population continues to soar over 7 billion and global consumerism expands, the demand for resources and pressure on the planet's ecosystem intensifies. Demographic pressure, urbanization, unequal access, shortages, and limited distribution of resources such as water, land, and energy exacerbate the potential for conflict. Further, the observed and predicted consequences of global warming and climate change on water availability, food security, disease vectors, ecosystem quality, and sea level will only serve to aggravate tensions and magnify disparities between the developed and developing world. The latter tend to be more dependent on natural resources and vulnerable to supply shocks, while developed countries are able to reach far and wide to meet the needs of their people. Yet, all places face struggles over who should have access to or how best to manage natural wealth.

Therefore, the primary purpose of this project is to take to heart the observations of *Our Common Future*—to provide a reference for students of geography and conflict studies that evaluates and debates the role of natural resources as either sources of dissension and violence or stability and peace. There are numerous examples from around the world wherein a natural resource is or has been disputed: diamonds in Africa, oil and natural gas in Canada and the United States, fisheries off the coast of New England, farmland in Central Asia, and seemingly water everywhere. Wherever there is a resource, there is a potential for conflict and cooperation and prosperity.

The book is organized into two volumes with both general and regional topics and case studies. Volume One's focus is on Asia, Africa, Oceania, and global issues. Sample topics in this volume include: climate change and drought in Australia; the transboundary hydropolitics of the Ganges, Mekong, Jordan, and Nile rivers; the influence of oil wealth on gender relations in the Middle East; the ubiquitous challenge of such valuable mineral resources as diamonds and coltan being used to support violence in sub-Saharan Africa; the biodiversity crisis; and the impacts of global warming on energy systems, geopolitics, and national security. The focus of Volume Two is on North, South, and Central America and the Caribbean. Topics of interest include petroleum politics and development in the Gulf of Mexico, Northern Alberta, the Falkland Islands, and Ecuador's Yasuni National Park; water disputes in the Colorado and Klamath river basins and drought-sensitive California; the role of international peace parks; and impacts on aboriginal peoples.

Each case in Volumes One and Two is framed as a question followed by a general overview of the topic and two discussion and/or debate essays. In general, the authors are seeking to answer these questions:

- What role do natural resources play in conflicts?
- When resources are in question, do stakeholders resort to violence or negotiation?
- For particular places and people, are natural resources used to promote development or destruction?
- How should natural resources be managed to avoid conflict?
- What is it about particular resources that make a situation contentious and more than just an economic issue?

The style is to be both informative in answer to the question and argumentative in support of a particular position. This approach allows the reader to ultimately decide which side has the more convincing argument. The book also contains supporting material on key concepts, people, places, and organizations germane to natural resource conflicts. The purpose is to increase the scope of the discussion and provide readers with avenues to expand and develop their understanding.

As a last word to the opening of this project, I turn to Kenyan environmental activist and Nobel Peace Prize–recipient Wangari Maathai, who observed: "In a few decades, the relationship between the environment, resources and conflict may seem almost as obvious as the connection we see today between human rights, democracy and peace" (Schmitz et al., 2013). There is a sense of concern in her prescient observation as well as hope—hope that akin to human rights and democracy, awareness of the relationship between environment and conflict will ultimately promote cooperation and peace.

REFERENCES

Brundtland, Gro Harlem, et al. (1987). *Our Common Future: World Commission on Environment and Development.* Oxford, UK: Oxford University Press, 290.

Schmitz, Cathryne L., Tom Matyok, Channelle D. James, and Lacey M. Sloan. (2013). "Environmental Sustainability—Education Social Workers for Interdisciplinary Practice," in Mel Gray, John Coates, and Tiani Hetherington (eds.), *Environmental Social Work.* New York: Routledge, 261.

UN Secretary-General's High Level Panel on Threats, Challenges and Change. (2004). *A More Secure World: Our Shared Responsibility—Report of the Secretary-General's High-Level Panel on Threats, Challenges and Change.* New York: United Nations General Assembly.

INTRODUCTION

M. Troy Burnett

NATURAL RESOURCE CONFLICTS—THE CONTEXT

Though an extensive two-volume text with numerous case studies from around the world, the premise of this book is straightforward—to explore the connections between natural resources and conflict. The accepted definition of natural resources is materials that occur in nature and are essential or useful to humans, such as water, air, land, forests, fish and wildlife, topsoil, and minerals. Often referred to as the Earth's gift to humanity, natural resources provide basic sustenance, economic and social development, and cultural identity. Beginning with the agricultural revolution, complex civilizations have been built and sustained through the conversion and usage of the natural world. Yet, as Jared Diamond explored in his best-selling book *Collapse: How Societies Choose to Fail or Succeed* (2005), societies that mismanage and fight over their natural resources more often than not doom themselves, as the Polynesians on Easter Island tragically discovered watching their complex civilization of 20,000 people dwindle to a meager, cannibalistic population of 2,000 by the time Europeans arrived in the 18th century. Deforestation was the primary cause of the Easter Island conflict and collapse, and the fate of its people provides a sobering warning for our own Earth Island.

Two primary theories have emerged to explain the role of natural resources in conflict, one focused on scarcity and the other concerned with abundance. The contravening theories posit that either too little of a resource may lead to conflict as people become desperate or an abundance of a resource can promote conflict as groups struggle to capture and control the wealth.

The first view, called the "Malthusian perspective" (named after the English demographer Thomas Robert Malthus), states that the potent mix of population pressure and resource scarcity will combine to increase poverty, desperation, and inequality. What follows, according to Malthus, are rebellion, social conflict, and environmental destruction.

On the other hand, some argue that resource abundance, rather than scarcity, is the challenge. Certain countries, though geographically blessed by abundant natural resources such as oil or diamonds, often experience social dysfunction, underdevelopment, corruption, stagnation, and regular cycles of violent conflict. In such a context, resources are viewed as "lootable" by either the self-serving greedy or the politically violent. Dysfunctional and sociopathic elements in a society are then able to fund their activities using the looted resource.

Admittedly, environmental factors are rarely the primary source of violent conflict. More often conflicts are rooted in ethnic and religious tensions, adverse economic conditions, low levels of development, and political instability. Yet, exploitation of natural resources and related environmental impacts can, and do, act as facilitators of conflict that magnify existing tensions or pushing antagonistic groups into full-scale violence. Indeed, as scholars have shown, many conflicts since 1990 have been fuelled by natural resource exploitation (Table I.1). A 2008 report from the Uppsala Conflict Data Program showed that close to 40 percent of all intrastate conflicts since World War II can be directly tied to natural resources (Uppsala, 2008). Civil wars in Liberia, Angola, East Timor, Afghanistan, and the Democratic Republic of Congo have centered on resources such as gold, diamonds, timber, oil, and other minerals. Along with the religious and ethnic differences, the ongoing struggles in Darfur (South Sudan) and the Middle East involve the control and appropriation of scarce resources such as water and fertile land.

As these and the many other examples explored in this two-volume book show, the relationship between natural resources, the environment, society, and conflict is complex and unpredictable; though three principal pathways can be discerned: natural resources act to (1) directly instigate the conflict; (2) fund the conflict; and (3) undermine peacemaking, institution building, and governance.

Instigating the Conflict

Allocation and the unsustainable use of natural resources are challenges in both developed and developing countries. Tensions inherently arise from competing demands. Often it is a failure related to ineffective governance that privileges certain economic groups and ideologies over others. In other cases, such as the global trafficking of wild species like the African elephant, it is the wanton and illegal exploitation of natural wealth for profit.

Table I.1 Recent Conflicts Fueled by Natural Resources

Country	Duration	Resources
Afghanistan	1978–2001	Gems, opium, timber
Angola	1975–2002	Oil, diamonds
Burma	1949–	Timber, tin, gems, opium
Cambodia	1978–1997	Timber, gems
Colombia	1984–	Oil, gold, cocoa, timber, emeralds
Congo, Democratic Republic	1996–2008	Copper, coltan, diamonds, gold, cobalt, timber, tin
Cote d'Ivoire	2002–2007	Diamonds, cocoa, cotton
Indonesia-Aceh	1975–2006	Timber, natural gas
Indonesia-West Papua	1969–	Copper, told, timber
Liberia	1989–2003	Timber, diamonds, iron, palm oil, cocoa, coffee, rubber, gold
Nepal	1996–2007	Yarsa gumba (fungus)
Papua New Guinea	1989–1998	Copper, gold
Peru	1980–1995	Coca
Senegal	1982–	Timber, cashew nuts
Sierra Leone	1991–2000	Diamonds, cocoa, coffee
Somalia	1991–	Fish, charcoal
Sudan	1983–2005	Oil

Source: Adapted from Ross 2003.

Invariably, there is competition for high value extractive resources like hydrocarbons, diamonds, timber, and precious metals. Greed, acute poverty, underdevelopment, and power create incentives to capture and control—often through violence—resource-rich territories. In many cases, powerful actors are able to undermine or hijack the state to serve their purpose. For instance, a key demand by Uniao Nacional para a Independencia Total de Angola (UNITA) in the agreement to halt the Angolan civil war in 1994 was to create the position of minister of geology and mining in order to consolidate its hold of the country's diamond mines. After the Cold War ended, when each side had received support from either the United States or the Soviet Union, diamonds and oil became the lifeblood of the civil war, such that the conflict was dubbed "the ultimate resource war" (Collier, 2007).

Conflicts frequently develop in situations of scarcity wherein the demand for land, water, and other resources, far outstrips the supply, a situation made worse by demographic pressures, social inequality, natural disasters, and climate change. The situation in South Sudan and Darfur highlight how the loss of fertile land, population increase, and drought have driven the region into decades-long civil conflict. The 1994 attempted genocide of the Tutsi people in Rwanda by the Hutus has been directly linked to the scarcity of resources as well.

Lastly, states whose economies are overly dependent on a few primary commodities (e.g., diamonds, timber, oil) tend to be economically and politically fragile and highly susceptible to the fluctuating nature of the capitalist world system. This situation is common and predictable enough to have earned the name of the "resource curse. " In such cases, local economic and political systems are held hostage to the capitalist world and its unsteady and fluctuating markets. Unable to fully develop alternative economic opportunities;, the state becomes politically and socially wedded to one industry to the extent that maximum effort is given to making "it" happy at the expense of the general society. The supposed valuable resource becomes a curse, wherein exploitation, revenue mismanagement, extrajudicial violence, and corruption become the norm.

Seemingly, a common trait in situations where natural resources instigate conflict is the challenge faced by states that lack the institutional capacity or the will to address resource-based tensions before they erupt into violent conflict. This challenge is compounded in illiberal societies that lack a democratic culture and civil society.

Funding the Conflict

Once tensions have built or violence has ensued, natural resources can be used to facilitate and deepen the conflict. High-value commodities can be used to generate the necessary funds to equip and maintain militias and armies. Invariably, these high-valued resources become strategic objectives and whoever controls them often wins the war. As the examples in Table I.1 reveal, many civil conflicts have been sustained for extended periods by natural resource wealth. Armed militias and government forces in Sierra Leone, Ivory Coast, Liberia, Cambodia, and Angola have all used the proceeds from high-value resources, called "conflict resources," to support their militaristic and political activities. Such conflicts long would have exhausted without the wealth provided by the valuable resource. From an outsider's perspective, these wars often transform into economic affairs rather than political-ideological contestations. The violence appears to be rooted in greed rather than grievance.

Undermining Peacemaking and Institution Building

The incentives and wealth associated with valuable resources can frustrate efforts to promote peace and conflict resolution. This is especially the case when particular groups or individuals feel threatened or stand to lose revenues from peace agreements and new institutional arrangements. To some actors, discussions of regulation, sustainability, or equitable re-distribution often serve as major spoilers to the process, undermining political agreement. For example, in 2005 a UN panel of experts that explored the conflict in the Ivory Coast found that the unregulated, economic benefits from diamonds, cocoa, and cotton acted as clear and unfortunate disincentives for both sides to negotiate peace (UNSCGE, 2005).

Indeed as the Uppsala University Conflict Data Program and Center for the Study of Civil War has shown, conflicts associated with natural resources are twice as likely to relapse into fighting within five years without effective resource management frameworks.

THE SILENT VICTIM OF NATURAL RESOURCE CONFLICTS—THE ENVIRONMENT ITSELF

To compound the problem, conflicts over resources not only affect groups of people but also have direct and indirect impacts on natural environments themselves. Conflicts of any sort are harmful to the environment and often compound and entrench existing problems creating endless cycles of destruction and despair.

Whether to secure tactical advantage or subdue and discourage resistance, competing groups will actively target natural resources by burning crops and grazing lands, cutting forests, poisoning soils and wells, or slaughtering livestock. In 1991, following his defeat and expulsion from Kuwait in the first Gulf War, Saddam Hussein had his military commanders dump millions of tons of oil into waterways and deliberately set fire to Kuwaiti oil fields. The United States was guilty of such practices during the Vietnam War, in which the government authorized the destruction of forest and farmland through the dumping of the dioxin-containing defoliant Agent Orange. Entire regions were stripped of vegetation and remain unsuitable for use to this day.

In general, the impacts of conflicts on natural resources can be grouped into three categories. The first is direct impact, the active, physical destruction of ecosystems and natural wealth. The second is indirect impact, that which results from the survival strategies of local and displaced peoples. With their ways of life disrupted, desperate people often turn to the liquidation of natural assets. Commitment to sustainability and long-term environmental stability wanes as people struggle to survive. The third type of impact conflicts cause is the major disruption to governing institutions and the rule of law as societies descend into chaos and illegality. Environmental rules, supports, and protections that existed prior to the violence are re-prioritized or discarded altogether.

The situation in Afghanistan is one example that reflects very starkly how conflict destroys the environment, setting the stage for vicious cycles of conflict and degradation. More the 80 percent of the Afghan people base their livelihoods on natural resources. The decades-long pressures of war, political upheaval, failed state institutions, religious fragmentation, climate change, drought, and the breakdown of traditional, community-based systems have resulted in a denuded and toxic landscape. Communities struggling to survive have been forced to deforest woodlands that had been collectively managed and sustained. As erosion and drought spread, many people are forced to search farther and wider for water and grazing lands, potentially coming into contact with neighboring peoples who also may be facing resource strains. As in South Sudan, peace and stability in Afghanistan will depend on reclaiming and restoring the natural resource wealth and addressing conflicts associated with access and usage.

COOPERATION, RESOLUTION, AND MANAGEMENT

While conflict and violence often occur when natural resources are in question, resource disputes have also led to cooperation, compromise, and sustainable management. Indeed, as many of the authors in these two volumes argue, scarcity or high-value natural resources can resolve disputes between adversarial groups and promote long-term peace rather than instigate or sustain violence. While there is no magic formula for cooperation, the key ingredients involve a combination of stakeholder willingness and a functioning, institutional framework that is viewed to be both transparent and fair.

Natural resource management is shaped by a variety of internal and external pressures. Global demand determines the value of many natural resources and demand is fickle and susceptible to marketing strategies. International organizations, consumers, investors, and trade regimes can act in concert to influence local markets and governance structures. Where conflict is perceived to be sustained or driven by natural resources, such as diamonds in Liberia, these actors can use their financial power to demand a peaceful resolution to the dispute. Outside parties can help facilitate negotiations and agreements, suggest mutually agreeable solutions such as parks, sustainable development, conservation mechanisms, open markets, and international standards. High-value resource and the groups who fight over them in particular are susceptible to global market influences and institutional incentives, lest they each in turn lose out on the potential wealth as trade embargoes are slapped on their precious commodity.

The UN, for instance, frequently uses its leverage to pass resolutions and organize embargoes and sanctions to directly influence conflicts associated with natural resources. The United Nations Environmental Program (UNEP), Convention on International Trade in Endangered Species (CITES), Convention on Biological Diversity (CBD), the Millennium Development Goals, and Agenda 21 are all examples of how the UN consolidates global concerns and exerts its influence to minimize conflict and promote sustainable development. Further, UN inspectors and peacekeepers have been deployed to monitor resource disputes and establish peace zones and protective barriers around disputed territories and resource-rich lands, water sources, oil fields, and mineral deposits. Such third-party intervention compels the competing groups to address their grievances in a less violent manner and promote resource-specific agreements and institutions to help prevent a return to fighting.

Such international development institutions as the World Bank and World Trade Organization can provide business standards and financial support as well as advice on revenue transparency, economic stability, and debt restructuring. The debt-for-nature swap program was inspired by such thinking. For instance, Costa Rica has taken advantage of debt-for-nature swaps to both reduce its financial burden and develop its renowned park system and ecotourism industry.

The international business community and transnational corporations in particular play a role by recognizing illicit economic activity and developing certification schemes to discourage resource markets that serve to sustain conflicts. The World Business Council for Sustainable Development (WBCSD) and many other NGOs provide forums to discuss resource exploitation and trade as well as and methods to promote cooperation and sustainability rather than conflict. In one notable case, starting in the 1990s, NGOs, governments, and the diamond industry banded together to address diamond-funded conflicts in Africa. Known as the Kimberley Process (KP), the certification scheme promotes international standards on the import, export, and sale of diamonds. Though not perfect, the process has undercut funding sources for many rebel groups and helped alleviate conflict in such African countries as Sierra Leone and Liberia. The KP also encourages and rewards places like Botswana to continue its more sustainable mineral industry.

To further combat the misuse of natural resource wealth, in 2002 the Extractive Industries Transparency Initiative was formed. First introduced at the World Summit on Sustainable Development, the initiative established guidelines and a monitoring system to ensure that the revenues from certain industries like mining and oil and gas are not used to fund conflicts but rather to promote development. With 48 member countries and a motto of "seeing results from natural resources," its primary goals are to mitigate conflict and address the problems of resource curse.

Indeed, there are many instances where global and local government and nongovernmental organizations have successfully invoked the rule of law to address resource-based disputes. From the Nile Basin Initiative to the CITES, negotiation, compromise, and binding agreements often are the chosen path. The Jordan River, a resource shared by Lebanon, Syria, Jordan, Palestine, and Israel, is a bellwether example that many agree should have led to greater conflicts and violence than has been the case. Despite profound ethno-religious differences, the people of the Jordan Basin have negotiated a series of transboundary water-management compacts that focus on conservation and fair allotment. In 1993, the Israelis and Palestinians established the Joint Water Committee to act as a dispute resolution body to address water issues. Again, though not perfect, with its history of mitigating disputes it is a step in the right direction.

Transboundary Biosphere Reserves and International Peace Parks are another mechanism that has been used to minimize conflict and address conservation concerns. The Glacier-Waterton International Peace Park between Canada and the United States is a model for cooperative, transboundary park management. Similarly, Guatemala and Mexico, in an effort to stem a long history of deforestation, cattle ranching, illicit drug smuggling, and political conflict, have established a biosphere reserve system along their border. In collaboration with the local people and environmental organizations, the reserve system encompasses a vast, tropical forest with high rates of biodiversity and natural resources wealth as well as a rich cultural history.

CONCLUSION

Natural resources present some of the most intractable and complicated challenges facing the international community today. States and people struggle to manage their natural resources and direct wealth gains into positive development. Conflict and violence often erupt in cases of scarcity or abundance fomenting cycles of social desperation and environmental destruction. Yet cooperation and stability may be found in situations where one would expect violence. While growing demand for natural resources combined with scarcity has made conflict management and resolution difficult, in our highly globalized and connected world there is more incentive for states and communities to negotiate and compromise. From the Colorado River basin to the Arctic Council, many of the authors in the volumes show this to be the case. Most competing groups realize that war and violence are unsustainable in the long term for all the stakeholders involved and the environment itself. Beyond the most desperate of situations where violence is viewed as the only option, stakeholders prefer compromise and accept that the challenge is to find appropriate mechanisms for resolving disputes and promoting conservation.

Indeed, the reader of the numerous cases presented in this two-volume book will quickly discover that there is both cause for despair and hope.

> "The difference between hope and despair is a different way of telling stories from the same facts."
>
> —Alain de Botton

REFERENCES

Collier, Paul. (2007). *The Bottom Billion*. Oxford, UK: Oxford University Press.

Ross, Michael. (2003). "The natural resource cures: How wealth can make you poor," in Ian Bannon and Paul Collier (eds.), *Natural Resources and Violent Conflict*. Washington, DC: World Bank.

UN Secretary-General's High Level Panel on Threats, Challenges and Change. (2004). *A More Secure World: Our Shared Responsibility—Report of the Secretary-General's High-Level Panel on Threats, Challenges and Change*. New York: United Nations General Assembly.

UN Security Council Group of Experts. (2005). *Report of the Group of Experts Submitted Pursuant to Paragraph 7 of Security Council Resolution 1584 Concerning Cote d'Ivoire*. New York: United Nations.

Uppsala Conflict Data Program, Uppsala University. (2008). *Conflict Termination Dataset* 2(1), 1946–2007. Accessed March 22, 2016, at http://www.pcr.uu.se/research/ucdp/datasets/ucdp_conflict_termination_dataset/.

RECOMMENDED READINGS

Woodrow Wilson Center for Environmental Change and Security: https://www.wilsoncenter.org/program/environmental-change-and-security-program.

VOLUME I

Alao, Abiodun. (2007). *Natural Resources and Conflict in Africa: The Tragedy of Endowment*. Rochester, NY: Rochester Press.

Bavinck, Maarten, Lorenzo Pellegrini, and Erik Mostert. (2014). *Conflicts over Natural Resources in the Global South: Conceptual Approaches*. Leiden, Netherlands, and London: CRC Press/Taylor & Francis.

Eichstaedt, Peter. (2011). *Consuming the Congo: War and Conflict Minerals in the World's Deadliest Place*. Chicago, IL: Chicago Review Press.

Kameri-Mbote, Patricia. (2007). *Navigating Peace: Water, Conflict, and Cooperation, Lessons from the Nile River Basin*. Washington, DC: Woodrow Wilson International Center for Scholars.

Le Billon, Philippe. (2005). *Fuelling War: Natural Resources and Armed Conflict*. New York: International Institute for Strategic Studies.

Le Billon, Philippe. (2012). *Wars of Plunder: Conflicts, Profits and the Politics of Resources*. New York: Columbia University Press.

Ochola, Washington Odongo, P. C. Sanginga, and Isaac Bekalo. (2011). *Managing Natural Resources for Development in Africa: A Resource Book*. Nairobi: University of Nairobi Press in association with International Development Research Centre, International Institute of Rural Reconstruction, Regional Universities Forum for Capacity Building in Agriculture.

Rahaman, M. M. (ed.). (2012). "Special Issue: Water wars in 21st century along international rivers basins: speculation or reality?," *International Journal of Sustainable Society* 4(1/2).

Renner, Michael. (2002). *The Anatomy of Resource Wars*. Volume 162. Washington, DC: Worldwatch Institute.

Shiva, Vandana. (1991). *Ecology and the Politics of Survival: Conflicts over Natural Resources in India*. New Delhi, India, and Tokyo, Japan: United Nations University Press.

Vajpeyi, Dhirendra K. (ed.). (2012). *Water Resource Conflicts and International Security: A Global Perspective*. Lanham, MD: Lexington Books.

VOLUME II

Brauch, Hans Günter, Úrsula Oswald Spring, John Grin, Czeslaw Mesjasz, et al., (2009). *Facing Global Environmental Change: Environmental, Human, Energy, Food, Health and Water Security Concepts*. First edition, Volume 4. New York: Springer.

Collier, Paul, and Ian Bannon. (2003). *Natural Resources and Violent Conflict: Options and Actions*. Washington, DC: World Bank Publications.

Conca, Ken, and Geoffrey D. Dabelko (eds.). (2003). *Environmental Peacemaking*. Washington, DC: Woodrow Wilson Center Press.

Diehl, Paul F., and Nils Petter Gleditsch (eds.). (2001). *Environmental Conflict*. Boulder, CO: Westview Press.

Dinar, Shlomi. (2011). *Beyond Resource Wars: Scarcity, Environmental Degradation, and International Cooperation*. Cambridge, MA: MIT Press.

Dobkowski, Michael N., and Isidor Walliman (eds.). (2002). *On the Edge of Scarcity: Environment, Resources, Population, Sustainability, and Conflict*. Second edition. Syracuse, NY: Syracuse University Press.

Herda-Rapp, Ann, and Theresa L. Goedeke (eds.). (2005). *Mad about Wildlife: Looking at Social Conflict over Wildlife*. Leiden, Netherlands: Brill Academic Publishers.

Homer-Dixon, Thomas F. (2001). *Environment, Scarcity, and Violence*. Princeton, NJ: Princeton University Press.

Humphreys, Marcartan, Jeffrey D. Sachs, and Joseph E. Stiglitz (eds.). (2007). *Escaping the Resource Curse*. New York: Columbia University Press.

Klare, Michael T. (2001). *Resource Wars: The New Landscape of Global Conflict*. First edition. New York: Metropolitan Books.

Matthew, Richard Anthony. (2010). *Global Environmental Change and Human Security*. Cambridge, MA: MIT Press.

Vasquez, Patricia I. (2014). *Oil Sparks in the Amazon: Local Conflicts, Indigenous Populations, and Natural Resources*. Athens: University of Georgia Press.

Volume 1
List of Entries by Region

NATURAL RESOURCE CONFLICTS

International

Is the world's increasing population stressing the Earth's resources and becoming a major source of conflict?
How have natural resource conflicts led to the demise of past civilizations?
As the world's population becomes more urbanized, how are cities being designed to avoid conflicts?
How have global warming and climate change promoted conflict in pastoral communities?
Will air quality be a source of regional conflict?
What role does ecotourism play in natural resource conflicts?
How does global warming and climate change influence a nation's security policy?
Is nuclear the right option to avoid future energy conflicts?
Could conflicts over water actually promote peace and stability?
What steps should be taken to help provide access to clean water for more people in the world?
To mitigate conflicts over water, is it better to treat water as a commodity or human right?
Which water basins are presently sites of the highest potential for conflict?

Will the international trade in hazardous waste promote stability or conflict?
With future conflicts seemingly guaranteed, is a technological breakthrough needed to avert the climate crisis?
To mitigate conflicts over natural resources, is it better to promote preservation or conservation?
How does the illicit trade in endangered species promote regional conflict?
Should cultural exceptions be made in whaling laws?
How are issues and conflicts over invasive species being addressed?
How does the loss of biodiversity promote conflict?
Are debt-for-nature swaps a viable means to promote stability in the developing world?

Africa

Was the Rwandan genocide of 1994 a result of conflict over natural resources?
What role have natural resources played in the Sudanese civil war?
Do diamonds have a negative influence on development in Africa?
Will the mining of coltan in the Congo further destabilize the region?
How will the Grand Ethiopian Renaissance Dam affect peace in the region?
Does the Kimberley Process work?
How does China's increasing demand for natural resources affect stability in Africa?
How have large-scale conservation efforts promoted conflict in Sub-Saharan Africa?

Asia, Oceania

Can it be argued that the wealth generated from oil is a primary cause of the disempowerment of women in the Middle East?
Is the Jordan River a source of regional conflict or stability?
What impact does control of valuable resources have on politics in the Middle East?
Is China's Green Great Wall an adequate solution to desertification?
What conflicts have arisen as a result of China's building of the Three Gorges Dam?
How can conflicts be avoided with Japan's fishing industry?
Is the crisis in Australia's Murray-Darling Basin the result of climate change or the decisions and actions of humans?

Is sustainable development and conservation or further resource exploitation and conflict the future in Borneo?
Was the conflict in East Timor, Indonesia, the direct result of natural resources?
Is the resource of the Mekong River Basin a potential for regional conflict?
Will the Ganges River be a source of regional conflict between India and Bangladesh?
How have natural resources caused political instability in post-communist Central Asia?

Volume 1
List of Entries by Topic

NATURAL RESOURCE CONFLICTS

Water

    Could conflicts over water actually promote peace and stability?
    What steps should be taken to help provide access to clean water for more people in the world?
    Which water basins are presently sites of the highest potential for conflict?
    How will the Grand Ethiopian Renaissance Dam affect peace in the region?
    Is the Jordan River a source of regional conflict or stability?
    What conflicts have arisen as a result of China's building of the Three Gorges Dam?
    How can conflicts be avoided with Japan's fishing industry?
    Is the resource of the Mekong River Basin a potential for regional conflict?
    Will the Ganges River be a source of regional conflict between India and Bangladesh?
    To mitigate conflicts over water, is it better to treat water as a commodity or human right?

Land

    Was the Rwandan genocide of 1994 a result of conflict over natural resources?

Will the international trade in hazardous waste promote stability or conflict?

How have large-scale conservation efforts promoted conflict in Sub-Saharan Africa?

Is China's Green Great Wall an adequate solution to desertification?

Is sustainable development and conservation or further resource exploitation and conflict the future in Borneo?

Was the conflict in East Timor, Indonesia, the direct result of natural resources?

Are debt-for-nature swaps a viable means to promote stability in the developing world?

As the World's population becomes more urbanized, how are cities being designed to avoid conflicts?

How have national park systems fomented conflict with Aboriginal peoples?

Atmosphere

How have global warming and climate change promoted conflict in pastoral communities?

Is the crisis in Australia's Murray-Darling Basin the result of climate change or the decisions and actions of humans?

With future conflicts seemingly guaranteed, is a technological breakthrough needed to avert the climate crisis?

Will air quality be a source of regional conflict?

How does global warming and climate change influence a nation's security policy?

Mineral and Energy Resources

Do diamonds have a negative influence on development in Africa?

Will the mining of coltan in the Congo further destabilize the region?

Does the Kimberley Process work?

How does China's increasing demand for natural resources affect stability in Africa?

Can it be argued that the wealth generated from oil is a primary cause of the disempowerment of women in the Middle East?

What impact does control of valuable resources have on politics in the Middle East?

Is nuclear the right option to avoid future energy conflicts?

Biodiversity and Wildlife

   How does the illicit trade in endangered species promote regional conflict?
   How does the loss of biodiversity promote conflict?
   How are issues and conflicts over invasive species being addressed?

General (Sustainable Development)

   Is the world's increasing population stressing the Earth's resources and
      becoming a major source of conflict?
   How have natural resources caused political instability in post-communist
      Central Asia?
   To mitigate conflicts over natural resources, is it better to promote
      preservation or conservation?
   How have natural resource conflicts led to the demise of past civilizations?
   What role does ecotourism play in natural resource conflicts?
   Should cultural exceptions be made in whaling laws?

Part I
International Conflicts

1

Is the World's Increasing Population Stressing the Earth's Resources and Becoming a Major Source of Conflict?

OVERVIEW

M. Troy Burnett and Max Lu

On October 31, 2011, according to an estimate by the United Nations (UN), the world population passed 7 billion people, just a dozen years after reaching 6 billion in 1999. News of the milestone set off renewed debate on whether that figure—or the 9 billion people expected by mid-century—is sustainable for a planet with limited resources and whether conflicts will result if the world is becoming overpopulated.

Concerns about overpopulation peaked in the late 1960s, particularly with the publication of American biologist Paul Ehrlich's 1968 book *The Population Bomb*, which contained dire warnings of looming and massive famines trigged by unsustainable population. Though the scale and timing of Ehrlich's predictions did not come true, he continues to defend his argument that the world's rising population poses grave threats to environmental sustainability and even human survival. There are dissenting voices, however. The world's overall population growth rate has slowed, from 2.2 percent in the 1960s to 1.1 percent today, and the breakthroughs in agricultural production called the Green Revolution have helped countries such as India feed larger numbers of people. Economic globalization continues to improve the lives of millions, political stability is the norm rather than the exception, and with ever-improving global democratic institutions the world's people have mechanisms to find cooperative solutions to problems. Still, many wonder if the world environment is approaching—or has already surpassed—its "carrying capacity" for human population and whether future conflicts are seemingly unavoidable.

In the first essay, Jeffery Gentry takes what he characterizes as a contrarian view that the world is not overpopulated, nor will it ever be. He argues that technology-driven increases in agricultural production are sustainable and further advances will result in less waste and carbon emissions. Moreover, statistics indicate that world population will level off and begin to decline after 2050. In the second essay, Max Lu argues that the surging population continues to trigger rising consumption that is unsustainable for the Earth's ecosystems. This is particularly true, Lu states, given that the prevailing ethos of economic health is based on continued growth of gross domestic product (GDP), which involves ever-increasing industrialization, urbanization, and consumption. The world's growing population is sustainable only if we are comfortable with the very steep inequality in living conditions in the world, or if those living in wealthier countries are willing to lower their standard of living in efforts to reduce the inequality, which he concludes is not a likely scenario. He argues that the world would not be able to sustain 7 billion people living (and consuming) at levels seen now in the United States and Europe, levels that also prompt tensions between the so-called "haves and have nots."

BACKGROUND

At the beginning of the 19th century, at the birth of the Industrial Revolution, there were 1 billion people on the planet, and it had taken all of human history—perhaps as long as 2 million years—to get to that point. It took only another 127 years to reach 2 billion (1927); then another 33 years to hit 3 billion (1960); 14 more years to reach 4 billion (1974); 13 more to get to 5 billion (1987); another 13 to reach 6 billion (2000); and a short 11 years to arrive at 7 billion (2011). Luckily, that breakneck pace seems to be slowing as current levels of fertility continue to decline around the world. Even with a declining rate of fertility, the UN Population Division believes that it will take us only until 2025 to reach 8 billion (a 14-year gap since 7 billion), and then another 20 years to reach 9 billion. The last 200 years, especially the past few decades, then, have seen a virtual explosion of people sharing the planet that has put us in genuinely uncharted territory.

For virtually all of human history up to the 19th century, population growth was kept in check by very high death rates. Life expectancy at most times and places was somewhere between 20 and 30 years. Keep in mind that when life expectancy is 20 years, nearly half of all children die before reaching age 5, which means the average woman must give birth to 6 children just to keep the population from declining. To complicate matters, childbearing in a high-mortality society was, and sadly still is in many parts of the world, a very risky business. Achieving that 6-child average means that some women will give birth to 12 children while others will die giving birth to their first. This was a fact of life for most of human history.

However, factors were in play in Europe at the beginning of the 19th century that would lead to improving health and longer lives. The first was the gradual receding of the Little Ice Age (1300–1850) in northern Europe, which allowed more land to be put into agricultural production throughout the region, leading to more food per person and thus healthier populations. Secondly, and equally important, was the receding of the plague, which had kept death rates high in Europe for centuries. The plague retreated (rather than disappeared) in the 14th century as a result of changes in housing, shipping, sanitary practices, and similar factors affecting the way rats, fleas, and humans encountered one another. The third and really most important long-term factor leading to a drop in death rates was the Enlightenment, a movement that championed the rights of individuals and espoused the cause of science instead of tradition and religion as a way of understanding the world around us. Our modern era truly emerged from the ideas and methods of the Enlightenment.

The means by which death rates can be lowered have now been spread all over the world, and pushing back death is the key underlying reason for population growth. By the time life expectancy reaches into the 50s (above the age at which women can bear children), only 2.1 children per woman are necessary to replace the population. Perhaps not surprisingly, since for all of human history societal survival depended upon women having six children, it has not been easy to change that mindset in the same short span of time in which we have raised life expectancy to unprecedented levels. Simply put, people in many parts of the world continue to have more children than are needed for replacement. Currently, the average life expectancy in the world is 70 years, whereas the average woman is having 2.5 children. It is for this reason that we have had such dramatic population growth.

The issue regarding how many people our planet can support has been debated for centuries. Scholars have put forward very different views about the implications of rapid population growth. Population pessimists ("doomsters") have hurled many apocalyptic warnings throughout history about what might happen if humans fail to curb our urge to procreate. In his seminal 1798 essay on population, Thomas Malthus asserted that population would necessarily grow faster than the food supply and, consequently, war, disease, and famine would emerge as inevitable ways to reduce the number of people. He warned, "The power of population is so superior to the power of the earth to produce subsistence for man that conflict and premature death must in some shape or other visit the human race" (Malthus, 1798). The Malthusian view of population has had its share of followers and detractors. Among neo-Malthusians, Stanford University population biologist Paul Ehrlich may be the most influential. His writings have informed and shaped public opinion about the global population issue for almost half a century. In his 1968 book *The Population Bomb*, he predicted that "hundreds of millions of people are going to starve to death" (Ehrlich, 1968). The titles of that book and his 1990 book with Anne Ehrlich *The Population Explosion* became popular metaphors used in negative discussions of population growth.

Optimists ("boomsters"), such as economists Ester Boserup and Julian Simon, on the other hand, emphasize the benefits of population growth in stimulating innovations and promoting economic growth. Boomsters do recognize problems that may stem from rapid population growth but believe humanity will find ways to cope, and that such pressures tend to result in cooperation rather than conflict (Lappé and Schurman, 1990)

REFERENCES

Ehrlich, Paul R. (1968). *The Population Bomb*. New York: Ballantine Books.
Lappé, Frances Moore, and Rachel Schurman. (1990). *Taking Population Seriously*. San Francisco: The Institute for Food and Development Policy.
Malthus, Thomas. (1798). *An Essay on the Principle of Population*. London: J. Johnson, in St. Paul's Church-Yard, Electronic Scholarly Publishing Project (1998), 44. Accessed March 7, 2016, at http://www.esp.org/books/malthus/population/malthus.pdf.

FURTHER READING

Kunzig, Robert. (2011, January). "Population 7 billion." *National Geographic 219*, 62.
McKee, Jeffrey Kevin. (2003). *Sparing Nature: The Conflict Between Human Population Growth and Earth's Biodiversity*. Piscataway, NJ: Rutgers University Press.
Santos, Filipe Duarte. (2012). *Humans on Earth: From Origins to Possible Futures*. Volume 1612–3018. New York: Springer.

THE EARTH'S "POPULATION PROBLEM" IS OVERSTATED AND WRONG
Jeffery Gentry

There are two sides (or more) to every story—every story except the one about human population. Most people have heard only one side: that population is too high and headed for disaster as the Earth's resources are rapidly depleted and humanity descends into group-on-group fighting. The preponderance of facts makes the truth clear, however. Our planet has never been and *never will be* overpopulated. Not only can Planet Earth sustain today's 7.4 billion humans, it will nicely manage the coming peak of 9 billion plus. The future is stability and peace, not conflict and chaos.

The population-bomb argument begins with British scholar Thomas Malthus. In 1798 he observed that nature limits the populations of all species. This process is beneficial. If populations somehow went unchecked they could rise geometrically (2-4-8-16), whereas resources rise only arithmetically (1-2-3-4). Malthus' theory entailed, however, that this law is inviolable: "[T]he increase of the human species can only be kept commensurate to the increase of the means of subsistence by the *constant operation* of the strong law of necessity acting as a check upon the greater power" (Malthus, 1798, emphasis mine). Malthus aptly explains why poverty persists in wealthy nations, and his essay makes plain that exponential growth could never actually happen.

Many modern scholars misconstrued Malthus as inviting the possibility of a population catastrophe (Elwell, 2009) because he mused counterfactually, "suppose that the restraints to population were universally removed." One of these authors was Paul Ehrlich, who became a media darling in the 1970s with his quasi-Malthusian claim of an imminent population disaster. The drastic human die-off of 4 billion people would occur between 1970 and 1990, including 65 million Americans. The nation of India was doomed and Great Britain would become an island filled with hungry people by 2000. The most draconian of forced population measures could not stop the coming famine, pandemics, and food wars (Ehrlich, 1996).

This global tragedy failed to materialize. The Green Revolution was one reason population was permitted to spike upward in the late 20th century. Led by American agronomist Norman Borlaug, hybrid varieties of maize, wheat, and rice more than kept pace with the growing world population. According to the United Nations, today's people are richer, live longer, and are better fed than ever before (United Nations Development Programme, 2010). This unprecedented health explosion has lifted life expectancy to historically mind-boggling levels.

Contrary to the neo-Malthusian case, sustainable food and water are here to stay. Zoologist Charles Godfray and colleagues note that grain production more than doubled after 1960 when arable land increased only 9 percent. The potential for further "sustainable intensification" in developing nations is vast (Godfray et al., 2010). No new technologies are needed to drastically increase food production again while reducing waste and carbon emissions. The yield gap between rich and poor nations is closing further due to the globalization of our food systems, allowing poor countries to specialize in growing foods best suited to their soils and climate. The twin virtues of technology-sharing and market globalization ensure continued declines in the proportion of those threatened by hunger.

Water is another key element of the population disaster. Alarmists forecast pandemic famines from water scarcity, emphasizing that we will never have more water than we do right now. This sounds frightening until one realizes we will never have any *less* water, either. Water is never lost, only redirected. Resource expert Jonathan Chenoweth observes, "It no longer makes sense to use self-sufficiency in food production to define water scarcity" (Chenoweth, 2008). Water enjoys a global market via the agricultural trade, as noted above. Water-poor nations, even the least-developed, now "buy" water by importing food. Chenoweth affirms that we have plenty of water for all global uses in the long term, especially considering that we extract just 10 percent of the renewable water in our lakes, rivers, and aquifers.

American women now average 2.0 babies, which is below replacement level. Only population momentum and immigration keep our numbers slowly rising. More than half of the world's people now live in nations experiencing sub-replacement birth rate, and depopulation already affects such countries as Russia, Japan, and Italy due to birth rate rates under 1.5.

Listening to the doomsayers, one might think that world population growth is accelerating. But the planet's total birth rate rate has tumbled for two generations: from 4.9 births-per-woman (of child-bearing years) in 1970, to 3.4 in 1990, to 2.5 in 2010. This figure is just above replacement. As soon as Earth's women dip below a long-term average of 2.1 children, the population will decline. Whereas growth averaged 20 percent per decade from 1950 to 1980, it slipped in the succeeding three decades to 15 percent, then 12 percent, then 10 percent.

Falling birth rates are attributed to rising wealth, health, and educational attainment. As women gain access to education, they prefer fewer children. Most people don't realize, however, that birth rate is falling everywhere. Latin America and the Caribbean now experience below-replacement birth rate despite widespread poverty. The same is true in poorer areas of Asia and the Middle East. The final holdout is Sub-Saharan Africa, where total birth rate remains above 4.5. But these are precisely the nations consuming the least natural resources and their birth rates are falling as well.

Africa is not overpopulated, especially considering its enormous natural resources. At 88 people per square mile, Africa is only slightly more populated than United States. (The world average is 135.) Europe is far more crowded than Africa, in fact *doubly* so. To say Africa's agrarian societies cannot manage greater density is false, as pre-industrial England thrived with 115 people per square mile. Despite steady gains in health and wealth, Africa has long been targeted by paternalistic population control measures. Elites from congested European countries relentlessly push birth control on Black Africa—a soft eugenics that many African leaders resent. In essence they are being told, *we Europeans have had our fun spawning children; you have no right to do the same*. But no one seems willing to put the demographics in perspective. Is Europe overpopulated? No. Is Africa overpopulated? No. Like the rest of the world, it just needs greater peace and prosperity.

To summarize today's realities, the human population will peak then slowly decline after 2050, and we have enough food and water to last for the rest of the epoch. Eventually, the doomsayers will have to turn their attention to the real problems we face. For example, if we want to help poor people everywhere, the West should abandon agricultural subsidies and land-consuming biofuels—corporate welfare programs that serve only to inflate food prices. Actions do matter, far more than our sheer numbers.

The prospect of a healthy and resource-stable planet beyond 2050 is not only possible but likely. It requires no new technologies, only processes already in motion. Demonstrated by economist Nicholas Eberstadt and others, a long era of slow economic growth has begun due to population aging (Eberstadt, 2010). Older people buy less and consume fewer resources. This lowers per-capita incomes and tax revenues, creating an expensive dependency ratio. In austere times, it's in everyone's selfish interest to drive shorter commutes and waste less food. Urban sprawl will peak and reverse itself because of its unaffordability and the smaller population. Reforestation is already happening in contracting regions of Europe, portending a healthier global environment in the year 2100.

We can summarize key elements of Earth's population history. Brutal conditions faced by early humans suppressed population growth for millennia, but we weren't driven into extinction like all other hominids. By 1900 the Industrial Revolution fueled population growth as death rates fell and birth rates remained high. Dramatic gains in prosperity and population perpetuated each other. Prosperity also lifted women educationally, dramatically lowering birth rates in the West after 1960. The resulting generational inversion induced population aging, halting the advance of first-world prosperity by 2010. Next, sluggish growth long-term will prompt incentives to conserve resources, followed by lower consumption itself. Finally, world population will crest after 2050 and then slowly, peacefully, decline.

REFERENCES

Chenoweth, Jonathan. (2008, August 23). "Water, water everywhere," *New Scientist* 199, 28–32.

Eberstadt, Nicholas. (2010). "The demographic future," *Foreign Affairs* 89(6), 54–64.

Ehrlich, Paul. (1996). Quoted in Julian Simon, *The Ultimate Resource 2*. Princeton, NJ: Princeton University Press, 35.

Elwell, Frank W. (2009). *Macrosociology: The Study of Sociocultural Systems*. Lewiston, NY: Edwin Mellen Press, 320–321.

Godfray, H. Charles, John R. Beddington, Ian R. Crute, Lawrence Haddad, David Lawrence, et al. (2010, February). "Food security: the challenge of feeding 9 billion people," *Science 327*, 813.

Malthus, Thomas R. (1798). *An Essay on the Principle of Population.* Public Domain Books: Kindle Edition, 9–10.

United Nations Development Programme. (2010). *The Real Wealth of Nations: Pathways to Human Development.* New York: Palgrave Macmillan, 1.

OVERPOPULATION STRESSES RESOURCES, WHICH IN TURN STRESSES PEOPLE

Max Lu

Can the planet support 7 billion or more inhabitants on a sustainable basis? Is the Earth overpopulated? How much is too much? Will an overpopulated Earth and the struggle for resources promote violent conflict? Questions such as these always arouse human passion and curiosity, but answers are inevitably fraught with uncertainties because the outcome of the people-versus-planet debate depends to a large extent on choices individuals have yet to make as well as ideas people do not yet have. Joel Cohen, a demographer at Columbia University's Earth Institute, published a book in 1995 on this very topic (Cohen, 1995). Cohen concludes that the question about how many people the Earth can support is unanswerable at the present state of our knowledge because it is difficult to predict what people will do in the future.

The difficulty in predicting the future course of demographic events, however, does not constitute a good reason for ignoring the issue altogether and "letting nature take its own course." A general consensus has emerged among scholars that the current path of development that humans are on—one blazed by today's developed countries—is not sustainable. The critical issue is not so much the increasing numbers of people as their profligate consumption of the planet's dwindling natural resources and the waste and pollution generated in the process. The world community needs to get together to make some serious changes in the way we use resources, manage our economy, and live our lives if we hope to transition to a more sustainable path for the planet.

It is one thing to keep 7 billion or more people alive; it is quite another to ensure that every member of the human race enjoys a healthy and fulfilling life. Achieving the latter is far more challenging than the former under any circumstances. Having so many of us on Earth just makes it so much harder and the potential for conflict that much greater. Unless we change the way we do things, the chances of eliminating poverty, malnutrition, and premature deaths are not good. We have been lucky that the doomsday scenarios predicted by population pessimists have not played out so far, but there is no guarantee that they will not happen in the future.

An important factor that calls into question the stability of human civilizations is our enormous impact on the ecosystem and whether the planet can take the strain as population continues to grow. More than half of the terrestrial biosphere is now intensively used by humans. A 1987 study shows humans then used about 40 percent of the net primary production in terrestrial ecosystems. The largest cities on Earth now contain tens of millions of residents each. Few if any areas on Earth remain untouched by humans. Because of the massive impact humans have had on the planet, scientists Paul Crutzen and Eugene Stoermer in 2000 coined a new term—Anthropocene (the Age of Man)—for a new geologic epoch (Crutzen and Stoermer, 2000).

Many of these changes are clearly positive. They have helped to improve human life. However, a host of other changes are detrimental to human well-being: air and water pollution, soil degradation, depletion of groundwater, exhaustion of mineral resources and fossil fuels, loss of biodiversity, ocean acidification, climate change, and the list goes on. One wonders how sustainable the current practices are and how much more beating the ecosystem can take before it snaps.

Some scholars believe humans are already using more natural resources than can be regenerated. According to the Global Footprint Network, with the current lifestyle, humanity as a whole is using 40 percent more renewable resources than can be replaced each year (Ryerson, 2010). Lester Brown, president of the Earth Policy Institute in Washington, D.C., argues that human beings have been eroding soil and depleting groundwater faster than they can be replenished, which may soon affect food production (Kunzig, 2011). There is a real concern about whether the world will be able to feed 9 billion people. Even if it is possible to produce enough food, how to do it without exhausting the planet's finite resources, especially water, will be a serious challenge.

Speaking of limits, in a 2009 study published in the journal *Nature*, a team of more than two dozen scientists from around the world identified nine "planetary boundaries" that humanity needs to stay within to avoid deleterious or even catastrophic environmental changes. They include climate change, ocean acidification, stratospheric ozone depletion, nitrogen and phosphorous cycle, global freshwater use, change in land use, biodiversity loss, atmospheric aerosol loading, and chemical pollution. All of these systems are related to the interacting chemical, physical, and biological processes on which life on Earth, including humans, depends. The authors believe we have already crossed three boundaries (climate change, rate of biodiversity loss, and human interference with the nitrogen cycle) (Rockström et al., 2009).

Arguably, population size still matters, but it is no longer considered the dominant factor affecting the planet's ecosystem. A bigger threat to sustainability is the rising consumption of people in many parts of the world. As people's income levels rise, they usually eat less grain-based food but more meat and dairy products. They also tend to buy more consumer goods. Urban residents generally also consume more than their rural counterparts. Not surprisingly, wealthy countries use many times more resources per capita than poorer nations and have a bigger environmental impact. With only 5 percent of global population, Americans consume a quarter of the world's energy and emit about 16 percent of the world's CO_2.

Here lies the main problem. One thing we know for sure is that the world will continue to industrialize and urbanize. More and more people will enjoy higher incomes and live in cities. According to the World Bank, more than 1 billion people in the developing world will be in the middle class by 2030, compared with just 400 million in 2005. Only about 3 percent of the world's population was urban when Thomas Malthus published his notable essay on population growth. The proportion of urban population stands at just over 50 percent now, and is projected to reach 69 percent in 2050. This means that in the next few decades, a significantly larger number of people worldwide will be consuming more. All the consumption translates into a higher demand for natural resources, from minerals and water to land for food production. If humans are already stressing Earth's finite resources as it is, can the planet take the strain in the future, particularly if people in developing countries all emulate the way Americans and Europeans live today, eating more meat, driving cars, and living in single-family homes?

CONCLUSION

The current development path that humans are on is clearly unsustainable. The GDP-based model drives ever-increasing consumption. There are just not enough resources for 7 billion or more people to achieve the lifestyles enjoyed in most developed countries. Humans need to change the way they consume resources and live their lives in order to put society on a sustainable path, but the issues facing developed and developing countries are very different. As a 2012 Royal Society report on people and the planet points out, most developed countries need to reduce their per capita consumption to a more sustainable level, but the 1.3 billion poorest people in the world need to consume more to be lifted out of extreme poverty. These are very challenging tasks and will require the adoption of new policies, institutions, and practices, as well as different ways of thinking of the future. Exactly how the necessary changes may be made is yet to be seen.

REFERENCES

Cohen, Joel E. (1995). *How Many People Can the Earth Support?* New York and London: Norton.

Crutzen, Paul J. (2002). "Geology of mankind," *Nature 415*, 23

Crutzen, Paul J., and Eugene F. Stoermer. (2000). "The 'Anthropocene,'" *Global Change Newsletter 41*, 17–18.

Kolbert, Elizabeth. (2011, March). "Enter the age of man," *National Geographic 219*, 60–85.

Kunzig, Robert. (2011, January). "Population 7 billion," *National Geographic 219*, 62.

Rockström, Johan, Will Steffen, Kevin Noone, Asa Persson, et al. (2009). "A safe operating space for humanity," *Nature 461*, 472–475.

Ryerson, William N. (2010). "Population, the multiplier of everything else," *The Post Carbon Reader Series: Population*, 3. Accessed March 7, 2016, at http://www.postcarbon.org/Reader/PCReader-Ryerson-Population.pdf.

2

HOW HAVE NATURAL RESOURCE CONFLICTS LED TO THE DEMISE OF PAST CIVILIZATIONS?

OVERVIEW
Mia Bennett

Narratives of past civilizations typically frame their citizens as having lived in harmony with their surrounding environments. A popular misconception is that mankind lived in peace with nature among untouched forests, pristine lakes, and wild mountains. No stream went overfished and no rainforest overharvested. But in fact, humans have made use of Earth's natural resources since the dawn of time—and not always sustainably. While it is difficult to attribute civilizational demise solely to poor decisions over natural resource management, they can certainly play a leading role. Misuses of resources such as forests, soils, and water have all turned what were once flourishing societies into archeological ruins. External factors such as climate change have also transformed resources that were once taken for granted into a scarce commodity, sending civilizations unable to adapt into a downward spiral.

UCLA geographer Jared Diamond, author of the seminal book *Collapse*, defines the collapse of a civilization as "local drastic decrease in human population numbers and/or in political, economic, or social complexity" (Diamond, 1994). Collapse usually does not happen overnight or even in the span of a few years; rather, it tends to be a drawn out process occurring over decades or even centuries, ending generally in decline but sometimes in complete extinction (Dugmore, 2012). Civilizations such as the Ancient Pueblo peoples (Anasazi) of the southwestern United States and the Polynesians of Easter Island, for instance, have disappeared completely from the face of the Earth.

The Norse Greenlanders were another such society that disappeared. In 986 CE, 14 boats filled with settlers from Iceland landed on the southwest coast of Greenland. Archaeological records demonstrate that they were the first people to inhabit the area, as the Inuit did not make their way there from northern Canada until around 1200. In a climate that was more conducive to agriculture than it is today, the Norse Greenlanders established two large settlements with dairy, sheep, and pig farms. Yet the pig farms caused severe erosion, worsening conditions for agriculture. Coupled with unfavorable changes in climate, including sea level rise, which reduced available pasture area, the Norse Greenlanders began to rely heavily on seal hunting. Coupled with other adaptations, this switch temporarily allowed them to withstand numerous climate fluctuations until conditions became too severe. By the middle of the 15th century, both settlements are believed to have ceased to exist. The Little Ice Age (1300–1850), a period of colder temperatures, is presumed to have made southern Greenland unfit for humans, as sealing became impossible given the increased sea ice. Norse Greenland is therefore often seen as a classic example of maladaptation by an inflexible temperate climate society extending into the arctic. Recent research, however, has found contrary results, explaining that the Norse Greenlanders were in fact resilient and adapted to numerous changes—but the switch to seal hunting they made in the 13th and 14th centuries in order to adapt actually engendered their downfall in the 15th century, when they could no longer hunt this crucial resource for sustenance (Dugmore, 2012). Economically induced isolation from former trade networks in the North Atlantic also worsened the situation, leaving Norse Greenlandic society to disappear into the chilly mists.

As the case of the Norse Greenlanders reveals, more than just mismanagement of natural resources has caused the ruin of a past society. Throughout history, phenomena such as drought or flooding, often induced by climate change, have significantly altered the landscape to the degree that humans could no longer successfully reside there. Political and economic decisions, too, have made already difficult living situations even more challenging. On the other side of the planet from Greenland lie the ruins of Angkor Wat, Cambodia. The stone temples that rise above a jungle filled with vines and trees once formed the bustling urban capital of the Khmer Empire. The kingdom ruled a large swath of Southeast Asia from the ninth through the 14th centuries and depended on annual monsoon flooding to irrigate its complex and extensive agricultural system. While written records about the Khmer Empire disappear after the 13th century—often a problem with ancient civilizations in decline—scientists have reconstructed the hydroclimate record using tree rings. They discovered that a weakened monsoon period lasting over several decades coincided with the collapse of the empire (Buckley et al., 2010) Without enough water, despite all its agricultural and hydraulic innovations, the Khmer Empire could not adapt to the drier climate. Consequently, a complex civilization based at Angkor Wat could no longer be supported. Of course, other geopolitical and economic factors helped bring about its decline as well—but lack of water likely was one of the chief instigators.

The Norse colonies in Greenland and the Khmer Empire in Cambodia differed drastically in terms of scale, complexity, and extent, yet the two societies met the same fate. The demise of societies due to the misuse or lack of natural resources is a trend that continues into the present day. The main difference between ancient times and today is that the present level of industrialization and globalization has dramatically amplified demand for natural resources. This has led to conflicts in places like the Amazon rainforest, where indigenous peoples, farmers, ranchers, and logging companies are all clamoring for access to natural resources (Hall, 2006). One researcher has found resources like oil, minerals, and drugs are the most likely commodities to cause conflict (Ross, 2004). In the Horn of Africa, the Second Sudanese Civil War, which lasted from 1983 to 2005, was partly instigated by fights over who would control the extensive oil fields (Johnson, 2003). The conflict drove millions of people to their deaths and embroiled numerous foreign actors, from the United Nations to individual states like China, which sold arms to Sudan (Large, 2008). Whereas societies could once collapse in isolation, globalization has greatly interconnected people on opposite sides of the world. A crisis in one society now reverberates with ill effects throughout many others.

REFERENCES

Buckley, Brendan M., Kevin J. Anchukaitis, Daniel Penny, Roland Fletcher, et al. (2010). "Climate as a contributing factor in the demise of Angkor, Cambodia," *Proceedings of the National Academy of Sciences* 107(15), 6748–6752.

Diamond, Jared. (1994). "Ecological collapses of past civilizations," *Proceedings of the American Philosophical Society*, 363–370.

Dugmore, Andrew. J., Thomas H. McGovern, Orri Vésteinsson, Jette Arneborg, et al. (2012). "Cultural adaptation, compounding vulnerabilities and conjunctures in Norse Greenland," *Proceedings of the National Academy of Sciences* 109(10), 3658–3663.

Hall, Anthony. (2006). "Extractive reserves: building natural assets in the Brazilian Amazon," in James K. Boyce, Sunita Narain, and Elizabeth A. Stanton (eds.), *Reclaiming Nature: Environmental Justice and Ecological Restoration*. Anthem: London.

Johnson, Douglas H. (2003). *The Root Causes of Sudan's Civil Wars*. Volume 5. Bloomington: Indiana University Press.

Large, Daniel. (2008). "China and the contradictions of 'non-interference' in Sudan," *Review of African Political Economy* 35 (115), 93–106.

Ross, Michael L. (2004). "How do natural resources influence civil war? Evidence from thirteen cases," *International Organization* 58(01), 35–67.

FURTHER READING

Diamond, Jared M. (2005). *Collapse: How Societies Choose to Fail or Succeed*. New York: Viking.

Schwartz, Glenn M., and John J. Nichols. (2010). *After Collapse: The Regeneration of Complex Societies*. Tucson: University of Arizona Press.

THE COLLAPSE OF EASTER ISLAND—A VALUABLE LESSON FOR OUR MODERN WORLD

M. Troy Burnett

There is a well-known truism relevant to this case: those who ignore history are doomed to repeat it. This rings true more than ever as the Earth and its inhabitants enter a new era of resource crisis and mass extinction. It was once thought that humanity's past history could not shed light upon the quandaries facing the human population today, but new insights into previous civilizations have enlightened us to their mistakes. As Jared Diamond shows in his best-selling book *Collapse: How Societies Choose to Fail or Succeed*, there are plenty of examples of how environmental mismanagement and natural resource conflicts resulted in civilizational collapse, including the Anasazi of the Southwest United States, the Vikings in Greenland, and the Mayans of Mesoamerica. One case in particular, Easter Island and its Polynesian inhabitants, offers a warning to what can happen if a civilization fails to recognize, acknowledge, and address the declining quality of the environment.

Located in the southeastern Pacific Ocean, off the coast of Chile, Easter Island (Rapa Nui) is a land of isolation and mystery. Beginning with the arrival of European explorers in 1722, questions have arisen regarding the nature and fate of the island and its civilization. This small, 62.1-square-mile island is more than 1,200 miles away from its closest neighbor, the island of Pitcairn, and more than 2,100 miles away from the nearest continental point. This raised the question of how the island became inhabited in the first place. Travelling by leaky canoes, the Polynesian settlers needed to cover vast distances with limited supplies. However,

Moai on Easter Island. The staggering architectural achievement of the people of Easter Island was the creation, especially the transportation and erection, of hundreds of *moai* monoliths. (iStockPhoto.com)

an even greater mystery came in the form of the enormous statues, called "moai." Weighing anywhere from 10 to 270 tons, 887 stone monuments have been catalogued, each representing a long-eared or short-eared, legless human male torso. To the Europeans, this represented a staggering feat of artistry and engineering; but how could this have been possible, for when they arrived on Easter day 1722, the island was in a state of profound collapse.

The captain of the first European vessel to arrive, Jacob Roggeveen, noted that to create such enormous stone monuments the islanders must have required thick timber for creating pulley machines, as well as strong ropes. However, Easter Island was barren, with not a single tree or bush over 10 feet tall. Furthermore, a complex society would be necessary to organize the carving, transport, and erecting of these monuments (Diamond, 2005). Again, when the European visitors arrived, they were greeted by only a small population of inhabitants, many of whom were suffering from malnutrition and other ailments. Recent research has led scientists to believe that at one point, upwards of 30,000 Polynesians resided on Easter Island. This was a far cry from the estimated 2,000 to 3,000 inhabitants that greeted Roggeveen. What were the events leading to the collapse of Easter Island and could it have been avoided?

First and foremost, Easter Island is not alone in Polynesian island collapses. The islands of Henderson, Pitcairn, Kahoolawe, and several others represent island civilizations that underwent a stunning decline. Like Easter Island, these islands are geographically isolated and contain several similar characteristics that make them vulnerable to deterioration. First, isolation of these islands restricted communication with other societies, thus preventing trade and valuable information from being exchanged. Second, with this isolation came a society's ability to unwittingly dwindle resources. The term "land amnesia" was coined to represent a society's inability to recognize the changing landscape before them. For example, a person who lives close to a glacier may not notice the small amount that it recedes yearly, compared to what someone who has not seen the glacier for many years may detect. In the case of Easter Island, inhabitants could not see the shrinking resource base upon which they relied. As forests were logged to help erect the monuments of Easter Island, precious timber resources dwindled, leaving the island bare of necessary vegetation. Ultimately, the forests of Easter Island were so completely devastated that the tree species became extinct, and with them so did all the land birds and several types of sea birds (Diamond, 2005). Without that necessary vegetation, the topsoil eroded, agricultural yields fell, and fuel sources vanished. The lack of timber also created a shortage of canoes used for deep sea fishing, further stressing the population's ability to sustain themselves, or, for that matter, abandon the island as the crisis worsened. The last circumstance attributing to the collapse of Easter Island was climate change. Unfortunately, Easter Island, like other islands susceptible to environmental degradation, is located in an area that receives modest rainfall. This results in a vegetation structure that needs to develop over long periods of time and is overly sensitive to disturbance.

As the environment declined, conflict ensued. The remaining population of Easter Island resorted to relocating into caves and stone sanctuaries as the resources became scarcer and threats from rival factions grew. Further, archeologists discovered that as food resources shrank, cannibalism became rampant as the inhabitants struggled to survive. Production of the moai statues abruptly ended, as quarries were seemingly abandoned overnight. Stone tools and unfinished monuments still buried line the quarries, leaving behind an eerie vision of a past thriving society.

A central thesis for those who study environmentally induced civilizational decline is that collapses often occur in environments that are recognized as ecologically vulnerable. Though it is true that civilizations in isolated regions like Easter Island are more apt to collapse due to ecosystem vulnerabilities, one cannot conclude that modern societies are more robust. Indeed, as Bahn and Flenley argue, the only difference between Easter Island and Earth Island is scale (Bahn and Flenley, 1992). The parallels between the Easter Islanders' over-consumption, environmental destruction, and inability to solve their resource crisis are striking. Similar to our situation, inhabitants of Easter Island may even have been aware of the environmental stresses, but were too heavily invested in their ideologies and social system to truly implement conservation. The most sobering fact is that akin to Easter Island, the population of Earth has no neighbors that can rescue us from a severely degraded ecosystem.

REFERENCES

Bahn, Paul G., and John Flenley. (1992). *Easter Island, Earth Island*. New York: Thames and Hudson.

Diamond, Jared M. (2005). *Collapse: How Societies Choose to Fail or Succeed*. New York: Penguin.

FURTHER READING

Diamond, Jared M. (1994). "Ecological collapses of ancient civilizations: The golden age that never was," *Bulletin of the American Academy of Arts and Sciences*, 37–59.

Diamond, Jared M. (1994). "Ecological collapses of past civilizations," *Proceedings of the American Philosophical Society*, 363–370.

SOIL AND THE COLLAPSE OF THE MIGHTY ROMAN EMPIRE
Mark Hecht

The world is littered with the remains of fallen civilizations. Scholars have long debated the causes of their demise, exploring the social, economic, and political factors. Along with these more common explanations, in many cases, from the Harappan of South Asia to the Mayans of Central America, a lesser-explored factor emerges—environmental sustainability. Indeed, conflict over natural resources often plays a role in the weakening, degradation, and eventual collapse of a dominant civilization.

Perhaps the most famous collapse is that of the mighty Western Roman Empire, effectively ending in 480 CE. Historians argue that this long-lasting, expansive empire collapsed due to invasion by external forces, increasing but unsustainable sociopolitical complexity, corrupt leadership, and the high cost of maintaining an empire. Added to this well-trod story is the role played by agriculture and soil quality.

The colonnaded *decumanus maximus*, one of two main streets in the Roman city of Timgad, present-day Algeria. At the top of the street is the Arch of Trajan, dating from the third century CE. (Dreamstime.com)

When Romulus founded Rome in 750 BCE the average farm size was between one and five acres. It was enough to feed a family on the locally managed and highly diversified farms. However, even though Romans had a strong grasp of agriculturally appropriate techniques, not all knowledge was at the level of today's agronomists.

A recognizable flaw among the Romans was an intense cultural focus on maximizing crop yield. Marcus Terrentisu Varro (116–27 BCE) emphasized this in his book *De re rustica*. He suggested that maximum crop yield could be attained through practices such as regular tilling of soil and not leaving lands fallow. Unfortunately, these practices, in combination with increasing centralization of land ownership, use of slaves, and other socioeconomic conditions, lead to rapid soil erosion. David Montgomery, a soil scientist from Washington State University, says that natural, pre-agriculture soil erosion in the area around Rome was about one inch every thousand years. However, during the era of the Western Roman Empire the rate of erosion was 10 times faster, about one inch per century (Montgomery, 2007).

The result of rapid soil erosion was higher input costs combined with decreasing crop yields. This led to adverse impacts on society such as increasing food prices and civil protest. When Varro wrote *De re rustica*, these problems had become self evident. About a century prior to Varro however, Marcus Porcius Cato (234–149 BCE) had written the Roman text *De agri cultura* in a time when centralization of land ownership was only just beginning. Centralization of land ownership, plus the increasing focus on cash crop production, the use of slaves, and absentee landlords, would all contribute directly and indirectly to increasing soil erosion. Socioeconomic conditions would become increasingly dire for the Roman Empire later, but Cato was already cognizant of a declining agricultural output among the Empire in his time. To add to his concern, across the Mediterranean Sea was the Carthaginian civilization, which Cato saw as both an agricultural and military rival to Rome. As an influential agricultural theorist, Cato was able to influence the political body of Rome to act upon the inevitable natural resource conflict that was about to arise. Rome basically did what Rome had done many times before—as its agricultural capacity and soil were literally being washed into the sea, it chose to invade and occupy all of North Africa.

Rome had actually fought a number of wars with Carthage, but it was during the Third Punic War (149–146 BCE) that Rome destroyed the city, but then turned around to rebuild it and settle many of its own citizens and soldiers in North Africa. Rome's goal was to supplement its own food supply, which it did successfully for the next 100 years. It was estimated that as much as two hundred thousand tons of grain a year were shipped from Egypt and North Africa to feed the million people in Rome (Montgomery, 2007). Supplies from North Africa were crucial because eventually the fields around Rome could not provide enough grain to feed the city.

Unfortunately, Rome had brought both imperial control as well as a complex set of agricultural theory and practices. Those unsustainable practices led to intensive cultivation of North African soils followed by rapid soil erosion. Effectively, Rome was repeating its agricultural mistakes in North Africa. The Roman town of Timgad, which had been settled in 100 CE, located in present-day Algeria, fell into ruin and had to be completely abandoned by 535 CE. The city held a 2,500-person theater and marble flush toilets. By the sixth century CE, very little existed in the surrounding desert landscape other than remnants of olive presses hinting at the former surplus of agricultural crops. Timgad was not unique. The Roman presence and its abandoned agricultural settlements litter the North African landscape from Algeria to Syria.

The Western Roman Empire commanded a presence across North Africa during the first century CE and beyond. However, the conflict over the most basic of natural resources, soil, left behind the carcass of the Carthaginian civilization and a graveyard of ruins from the once mighty Western Roman Empire. It would take many centuries for Italy to be repopulated but even today it is estimated the soil could not support as many people as it once had during the early years of the Roman golden age. Even today, North Africa is hardly a place we think of as an agricultural oasis of bountiful productivity. Instead, the urban ruins and denuded countryside of arid desert stand as fascinating signposts for long-ago, collapsed civilizations that fell from conflict over soil.

REFERENCE

Montgomery, D. R. (2007). *Dirt: The Erosion of Civilizations*. Berkeley: University of California Press.

FURTHER READING

Butzer, Karl W. (2012). "Collapse, environment, and society," *Proceedings of the National Academy of Science, 109*(10), 3632–3639. Accessed March 7, 2016, at http://www.pnas.org/content/109/10/3632.abstract.

Diamond, J. (2005). *Collapse: How Societies Choose to Fail or Succeed*. New York: Viking.

Good, David H., and Raphael Reuveny. (2009). "On the collapse of historical civilizations," *American Journal of Agricultural Economics 91*(4), 863–879. Accessed March 7, 2016, at http://ajae.oxfordjournals.org/content/91/4/863.

Tainter, J. (1988). *The Collapse of Complex Societies*. Cambridge, UK: Cambridge University Press.

3

AS THE WORLD'S POPULATION BECOMES MORE URBANIZED, HOW ARE CITIES BEING DESIGNED TO AVOID CONFLICTS?

OVERVIEW

Robin Morris Collin and Robert William Collin

As of 2015, the majority of the world's population lived in urban areas. That number grows by nearly 60 million each year and it's expected that by 2050, seven out of every ten people will live in cities. That many people living in a relatively small space can have a huge effect on the environment through resource depletion as well as pollution and even destruction of the environment. Sustainable urban initiatives, however, can mitigate some of those effects. For example, sustainable transportation initiatives such as the use of public transportation, walking, or riding bikes can reduce the impact to energy resources and reduce air pollution.

In the first essay on this question, Roman Cybriwsky, urban geographer at Temple University, guides us through three world cities (Copenhagen, Bogotá, and Singapore) to show how they are among the leaders in reducing the impact on their surrounding environments. In the second, he argues why and how, by focusing on transportation, Bogotá has emerged as the ideal model for the developing world.

Sustainable practices not only support the healthy use of natural resources and the survivability of the environment, they support the continuance of human life as well. Without a healthy environment, the quality of human life on the planet would be severely degraded at the very least. Without natural resources, human life couldn't exist.

BACKGROUND

Humans can comfortably live on only 20 percent of the Earth. Most live on land, between sea level and one mile in altitude. Fresh water, stable landmasses, and gentle climates are often the starting point of human habitation. By the year 2030, 60 percent of the world's population will be living in urban settlements—cities and towns. The majority of people will be living in less developed countries, and 84 percent of people living in developed countries will be living in cities.

Food insecurity is a major result of ecosystem degradation. Rural areas of poor countries are the most dependent on local ecosystems for food, but everyone is dependent on some ecosystem for food. Climate change greatly increases the risks to traditional agricultural production. Currently, the world population is slightly less than 6 billion people, with about 800 million overfed and 800 million underfed. Another 1 billion people are malnourished. With population increases, cumulative impacts on ecosystems from industrial agriculture and climate change, the threat to food security is increasing.

In many ecosystems, fresh water is in short supply. According to the Millennium Ecosystem Assessment, which was done at the request of the United Nations, more than 1 billion people do not have access to safe, fresh water. Only about 7 percent of the water on Earth is fresh water. Underground water supplies in aquifers usually become contaminated before they dry out, as chemicals and waste become more concentrated. Deaths from infectious diseases, caused by contaminated or unsafe water, account for about 6 percent of global deaths each year. This is about 1.8 million deaths a year, many of them small children. Fresh water is closely linked to quality of life and to economic development.

Air pollution from indoors and outdoors is beginning to erode ecosystems and public health in urban areas. In the United States, the average asthma rate is about 7 percent, but in urban areas like Portland, Oregon, it is about 14 percent in communities of color. In other countries indoor heating and cooking done with biofuels, like wood, unleash fine particles into the air that can create health hazards for those who breathe them in. Worldwide, about 3 percent of disease is attributed to indoor air pollution. Generally, the more concentrated the population, the more concentrated the pollution from this source. Increasing urbanization therefore increases the risk of air pollution-related diseases.

If biofuels are used for cooking and heating and those fuels become unavailable, then other health issues increase. Without the ability to keep warm or boil water or cook food thoroughly, other diseases take hold. In many countries, it is women's role to get the wood and the clean water used for cooking and cleaning. As forests are depleted, these women must walk farther and longer and lose time and the energy to resist disease, nurture children, tend crops, and attend school. Deforestation often leads to decreased water supply because the trees provide shade over water that slows evaporation and because the tree roots retain water and release it slowly.

As human populations increase and become more urbanized, threats from both naturally occurring poisons and human waste management practices increase. Some water sources may have high levels of natural, dangerous chemicals such as arsenic. In the push for fresh water, some of these sources may be tapped without adequate testing or purification. They may be used directly as drinking water or indirectly as irrigation water. They may also leech into another underground water source if that source becomes empty or low. Human sources of water contamination can result from pesticides that can linger in underground water systems long after their use.

Human societies greatly value culture and traditional practices. These vary enormously throughout the world. They include recreation, beauty, tourism, education, cultural preservation, and a sense of place. With ecosystem erosion, these values are also affected. In some cases, this can result in economic loss, in others losses of health quality. For example, fish have long been the center of the Japanese diet. In fact, Japan is the world's largest consumer and harvester of fish. The country has seen dramatically lower catch numbers over the last 20 years because fishermen have simply overfished Japan's waters. Japan must now depend on fish imports to make up for the shortfall, which has resulted in higher prices for consumers. Because of the depletion of Japan's fish supply, one of the country's main food sources is disappearing—the country's ecosystem loss has led to economic loss.

Food, water, energy, and culture are all affected by climate change. Fast changes can be disruptive to ecosystems. Rising ocean levels will cause salinization of fresh water supplies farther inland, and much of the world's urbanizing population is concentrated along a coast. Direct effects in the near future are most easily known, but indirect effects in the middle or distant future are less known. The lag time between human action and its effect on actual climate change is a major factor in the uncertainty. It is compounded by the lack of knowledge about direct and indirect impacts. Some facts are certain though. Human population growth in urbanized areas and poverty that is ignored will have negative impacts on global environmental systems.

Although this downward spiral is a serious challenge to sustainable development, there is opportunity for rapid reversal. Encouraging innovative approaches, from biking instead of driving whenever possible to creating new technologies to treat water, could be important steps toward reducing environmental degradation. Given the increasing population coupled with that population's growing desire to live in urban centers, and the fact that humans find only 20 percent of the planet fit for habitation, this is a high priority because ecosystem degradation will spread to global systems that affect everyone.

FURTHER READING

Kellogg, Scott T., and Stacy Pettigrew. (2008). *Toolbox for Sustainable City Living: A Do-It-Ourselves Guide*. Brooklyn, NY: South End Press.

Kidokoro, T., N. Harata, L. P. Subanu, J. Jessen, A. Motte, and E. P. Seltzer (eds.). (2008). *Sustainable City Regions: Space, Place and Governance*. New York: Springer.

Robertson, Melanie. (2012). *Sustainable Cities: Local Solutions in the Global South*. Ottawa, Canada: Practical Action Publishing.

COPENHAGEN, BOGOTÁ, AND SINGAPORE: THREE INSPIRING EXAMPLES OF SUSTAINABLE CITIES
Roman Adrian Cybriwsky

COPENHAGEN

European cities are generally recognized as world leaders in sustainable urban practices, and Copenhagen, the capital of Denmark, is a leader among the leaders. Like Stockholm, Oslo, Amsterdam, and other major cities in the region, Copenhagen has greatly reduced its impact on the environment with innovations in energy-efficient architecture and building techniques, reductions in carbon emissions and solid waste, and increased reliance on efficient and eco-friendly mass transit. However, the city stands out from the others as being extraordinarily bicycle friendly. Other Europeans use bicycles too, but in Copenhagen as many as one-half of people surveyed have reported that bicycling is their main means of transportation in the city, and nearly 40 percent of workers reported that it is their main way of commuting. This exceeds the total number of people who commute by bicycle in the entire United States. Indeed, we can say that this beautiful metropolis of nearly 2 million people is the bicycling capital of the world.

The popularity of bicycling in Copenhagen goes back to the late 19th century when it caught on as both a sport and a means of transportation. The first bicycle path opened in 1892 on Esplanaden, a waterside street in the urban center. Others

Copenhagen wind farm with harbor and lighthouse in the foreground, June 2009. (Tedholt/Dreamstime.com)

followed, especially in larger urban parks and along the shores of the city's prominent lakes. Before long, Copenhagen became Europe's—and the world's—biking leader. Biking's popularity continued to increase in the early 20th century, and in the 1930s, evolved as well into a spectator sport for both indoor and outdoor bike races. However, Denmark's prosperity after World War II and the rise of consumer society led to the rise of an automobile culture, and except for die-hard enthusiasts, biking fell by the wayside. As automobile ownership grew, street networks were built without bicyclists in mind, leading to a loss in biking's appeal and a loss of lives from car-bike accidents. By the 1970s, biking accounted for only 10 percent of transportation in the city. Danish cyclists took to painting white crosses on streets where bikers had died as a way to focus attention on the need to improve bicycle safety. The 1970s energy crisis hit Denmark especially hard, waking the public up once again to the possibility of cycling as an alternative, and eventually the city's bicycling culture was reborn.

Bicycling in Copenhagen benefits from the city's relatively flat terrain and high density of urbanization, meaning that distances people need to travel are often short and easy to negotiate. The appeal of bicycling is also tied to continued energy shortages in Denmark and a high cost for gasoline and other fuels. In order to maximize bicycle safely, the city has constructed an efficient network of dedicated bicycle paths and bicycle lanes along city streets, and times traffic lights according to the flow of what are called "green waves" of bicycle traffic. Some bike lanes have been widened to three tracks to allow for what is called "conversational" biking. The utility of getting around by bicycle has been enhanced by integrating the mode with transportation by train and bus by allowing riders to bring their bikes on board or to attach them to specially designed racks on the outside. The city's taxis are required by law to carry bike racks, and using them costs passengers only a little extra in addition to the fare.

Every day, Copenhagen residents bicycle nearly three-quarters of a million miles, resulting in a much quieter city than one that depends on buses and automobiles, cleaner air, and a measurably healthier public. This, in turn, produces tangible benefits to the economy and considerable savings in healthcare costs. Even the mail is delivered in Copenhagen by bicycle. There are also many bicycle rickshaws and "velo taxis" in the city, as well as quite a few bicycle rental shops and public bike-share systems that locals and visitors can use. In fact, bicycling is the recommended way for tourists to see the sights of Copenhagen. The city also has many bicycle messengers, as well as various vendors of coffee, ice cream, and other products that operate from what are known as cargo bikes. Furthermore, policing in Copenhagen employs bicycles as a fast and efficient way to patrol neighborhoods, and to enhance both visibility and contact with neighbors. Another benefit is that the design and manufacture of high-end bicycles has come to be a significant part of Copenhagen's economy. The down side, however, is that the city never seems to have enough parking spaces for bicycles, and that key street interchanges and popular shopping districts are chronically overcrowded with too many bicycles. Therefore, it sometimes becomes necessary for police to round up carelessly parked bikes and haul them away by truck.

BOGOTÁ

Bogotá is the capital of Colombia and, with a population of more than 7 million, one of the major metropolises of South America. Historically, the city was a prominent Spanish colonial capital and a center of Colombia's struggle for independence. As it grew, it prospered from the rich coffee production of the Colombian highlands. However, in the latter decades of the 20th century the city developed a reputation as one of the world's most dangerous urban areas, with high crime rates tied to violent gangs and narcotics trafficking. The situation is now much improved, due in significant part to an effective community-based policing system called Communidad Segura, or "Safe Community." Consequently, Bogotá is now considered much more favorably around the world, and has come to be known as a leader, especially in the developing world, of sustainable urban practices. Its most impressive achievements have been in urban transportation.

Like many fast-growing large cities, 20th-century Bogotá came to be choked by the automobile. A pall of air pollution hung over the metropolis and traffic on an inadequate street network became so congested that commuting became a nightmare. Enter new mayor Enrique Peñalosa in 1998, with an inspired plan for making things better. Instead of focusing on construction of superhighways and widening roads to ease traffic flow, as many cities have done to end congestion, Peñalosa's strategy was to discourage automobile use through a three-pronged approach: (1) the introduction of very specific restrictions on automobile usage in the city, (2) construction of an innovative new mass transit system, and (3) successfully turning Bogotá into a bicycle-friendly city.

The motor vehicle restrictions, called *pico y placa* (peak and [license] plate), regulate access to key streets during morning and evening commuter rush periods according to day of the week and the last digit of a car's license plate. This forces automobile owners to take alternative transportation on days that they are not permitted to drive. Once they do this, many drivers stay with the alternative travel mode even on days they could drive.

The new mass transit system is called TransMilenio. It is an integrated bus network that consists of large busses that move rapidly on dedicated "busways" along major streets, and smaller feeder buses and minivans called *colectivo* that operate in residential neighborhoods to bring passengers to major stops along the busways. Passengers are allowed to make transfers from bus to bus for a single fare. The larger buses are articulated, meaning that they are longer than normal buses and can bend at a central pivot, allowing for sharper turns.

The new bicycle network employs safe bicycle paths that have been constructed in the city, as well as dedicated bicycle lanes along major roads that have replaced thousands of curbside parking spaces. These dedicated bike lanes are called *ciclorrutas*. They now total more than 234 miles and serve as many as 400,000 riders each day. On Sundays, many of Bogotá's major streets are closed to motor vehicles altogether and are given to pedestrians and bicyclists. These *Ciclovía* Sundays, as they are known, are a further way to increase interest in bicycling among the public as an alternative to automobiles. As a result, the city has become noticeably quieter, the air is cleaner, and citizens benefit from good exercise. A side benefit is that many residents of Bogotá have gotten to know their city better, which in turn increases civic-mindedness and feelings of neighborliness between different communities.

Peñalosa's plans faced resistance from the beginning from some of Bogotá's wealthy elite residents and powerful business interests. The rich were accustomed to getting around the city in isolation in air-conditioned vehicles and were in no mood to switch to busses or bikes. In fact, some residents who could afford to do so actually purchased second automobiles with different license plate numbers in order to be able to drive every day. Bogotá's elites were also unhappy that the mayor had proposed to purchase a private country club where they were members in order to expand the city's public parkland. As a result of such opposition, Peñalosa was not reelected for a second term as mayor. However, the improvements to transportation that he initiated have not only survived but have grown. After long delays about funding and design, the city is now constructing its first-ever subway system, the Bogotá Metro. The first line will be nearly 15 miles long and have 27 stations. It is expected to start operations in 2019.

SINGAPORE

Singapore is a small city-state on an island off the southern tip of the Malay Peninsula in Southeast Asia. Its nearest neighbors are the country of Malaysia across a narrow strait to the north, and various small islands to the south belonging to Indonesia that can be seen on clear days from Singapore's tall buildings. Singapore covers only 274.1 square miles, but has a population that has grown to more than 5.4 million, resulting in one of the highest population densities of any country in the world. Although space is limited, Singapore has achieved one of the most advanced and highly educated societies in the world, an extremely high standard of living, and a disproportionately large economic impact both within its region and globally. However, because it is an island completely surrounded by seawater, and the catchment area for rainfall is so small, Singapore has always struggled to supply the population with fresh water. Yet, here too Singapore has succeeded admirably: despite the obstacles, this small, crowded country is a world leader in being able to provide its citizens (and the millions of foreign visitors who travel to this popular tourism and business destination each year) with a dependable supply of high-quality fresh water at affordable cost.

The history of Singapore's water works begins when the island was under British control with the 1868 containment of water from an earthen embankment to create the MacRitchie Reservoir. Other reservoirs were created in 1910 and 1940, also during British rule. In 1932 a pipeline was completed to transport fresh water to Singapore along a causeway across the strait from British Malaya, the predecessor of today's Malaysia. After the colonial period, there were tensions in the 1960s between Singapore and Malaysia, and it became clear that the newly independent city-state needed a water supply of its own. Therefore, Singapore's first prime minister, the greatly influential Lee Kuan Yew, made it a personal priority to achieve this.

Today, providing fresh water for Singapore begins with effective land-use planning. The government carefully controls where urban development is allowed in order to maximize open space and ground water conservation. It also conserves rainwater runoff and adds that water to its inventory of available supply. As was started under the British, much of the undeveloped land in Singapore has been engineered into an expanding network of reservoirs that retain the island's rainfall before it flows into the sea. The largest is the Marina Bay Reservoir near the city's downtown. It opened in 2008 in an estuary of a small river, and is bounded by a specially constructed barrage to keep out salt water. The city also adds to its water inventory by de-salting seawater, which now produces about 10 percent of the supply, although that is a costly, energy-consuming project. There is also continuation of water imports from Malaysia, but that country has been asking much higher prices in recent contract negotiations, causing Singapore to redouble its commitment to water independence.

Perhaps the most remarkable aspect of Singapore's water program is reclamation of wastewater, including sewage, into a high-grade water that is not only good for gardening, swimming pools, and industrial uses, but also is perfectly safe to drink. Known by the brand name NEWater, the recycled water was engineered locally and is a product of Singapore's highly educated population and leading-edge technologies. It is produced in four new treatment plants via four complementary and mutually reinforcing barriers of advanced membrane technologies and ultra-violet disinfection. The treatment plants have a total capacity of about 20 million U.S. gallons per day, and currently account for about 30 percent of local needs. The treatment plant, in a district called Bedok, has a visitors' center that allows residents to learn the details of the reclamation process. Despite being perfectly potable, most NEWater goes for industrial uses. There was initial skepticism among the public about drinking water that once ran in toilets, but those doubts have now passed as the public has become used to the idea and trusts it. The public relations campaign to promote NEWater makes use of a mascot named Water Wally, a smiling blue water droplet that encourages Singaporeans to conserve water by repairing leaky taps and keeping showers short. Plans are to make more than one-half of Singapore's water come from such recycling. Not surprisingly, Singapore has emerged as one of the world's leading centers for research about water technology, conservation, and safety.

MAKING SUSTAINABLE CITIES—THE NEED TO FOCUS ON TRANSPORTATION
Roman Adrian Cybriwsky

As I showed in my previous essay, we have three very different cities in distant and disparate parts of the world, and comparing their various approaches to sustainability is a bit like comparing apples and oranges. All three offer excellent examples of successful practices in urban sustainability. Nevertheless, we can argue that the sustainable urban initiatives we have described for Bogotá, Colombia will have the greatest long-term success and the greatest potential impact for other cities around the world.

The Bogotá experience is compelling because it shows a way for hundreds of other, similar cities to become more sustainable. The greatest rates of urbanization are taking place now in developing countries such as Colombia, and there are countless cities across Asia, Africa, and Latin America that are bursting with new residents transplanted from poor rural areas. There is also an explosion in these cities of automobile use by a rising middle class, creating added pressures on the planet's limited energy supplies and increasing pollutants into the atmosphere that feed global warming. If these cities choke on the traffic and pollution they create, then economic development will stall and people will stay poor. Many cities in the United States, Western Europe, and other places in the developed world learned these lessons the hard way, and are now struggling to wean themselves from fossil fuels and automobile lifestyles. Cities in the developing world can benefit from those lessons and turn, as Bogotá has admirably done, to a future with fewer cars and more transportation alternatives for more citizens.

Among the many reasons why the poor are often trapped in poverty for generation after generation in cities around the world is a geographical mismatch between those parts of the city where they live and those parts of the city with concentrations of jobs and economic opportunity. It makes sense, then, to finds ways to reduce this disadvantage, even while other causes of poverty are more complicated and difficult to address. Around the world, the basic geography of cities is one in which people with wealth and power live convenient to the centers of economy and government they command, either by virtue of short distances or by easy commuting by rail, private automobiles, or other means. In the cities of the developing world by contrast, including in the sprawling metropolis of Bogotá, poor people's communities generally are found at the urban border, some distance from the city core and better neighborhoods. Many of them are so-called squatter settlements: neighborhoods that newly arrived poor migrants from the countryside have built at the urban edge because the city's housing market is unaffordable for them and because, as poor people, they are not especially wanted. Thus, an additional feature of typical urban geography (in rich countries and poor countries alike) is limited interaction between rich and poor. Without good transportation links, a city's poor areas will be destined to remain poor and any goals for social integration will be doomed to failure. Dependable low-cost, efficient bus service, as well as a safe way to commute moderate distances by bicycle, levels the field of urban opportunity and gives poor people a better chance to find a place in the city's economy.

In restructuring urban space against the automobile rather than for it, Bogotá has provided the power of mobility to countless lower-income residents and enabled them to compete more effectively for toeholds in the city's prosperity. All but the poorest can afford the inexpensive new TranMilenio system to get around the city, while many other residents make use of the city's new *ciclorrutas*, and commute by bicycle. As a side benefit, they also improve their health and ride as equals with people of all classes. The Bogotá Metro that is under construction will also help conquer the disadvantages of geographical marginalization. So far, the

TransMilenio system and the new bicycle lanes do not reach most of the distant squatter settlements, so the benefits of better transportation are not yet universal. But the network is expanding, and now serves areas of Bogotá that had previously been isolated. There is room in the city transportation plan, too, for the automobile, so Bogotá is wisely offering a range of transportation alternatives. What is most important is that the transportation needs of the urban poor are being taken seriously in Bogotá, and that the city is becoming a shining example of social inclusion and environmental sustainability in transportation planning in developing countries.

The sustainability initiatives that we have described for Copenhagen and Singapore are very impressive too. In fact, both cities have transportation systems that are far superior to those in Bogotá, including better mass transit, bicycling, and roadways for private automobiles. Both cities also provide fresh water to their respective populations more successfully than Bogotá, and both cities have admirable programs to help the minority of their citizens who are needy. But both Copenhagen and Singapore are in very wealthy countries and have many more resources to work with than a city like Bogotá that is in a developing country with a very large poor population and a history of excessive privilege by the richest few. Therefore, we single out Bogotá from among the three cities precisely because of forward thinking about the relationships between the problems of social inequality and the problems of urban traffic congestion and accessibility. Bogotá is showing ways for countless other cities around the world to cope with the same problems, while Copenhagen and Singapore are being shown by the Bogotá experience how some of the foreign aid monies that their respective countries spend generously around the world can be used to simultaneously meet social and environmental goals.

4

How Have Global Warming and Climate Change Promoted Conflict in Pastoral Communities?

OVERVIEW
Troy Sternberg

Contemporary pastoral livelihoods are in a period of great transition. The world's 200 million pastoralists represent expanding populations, diverse development trajectories, inconsistent government support, and often encounter both direct and de facto efforts to settle. Pastoralism features in arid and semi-arid regions where mobility, ecological knowledge and seasonal pastures provide effective management of environmental risk. Today endemic physical threats—drought, plant growth, water, temperature (hot and cold), and precipitation patterns are exacerbated by climate change and global warming—new factors that disrupt livelihoods and can contribute to conflict in pastoral communities.

BACKGROUND

Customary herding livelihoods are predominantly located in an arc from Africa through the Middle East, South and East Asia, as well as parts of Australia and the highlands of South America. Pastoral communities depend on the natural landscape as animals efficiently convert limited ecological productivity into sustenance. Access to open rangeland and movement based on pasture condition, weather and seasonality are key features of pastoralism. Thus changes to the environment affect animals and challenge livelihoods. Climate directly impacts the land, water and vegetation resources herders use. The Intergovernmental Panel on Climate Change projects warming temperatures, precipitation variability, and more intense climate events in several arid and semi-arid regions pastoralists inhabit. Changes in climate alter pastoralism as herders search for new lands, alternate water sources and use less-palatable plant species for their animals. This process involves seeking access to larger pastures, competition for finite resources, shifts in types of animals raised, and greater household expenses that are driven by the cost of migration, emergency fodder, and acquiring access rights to pasture.

From afar the image of pastoralists is often of a nomad crossing the steppe or sand on horseback, a rugged individual recalling past lifestyles. The reality is more nuanced as herders deal with the needs of animals, household demands, and the pressures of climate, ecology, and water. Economics, government, and human engagement represent external forces in herders' lives and make pastoralists active members of society. As climate alters physical and environmental boundaries, pastoralists come into competition with both other herders and divergent land uses such as agriculture, resource extraction, and urbanization. The result can be several diverse groups interested in and claiming access to land, including farmers, miners, settlements, and developers. This can lead to conflict over land use and highlights the role of policy and governance in defining and implementing forms of land tenure. Enforcement of civic norms and laws can be through traditional methods (e.g., families, tribes, communities), economic factors (e.g., land ownership, user fees, profit motives, subsidies) and government representatives (e.g., rangers, police, army).

By their nature competing land uses are difficult to integrate. Herder needs directly conflict with farmers' cultivation, fencing and intensive water use. Resource extraction, particularly mining (e.g., coal, copper, gold, oil), is common in arid areas and requires infrastructure, such as pipelines, roads, and deep wells that intensively consume resources and disrupt pastoral patterns. The expansion of settlements, development and urbanization, and related growing populations further reduces open areas suitable for herding. The environmental exposure of herders means that changes instigated by climate often contribute to disputes over contested land.

Pastoralism is practiced in marginal environments often with no fixed abode and outside conventional state engagement and control. The large number of farmers, the wealth generated by mining, and pressing needs of towns and cities sideline the pastoral voice and constrain their political rights and engagement with national governments. Added to this are common herder differences of culture, tribe, landscape, language, and religion (e.g., Tuaregs, Tibetans, Bedouin) that may see them disadvantaged vis-à-vis other social groups. Lack of power in autocratic states (e.g., China, Syria, Oman, Sudan) and a lack of numbers in democracies (e.g., Botswana, Israel) further restrict herders' rights and power.

Against this background climate and global warming act as instigators and threat multipliers in pastoral communities. First, there is greater competition between herders for physical resources. More animals drinking at a well or grazing one pasture can lead to land degradation. With livelihoods at stake, conflict can arise, such as those seen in 2014 between herding groups in South Sudan and between herders and the state in Syria. At the next level are clashes with farmers over access to land. In years with good productivity farmers may expand cultivation in dry areas that are often traditional herding pastures. This affects the rangeland as tilling the soil uproots the natural vegetation and reduces forbs and grasses animals depend on. Water is used at a greater rate and even rudimentary roads, buildings, and fences reduce available rangeland as the human footprint increases. In dry years, if farmers retreat, the land conversion has already diminished pasture quality.

A third level of conflict is with resource extraction. This can reflect individuals (including herders) prospecting for gold (Mongolia, West Africa), small to medium scale operations (most countries) and large governments (e.g., China, Kazakhstan, Saudi Arabia) or international corporations (e.g., Rio Tinto, BHP, Chinalco). Mining alters the land surface, is known to pollute and divert water sources, and requires land rehabilitation to regain productivity, a process seldom undertaken in developing nations. At the small scale, this may mean streams and wells become unusable for herders, pasture is dug up, and money and labor are unavailable for herding. At larger scales the scope of land change resulting from mechanized extractive methods and mineral processing can be significant. The perceived power and money of mining interests is great compared to herders; their presence receives government support because of the tax income mining generates.

In isolation herders cope with climate change through their ecological knowledge, traditional skills, movement, and changes in both animal composition and herding practices. However, in today's interconnected world pastoralists are seldom as remote as in the past. Changing climates and global warming result in herding transition and frequent contact and engagement with settled populations, which at times may include former herders, conflict comes when divergent and conflicting lifestyles force interaction and competition. Open range and supportive policies can help mitigate the impact of climate change on pastoralists. More common is state encouragement of larger, more powerful groups and their desired land uses. In the 21st century, global warming and climate change stress and threaten pastoral communities. As a result climate-driven conflict will be a major challenge to millennia-old pastoral livelihood patterns.

FURTHER READING

Catley, Andy, Jeremy Lind, and Ian Scoones. (2013). *Pastoralism and Development in Africa: Dynamic Change at the Margins*. London: Routledge.

Kreutzmann, Hermann. (2012). *Pastoral Practices in High Asia: Agency of "Development" Affected by Modernisation, Resettlement and Transformation*. Dordrecht, Netherlands, and New York: Springer.

Parry, Martin, Osvaldo Canziani, Jean Palutikof, Paul van der Linden, and Clair Hanson. (2007). *Climate Change 2007: Impacts, Adaptation and Vulnerability: Working Group II Contribution to the Fourth Assessment Report of the Intergovernmental Panel on Climate Change*. Cambridge, UK: Cambridge University Press.

MONGOLIAN PASTORALISM, CLIMATE CHANGE, AND CONFLICT
Ariell Ahearn and Troy Sternberg

Pastoralists' intricate relationship with nature and the environment places climate at the center of herder lives in Mongolia. Climate patterns and physical factors such as the quality of water sources and pasture vegetation shape herder strategies for raising small and large livestock breeds, where mobility is a key factor. Extreme temperatures (from below 0°C to 40°C), variable precipitation, snow and ice, and storms comprise challenges for pastoralist livelihoods, on which one-third of the population depends. Thus as climate patterns change in the context of Mongolia's political economic system, herder households are affected and often disrupted. In extreme climate events, such as the 2009–2010 winter disaster, the unmitigated climatic risks lead to high livestock mortality, loss of livelihoods, health concerns, and food scarcity in rural areas. Climate conditions also contribute to competition and conflict over resources such as land, water, and services, both between pastoralists and between herders and other groups, such as miners and rural governments.

In the dry, remote Gobi-Steppe territories of Bayanhongor Province in central west Mongolia, an 85-year-old monk, who was formerly employed as a horse herder for a livestock collective in socialist Mongolia, related to us the following information about his region:

> In old times . . . we didn't have stable residential places. Since Mongolians are nomads we used to move around a lot. Each family had moved to a new area in each season—four areas for four seasons. This helped us to have healthy animals and keep nature in balance. We didn't have any problems with a lack of pasture. Also, another issue is the goatherds. The number of

goats increased rapidly due to the high increase in the cashmere price. They prevent grasses from growing nutritiously because they eat the roots. Secondly, is the issue of rain. It's not raining during the scheduled time. Now it rains after long sunny days.

The old man touched on a number of issues that are adversely affecting pastoral husbandry, including observed climate change, reduction in seasonal grazing and browsing territories, reduced access and freedom of movement, an unsustainable increase in the size of herds, and the growing presence and scale of mining. Collectively, these issues are linked with the rapid changes in Mongolian governance and society since the transition to a market economy in the early 1990s. Mongolian herders today are often caught in such contradictory positions as maintaining their pastoral traditions and managing investments in education, property, and other resources that are embedded in unfamiliar, urban institutions. The situation has been made more difficult and tense in the context of an extreme, changeable, and more unpredictable climate and environment.

Vegetation growth, groundwater levels, and access depend on highly variable precipitation in the arid region (50–400mm annually). Conflict over water and other pasture resources is acute in the Gobi, particularly around mining sites, where aquifers are tapped to accommodate large-scale extraction processes. The issue of systemic risk or negative feedback cycles becomes more apparent as herders become less financially secure and increasingly reliant on cashmere goats, which have the potential to further degrade pasture if their increased numbers are not accompanied by increased mobility. Lack of water may create conflict between herder households, especially as it relates to securing use rights to winter shelters through the new private property systems. These conflicts are more apparent in the Gobi region, where cashmere goats comprise a larger portion of the herd stock, large-scale mining operations are ongoing, and the lack of water combined with the frequent extreme winter weather events (which the locals call *dzud*) contribute to the risk households need to manage.

The conflicts between herders and mining enterprises have taken a variety of forms. In cases reported by environmental rangers in Bayanhongor province, former or current herders who temporarily migrate from adjacent counties have been illegally scouring pastureland for precious stones or gold using shovels and metal detectors. The systematic digging up of pasture by these opportunistic "miners," who themselves may have lost herds in *dzud* disasters or are in need of cash, has created serious conflicts between authorities and local herders as valuable pasture land continues to be degraded. At the other end of the spectrum, the mining industry has occupied, legitimately and illegitimately, herder's traditional pastureland claiming both the land and water rights for private use. For example, the Rio Tinto joint-mining venture at the Oyu Tolgoi site in the Gobi has staked out land once used as a commons for livestock grazing. The loss of pastureland, the noise and pollution such mining entails, the depletion of water, as well as the presence of foreign labor has created animosity and conflict.

The fundamental conflict that Mongolian pastoral society faces is framed by how climate change and the resulting new, unpredictable weather regime affect the ability to raise animals in a transitioning society. This was exemplified by the great hardship caused by the "worst ever" 2009–2010 winter *dzud* disaster in which 25 percent of the country's animals died. Dynamic social issues stress pastoralism as herders contend with labor shortages and a sense of uncertainty created by unstable currency regimes and fluctuating market prices for basic goods such as meat, dairy products, flour, rice, and cashmere. With a dearth of social services available in the countryside, rural households are often divided between urban and rural sites as members work to access and invest in resources such as education, technology, private property in settled districts as well as seasonal campsites, wage labor, and urban networks. These investments may be interpreted as a way to establish secure households in a complex physical and institutional environment, or may represent an everyday "triage" or mitigation of uncertainty. Nonetheless, it is apparent that Mongolian herders historically have an aptitude to contend with the conflict in their lives with skill and resilience. It is yet to be seen to what extent the Mongolian government will be able to establish the necessary sovereignty over its resources to effectively act as a stabilizing institutional force rather than another source of potential instability.

CONFLICT IN SYRIA—PASTORAL COMMUNITIES AND GLOBAL WARMING
Troy Sternberg

Pastoralism has been an integral part of Syria and the greater Fertile Crescent for millennia. Practiced by Bedouin and related tribes, herding animals has been an effective way to turn the desert's scarcity into productive livelihoods. In the past the ability to move, knowledge of the local environment, adaptive skills, and a thorough understanding of climate created strong pastoral communities. More recently, climate change and global warming have seriously affected pastoral livelihoods and contributed directly to social unrest and conflict. Concurrently there have been significant transformations in Syrian society, governance and land use that have significantly affected pastoral viability. The process began during World War I with the T. E. Lawrence-inspired *Revolt in the Desert* (1927) that resulted in maps being redrawn and the establishment of the Syrian nation based in the ancient city of Damascus. Once free-ranging pastoralism had been affected as the state grew in strength and control, agriculture was encouraged and borders, previously viewed as shifting lines in the sand by herders, solidified and animal movement was restricted. As a minority of the population and lacking political power, pastoralists lost influence and official support. This impacted herders' ability to continue traditional livelihood strategies and increased their exposure to weather events. When extreme drought hit in the late 2000s, herders were unable to cope with the disaster. The roots of the ongoing civil war (as of 2014) can be directly related to the long-term drought and resultant food insecurity, poverty, and out-migration from pastoral communities in northeastern Syria and surrounding regions.

The *Badia*, the local name for the northern Arabian desert, traces present sheep-herding tribes back to the 14th century with these groups later joined by long-distance camel herders (Chatty, 2014). As the Ottoman Empire drew to a close in the 20th century, politics and power structures gained importance when an independent Arab state was established. The transition away from a predominantly pastoral society began when the French set up semi-autonomous regions in the *Badia* in the 1920s. In the 1950s, the Syrian government made efforts to break tribal associations and educate the "wild" communities to be good citizens. This included abolishing tribal privileges and settling the Bedouin pastoralists who currently make up approximately 10 percent of the population. The result has been an ongoing struggle between the central government and tribal leaders that has resulted in the marginalisation of pastoralism in society.

Recent pastoral challenges in Syria have been exacerbated by the changing climate, politics, and governance. Since 1970, competition between social groups and tribes saw the minority Alawite government of President Assad (both father and son) neglect the plight of pastoral communities in rural areas such as the *Badia*. At the same time policy favored farming over herding, investment in extensive irrigation in arid regions, and settlement that resulted in water shortages, land degradation, and restrictions on herder movement. Expanding populations led to increased livestock numbers and compounded resource and livelihood stress. As a result of fragmented land use and overexploitation of natural resources, herder vulnerability to climate hazards and global warming intensified, culminating in a series of events that contributed to civil war.

From 2007 to 2011 severe drought covered much of Syria; in 2008, 97 percent of the country's vegetation was damaged (Erian, 2010). While drought is a recurring hazard, the multi-year event threatened herding viability as the lack of precipitation impacted pastoralists by reducing the natural resources animals depend on. This included less vegetation for animal fodder, reduced water supply, weakened livestock and high evapotranspiration rates (reflecting moisture loss) that contributed to competition for rangeland and thus overgrazing and conflict between herders and farmers for water and land access. The outcome was high animal mortality as 85 percent of livestock in the northeast region died, 75 percent of crops failed, and 1.5 million people were displaced from pastoral and agricultural regions. Up to 3 million people, 13 percent of the country's population, were affected (Em-Dat, 2014; Sternberg et al., 2014). As animals died in great numbers herders lost their livelihoods which led to out-migration to cities in search of work.

Globally drought is the most damaging natural hazard, leading to great human and economic costs; in Asia alone drought has contributed to 9.6 million deaths and affected 1.7 billion people since 1900 (Em-Dat, 2014). Against this background, it is not surprising to see the 2007–2011 drought's severe impact in Syria. In addition to the environmental crisis the drought had stark social implications. The striking outcome was the relocation of formerly independent pastoralists from the *Badia* to slums in and around Syrian cities such as Dara'a and Homs. A lack of jobs, negligible state support, and little recognition by the government of the problems internal refugees faced led to high poverty rates and fuelled discontent and unrest amongst displaced migrants. The combination of existing political tension and perceived inequalities, dissatisfied new urban populations, and disaffected rural communities contributed to an opposition movement, then protest and civil unrest spurred by notions of the Arab Spring emerging across the Middle East. The direct link between climate and conflict helped ignite Syria's civil war and saw the traditionally well-armed Bedouin tribesman drawn into the civil conflict.

The years of fighting in the *Badia* have greatly stressed pastoral livelihoods as herders became insurgents and fighters. This process shrank the rural labor force, made herding dangerous, and emptied the countryside, resulting in fewer animals, food scarcity, and further outmigration from pastoral areas. As of July 2014, the stark number of 9 million Syrian refugees included more than 6 million internally displaced people and more than 2.5 million refugees, predominantly located in Turkey, Jordan, Lebanon, and Iraq (EU, 2014). As the conflict shows little sign of resolution the role of climate change and ineffective governance in disrupting pastoralism becomes clear. The Assad government's inability, disinterest, or inept approach to dealing with the drought and climate-induced disaster in rural Syria was a key part of the equation that has led to civil war in the country. Events in Syria paint a dismal picture of the direct link between climate, global warming, and conflict. The nexus reflects the breakdown of traditional pastoralism, evolving climate patterns and government failure as the interaction between the state and pastoralists in Syria has collapsed.

REFERENCES

Chatty, Dawn. (2014). "Syrian tribes, national politics and the uprising." Accessed February 29, 2016, at dawnchatty.wordpress.com.

Em-Dat. (2014). The International Disaster Database. Accessed February 29, 2016, at www.emdat.be.

Erian, Wadid, Amjad Abbashar, and Luna Abo-Swaireh. (2010). *Drought Vulnerability in the Arab Region, Special Case Study: Syria, Ten Years of Scarce Water (2000–2010).* Geneva: U.N. International Strategy for Disaster Risk Reduction.

European Union. (2014). "Syrian Refugees: A Snapshot of the Crisis—in the Middle East and Europe." Accessed February 29, 2016, at syrianrefugees.eu/.

Femia, Francesca, Troy Sternberg, and Caitlin E. Werrell. (2014). *Climate Hazards, Security and the Arab Uprisings.* Eastbourne: Sussex Academic Press.

Lawrence, T. E. (1927). *Revolt in the Desert.* New York: George H. Doran and Company.

5

WILL AIR QUALITY BE A SOURCE OF REGIONAL CONFLICT?

OVERVIEW
Mia Bennett

In summer 2013, Hong Kong's decision to place a panoramic backdrop of the city's famous skyline with blue skies made headlines around the world (Neuman, 2013). The backdrop was installed so that tourists could take photographs of themselves with a prettier sight than the constant smog-filled skies that bedevil the Asian metropolis and almost render the skyscrapers invisible. The story made news for its seeming ludicrousness, but it was also emblematic of the severe air pollution facing Hong Kong and many places around the world today.

The atmosphere consists of 78 percent nitrogen, 21 percent oxygen, 1 percent argon, small, varying amounts of water vapor, and 0.04 percent carbon dioxide and other trace gases. It is humans' addition of greenhouse gases, toxins, and other pollutants to the minute percentage of other trace gases, particularly since the Industrial Revolution, that has worsened air quality in many places, exerting dramatic tolls on human health and life. Although the air we breathe makes life possible, it can also in certain circumstances prove fatal. In 2014, the World Health Organization (WHO) determined that in 2012, 7 million deaths—one in eight globally—was linked to air pollution (WHO, 2014). Exposure to pollutants like soot, persistent free radicals, chlorofluorocarbons, and volatile organic compounds can lead to respiratory, cardiovascular, and dermatological diseases. The

WHO report went so far as to call air pollution "the world's largest single environmental health risk" (WHO, 2014).

BACKGROUND

There are four main sources of air pollution: mobile sources (e.g., automobiles, airplanes, and trucks), stationary sources (e.g., power plants, oil refineries, and factories), area sources at a range of scales (from wood-burning stoves to agriculture), and natural sources (e.g., volcanoes and wildfires) (National Park Service, 2013). The first three sources are all anthropogenic, in that humans are responsible for them. Still, not all societies share the burden of responsibility equally. While air pollution is diffuse and dispersed, it ultimately comes from specific sources on the ground. The possibility of being able to assign blame means that the possibility of regional and international conflict over air quality exists. Air pollution therefore poses not just environmental risks, but geopolitical ones, too. Unlike on the Earth's surface, where countries can erect fences and walls to demarcate their borders, no such lines can be drawn in the air. Problems associated with air quality therefore exemplify the type of border-crossing environmental problems facing societies in the 21st century.

There is a definite geography to air pollution, for some countries disproportionately emit certain types of pollutants into the atmosphere. Industrial economies such as the United States, Australia, and Canada, for instance, have many mobile and stationary sources of air pollution with millions of cars and numerous power plants. These types of countries regularly top the list of the world's largest greenhouse gas emitters despite efforts to reduce emissions. The pumping of carbon dioxide, a greenhouse gas, into the air is one of the main mechanisms driving climate change. Developing countries like China, India, and Indonesia also have an increasing number of automobiles, factories, and power plants, many of which still rely on coal, a "dirty" fuel that introduces large amounts of soot and carbon into the air. Even less developed countries still cause air pollution. In some countries in Africa and Eastern Europe, continued reliance on wood-burning stoves introduces large amounts of soot into the air, which can dramatically reduce air quality. Additionally, in many low- to middle-income countries like Brazil and Indonesia, forests are burned down to make room for agriculture and pasture—a strategy that may render the land clear but the air dirty for hundreds of miles around.

One of the primary challenges with tackling air pollution is that once pollutants and toxins enter the air, atmospheric currents can carry them far from the original emission site. As a result, some argue that air quality could cause regional conflicts. In the first essay, I examine three cases that show how air pollution is already straining international relations. In 1986, the Chernobyl incident sent radioactive material across 40 percent of Europe and even as far as China and North America (Yablokov and Nesterenko, 2009). Less dramatically but more regularly, every year forest fires in Indonesia lit to clear land blanket Singapore and Malaysia in smog. The problem was so severe in the summer of 2013 that a major diplomatic row erupted. Even when the problem of air pollution is more confined within a country's borders, as with China's poor air quality resulting from the factories and power plants often built right near cities, attempts by the U.S. embassy in Beijing to monitor and report air quality have caused a rift in relations, with Beijing perceiving the Americans to be hypocritical and meddlesome in what the Chinese view as a domestic issue.

On the other hand as the second essay on this question highlights, some argue that the diffuse nature of air quality is actually motivating countries to cooperate to find solutions. The ozone hole over Antarctica, which for years was growing larger due to pollutants like chlorofluorocarbons (CFCs) often found in old refrigerators, is now shrinking as a result of the 1987 Montreal Protocol. The multilateral treaty prohibited signatories from producing CFC-like compounds. Underscoring its success, former United Nations Secretary General Kofi Annan called the protocol the single most successful international agreement to date (U.S. Department of State, 2015). With the ozone hole decreasing in size, people in Australia have to worry less about sunburn and skin cancer, demonstrating the public health benefits of coordinated international action on air pollution. Despite the accomplishments of the Montreal Protocol, however, air pollution is a problem that requires collective action to tackle.

From space, the atmosphere may look like a giant, protective blanket encircling the Earth. Yet certain parts of it are more polluted than others, like the ozone hole over Antarctica and the thick smog over Beijing. There is thus an uneven geography to air pollution, but it is still a problem that does not discriminate based on borders. Big cities, small villages, rich countries, and poor ones all suffer from problems associated with poor air quality. The crosscutting, border-spanning nature of the issue means that solutions to improve air quality will require at the very least regional coordination, and at the most a global agreement when it comes to reducing greenhouse gas emissions. Without any sort of cooperation, conflict could very well emerge.

REFERENCES

National Park Service. (2013). "Where Does Air Pollution Come From?" Accessed February 26, 2016, at http://www.nature.nps.gov/air/AQBasics/sources.cfm.

Neuman, Scott. (2013). "Have Your Picture Taken with Hong Kong's (Smog-Free) Skyline." *The Two-Way*. National Public Radio. Accessed May 1, 2015, at http://www.npr.org/blogs/thetwo-way/2013/08/29/216802749/have-your-picture-taken-with-hong-kongs-smog-free-skyline.

U.S. Department of State. (n.d.). "The Montreal Protocol on Substances that Deplete the Ozone Layer." Accessed May 1, 2015, at http://www.state.gov/e/oes/eqt/chemicalpollution/83007.htm.

World Health Organization. (2014, March 25). "7 Million Premature Deaths Annually Linked to Air Pollution." Accessed May 1, 2015, at http://www.who.int/mediacentre/news/releases/2014/air-pollution/en/.

Yablokov, Alexey V., and Vassily B. Nesterenko. (2009). "1. Chernobyl contamination through time and space," in Alexey V. Yablokov, Vassily B. Nesterenko, Alexey V. Nesterenko (eds.)., *Chernobyl: Consequences of the Catastrophe for People and the Environment*. Volume 1181. New York: Annals of the New York Academy of Sciences.

FURTHER READING

Phalen, Robert F. (2007). *The Particulate Air Pollution Controversy: A Case Study and Lessons Learned*. Boston: Kluwer Academic Publishers.

Sethi, Rajat. (2013). *Air Pollution: Sources, Prevention, and Health Effects*. Hauppauge, NY: Nova Science Publishers.

CONFLICTS AND AIR POLLUTION—THE FUTURE IS HERE
Mia Bennett

For those wondering whether air quality will be a source of regional conflict, the future is already here. Air pollution has been causing international disputes both regionally and globally for decades. Often an externality associated with industrial activities, air pollution can impact countries far beyond the original sites of emission. While a handful of treaties have been successful in both reducing international conflict and avoiding air pollution in the first place, many more conflicts have arisen and will likely come to the fore in the future as industrialization proceeds around the world.

In Central and Eastern Europe, "dirty industrialization" in the 1960s caused acid rain to fall over much of Europe, especially in Scandinavia, damaging their forests and water. Acid rain occurs when gases from fossil fuel combustion combine with water vapor to produce sulfuric and nitric acid. To combat this problem, 34 European countries signed the Long Range Transboundary Air Pollution Convention (LRTAPC) in 1979 in order to collectively reduce emissions (Braden and Shelley, 2014). Levels of sulfuric and nitric acid have since fallen significantly in Europe, and the treaty has been extended to include countries in North America and Asia (UNECE, 2015). According to the United Nations Economic Commission for Europe (UNECE), the convention was "the first international

Chernobyl Nuclear Power Plant in the town of Pripyat, in Ukraine. The catastrophic nuclear meltdown occurred on April 26, 1986. (Shutterstock)

legally binding instrument to deal with problems of air pollution on a broad regional basis" and has "served as a bridge between different political systems and as a factor of stability in years of political change" (UNECE, 2015). From this point of view, air pollution indirectly improved international relations in Cold War Europe by forcing countries to cooperate if they wanted to improve their environments.

While diplomatic efforts and binding treaties helped curtail acid rain in Europe and the LRTAPC is hailed as a victory for international cooperation, beginning in the 1980s the region has experienced massive de-industrialization. The end of the Cold War and the expansion of the EU has also ushered in an era of peace and cooperation. It is a different story in Asia, where industrialization and economic growth combined with political tensions makes air pollution a viable catalyst for conflict.

AIR POLLUTION IN ASIA

In November 2010, an air-quality monitoring device at the U.S. embassy in Beijing reached 755ppm—well above 500ppm, the supposed top of the scale. An embassy official tweeted that the air pollution had become "crazy bad" (Wong, 2015) before his message was deleted. The embassy reported similarly high levels in January 2013 with the more diplomatic reading of "Beyond Index." Aside from the Americans living in Beijing, the thick smog and haze that blanketed the Chinese capital that month did not directly affect the United States. Yet the United States still felt the need to issue data on Beijing's air quality, which a Chinese Foreign Ministry official in 2009 called "insulting." The Chinese government, keen to promote its policy of non-interference in other countries, was therefore offended when it perceived the United States to be meddling in its domestic affairs. No severe conflict erupted, but air quality—or lack thereof—has proven to be yet another bone of contention between the two superpowers.

Thousands of miles to the south of Beijing, yearly forest fires in Indonesia send plumes of smoke to neighboring Singapore, Malaysia, Brunei, and Thailand (Quah, 2002). The fires are set deliberately to clear land for agriculture and paper and palm oil plantations. In June 2013, smoke from the fires was so severe that it sparked a diplomatic row, which became known as the "haze crisis." Pollution in Singapore reached a record level of 371ppm, surpassing the "hazardous" classification. The Singaporean environment minister wrote, "no country or corporation has the right to pollute the air at the expense of Singaporeans' health and wellbeing" (Agence France-Presse, 2015). In response, Indonesia accused Singaporean and Malaysian companies of having started the fires on Sumatra and Borneo. While no armed conflicts erupted over the air pollution, the diplomatic dispute strained political and commercial relations in Southeast Asia that summer.

CHERNOBYL

Tensions over air pollution have occurred in Europe, too, despite existing treaties like the LRTAPC. This convention could not have prevented the catastrophic nuclear power plant accident at Chernobyl in 1986. The meltdown of the Soviet nuclear power plant in Ukraine sent large amounts of radionuclides such as iodine-131, caesium-134, caesium-137, and strontium-90 into the atmosphere. Wind patterns at the time of the meltdown caused Sweden and Finland to be greatly affected, with more than 5 percent of their territory accumulating high levels of caesium-137 contamination (Fairlie and Sumner, 2006). Scandinavian experts were some of the first to detect the radiation cloud, while the Soviets continued to deny the severity of the problem. Soon after the disaster, Soviet official Vitalii Churkin testified at a Senate subcommittee hearing, "It is my opinion that there was no real harm to other countries" (McConnell, 2011), a denial that angered many. Indeed, lack of transparency and acceptance of responsibility can be an enormous source of tension between countries dealing with air pollution, especially those on the receiving end.

The international tensions that resulted from Chernobyl disrupted more than just relations between national governments. It also affected people's relationship to the land, air, and water. Radionuclides carried by the northerly winds threatened the indigenous reindeer-herding Sami people of northern Scandinavia because their animals eat lichen, a plant that soaks up radiation like a sponge. The Sami were forced to confiscate much of their reindeer meat after Scandinavian governments introduced strict limits on permissible levels of radiation following Chernobyl. One reindeer herder noted, "This is not just a matter of economics but of who we are, how we live, how we are connected to our deer and each other" (Stephens, 1995).

Despite the attempts of countries such as Germany, which sought reparations for the incident but was rebuffed, the USSR did not have to pay for other countries' economic damages since the country did not belong to any international liability and compensation regime relating to nuclear damage (Schwartz, 2006). Even today, it is still hard for governments to obtain reparations from the country responsible for their air quality woes. So far, international conflict has been restricted to the exchange of hot air by diplomats for the most part, even in the worst instances like Chernobyl. But it is still conflict nonetheless.

CONCLUSION

As globalization and industrialization continue to expand, air pollution will seemingly worsen. Invariably this will create tensions within and between countries. So far, diplomatic efforts have succeeding in addressing some of the most pressing air pollution threats (e.g., ozone depletion, acid rain), effectively diffusing the potential for violent conflict. However, in regions such as Southeast and East Asia there is no legitimate transboundary mechanism for dealing with air pollution so conflict remains a distinct possibility. Further, at the global scale, though there have been numerous attempts to curtail greenhouse gas emissions (e.g., Kyoto Protocol, United Nations Framework on Climate Change), they have each in turn failed to reduce the amount and stem global warming. As the temperature of the Earth and sea levels rise, so too will tempers rise.

REFERENCES

Agence France-Presse (AFP). (2015, September 16). "Indonesia moves to stop forest fire pollution as haze grips Singapore," *The Guardian*. Accessed May 1, 2015, at http://www.theguardian.com/environment/2014/sep/16/indonesia-forest-fire-pollution-haze-singapore-palm-oil.

Braden, Kathleen E., and Fred M. Shelley. (2014). *Engaging Geopolitics*. New York: Routledge.

Fairlie, Ian, and David Sumner. (2006). *The Other Report on Chernobyl (TORCH)*. The Greens/European Free Alliance in the European Parliament. Accessed May 1, 2016, at http://www.greens-efa.eu/the-other-report-on-chernobyl-torch-206.html.

McConnell, Robert. (2011, April 26). "Remembering the Soviet response to Chernobyl," *The National Review*. Accessed May 1, 2015, at http://www.nationalreview.com/corner/265612/remembering-soviet-response-chornobyl-robert-mcconnell.

Quah, Euston. (2002). "Transboundary pollution in Southeast Asia: the Indonesian fires," *World Development, 30*(3), 429–441.

Schwartz, Julia A. (2006). "International nuclear third party liability law: the response to Chernobyl," *International Nuclear Law in the Post-Chernobyl Period*, 41–44. Accessed May 1, 2016, at https://www.oecd-nea.org/law/chernobyl/SCHWARTZ.pdf.

Stephens, Sharon (ed.). (1995). *Children and the Politics of Culture*. Princeton, NJ: Princeton University Press, 300.

United Nations Economic Commission for Europe (UNECE). (n.d.). "Environmental Policy: Air: Introduction." Accessed May 1, 2015, at http://www.unece.org/env/lrtap/30anniversary.html.

United Nations Economic Commission for Europe (UNECE). (n.d.). "The Convention: The 1979 Geneva Convention on Long-range Transboundary Pollution." Accessed May 1, 2015, at http://www.unece.org/fr/env/lrtap/lrtap_h1.html.

Wong, Edward. (2015, January 12). "On a scale of 1 to 500, Beijing's air quality tops 'crazy bad' at 755," *New York Times*. Accessed May 1, 2015, at http://www.nytimes.com/2013/01/13/science/earth/beijing-air-pollution-off-the-charts.html.

AIR QUALITY: HARDLY EVER A SOURCE OF REGIONAL CONFLICT

Bryan Comer

Severe air pollution episodes have made headlines throughout history. Perhaps the most famous air pollution episodes occurred in Donora, Pennsylvania, and London, England. First, in 1948, a three-day temperature inversion coupled with intense industrial air pollution resulted in the deaths of 20 people in Donora, Pennsylvania, and approximately 6,000 others became seriously ill (Bachmann, 2007; Franek and DeRose, 2003). Then, in 1952, more than 4,000 Londoners died from cardiac and respiratory problems during the "London Fog," when a five-day temperature inversion drove concentrations of air pollutants to unprecedented levels (Bachmann, 2007). We now know that total deaths were closer to 12,000 as people died from complications in the six months following the initial event (Griffin, 2007). More recently, consistently poor air quality in places like Beijing, China, remind us that the price of industrialization often includes exposing people to dangerous levels of air pollution. Decades of research have confirmed the link

A woman wears a face mask in the subway on October 8, 2014, in Beijing, China. (Fred Dufour/AFP/Getty Images)

between air pollution and serious human health problems including respiratory illnesses and premature death from lung cancer (Dockery et al., 1993; Pope et al., 2002). Air pollution also has negative environmental impacts and can damage crops, acidify lakes, and drive climate change. Unfortunately, air pollution can affect locations far from the emissions source as it is transported regionally or even across oceans (Birmili et al., 2010; Li et al., 2002). Despite the health and environmental impacts of air pollution, air quality rarely leads to regional conflict. In my view, there are two main reasons for this: (1) the true source of air pollution is difficult to identify; and (2) other types of environmental degradation overshadow the problems caused by poor air quality.

First, while the main sources of air pollution in the Donora and London episodes were industrial and residential fossil fuel combustion, the health consequences were localized and did not significantly impact their broader regions. Often the specific sources of regional air pollution are less obvious, especially when compared to other types of environmental degradation like poor water quality and water scarcity. "Airsheds" are dynamic and change with the climate, the season, and the weather, making it difficult to pinpoint consistent sources of air pollution. Also, while some forms of air pollution are visible (e.g., smoke and smog), other forms are not (e.g., carbon monoxide). The fact that air pollution can be invisible means it is often "out of sight, out of mind." While water pollution may be invisible in some cases, when pollution is discovered, its source is easier to identify since watersheds can be delineated more accurately than airsheds. This bounds the potential sources of pollution and degradation. When drinking-water supplies are polluted or water needed for agriculture is diverted by upstream neighbors, the source of the problem tends to be obvious and the consequences immediate. On the other hand, when air is polluted by upwind neighbors, the source of the problem is less obvious and the consequences may take years or decades to materialize. As the lag between cause and effect increases, it becomes harder to blame the "bad actors" creating the pollution, limiting air quality's ability to cause conflict.

Second, other types of environmental degradation may play a more direct role in generating conflict than air pollution. While it may be possible for air quality to be a source of regional conflict, access to other natural resources like arable land, timber, coal, oil, water, and even diamonds seem to have a stronger influence. Perhaps the most dramatic and disturbing example is the extraction of conflict resources like timber, minerals, and diamonds in Africa to fund the activities of rebel groups who perpetuate violent regional conflicts (Bannon and Collier, 2003). When these types of regional conflicts occur, there are often multiple (and intertwined) non-environmental and environmental causes. For example, what began as a struggle over water and land for cattle grazing in the embattled state of Jonglei, South Sudan devolved into violent ethnic conflict between the Lou Nuer and Murle groups: a shift from "resource-driven conflict to identity-driven conflict" (Yoshida, 2013). As another example, the 1967 Six-Day War, which has historically been viewed as an ethnic conflict between Arabs and Israelis over disputed territory in the West Bank, can also be viewed as a natural resources conflict over access to the Jordan River's fresh water supply (Asser, 2010).

Air quality degradation does not seem to cause similar regional conflicts. For instance, when it was discovered that air pollution from China was degrading air quality in Japan in 2013, it led Japanese "officials to consider international cooperation to deal with the problem" instead of causing conflict (Okudera, Hayashi, and Yoshioka, 2013, para 1). In fact, it seems that air pollution can lead to regional cooperation rather than conflict in many cases. In the United States, the Western Regional Air Partnership (2010) brings together states and tribes in the western United States to tackle common air quality problems. In Africa, the Air Pollution Information Network for Africa, coordinated by the Stockholm Environment Institute (2008), helps southern African countries collaborate on reducing regional air pollution. When we consider the threats to social and economic prosperity, or even survival itself, poor air quality is low on the list of concerns. The availability of land, timber, fuel, and water are often necessary ingredients to economic growth, but air cannot be extracted, cut down, bottled, or sold for economic gain. However, the long-term cumulative impact of air pollution (including climate change) has real social, economic, and environmental consequences that reduce well-being and quality-of-life.

Though poor air quality has been linked to human and environmental harms, it is rarely a source of regional conflict. I have argued that the difficulty of assigning blame to the sources of air pollution and the relative influence of other environmental drivers of conflict mediate air quality's ability to cause regional conflict. Even when air pollution is identified as a problem, it is often seen as a necessary evil or side effect of economic growth. Thus, people are willing to trade off long-term health consequences in favor of short-term economic prosperity. This is not to suggest air quality has been ignored or that steps have not been taken to curb regional air pollution. If history is any indication, air quality concerns are more likely to result in regional cooperation than conflict.

REFERENCES

Asser, Martin. (2010, September 2). "Obstacles to Arab-Israeli peace: water," *BBC News*. Accessed March 29, 2014, at http://www.bbc.com/news/world-middle-east-11101797.

Bachmann, John. (2007). "Will the circle be unbroken: a history of the U.S. national ambient air quality standards," *Journal of the Air & Waste Managment Association* 57, 652–697.

Bannon, Ian, and Paul Collier. (2003). *Natural Resources and Violent Conflict: Options and Actions*. Washington, DC: World Bank Publications.

Birmili, Wolfram, Tina Gobel, Andre Sonntag, Ludwig Ries, Ralf Sohmer, et al. (2010). "A case of transatlantic aerosol transport detected at the schneefernerhaus observatory (2650 m) on the northern edge of the Alps," *Meterologische Zeitschrift* 19(6), 591–600.

Dockery, Douglas W., C. Arden Pope III, Xiping Xu, John D. Spengler, et al. (1993). "An association between air pollution and mortality in six U.S. cities," *New England Journal of Medicine* 329, 1753–1759.

Franek, William, and Lou DeRose. (2003). *Principles and Practices of Air Pollution Control: Student Manual*, second edition. Research Triangle Park, NC: Air Pollution Training Institute.

Griffin, Roger D. (2007). *Principles of Air Quality Management*, second edition. Boca Raton, FL: Taylor & Francis.

Li, Qinbin, Daniel J. Jacob, Isabelle Bey, Paul I. Palmer, et al. (2002). "Transatlantic transport of pollution and its effects on surface ozone in Europe and North America," *Journal of Geophysical Research* 107, D13.

Okudera, Atsushi, Nozomu Hayashi, and Keiko Yoshioka. (2013, February 1). "Air pollution from China reaches Japan, other parts of Asia," *The Asahi Shibun*. Accessed March 31, 2014, at http://ajw.asahi.com/article/sci_tech/environment/AJ201302010087.

Pope, C. Arden, Richard T. Burnett, Michael J. Thun, Eugenia E. Calle, et al. (2002). "Lung cancer, cardiopulmonary mortality, and long-term exposure to fine particulate air pollution," *Journal of the American Medical Association* 287(9), 1132–1141.

Stockholm Environment Institute. (2008). "Regional Air Pollution in Developing Countries." Accessed March 30, 2014, at http://www.sei-international.org/rapidc/apina.htm.

Western Regional Air Partnership. (2010). "Welcome to the WRAP." Accessed March 31, 2014, at http://www.wrapair2.org/.

Yoshida, Yuki. (2013). "Interethnic conflict in Jonglei state, South Sudan: emerging ethnic hatred between the Lou Nuer and the Murle," *African Journal on Conflict Resolution,* *13*(2), 39–57.

6

WHAT ROLE DOES ECOTOURISM PLAY IN NATURAL RESOURCE CONFLICTS?

OVERVIEW
Barbara McNicol

The International Ecotourism Society defines ecotourism as responsible travel to natural areas that conserves the environment and improves the well-being of local people. Geoffrey Wall pronounced that "Ecotourism, under whatever definition, is an instigator of change" (Wall, 1996). Ecotourism is thought of as a non-extractive form of economic generation for a country. It is hailed as promoting alternative livelihoods different from the income-generating but extractive natural-resource initiatives of forestry, mining, ranching, or oil and gas production.

Much current study promotes the concept that ecotourism and extractive natural resource industries are polar opposites. One suggestion is that successful ecotourism activities either displace or are mutually exclusive of other natural resource activities. Bram Büscher and Veronica Davidov suggest that there exists an *ecotourism-extraction nexus* where the activities of ecotourism are compatible with extractive resources, especially mining or oil and gas production, and that these activities often take place side by side, sometimes supported by the same institutions (Büscher and Davidov, 2014).

BACKGROUND

Tourism geographers have come to view the ideal of ecotourism as having four conditions: (1) the experience is nature-based, (2) it has an educational component, (3) it is sustainable, and (4) its process contributes toward conservation of the natural land base and ecosystem in which it occurs. This final component, of incorporating conservation, implies the ability of the processes of ecotourism to achieve specific goals of conservation and sustainable tourism development. For example, contributing to local environmental management initiatives or paying fees to use an area that then contribute toward conservation goals, all meet this criteria.

At its simplest, this may mean that ecotourism activities will generate greater economic benefits than alternate forms of extractive natural resource use such as forestry or mining. In other words, ecotourism managers must balance economic profitability with ecological health and conservation of locally used natural resources. If conservation is not an outcome of the ecotourism process, then the ideal of ecotourism has not been achieved, and the land may be better used for other resource activities. At the same time, ecotourism may exist in co-operation with other natural resource uses, where non-extractive vs. extractive uses are not labeled as either "good" or "bad" but as economically appropriate for a specific land base. For example, a marine environment can be used for fish farming or shellfish production while it is still successfully supporting recreational activities such as kayaking or scuba diving. In the end, cooperation between different uses of natural resources becomes directly dependent upon communication between stakeholders and the implementation of effective knowledge and education programs.

To include all four conditions of ecotourism, especially sustainability and conservation, requires long-term planning and an understanding of critical or sensitive natural resources. In developing countries, communities continue to bear a disproportionate amount of the costs associated with conservation, especially those close to protected areas that are meant to protect biodiversity. These protected ecosystems are often in conflict with traditional community livelihoods where activities such as hunting, logging, and plant harvesting are seen as threats to pristine environments that bring in necessary regional and national tourist dollars. Ecotourism, however, is not about establishing control over natural resources and the people that use them. Economic growth and environmental conservation can be compatible and should become more compatible through the longer-term implementation of ecotourism initiatives.

In the end, tourism is a process that requires consideration of all natural resources. As a non-extractive activity, ecotourism is often in conflict with extractive resources of forestry, mining, and oil and gas production, to name a few.

However, it is often the large size of a tourism project or the intensive nature of the natural resource extraction that may be incompatible with community livelihoods. Not all ecotourism is "good tourism" and it is generally accepted that the only form of impact-free tourism is "no" tourism. All tourism will create some form of impacts, both positive and negative, but successful ecotourism will always ensure that the goal of ecological conservation is met. If successful environmental conservation is not the outcome, then there are alternative forms of natural resource use that may better fit the land base.

REFERENCES

Büscher, Bram, and Veronica Davidov. (2014). "The Ecotourism-Extraction Nexus," in Bram Büscher and Veronica Davidov (eds.), *The Ecotourism-Extraction Nexus, Political Economies and Rural Realities of (Un) Comfortable Bedfellows*. Routledge ISS Studies in Rural Livelihoods. London and New York: Routledge, 1–16.

Wall, Geoffrey. (1996). "Change, impacts and opportunities," in Joseph A. Miller and Elizabeth Malek-Zadeh (eds.), *The Ecotourism Equation: Measuring the Impact*. Bulletin Series 99, Yale School of Forestry and Environmental Studies. New Haven, Connecticut, 108–117.

FURTHER READING

Hill, Jennifer, and Tim Gale. (2012). *Ecotourism and Environmental Sustainability: Principles and Practice*. Burlington, VT: Ashgate.

Holden, Andrew. (2008). *Environment and Tourism*, second edition. New York: Routledge.

ECOTOURISM: COOPERATION OR BUST?
Edward Jackiewicz and Olga Govdyak

On the surface, ecotourism appears to be a highly palatable aspect of the increasingly diverse and often contentious tourism industry. Ecotourism has also become a highly marketable concept for destinations seeking to increase revenue and, according to some, misuse the term to their advantage, or "greenwash." In practice, ecotourism must protect the very resources it markets to potential tourists and in order to do this there must be collaboration among the various actors or stakeholders who play a role in designing and implementing the nature-friendly experience.

According to The International Ecotourism Society (TIES), ecotourism is defined as "purposeful travel to natural areas to understand the culture and the natural history of the environment; taking care not to alter the integrity of the

Sign for the 3 Rivers Eco-Lodge, a supposed "environmentally friendly retreat" near Dominica's wild east coast. (AP/Wide World Photos)

ecosystem; producing economic opportunities that make the conservation of the natural resources beneficial to the local people" (TIES, 2009). Other definitions have emerged over the years and include terms like self-sustaining, small scale, and low impact. Despite some definitional variability most observe that for ecotourism to be a sustainable venture it must balance economic and cultural as well as environmental dimensions, which has proven to be a significant challenge because it involves multiple organizations and individuals with varying perspectives and objectives. However it is defined, it is undoubtedly one of the fastest-growing sectors of the increasingly vast tourism industry, and in order for it to achieve its stated goals, a collaborative model is integral.

According to Kevin Hannam and Dan Knox (2010), ecotourism should be viewed as "a tourism product and a consumer desire" (Hannam and Knox, 2010), a relationship that is mutually reinforcing. Within this duality, there are several interrelated elements that need to be incorporated for the enterprise to be sustainable; namely, environmental conservation, economic growth, cultural preservation, local involvement and control, and environmental education (Hannam and Knox, 2010). To simplify a bit, there must be a negotiation and integration between economic, environmental, and cultural priorities at different geographic scales.

Ecotourism should be considered within the broader framework of sustainability that compels us to live in a manner that does not jeopardize future generations to live in a similar way. The reality of contemporary tourism and travel is that it is not very sustainable, although ecotourism, when practiced correctly, aims to alleviate many of the negative impacts associated with standard or more traditional types of tourism. It is clear that the way the majority of the world's tourists currently travel is not sustainable nor does it qualify as ecotourism. In order to achieve economic, cultural, and environmental sustainability, tourism must concern itself with the interconnections between the three as well as implement practices that help the less fortunate of the world.

Criteria for eco-tourist resorts/destinations are numerous and wide-ranging, including: minimizing impact, environmental and cultural awareness, providing positive experiences for both the tourist and the locals, providing financial benefits for conservation and for the empowerment of the local people, and raising sensitivity to the countries' political, environmental, and social climate (TIES, 2014). Simultaneously meeting all of these criteria is challenging for the destination stakeholders because there are varied interests and demands. For example: If a destination hotel or resort wants to provide a comfortable experience for tourists, can it do so without placing too much stress on the local environment? What is the threshold where too many visitors cause irreparable harm to the local ecosystem simply by trying to meet such basic needs as hot water, sewage and trash disposal, and food and beverage, not to mention the impact of traveling to the destination whether by bus, boat, auto, plane, or foot? Additionally, do the resort proprietors need to consult with others in the community about whether their business practices meet the ecotourism criteria? Regulations, if they exist at all, aren't strictly enforced and allow for many resorts to claim they are eco-friendly while engaging in practices that may be detrimental to the environment they are claiming to protect. This brings to light another matter: just how feasible is ecotourism and what determines whether or not it is successful? And, for that matter, how do we determine success?

Ecotourist resorts frequently market their small footprint, large contribution to the local community, green energy programs, and preservation of local flora, fauna, and cultural resources, but how well and to what extent they adhere to these policies or criteria is questionable. As we attempt to illustrate here, identifying and measuring success can be challenging but if stakeholders cooperate and agree to work toward common goals specific to their local environment then successful ecotourism practices are within reach. In sum, a successful ecotourism destination will be able to merge environmental, cultural, and economic goals, which can be viewed by some as in conflict, but we suggest that they must integrate and cooperate to achieve the long-term goal of sustainability.

CONFLICTING INTERESTS

To effectively address economic, environmental, and cultural priorities in marginal nations, negotiation and integration with local governments and their residents must first be outlined to develop strategies that seek to benefit each factor. Though ecotourism as a general form of visitation is fondly perceived, details as to the exact meaning of ecotourism are arbitrarily defined, making it difficult to establish a set of uniform guidelines.

There is a universal understanding of the idea that most ecotourists travel from wealthy countries to poorer countries that rely heavily on the consistency of seasonal arrivals. Local economies prosper from the influx in spending but struggle if the tourism count exceeds forecasted travel because of their inability to cater to pressures for increased accommodations and resources. Local communities of host nations often find themselves on the cusp of integration with the developed world but the livelihoods of local residents who do not participate in tourism-based activities are compromised as the side effects of tourism establishments cripple their means of production. Circumstances in Costa Rica lend first-hand insights into the adverse effects the nation is forced to handle as a result of the recent boom in visitation. Southwestern Costa Rica's Osa Peninsula first gained popularity as a destination for ecotravelers who ventured "off the beaten path," but within a decade word reached the mainstream ecotourism channels where by 2000 visitation increased more than tenfold (Horton, 2009). Over half of some 20,000 travelers who came to the peninsula visited at least one of its ecotourism-based wilderness locations and the Osa Peninsula now ranks as the country's leading ecotourism destination.

Places like Costa Rica's Osa Peninsula receive attention and assistance from their governments for expansion projects aimed to boost traveler visitation; however, the key players in these types of opportunities are private sector stakeholders who envision success in years to come in places otherwise untouched by larger chain operations such as transnational hotels. The downside of foreign investor introductions to places like the peninsula fall on the side of the local residents, who often possess similar interests for development but fail to recognize the full potential of a location due to lack of international experience in tourism oriented markets (Horton, 2009). At the same time, well-rounded foreign investors rarely extend a dialogue that provides transparency regarding new projects while limited funding and loan access make it impossible for locals to embark on an ecotourism-based project of their own. Limited communication and therefore collaboration among the key stakeholders further cripples the overall process of creating uniformity in economic, cultural, and environmental sustainability through ecotourism.

Far too often we find that due to a lack of communication between the various stakeholders, mutual agreement is not fulfilled. This leads to the disempowerment of local populations in areas where subsistence living often serves as the only means by which people may fundamentally balance their lifestyle. Resettlement agendas often disregard the need for continuity of traditional practices where farmers might suddenly find themselves learning new methods such as fishing in order to survive, and vice versa. Meanwhile, the projects of private and mostly internationally based stakeholders continue to be carried out, and regardless of whether aims are geared toward sustainable or traditional visitation, the trend of displacement of local populations is one that will certainly prove detrimental to conservation and cultural preservation efforts in years to come.

COOPERATION IS NECESSARY

Because ecotourism is multifaceted and needs to be addressed as such, to be successful, collaborative efforts must be pursued. Broadly speaking, tourism, as any human activity, will adversely impact the place where that activity occurs. The goal of ecotourism is to mitigate those impacts and, even better, provide an impetus to protect and/or improve the natural environment where this activity occurs. Tourism is a multifaceted, complex industry that involves many actors and for ecotourism to attain its goals of ecological, cultural, and economic sustainability, these actors must act in concert or at least make compromises so that all parties are in agreement. Among the actors involved in promoting and delivering a successful ecotourism industry are: tour operators (both local and abroad), hotel/restaurant owners and operators, government agencies, community organizers, local residents, and tourists. If, and it's a big *if*, these actors can agree on a set of goals and principles that will necessarily require compromises, then the potential for a sustainable enterprise is possible. Without such an agreement, the enterprise is doomed.

For ecotourism to succeed there is a need to examine the supply and demand side of this equation. In other words, for optimal results both the tourist and tourism providers must interact in ways that sustain and promote the economic, cultural, and environmental health of the destination. In understanding the role of the tourist, it is important to understand what motivates someone to travel to a specific locale, in this instance an ecotourism site. As most types of tourism have become accessible to the middle class, tourism has become an increasingly diverse industry and consequently the appetite for varied tourism experiences has kept pace. Many individuals travel to places to build their "cultural capital," which can center around the unique experiences that ecotourism can provide. On the flip side, tour operators, hotel and restaurant owners, and government organizations are increasingly trying to make their products unique or at least sell them as unique. Potential tourists now have many options where to spend their tourism dollars and while many elements factor into the decision of where to spend their holiday, cost and uniqueness would certainly rank near the top.

REFERENCES

Hannam, Kevin, and Dan Knox. (2010). *Understanding Tourism: A Critical Introduction.* Thousand Oaks, CA: SAGE Publications, 16.

Horton, Lynn R. (2009). "Buying up nature: economic and social impacts of Costa Rica's ecotourism boom," *Latin American Perspectives,* 36(3), 93–107. Accessed March 1, 2016, at http://www.jstor.org/20684606.

International Ecotourism Society. (2009). "What Is Ecotourism?" Accessed February 27, 2016, at https://www.ecotourism.org/what-is-ecotourism.

FURTHER READING

Hiponia, Malcolm C., and Enrique G. Oracion. (2009). "Nature and people matter: conservation and ecotourism in Balanan Lake, Negros Oriental," *Philippine Studies: Chinese Filipinos and Citizenship* 57(1), 105–136. Accessed March 7, 2016, http://www.jstor.org/stable/42633990.

Wang, Guangyu, John L. Innes, Sara W. Wu, Judi Krzyzanowski, Yongyuan Yin, Shuanyou Dai, Xiaoping Zhang, and Sihui Liu. (2012). "National park development in China: conservation or commercialization?" *Ambio.* 41(3): 247–261. Accessed March 7, 2016, http://www.jstor.org/stable41510579.

Wright, Pamela A. (1993). "Sustainable ecotourism: Balancing economic, environmental and social goals within an ethical framework," *The Journal of Tourism Studies* 4(2), 54–66. Accessed March 7, 2016, at http://jtr.sagepub.com.libproxy.csun.edu/content/33/2/59.6.

SUCCESSFUL ECOTOURISM: INAUTHENTIC TOURISM EXPERIENCE VERSUS INTEGRATING ENVIRONMENTAL MANAGEMENT AND CONSERVATION

Barbara McNicol

Ecotourism and the non-extractive activities and infrastructure associated with it are controversial and will remain controversial until professional standards and principles, certification, and government/industry partnerships are prioritized over false images and marketing. Relevant questions for environmental and natural resource managers include: Are the changes that occur through the activities of ecotourism beneficial to the conservation of ecosystems, communities, and natural environments or do these activities degrade sensitive natural and community ecologies? Are there better forms of natural resource use and economic generation than ecotourism activities for a given land base?

The main barrier to examples of successful ecotourism is the nature of tourism as a consumptive activity. It doesn't matter how "eco" the tourism is, it is still part of the cycle of production and consumption and tourists consume natural resources and ecosystems as part of the cycle. Examples of poor ecotourism planning and management are usually those that place emphasis on marketing a product as "ecologically sensitive" with little understanding of the components of sustainability or conservation. This approach to tourism has been referred to as green consumerism in the environmental literature (Holden, 2008) and produces an ecotourism experience that places emphasis on mostly information rather than environmental understanding. In other words, the educational component is in the form of marketing the tourism landscape and the associated natural resources by using an image-making brochure, often based on inauthentic images. Poorer ecotourism, therefore, can often be equated with the move to greener consumer products where the image is used as a marketing tool rather than to produce a quality visitor experience accompanied by conservation-based development. Superimposing inauthentic ecotourism experiences onto critical or fragile ecosystems can initiate some very negative impacts.

Successful sustainable tourism initiatives often use the tools of environmental management such as foundational theories of carrying capacity, limits of acceptable change and environmental assessment, and different evolving forms of these. Applications of these place emphasis on the identification and mitigation of negative impacts that are embedded in the practices of appropriate ecotourism. At the same time, the ecotourism industry requires standards that can be enforced by a governing body with authority. Currently, most companies operate with guidelines that are regulated by the tourism industry as voluntary codes of conducts for both commercial operators and their visitors. These include little government regulation and enforcement. Unfortunately, this leaves a substantial amount of room for corruption by both business and state. The implementation, regulation and monitoring of ecotourism standards need to be enforced and monitored by partnerships between communities, the tourism industry, natural resource managers, environmental organizations (such as environmentally focused NGOs, or ENGOs) and all levels of governments.

The more visitors that are given access to sensitive or critical ecologies, without professional standards and committed partnerships, the greater the impacts will be. In the end, effective ecotourism is about the balance between sustainability of the natural resources and ecosystems and the profitability of the tourism activities. The establishment of professional standards and an ecotourism certification program may ensure a move toward better and comprehensive ecotourism that encompasses key components of a quality nature-based tourist experience, an education component, and the focuses of sustainability and conservation.

Community-based ecotourism can lead to a more sustainable long-term use of land in the form of continual economic revenue over other forms of resource extraction or land use such as, for example, cattle ranching. Cattle ranching may initially generate high economic returns but ultimately will remove vegetation, degrade the soil and contribute to less potable water sources. Community-based ecotourism projects provide avenues for the conservation of natural resources and the development of rural communities through alternative uses of natural assets resulting in collaboration and interactions between resident and other, often specialist, groups. It is also not inconceivable that ecotourism and cattle ranching can exist side by side with the proper communication and partnership.

Many current ecotourism initiatives rely on protected areas as pristine environments. Ecotourism, however, can be incorporated into regional land use protection and planning through the designation of a biosphere reserve. The model of a biosphere reserve incorporates zones of multiple uses: community uses transition into a natural resource buffer zone, with stronger preservation goals in the core of the reserve. This allows for the integration of forestry and mining outside and ecotourism in the buffer and core zones to help improve the economy of local communities. Many developing countries, notably in Africa and South America, are moving from traditional land management models that protect strict biodiversity, often in reserves, toward models that incorporate the improvement of local livelihoods that are integrated with environmental conservation that include ecotourism initiatives. For example, in Bwindi National Park in Uganda, Africa, more money can be made by taking ecotourists on tours to see mountain gorillas than local people can gain by poaching them. Ultimately, protecting endangered single species as well as sensitive ecosystem biodiversity is a concern of many successful ecotourism initiatives.

At the same time, there is a popularly held image of ecotourism that it only occurs in tropical or developing countries and that these are the most important destinations for ecotourism markets. In fact, the demand for ecotourism in Canada and the United States is high, especially from North American and European travelers. Activities may include learning about other cultures (especially First Nations and Native American cultures), visiting heritage sites and learning about the history of an area, visiting villages, and talking to local people as well as traditional ecotourism activities such as bird and wildlife watching. This "developed" notion of ecotourism emphasizes the need for sound tourism management through the identification of appropriate visitor behaviors, acceptable group sizes, land access limits, and a strong educational component focused on local community, heritage, and biodiversity conservation. A profile of Bald Eagle tours along Washington state's Skagit River, for instance, is an example of foresters, conservationists, local communities, and commercial tour operators coming together to allow tourists access to birds through compromise that keeps both the visitors and animals safe.

In the end, there exist examples of both bad and good ecotourism around the globe but successful ecotourism will incorporate key components of a nature-based, educational experience that ensures a sustainable tourism experience and the goal of ecological conservation. A main goal is that economic growth from natural resource development and the goal of conservation of biodiversity can co-exist and possibly complement future initiatives in both the developing and developed world.

REFERENCE

Holden, Andrew. (2008). *Environment and Tourism*, second edition. New York: Routledge.

7

How Do Global Warming and Climate Change Influence a Nation's Security Policy?

OVERVIEW
Bruce E. Johansen

A warming climate is provoking examination of military strategy from location of bases to the military's basic role in the world. As a result, the U.S. military has become a major source of risk assessments on climate change during the last decade. Global warming is forcing forward-thinking military strategists to question the military's role in shaping its position toward assistance in natural disasters that produce large numbers of climate refugees who need assistance with basic survival (CNA, 2014).

"Unlike the problems that we are used to dealing with, these will come upon us extremely slowly, but come they will, and they will be grinding and inexorable," said Richard J. Truly, a retired United States Navy vice admiral and former NASA administrator (Revkin and Williams, 2007). Consultants' reports to the government have warned that effects of global warming could provoke large-scale migrations, increased tensions across borders, spread of diseases, and intensifying conflicts over food and water. All could involve military forces of the United States and other nations.

A board of 11 retired generals and admirals first issued an advisory report to the Pentagon in 2007 and updated it in 2014, finding that:

> Actions by the United States and the international community have been insufficient to adapt to the challenges associated with projected climate change. Strengthening resilience to climate impacts already locked into the system is critical, but this will reduce long-term risk only if improvements in resilience are accompanied by actionable agreements on ways to stabilize climate change. . . .The update serves as a bipartisan call to action. It makes a compelling case that climate change is no longer a future threat—it is taking place now. It observes that climate change serves as a catalyst of conflict in vulnerable parts of the world, and that projected changes in global migration patterns will make the challenges even more severe. It identifies threats to elements of national power here at home, particularly those associated with our infrastructure and our ability to maintain military readiness. (CNA, 2014)

For example, the United States and other national naval forces require location on bases near oceans and are vulnerable to sea-level rise. The U.S. Navy's largest concentration of stationary assets, in Norfolk, Virginia, is located in an area that is the second most likely to flood (after New Orleans) in the United States as oceans rise. Rising sea level is compounded in this area by a subsiding land surface and the low, flat nature of the Tidewater area.

The Pentagon has linked intensifying drought in the Middle East to conflict over food and water that has overturned several governments. In the Mekong Delta Bangladesh, eastern India, and other regions, Pentagon reports also assert that flooding provoked by rising seas could lead to increasing numbers of refugees. U.S. Secretary of State John Kerry said that U.S. national security policy would be shaped by trends identified in the Pentagon's reports: "Tribes are killing each other over water today," Kerry said. "Think of what happens if you have massive dislocation, or the drying up of the waters of the Nile, [and] of the major rivers in China and India. The intelligence community takes it seriously, and it's translated into action" (Davenport, 2014). "The [U.S. Defense] Department certainly agrees that climate change is having an impact on national security, whether by increasing global instability, by opening the Arctic or by increasing sea level and storm surge near our coastal installations," said John Conger, the Defense Department's deputy under secretary of defense for installations and environment. "We are actively integrating climate considerations across the full spectrum of our activities to ensure a ready and resilient force" (Davenport, 2014).

The Pentagon's *Quadrennial Defense Review*, issued in March 2014, came to similar conclusions, with a notable emphasis on extreme weather's role as a "threat multiplier" in destabilizing societies in ways that increase the appeal of ideologies that inspire acts of terrorism. The Pentagon's reports have reached the level of associating climate change in specific African countries, such as Mali (where the Sahara desert is spreading and devastating agriculture) as contributing to a jihadist uprising. By 2014, Al Qaeda in the Islamic Maghreb had seized much of northern Mali, and was acquiring influence in the country's government.

The Pentagon's reports link national security to climate security. The Pentagon also has recognized climate change as a national-security threat, and found it useful for seeking increases in defense spending. Every four years, the U.S. Defense Department reviews its mission as rationale for its budget. In 2010, and years following, climate change has found its way into this document as a "preparedness mission . . . occurring in multiple and unpredictable combinations." Defense Secretary Robert Gates justified the department's $553 billion budget (as of 2011) in part by calling climate change "an accelerant of instability" (Pentagon Budget, 2011).

REFERENCES

Center for Naval Analyses Advisory Board (CNA). (2014). *National Security and the Accelerating Risks of Climate Change*. Washington, DC: U.S. Department of Defense. Accessed March 1, 2016, at http://www.cna.org/sites/default/files/MAB_2014.pdf, 1.

Davenport, Carol. (2014, May 13). "Climate change deemed growing security threat by military researchers," *New York Times*. Accessed May 22, 2014, at http://www.nytimes.com/2014/05/14/us/politics/climate-change-deemed-growing-security-threat-by-military-researchers.html.

Revkin, Andrew C., and Timothy Williams. (2007, April 15). "Global warming called security threat," *New York Times*. Accessed May 20, 2014, at http://www.nytimes.com/2007/04/15/us/15warm.html.

FURTHER READING

Campbell, Kurt M. (ed.). (2008). *Climatic Cataclysm: The Foreign Policy and National Security Implications of Climate Change*. Washington, DC: Brookings Institution Press.

McClatchy Newspapers, Omaha (eds.). (2011, February 13). "Pentagon budget reflects growth of security needs," *World-Herald*, 2-A.

Moran, Daniel. (2011). *Climate Change and National Security: A Country-Level Analysis*. Washington, DC: Georgetown University Press.

Scheffran, Jürgen. (2012). *Climate Change, Human security and Violent Conflict: Challenges for Societal Stability*. New York: Springer Verlag.

CLIMATE CHANGE: AN EMERGING CONCERN OF NATIONAL SECURITY
M. Troy Burnett

"For four decades, security has been defined largely in ideological terms . . . the threat posed by continuing environmental deterioration is no longer a theoretical one."

—Brown et al., 1988

Climate change has recently been labeled a pressing security concern for governments, with many arguing that global warming and the resultant climate change will increase the risk of social instability and violent conflict (Barnett and Adger, 2007). According to the International Panel on Climate Change (IPCC) there is widespread consensus that climate change is the source of many kinds of rapid environmental change: soil desiccation and desertification, sea level rise and coastal flooding and erosion, more intense storms, loss of biodiversity and extinction, and extremes of hot and cold, especially in urban areas. Long the purview of scientists and environmental policy makers, these impacts have gained the attention of government security and intelligence branches, such as the U.S. Department of Defense. For security experts, global warming and climate change act as threat multipliers in conjunction with other traditional threats to national security. As a result, state governments and national security experts have increasingly developed and deployed their security apparatus to actively prepare for ecological crisis and conflict—many calling the 21st century the era of environmentally induced conflicts.

Broadly speaking, there are two means by which conflict might arise as a result of changing climates: (1) conflict arising through shifts in the economics and politics of energy resources as the international community acts to mitigate the causes of global warming, and (2) conflict arising from dramatic local and regional environmental changes that has the potential to stress social systems and foment antagonistic internal and external relations. From the national security perspective, rapid climate change arguably has the potential to undermine human security by reducing access to and degrading the quality of natural resources, such as water and arable land. Further, it can undermine the ability of States to act in a manner that promotes peace and development. There is also the simple fact that the vulnerability of people to climate change is related to their dependency on natural resources and ecosystem services, the extent to which the resources and services are affected by climate, and their ability to adapt to the changes in these services. According to Barnett and Adger, "The more people are dependent on climate sensitive forms of natural capital, and the less they rely on economic or social forms of capital, the more at risk they are from climate change" (Barnett and Adger, 2007). In other words, the potential for conflict is related to a variety of social factors, including levels of poverty, access to economic opportunities, levels of support from the state, effectiveness of decision-making, and the depth of community support mechanisms.

The United States security community in particular began to take note of the security implications of climate change with the publication of a landmark report in 2007 (updated in 2014) by the Center for Naval Analysis (CNA). Comprising climatological experts and U.S. military officers, the report concludes that in spite of the uncertainty over the specific causes and consequences of global warming the changes have already and will continue to foment civil instability. It goes on to warn that these developments will continue to contribute to state failure, international conflict, regional strife in historically unstable regions, and even terrorism and genocide—each of which may require further intervention by an already overburdened U.S. military. Many of the aforementioned observed and predicted meteorological changes (increased storm intensity, flooding, extremes of heat and cold, sea level rise) could also complicate existing and future military operations. For example, the U.S. Naval supply station on the Indian Ocean atoll of Diego Garcia, with a high point of only 30 feet, is under serious threat from sea level rise.

Along with the broad security concerns, the consensus from the U.S. national security establishment is that there are 10 highly consequential implications of climate change that require immediate preparation and planning:

1. Developing World—Because of the stark differences in wealth and technological capacity, climate change and its stresses will further increase tensions between the developed and developing worlds, especially as the former, with its high levels of greenhouse gas emissions, is viewed as the cause of global warming.
2. Increased Migration—Invariably desperate individuals will migrate from those areas most affected by the rapid changes. This will inevitably strain the existing, overburdened immigration system. Most countries, even the United States, are lukewarm towards migrants in the best of times let alone towards desperate environmental refugees.
3. Health Consequences—Potential health crises especially concerning vector-born diseases (e.g., malaria), storms, flooding, and heat and cold waves.
4. Water Scarcity—Resource availability for agriculture and domestic consumption will shrink in some of the most populous regions on the Earth, such as the Sahel and semi-arid Asia.
5. Nuclear Energy—As countries shift towards non-carbon based energy generation, there is the likely possibility of a renaissance in nuclear. The

concern is the sizable increase in the dangers of an accident and the increased availability of fissile materials for weapons proliferation.

6. International Relations—This category concerns social and political changes to international relations and the burdens and potential conflicts in politically unstable regions, authoritarian systems, and even stable democracies to cooperate. The United Nations and other such international institutions will have difficulty managing adverse consequences in the world's more susceptible regions.

7. Governmental Viability—Existing governments and political systems will face mounting unrest if viewed as being ineffective at managing climate-induced challenges. Crisis can lead to authoritarianism, and violence has often been the last resort of the desperate.

8. World Political Disequilibrium—Climate change is likely to create unanticipated shifts in global and regional power. Again, climate stresses may create regional power vacuums and encourage territorially aggressive actions by expansionary governments.

9. The Role of China—China has recently surpassed the United States as the world's largest source of greenhouse gas emissions, has 16 of the 20 most polluted cities on Earth, and has an authoritarian system of government that actively denigrates democracy and bullies its neighbors. China also is the world's largest producer of nonrenewable energy technologies. As a result, the country represents an ambiguous X factor in regards to global warming and climate change.

10. The Leadership Role of the United States—Unfortunately, politics have dominated the discussion surrounding global warming and climate change much to the frustration of the American people and the global community. One can hope that the United States will take a leadership position on the challenges ahead, but the country could very well turn in on itself and worry only about its own borders and security challenges. (Campbell, 2008)

In conclusion, there are many current and existing challenges associated with global warming and climate change. Governments such as the United States have taken note and accepted that efforts to mitigate climate change and the consequences of those changes represent stresses to national security. Strategic plans are being drafted, security personnel and militaries are being mobilized, for as Winston Churchill famously observed at the advent of World War II, "the era of procrastination, of half-measures, of soothing and baffling expedients, of delays is coming to its close . . . in its place we are entering a period of consequences."

REFERENCES

Barnett, Jon, and W. Neil Adger. (2007). "Climate change, human security, and violent conflict," *Political Geography 26*, 639–655.

Brown, Lester, William U. Chandler, Alan Durning, Christopher Flavin, et al. (1988). *Worldwatch Institute Report—State of the World 1988*. Washington, DC: Worldwatch Institute.

Campbell, Kurt M. (ed.). (2008). *Climatic Cataclysm: The Foreign Policy and National Security Implications of Climate Change*. Washington, DC: Brookings Institution Press.

Center for Naval Analyses Advisory Board (CNA). 2014. *National Security and the Accelerating Risks of Climate Change*. Washington, DC: CNA Analysis and Solutions, U.S. Department of Defense. Accessed March 1, 2016, at http://www.cna.org/sites/default/files/MAB_2014.pdf

WAR IS ENVIRONMENTALLY OBSOLETE
Bruce E. Johansen

We are familiar with the lethal toll of war, and the many good reasons for opposing its use in international diplomacy until all other avenues have been exhausted. Most war is waged in a self-justifying gale of hatred-fueled nationalistic rage that disregards all collateral damage as nasty but necessary. The environmental unfriendliness of war is no state secret. Four decades ago, Vietnam was being sprayed with Agent Orange (with consequent birth defeats) even as citizens of the United States celebrated their first Earth Day.

Modern warfare, waged over long distances with battleships, tanks, and jet-propelled aircraft, is immensely carbon-intensive. While the U.S. Defense Department has recognized global warming as a factor in international conflict and has taken some of the same steps as the larger society to reduce its energy consumption (e.g., low-flush toilets, cutting off the lights in the war room when not in use) it has yet to recognize that war, itself, contributes to global warming. I am not talking here about improving the atrocious gas mileage of tanks and fighter jets. I am asking whether we can de-carbonize international relations by changing the role of the military so that we don't solve problems with war. If we want to retain a military establishment, it will have its hands full in coming years dealing with climate refugees.

War has become progressively more mechanized, using more fossil fuels, with the passage of time. Less than a hundred years ago, at the beginning of World War I in Europe, the main motive force in battle was the horse and shoe leather, as troops in Europe marched off to battle on foot or horseback. World War I quickly witnessed a dramatic escalation in war's carbon-dioxide production with the advent of aerial bombardment, as well as increasing use of tanks. War is often a powerful technological motor and carbon-consumption innovator. World War II began with quarter-century-old bi-planes, and ended with jet-propelled fighters, a massive increase in fuel consumption. Global preparations for war (excluding war's actual conduct) have been estimated to produce as much as 10 percent of carbon-dioxide emissions (Bidlack, 1996; Biswas, 2000; Majeed, 2004). Analysis of paleoclimatic data correlated with historical records of warfare around the world between 1400 and 1900 suggests substantial association of temperature change with frequency of war (Zhang et al., 2007).

Energy efficiency has never received much thought in warfare. World War II's Sherman tank, for example, got 0.8 miles per gallon. Seventy years later, tank mileage had not improved: the 68-ton Abrams Tank got 0.5 miles per gallon. Fighter jets' typical fuel consumption is 300 to 400 gallons per hour at full thrust, or 100 gallons per hour at cruising speed during training and combat missions. Blasting to supersonic speed on its afterburners, an F-15 Fighter can burn as much as four gallons of fuel per second. The B-52 Stratoscruiser, with eight jet engines, consumes 86 barrels of fuel per hour (3,784 gallons). The United Kingdom's Green Party estimated that the United States, Britain, and the minor parties of the "coalition of the willing" burned the same amount of fossil fuel in the Iraq war (40,000 barrels a day) as the 1.1 billion people of India. The Iraq War by itself added more greenhouse gases to the atmosphere than 60 percent of the world's nations.

Reports coming out of the Pentagon now consider climate change a "threat multiplier" that affects national security and postwar rehabilitation of ecosystems (CNA, 2007; Machlis and Hansen, 2008). The U.S. Defense Department also now includes climate change in its assessments of global security. Likewise, the Intergovernmental Panel on Climate Change (IPCC) anticipates that effects of global warming will contribute to declining water resources, reduced food security, and increasing migrations of "environmental refugees," all sources of conflict (IPCC, 2007; Johansen, 2009).

The de-carbonization of war will require reconsideration of nationalistic, political, and religious concepts that usually aggravate conflict and lead to war. A sustainable future requires a worldwide re-fit of the military's mission that requires more than a change of technology. It requires a re-definition of nationalism that conforms with requirements of Earth sustainability, sharply reducing greenhouse-gas emissions. The "green" armed forces will become service organizations that react to environmental threats in a future in which war as we know it today has become illegal on environmental grounds. War waged in a self-justifying gale of hatred-fueled nationalistic rage that disregards all collateral damage as nasty but necessary must become an artifact of the past. The Earth can no longer afford fossil-fueled war.

REFERENCES

Bidlack, Harold W. (1996). "Swords as Plowshares: The Military's Environmental Role." PhD dissertation, University of Michigan, Ann Arbor.

Biswas, Asit K. (2000). "Scientific assessment of the long-term consequences of war," in Jay E. Autsin and Carl E. Bruch (eds.), *The Environmental Consequences of War*. Cambridge, UK: Cambridge University Press, 303–316.

CNA Corporation Military Advisory Board and Study Team. (2007). "National Security and the Threat of Climate Change." Alexandria, VA: CNA Corp.

Intergovernmental Panel on Climate Change (IPCC). (2007). *Climate Change 2007: Synthesis Report*. Geneva, Switzerland: IPCC.

Johansen, Bruce E. (2009). "The carbon footprint of war," *The Progressive*, October, 27–29.

Machlis, Gary E., and Thor Hanson. (2008, September). "War ecology," *BioScience 58*(8), 729–736.

Majeed, Abeer. (2004). *The Impact of Militarism on the Environment: An Overview of Direct and Indirect Effects*. Ottawa, Canada: Physicians for Global Survival.

Zhang, Davd D., Peter Brecke, Harry F. Lee, Yuan-Qing He, and Jane Zhang. (2007). "Global Climate Change, War, and Population Decline in Recent Human History." *Proceedings of the Academy of the National Academy of Sciences, 104*(19), 214–219.

8

IS NUCLEAR THE RIGHT OPTION TO AVOID FUTURE ENERGY CONFLICTS?

OVERVIEW
Robert Goble and M. Troy Burnett

The nuclear disasters at Three Mile Island, Chernobyl, and most recently at Fukushima Daiichi not only brought new life to anti-nuclear movements, they caused governments worldwide to reassess the safety of their nuclear power programs. Many countries canceled nuclear energy projects in light of the disasters, but overall, the technology is growing. By 2013, more than 400 nuclear energy plants were in operation around the world, with 68 plants under construction in 15 countries. The growing demand for electricity and the potential inability of conventional sources of power to supply the need is the primary reason countries are pursuing nuclear energy. Globally, the demand for electricity is predicted to grow by 50 percent by 2030. Nuclear energy production has the capability to answer that demand in short order, unlike other renewable energy sources such as wind, solar, and geothermal. In addition, the technology enables many countries to eliminate their dependence on other countries for energy. Opponents of nuclear point to the well-known disasters, however, and ask, at what risk, and is it the right option?

  In the first essay, Duane Bratt points out the possibility of risk in all forms of energy production, as well as the improvements in nuclear safety procedures to support the future development and growth of nuclear energy production around the world. M. Troy Burnett, however, compares nuclear energy to a Faustian bargain, warning that the risks far outweigh the benefits and that the conflict potential is too high to depend on to meet future demand.

BACKGROUND

Nuclear power plants are now used in 31 countries around the world to provide electricity. In many ways, nuclear plants are similar to the coal-burning and other fossil-fuel power plants that generate the largest portion of the world's electricity. A large thermal power plant produces electricity by using a heat source to boil water; the resulting steam runs an engine to turn a generator that makes the electricity. The difference between a nuclear power plant and a coal-fired plant is that nuclear power uses heat from the nuclear energy released in a controlled splitting (fission) of uranium nuclei instead of heat from the chemical energy released when coal is burned to produce carbon dioxide. The steam engine and generator are pretty much the same.

As of 2012, there were about 440 large civilian reactors operating worldwide, producing about 15 percent of the world's electricity. The United States has the largest number of plants, with 104 reactors producing about 20 percent of U.S. electricity. France is most heavily invested in nuclear power, with 58 reactors producing about 75 percent of the country's electricity.

The impacts of nuclear electricity generation neither begin nor end with the power plant.

Mining and Milling of Uranium Ore

Uranium ore is removed from the ground, and the ore is crushed and leached to extract uranium in the form of uranium oxide. The remaining waste stream, called tailings, contains radioactive materials and toxic metals.

Conversion and Enrichment of the Uranium

To obtain the enriched uranium that is needed (except for reactors that burn natural uranium as fuel), the uranium oxide is converted to uranium hexafluoride, and then either gaseous diffusion or centrifuges are used to create enriched uranium and a second stream of depleted uranium. These are then converted back to uranium oxide. The wastes to be coped with include hydrogen fluoride and uranium fluoride residues and the depleted uranium; there are, however, some practical uses for depleted uranium.

Fabrication of Fuel Elements

Uranium oxide is baked into pellets that are then put in metal rods. The fuel rods are bundled to make fuel assemblies for use in reactors.

Operation of a Power Reactor

A large reactor might produce roughly 7 to 8 TerraWatt hours (Twh) per year (1 Twh equals a thousand million kilowatt-hours [kWh]). In doing this, it will use roughly 20 metric tons of enriched uranium, requiring about 160 metric tons of natural uranium. That latter amount might be compared to the roughly 3 million metric tons of coal that must be burned to produce the same amount of electricity. The primary waste from reactor operations is the spent fuel; additionally, there will be routine and accidental releases of radioactive materials to air and water. Severe accidents have occurred in which cooling of the fuel failed, the core melted, and there was potential or actual uncontrolled release of large amounts of radioactive material. After reactor operations cease, the site itself is severely contaminated with radioactive materials and thus represents a long-term waste stream.

Storage, Processing, and Long-Term Disposal of Spent Fuel

Fuel assemblies that have completed their useful operation in the reactor must be removed. They contain high amounts of short-lived radioactive elements and thus require careful attention to cooling and radiation shielding. Pools of circulating water provide both cooling and shielding for an initial few years. Afterward they can be transferred for storage to ventilated dry casks; so far there has been limited use of dry cask storage, and by now many pools around the world can be considered overcrowded. After a period of temporary storage during which much short-lived radioactivity has decayed, two basic options for the spent fuel are under consideration. One is long-term disposal of the spent fuel rods themselves. The other is to use a further processing cycle in which fission products are separated from the heavy elements, such as uranium and plutonium. The idea is that some plutonium and enriched uranium can be used for fuel, while the fission products and other heavy elements will be placed in long-term disposal sites. At present there are no facilities available for long-term disposal of most spent fuel around the world. Reprocessing creates the fission product and heavy metal waste streams for which, as noted, there are presently no facilities for long-term disposal. This involves trade in plutonium, which could potentially be diverted to produce nuclear weapons, and requires additional reprocessing plants that will be a source of further contamination.

There have been very few new plants installed since 1990, and very few nearing completion. Important reasons for the slowdown are that costs of power plants are high, routinely exceed predictions, and continue to escalate and that there has been persistent distrust of and resistance to nuclear technology by substantial numbers of people worldwide. Distrust stems from many factors: nuclear technologies are linked consciously or unconsciously to nuclear weapons; radiation evokes dread because it is invisible, unfamiliar, and causes cancer; and despite years of study and promises, governments and industry have failed to put forward a credible program for long-term management of nuclear waste. Three major nuclear power plant accidents involving a core melt have also shaken public confidence. They took place at the Three Mile Island Plant in Pennsylvania in 1979, the Chernobyl Plant in the Ukraine in 1986, and three reactors at the Fukushima Plant in Japan in 2011. Each time the events unfolded slowly, and the response by plant operators, government agencies, and other observers was confused as the world watched. All three accidents leave behind a contaminated plant site and unusable reactors; radiation exposures from Chernobyl were sufficient to cause many thousands of cancers. It is too early as of this writing to estimate health consequences from Fukushima. Both Chernobyl and Fukushima leave a legacy of contaminated land extending well outside the plant boundaries.

During the 20-plus–year slowdown in nuclear power plant construction, three trends are significant. There have been numerous design advances for reactor technology, offering some prospects for more flexible configuration and use and possibly some significant safety advantages. There has been a strong effort to relicense and extend the life of older reactors beyond their design lifetimes. And there has been a strengthened call by governments, the nuclear industry, and some environmental groups for considering renewed investment in nuclear power in spite of its high costs as part of the effort to limit greenhouse gas emissions that cause global warming. Discussion will likely take place as countries around the world reexamine the state of their nuclear industry in light of the experience of Fukushima.

FURTHER READING

Marcus, Gail H. (2008). "Innovative nuclear energy systems and the future of nuclear power," *Progress in Nuclear Energy, 50*(2), 92–96.
Sovacool, Benjamin K. (2011). *Contesting The Future of Nuclear Power: A Critical Global Assessment of Atomic Energy.* Hackensack, NJ: World Scientific.
Whitfield, Stephen C., Eugene A. Rosa, Amy Dan, and Thomas Dietz. (2009). "The future of nuclear power: value orientations and risk perception," *Risk Analysis, 29*(3): 425–437.

HOW TO AVOID FUTURE ENERGY CONFLICTS? PROMOTE NUCLEAR!
Duane Bratt

The nuclear accident at Japan's Fukushima Daiichi power plant in March 2011 has rekindled the controversy over nuclear energy. As a result of this accident, both Japan and Germany, two of the most nuclear-intensive countries in the world, have initiated a phase-out of nuclear energy. There are risks with nuclear energy,

View of the damaged Unit 4 reactor at the Fukushima Daiichi nuclear power plant in Okumamachi, Fukushima prefecture, northern Japan, November 12, 2011. A tsunami hit the facility following a massive earthquake on March 11, 2011, resulting in a large release of radiation. (David Guttenfelder/AP Photo)

but as both Japan and Germany are already discovering, there are more risks in not using nuclear energy. For example, Germany is replacing its nuclear generation not with increased use of wind and solar as was promised, but an expansion of coal supplemented by imports of French nuclear, Polish coal, and Russian natural gas. In the case of Japan, shutting down the vast majority of its nuclear fleet has led to billions of dollars being spent to import liquefied natural gas as well as instituting electricity rationing. The risks of not pursuing nuclear energy can be further emphasized by the fact that there are more countries that are either expanding their use of nuclear energy (e.g., China, India, Russia, and South Korea) or introducing nuclear energy to their electricity system (e.g., United Arab Emirates). In total, more nuclear reactors are being built than are being shut down. This essay explains why nuclear energy is worth the risk.

DRIVERS FOR NUCLEAR ENERGY

There are three major drivers for nuclear energy. First, nuclear energy is needed to address the growing global demand for electricity. Much of this growth will come from developing countries, with China and India accounting for almost half the increase. Heightened demand will come from several interrelated sources. There is an expectation of increased population growth. There will also be an increased demand for a higher standard of living for many people in developing countries. This is especially true for the 1.6 billion people currently lacking access to electricity. Finally, electricity has been consistently increasing its share of energy consumption throughout the world because of urbanization, information technology, electricity-driven urban transportation systems including electric cars, and automated manufacturing.

A second driver is that nuclear energy can help mitigate the problem of greenhouse gases (GHGs), like carbon dioxide (CO_2), contributing to climate change. Most electricity is generated using fossil fuels (e.g., coal, oil, and natural gas) that emit large amounts of GHGs. The IEA predicts that energy-related CO_2 emissions will rise from 28.8 gigatonnes (Gt) in 2007 to 34.5 Gt in 2020 and 40.2 Gt in 2030. The environmental consequences of this sustained rate of emissions will be dire.

The world's people have realized that electricity generation must move away from fossil fuels. According to the Accenture multinational poll on nuclear power, 88 percent believed that it was important that their country "reduce its reliance on fossil-fueled power generation (i.e., coal, oil or gas generated power)." In addition, only 39 percent believed that "renewables alone can fill in the gap, in order to reduce [their] country's reliance on fossil-fueled power generation" (Accenture, 2009). Because it does not emit greenhouse gases, a move toward greater utilization of nuclear energy is better for the environment.

A final driver is the need to provide a country with energy security. Fossil fuels will continue to be a primary source of electricity for decades to come. However, price volatility and concerns over the security of supply are leading countries to shift toward nuclear power. In the past, the lack of domestic fossil fuels was the key driver that led countries like France and Japan to focus their electricity generation on nuclear power. Converting to nuclear power meant that they did not have to rely on imports of coal, oil, or natural gas. It was the 1973 oil shocks that highlighted French dependence on imported Middle Eastern oil and from that moment forward, France shifted its electricity generation from oil to nuclear. Today, France has the world's highest percentage of electricity produced by nuclear power (over 76 percent). In the case of Japan, it cannot "exchange energy with neighboring countries through power transmission lines or pipelines" because it is an island. Japan also lacks many natural resources, meaning that it depends "on foreign countries for about 80 percent of its energy resources." For this reason Japan had traditionally believed that "nuclear power generation contributes to improved energy sufficiency and to the stability of the energy supply" (Japan Nuclear Power, 2002). At the time of the Fukushima Daiichi accident, Japan had about 30 percent of its electricity produced by nuclear power.

There are two aspects to energy security. First is the price of fossil fuels. Although the recession of 2008–2010 led to a temporary decline in oil and natural gas prices, the trajectory has been mostly upward. High prices motivate countries with high shares of imported fuels for their electricity generation to look for substitutes. A related concern is price volatility. As the IAEA (2008) has stated, "all elements of the energy supply infrastructure are long lived. Similarly, energy-intensive industries base their investment decisions on cautious expectations about future energy and electricity prices. A reasonable degree of stability and predictability of resource prices is crucial for such decisions" (IAEA, 2008). All fuel prices fluctuate, but in the case of nuclear power, fluctuation has been mitigated because the cost of fuel as a percentage of production costs is only 10 percent for nuclear power plants, compared with 93 percent for natural gas plants, and 77 percent for coal plants.

The second aspect is security of supply. Political conflicts in key supply regions raise severe concerns over the security of supply. For example, in 2006 and again in 2008 Russia shut off natural gas shipments to Ukraine because of disputes over natural gas supplies, pricing, and debts. The aftermath of Ukraine's Orange Revolution in 2004–2005 and its impact on relations with Russia was also a factor. In the process, other European Union (EU) states were also affected because about 25 percent of all natural gas consumed in the EU comes from Russia and 80 percent of it was transported through pipelines in Ukraine. Energy security has often been identified in public surveys as a reason to pursue nuclear energy.

Critics of nuclear energy often tout the great benefits of renewable sources such as wind and solar energy. However, this needs to be viewed with some skepticism because there are a number of significant flaws with renewable energy sources. Most importantly, they cannot provide the sustained high base load of electricity that nuclear energy provides. Renewables also require backup power systems (usually natural gas) when the sun is not shining or the wind is not blowing. Furthermore, because of the substantially greater efficiency of nuclear power, it has a smaller environmental footprint.

CONCLUSION

Nuclear energy, like all forms of electricity, has its risks. However, the benefits of nuclear energy in producing high amounts of electricity, mitigating the effects of climate change, and producing energy security outweigh these risks. In addition, many of the risks—fear of accidents, nuclear waste, and the perceived benefits of renewable energy—have often been exaggerated by critics of nuclear energy.

There are additional reasons to pursue nuclear energy. First is the fact that since the 1970s nuclear reactors have steadily become safer and more efficient. International organizations such as the International Atomic Energy Agency (IAEA) and the World Association of Nuclear Operators (WANO) have created peer review systems that have improved reactor safety, security, and performance. Second, there is ongoing research and development into nuclear technologies. Examples include small modular reactors (between 10 and 300 megawatts), which are ideal for such smaller jurisdictions and remote locations as the Canadian Arctic, Antarctica, and Russian Siberia; thorium-based reactors that do not use uranium; and reprocessing fuel technology that reuses spent fuel and thereby reducing the amount of nuclear waste.

Nuclear energy, through a cost-benefit analysis with other energy sources, and the opportunities of future advances, is definitely worth the risk.

REFERENCES

Accenture. (2009). *Multinational Nuclear Power Pulse Survey*, 8–11.
International Atomic Energy Agency. (2008). *Climate Change and Nuclear Power*. Vienna, Austria: IAEA, 14.
Japan Nuclear Power. (2002). "Japan's Nuclear Program." Accessed November 30, 2009, at http://www.japannuclear.com/nuclearpower/program/.

NUCLEAR ENERGY IS A CONFLICT MULTIPLIER
M. Troy Burnett

Nuclear energy is a dangerous Faustian bargain—an overhyped cornucopia that while living up to its peril has never lived up to its promise. Or perhaps, the more apt metaphor is Frankenstein, that human-created monster of scientific possibility hatched in the mind of Mary Shelley that represents the quintessential cautionary tale of unintended consequences and lack of foresight. This is nuclear energy: great in a theoretical physics laboratory, but destructive and dangerous in the messy, less-controllable real world. Atomic energy also provides the source of the most potent, biosphere-destroying weapons humanity has ever devised—plutonium. One should also understand that some of the risks of nuclear energy are transgenerational and historical, seemingly for the lifespan of the human species, let alone the lifespans of one's grandchildren. Nuclear is an energy source that will continue to serve as a conflict multiplier rather than mitigator.

The resurgence of attention on nuclear energy is directly related to concern with global warming and climate change. The nuclear industry and its advocates have, in my opinion, quite immorally taken advantage of the world's concern with global warming and greenhouse gases to promote nuclear energy as a more

Nuclear power plant at Three Mile Island, Pennsylvania. The facility experienced a partial nuclear meltdown of Reactor 2 on March 28, 1979. (iStockPhoto.com)

environmentally friendly "carbon-free" option. This 21st-century public-relations term is misleading, and to some degree, just plain wrong. The building and eventual decommissioning of nuclear power stations is not carbon free; the mining, extraction, and transportation of fissile materials is not carbon free; the disposal and storage of radioactive waste is not carbon free. Would your average household want its nearby power station generating carbon dioxide, which isn't toxic and in truth one of the least potent of the greenhouse gases, or plutonium, which, while not a greenhouse gas, is one of the most toxic substances on Earth as well as the source for the most powerful, city-annihilating weapons?

THE PROBLEMS WITH NUCLEAR—THE RISKS AND DANGERS MASSIVELY OUTWEIGH THE BENEFITS

To viscerally know the dangers of nuclear power one only has to reflect on Japan's Fukushima Daiichi disaster, which began in 2011. The saga dramatically unfolded on live television, revealing that even with precautions and advanced engineering safety mechanisms and systems, disasters can and do happen. While the initial accident was not human error or malfunctioning reactors but rather an earthquake and resultant tsunami, it remains that the Daiichi reactor exploded, releasing radioactive gases into the surrounding towns and environment. Not surprisingly, the nuclear industry has been denounced for this accident.

Doubtless, the ecological and economic consequences of such accidents are devastating and enduring. The Ukrainian Chernobyl nuclear plant, which melted down in 1986 as a result of both technological and human failure, is presently encased in a massive cement sarcophagus that will have to be monitored and maintained for hundreds of years to avoid further radiation leaks. More than 350,000 people had to be forcibly resettled from the region and the ghostly, abandoned village of Prypiat serves as a stark reminder to the consequences of accidents. This disaster, though having begun 30 years ago, is still an ongoing source of tension between European countries.

Though the industry repeatedly claims that nuclear accidents are quite rare, Benjamin Sovacool has reported that globally there have been 99 serious accidents at nuclear facilities, including the most dramatic examples of Windscale (1957), Idaho Falls SL-1 (1961), Three Mile Island (1979), Tokaimura (1999), and the aforementioned Chernobyl (1986) (Sovacool, 2012). Astoundingly, this is almost two accidents per year since nuclear energy became a serious energy provider in the 1950s, and 56 of the 99 have occurred in the United States. Effectively, the Fukushima disaster puts the number at an even 100.

The tragedy of a nuclear accident is the slow, persistent way it disrupts and destroys whole communities. Long after the immediate drama has passed residents in and around the exposure zone continue to suffer. According to long-time industry journalist Stephanie Cooke:

> You have people in Japan right now that are facing either not returning to their homes forever, or if they do return to their homes, living in a contaminated area . . . And knowing that whatever food they eat, it might be contaminated and always living with this sort of shadow of fear over them that they will die early because of cancer . . . It doesn't just kill now, it kills later, and it could kill centuries later . . . I'm not a great fan of coal-burning. I don't think any of these great big massive plants that spew pollution into the air are good. But I don't think it's really helpful to make these comparisons just in terms of number of deaths. (2011)

Nuclear power, according to Amory Lovins of the Rocky Mountain Institute, "is the only energy source where mishap or malice can destroy so much value or kill many faraway people; the only one whose materials, technologies, and skills can help make and hide nuclear weapons; the only proposed climate solution that substitutes proliferation, major accidents, and radioactive-waste dangers" (Interview with Annabelle Quince, 2011). Even "normally" functioning reactors are associated with greater risk of unexplained human deaths and cancer. More than 100 radioactive chemicals (e.g., strontium90, iodine131, and cesium137) are produced by nuclear reactors.

NUCLEAR ENERGY AND SECURITY

Along with the environmental and health costs and risks of nuclear power, there are a host of security issues. The industry presently relies on a fragile and inefficient transmission and distribution network that is highly centralized. This makes it susceptible to accidents, sabotage, and attack. The International Energy Agency (IEA) has noted that terrorists would only need to attack a few, poorly guarded facilities to cause a cascade of power failures costing billions of dollars. Reactor cores themselves make tempting targets, and the fissile material produced from nuclear reactions can be used to make weapons of mass destruction. This is hardly a theoretical exercise. Over the past 50 years there have been numerous attacks on facilities. The International Policy Institute for Counter-Terrorism lists some 165 incidents from 1970 to 1999. In order to test security systems, the U.S. Navy SEALs have conducted mock attacks on various facilities and concluded that they could effectively cause a meltdown at more than 50 percent of them.

Greenpeace activists are fond of saying that nuclear power and nuclear weapons have grown up like Siamese twins. To make a nuclear bomb requires fissile material, usually uranium235 or plutonium239. Despite all the efforts of the global community and its non-proliferation institutions it has proven difficult to monitor and secure the generated plutonium and prevent its dispersion for weapons usage. The stark reality is that any country with a basic nuclear reactor can produce nuclear weapons very quickly. At a minimum, they could sell the generated plutonium for a hefty sum. Indeed, this has been the case with countries such as Israel, India, Pakistan, and North Korea that have all constructed nuclear weapons from their "civilian," electricity generation nuclear reactors. Seemingly, it is only a matter of time before Iran declares itself nuclear-capable.

CONCLUSION

Arguments against assuming the risks of nuclear energy are quite clear. Furthermore, there are clear alternatives: (1) a more conservation-based approach to the existing, fossil fuel based energy system; and (2) a continuations of aggressively moving towards renewable, low-impact energy sources (e.g., solar, wind, cogeneration, geothermal) to the point where those technologies can achieve economies of scale with the present, fossil fuel-based system and heavily subsidized nuclear option.

Faust lost everything that was dear to him with his deal with the devil, and everyone is familiar with the chaos and destruction wreaked by Dr. Frankenstein's hubristic creation. In short, don't be fooled by the allure—nuclear energy is dangerous, expensive, ecologically destructive and a red herring for better solutions. The world will be a safer place the sooner we realize this.

REFERENCES

Cooke, Stephanie. (2011, June 8). "Japan says it was unprepared for post-quake nuclear disaster," *Los Angeles Times*. Accessed May 1, 2016, at https://web.archive.org/web/20110608222345/http://www.latimes.com/news/nationworld/world/la-fg-japan-nuclear-report-20110608,0,7481490.story?track=rss.

Quince, Annabelle. (2011, March 30). "The history of nuclear power," Interview, *ABC Radio National*.

Sovacool, Benjamin K. (2012). *Contesting the Future of Nuclear Power—A Critical Assessment of Atomic Energy*. Hackensack, NJ: World Scientific.

9

COULD CONFLICTS OVER WATER ACTUALLY PROMOTE PEACE AND STABILITY?

OVERVIEW
J. C. Veilleux and M. Troy Burnett

There is a simple truth—water resources are finite yet vital for all aspects of human society and ecosystem functioning. A debate has emerged over the role of water resources as an instigator of conflict or rather, whether the stresses over water promote negotiation and compromise. Compounding the problem is climate change and its impact on the spatial and temporal distribution of water making it more difficult to store and transport. Furthermore, as more of the planet moves to the free market model, there is the debate over whether water is a universal human right or just another tradable, resource commodity.

Agriculture accounts for the highest percentage of water resources use worldwide—estimates ranging between 70 to 90 percent (Siebert et al., 2010). Geographically, there are over 280 internationally shared surface water resources worldwide (TFDD, 2015). A recent infographic designed by UNESCO indicates that there are upwards of 3 billion people who lack access to safe drinking water and another 2.5 billion without access to sanitation (UNESCO, 2015). A growing human population, with a sizable number already at risk for safe water access, with a need for increased agricultural production in an era of unpredictably changing climate results in conflicting needs and uses of available water resources (Dabelko, 2008).

There are three schools of thought as to where the mounting complexity surrounding water resources may lead: (1) countries will go to war over water,

(2) water tensions will result in a global hegemony of control and distribution, and (3) water as vital to human survival will promote negotiation, compromise, and global stability. The last scenario clearly suggests that water resources can offer a diplomatic platform for peace and stability. This essay will explore these ideas and their basis, and give a few case study examples.

BACKGROUND

War over Water

In the early 1990s the Cold War officially ended with the dismantling of the Soviet Union and its communist inspired economic and social ideology. As a result, securities scholars began to shift their focus to other threat sources (Buzan et al., 2001). Natural resources, such as oil and water, were identified as potential destabilizers and conflict starters. Typically, when experts refer to water wars, they point to a few prime examples, such as the Brahma-Putra River (China and India), the Jordan River (Israel, Jordan, and Palestine), Africa's Nile River basin shared by 11 countries, and the Tigris-Euphrates rivers (Turkey and Iraq) (Gleick, 1993; Homer-Dixon, 1991; Brown, 2013; Kaplan, 1994). Each of these cases features existing geopolitical tensions or existing conflict.

The Pacific Institute, a not-for-profit environmental-research organization, developed a Water Conflict Chronology that seeks to document all water-related conflict (Glieck, 2015). Water, the institute argues, may not be the sole cause of a conflict, but it is often a contributing factor. The civil war in Sudan is cited as an example of a war partly caused by water and drought. Conflict between Israel and its neighbors is cited as another struggle over securing water resources. In another case a conflict arose in Bolivia called the Cochabamba Water War, where local farmers protested government proposals to commodify the water resources. Ultimately, after tense protests involving rocks and Molotov cocktails, the farmers were able to overturn these efforts (Shultz, 2005).

Hydrohegemony: Coerced Control of Water Resources

Some scholars argue that water tensions invariably promote instability, yet instead of direct violence they result in domination and coercion. This perspective is termed "hydrohegemony." Hegemony is a geopolitical term used to describe the dominance of one group, country, and/or ideology over another. The root of this perspective is that there will not be direct, violent conflict over water, but rather a diplomatic domination with implied threat. Water resources do not lead to violence or fair cooperation, but rather regional asymmetry related to power structures and information sharing between the stakeholders in question (Zeitoun, 2006; Wegerich, 2008).

Examples of existing hydrohegemony include water resources shared between the United States and Mexico, or on the Nile River, which is dominated by Egypt. Other examples include Israel-Palestinian relations, China's water domination in east Asia, and the hydropolitics in the Aral Sea basin, which is still dominated by Russia. In these cases, it is recognized that one country has more power than another and uses that power to exploit water resources sometimes with full consent, however derived, from the other stakeholders.

In the case of the United States, the country has used treaties and water development schemes to dominate water resources with its neighbor, Mexico. The United States has more power—economically, diplomatically, and militarily—to force Mexico to comply with its decisions regarding a shared water resource (e.g., the Colorado River). The result is that while the United States develops and uses the resource, Mexico must make due with the leftovers.

Water for Peace and Stability

Finally, the idea that water conflict can result in increased global peace and stability stems from the idea that water resources bring stakeholders to the table; that water issues actually necessitate negotiations, diplomacy, and compromise rather than perpetual conflict (Wolf, 1998; Wolf, 2004). Contrary to the two conflict schools of analyses, this research emphasizes that there are many more shared water resources where coordination and stability are the norm. For instance, Oregon State University's Transboundary Freshwater Dispute Database has catalogued over 280 shared, stable, and peaceful basins (OSU, 2015). As Wolf argues, despite water scarcity, climate change impacts, or any other physical threat to water supply, countries resort to peaceful negotiations when there is institutional capacity to do so (Wolf, 2003). Institutional capacity includes existing precedent including international agreements, treaties, organizations that manage water resources, and/or international bodies that manage water resources. This capacity provides a regular platform to allow for open dialogue that avoids conflict and promotes peace and stability (Wolf, 1998; Kramer, 2008; Veilleux, 2013).

Recent negotiations on the Nile River between Egypt, Sudan, and Ethiopia are an example of peaceful diplomacy (Davidson and Feteha, 2015). Ethiopia started construction of a large-scale dam on its portion of the Nile River, the Abey or Blue Nile, unilaterally. The existing Nile Treaty signed during the colonial era states that only Egypt and Sudan are legally guaranteed 100 percent of the water and there should be no upstream development on the water resources. Ethiopia was never colonized and did not sign this treaty. Ethiopia's move to develop a dam is legal, but would disrupt the flow of the Nile for a period of time to fill the reservoir behind the dam. Because of this, diplomatic talks between the Egyptian, Ethiopian, and Sudanese governments began in 2013 and have resulted in preliminary conclusions in 2015 that allow Ethiopia to continue with the dam, while guaranteeing Egypt a portion of the generated electricity as well as technical say in the filling of the reservoir.

CONCLUSION

The future of shared water resources is a contentious issue. While some find that dwindling water resources will result in violence, instability, or asymmetrical domination within and between countries, others argue that water tensions offer the ability and opportunity for stakeholders to communicate and negotiate. With increasing demand and dwindling supplies, water resource disputes will be magnified. How we choose to handle them as a global community remains to be seen.

REFERENCES

Brown, Lester. (2013, July 10). "The real threat to our future is peak water," *The Guardian*. Accessed March 7, 2016, at http://www.theguardian.com/global-development/2013/jul/06/water-supplies-shrinking-threat-to-food.

Buzan, Barry, Ole Wæver, and Jaap De Wilde. (1998). *Security: A New Framework for Analysis*. Boulder, CO: Lynne Rienner Publishers.

Dabelko, Geoffrey. (2008). "An uncommon peace: environment, development and the global security agenda," *Environment: Science and Policy for Sustainable Development, 50*, 32–45.

Davison, William, and Ahmed Feteha. (2015, March 24). "Egypt, Sudan edge toward cooperation on Ethiopia's Nile Dam," *Bloomberg*. Accessed March 7, 2016, at http://www.bloomberg.com/news/articles/2015-03-24/egypt-and-sudan-edge-toward-cooperation-on-ethiopia-s-nile-dam.

Gleick, Peter H. (1993). "Water and conflict: fresh water resources and international security," *International Security 18*, 79–112.

Gleick, Peter H. (2015). Pacific Institute Water Conflict Chronology Database. Accessed March 7, 2016, at http://worldwater.org/water-conflict/.

Homer-Dixon, Thomas F. (1991). "On the threshold: environmental changes as causes of acute conflict," *International Security 16*(2), 76–116.

Kaplan, Robert D. (1994). "The coming anarchy," *Atlantic Monthly, 273*, 44–76.

Kramer, Annika. (2008). "Regional Water Cooperation and Peacebuilding in the Middle East." Initiative for Peacebuilding. Accessed March 7, 2016, at http://nl.ircwash.org/sites/default/files/Kramer-2008-Regional.pdf.

Oregon State University (OSU). (2015). Transboundary Freshwater Dispute Database, College of Earth, Ocean and Atmospherics Sciences. Accessed March 7, 2016, at http://www.transboundarywaters.orst.edu/.

Shultz, Jim. (2005, January 28). "The politics of water in Bolivia," *The Nation*. Accessed March 1, 2016, at http://www.thenation.com/article/politics-water-bolivia.

Siebert, Stefan, J. Burke, J. M. Faures, K. Frenken, et al. (2010). "Groundwater use for irrigation—a global inventory," *Hydrology and Earth System Sciences*, 14(10), 1863–1880.

United Nations Educational, Scientific and Cultural Organization (UNESCO). (2015). World Water Day infographic. Accessed March 1, 2016, at http://www.unesco.org/new/en/world-water-day.

Veilleux, Jennifer C. (2013). "The human security dimensions of dam development: the grand Ethiopian renaissance dam," *Global Dialogue* 15(2), 1–15.

Wegerich, Kai. (2008). "Hydro-hegemony in the Amu Darya basin," *Water Policy*, 10(2), 71–88.

Wolf, Aaron T. (1998). "Conflict and cooperation along international waterways," *Water Policy*, 1(2), 251–265.

Wolf, Aaron T. (2004). *Regional Water Cooperation as Confidence Building: Water Management as a Strategy for Peace*. Berlin: Adelphi Research.

Zeitoun, Mark, and Jeroen Warner. (2006). "Hydro-hegemony—a framework for analysis of trans-boundary water conflicts," *Water Policy*, 8(5), 435–460.

FURTHER READING

Pachauri, Rajendra K., and Andy Reisinger. (2007). *IPCC Fourth Assessment Report*. Geneva, Switzerland: IPCC.

COUNTRIES DO NOT GO TO WAR OVER WATER

J.C. Veilleux

Water resources are finite and necessary, and as such represent a potential for conflict. Scholars and practitioners have outlined a hierarchy of needs related to water resources: ecosystem functioning, domestic household use, small-scale agriculture, commercial agriculture, industrial use, municipal use, and national projects, such as a dam. Users in this suite of needs include flora and fauna, individuals, communities, cities, parks, governments, and corporations. Such a range of uses and users for finite water resources can lead to conflicting uses that change access, quality, and quantity of the resources for all involved. In many cases, a fine balance between stakeholders exists that may be disrupted when a change event occurs such as a drought, population increase, economic policy shifts, governmental changes, or a dam development project. Change can lead to potential conflict scenarios over shared water resources. However, given communication, diplomacy, and existing frameworks for management, there is an opportunity for water conflict to turn into opportunities for peace and stability.

The Danube River passes through Bratislava, the capital of Slovakia. The river has historically been the site of contention between neighboring Slovakia, Austria, and Hungary. (European Commission)

Despite the fear, historically there have been no documented international violent conflicts exclusively over water resources. Indeed, countries have frequent disputes over shared water, but governments will typically negotiate and compromise. When a water resource crosses international boundaries, interest for diplomacy in the form of a treaty or other equivalent agreement is high, for the alternative would be a state of perpetual mistrust and conflict.. However, there is no international water law, so when countries meet to discuss water sharing ideas the decisions are highly contextual. Countries that share water resources have different economic, social, cultural, and political goals for and uses of the water resources. Some level of sharing water resources is almost always agreed upon in some fashion, at some point, though the outcomes are not always fair.

Some scholars observe that relationships on shared water resources—such as China upstream of Laos, or the Navajo Nation within the territory governed by the United States—are imbalanced, or hegemonic, relationships. However imbalanced, water sharing allows for the opportunity of asymmetric powers to engage, something that could lead to expanding the diplomatic conversations to other topics. Recently, in the Nile River basin, diplomatic meetings that originated about shared water resources gave the opportunity for Egypt and Ethiopia to discuss common terrorist threats and how to manage these together. Water resources discussions between Israel and the Palestinian State have continued despite surrounding violent conflict in the region. Agreements made official through written documents are considered peaceful and stable agreements by nature, and in the case of water, by necessity.

Treaties and other agreements about water resources often include elements about using the shared water resources that are peripheral. The treaty between the United States and Canada regarding the Columbia River watershed includes text pertaining to electricity generation and flood control, and a U.S. congressional amendment (S 2024 and HR 2024) will include consideration for riparian ecosystems. The highest *consumption* of water resources worldwide is for agriculture, but one of the highest *uses* is for power generation—directly in generating hydropower and indirectly to create steam to drive turbines in coal, oil, and nuclear power plants, as well as cooling in these plants. Water is used in industrial processes from creating plastic goods to jeans to metal works. One scholar posits that everything we consume and use, from the moment we wake up in the morning to the time we go to sleep at night, has water imbedded in the product. This is called virtual water. For this reason, water agreements may include trade agreements for goods or energy, transportation routes, and a myriad of diplomatic decisions that may not make it into the water agreement but are fostered by the conversation.

Water conflicts have been found to occur at local and regional levels, and subsequently are often resolved through local or regional mechanisms. When there are institutions, mechanisms, and diplomatic norms to manage resources (e.g., treaties, agreements, traditions, organizations) the likelihood for negotiation and conflict resolution is much higher. This is because of an established method of communications and understood power dynamics sets a precedent for how to communicate across stakeholders' interests. Organizations that manage water usually have dispute resolutions methods by which to handle conflicts when they arise. These methods can include fines for users, specialized lawyers and experts for court proceedings, and meetings for ongoing communications between potentially conflictive parties. An example is the *acequia* system in Northern New Mexico. The acequia canal system is a water management system that includes an institutional structure of negotiation and dispute resolution. Participants in the water compact meet frequently and the system even includes a *mayordomo*—a yearly, rotating leadership-overseer position. The *mayordomo* oversees water flow through a series of engineered water systems, is in charge of inspiring users to keep their sections clear of obstruction, and if users are found to be taking more than their designated share, they are fined.

When conflicts of use occur, salient issues of economic, cultural, social, and environmental reasons are elevated. Sometimes these issues may lead to discoveries that cause some serious policy changes and water-use culture changes. The recent drought in California has included new dialogue about people's personal water bills, filling swimming pools, watering golf courses, and what types of crops are grown. Farmers have considered changing from water-intensive crops (e.g., cotton) to less water-intensive crops (e.g., beans and cabbage). Towns are exploring new methods for how water consumption is metered. Homeowners may decide to zero-scape their previously green lawns and industries may decide to implement water efficient technologies. In 2015, to allay fear and mitigate conflict, the state of California enacted a comprehensive policy to encourage reduction and efficiency in usage.

Conflicts, while potentially explosive, often serve to promote awareness, responsibility, and conservation. Water disputes can lead to independent studies and important questions, such as: Is this water use sustainable? Is this water use necessary? How can we maintain current use with less so that other stakeholders may also benefit from our shared resources? Often times what starts out as a resource dispute with a winner-take-all attitude, results in a win-win scenario, due to the forced dialogue between potentially competing parties.

Tensions over water resources will continue as population grows and water and land development increase. Doubtless, the disputes will be exacerbated by the unknown hydrologic impacts of climate change. If past precedent is any indication though, there is hope that society will, in general, use water resource dispute as opportunities for negotiation, compromise, innovation, peace and stability.

TRANSBOUNDARY WATER MANAGEMENT—SOME SUCCESS STORIES
Mia Bennett

When a river, sea, lake, drainage basin, or any other body of water crosses international borders, it is commonly assumed that conflict will result. This is especially the case when water resources overlap with already tense borders. In arid Central Asia, upstream Kyrgyzstan and Tajikistan are planning to build dams that could limit downstream Uzbekistan's water resources. Uzbek President Islam Karimov seethed that the upstream countries' presidents "forget that the Amu-Darya and Syr-Darya are trans-border rivers" (Lillis, 2012). And in Africa, the now ousted president of Egypt, Mohammed Morsi, threatened action over a $4.2 billion hydroelectric dam Ethiopia has proposed to build upstream on the Nile. "If it loses one drop, our blood is the alternative" (Al Jazeera, 2013), he declared, referring to the river that makes agriculture—and indeed, human civilization—possible in Egypt.

Despite these headline stories, even as drought and increasing population have strained global water supplies, cooperation rather than conflict still persists in water management—including in the Middle East and North Africa

(De Stafano et al., 2010). As such, we may be able to paint a rosier picture of hydropolitics than the media commonly portrays. Stories of cooperation do not sell as many newspapers as stories of bloodshed over watersheds, but that does not mean they do not exist. Indeed, highlighting stories of cooperation is essential to show that successful international management is possible—and necessary. As Irina Bokova, director-general of the United Nations Educational, Scientific and Cultural Organization (UNESCO), urged, "With transboundary river basins and aquifer systems representing almost half the earth's surface, water cooperation is vital for peace." (UN Department of Economic and Social Affairs, 2014) In total, there are 276 transboundary river basins in the world, with 256 of those being shared by two to four countries (UNESCO, 2013). Indeed, with freshwater resources being so vital for human life, transboundary resources can even bring countries to the table to work towards a mutually beneficial solution—perhaps showing, as the United Nations has suggested, that "water more often unites than divides people and societies" (United Nations Department of Economic and Social Affairs, 2014).

In Europe, trans-border water management has been fairly successful for a number of reasons. Compared to Africa, Asia, and South America, Europe enjoys relatively low tensions, while the existence of the European Union (EU) has brought countries closer together. In fact, the EU Water Framework Directive (WFD) has established a legal framework to enhance water quality status in member states. They are each individually required to obtain good status in all of their surface water by 2015 and all of their groundwater by 2027 (International Commission for the Protection of the Danube River, 2009). In order to meet these requirements, EU countries have had to work together as they have done along the Danube River Basin.

Located in Central Europe, the Danube River basin crosses more countries than any other basin in the world—19 in total, including both EU and non-EU members. The Danube River Basin Management Plan, adopted in 2000, emerged directly out of the EU WFD, which requires member states to "endeavour to produce a single river basin management plan" (International Commission for the Protection of the Danube River, 2009). Although the non-EU countries of Bosnia and Herzegovina, Montenegro, Serbia, Slovakia, and Ukraine are not legally obligated to join or to improve their water quality, they have still provided data in the same way on everything from wastewater collecting systems to the number of protected areas. This sort of cooperative work helps harmonize standards of water quality and access across entire river basins, a method which can go a long way towards managing what is ultimately an international environmental resource. The International Commission for the Protection of the Danube River (ICPDR) has turned into "one of the largest and most active international bodies of river basin management expertise in the world" (ICPDR, 2009), and it may be able to export its knowledge to other countries seeking advice. As nature does not respect political borders, successful management must inevitably be trans-border, too.

Transferring management advice to other contexts, however, is fraught with challenges. Referring to issues in India, an International Water Management Institute briefing warned, "The problems that river basin institutions in the developed world successfully address—such as pollution, sediment buildup in rivers and the degradation of wetlands—are not the top priorities for Indian policy makers and people" (International Water Management Institute , 2002). Indeed, in Asia, no organization exactly like the ICPDR has yet emerged. Other more loosely organized groups like the Mekong River Commission in Southeast Asia may be signs of better management to come, but then again, this commission only includes the downstream countries of Thailand, Lao, Cambodia, and Vietnam. The upstream countries of China and Burma are merely observers. Without both upstream and downstream countries coming to the table, as they have done along the Danube, fully integrated management will not be possible.

Thus, some caution should be exercised in thinking that tussles over water management can ultimately promote peace and stability. In the Middle East, while geographer John Allan determined that conflicts over water have actually lessened since the 1970s, this is largely because countries in the region have been able to import "virtual water" from other places around the planet. By importing grain grown abroad, Middle Eastern countries are essentially purchasing crops grown with water elsewhere, lessening the burden on their own resources (Allan, 2002). Seen in another light, however, the international trade of water has served as a temporary band-aid that has allowed countries to avoid solving water management conflicts in their own neighborhood. Uzbek President Karimov, the leader who is so concerned about the dams his neighbors on higher ground are building, warned, "Everything can be so aggravated that this can spark not simply serious confrontation but even wars" (Lillis, 2012). When tensions become so high that outright war rather than cooperative management of a water basin seems more appealing, even virtual water will not be an apt substitute. Yet hopefully, statements such as Karimov's will remain heated rhetoric and the global trend of cooperation rather than conflict will prevail.

REFERENCES

Al Jazeera (eds.). (2013, June 11). "Egypt warns Ethiopia over Nile dam." Al Jazeera News: Africa. Accessed March 1, 2016, at http://www.aljazeera.com/news/africa/2013/06/201361144413214749.html.

Allan, John A. (2002). "Hydro-peace in the Middle East: Why no water wars? A case study of the Jordan River Basin," *SAIS Review 22*(2), 255–272.

De Stefano, Lucia, Paris Edwards, Lynette De Silva, and Aaron Wolf. (2010). "Tracking cooperation and conflict in international basins: Historic and recent trends," *Water Policy 12*(6), 871–884.

International Commission for the Protection of the Danube River. (2009). Danube River Basin District Management Plan. Document Number IC/151. Vienna: ICPDR Secretariat.

Lillis, Joanna. (2012). "Uzbekistan Leader Warns of Water Wars in Central Asia." EurasiaNet.org. Accessed September 7, 2015, at http://www.eurasianet.org/node/65877.

United Nations Department of Economic and Social Affairs. (2014). "International Decade for Action 'WATER FOR LIFE' 2005–2015.'" Accessed October 24, 2015, at http://www.un.org/waterforlifedecade/water_cooperation.shtml.

United Nations Educational, Scientific and Cultural Organization (UNESCO). (2013). "UN Water World Water Day 2013: International Year of Water Cooperation." Accessed March 1, 2016, at http://www.unwater.org/water-cooperation-2013/water-cooperation/facts-and-figures/it/.

Vidyanagar, Vallabh (ed.). (2002). "The challenges of integrated river basin management in India: issues in transferring successful river basin management models to the developing world." *Water Policy Briefing*, International Water Management Institute, IWMI-TATA Water Policy Program. Gujarat, India: International Water Management Institute, 1–6.

10

What Steps Should Be Taken to Help Provide Access to Clean Water for More People in the World?

OVERVIEW

Dennis Moran and M. Troy Burnett

"Whiskey is for drinking; water is for fighting over."

—Mark Twain

Over the past several years, the lack of access to freshwater in many parts of the world has come to be regarded as the most serious and immediate environmental crisis facing the world. Other crises may draw more headlines—for example, pollution and overfishing of oceans, or global warming—but water scarcity is already a deadly crisis, responsible for thousands of deaths per year as people in developing countries are forced to drink from contaminated water supplies. Competition over stressed water sources has played a large role in many world conflicts and is expected to be a trigger for many more as the problem gets worse. Water scarcity is also one of the most prominent ways that global climate change is felt as droughts become more frequent and severe in many areas. For these reasons and others, such organizations as the United Nations, the World Bank, and the European

Union are devoting increasing amounts of money and research time to the problem. Yet, providing access to clean water to the millions who lack it is a formidable task with many components to account for and many obstacles to overcome.

The crisis disproportionately affects many parts of the developing world, places where governments and people are least equipped to cope with it. In some of those areas, such as arid parts of Africa, the problem is both a resource crisis, meaning that such water sources as rivers and aquifers are overburdened and drying up; and a service crisis, meaning that even the potential resources that exist are not being effectively delivered due to poor management, lack of funding, and governmental corruption. Often the water that is delivered is contaminated due to pollution and a lack of proper sanitation and water-treatment facilities. In addition, climate change is exacerbating the resource crisis—increasing the frequency and severity of droughts in many semi-arid parts of the developing world—while population growth is putting further strain on limited available resources and inadequate services. The UN estimates that 90 percent of the 3 billion people projected to be added to the world population by 2050 will be in developing countries, most in areas that lack (or by then will lack) access to clean water. The increase in population will mean more demand for agricultural irrigation, which accounts for 70 percent of human water use. Beyond the figures provided by international water resource managers, the sight of thirsty faces and lands may best prompt world citizens to ask, what's the best way we can provide access to clean water for more people?

In the first essay, Nathan Eidem identifies the need for education at the grassroots level in those areas suffering the most, providing information on such basic concepts as the links between water quality and human health. He notes a further need for governments, nongovernmental organizations, and private businesses to work together to create a cost-efficient water supply infrastructure for communities lacking access to clean water. Once these goals have been accomplished, planning can shift to stress localized management of water resources, with regional and national governments providing regulatory standards on water quality.

In the second essay, Coralie Noël also stresses the need for infrastructure development, citing the problem of untreated wastewater and industrial discharge into water supplies in developing countries. She outlines the need for planning and coordination at various levels of water resource management, and the importance of self-sustaining water services. Noël contends that water management within a country should be better coordinated—most effectively via implementation of an approach called integrated water resources management—but also that international cooperation on water issues must be enhanced since many countries share water resources.

BACKGROUND

Throughout history, human populations have had to take elaborate measures to compensate for nature's uneven distribution of the freshwater that people need to drink, bathe, and grow food. Elaborate distribution and irrigation systems were often among the most impressive engineering feats of the ancient world, devised by groups in the Middle East, China, India, Mesoamerica, and Europe. Many early civilizations developed in arid areas and could not count entirely—or at all—on rainfall to provide the water they needed. Thus, early irrigation systems tapped into such fabled rivers as the Nile, Yellow, Indus, Euphrates, and Tigris, or springs such as Israel's spring of Jericho. Inevitably, conflicts over water sources arose. In the 19th century, water was the defining issue in the white settlement of the arid western United States, prompting a popular quote attributed to Mark Twain: "Whiskey is for drinking; water is for fighting over."

Added to the age-old problems of uneven distribution, pressures on freshwater availability have been increasingly affected by population growth, increasing pollution, poverty, corrupt or ineffective governments, and climate change. All of these impact parts of the developing world where lack of infrastructure is already a problem. While water scarcity has been a source of hardship and conflict through history, these factors are combining to pose what many authorities studying the problem consider the most severe crisis the world will face in the 21st century. For poor nations sharing overtapped rivers and aquifers, the threat of wars over water is real. In many cases, the role of water supplies in world conflicts in such areas as Darfur and the Middle East is underappreciated, according to many experts.

The distribution of water through evaporation and precipitation is more or less a constant amount—about 24,000 cubic miles of rainfall per year—but the distribution has always been inconsistent. In some countries, up to 90 percent of the year's rain may fall in a few major storms during a short monsoon season. Rainforests receive a huge amount of the world's rainfall; the Amazon River watershed accounts for one-fifth of the world's freshwater flow, but the area is largely made up of inaccessible forest (and the more that trees are cut down to access the area, the less rain falls due to the loss of evapotranspiration).

For areas that need more water, there are a limited number of ways of getting it. Dams can be built on rivers and streams, and water can be stored in reservoirs. Wells can reach down and tap water stored in underground aquifers. Water can be brought in from somewhere else. In coastal areas, seawater can be desalinated. Another measure sometimes counted as a water source is conservation—people learning to cut back on unnecessary water use and adopting such methods as drip irrigation to cut down on waste. The water saved can then be counted as a sort of "new" supply.

Some of those methods can have severe drawbacks in certain areas. Building dams has become increasingly controversial, especially larger projects that are seen as damaging to the environment and that often displace communities of people who live in valleys that must be flooded to become reservoirs. Desalinating seawater is an expensive option and is in very limited use. Drawing on groundwater poses risks because in some areas it is essentially a nonrenewable source.

Currently about 20 percent of the water people use comes from groundwater, and that proportion is rising. With continued extraction, groundwater tables in some areas become lower, requiring deeper wells and higher costs.

There are proposals in water-rich Canada to export bulk quantities of freshwater. Canada, with 0.25 percent of the world's population, stores an estimated 20 percent of the world's total freshwater supply and circulates about 9 percent of the world's "renewable" freshwater—the water that flows in rivers and falls as precipitation. There are business interests that would like the country to allow freshwater to be transported to the U.S. Southwest, and possibly shipped overseas in tankers or huge bags that would be towed by ships to parched countries on other continents. Proponents say that for Canada to market water is no different from Saudi Arabia marketing oil. These proposals have critics, however, who feel that water should not be treated as a for-profit commodity, and that selling it to developing nations could cause conflicts over who gets the water, possibly widening divisions between rich and poor in countries receiving the water. Many critics also oppose such proposals on environmental grounds. The Canadian government hasn't approved anything yet.

Another element of the looming crisis is poor management of water resources. The problem was dramatized in July 2009 when inhabitants in five villages in Nigeria's Kano state organized a protest, saying they had waited 15 years for the state government to provide wells. The villagers must carry water containers many miles and often take water from contaminated ponds, which led to six deaths from cholera in one month alone. Nigeria, Africa's most populous nation with 170 million people, is one of four West African nations in which fewer than half of the residents have access to safe drinking water, according to the United Nations.

Corrupt and inefficient national and local governments and a lack of resources and technological expertise have hampered efforts in such places as rural Nigeria. The UN, World Bank, European Union, and other international agencies have put forth models for alleviating such obstacles, including a concept called Integrated Water Resources Management, which involves coordinating different uses of water (e.g., agriculture, industry, home use, the environment) as well as all the different entities involved in construction, development, and delivery of any services that involve water. With better management, available resources can be used more efficiently and safely.

However, management issues are very difficult to solve, and it is even harder to fruitfully address the problems posed by population growth and climate change. It is therefore perhaps not surprising that a multinational public opinion poll conducted in August 2009 by an organization called Circle of Blue, which surveyed 1,000 people each in 15 countries, identified freshwater availability as the world's top environmental concern.

FURTHER READING

Figuères, Caroline, Cecilia Tortajada, and Johan Rockström (eds.). (2012). *Rethinking Water Management: Innovative Approaches to Contemporary Issues.* New York: Routledge.

Mulder, Michelle. (2014). *Every Last Drop: Bringing Clean Water Home.* Victoria, BC, Canada: Orca Book Publishers.

INFRASTRUCTURE FIRST, THEN BETTER MANAGEMENT
Nathan Eidem

Although water is abundant on Earth, less than 3 percent of all water on the planet is freshwater, and the majority of that freshwater is trapped as ice in glaciers and ice sheets. According to the World Bank and UNICEF, nearly 750 million people around the world do not have access to safe drinking water. Additionally, the world's population is increasing ever more rapidly. The world's population has grown from 1 billion in 1804 to 6 billion in 1999 to over 7 billion in 2016 thanks to better medicine and better agriculture. The fastest population growth is happening in developing nations. These same countries are in the greatest need of improved access to clean water. Further, water consumption is increasing worldwide. Currently, an average of five to eight gallons per person per day of clean water is sufficient to meet basic human needs in the developing world, as opposed to such developed nations as the United States and Germany, which have rates of 100 and 34 gallons per person per day, respectively. As developing nations industrialize, standards of living rise and water consumption increases. As consumption increases, the amount available to other animals and plants decreases. This in turn limits ecosystems' ability to naturally filter pollutants from water, ultimately posing health risks to humans. Considering all of these factors, the problem of providing access to clean water to more people around the world is a complex and multifaceted one. A variety of strategies should therefore be employed to address the issues of freshwater access and quality.

The first step toward increasing access to clean water begins at the local level. People living in communities without basic water and sanitation infrastructure need to be educated about the links between water quality and human health in order to promote a change in behavior. For example, in many parts of the developing world, especially in crowded slums, water sources are often polluted by human waste, which leads to deaths from preventable diseases. Nongovernmental organizations (NGOs) such as the World Bank would be well suited to train local leaders on these issues. Local officials, such as council members and teachers, could then provide training to the general public through meetings and schools. All citizens need to be educated on water-quality issues, as it may take years to change behavior at the community level. Utilizing established local leaders will increase local buy-in to the program.

Governments, NGOs, and private companies also need to work together to extend basic water-supply infrastructure to the people currently without it. When building this infrastructure, it is essential that it be cost-efficient, as these communities are generally very poor and will need to be able to afford the necessary operation and maintenance costs. Increasing access to clean water will help to improve the economies of the developing world by increasing productivity by decreasing illness. An example of this type of partnership is the World Bank's project to increase rainwater harvesting in drought-stricken municipalities in India. For this project, the World Bank partnered with a university and various government officials to develop and construct a rainwater harvesting system that connected tanks on each house to larger community-wide storage tanks. These tanks lead to a village tank, which is used to replenish the well. In regions that sit atop aquifers, low-cost tube wells are a quick way to increase domestic water supplies. This technology is common in Africa and Asia, and the World Bank has been involved with funding some of these projects. If a tube well program is implemented, however, appropriate groundwater extraction regulations need to be established to prevent depletion of the aquifer.

Once basic infrastructure is constructed, local governments or councils need to be created to manage and protect the new water supply systems. A study in the former Soviet Union showed that community-based management of infrastructure is more effective than a centralized government management approach. Water users who are also responsible for maintenance are more proactive in routine maintenance, and community members are less likely to vandalize infrastructure when they have an important role in its upkeep. Additionally, any fees associated with maintaining the infrastructure are more easily collected by community members. Along with the creation of local governing bodies, additional education is needed on water conservation in order to promote the long-term sustainability of the freshwater resource for the community.

While local government should take the lead in managing water resources, there are important steps that need to be taken at higher levels of government. National and regional water-quality standards must be established, as water is a common-pool resource, meaning that it is accessed by many users. Surface water travels from place to place, and pollution from users upstream impacts users downstream. Groundwater moves at a much slower rate than surface water, but here too pollution in one region of an aquifer can impact water quality in other regions. Many developed nations have long-standing water-quality standards that could provide models for the developing world to follow. The major obstacle to these large-scale standards is funding. There is a lack of money in the developing world, and environmental quality monitoring and regulation is not a top priority for spending when budgets are limited. This is why education at the local level in all communities is critical. If everyone maintains clean freshwater supplies locally, then there is not as great a need for top-down water quality regulation.

Providing access to clean water to more people is important from many standpoints. From a humanitarian perspective, all humans should be able to access clean water, as it is essential for life. In this age of globalization, it is in everyone's best interest to help maintain high standards of hygiene and sanitation, as diseases can rapidly spread around the world. Further, expanding access to clean water can help to stabilize communities and improve global security. Finally, from an environmental perspective, maintaining good water quality will keep ecosystems healthy and allow them to provide the ecosystem services that humans often take for granted long into the future.

INFRASTRUCTURE IS FINE, BUT WE NEED TO FOCUS ON REGULATION, MANAGEMENT, AND INTERNATIONAL COOPERATION

Coralie Noël

Overexploited and polluted by human activities, water has become a fragile resource, in quantity and in quality, everywhere in the world. Rampant population growth, increasing urbanization, economic growth, and changing consumption put more and more pressure on water resources. During the last 50 years, world water consumption has tripled as the population has doubled. With a world population projected to be 8 billion by 2030 and 9 billion by 2050, the need will increase considerably; for example, it will be necessary to increase irrigated agricultural lands to feed this population. It is necessary to take into account the increasing need related to the development of India and China, and in several areas of the world geopolitical problems can lead to tensions over the use of transboundary aquifers and rivers. Lastly, the effects of climate change on water resources are already being felt and will likely worsen such situations. This is why it is all the more necessary to make efforts to provide clean water to more people in the world.

Developing and financing infrastructures for access to drinking water and sanitation for all is a prime objective. In developing countries, 85 percent of domestic wastewater and 70 percent of industrial waste are directly discharged untreated into the aquatic environment, where they pollute the water supply, leading to dire health consequences. Public authorities, either national or local, must develop infrastructural elements such as drinking-water production plants, wastewater treatment plants, and delivery networks, and make sure they are well operated and maintained. Wastewater treatment can be either collective (for urban areas) or on-site (for rural areas).

As water must be locally managed, it is important that national authorities give to local authorities the necessary powers and skills to organize water and sanitation services. To optimize the development of infrastructures, objectives, deadlines, and actions should be defined in management plans. This requires political will and financing. For developing countries, access to clean water should be the priority for bilateral aid and international funding institutions.

Even in developing countries, it is absolutely necessary for decision-makers to develop the economic autonomy of water services to guarantee the financing of investments and functioning in the long term. The viability of water utilities requires a detailed, balanced budget, whether the management system is public or delegated to a private operator. Income must come from water bills paid by the users by setting a price for the service, setting cooperative mechanisms to provide for the poorest, if necessary. Even if the water price is low, it is important to give an economic value to water to motivate people to conserve. Revenue from water bills should be used to invest in improvements so that "water pays for water." Providing water for human consumption should be the top priority, and allocation for other uses (e.g., irrigation, industry) should be defined through participative processes to take account of local needs.

Water resources should be better regulated, in quality and quantity, following a cross-sectoral approach called integrated water resources management at the river-basin level. In most cases, the legal framework should be strengthened by setting standards for water use and water pollution, and by enforcing compliance. Then it is necessary to adopt a comprehensive approach toward all pressures on water resources, thus allowing everyone to have access to safe water and sanitation, ensuring agricultural production and industry, preserving water resources and aquatic environments, and managing floods and droughts. These interests often compete and can no longer be individually solved in a sectoral way.

As stated by the International Network of Basin Organizations, we need coordination among the different water uses, between upstream and downstream, between quantity and quality, between surface water and groundwater. Since water has no national and administrative boundaries, river basins are the most logical territories for organizing water management. Integrated water management at the river-basin level means defining specific administrative arrangements, river basin management plans, programs for action, networks for monitoring water status, financing mechanisms, and other elements. Users' participation should be organized within specific bodies, for example through river basin committees, gathering representatives of state and local authorities and of the different categories of users.

Capacity building is also a key factor. Developing infrastructure alone is not sufficient. Providing clean water to more people in the world is also a question of governance and institutional capacities. It implies improving countries' entire organization toward water management, through policy reforms and clarification of responsibilities. It also implies improving the skills of technicians, engineers, and decision-makers. The technical nature of water professions requires very precise qualifications, and personnel costs represent the highest item of expenditure in water supply and sanitation utilities. Basic and continuing vocational training for all personnel involved is central for the successful management of water utilities.

Finally, international cooperation should be reinforced. Cooperation should be strengthened between countries sharing the same river or aquifer. There are about 263 transboundary rivers and several hundred transboundary aquifers. As co-riparian countries share responsibility, the signing of international agreements and the creation of international commissions should be supported where they do not exist. In Europe, the Water Framework Directive represents a very important step for the joint management of water resources: it constitutes an operational framework for multilateral coordination on a river-basin scale with common objectives and principles that can be exported to other parts of the world. The 1992 United Nations Economic Commission for Europe Convention on the protection and use of transboundary watercourses and international lakes, also known as the Helsinki Convention, developed key principles for cooperation across a broader geographical area than just the European Union—in Central Asia, for example. The 1997 United Nations Watercourses Convention, which entered into force in 2014, only ratified by 36 nations, also provides a global framework for transboundary water cooperation.

International cooperation should also be reinforced through assistance programs to Africa, Asia, and Latin America. The financial resources devoted by international and bilateral donors to cooperation programs and capacity building should significantly increase and prioritize water issues. To conclude, common cause is necessary to meet water challenges, and both developed and developing countries have a stake in avoiding a crisis. The role of the European Union and the United States is therefore particularly essential.

11

TO MITIGATE CONFLICTS OVER WATER, IS IT BETTER TO TREAT WATER AS A COMMODITY OR A HUMAN RIGHT?

OVERVIEW
M. Troy Burnett and William Osei

Water, like air, is a basic need for human survival. Unlike air, however, water is not evenly distributed, and population growth, climate change, and other factors are increasingly stressing the availability of clean, freshwater to many parts of the world. According to the United Nations (UN), about 900 million people in the world lack access to clean, fresh water, and the UN's Human Rights Council in 2010 declared that such access is a human right that national governments must ensure. There is debate, however, whether the delivery of water should be in the hands of private corporations that would market and sell water as a commodity. Some believe that this model best ensures the that water will be provided—and won't be wasted if people have to pay a market price for it—while others believe that treating water as a commodity is incompatible with the view that water is a basic human right.

In his essay, Mark Hecht argues that treating water as a commodity has been the basis for successful and efficient water management systems for a long time, citing water markets devised by the ancient San culture of the Kalarahi Desert in southern Africa. The marketing of water should be regulated to ensure the delivery of water for basic needs, but beyond that, treating it as a "tradable good" helps ensure against wasteful and inefficient use as well as excessive demands on ecosystems, he contends. John Agnew, in his essay, argues that viewing water as a human right is fundamental to human society, which is based on the need for cooperation. Cooperative management, therefore, and not private ownership of water as a commodity is essential to the maintenance of civil society, even as management systems can be improved by political means to reduce waste and improve distribution.

BACKGROUND

The situation appears to be getting direr. Latest figures suggest that more than 1 billion people on Earth do not have access to safe drinking water and more than double that number lack water for basic sanitation. According to the Millennium Development Report of 2011, an urban dweller in Sub-Saharan Africa is 1.8 times more likely to use an improved drinking water source than a person in the rural area of that region. On the other hand, the poorest urban households are 12 times less likely than the richest households to have the benefits of a piped drinking water supply on premises. It is doubtful whether Sub-Saharan Africa will reach its estimated Millennium Development target of 75 percent access to safe drinking water by 2015, as progress toward that target stalls or deteriorates (see Table 11.1). This region is abundantly endowed with untapped water resources, as only 3 percent of its estimated sustainable water supply potential had been exploited by 2005. Financing for water development projects, infrastructure for distribution, and poverty are among major factors that hinder universal access to quality water in the region. The gross internal sustainable water supply potential remains close to the estimated levels of a decade ago. In comparison, the Netherlands, a wealthy but water-deficit jurisdiction, imports over 75 percent of its water but manages to provide universal access to clean water for all of the country's citizens.

Limited access to good quality water has reversed modest gains in living standards and general productivity in economies. Water and sanitation affect health, disease, economic growth, and social development and amplify their negative impacts. According to a 2009 draft document by the Institute for Human Rights and Business, when people have to travel long distances to collect water, or spend a disproportionate portion of their income on water, they are deprived of time and resources to pursue other activities meaningful to improving or even maintaining their livelihoods (Institute for Human Rights and Business, 2009). In the foreword to a publication by the World Health Organization, Kofi Annan, a former secretary-general of the United Nations, wrote that "access to safe water is a fundamental human need and . . . a basic human right" (World Health Organization, 2003).

Table 11.1 Millennium Development Goals: Progress on Access to Safe Drinking Water by Region

	1990			2004			2015 Target			On Target?
	Urban	Rural	Total	Urban	Rural	Total	Urban	Rural	Total	
Northern Africa	95	82	89	96	86	91	98	91	95	On target
Sub-Saharan Africa	82	36	49	80	42	56	91	68	75	No progress or deterioration
Latin America & Caribbean	93	60	83	96	73	91	97	80	92	Target met or close to being met
Eastern Asia	99	59	71	93	67	78	100	80	86	On target
Southern Asia	90	66	72	94	81	85	95	83	86	Target met or close to being met
Southern-Eastern Asia	93	68	76	89	77	82	97	84	88	On target
Western Asia	94	70	85	97	79	91	97	85	93	Target met or close to being met
Oceania	92	39	51	80	40	51	96	70	76	No progress or deterioration
Commonwealth of Independent States*	97	84	92	99	80	92	99	92	96	Target nearly met in Europe but no progress or deterioration in Asia

*CIS: Russia, Armenia, Azerbaijan, Belarus, Kazakhstan, Kyrgyzstan, Moldova Tajikistan, Uzbekistan, Turkmenistan, Ukraine.

Contaminated water jeopardizes both the physical and social health of all people. Waterborne diseases are estimated to cause three million to five million deaths a year and many more illnesses (Policy Research Division, 2008). Hutton and Haller (2004) noted major economic benefits, direct and indirect, from water and sanitation improvements; benefits that also extend to non-health targets (Hutton and Haller, 2004). The health sector, patients, consumers, and the agricultural and industrial sectors accrue benefits when improvements are made to water and sanitation facilities.

Ziganshina wrote that "the human right to water exists without requiring any legal recognition, if one admits that water is vital to life" (Ziganshima, 2008). Biswas argued that using the approach of water as a human right would pave the way for translating the right to water into specific national and international obligations and responsibilities (Biswas et al., 2008). McGaw argued to the extent that realization of water's fundamentality and rise in its scarcity constituted the ethical justification for a(n) human right to water: "If it is truly essential for all life, to whom can it be denied?" or "should anyone be denied?" (McGaw, 2010).

To raise awareness of the fundamental importance of water and draw attention to issues of supply and distribution, the Generally Assembly of the United Nations took a position and declared water a universal human right in 2010. This represented a turning point in the search for fairness, equal opportunity, and unhindered access to and for the sustainable development of water resources (UN General Assembly, 2010; de Albuquerque, 2011). Specifically, the United Nations publication, *The Right to Water* (United Nations, 2010) articulated that the right to water contains clauses that include access to a minimum amount to sustain life and health. However, the fact that water has been declared a human right and that more attention has been given to it as a result does not mean that the problem is solved, or that there is an adequate system to provide for this right. In other words, the real issue is whether it is practical or effective in the provisioning of water to consider it a human right or a commodity?

REFERENCES

Biswas, Asit K., Eglal Rached, and Cecilia Tortajada (eds.). (2008). *Water as a Human Right for the Middle East and North Africa*. London: Routledge.

De Albuquerque, Catarina. (2011, March 4). Statement of UN Independent Expert on the Human Right to Water and Sanitation at the conclusion of her mission to the United States (February 22 to March 4, 2011). Accessed May 1, 2016, at http://aquadoc.typepad.com/files/un-ie-end-of-mission-statement-mar-4-2011.pdf.

Hutton, Guy, and Laurence Haller. (2004). "Evaluation of the Costs and Benefits of Water and Sanitation Improvements at the Global Level." Water, Sanitation and Health: Protection of the Human Environment. Geneva, Switzerland: World Health Organization. Accessed May 1, 2016, at http://www.who.int/water_sanitation_health/wsh0404.pdf.

Institute for Human Rights and Business. (2009). "Draft: Business, Human Rights and the Right to Water Challenges, Dilemmas and Opportunities." Roundtable Consultative Report, January.

McGaw, George. (2010). "Water for life: the challenge posted by un-codified human right to water in international law," *University for Peace Law Review* 1(30), 39–51.

Policy Research Division of the Department of Foreign Affairs and International Trade Canada. (2008). *The Global Water Crisis: A Question of Governance*. Ottawa, Canada: Foreign Affairs and International Trade.

UN General Assembly. (2010, August 3). "The human right to water and sanitation." Resolution adopted by the General Assembly, 64th session, Agenda item 48 A/RES /64/292. New York: United Nations.

United Nations. (2010). "The Right to Water." Fact Sheet No. 35, Office of the United Nations High Commissioner for Human Rights, New York, Geneva, Switzerland: United Nations, 7.

World Health Organization. (2003). *Emerging Issues in Water and Infectious Disease*. Geneva, Switzerland: World Health Organization.

Ziganshima, Diana. (2008). "Rethinking the concept of the human right to water," *Santa Clara Journal of International Law* 1 113–128.

FURTHER READING

Roth, Dik, Rutgerd Boelens, and Margreet Zwarteveen. (2005). *Liquid Relations: Contested Water Rights and Legal Complexity*. Piscataway, NJ: Rutgers University Press.

Sultana, Farhana, and Alex Loftus. (2013). *The Right to Water: Politics, Governance and Social Struggles*. London: Routledge.

WATER IS, AND ALWAYS HAS BEEN, A COMMODITY
Mark Hecht

Declaring water to be a human right is not only unrealistic but is likely to lead to unintended, negative consequences and future conflicts. How to manage water as a commodity, though, is debatable.

The United Nations (UN) has not formally recognized water as a human right, nor should it. While lives, liberty, freedom from torture, and access to education are all included in the UN International Declaration on Human Rights, water remains absent. Some of the previously mentioned items are inherent concepts that cannot be traded. We cannot trade freedom. We cannot trade respect for life or the concept of liberty. However, we can trade physical entities such as water.

A water vendor in Indonesia is seen in this undated handout photo from the World Bank. Small-time vendors make a modest living selling the world's most basic commodity. But a new global water commission said on August 5, 1999, it's a system that has the world's poorest people paying up to 100 times more for water than wealthier users who draw their baths from subsidized water systems. (Curt Carnemark/World Bank/AP Photo)

We can also trade entitlements or access to things such as access to education, access to resources, and of course access to water. Since water is fundamentally different than standard physical resources, and forms the foundation for all life just as air does, we need to treat water with special consideration. In light of this special condition, the UN Human Rights Council declared in September of 2010 that access to water is a basic human right, though water by itself is not.

While access to water for basic needs is critical and formally recognized by the United Nations, water as a commodity has always been an integral part of any successful management system beyond basic needs. In one of the driest parts of the world, the San Bushmen of the Kalahari Desert have developed complex management systems that sustain life and the ecosystem. James G. Workman argues that the San, who've had minimal impact from outside influences for thousands of years, have created "subtle and highly complex markets (that) exist for the vital exchange of water resource goods, services or information" (Workman, 2010). Access is not random nor is it considered a human right. It is instead "self-regulated by defining the terms of individual and group territorial rights: who, how, when and where people could, for example, drink water" (Workman, 2010). And of course this is no different from any other society. How we design water management systems is defined by laws and customs that tell us who, how, when, and where the individual and the society can have water, and how much. While the San have perhaps the longest continuous system of water management of any current society on Earth, which includes the marketing of water commodities, Australia is considered to be the first nation state to implement a highly complex system of water trading. And trading involves the understanding that water can be bought and sold just as any other commodity. Australia's experimentation comes from its experience with the problems inherent in "public" water.

According to water laws and doctrines that have been passed down through time in such countries as Australia, Canada, New Zealand, the United Kingdom, and the United States, the "public" governing bodies have typically attached water rights to land rights in common law. Or those who come first get full access to first use, known as prior appropriation. The many problems inherent in these laws or doctrines are that water rights attached to property ownership leads to problems when there is a need for transferring only the water without owning the land. And prior appropriation is often conditional on use. In other words, the owners of the water rights can only keep the rights as long as they use the water. Under such conditions, water is often used excessively and inappropriately simply to maintain indefinite ownership. Australia has taken the lead in recognizing the inherent flaws in its public system and instead has taken a modified commodity approach. As opposed to a full open market like that implemented in Chile, Australia has recognized the need for treating water with special consideration. Water for basic needs is recognized, as is the need for minimum water flows for fish and other wildlife. Beyond this, however, "water reforms required the separation of water rights from land [so] water can be traded with market fluctuations in price and quantity" (Australian Government, n.d.).

With this in mind we can recognize that basic water needs for sustaining life can be considered beyond the realm of pure commercialization. Excess water beyond basic human needs, however, can be considered a tradable good, a commodity. Of course the real question is, what do we mean by water being a commodity? In this sense, the Merriam-Webster dictionary defines commodity as "something useful or valued." And all societies have found water to be useful or valued. And value comes with a price. If we put a low value on water or subsidize it because we consider it a human right, we will end up using it excessively and without care.

So if water is considered to be a human right, how will we define that? Is it a human right to take water for drinking? Is it a human right to take water out of the ecosystem for washing and bathing? Is it a human right to take water out of the ecosystem to the detriment of fish for growing crops? Is it a human right to take water out of the ecosystem to the detriment of fish and all other non-human life for manufacturing? At what point does a human right conflict with the rights of other non-human users? This is a point that virtually all indigenous groups and any society that considers long-term consequences brings to the discussion and to their management system. At no point do they take a self-centered anthropocentric viewpoint that says water is a human right. Instead it is understood that the voice of those who cannot speak for themselves must be heard. And this involves being practical in a holistic manner. Practicality includes treating water to a certain extent as a commodity. Who, how, when, and where—these are the true issues, not "human rights."

Indeed, a debate that pits the issue as one of rich versus poor, equal versus unequal, public versus private, north versus south, commodity versus human right, is a misleading debate. The true debate is over management and practicality for the long term. Any society that has existed sustainably seems to share a few common similarities:

1. It treats water as an entity owned by all creatures, not just humans as a human right.
2. Access for basic needs is universal.
3. Management and control is usually watershed based.
4. Water-based goods, services, and access to water are to varying degrees treated as commodities to be traded through money, barter, debt, reciprocity, and other means of valuation.

In this context, water should not be treated in a narrow sense as a human right but viewed instead as an entity that is understood to have a commodity role in any meaningful and long-term management system.

REFERENCES

Australian Government. (n.d.) "Water Trading." National Water Commission. Accessed March 3, 2016, at http://www.nwc.gov.au/www/html/?a=23333.

Workman, James G. (2010). "Water challenges and solutions, H2Ownership: ancient, equitable traditions of efficient water resource trading in desert cultures," *Globalwater.* Accessed March 1, 2016, at http://globalwater.jhu.edu/magazine/article/h2ownership_ancient_equitable_traditions_of_efficient_water_resource_tradin/.

WATER SHOULD BE A HUMAN RIGHT!
John Agnew

At one time water was regarded everywhere as a basic need for sustaining human life, along with air and essential sustenance. Society, by definition, approved of this arrangement as a central feature of social reproduction and provided it in a myriad of ways for those who could not readily provide it for themselves. I argue that there is still a compelling logic to this view. In fact, it is only since the 1970s that the idea of water as a commodity like any other has become widespread. This was a consequence of the diffusion of neo-liberal ideas claiming that private firms and markets (and therefore prices) allocate all goods, including such public goods as water, more efficiently than do government-run bureaucracies. In Britain and some other countries this led to the privatization of hitherto municipal and other public water authorities. Around the world, international organizations such as the World Bank have encouraged a similar approach, arguing that more money will be invested in water pipelines and reservoirs and other supply technologies and less water will be wasted by consumers during delivery if water is priced such that consumers must pay for the privilege of using water that now belongs to private water companies. Property rights in water, therefore, will provide a market-based solution to the so-called tragedy of the commons (Hardin, 1968). That water provision illustrates: people will consume more responsibly and will receive better quality water if they have to pay private companies for it.

At first sight, this argument can seem persuasive. As the world's overall population has grown, as pollution has increased because of industrialization, and as more people crowd into increasingly congested and ill-planned cities, both the quantity and the quality of readily available water has gone down. The conjunction between this reality and the spread of market thinking is what has produced the seeming inevitability of regarding water as just another commodity. This thinking, however, is fallacious. The world water issue is a political-managerial problem more than a simple economic one. Managing the flow of water to consumers can be done in a variety of ways other than through giving over ownership of water to private businesses. As a result, the traditional view of water as a human right can be maintained in practice as well as in theory.

First of all, then, it is important not to abandon the view of water as a human right. If we do, we abandon our very humanity based as it is on mutual aid: only those who think that there is no such thing as society can find much comfort in seeing water entirely as a commodity. Those who believe in the reality of human cooperation and the consequent social necessity of caring for others that this implies must see water as a human right. Cooperation is as fundamental a feature of human biological evolution as is conflict. Yet, it has never received as much emphasis. In liberal evolutionary theory, natural selection is all about conflict: if someone wins someone else always loses. Yet, the simple Prisoner's Dilemma Game shows clearly that all participants in struggles over access to such resources as water are relatively better off if they cooperate. If you trust others by cooperating, all involved will be better off than if each acts selfishly. By cooperating, if each individual pays a cost so that others receive a benefit, though they may forfeit the absolute best outcome as isolated individuals, in the absence of information about what others will do everyone on the whole gets a better result by cooperating than they would if each went it alone (Nowak, 2011). For relatively "pure" public goods like water that are necessary for life and generally difficult to exclude people from consuming, cooperative management rather than privatized provision, therefore, is the best approach to provision. Second, even as the provision of water comes under strain for the reasons listed previously—population growth, congested cities, etc.—better public management can do a more effective and equitable job than placing provision in the hands of private companies to resolve the real difficulties that do face water provision in many parts of the world today. In many places intensely politicized specialized bureaucracies staffed by timeserving cronies of politicians and local aristocracies often dominate the provision of water to local populations. This chronic public mismanagement, more than the inherent logic of private ownership—which I have argued is in fact inappropriate for water—and as often the desire to sell public assets to private political allies account in large part for the appeal of water privatization. I now develop the two crucial points about cooperation and management at greater length.

Numerous international meetings and subsequent declarations have proclaimed water to be a basic human right. These range from the 1998 Water Contract and 2000 Cochabamba Declaration to the UN General Comment on the Right to Water of 2002. They all reflect the view in one way or another that, in the words of the Accra Declaration on the Right to Water of 2001:

- Water is a fundamental human right, essential to human life to which every person, rich or poor, man or woman, child or adult is entitled.
- Water is not and should not be a common commodity to be bought and sold in the market place as an economic good.
- Water is a natural resource that is part of our common heritage to be used judiciously and preserved for the common good of our societies and the natural environment today and in the future.
- Water is an increasingly scarce natural resource, and as a result crucial to the securities of our societies and sovereignty of our country. For this reason alone, its ownership, control, delivery, and management belong in the public domain today and tomorrow. (Sierra Club, 2011)

This is all very well, critics may say, but providing potable water to people around the world remains a massive problem. By way of example, perhaps two-fifths of the people in Asia's cities do not have access to piped water. Many people worldwide have only intermittent supplies of unsafe water. International organizations such as the World Bank and IMF have been major proponents of the idea that only privatization of water provision can possibly address this massive problem. The potential profits in water will provide an incentive to invest in the infrastructure and management necessary to produce a positive outcome. In fact, schemes based on such principles are beside the point. The main issue is management not commoditization. Private management is not inherently more efficient than is public when the provision in question involves a technical monopoly such as that of area-based water provision. There is thus no good managerial case for privatization. Indeed, the case for privatization, while hiding behind nostrums about private efficiency and market discipline (even in the absence of competition between providers), is largely one of giving economic rents to political allies and campaign contributors as has been the case with privatization of water utilities in Italy (Marino, 2010).

The basic evolutionary logic of cooperation as indicated by the Prisoner's Dilemma and simple managerial changes that can make provision more reliable and of higher quality suggest that there are practical more than moral grounds for thinking of water as a human right. Everyone needs water to survive. There is absolutely no case for why this requires privatized provision. Indeed, the logic of human cooperation and the at least equivalent efficiency of public management to private in the face of technical monopoly point in absolutely the opposite direction. Water is a public good that can be best managed publicly.

REFERENCES

Hardin, Garrett. (1968). "The tragedy of the commons," *Science 162*, 1243–1248.

Marino, Giuseppe. (2010). *La Casta Dell'acqua—Come la Privatizzazione Sta Assetando L'Italia*. Modena, Italy: Nuovi Mondi.

Nowak, Martin, with Roger Highfield. (2011). *SuperCooperators: Altruism, Evolution, and Why We Need Each Other to Succeed*. New York: Free Press, 11.

Sierra Club. (2011). "Accra Declaration on the Right to Water of 2001." Accessed April 18, 2011, at http://www.sierraclub.org/committees/cac/water/human_right/.

12

WHICH WATER BASINS ARE PRESENTLY SITES OF THE HIGHEST POTENTIAL FOR CONFLICT?

OVERVIEW
Mia Bennett

Water is necessary for human life. Aside from the eight recommended glasses a day, agriculture, sanitation, cooking, transportation, and many other activities would be impossible without water. The liquid often seems to be all around us. "Water, water, everywhere," goes the refrain inspired by English poet Samuel Coleridge's "Rime of the Ancient Mariner," ominously concluding, "and not a drop to drink." Although the mariner in the poem is at sea, there is a growing lack of drinking water on land as well. A 2014 report from the United Nations underscored the global decrease of fresh water per capita, attributing the decline to both climate change and increasing population pressures (United Nations, 2014). With water becoming ever scarcer, particularly since water basins—the term used to describe an area of land in which all of the rivers, streams, and rainfall inside drain to the same common outlet, be it a sea, ocean, or lake—often cross international borders, effective multilateral management is more important than ever. The neologism "hydropolitics," first coined by political scientist John Waterbury, is used to describe the study of the management of water, particularly when the resource spans more than one country (Waterbury, 1979). The irony, however, is that in times of scarcity, hydropolitics becomes all the more tense as countries become more defensive of their precious water resources.

BACKGROUND

Within water basins, especially those that cross international borders, conflicts can arise over water allocation. These types of watersheds are known as transboundary basins. Peter Gleick, a leading researcher on water and security issues, has posited that "water wars" could foment as a result of all of these pressures, which are driving water scarcity (Gleick, 1993). Others are more cautious, asserting that cooperation is more likely and that no wars have yet come about directly as a result of water. A team of researchers from Oregon State University's Program in Water Conflict Management and Transformation determined that "despite the current global water crisis, tendencies towards international cooperation over water are more prevalent than conflict," even in the contentious and drought-prone Middle East and North Africa. They did, however, note an increasing tendency in recent years towards "less cooperative interactions" (De Stefano et al., 2010).

Wars or no wars, the potential for conflict can be exacerbated by a number of factors, including increasing population, climate change, and existing geopolitical tensions. Take the Ganges-Brahmaputra-Meghna (GBM) Basin, for example, which lies between the Himalayas and the Bay of Bengal in the Indian Ocean. India, China, Nepal, Bangladesh, and Bhutan all have territory within the GBM. This transboundary basin supplies water to the 630 million people who live within its bounds—just a little under 10 percent of the global population (Food and Agriculture Organization of the UN, 2015). The population is growing quickly here, too, particularly in Bangladesh, a low-lying and densely populated country that is also vulnerable to sea level rise. Yet existing rivalries between India and China, and India and Bangladesh, make it even more difficult for the countries to come to bilateral or multilateral agreements on how water should be reliably and fairly allocated to the hundreds of millions of people lying within the basin.

Topography is also a determining factor in water-basin management. Because they essentially control the source of the water, upstream states tend to have the advantage in any discussion over how rights and resources are allocated. Though they cannot control precipitation, they can control water flow, availability, and quality, especially through the construction of dams and reservoirs. Furthermore, in the GBM Basin, torrential monsoons cause flooding every year that is exacerbated in already-saturated Bangladesh. As the country lacks proper infrastructure like reservoirs and drainage systems, the rainfall cannot be saved to use during drier months. Compounding the problem, Bangladesh is often caught off guard by floods because India fails to share information about upstream flow. Bilateral issues within water basins concern more than just traditional forms of conflict over quantity and quality, they also encompass issues such as information sharing (or lack thereof).

Even when a water basin falls within a single country, questions over the allocation can still cause conflict between states or counties. In China, the Yangtze River was dammed and over two million people forcibly relocated in order to build the Three Gorges Dam (Harris, 2011), which diverts water from the country's monsoon-soaked southern region to the arid economic centers of the northwest. And in the southwestern United States, the heavily overtaxed Colorado River Basin constitutes a problem that will need to be resolved between several states in the southwestern United States (Reisner, 1993). Any decisions will also affect the downstream country of Mexico, too.

It is also important to remember that the rivers and streams in watersheds bring more than just water to the surrounding communities both upstream and downstream. They also transport nutrients that enrich riverbank soil, making agriculture possible. On the other hand, the chemicals, runoff, and pollutants contained within poorly managed rivers can poison watersheds and have detrimental effects on human health and environmental quality. The multiple roles played by watersheds mean that more than just avoiding conflict, successful water basin management involves scientifically informed, holistic ecosystem-based decision-making that is carried out by all of the involved countries or states. The concept of "integrated water resources management" has arisen as a recommended practice. The Global Water Partnership defines this strategy as "a process which promotes the coordinated development and management of water, land and related resources, in order to maximize the resultant economic and social welfare in an equitable manner without compromising the sustainability of vital ecosystems" (United Nations, 2015).

The two essays on this question will illustrate examples of water basins that have had varying outcomes due to the way in which they were managed. One will go deeper into the issues surrounding the damming of the Yangtze River, while the other will explore Central Asia's Aral Sea. Here, environmental mismanagement by multiple states has led an entire inland sea to dry up, leaving dust and rusting ships in its dusty wake. Not a drop to drink, indeed.

REFERENCES

De Stefano, Lucia, Paris Edwards, Lynette de Silva, and Aaron T. Wolf. (2010). "Tracking cooperation and conflict in international basins: Historic and recent trends," *Water Policy* 12(6), 871–884.

Food and Agriculture Organization of the United Nations. (2015). Ganges-Brahmaputra-Meghna Basin. AQUASTAT. Accessed February 28, 2015, at http://www.fao.org/nr/water/aquastat/basins/gbm/index.stm.

Gleick, Peter H. (1993). "Water and conflict: fresh water resources and international security," *International Security* 18(1), 79–112.

Harris, Stuart. A. (2011). "Mega-hydroelectric power generation on the Yangtze River: the Three Gorges Dam," in Stanley D. Brunn (ed.), *Engineering Earth: The Impacts of Megaengineering Projects*, 1569–1581. New York: Springer.

Reisner, Marc. (1993). *Cadillac Desert: The American West and Its Disappearing Water*. London: Penguin.

United Nations. (2014). "The United Nations World Water Development Report 2014." New York: United Nations.

United Nations Department of Economic and Social Affairs. (2015). "International Decade for Action 'Water for Life' 2005–2015." Accessed October 24, 2015, at http://www.un.org/waterforlifedecade/water_cooperation.shtml.

Waterbury, John. (1979). *Hydropolitics*. Syracuse, NY: Syracuse University Press.

FURTHER READING

Brichieri-Colombi, Stephen. (2008). *The World Water Crisis: The Failures of Resource Management*. New York: I. B. Tauris.

De Stefano, Lucia, Paris Edwards, Lynette de Silva, and Aaron T. Wolf. (2010). "Tracking cooperation and conflict in international basins: historic and recent trends," *Water Policy* 12(6), 871–884.

Vajpeyi, Dhirendra K. (ed.). (2012). *Water Resource Conflicts and International Security: A Global Perspective*. Lanham, MD: Lexington Books.

FROM ARAL SEA TO ARAL DESERT
Mia Bennett

Central Asia's Aral Sea was once one of the four largest lakes in the world. Lying between Kazakhstan and Uzbekistan, it has historically served as an important water basin for a number of other Central Asian countries, including Turkmenistan, Afghanistan, Tajikistan, and Kyrgyzstan. The Aral Sea lies in a basin that has been alternately flooded and desiccated for millions of years, but it is now at its lowest point in 1,300 years (Micklin, 1988). Much of this diminution can be attributed to anthropogenic factors. Today, the sea is nothing but a dusty glimmer of its former self. Vast stretches of salty, toxic sand dotted with eerily exposed shipwrecks cover most of the 68,000 square kilometers that were once water. Already in 1990, the Royal Geographical Society (RGS) called the Aral Sea "the world's worst ecological disaster" (BBC, 1990). One year later, the Soviet Union collapsed, turning management of the Aral Sea into an international rather than domestic issue. Twenty-five years after the RGS' declaration, the sea has shrunk

Abandoned ships near the Kazakh city of Aralsk sit on sand that was once part of the Aral Sea. Formerly one of the four largest lakes in the world, the Aral Sea has been steadily shrinking since the 1960s. By 2007, it had declined to 10 percent of its original size, splitting into four lakes. It is considered one of the world's worst, human-induced ecological disasters. (AFP/Getty Images)

even further, although there are some signs that a minor recovery is underway at least in one section of the sea-turned-desert.

In the 1960s, driven by the Soviet obsession with central planning of the economy, the Politburo decided to turn swaths of the steppes of Central Asia into fertile farmland. Millions of hectares of land were irrigated in order to grow cotton, called "white gold," and turn the USSR into a major cotton exporter. To carry out this feat in such an arid environment required enormous hydroengineering projects. The USSR's Hydropower Institute oversaw the construction of more than 20,000 miles of canals, 45 dams, and 80 reservoirs in order to deliver precious water to parched Kazakhstan and Uzbekistan (Howard, 2014). To irrigate the desert, the Amu Darya and Syr Darya, two rivers that once fed the Aral Sea, were diverted. Ships could now sail across the desert via the canal, while fishery farms and fields of cotton and melons sprung up from the sands (Zonn, 2014).

If all of this seems like a mirage, that's because it was in fact too good to be true and proved to be unsustainable. The diversions set in motion a chain of events that led to the drying up of the Aral Sea—a problem actually foreseen by Soviet engineers. However, they believed that a cubic meter of water used to irrigate land would prove more valuable than a cubic meter of water flowing into the Aral Sea

(Micklin, 1988). But this myopic mindset took into account short-term economic gains rather than long-term environmental consequences. The Aral Sea disaster has become a cautionary tale and demonstrates the folly that can result from a single government trying to reengineer an entire water basin, especially when it flies in the face of sound ecosystem-based management.

The drying up of the Aral Sea has exposed unfertile sand as well as toxic chemicals and residue from weapons testing. The rapid evaporation of water has increased the lake's salinity from 10 grams per liter (g/l) before diversion schemes began to 100g/l now (Micklin, 2007). Winds whip up this poisonous brew of salt and toxins, exacerbating already harsh climes and making the seasons more extreme. Once-profitable fishing towns now sit tens of kilometers from shore with rusting boats permanently moored in the sand.

International and national efforts have attempted to restore this apocalyptic landscape. In 1992, just one year after the Central Asian republics won independence from the Soviet Union, five of the states (Kazakhstan, Uzbekistan, Turkmenistan, Kyrgyzstan, and Tajikistan) formed the Interstate Commission for Water Coordination (ICWC) of Central Asia. Three years later, these five countries within the Aral Sea water basin created the Aral Sea Program, which also involved the World Bank, the European Union, the United Nations Development Program, and a number of national governments, all of which were supposed to donate money. Yet due to lack of adequate funding, the program's goal of restoring the Aral Sea to its former level has clearly not been achieved. Instead, national governments may be better equipped to enact smaller-scale solutions to save parts of the Aral Sea. For instance, some respite may be found in Kazakhstan's efforts to salvage the North Aral Sea, one of the four remnants of the original body of water left by 2007. With financial assistance from the World Bank, the country built a dam that has led to a better-than-expected rise in the water level and a decrease in salinity (World Bank, 2014).

The Aral Sea exemplifies the severe environmental, economic, and human health problems that can result when a water basin is mismanaged. Furthermore, its mismanagement under a single country, the USSR, and continued degradation under the oversight of several sovereign countries demonstrates that no single political set-up can guarantee the successful management of a water basin. With five countries trying to manage a single water basin, any region-wide plan would inevitably require some countries to make more sacrifices than others. Hydropolitics is complicated no matter how the borders are drawn, but it is even more complex when a large number of countries are involved. As Victor Dukhovny, the director of the ICWC's Scientific Information Center, warns, "The national 'egoistic' scenario orients each country toward the satisfaction of its own interests without taking account of other riparian partners" (Dukhovny, 2003). Dukhovny, however, is ultimately optimistic. He believes that if interstate cooperation succeeds, the Aral Sea could become "the world model of rational use of transboundary water resources on a large scale" (Dukhovny, 2003). Yet for this to happen, the five countries involved would actually have to work together and aim for what's best for the region rather than what's best for the state—and that is a difficult pill for any government to swallow, particularly those led by narcissistic Central Asian dictators. As Turkmenistan's leader oversees the construction of a large man-made lake in the Karakum desert to improve irrigation—a plan that has been criticized by environmentalists and could also lead to tensions with neighboring Uzbekistan, as it would require diverting water from the Amu Darya river (Stone, 2008)—a day of rational transboundary water management seems like a distant dream.

REFERENCES

BBC. (1990, October 22). "Aral Sea is 'world's worst disaster,'" *On This Day*. Accessed October 22, 2015, at http://news.bbc.co.uk/onthisday/hi/dates/stories/october/22/newsid_3756000/3756134.stm.

Dukhovny, Victor. A. (2003). "The Aral Sea basin—rumors, realities, prospects," *Irrigation and Drainage 52*(2), 120.

Howard, Brian C. (2014, October 2). "Aral Sea's eastern basin is dry for the first time in 600 years," *National Geographic*. Accessed March 1, 2016, at http://news.nationalgeographic.com/news/2014/10/141001-aral-sea-shrinking-drought-water-environment/.

Micklin, P. (2007). "The Aral sea disaster," *Annual Review of Earth and Planetary Science 35*, 47–72.

Micklin, Philip. (1988). "Desiccation of the Aral Sea: a water management disaster in the Soviet Union," *Science 241*(4870), 1170–1176.

Stone, Richard. (2008). "A new great lake—or dead sea?," *Science 320*, 1002–1005.

World Bank. (2014, July 10). "World Bank and Kazakhstan Plan Further Improvements in the Northern Aral Sea Area." Accessed March 1, 2016, at http://www.worldbank.org/en/news/press-release/2014/07/10/world-bank-and-kazakhstan-plan-further-improvements-in-northern-aral-sea-area.

Zonn, Igor S. (2014). "Karakum Canal: Artificial river in a desert," in Igor Zonn and Andrey Kostianoy (eds.), *The Turkmen Lake Altyn Asyr and Water Resources in Turkmenistan*. Berlin, Germany: Springer-Verlag, 95–106.

MOVING PEOPLE, MOVING EARTH: THE YANGTZE RIVER AND THE THREE GORGES DAM

Mia Bennett

The Yangtze is a river of superlatives. It is the longest river in China and the third longest in the world, cascading down from the mountains to the north of the Tibetan Plateau and then coursing some 6,500 kilometers before flowing out into the East China Sea near Shanghai. Some 480 million people, a third of China's

China's Three Gorges Dam, the world's largest hydroelectric dam. The dam's construction had long been supported by Chinese officials for its financial benefits, and long been opposed by environmentalists, historians, and human rights groups for the flooding of the gorges and Chinese villages along the Yangtze River. (Shutterstock)

population, live in the Yangtze River Basin, which stretches over 1.8 million square kilometers. The basin also supplies some 40 percent of China's freshwater resources, providing crucial water for the bulk of the country's rice, grain, and fishery production (World Wildlife Fund, n.d.). It is also an extremely powerful river that flows towards China's powerhouse coastal cities. For over a hundred years, Chinese leaders have dreamed of harnessing the river's energy. Finally, after a period of construction lasting 12 years, the dam opened in May 2006, with the final stage of installation drawing to a close in 2009. Although management of the Yangtze River Basin is largely a domestic issue since it lies entirely within China's borders, the dam has also generated international controversy due to its enormous social, environmental, and economic ramifications.

SOCIAL EFFECTS

Ten times more powerful than the Hoover Dam, the Three Gorges Dam is the world's largest hydroelectric power generator. It is also the world's largest resettlement project. 1.3 million people were forced out of their homes to make room for the dam and its massive reservoir, which inundated 13 cities, 140 towns, and 1,350 villages (International Rivers, 2012). While the government compensated displaced people with small sums of money or new apartments elsewhere, little was done to provide people with new, sustainable livelihoods. The forced uprooting of so many people would likely have been impossible in a democracy, yet given that China is an authoritarian state, enactment of such a policy was feasible. Electricity generation, flood control, and the creation of more reliable shipping opportunities were all prioritized over the well-being of the people living in the Three Gorges area (Heming, Waley, and Rees, 2001).

ENVIRONMENTAL EFFECTS

Chinese officials have highlighted the environmental benefits of the Three Gorges Dam. Hydropower is a form of renewable energy, and its generation allows China to burn less coal without having to rely, for instance, on nuclear power. Yet there have been a large number of negative environmental effects. First, with the creation of the reservoir, large swaths of arable land in China have been lost; this in a country that already has a lower amount of area available for agriculture per person compared to the global average. Second, the dam's construction has caused more landslides, fragmented ecosystems, and decreased sediment loads in downstream rivers. So much water has been displaced that it has even led to crustal deformation in the Three Gorges area and slightly shifted the earth's gravity field (Zhang et al., 1996). Environmental concerns have become so serious that in 2008, Wang Xiaofeng, supervisor for the Three Gorges Dam project for China's State Council, admitted, "We simply cannot sacrifice the environment in exchange for temporary economic gain." Despite this sentiment, China continues to build more dams at great social and environmental costs but with certain economic gains. Indeed, the Three Gorges Dam is the lynchpin in a larger series of dams that China is building along the Yangtze River.

ECONOMIC EFFECTS

The Three Gorges Dam cost $37 billion to build (Reuters, 2009). Despite the colossal outlay of money required, the dam's generation of approximately 100 billion kilowatt hours per year of electricity (equivalent to 2.85 percent of China's electrical power usage in 2013) makes it an undeniably important source of power for an energy-hungry country (Natali et al., 2013). Further, aside from power generation, the Three Gorges Dam has also improved access to the inland port city of Chongqing, which sits ashore the Yangtze some 600 kilometers upstream of the dam (Chinafolio, 2014). Similar to the case study about the decision to divert inflow to the Aral Sea in order to create fertile, economically valuable agricultural land, economic benefits triumphed over environmental ones.

CONCLUSION

Although the Yangtze River Basin is confined to China, its construction is still sparking international concern. First, China, with its enhanced expertise in dam building and financing, is planning an additional number of hydroelectric power projects, several of them on transboundary rivers like the Mekong, Salween, Brahmaputra, and Amur (Chinafolio, 2014). All of these rivers flow south from the Himalayan Plateau to downstream countries in Southeast Asia—again a case of hydropolitics at play where the upstream country holds leverage over the downstream country. Second, China can export its hydro-engineering knowledge to other countries interested in exploiting this energy source. Already, China has helped to finance and build dams in Vietnam, Laos, Myanmar, and Cambodia. This strategy helps placate countries that might otherwise protest the construction of upstream dams that would benefit China at the cost of reducing river flow into their own countries. Even farther afield, a Chinese consortium was awarded a $4.7 billion contract to construct two hydroelectric dams in Patagonia, Argentina (Reuters, 2013), underscoring the global reach of Chinese hydropower expertise. Indeed, it could go so far as to spark a new global wave of dam building. The century-old Chinese dream of damming a river for energy is becoming a goal for countries around the world; the hope is that such ventures by the Chinese people will bring stability and prosperity to the regions affected.

REFERENCES

Chinafolio. (2014). "Hydro-power and Hydro-Hegemony: China's Prolific Dam-Building." Accessed March 1, 2016, at http://www.chinafolio.com/hydro-power-and-hydro-hegemony/.

Heming, Li, Paul Waley, and Phil Rees. (2001). "Reservoir resettlement in China: past experience and the Three Gorges Dam," *The Geographical Journal, 167*(3), 195–212.

International Rivers. (2012). "Three Gorges Dam: A model of the Past." Accessed March 5, 2016, at http://www.internationalrivers.org/files/attached-files/3gorgesfactsheet_feb2012_web.pdf.

Natali, J., Philip Williams, Rachel Wong, and G. M. Kondolf. (2013). "After Three Gorges Dam: What have we learned?," *AGU Fall Meeting Abstracts, vol. 1*, 1155.

Reuters. (2013, November 1). "China's Gezhouba to build dams in Argentina worth $4.7 billion," Accessed March 1, 2016, at http://www.reuters.com/article/2013/11/01/us-gezhouba-argentina-idUSBRE9A00KH20131101.

Reuters. (2009, September 14). "China says Three Gorges Dam cost $37 billion." Accessed March 1, 2016, at http://www.reuters.com/article/2009/09/14/idUSPEK84588.

World Wildlife Fund. (n.d.). "Yangtze River." Accessed March 1, 2016, at http://wwf.panda.org/about_our_earth/about_freshwater/freshwater_problems/river_decline/10_rivers_risk/yangtze.

Zhang, Kefei, Will Featherstone, S. F. Bian, and B. Z. Tao. (1996). "Time variations of the Earth's gravity field and crustal deformation due to the establishment of the Three Gorges reservoir," *Journal of Geodesy*, *70*(7), 440–449.

13

WILL THE INTERNATIONAL TRADE IN HAZARDOUS WASTE PROMOTE STABILITY OR CONFLICT?

OVERVIEW
M. Troy Burnett

In the last two decades with the era of globalization and the expansion of international trade, the generation and transboundary movement of hazardous waste and its disposal has emerged as a contentious environmental issue. As the contributing authors in this section emphasize, at root is the debate over whether or not wealthier places can or should be able to dump their waste on poor places and whether this trade will promote conflict.

BACKGROUND

Hazardous waste can be defined as any material that poses a substantial threat to either human health or the environment when being improperly handled (Singh and Lakhan, 1989). Examples of these include: acids, cyanides, pesticides, solvents, compounds of lead, mercury, arsenic, cadmium, zinc, polychlorinated biphenyls and dioxins, fly ash from power plants, infectious waste from hospitals, herbicides, obsolete explosives, nerve gas, radioactive materials, sewage sludge, and other materials containing toxic and carcinogenic organic compounds. The United States is the biggest producer of hazardous waste with over 350 million metric tons being produced each year. According to the Organization for Economic Co-operation and Development's (OECD) own stats, over 90 percent of the generated hazardous waste originates in OECD countries (i.e., the developed world). Prior to the era of globalized trade, the transboundary movement of hazardous waste was mostly between developed countries (e.g., the United States and Canada). Yet, as disposal has become more costly and suitable sites more difficult to find, lesser-developed countries, which often lack the capacity to handle hazardous waste, have been targeted as dumping grounds. This practice has been contentious, with many decrying it as "environmental injustice" or "environmental racism" on a global scale as essentially poorer, more politically marginalized communities are required to bear the burden of industrialization without have reaped many of its benefits (Marbury, 1995).

A notable case of unsound dumping occurred in Nigeria in the 1980s. An Italian businessman, working under a general product import license, covertly substituted shipments of several thousand tons of toxic and radioactive waste, including the highly carcinogenic polychlorinated biphenyls. The hazardous waste, over 3,800 tons, was taken to an unmanaged storage site in Koko, where many of the drums were damaged and leaking. Uninformed and ill-prepared workers suffered severe chemical burns, paralysis, impaired vision, nausea, and over time, symptoms of cancer. Even after the waste was removed, the land within a half-kilometer radius was declared toxic with severely contaminated surface and groundwater (Vir, 1989).

In another case, in 1988, European firms offered Guinea-Bissau $600 million dollars to dispose of 16 million tons of toxic waste over a five-year period. While modest for the exporting corporations, the amount was equal to four times the gross national product of the small African nation making it a highly appealing trade-off for the economic elites of Guinea-Bissau. Similar arrangements were reported in the 1980s in other African countries such as Namibia, Guinea, Angola, and Sierra Leone (Vir, 1989). Whether the dumping takes place with the consent of the government or as part of an illegal operation, often the general public is powerless to resist and inevitably bear the health and environmental consequences.

The motivation for exporting hazardous waste to developing countries is mainly economic, rooted in the logic of colonial and neocolonial exploitation. Lawrence Summers, the former vice president and chief economist of the World Bank, even directly encouraged the trade in hazardous waste. In an oft-cited 1991 memorandum on trade liberalization, Summer's wrote: "I think the economic logic behind dumping a load of toxic waste in the lowest wage countries is impeccable and we should face up to that." While ethically questionable, Summer's capitalist inspired, profit seeking motive is sound, for he is simply suggesting that places with the lowest costs and lowest wages are "ideal" sites in that they have a comparative advantage in waste storage.

Inspired by the 1962 publication of Rachel Carson's *Silent Spring*, industrialized countries, such as the United States, have become more aware of the dangers of unsound disposal of hazardous waste. As a result, these countries, especially the more democratic ones, have implemented more stringent environmental and safety regulations that have effectively made disposal extremely costly and politically difficult. On the other hand, developing countries that often lack political and economic stability provide a disposal option at prices a mere fraction of those in the country of origin. According to one study in the late 1980s, the average disposal costs for one ton of hazardous wastes in Africa was between $2.50 and $50, while costs in Europe and the United States ranged from $100 to $2,000 (Kummer, 1995). To reiterate, the lower costs generally reflect the lack of environmental standards, less stringent laws, and absence of public opposition due to lack of information concerning the dangers involved. The contention and controversy is that without regulation developing countries will continue to be increasingly susceptible to exploitation and environmental injustice, since: "like water running downhill, hazardous wastes invariably will be disposed of along the path of least resistance and least expense" (Porterfield, and Weir 1989).

The Basel Convention on the Control of Transboundary Movements of Hazardous Wastes and Their Disposal (Basel Convention) has emerged as an important international treaty and global mechanism to better and more fairly regulate the transboundary movement of hazardous waste. Implemented in 1989, it now has 182 signatories. However, it has only modestly worked and been criticized for a host of reasons, including: (1) the difficulty to enforce obligations, (2) the failure of the United States as the largest generator of hazardous waste to commit to it, (3) the general and ambiguous definitions of key terms such as "hazardous waste" and "environmentally sound management," and (4) the many loopholes that continue to permit hazardous waste exports for "recycling."

REFERENCES

Kummer, Katherine. (1995). *International Management of Hazardous Wastes*. Oxford, UK: Oxford University Press.

Marbury, Hugh R. (1995). "Global Environmental Racism," *Vanderbilt Journal of Transnational Law 251*, 293.

Porterfield, Andrew, and David Weir. (1989, October 3). "The export of U.S. toxic waste," *The Nation*.

Singh, Jang B., and V. C. Lakhan. (1989). "Business ethics and the international trade in hazardous wastes," *Journal of Business Ethics, 8*(11), 889–899.

Vir, Arti K. (1989). "Toxic trade with Africa," *Environment, Science & Technology Journal 23*(1).

FURTHER READING

Asante-Duah, D. Kofi, and Imre V. Nagy. (1998). *International Trade in Hazardous Wastes.* Oxford, UK: Taylor & Francis.

MacLeod, Melissa. (2013, January 5). "Transnational trafficking of hazardous waste from developed to developing nations: policies and recommendations," *Interdisciplinary Journal of Health Sciences* 3(1).

National Geographic (eds.). (2015). "Toxic Waste:, Man's Poisonous Byproducts." *National Geographic.* Accessed March 5, 2016, at http://environment.nationalgeographic.com/environment/global-warming/toxic-waste-overview/.

Sánchez, Roberto. (1994). "International trade in hazardous wastes: a global problem with uneven consequences for the third world," *The Journal of Environment & Development* 3(1), 139–152.

CONTROVERSY AND CONFLICT WITH THE TRADE IN HAZARDOUS WASTE
Tera Trujillo

The dumping of hazardous waste around the world creates not only environmental concerns, but economic and political ones as well. The presence of the most toxic forms of hazardous waste can be traced back to the beginning of the Industrial Revolution when the by-products of mass production began to noticeably impact human health and degrade the air and water. What's changed is the both the scale of the waste and the ability via the processes of globalization and international shipping to move the waste greater distances from its point of origin. Further, the technological age has added a whole new type of toxic waste—dubbed "e-waste." These new technologies and their short lifespan have placed added pressure on already stressed environments in both the developing and developed worlds. The result is a system that is neither sustainable nor healthy and in many situations, a source of conflict.

To get a sense of the magnitude of the problem, in the United States alone, according to the Environmental Protection Agency about three pounds of household hazardous waste is accumulated each year for a total of about 530,000 tons per year (EPA, n.d.). Current global levels of waste generation have risen with economic development and urbanization to an average of almost three pounds per person per day. One can really get a sense of the scale of the problem with the fact that this rate is expected to double by 2025.

Health risks are an obvious problem when dealing with hazardous waste, and the people at risk are typically those living near or on top of hazardous waste landfills. For example, studies conducted at the Love Canal landfill site in Niagara, New

Cleanup efforts in 1981, after toxic waste was detected in a New York neighborhood called Love Canal. In 1978, a State of Emergency was declared in Love Canal, New York, after the discovery of environmental toxic chemicals, whereupon the Centers for Disease Control along with the Environmental Protection Agency participated in a cytotoxicity study on local residents. (Centers for Disease Control and Prevention)

York, showed that by the mid-1970s, toxic chemicals leaking from the site were detected in local streams, sewers, soil, and regional air and was severely affecting the health of the residents (Rushton, 2003). Upon learning of these impacts, the local people and their supporters rose up in protest to demand retribution and remediation. The conflict and its resolution has since become a seminal moment for toxic waste activism and the environmental justice movement.

Studies inspired by the Love Canal incident continue to reveal the adverse health impacts associated with the hazardous dumping, including low birth weight, spontaneous abortion, and birth defects. Cancer is also a common threat associated with proximity to hazardous waste. For example, there were reports of cancers of the liver, kidney, pancreas, and non-Hodgkin's lymphomas among persons living near the Miron Quarry site, the third largest in North America (Rushton, 2003). This problem continues to escalate and is seemingly found throughout the country. The eating of fish containing mercury from hazardous waste dumping into the oceans has been a persistent problem causing health risks for the people and animals that are eating these contaminated fish (National Geographic, 2015).

In terms of the hazardous waste trade, Walmart provides a recognizable example. After a series of lawsuits, the company had to plead guilty in May 2013 to dumping hazardous waste improperly in California and Missouri. The case included six counts of violating the Clean Water Act in California and one count of violating a federal law related to pesticide disposal in Missouri (Clifford, 2013). This is just one example of how big corporations, either directly or indirectly, may circumvent laws to increase profits with seemingly little concern about the health and environmental implications. The $110 million spent on resolving these issues will have no effect on the $128 billion made in revenue during the year of 2012 (Clifford, 2013). Economic power often seems to matter more to the people in power than the health and safety of our people and our ecosystems.

To make matters worse, the hazardous waste trade has become a global phenomenon with high environmental and health impacts, high profits, and a high potential for inter- and intra-state conflict. Despite international agreements such as the Basel Convention on the Control of Transboundary Movements of Hazardous Wastes and Their Disposal (Basel Convention), developed countries continue to legally and illegally export their hazardous waste to the most economically disempowered and politically weak places. For example, ten European countries, five Asian countries, and five African countries are currently illegally trafficking hazardous waste to war-torn Somalia. Over a period of 20 years, about 500,000 tons of toxic waste has been dumped on the coast of Somalia (Lutke, 2013). It should be noted that the trade in hazardous waste occurs not only from wealthy to less wealthy countries. In fact, the United States is a net importer of hazardous waste, receiving 48,091,380 more tons than it exported between the years of 1997 and 1999

In conclusion, the terrain of hazardous waste is a conflicted one. Governments, corporations, and individuals try to maintain their economic imperatives while giving the impression that they are acting with a conscience. Invariably, civil society has demanded governmental and corporate accountability creating a tense situation with threats, lawsuits, and duplicity from both sides. Social instability and conflict will only increase as the global trade in hazardous waste continues to expand.

REFERENCES

Clifford, Stephanie. (2013, May 28). "Wal-Mart is fined $82 million over mishandling of hazardous wastes," *New York Times*. Accessed March 1, 2016, at http://www.nytimes.com/2013/05/29/business/wal-mart-is-fined-82-million-over-mishandling-of-hazardous-wastes.html?_r=0.

Environmental Protection Agency. (n.d.). "Household Hazardous Waste." Accessed March 5, 2016, at http://www3.epa.gov/epawaste/conserve/materials/hhw.htm.

Lutke, Elin. (2013, June 14). "Illegal Trafficking of Hazardous Waste from Europe to Somalia." *Prezi*. Accessed February 27, 2015, at https://prezi.com/spwyprjbjuez/illegal-trafficking-of-hazardous-waste-from-europe-to-somalia/.

National Geographic (eds.). (2015). "Toxic Waste: Man's Poisonous Byproducts." *National Geographic*. Accessed March 5, 2016, at http://environment.nationalgeographic.com/environment/global-warming/toxic-waste-overview/.

Rushton, Lesley. (2003). "Health hazards and waste management," *British Medical Bulletin, Oxford Journals*. Accessed March 5, 2016, at http://bmb.oxfordjournals.org/content/68/1/183.full.

FURTHER READING

Baiamonte, Valentina. (2015, February 22). "Environmental crime and instability: the role of criminal networks in the trafficking and illegal dumping of hazardous waste," *Freedom from Fear Magazine 9*. Accessed March 1, 2016, at http://f3magazine.unicri.it/?p=600.

INTERNATIONAL TRADE OF HAZARDOUS WASTE CAUSES STABILITY
Nicole Lomba

Hazardous waste and its improper disposing techniques is a contentious issue for many countries, businesses, and local communities. As countries expand their economic base through industrialization, more hazardous waste is created while places to dump it have become increasingly scarce or politically contentious. The result has been an increase in the trade of toxic material—wherein the bulk of this trade involves wealthier countries that export their waste, often due to political and environmental concerns or economic gain, to poorer countries that begrudgingly receive the hazardous waste in exchange for small monetary gain. This situation has led to disagreements and cries of exploitation and toxic colonialism. Yet, despite the outlier experiences of illegal hazardous waste dumping, the fact is that the trade in hazardous waste is an emerging global market with beneficial opportunities for both the exporter and the importer. Further, with the ratification of the Basel Convention by 182 countries, there exists an international framework to better manage the trade and reduce the potential for conflict.

Hazardous waste trade has a long history, though mainly with industrial chemicals such as acids, cyanides, lead compounds, mercury, and arsenic as well as sewage sludge and other materials that include toxic and carcinogenic organic compounds. With the advent of the technological age, there has emerged a new

Bidjan youths block a street and burn tires to protest the dumping of toxic waste from the *Probo Koala*, a Panamanian-registered tanker ship, September 15, 2006. The waste caused 10 deaths and thousands more were hospitalized. (AP/Wide World Photos)

form of toxic waste—e-waste. Products such as cell phones, computer monitors, audio and stereo equipment, wireless devices, cameras, telephones, and many other electronics are loaded with hazardous materials that require proper handling and disposal. The global trade and ultimate disposal of these products have become a serious problem for developed and developing countries.

The poorer and more political marginalized a place is the more vulnerable it is to the negatives of the hazardous waste trade. One particular study that focused on West Africa revealed a long history of legally and illegally imported industrial waste and its negative health and environmental impacts (Macleod, 2013). Macleod highlights a variety of situations including the case of Kassa Island, Guinea. In March 1988, a Norwegian shipping company dumped 15,000 tons of incinerator ash into a deep pit. Within a few years, the residents of Kassa Island noticed that their island's vegetation began to die, yet they were not compensated for their losses and many were forced to abandon their farms.

In another case, in 1988, business leaders in Koko, Nigeria, imported 900 tons of waste from Italy, 150 tons of which were chemicals including formaldehyde and methyl melamine, both carcinogenic. A conflict ensued as a result of the improper listing of the chemicals that were being exported. Macleod also examined a more recent incident in 2006 in Abidjan, Ivory Coast (Macleod, 2013). In this case, 17 people died and more than 80,000 were forced to seek medical attention due to vomiting, nosebleeds, and difficulty breathing. The source of the malady was directly linked to 500 tons of toxic waste that was dumped in 14 sites around the city. These dumping sites were also near water and other agricultural sources, and though the waste was labeled as petroleum, it included the highly toxic sulphur hydrocarbon. Estimates showed that it would have taken $250,000 for the exporting country to properly treat the waste in their own country, while in Africa they were charged only $18,500.

Since 1992 and the ratification of the Basel Convention on the Control of Transboundary Movements of Hazardous Wastes and Their Disposal (Basel Convention), the trade in traditional industrial, toxic waste has been better regulated. Presently, the focus has been on better managing systems for e-waste, which the Basel Convention only marginally regulates. In research done by Shumeng Liu at Columbia University, it was reported that in 2012 the generated amount of electronic waste in the United States was about 9.4 million tons and in China 7.3 million tons. The global e-waste generation amount in the same year was 49 million tons (Liu, 2014). Liu noted that the problem at hand is the illegal export of e-waste from developed countries to underdeveloped countries such as China. Although they are the second largest exporter of e-waste they are also the largest importer as well. In short, China has become the major sink of the world's electronic waste taking on about 20 percent of the e-waste generated globally. Further, despite efforts, approximately 38 percent of e-waste is recycled irresponsibly by individuals and companies using primitive, unsafe methods.

The fact is, in the global economy the trade in hazardous waste is a large and profitable market. To make the trade in waste more responsible to minimize conflict and exploitation, it must be tackled from the perspectives of both regulation and technology (Liu, 2014). Further, invoking fair trade standards that promote equitable market practices as well as responsible recycling is necessary to avoid exploitation and toxic colonialism.

REFERENCES

Liu, Shumeng. (2014). "Analysis of Electronic Waste Recycling in the United States and Potential Application in China." Master's thesis, Earth Engineering Center, Columbia University.

Macleod, Melissa. (2013, January 5). "Transnational trafficking of hazardous waste from developed to developing nations: policies and recommendations," *Interdisciplinary Journal of Health Sciences* 3(1).

14

WITH FUTURE CONFLICTS SEEMINGLY GUARANTEED, IS A TECHNOLOGICAL BREAKTHROUGH NEEDED TO AVERT THE CLIMATE CRISIS?

OVERVIEW

M. Troy Burnett

As the idea of a coming global climate crisis and ensuing conflicts at a multitude of scales continues to gain prominence in both academic circles and society at large, the question of how to prevent or cope with such a crisis has loomed large. In parallel with the debate over the causes of global climate change, a discussion of the potential solutions to the problems posed by such change is engaging both policymakers and scientists around the world. As with so many aspects of the topic of global warming and climate change, however, disagreement often stems from incomplete knowledge or the existence of competing models.

According to some of the bleakest proposed scenarios, it is already too late to change the course of the Earth's climatic trends. Such models have the planet slated for changes that could greatly disrupt human societies and alter the environmental and ecological balance worldwide. These sorts of predictions have led some to wonder whether the only way to avert crisis is to develop new, game-changing technology with the potential to correct or even reverse the climatic trends observed by climate scientists. Some experts believe that such technology is possible and necessary, while others believe such innovation is either unnecessary or even a dangerous crutch that might prevent countries around the world from doing all they can to limit the anthropogenic (human-caused) causes of climate change. This debate often takes the form of a conversation between the sciences and the humanities.

BACKGROUND

From the beginning of international efforts to address anthropogenic climate change, negotiators recognized that the greatest burden to cut greenhouse gas emissions believed to be responsible for the phenomenon fell upon the industrialized world. The concept of "differentiated responsibilities" between developed and developing countries was included in the United Nations Framework Convention on Climate Change (UNFCCC) produced by the Earth Summit in Rio de Janeiro in 1992, which recognized not only contemporary levels of carbon emissions into the atmosphere, but also the historical record dating to the era of the Industrial Revolution. The concept of differentiated responsibilities recognized that the proportion of global emissions from developing countries would continue to grow to meet those countries' development needs, even as industrialized countries would begin to cut back.

The Kyoto Protocol (1997) mandated reductions in the emissions of six greenhouse gases for 37 industrialized countries, from 2005 to 2012. The United States, until 2006 the world's largest emitter of greenhouse gases, has never ratified the Kyoto Protocol (though 187 other countries have), and U.S. presidents Bill Clinton and George W. Bush never even sent it to the U.S. Senate for ratification. Bush complained that the protocol would place too great a burden on the U.S. economy, and that such large, developing countries as China and India should have been required to cut back emissions as well. Around 2006, China became the largest emitter of greenhouse gases, though its per-capita emissions of carbon dioxide, by far the most prevalent greenhouse gas, remain less than one-third of those emitted by the United States. In the days preceding the Copenhagen UNFCCC conference in December 2009, the leaders of both the United States and China—which together account for 40 percent of global carbon dioxide emissions—were citing figures for emissions cutbacks, which observers considered a hopeful sign from two countries whose emissions have continued to rise, and that haven't previously earmarked reduction targets.

No binding agreements were produced in Copenhagen, but the conference did produce the Copenhagen Accord (2009), a non-binding agreement reached in a closed-door session on the last day of the conference by the leaders of the United States, China, and several other countries. The document set only broad goals for emissions reduction, and it was not formally approved by the conference at large. Although more than 100 countries ratified the accord in the months following the conference, several developing countries rejected it on the grounds that industrialized nations were skirting their responsibilities by not committing to specific targets.

Despite the persistence of a skeptical minority, the evidence of global warming continues to accumulate. Scientific evidence that certain gases hold heat from the sun in the atmosphere (much like a glass-enclosed greenhouse) dates to the early 19th century, and by the mid-20th century, scientists were documenting increased levels of carbon dioxide in the atmosphere. Some also began to consider that such human activities as the burning of fossil fuels might be at least partly at fault. By the 1980s, evidence of generally warming temperatures and increased levels of atmospheric carbon dioxide and other greenhouse gases prompted the start of international efforts to address the issue. In 1988, the United Nations and the World Meteorological Organization created the Intergovernmental Panel on Climate Change (IPCC), and 1992's Earth Summit followed the IPCC's first assessment report on the issue.

In 2007, the IPCC's fourth assessment report stated that evidence of global warming was "unequivocal" and that increases in average temperatures was very likely due to the observed increase in anthropogenic greenhouse gas concentrations. Report authors specified that the wording "very likely" translated to a better than 90 percent probability that human activities were largely to blame. The report noted that 11 of the 12 years prior to 2007 ranked among the top 12 warmest years since reliable record-keeping began in 1850, and that in 100 years the global average temperature rose by 0.74°C. Though that rise may seem small, it is believed to be the cause of a number of observable effects, including the melting of glaciers and rising sea levels.

The IPCC report, as well as other reports from the United Nations and other organizations, have documented that the effects of climate change will take a disproportionate toll on poor countries—which ironically have done the least to cause it. For example, climate change is expected to increasingly exacerbate extreme weather conditions, causing more droughts and flooding in areas already prone to such phenomena. That means increasing desertification in African countries bordering the Sahara Desert, and more frequent and severe tropical storms in poor areas of East Asia, Southeast Asia, and South Asia. Many developing countries have weak infrastructure and social institutions, and climate change will also put further stress on the availability of clean water. The United Nations estimates that between 75 million and 220 million people will face more severe water shortages due to climate change in Africa, a continent where lack of access to clean water in many areas is already considered a crisis.

The international effort to combat climate change has two broad divisions: mitigation, efforts to reduce greenhouse gas emissions; and adaptation, measures to protect ecosystems and populations from the effects of climate change already underway. (Because greenhouse gases remain in the atmosphere for a long time, global warming will continue to increase even if all greenhouse gas emissions were stopped immediately.) Proposed aid to developing countries incorporates both mitigation and adaptation measures.

To mitigate the threat from emissions, industrialized countries are expected to help developing nations develop sustainable energy sources utilizing such "green" sources as wind and solar power. Thus, reliance on the burning of fossil fuels can be greatly lessened as those countries strive to develop economically and provide for their citizens' needs. Mechanisms are also being developed to provide funding to tropical countries as an incentive to stop destroying rainforests.

In addition to condemning the lack of a binding agreement from industrialized nations to sharply cut emissions, representatives of developing nations meeting in Bolivia in April 2010 agreed that the funding for mitigation targeted in the Copenhagen Accord does not go far enough. The general sentiment of the participants of this summit, dubbed the World People's Conference on Climate Change and the Rights of Mother Earth, was that either capitalism dies or Mother Earth dies. A "Peoples Agreement" was reached at the conference that demanded developed countries must allocate a minimum of 6 percent of their gross domestic products to addressing climate change.

Even as industrialized nations and such larger developing nations as China, India, and Brazil struggle to agree on emissions reductions and invest in alternative energy to help them meet targets, they also continue to rely on global trade to fuel desired economic growth. Yet, since many activists and some leaders of poorer countries believe that the system itself is to blame, it is likely that disagreements over solutions to climate change will persist.

FURTHER READING

Brown, Marilyn A., and Benjamin K. Sovacool. (2011). *Climate Change and Global Energy Security: Technology and Policy Options*. Cambridge, MA: MIT Press.

Murphy, Deborah. (2005). *Climate Change and Technology*. New York: International Institute for Sustainable Development.

Tremblay, William O. (2011). *Barriers to Climate Change Mitigation Technologies and Energy Efficiency*. New York: Nova Science Publishers.

NECESSITY WILL COMPEL TECHNOLOGICAL INNOVATION
Bruce E. Johansen

Before the end of this century, the urgency of global warming will become manifest to everyone. Solutions to our fossil fuel dilemma—solar, wind, hydrogen, and others—will evolve during this century. Within our century, necessity will

Collecting troughs of a Solar Energy Generating System (SEGS) in the Mojave Desert, California. These hybrid power plants operate on a parabolic trough system for collecting and generating solar energy. (iStockPhoto.com)

compel invention. Other technologies may be developed that have not, as yet, even broached the realm of present-day science fiction, any more than digitized computers had in the days of the Wright brothers a century ago. We will take this journey because the changing climate, along with our own innate curiosity and creativity, will compel a changing energy paradigm.

Such change will not take place at once. A paradigm change in basic energy technology may require the better part of a century, or longer. Several technologies will evolve together. Oil-based fuels will continue to be used for purposes that require them. Air transport comes to mind, although engineers already are working on ways to make jet engines more efficient.

J. Craig Venter, the maverick scientist who compiled a human genetic map with private money, has decided to tap a $100 million research endowment he has created from his stock holdings to scour the world's deep ocean trenches for bacteria that might be able to convert carbon dioxide to solid form using very little sunlight or other energy. Failing that, Venter proposes to synthesize such organisms via genetic engineering. He would like to invent two synthetic microorganisms, one to consume carbon dioxide and turn it into raw materials composed of the kinds of organic chemicals that are now made from oil and natural gas. The other microorganism would generate hydrogen fuel from water and sunshine.

The coming energy revolution will engender economic growth and become an engine of wealth creation for those who realize the opportunities that it offers. Denmark, for example, is making every family a shareowner in a burgeoning wind-power industry. The United Kingdom is making plans to reduce its greenhouse-gas emissions by 50 percent in 50 years. The British program begins to address the position of the Intergovernmental Panel on Climate Change (IPCC) that emissions will have to fall 60–70 percent by century's end to avoid significant warming of the lower atmosphere due to human activities. (Many scientists assert that such reductions will need to be realized in half a century).

EVOLUTION OF SOLAR POWER

Solar power has advanced significantly since the days of inefficient photovoltaics. With solar power still three to five times as expensive per kilowatt hour as coal, inventors are working on new technologies and mass production to reduce that gap. In California, solar power is being built into roof tiles, and talk is that nanotechnology will some day make any surface the sun hits a source of power—windows, for example. Experiments have been conducted with a new form of solar energy—Concentrating Solar Power (CSP). "[CSP uses] a mirror in the shape of a parabola to focus light onto a black pipe with a heat-transfer fluid inside. The fluid is used to boil water into steam, which turns a generator that can produce 64 megawatts. The newest solar-thermal technology involves building a 'power tower,' a tall structure flanked by thousands of mirrors, each of which pivots to focus light on the tower, heating fluid. That design can work even in places with weaker sunlight than a desert" (Wald, 2008).

Solar power is growing to industrial scale. In 2008, photovoltaic solar power installations were planned and built in California's San Luis Obispo County. The Topaz Solar Farm, as it is known, produces 550-megawatts. Presently, Topaz is the world's largest solar facility. Indeed, the cost of solar power has been declining sharply, from $22 per watt in 1980, to $6 per watt in 1990, to $2.70 in 2005. Economies of scale as well as improvements in efficiency and availability of less expensive construction materials may bring solar energy down to a cost that can compete with fossil-fuel generation by about 2015.

The silicon solar panels that dominate the industry today may be replaced by new technologies that combine several light-absorbing materials that capture different portions of the solar spectrum, or solar cells manufactured in rolls of thin copper indium gallium selenide (CIGS) film atop a metal foil. Nanotechnology plays a role in some designs for future solar-generating technology that is theorized but has not yet been commercialized. While today's silicon cells convert about 15–20 percent of sunlight to electricity in the field (up to 24 percent under perfect laboratory conditions), new technologies that have broached the realm of theory (and some being designed) raise that figure to 40 percent, 60 percent, even 80 percent (Service, 2008). Photovoltaics made of plastic may dramatically reduce manufacturing costs.

TECHNOLOGY IS NOT THE ENTIRE TICKET

A technological game-changer for global warming would certainly help deal with a problem that is bound to have many solutions. Technology by itself, however, will not be the entire ticket to a new world in which greenhouse gases can be reduced to sustainable levels, and stay there. By sustainable, many scientists now believe that a carbon dioxide (CO_2) level of 350 parts per million (and gradually falling) will solve the problem—a tall order in a world in which the level is already 10 percent above that level, at about 385 parts per million.

In addition to new technology, from the prosaic (including such low-tech adaptations as light-colored roofs) to advanced forms of alternative energy and those wonderful concepts that have barely broached science fiction today, human attitudes must change. The climate change issue is so daunting in part because it requires fundamental changes not only in technology, but also to our basic behavior, individually and collectively. Technology exists within a human context that includes such intangible factors as human nature, as world-enveloping plans face off with religious preferences and nationalistic political inclinations.

We are overdue for an energy system paradigm shift, and surprising technological changes could be part of it. Limited supplies of oil and their abundance in the volatile Middle East argue for new sources, along with accelerating climate change from greenhouse gases accumulating in the atmosphere. According to an editorial in *Businessweek*, "[a] national policy that cuts fossil-fuel consumption converges with a geopolitical policy of reducing energy dependence on Middle East oil. Reducing carbon dioxide emissions is no longer just a 'green' thing. It makes business and foreign policy sense, as well. . . . In the end, the only real solution may be new energy technologies" (2004).

REFERENCES

Bloomberg Businessweek (eds.). (2004, August 16). "How to combat global warming: in the end, the only real solution may be new energy technologies," *Bloomberg Businessweek*, 108.

Service, Robert F. (2008, February 8). "Solar power: can the upstarts top Silicon?," *Science* 319, 718.

Wald, Matthew. (2008, March 6). "Turning glare into watts," *New York Times*. Accessed March 1, 2016, at http://www.nytimes.com/2008/03/06/business/06solar.html.

HOW CAN SOCIETY RESPOND TO THE CLIMATE CRISIS? BY CHANGING OUR OWN BEHAVIOR

Benjamin K. Sovacool

We do not necessarily need new technologies to avert the climate crisis. Instead, historical and contemporary examples suggest that changes to individual behavior can do much to lower greenhouse gas emissions and respond to climate change.

Three examples—electricity, gasoline-powered automobiles, and nuclear reactors—all show how new technologies can provoke optimistic fantasies regarding their widespread use, moving visions revolving around grand future utopias. They also show that many of the downsides—such as the expense of electricity at the time and its reliance on fossil fuels, congested traffic and air pollution created by cars, or nuclear waste and the proliferation of nuclear weapons—were undervalued and discounted. People gave such little thought to the health risks of radiation in the 1950s that many even sported radium watches with dials that shined a warm green in the dark.

The implication for current discussions about energy technology and policy are that the challenges faced by new systems are frequently discounted in the face of much more compelling (and exciting) fantasies. Put in context of the climate crisis, it implies that people can often get caught up in the hype of certain technological solutions, leading them to overestimate the ability for that technology to induce positive change.

Second, the technologies that have the most potential to help homeowners, businesspeople, and captains of industry save money, improve energy security, and fight climate change are ironically rejected by those very consumers. Why? The three cleanest forms of electricity supply on the market today are renewable power generators (think solar panels, wind turbines, hydroelectric dams, geothermal power plants, and biomass electricity stations), energy efficiency programs, and distributed generation technologies (think small-scale power plants like fuel cells or micro-turbines).

Yet utility operators reject these technologies because they are trained to think only in terms of big, conventional power plants. Consumers practically ignore renewable power systems because they are not given accurate price signals about electricity consumption. Intentional market distortions (such as subsidies) and unintentional market distortions (such as split incentives) prevent consumers from becoming fully invested in their electricity choices. As a result, newer and cleaner technologies that may offer social and environmental benefits but are not consistent with the dominant paradigm continue to find little use.

How can society respond to the climate crisis? By changing our own behavior. Individual behavior is a discrete and often overlooked source of greenhouse gas emissions. Individuals are not listed in government reports as a source of emissions, yet some studies have noted that individual behavior—actions under the direct, substantial control of a person but not undertaken in the scope of their employment—accounts for 32 percent of annual carbon dioxide (CO_2) emissions in the United States (Vandenbergh and Steinemann, 2007). Individual behavior, such as driving personal automobiles, eating food, taking vacations, and using electricity in the home, was responsible for 4.4 trillion pounds of carbon dioxide emissions in the United States in 2000, while the entire industrial sector emitted only 3.9 trillion pounds. When put into an international context, the emissions from such individual behavior in the United States accounted for about 8 percent of the world's carbon dioxide emissions, larger than the total emissions from such developed countries as Canada, South Korea, and the United Kingdom, as well as chemical manufacturing and petroleum refining.

The importance of individual, behavioral change has been confirmed in two recent studies. One 2009 study found that three types of simple, low- to no-cost actions could save immense amounts of energy and therefore abate copious amounts of greenhouse gas emissions. Three sets of changes were deemed most important:

- Infrequent actions like installing compact fluorescent light bulbs, placing weather stripping on windows and doors, and inflating automobile tires to correct pressures.
- More frequent actions like slower highway driving, air-drying household laundry, and turning off unneeded lights and appliances.
- Making informed purchases and investment decisions for more efficient windows, appliances, and automobiles.

The study found that these three sets of changes alone could reduce total energy use among individuals and homes by 23 percent, reducing about 12 percent of total U.S.-delivered energy use in 2008 (Laitner, Ehrhardt-Martinez, and McKinney, 2009).

Another investigation found that the majority of energy consumed by an average U.S. household was directed at two purposes: running a private motor vehicle and controlling the temperature within a home. Relatively little energy is used for lighting, cooking, running computers, and so on. The authors found that if individuals were to switch to more fuel-efficient automobiles, upgrade their furnaces, purchase more efficient light bulbs, and also turn their thermostats down during the winter (or up in summer), turn off lights when not in use, and watch less television, they could cut household energy use by more than 50 percent (Gardner and Stern, 2008).

Individuals, in other words, can alter many of their daily practices to substantially reduce emissions: they can, for instance, use less energy-intensive goods and services, drive more efficient cars, and purchase better electric appliances. They should not be viewed as passive recipients loosely connected to climate change, but as active participants whose lifestyles play a central (and disturbing) role in contributing to energy and climate problems.

To conclude, we do not need technology to get us out of the climate conundrum; we need to take responsibility for our own actions. Individuals making relatively simple changes to their lifestyles, such as consuming less energy at home, cycling instead of driving to work, and air-drying laundry can in aggregate add up to significant climatic benefits. Put another way, our own individual behavior can be just as important as developing new technology. The situation brings to mind the words of Rachel Carson, who wrote in 1962 that "the human race is challenged more than ever to demonstrate our mastery—not over nature, but of ourselves" (Carson, 1962).

REFERENCES

Carson, Rachel. (1962). *Silent Spring*. New York: Houghton Mifflin, ix.

Gardner, Gerald T., and Paul C. Stern. (2008, September/October). "The short list: the most effective actions U.S. households can take to curb climate change," *Environment*. Accessed May 7, 2016, at http://www.environmentmagazine.org/archives/back%20issues/september-october%202008/gardner-stern-full.html.

Laitner, John A. "Skip," Karen Ehrhardt-Martinez and Vanessa McKinney. (2009). "Examining the Scale of the Behavior Energy Efficiency Conundrum." Paper presented to the 2009 American Council for an Energy-Efficient Economy Summer Study, Washington, D.C.

Vandenbergh, Michael P., and Anne C Steinemann. (2007). "The carbon-neutral individual," *New York University Law Review 82*, 1673–1745.

15

TO MITIGATE CONFLICTS OVER NATURAL RESOURCES, IS IT BETTER TO PROMOTE PRESERVATION OR CONSERVATION?

OVERVIEW

M. Troy Burnett

There are many ways to approach environmental protection. One can opt to prevent humans from interfering with nature at all (preservation) or utilize resources with as little damage and waste as possible (conservation). Modern preservationists place a premium on wilderness, seeking to have additional lands designated by the government for protection in their natural condition, and unimpaired for the public's future use and enjoyment. Many groups are less strict, believing that a certain amount of use of the land is permissible. But some of these groups do not believe that the federal government can be relied upon to monitor the situation. Many conservation groups, such as the Sierra Club or the Natural Resources Defense Council, act as government watchdogs. Still others argue that each municipality and state should decide whether it wants to preserve or conserve the natural resources within its jurisdiction. Some who advocate for local management also see it as a way of opening up land for recreation, arguing that since many natural areas are public property, the public should be able to utilize those resources for enjoyment—an argument popular with recreationists such as ATV riders and off-roading groups.

The wide array of opinions on the environment helps to explain why our authors, all very much in favor of taking care of nature, reach such different conclusions. Peter Jacques favors strict preservation under federal control. Jacqueline Vaughn advocates federal control to enforce a balance of preservation and conservation.

BACKGROUND

In 1912, environmentalist John Muir wrote: "These temple destroyers, devotees of ravaging commercialism, seem to have a perfect contempt for Nature, and, instead of lifting their eyes to the God of the mountains, lift them to the Almighty Dollar" (Browning, 1988). The "temple" to which Muir was referring was Hetch Hetchy Valley, a lush, blooming canyon located in Yosemite National Park. Muir's scathing criticism was directed towards supporters of a proposed plan to build a dam and flood Hetch Hetchy in order to supply the city of San Francisco with water and electricity. Muir, who eventually lost the battle to prevent the dam's construction, was concerned that damming and flooding the valley would destroy its natural beauty. While some may agree that Muir was correct, millions of people currently residing in northern and central California benefit from the water and electricity produced by O'Shaughnessy Dam.

Clearly, the need to protect nature often conflicts with the needs of humans. There appear to be two main options for dealing with the situation: preservation, the maintenance of the natural world with the bare minimum of human intrusion, and conservation, the wise and judicious management of natural resources that allow human use. The debate between preservation and conservation was brought into sharp focus during the conflict over the Hetch Hetchy Valley. It highlighted a developing rift within the environmental movement and led to the collapse of Muir's friendship with Gifford Pinchot, the first chief of the U.S. Forest Service. Muir was a staunch preservationist who believed that all public lands should be left in their original state with no human interference, while Pinchot was a conservationist who believed that natural resources could be used responsibly through active management by the government.

Muir and Pinchot's contrasting philosophies have carried on to the present day. In terms of public policy, preservationists generally support the creation of parks or nature reserves that ban potentially harmful practices like fishing, hunting, or logging. Forest areas would be preserved not only to protect their natural beauty and biodiversity, but also to serve as places for scientific study and peaceful recreation. On the other hand, conservationists endorse policies that allow for the sustainable use of natural resources through commercial activities and public recreation.

The federal government's stance on the environment tends to shift from administration to administration depending on its political philosophy—a situation that makes long-term solutions to environmental questions very difficult. Over the course of the past few decades, conservative administrations have been inclined to favor conservation, endorsing policies that lessen government regulation while allowing businesses to develop natural resources. For example, in the early 1980s, the Reagan administration rolled back its enforcement of existing environmental laws and permitted access to public lands for oil drilling and coal mining. Meanwhile, more liberal administrations have often supported policies that hedge toward preservation by seeking increased government protection for public lands. In 1978, President Jimmy Carter designated millions of acres of land in Alaska as national monuments to protect them from the interests of oil companies. In the 1990s, Bill Clinton sparked a great deal of controversy by designating 21 areas as protected national monuments during his term in office. Critics claim that such designations, which greatly limit how land is used and developed, infringe on states' rights and hinder local economies.

Although during his administration President George W. Bush placed two areas under federal protection—the African Burial Grounds National Monument in New York and the Northwestern Hawaiian Islands National Monument—his administration largely displayed the conservative reliance upon conservation. For instance, the Bush administration expressed support for oil drilling in the Arctic National Wildlife Refuge (ANWR), a protected region in northeastern Alaska that shelters a diversity of animal and plant life. While drilling in ANWR could help sustain the United States in terms of its energy needs, environmentalists have raised concern over the potential disruption of wildlife in the area. In addition, President Bush also advocated a plan to expand snowmobile traffic in Yellowstone National Park—a plan that eventually failed. While President Bush's plan would have required the gradual use of snowmobiles with cleaner engines, critics still voiced concerns over the impact of snowmobile pollution and noise on the park. Perhaps the most controversial of the Bush administration's policies has been the Healthy Forests Initiative, passed by Congress and signed by President Bush in 2003. Supporters of the Healthy Forests Initiative said that the law, which allows the logging industry to thin areas of forests deemed a fire risk, will help decrease the occurrence of large-scale forest fires. Meanwhile, detractors called the Healthy Forests Initiative a means to give logging companies unhindered access to the nation's forests under the guise of an environmentally friendly name.

Undoubtedly, the relationship between the U.S. government and the environment has often proved complicated and controversial during the different administrations that have come and gone. Because there are so many ways to handle environmental protection, coming to a solution that will provide the best outcome for all sides will not be an easy task.

REFERENCE

Browning, Peter (ed.). (1988). *John Muir in His Own Words: A Book of Quotations*. Lafayette, CA: Great West Books, 65.

FURTHER READING

del Mar, David Peterson. (2014). *Environmentalism*. London: Routledge.

PRESERVATION OR CONSERVATION, THE GOVERNMENT MUST PLAY THE KEY ROLE

Jacqueline Vaughn

The federal government should be trusted to preserve natural resources because state and local governments do not have the financial capacity to do so and because these issues require a national response, rather than a regional or local one. While the federal government does not have a stellar track record on environmental issues, that of the states is far worse. There is no other real option to get the job done.

When the founders of the United States wrote the U.S. Constitution in 1787, the federal government was given only a handful of responsibilities in governing the new nation, and the preservation of natural resources was not one of them. As a result, each state and local jurisdiction usually developed its own policies regarding hunting wildlife, logging, mining, and, much later, setting aside land to be protected. The result has been a crazy quilt of regulations and statutes that lacks continuity and that often fails to protect our natural resources.

Historically, the argument has been that state and local governments should control the lands and resources within their boundaries, but that concept is no longer appropriate. Instead, we see an uneven pattern of involvement where the economic resources and commitment to environmental values varies considerably. One study found that some progressive states, led by Oregon, New Jersey, Minnesota, Maine, and Washington, have made substantial progress in preserving forests or natural areas as part of the states' overall policies for environmental protection. But the bottom five states by environmental criteria (Oklahoma, Arkansas, New Mexico, Wyoming, and Alabama) have made little effort to protect natural resources. State expenditures for environmental and natural resource programs in 2003 ranged from $100 or more per capita in 10 states to $50 or less per capita in 15 other states. With such variations in the amount of money states spend, there are going to be vast regions of the country where natural resources are less protected than in others.

It is doubtful that states have the level of fiscal resources needed to maintain the operation of agencies that are responsible for natural resources since the economic recession has reduced revenues, resulting in spending cuts. The public is more interested in key services such as education, health care, and public safety, which means environmental agencies are likely to be hit hardest by reductions in staff and operations such as enforcement. State-level natural resource policies are also at risk due to the increasing influence of conservative-oriented, rather than conservation-oriented, leaders. Due in part to economic pressures and the influence of industry interests, the majority of states have adopted legislation that waters down preservation laws and programs, rolling back many of the protective policies that had been enacted in the 1990s.

One of the factors that make local and state level natural resource protection efforts difficult to achieve is the reality that wildlife migrate and forests do not recognize state borders. One state might have developed a substantial plan for protecting its public lands, while an adjacent state takes a much less restrictive view of mining or logging. Even on a regional level, cooperation among states has not resulted in many effective partnerships. Despite the hope that states facing common problems would join together to solve problems that affect them, regional approaches are more often the exception than the rule.

The lack of financial capacity and the need for uniform standards and laws makes it imperative that the states relinquish at least some of their sovereignty in this policy area. Natural resource protection should be shifted to the federal government to insure that those resources are a legacy left to generations throughout the country, not just a handful of states that consider conservation a priority.

PRESERVATION FIRST!
Peter Jacques

The U.S. government should manage natural resources by making preservation, not conservation, its priority.

There are several reasons why the U.S. federal government should make restoration and preservation a priority for both the land it controls and for private land subject to federal laws (e.g., the Clean Water Act and the Endangered Species Act). Preservation refers to preventing human impositions and use in areas currently not subject to human modification. Restoration occurs when important ecological elements are reconstructed, such as the introduction of corridors for animal migration in places where natural migration routes have been blocked by human

A clearcut area of a forest. Clear-cutting is a harvesting method in which all the trees in a given area are cut down at one time, leaving once-plentiful old-growth forests a field of stumps, broken saplings, and rotten logs. A once-common technique, it is criticized by forestry experts for reducing the biological diversity and resilience of a forest. (U.S. Fish & Wildlife Service)

development. Since development and use of land is the norm in America, places not permanently set aside are eventually developed and modified, sometimes irreversibly. Freedom for the land and its plants and animals and for people wishing to experience this freedom will be lost if restoration and preservation are not the priorities. It is left to governments to choose preservation, or preservation will go largely unrealized.

The minimum duty to the living world, under human control, is to let it exist. However, when humans use resources in places, even when this is done with a "light touch," it changes the functional relations of the land to the flora and fauna and harms the ability of species to exist. This partially explains why the world faces the "Sixth Great Extinction" in geological time. Until now there have been five tremendous eras of loss of life on the Earth. We are now in the midst of the next one, the sixth, in which the extinction rate is 100–1,000 times as great as the normal rate at which species usually go extinct. This extinction era is believed to be driven by human change to the environment, such as through development and modification of land and land cover. Restoration and preservation of land is an essential duty to life on Earth.

One reason that preservation is so critical to the survival of life on Earth is the fact that there are invisible elements at work in ecosystems. Disruption of these elements can have unforeseen consequences. The most important element is energy. As humans use elements of nature, as when we turn trees and forests into lumber, energy is lost in the process. Humans depend on this energy to survive. However, if we use too much, we may endanger our own well-being. The loss of matter and energy depletes options for the ecosystem. Ecosystems are highly interdependent systems where small changes can set off expanding chain reactions. The ultimate and precise effects of changes cannot be predicted, even by the best models. Even under very careful conservationist management, mistakes often driven by human greed are made. Energy in the ecosystem is lost as a regular and predictable element of conservationist/human-centered management. Preservation, not conservation, is the best approach.

16

HOW DOES THE ILLICIT TRADE IN ENDANGERED SPECIES PROMOTE REGIONAL CONFLICT?

OVERVIEW
Ariana Tran and M. Troy Burnett

The international black market trade in endangered species is a global problem with environmental, economic, and political implications. In fact, The International Criminal Police Organization (INTERPOL) estimates the value of the illegal animal trade to be between $10 billion and $20 billion per year. Even though this is just an estimate, it is believed to only trail drugs and weapons in the global illicit marketplace. Not surprisingly, this illegal trade has led to frequent conflict within those countries where the wildlife is found, many of which have weak economies and unstable political climates. The illicit trade is most prevalent in countries of Asia and Africa for two reasons: (1) they possess the greatest supply of exotic animals; and (2) they possess a high number of consumers who believe in the mystical powers of animals and their by-products. It is important to make clear however that this is a both a regional and a global industry with consumers and traders found in every country.

BACKGROUND

Rhinos, elephants, sharks, lizards, crocodiles, tigers, snakes, monkeys, and various birds are among the highest-profile species under threat by hunters and poachers. The tiger, for example, is widely sought because each part of the animal has potential value. The skin, bones, and body parts of the tiger are often used in traditional Chinese medicine because of the perceived health benefits, including enhanced virility. Tiger teeth and claws are believed to possess mythical powers providing potency or protection to those who wear them. According to Weirum (2007), tiger bone wine, made from soaking tiger skeletons in alcohol, is coveted in China for its many healing properties. As a result, and in spite of laws and strict penalties, the number of tigers has dwindled to less than 5,000 from the nearly 100,000 that existed in the 1990s.

Another example is the rhino horn, which is shaved or ground into a powder to treat many illnesses throughout Asia. It is also commonly assumed that rhino horn powder will enhance male virility. According to Stelley (2013), some traders actually inject Viagra into the horn to give consumers the false impression that the enhancement is coming from the horn powder. He adds that these absurd beliefs, reinforced by the shady practices of the suppliers, drive the trade of endangered species. The problem with rhinos has become so severe that conservationists will tranquilize the animal and saw off its horn so that it becomes worthless to poachers. These horns do not grow back.

Those involved in the illicit trade are ignorant or indifferent to the problem that the species they trade are endangered. The trade in endangered species has become a network woven together with crime, greed, and ignorance. An exotic fish from Australia, the Philippines, or the United States smuggled through Hong Kong can be worth as much as $10,000 in China (Stelley, 2013). That one fish has undergone a complicated path involving multiple actors poaching, smuggling, or selling in the underground market in China. Indeed, these illicit businesses thrive off of rare amenities—the rarer the fish or animal part the more valuable. The money and perceived benefits involved with endangered species is substantial, encouraging suppliers and demanders to take great risks. In some instances, the illegal activity is not even hidden. Guangzhou, for example, a city close to the Hong Kong border, has wild game restaurants where customers can choose their exotic meal, many choosing crocodile plucked straight from plastic bins (Stelley, 2013).

The illicit trade is not just limited to countries in the Eastern hemisphere. Some American states do not enforce existing laws regarding exotic animals, including lions, tigers, cougars, leopards, and chimpanzees (VICELAND, 2014). For example, Ohio has little to no regulation. As a result, in 2012 a man with a collection of large wild cats let them loose before committing suicide. Though most of the cats were trapped and then killed, they posed a risk to the community while they were at large (VICELAND, 2014). Within the United States, there are also large reservations made for hunting exotic game. Exotic animals are purchased in the illicit market and covertly transferred to large parcels of land where people can pay to hunt.

Auctions also take place, with no restrictions and oversight, where animals go to the highest bidders, whoever they may be (VICELAND, 2014). Further complicating the issue is the growth of online trading, escalating the market and reducing the trade barriers (IFAW, 2013).

Though there is widespread consensus that this is an important environmental and political issue, as the essays in this section highlight, it is unclear whether addressing the problem often inspires regional cooperation and conflict. Numerous institutions, both local and global, have formed to address this problem. The Convention on International Trade in Endangered Species of Wild Fauna and Flora (CITES) is a voluntary international agreement between governments. The agreement was enacted in 1973 to protect nearly 5,000 species of animals against overexploitation and trade. Other organizations involved in this battle are the World Wildlife Fund, The Nature Conservancy, and The International Fund for Animal Welfare. Despite their efforts, trade continues to expand.

REFERENCES

Hastie, Jo, and Tania McCrea-Steele. (2014). "Wanted—Dead or Alive: Exposing Online Wildlife Trade." International Fund for Animal Welfare. Accessed March 1, 2016, at http://www.ifaw.org/sites/default/files/IFAW-Wanted-Dead-or-Alive-Exposing-Online-Wildlife-Trade-2014.pdf.

Stelley, Santiago. (2013, January 8). "Documenting Asia's Illegal Animal Trade." YouTube video. Accessed March 1, 2016, at https://www.youtube.com/watch?v=PQC3jp1udUg.

VICE. (2014). "An Inside Look at the Exotic Animal Trade: Profiles by VICE." YouTube video. Accessed March 1, 2016, at https://www.youtube.com/watch?v=LSQ8blCdAtA.

Weirum, Brian K. (2007, December 29). "Tiger Bone Wine." Big Cat Rescue. Accessed January 14, 2015, at http://bigcatrescue.org/tiger-bone-wine/.

FURTHER READING

The Economist (eds.). (2013, March 16). "The endangered species trade: on the way out," *The Economist*. Accessed January 13, 2015, at http://www.economist.com/blogs/banyan/2013/03/endangered-species-trade.

Williams, Horace O., and Viktor T. Grante (eds.). 2011. *Illegal Trade in Wildlife*. New York: Nova Science Publishers.

World Wildlife Fund. (2011). "Closing a Deadly Gateway." World Wildlife Fund International. YouTube video. Accessed March 1, 2016, at https://www.youtube.com/watch?v=uc1XbBvcFqo.

Wyler, Liana Sun, and Pervaze A. Sheikh. (2008). *International Illegal Trade in Wildlife*. New York: Novinka Books.

THE LINK BETWEEN ILLICIT TRADE IN ENDANGERED SPECIES AND REGIONAL CONFLICT

Ariana Tran and M. Troy Burnett

The illicit trade in endangered species has far-reaching implications at both the regional and global scales. The international wildlife trade is estimated to be worth over $330 billion annually, with $10 billion to $20 billion of that total derived from illegally trafficked wildlife (Douglas and Alie, 2014). Given the large amount of money to be gained through unsanctioned trade, it is not surprising that it has been linked to other illicit activities such as money laundering, corruption, and terrorism. The problem is magnified in the developing world where economic desperation co-exists with high species and habitat diversity. Further, many developing areas are burdened by ongoing political conflict, with rival groups finding the quick revenues to be generated by wildlife trafficking an easy fix to their funding problems. With the growth of the Internet, the illicit market has greatly expanded, globally linking suppliers with demanders (Hastie and McCrea-Steele, 2014). The

Rangers stack elephant ivory at the Kenya Wildlife Headquarters. (Khalil Senosi/AP Photo)

International Fund for Animal Welfare (IFAW) found 280 illegal online wildlife market sites in 16 countries. Criminal networks have formed to promote and facilitate wildlife trade, becoming a threat to regional and global security. Along with the economic power of the criminal trade networks, efforts at international cooperation to eradicate this trade are undermined by corruption, suspicion, and mistrust.

It is not only live animals that are traded, but various animal parts that are valued for their perceived medicinal properties or simply as unique souvenirs to place on a mantle. Such trade is most prevalent in Southeast Asia and Africa. China is known to be the largest consumer of these exotic products with supply derived from the countries of Southeast Asia and Africa. The Bengal tigers, for instance, are hunted and systematically slaughtered then parceled into segments to be used to make pseudoscientific medicines or trinkets for consumers in China. One such exotic product, tiger bone wine, is made by soaking the animal's skeleton in a vat of wine. For the consumer paying an exorbitant amount, the wine is imagined to cure illness and increase virility (Weirum, 2013). According to Brian K. Weirum, China is by far the world's largest market for illicit tiger parts. Demand has accelerated as China's economic growth enriches many of its citizens. The result has been an increase in the illegal trade and the further endangerment of tigers in India and Nepal.

Laws often exist to protect endangered species, such as the Bengal tiger. Yet, because of the economic or political instability in the countries involved, enforcement has been difficult. Economic incentives and corruption readily trump mechanisms to limit trade. Officials have been documented to accept bribes to certify paperwork (Anderson and Jooste, 2014). For example, in the case of South Africa police and military units have themselves been involved in rhino horn trafficking. In Uganda in March of 2014, it was discovered that Ugandan soldiers killed and traded more than 22 elephants—producing more than $1 million worth of ivory (Anderson and Jooste, 2014). Even when there is evidence presented, the guilty parties are rarely taken to trial. In Kenya, 70 percent of case files were found to be "misplaced" by an independent Kenyan conservation group. Where cases actually go to trial in Kenya, only 8 of the known 224 defendants were convicted of animal trafficking (Anderson and Jooste, 2014).

It is not just the trade in specific wildlife that is the source of conflict, but control over their habitats as well. As noted by Leo Douglas and Kevin Alie (2014), viewing them as a threat to their operations, Congolese rebels murdered wildlife rangers. Illicit traders and rebel factions have seized control over regions known for ecotourism to then clandestinely run the operations and pocket the proceeds from unwitting tourists. Ecotourism and trophy hunting generate large sums of money for many African countries, yet the current corruption in this area suggests that the benefits, at least in certain regions, are realized mostly by rebel groups and corrupt government officials. The mismanagement also jeopardizes the long-term viability of these lands because ecotourism will no longer exist if the population of these exotic species continues to dwindle. For example, Kenya currently earns more than $1 billion annually from ecotourism (Douglas and Alie, 2014).

Another insidious aspect of this issue involves the wanton massacre of valuable species by rebel groups for the simple goal of destabilizing legitimate governments. They are keenly aware of the economic potential species preservation and ecotourism provide, and without moral qualms wantonly slaughter species in order to degrade the industry and promote fear. An example of this behavior comes from the Democratic Republic of the Congo's Virunga National Park where Mai Mai rebels slaughtered hundreds of hippopotamuses, leaving their rotting carcasses as a warning to the government and would-be tourists (Douglas and Alie, 2014). These same rebels, in a type of hostage bargaining, have also threatened to slaughter the endangered mountain gorillas if their demands are not met (Wadhams, 2007).

In short, the most dangerous sources of conflict resulting from the illegal trade of endangered species seemingly lies with rebel militias promoting civil conflict and groups involved in terrorism. Similar to diamonds, valuable wildlife has become a "conflict resource" to political groups in need of funding. Douglas and Alie (2014) point to several examples illustrating this connection. Accounts from fugitives of the Lord's Resistance Army led by warlord Joseph Kony in northern Uganda have revealed links of trading ivory with Arab businessmen and officers in the Sudanese military for other commodities including guns and medical supplies. Ivory in the rhino horn trade is traced to Congolese, Sudanese, and Ugandan civil conflicts. The Taliban in Afghanistan and Pakistan are beneficiaries of the illicit falconry trade, while Somali warlords and Indian Islamic extremist groups loyal to Al Qaeda are involved in wildlife trade as well.

Sadly, the situation does not appear to be improving despite the long list of local laws and global institutions such as the United Nations' Convention on International Trade in Endangered Species of Wild Fauna and Flora (CITES). The economic incentives are too high and the criminal networks are well established. In developing countries, corruption and bribery are administrative facts and, more often than not, those involved in pre-existing civil conflicts either exploit the demand for select wildlife or wantonly slaughter species in order to destabilize their opponents.

REFERENCES

Anderson, Bradley, and Johan Jooste. (2014, May). "Wildlife poaching: Africa's surging trafficking threat," *Africa Security Brief: A Publication of the Africa Center for Strategic Studies 28*, 1–8.

Douglas, Leo R., and Kevin Alie. (2014, January 17). "High-value natural resources: Linking wildlife conservation to international conflict, insecurity, and development concerns," *Biological Conservation, 171*, 270–277.

Hastie, Jo, and Tania McCrea-Steele. (2014). "Wanted—Dead or Alive: Exposing Online Wildlife Trade." International Fund for Animal Welfare. Accessed March 1, 2016, at http://www.ifaw.org/sites/default/files/IFAW-Wanted-Dead-or-Alive-Exposing-Online-Wildlife-Trade-2014.pdf.

Wadhams, Nick. (2007, October 28). "Endangered gorillas 'held hostage' by rebels in Africa park," *National Geographic News*. Accessed March 1, 2016, at http://news.nationalgeographic.com/news/2007/05/070523-gorillas-hostage.html.

Weirum, Brian K. (2007, December 29). "Tiger Bone Wine." Big Cat Rescue. Accessed January 14, 2015, at http://bigcatrescue.org/tiger-bone-wine/.

THE NEED FOR COOPERATION IN THE ILLICIT WILDLIFE TRADE

Cynthia Tafoya and M. Troy Burnett

As the number of animal species rapidly dwindles, the race to conserve these creatures and their habitat has become urgent. With over 180 signatories to the Convention on International Trade in Endangered Species of Wild Fauna and Flora (CITES), it has become clear that the international community is serious about biodiversity and the need to stem the trade in endangered species. Though challenging to coordinate and enforce, efforts to eliminate the illicit trade has presented opportunities for political unity between countries that either don't engage with each other or who may even be antagonistic. The illegal trade in exotic wildlife is transboundary and subsequently to eliminate the practice requires a transboundary regulatory framework as well as global/local enforcement mechanisms, cooperation, and transparency from the international community.

Widely regarded as a symbol and source of strength and healing in China and elsewhere, the tiger is at the heart of the issue. Traditional Chinese medicinal practices has longed used tiger parts to treat an array of ailments to the liver and kidneys, as well as afflictions such as epilepsy, baldness, toothaches, joint pain, ulcers, nightmares, fevers, and headaches. When pulverized and consumed in teas, tiger parts are believed to promote longevity, and increase stamina and virility. As a result of such cultural beliefs, according to the International Union for the Conservation of Nature, the South China tiger (*Panthera tigris amoyensis*) is considered functionally extinct—one has not been seen in China for over 25 years. Yet, demand for tiger parts is still high and in order to provide the supply, poachers must hunt and slaughter tigers elsewhere and transport them illegally into China.

While the demand remains steady, the scarcity has driven the value of the parts up, creating more allure for poachers and higher status for consumers.

From the example of the Chinese tiger and other tiger species, it is clear that no one country has the power to stop the illicit trade of animal parts and that entire regions must assume accountability for the ways in which such activity occurs. While it seems like an impossible feat to get government leaders to collaborate on issues of conservation, there have been cases where separate ruling bodies have put aside their differences and made wildlife conservation a priority. In 2011, the World Bank developed a groundbreaking project in South Asia called the Strengthening Regional Cooperation for Wildlife Protection in Asia (SRCWP) as an attempt to combat the illicit trade of animal parts throughout the continent. The project assists participating governments in building and enhancing shared capacity, institutions, knowledge, and incentives to collaborate on tackling the illegal wildlife trade and other selected regional conservation threats. According to the World Bank, the benefits of the project have already become evident in Bangladesh where it has helped the Bangladesh Forest Department establish a Wildlife Crime Control Unit (World Bank, 2015). The Unit is equipped with a forensics lab, a legal support arm, and a wildlife crime control group. Under the assistance of the SRCWP, this new control unit coordinates with many international agencies such as INTERPOL and the International Consortium on Combating Wildlife Crime. These projects are vital, for, along with being one of the least developed countries in the world, Bangladesh is 1 of only 13 regions in which tigers still roam. Poachers and traders view such conditions as easy to exploit.

The complex nature of the conflict around the illicit trade in wildlife is also illustrated in Africa. Poachers and traffickers of wildlife often engage in other nefarious activities such as drugs, arms trafficking, political conflict, and as funding sources for terrorist groups. The very real connection between wildlife poaching and terrorism is captured in award-winning director Katheryn Bigelow's the *Last Days of Ivory*. The 2014 animated film unveils the connections between the slaughter of African elephants and the funding of terrorist organizations such as the Lord's Resistance Army, Janjaweed, and Boko Haram (Bigelow, 2014). According to a 2014 article in the *Washington Post*: "illegal ivory funds as much as 40 percent of the operations of al-Shabab, the group behind the attack at a Nairobi shopping mall where 60 people were killed" (Bergenas, 2014). The rising awareness of these linkages has spurred both local authorities and the international community to take direct action. Along with stronger local laws, the United States in particular has been actively combating the Lord's Resistance Army's poaching and trafficking activities.

Admittedly, many of these countries involved in this conflict have difficulty enforcing anti-wildlife trafficking laws as they are plagued by political and economic instability. Thus, the elimination of the increasingly globalized network of illegal activities requires an equally globalized regulatory system. There can no longer be cultural loopholes and regulatory safe havens for illegal poachers and traders. Further, international efforts must go beyond stopping poachers and traffickers (the suppliers) and address the role that traditional cultural norms play in creating such a high demand for these illicit products. One way this can be achieved is through education and the promotion of scientifically based alternatives that effectively dispel the cultural belief in the "potency" of tiger and other exotic animal parts. The simple fact that needs to be conveyed is that animal parts, such as tiger bones and rhino horns, do not provide any real healing qualities beyond a placebo effect and that any perceived benefit of such remedies can be gained through legitimate pharmaceutical means. The survival of many unique species such as tigers, elephants, rhinos, and monkeys among many others is contingent upon this awareness coupled with the participation of political and economic leaders.

Younger generations, educated in this more globalized world that values biodiversity, are starting to appreciate more their biological heritage and realize the economic, social, and ecological benefits of protecting threatened species and their habitats.

REFERENCES

Bergenas, Johan, and Monica Medina. (2014, January 31). "Break the link between terrorism funding and poaching," *Washington Post*. Accessed March 1, 2016, at https://www.washingtonpost.com/opinions/break-the-link-between-terrorism-funding-and-poaching/2014/01/31/6c03780e-83b5-11e3-bbe5-6a2a3141e3a9_story.html.

Bigelow, Kathryn (dir.). (2014). *Last Days of Ivory*. Film. Accessed March 1, 2016, at http://www.lastdaysofivory.com/#the-film.

World Bank. (2015, October 22). "Regional Collaboration for Combating Illegal Wildlife Trade in Bangladesh." Accessed March 1, 2016, at http://www.worldbank.org/en/news/feature/2014/10/14/regional-collaboration-for-combating-illegal-wildlife-trade-in-bangladesh.

FURTHER READING

Guynup, Sharon. (2014, April 29). "Tigers in traditional Chinese medicine: A universal apothecary," *National Geographic*. Accessed March 1, 2016, at http://voices.nationalgeographic.com/2014/04/29/tigers-in-traditional-chinese-medicine-a-universal-apothecary/.

17

SHOULD CULTURAL EXCEPTIONS BE MADE IN WHALING LAWS?

OVERVIEW
Mia Bennett

Whales are some of the largest creatures on Earth. Their high levels of intelligence and sociability have made them Hollywood stars and poster children for the environmental movement. These marine mammals can be found in nearly every ocean, and societies around the world have found use for them. Due to their size—a blue whale can reach up to 100 feet in length (Northeast Fisheries Science Center, 2011)—and versatility, cetaceans have long been hunted as a source of food and resources. The earliest evidence for dolphin hunting dates back to 6300–5300 BCE on Santa Cruz Island off California. Archaeologists have found similarly ancient signs of whaling along the North Pacific Rim and nearby Arctic regions in places like Japan and Chukotka, Russia (Savelle and Kishigami, 2013), areas where people have continued to hunt whales into the modern era for commercial and subsistence purposes.

BACKGROUND

Today, whaling can be placed into three main categories. First, there is commercial, for-profit whaling, begun by the Basques in the 11th century. Living in present-day Spain and France, these people hunted right whales and bowhead whales as far west as Newfoundland, Canada, and as far north as Svalbard, in the Arctic Ocean (Savelle and Kishigami, 2013). Whaling became modernized in the 19th century, when harpoon gun-fired grenades allowed boats to swiftly kill large numbers of whales for their oil, blubber, and baleen, an activity that peaked in the 1960s.

Today, only Norway and Iceland officially carry out commercial whaling, objecting to the moratorium placed on the activity by the International Whaling Commission (IWC) in 1986. While these two Nordic countries are members of the IWC, their reservation against the moratorium contradicts what has become an increasingly accepted international norm. The adherence of most of the world's countries to the moratorium has massively reduced whaling, helping all whale species recover from the risk of extinction (Hurd, 2012). Whereas 66,000 whales were killed in 1961, only 326 were killed in 1989—but that number grew to 2,000 by 2008 (Hurd, 2012).

Part of the recent increase has taken place under the second of two categories: scientific whaling and indigenous, or aboriginal sustenance, whaling. So-called scientific whaling is permitted by the IWC, which allows countries to "kill, take, and treat whales for purposes of scientific research" (IWC, 1946). However, Japan's scientific whaling in the Southern Ocean off Antarctica was ruled illegal in March 2014 by the International Court of Justice in a case brought by Australia, which argued that the Asian nation was violating its obligations under international law (Strausz, 2014). No such ban, however, has followed for the country's scientific whaling in the North Pacific Ocean, though many environmentalists hope that one will follow suit.

Harder to justify on ethical grounds, yet arguably necessary in order to maintain the overall health of whale stocks, would be the banning of the second category: aboriginal subsistence whaling. The IWC explains that this practice "does not seek to maximize catches or profit," and the organization "ensures that hunts do not seriously increase the risk of extinction" while also allowing "native people to hunt whales at levels appropriate to cultural and nutritional requirements (known as 'need') in the long-term" (IWC, 2014). The multilateral organization manages indigenous whale hunts by the Inupiat and Yupiit in Alaska, the Chukchi and Yupiit in Russia, the Inuit in Greenland, and the indigenous peoples of Bequia in St. Vincent and the Grenadines (Savelle and Kishigami, 2013). The IWC also oversees whaling by the Makah in Washington State, but lawsuits brought by environmental organizations have halted this hunt (Savelle and Kishigami, 2013). Indigenous whaling also takes place outside the auspices of the IWC by communities in Canada, where the constitution guarantees the Inuit people's right to whale, and in Indonesia. Neither of these countries are members of the IWC.

Those opposed to indigenous whaling observe that a dead whale is still a dead whale regardless of the motives behind its killing. The first essay assesses the point of view of those who contest this activity, condemned as brutal and uncivilized. Contrary to popular belief, indigenous whaling has become modernized in many cases, with hunters using motorized boats and harpoon guns (Reeves, 2002). In places like Greenland, whale meat has been found being sold to tourists both on the island and as far away as Copenhagen, violating IWC regulations (Tripp, 2012). Thus, although indigenous whaling is smaller in scale than industrialized modernized whaling, environmentalists still protest it, particularly its creeping commercialization. They argue that just as indigenous peoples have adapted to the modern era by wearing high-tech parkas and driving snowmobiles, they can also adapt by discontinuing the archaic practice of whaling.

As the second essay explores, those in favor of aboriginal whaling highlight the practice's sustainability. Indigenous peoples use the whole body of a whale, from its flesh to its rib bones, which have even been used as structural supports for dwellings in Chukotka (Gusev et al., 1999). It was not until the advent of industrialized whaling that species began to precipitously decline. Furthermore, if indigenous peoples cannot hunt whales, it might be difficult and costly to fly in supplies to make up for the amount of sustenance and materials that would otherwise come from a whale. Aside from just simple nutrition, whales have important cultural and spiritual meaning to indigenous peoples such as the Inupiat, who call themselves the "People of the Whales" (Sakakibara, 2010). To deprive these peoples of their ability to hunt whales would be to deprive them of their way of life.

The two essays reveal that while aboriginal subsistence whaling enjoys somewhat more sympathy from the global community than commercial whaling, it is still a highly contentious issue especially since the distinction between subsistence and commercial whaling is not always clear. Still, unlike in the waters off Antarctica, where Sea Shepherd boats have rammed into Japanese whaling boats in heated conflicts, environmental activists have so far refrained from entering into open skirmishes with indigenous subsistence hunters. Yet the issue remains a bitterly divided one, entangled with fights over indigenous rights and animal rights. Both sides have vocal proponents, ensuring that the debate over aboriginal subsistence whaling will rage into the 21st century.

REFERENCES

Gusev, Sergei V., Andrey V. Zagoroulko, and Alexsey V. Porotov. (1999). "Sea mammal hunters of Chukotka, Bering Strait: recent archaeological results and problems," *World Archaeology* 30(3), 354–369.

Hurd, Ian. (2012). "Almost saving whales: the ambiguity of success at the International Whaling Commission," *Ethics and International Affairs* 26(1), 103–112.

International Whaling Commission. (2014). "Aboriginal Subsistence Whaling." Accessed March 2, 2016, at http://iwc.int/aboriginal.

International Whaling Commission. (1946). "International Convention for the Regulation of Whaling." Accessed March 5, 2016, at http://avalon.law.yale.edu/20th_century/whaling.asp.

Northeast Fisheries Science Center. (2011). "NEFSC Fish FAQ." Accessed March 2, 2016, at http://www.nefsc.noaa.gov/faq/fishfaq9.html.

Reeves, Randall. (2002). "The origins and character of 'aboriginal subsistence' whaling: A global review," *Mammal Review 32*(2), 71–106. Accessed March 2, 2016, at http://onlinelibrary.wiley.com/doi/10.1046/j.1365-2907.2002.00100.x/full.

Sakakibara, Chie. (2010). "Kiavallakkikput agviq [into the whaling cycle]: Cetaceousness and climate change among the Iñupiat of Arctic Alaska," *Annals of the Association of American Geographers 100*(4), 1003–1012. doi:10.1080/00045608.2010.500561.

Savelle, John, and Nobuhiro Kishigami. (2013). "Anthropological research on whaling: prehistoric, historic and current contexts," *Senri Ethnological Studies 84*(1), 1–48.

Strausz, Michael. (2014). "Executives, legislatures, and whales: the birth of Japan's scientific whaling regime," *International Relations of the Asia-Pacific*. Accessed March 2, 2016, at http://irap.oxfordjournals.org/content/14/3/455.abstract.

Tripp, Emily. (2012, December 11). "Whale meat being sold illegally in Greenland and Denmark," *Marine Science Today*. Accessed March 2, 2016, at http://marinesciencetoday.com/2012/12/11/whale-meat-being-sold-illegally-in-greenland-and-denmark/.

FURTHER READING

Burnett, D. Graham. (2012). *The Sounding of the Whale: Science & Cetaceans in the Twentieth Century*. Chicago, IL: The University of Chicago Press.

Freeman, Milton M. R., Lyudmila Bogoslovskaya, Richard A. Caulfield, Ingmar Egede, et al. (1998). *Inuit, Whaling, and Sustainability*. Contemporary Native American Communities Volume 1. Walnut Creek, CA: Altamira Press.

Hunter, Emily. (2009, May 5). "Whaling: the latest culture war," *This Magazine*. Accessed May 5, 2016, at http://this.org/magazine/2009/05/05/whaling-culture-war/.

NO! A DEAD WHALE IS STILL A DEAD WHALE

M. Troy Burnett

From Pinocchio's Monstro to Captain Ahab's Moby Dick to the Biblical Leviathan that consumed Jonah, it is not that long ago that whales were viewed as monsters, sinister forces that lurked in the deep, dark oceans. The imagery shifted when it was discovered that whales had utilitarian value. Viewed as an exploitable resource, beginning in the 17th century, the creatures were hunted en masse. As technology and skills improved, by 1940 more than 50,000 whales were being killed annually. As our perception and understanding evolved, it was realized that whales were not monsters, but intelligent and long-living beings—in fact, sea mammals that are more akin to humans than fish. Global efforts to protect the

Members of the anti-whaling environmental group Greenpeace, wearing masks of Japan's Commissioner to the International Whaling Commission, Minoru Morimoto, stage a demonstration against Japan's government at the commission's meeting in May 2002. (AFP/Getty Images)

species soon took off as evidence of their looming extinction mounted. Defying death, conservationists from Greenpeace and Sea Shepherd courageously placed their boats and themselves between a whaler's harpoon and its target. "Save the Whales" emerged as the slogan of a massive awareness raising campaign that eventually helped inspire the worldwide ban on commercial whaling in 1986 as well as the formation of the International Whaling Commission (IWC) to oversee conservation efforts. Unfortunately, there are countries that have chosen to ignore the ban—Japan, Norway, Iceland—as well as countries who continue to hunt by invoking "cultural exemptions" (Denmark, Russia, United States, and St. Vincent and The Grenadines).

The current IWC regime governing the hunting of whales via cultural exceptions is flawed, corrupt, ineffective, and in serious need of reform. Frankly, so-called cultural exceptions, which include anything from science to religious ceremony, are thinly disguised attempts to continue the practice of commercial hunting. The time has come to ban all forms of and reasons for whale hunting. Culture and tradition are not reason enough to slaughter some of Earth's most majestic and threatened creatures. The lame excuse of "culture" has long been used to defend unsavory practices from slavery to racism to misogyny.

Further, the "subsistence" and "for food" arguments in support of whaling are weak and anachronistic. Due to the biomagnification of toxins up the food chain and into the flesh of whales and other marine mammals, the consumption of whale meat in aboriginal communities, such as the Inuit of Greenland, is at historic lows. Further, by exposing the cruel practice, awareness-raising efforts have been successful in dramatically decreasing the demand for whale meat in Japanese markets—for too long a popular delicacy in Sushi restaurants. The Norwegian and Icelandic publics as well, upon learning that the purpose of their tradition of whale hunting and IWC invoked cultural exception was to supply Japanese markets, have come out in droves to protest their countries' behavior and demand an end to the practice.

Since they resumed whaling in 1993, Norwegian commercial hunters have killed more than 10,000 whales. Fuelling the demand to end the hunt is that fact that despite considerable investment and research by the Norwegian government and whalers themselves, there is admittedly no humane way to "harvest" a whale. Indeed, the method for killing a minke whale, with a penthrite harpoon, has changed little in over 150 years. Visibility, swells, and movement make it difficult for even the most experienced whaler to kill instantly. According to Norwegian government statistics, 20 percent of the harpooned whales are hit in non-vital areas and end up suffering long and agonizing deaths.

In the case of Japan, proponents of whaling rationalize and defend the practice by invoking cultural tradition and national heritage. The Institute of Cetacean Research in Tokyo is the country's premier institution defending and monitoring the whaling industry. The institute claims it supports whaling for "scientific reasons," when the fact is that particular clause of the IWC regime is a smokescreen for the continued sale of whale meat to Japanese consumers. Moreover, ardent defenders believe that efforts to end Japan's whaling are nothing more than Western arrogance. As Jun Hoshikawa, director of Greenpeace Japan, observes, "The Japanese whaling industry has cunningly used the term 'culture' as a get-out-of-jail-free card—by framing this as an issue of culture or sovereignty, it aims to make any anti-whaling group look like they are colonialist and discriminatory" (Hunter, 2009). He and a small but vocal faction in Japan believe that "the hunt is senseless slaughter in service of fake science, a dead industry, and nationalist posturing . . . the whales should not bear the punishment for our foolishness" (Hunter, 2009). Hoshikawa and others are convinced that whaling is not even commercially viable but persists because it is framed as an issue of national sovereignty: "countries like Japan that still run whaling hunts now see it as a political defeat to cave in to international pressure" (Hunter, 2009).

CONCLUSION

The monetary value of whales—as much as $100,000 for a single minke whale—along with the stubborn invocation of national sovereignty and cultural tradition seemingly guarantee that they practice will continue. Though begun with good intentions, the IWC has proven to be a weak and ineffective body, its members prone to bribery and cajoling by Japan to support whaling or at least not make much of a diplomatic row when it flaunts the rules. The IWC defends its approach arguing that if it eliminates the cultural exceptions clause the whole agreement and general ban would unravel paving the way for a full-scale resumption of commercial whaling. While this may in a sense be possible, though unlikely, the real issue is not the survival of a failed bureaucracy, but the survival and flourishing of whales. Industrial-scale hunting when combined with habitat degradation and climate change has pushed many Cetacean species to the brink of extinction. Whales as mammals are slow to reproduce yet can live between 70 and 150 years. This makes them vulnerable to population collapses and extinction. The biggest animal to have ever existed, the blue whale, despite being protected has yet to recover to a stable population size. The West Pacific grey whale was hunted so effectively that it is presently the most endangered whale in the world with fewer than 100 individuals, though its close relative, the East Pacific grey whale, has recovered. If given enough time and space, many of the species may recover. To ensure this recovery, all forms of whaling should be banned and no country should be allowed to invoke cultural exemptions. Further, the world's non-whaling countries, such as the United States, should more vocally press for a complete and absolute ban. Doubtless, just as our present generation views slavery with malice, so too will our descendants feel about whaling.

REFERENCE

Hunter, Emily. (2009, May 5). "Whaling: the latest culture war," *This Magazine*. Accessed May 2, 2016, at http://this.org/magazine/2009/05/05/whaling-culture-war/.

IN DEFENSE OF CULTURAL EXCEPTIONS FOR WHALING
Mia Bennett

For thousands of years, people in a wide range of environments from the frigid Arctic Ocean to the warm waters off Indonesia have hunted whales for subsistence.

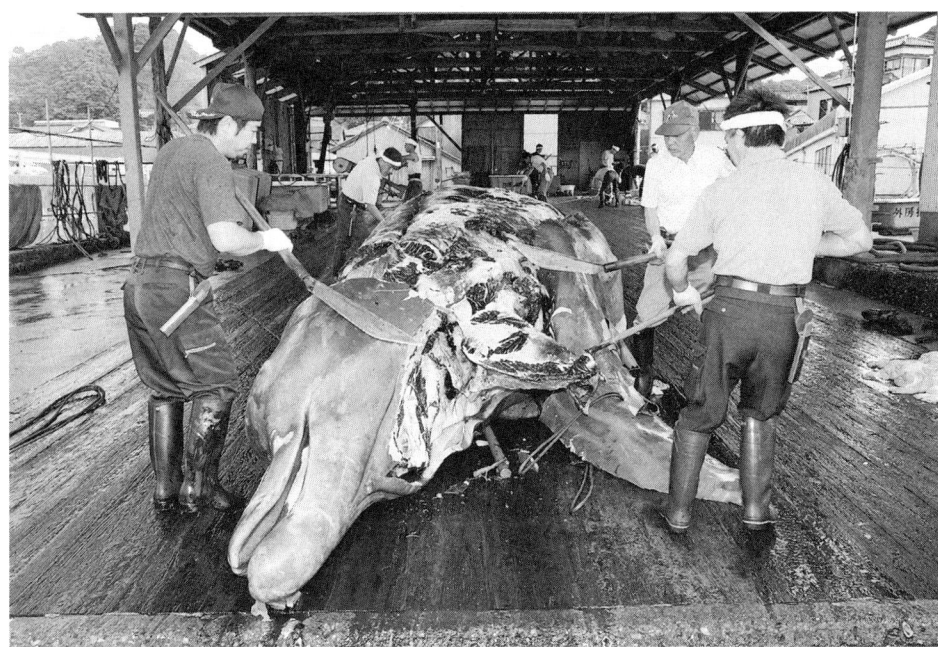

Japanese whalers clean and cut meat from a Baird's Beaked Whale at Wada Port, July 9, 2003, in Chiba-Prefecture, Japan. Whale meat remains an expensive gourmet food in Japan and its consumption is a national custom. The International Whaling Commission (IWC) set Japan's catch quota for Baird's Beaked Whales at 40 whales per year in 1983, and the species is believed to be in no immediate danger of extinction. (Koichi Kamoshida/iStockPhoto.com)

While it is mistaken to believe that indigenous peoples inhabit an ahistorical world untouched by modern civilization, in many cases, their practices still reflect ancient traditions closely tied to sustainable use of the Earth's resources. With numerous rights already taken away from indigenous peoples, they should not have to cease their remaining activities, such as whaling, due to the flagrant overhunting of whales by industrialized societies. As such, cultural exceptions should be made in whaling laws when the practice is carried out for aboriginal subsistence purposes. Yet close monitoring of indigenous hunts is required to ensure transparency and guarantee that they are being conducted for their stated purposes.

Whaling is integral to several indigenous societies around the world, as the practice allows them to provide for the needs of their communities. In Alaska's North Slope, the Inupiat Eskimo way of life revolves around the hunt of the bowhead whale (Chiropolos, 1994). In the town of Barrow (population 5,200), a single bowhead whale carcass can feed a community for at least a year. Whale meat is a welcome traditional and local addition to a diet that otherwise must rely upon expensive foodstuffs like milk flown in from hundreds of miles away (DeMarban, 2013).

In Indonesia, the Lamalera use every part of the approximately six sperm whales they catch annually for everything from food to currency (BBC, 2014). Without the ability to hunt whales, several cultures would lose their traditional ways of life along with a sustainable, local means of feeding themselves and providing for their needs.

Indigenous subsistence whaling thus differs starkly from commercial whaling. This industrialized practice has killed thousands of whales per year since the 17th century, expanding enormously in the 20th century to meet growing global demand for products like whale oil. In two Antarctic seasons alone (1959–1960 and 1960–1961), two Soviet ships killed 25,000 humpback whales (Clapham and Ivashchenko, 2009). In light of the decimation of whale stocks, the International Whaling Commission (IWC), established in 1946, placed a moratorium on whaling in 1986. The organization currently allows aboriginal subsistence whaling in Greenland, Russia's Chukotka Autonomous Okrug, St. Vincent and the Grenadines, Alaska, and Washington State (IWC, 2014).

Today, only Iceland and Norway, both of which object to the moratorium, whale for commercial purposes despite IWC resolutions asking them to cease. Japan, after ceasing its commercial hunt in 1988, has since carried out what it claims to be a scientific whaling program. After the cetaceans have been ostensibly analyzed, the whale meat is distributed in supermarkets and restaurants across Japan even though national consumption of the product has declined (Blok, 2008). While the argument could be made that Japanese whaling should be granted a cultural exception, in actuality, an "elite-driven countermovement, encompassing powerful actors and organizations from the bureaucratic, political, industrial and cultural spheres" (Blok, 2008) actually drives the whaling industry, which is no longer a tradition integral to contemporary Japanese culture. Japanese whaling in the Southern Ocean is an industrialized activity that kills up to 950 minke, fin, and humpback whales yearly while reaping a profit of $50 million (Gales et al., 2005), making commercial interests seem to be the real motivation—not cultural ones.

Reflecting the codification of anti-whaling sentiment into international law, in March 2014, the International Court of Justice ruled against Japan's scientific whaling activities in the Southern Ocean Whale Sanctuary off Antarctica, finding that "scientific output to date appears limited" (ICJ, 2014). So whereas Japan hunts whales for the benefit of a small group of politically powerful stakeholders, indigenous peoples hunt whales to fill dietary and cultural needs otherwise hard to meet.

Indigenous whaling is not without its issues. First, while cultural exceptions should be made for indigenous whaling, the claims justifying the right to whale and the activities themselves must be subject to close scrutiny and monitoring. The IWC, for instance, allows a total catch of 140 Eastern North Pacific gray whales by Chukotka's Yup'iit and Chukchi indigenous peoples and Washington

State's Makah people (IWC, 2014). Yet it was discovered that the gray whales caught in Chukotka were being fed to foxes (Reeves, 2002). It is unsurprising that the meat went to the dogs, so to speak, since Chukotka's indigenous peoples view gray whale hunting as less prestigious than bowhead whale hunting (Krupnik, 1987). This misuse of whale meat is worrying given that bowhead whaling, reintroduced after the collapse of the Soviet Union, has allowed the Yup'iit to allegedly "strengthen their cultural identity, self-sufficiency, and hence self-respect at this time of extreme social, physical, and emotional distress" (Freeman, 1998). The IWC and the indigenous peoples claiming a right to whale must therefore closely communicate to ensure mutually satisfactory policies that enable the continuation of sustainable aboriginal sustenance hunts while ensuring that no whales are killed unnecessarily.

A second issue with permitting cultural exceptions is that while some IWC limits pertain to the number of strikes a community can carry out—that is, how many whales they can legally hit with a harpoon or rifle—others pertain to the total number they can catch. Setting strike limits more effectively maintains whale populations than total catch limits, as struck, injured whales can still later die, depleting the population the same way a successfully hunted one would. The IWC should therefore turn all quotas into strike limits as a best practice. Ultimately, effective management of whale stocks affects more than just whales. The global decimation of these cetaceans has negatively affected other marine mammal populations, such as seals, sea lions, and otters (Springer et al., 2003), highlighting the need to maintain healthy whale stocks for the integrity of the entire marine ecosystem.

Allowing cultural exceptions for aboriginal substance whaling fosters the continued existence of traditional ecological knowledge, which has largely enabled a sustainable way of living with the earth unlike industrial practices. After all, whale populations did not begin to decline dramatically until the introduction of commercialized whaling. With indigenous peoples sustainably hunting whales for thousands of years prior, according them the right to continue their practices while adhering to a robust and scientifically informed management system does a small amount of justice to peoples whose ways of life have already been trampled by the relentless onslaught of capitalism, industrialization, and globalization.

REFERENCES

BBC. (2014). "Sustainable Fishing: Lamalera Whale-Hunters in Indonesia." BBC: Bitesize. Accessed April 30, 2014, at http://www.bbc.co.uk/learningzone/clips/sustainable-fishing-lamalera-whale-hunters-in-indonesia/11954.html.

Blok, Anders. (2008). "Contesting global norms: politics of identity in Japanese pro-whaling countermobilization," *Global Environmental Politics* 8(2), 39–66.

Chiropolos, Michael L. (1994). "Inupiat subsistence and the bowhead whale: can indigenous hunting cultures coexist with endangered animal species," *Colorado Journal of Environmental Law and Policy 5*, 213.

Clapham, Phil, and Yulia Ivashchenko. (2009). "A whale of a deception," *Marine Fisheries Review* 71(1), 44–52.

DeMarban, Alex. (2013, July 18). "Fermented 'stink whale' landed in Barrow, and it's a blessing during tough season," *Alaska Dispatch*. Accessed April 30, 2014, at http://www.alaskadispatch.com/article/20130718/fermented-stink-whale-landed-barrow-and-its-blessing-during-tough-season.

Freeman, Milton M. R., Lyudmila Bogoslovskaya, Richard A. Caulfield, Ingmar Egede, et al. (1998). *Inuit, Whaling, and Sustainability*. Contemporary Native American Communities Volume 1. Walnut Creek, CA: Altamira Press, 82.

Gales, Nichoas J., Toshio Kasuya, Phillip Clapham, and Robert L. Brownell. (2005). "Japan's whaling plan under scrutiny," *Nature* 435(7044), 883–884.

International Court of Justice (ICJ). (2014, March 31). "Whaling in the Antarctic (Australia v. Japan: New Zealand Intervening)." Reports of Judgments Advisory Opinions and Orders. Accessed April 30, 2014, at http://www.icj-cij.org/docket/files/148/18136.pdf.

International Whaling Commission (IWC). (2014). "Aboriginal Subsistence Whaling." Accessed April 29, 2014, at http://iwc.int/aboriginal.

Krupnik, Igor I. (1987). "The bowhead vs. the gray whale in Chukotkan aboriginal whaling," *Arctic*, 40(1), 16–32.

Reeves, Randall. (2002). "The origins and character of 'aboriginal subsistence' whaling: A global review," *Mammal Review* 32(2), 71–106. Accessed March 2, 2016, at http://onlinelibrary.wiley.com/doi/10.1046/j.1365-2907.2002.00100.x/full.

Springer, A. M., J. A. Estes, G. B. van Vliet, T. M. Williams, D. F. Doak, et al. (2003). "Sequential megafaunal collapse in the north Pacific Ocean: an ongoing legacy of industrial whaling?," *Proceedings of the National Academy of Sciences* 100(21), 12223–12228.

18

HOW ARE ISSUES AND CONFLICTS OVER INVASIVE SPECIES BEING ADDRESSED?

OVERVIEW

Susan L. Woodward and Joyce A. Quinn

BACKGROUND

Invasive species are associated with a variety of ecological, economic, public health, and aesthetic impacts. The costs and benefits are high, and there are many stakeholders involved at a variety of scales. The official definition of "invasive" in the United States includes reference to the harm a species can or does do. Yet it should be remembered that many species are initially introduced because someone foresees a benefit, be it a beautiful blossom, a challenging game animal, a fascinating pet, or a way to control a pest or ameliorate an environmental problem.

Estimates of the costs of invasive species to the United States are commonly reported at well over $100 billion per year, but it is impossible to know the exact figure, which is likely much higher. It is difficult to put a dollar value on ecological damages or to separate the financial impacts of the combination of factors affecting agriculture, forestry, fisheries, industry, land values, and human well-being, not to mention the price of control and measures directed at preventing introductions, managing invasive species, and implementing remediation measures to repair the damage.

With so much at stake, controversies and conflicts are common as management policies are being formulated, debated and implemented.

ECOLOGICAL IMPACTS IN NATURAL AND SEMI-NATURAL ECOSYSTEMS

As new species spread into the wild and semi-wild habitats of the United States, they have the potential to affect life in our forests, grasslands, and deserts at all biological/ecological levels. Native organisms may respond as individuals to a new predator or competitor by altering their behavior. A case in point is the avoidance of some rodents to areas infested by the red imported fire ant. As a result of fire ant presence, mice may forage in less protected areas and become more vulnerable to predation by owls.

Individual organisms can also be affected by introduced pathogens, predators, or competitors for limited resources to the extent that the impact becomes evident at the population level, when increased mortality rates threaten the survival of the entire population of a given organism. Avian malaria threatens to decimate several endemic honeycreepers in Hawai'i. West Nile virus caused significant population declines in crows and chickadees when it first spread through eastern states. In the Great Lakes, the round goby displaces such native fish as the mottled sculpin from its customary spawning grounds and competes with it and other fish for food. Certainly the most notorious recent invader is the predatory brown tree snake, which arrived in Guam sometime between the end of World War II and 1952, and in the next 20 years caused the extinction of 10 species of native forest birds and decimated lizards, causing the local extinction of 4 species. In addition, the brown tree snake is implicated in the loss of two species of bat from Guam. While the example of the brown tree snake is unusually dramatic and illustrative of what can happen when a new predator is introduced to an island previously lacking predators, it does serve as a cautionary tale of how wrong things can go.

The zebra mussel, through its rapid population growth and ability to grow on the shells of native unionid mussels, can physically overwhelm the host and reduces its access to nutrients. Among plants, spotted knapweed, a perennial forb, is an introduced competitor species. It produces an allelopathic chemical that depresses the germination or growth of native plants, such as the endemic Mt. Sapphire rockcress, and thereby preserves a greater share of light, water, and nutrients for the invader.

Native populations may also be affected at the genetic level through hybridization and introgression. Hybridization involves the crossbreeding of members of two species. When viable offspring are produced they may exhibit hybrid vigor and grow faster or larger than either parent and reproduce more quickly than either. If sterile offspring are produced, the parent species have wasted their gametes, a practice that may be costly if their numbers are already low. The rainbow trout, a native transplant to western waters, produces fertile offspring when it mates with the California golden trout and the threatened Paiute cutthroat trout. Hybrid rainbow trout/golden trout also can backcross with both parent species and contaminate the gene pool of golden trout by introducing genes of rainbow trout, a process known as introgression. Through this means the native genotype can disappear. Smooth cordgrass, another native transplant to California, readily hybridizes with the native California cordgrass. The first generation hybrids have higher growth rates and greater reproductive success than either parent. The hybrids also tolerate a broader range of salinity and invade open mudflats, changing the physical environments in an estuary.

The loss of one or more species as well as the addition of new species has repercussions for an entire ecological community. Mutualistic relationships such as predator/prey and pollinator/host can be disrupted. Niche shifts can occur as new species are accommodated: where the brown anole is present, the native green anole, which customarily seeks prey on the ground or lower regions of tree trunks, forages higher in the tree canopy. Chestnut blight fungus essentially eliminated the American chestnut from the tree layer of eastern forests. The species' relative abundance of other trees in the forests changed as white oak, chestnut oak, and red oaks increased in the absence of chestnut.

When abiotic as well as biotic elements are affected, impacts are occurring at the ecosystem level. Two important ecosystem-level changes involve nutrient cycles and disturbance regimes. By filtering such huge amounts of water, dense populations of zebra mussel increase the amount of nitrogen and phosphorus in the water column and reduce the amount of carbon, which migrates down to the bottom-dwellers in the mussels' pseudofeces. In Hawai'i, a plant alters the nitrogen cycle, with ecosystem-wide consequences. The fire tree fixes nitrogen from the atmosphere, which allows it—unlike any native trees—to live on the nitrogen-poor volcanic substrates of the islands. Fire trees add nitrogen to the soil and provide suitable conditions for a variety of other plants to colonize the area, thereby giving rise to a whole new community of plants.

At a regional or landscape scale the mixing of species from all over the globe leads to the homogenization of the world's biota and a loss of global biodiversity. While locally the number of species may increase, the same species tend to be added everywhere. And it is the locally restricted and unique species that tend to be disappearing. This impoverishment of the variety of life on earth is viewed with alarm, for homogenization is occurring at all levels—genetic, species, community, and ecosystem—potentially interfering with ecosystem functioning, ecosystem services, and the ability to evolve and adapt to changing environmental conditions. Furthermore, the world becomes a less interesting place as a great sameness spreads across not only our human-made townscapes and cityscapes, but the natural world as well.

ECONOMIC IMPACTS

In agriculture, direct damage to crops and pastures affects yields and the quality of the product, which in turn can have repercussions on market value. Weeds, insects, and pathogens cost agriculture about $25 billion each year in lost production and another $3 billion for pesticides to control them. Measures set up to protect plant and animal life and human health in the United States can become trade barriers and violate World Trade Organization agreements, causing costly boycotts among international buyers. The inspections, quarantines, monitoring, and response to introduced insects and pathogens are all expensive but necessary to protect our food supply as well as our farmers. Forestry suffers financial loss not only when trees sicken and die but also when quarantines prevent sales of wood products. Some 9 percent of lumber, pulpwood, and other forest products are thought to be lost to insect damage at an annual cost of $7 billion. The "Slow the Spread Program" targeting the gypsy moth costs the federal government $8 million to $10 million a year, with additional funds provided by affected states. Similar programs are needed for the emerald ash borer and other invasive insects. The green crab is assumed to have caused the demise of the soft shell clam fishery in New England in the 1950s and is also implicated in declines of the commercially important northern quahog, a scallop, and other shellfish with annual harvests worth $44 million in 2000. Fouling damage by Asian clams in the United States reportedly amounts to $1 billion a year. The damage by zebra mussels and control of those mollusks at raw water-using and electricity-generating industries in the Great Lakes region are estimated by the Wisconsin Department of Natural Resources to cost more than $100 million year. Other Great Lakes invaders affect the recreation industry in the region, where losses from sport fishing alone reach an estimated $200 million per year. In Florida, hydrilla clogs waterways and costs $14.5 million per year to control, but there are also financial impacts on the recreation and tourism industries.

PUBLIC HEALTH AND WELL-BEING

The most obvious impacts to human health are new pathogens. Global epidemics are expected to become more common with ever-increasing international travel and the globalization of world trade. Such pathogens, past and future, have followed or will follow the same pathways as other invasive species. For some, their virulence depends on finding reservoirs and transmitters among both native and nonnative animals, as in the case of the West Nile virus and the bacterium that causes Lyme disease. A warming climate and invasive mosquitoes likely mean the establishment of (currently) tropical diseases like dengue fever in the near future, but the ubiquity and rapidity of air travel opens the U.S. population to all sorts of emerging infectious diseases.

A host of simply annoying species have invaded the United States. Asian multicolored lady beetles and brown marmorated stink bugs are two recent examples, while the common bed bug represents a very old traveler now experiencing a resurgence. For folks living in parts of Hawai'i the noisy coqui can be added to the list, and for people in Florida the Cuban treefrog lurking in the toilet fits the bill.

Such annoyances can be expensive. The din of calling coquis can lower property values. Bed bug–bitten customers sue hotels and landlords, adding to the costs incurred trying to eradicate bed bugs.

As the essays in this section highlight, the issue of invasive species is complex, with no single, simple solution. It's going to require less bickering and legal wrangling and more awareness, education, cooperation, and coordination especially as the world's biodiversity continues to decline at alarming rates.

FURTHER READING

Clout, Michael N., and Peter A. Williams. (2009). *Invasive Species Management: A Handbook of Principles and Techniques.* Oxford and New York: Oxford University Press.

Mooney, Harold A., and Richard J. Hobbs. (2000). *Invasive Species in a Changing World.* Washington, DC: Island Press.

INVASIVE SPECIES—A COMPLEX ISSUE WITH NO SIMPLE SOLUTIONS
Joyce A. Quinn

Invasive plants number in the hundreds. While many cause no harm in some regions of the United States, others wreak havoc on natural ecosystems or detrimentally affect human well-being, such as health, crops, recreation, or economics. It is a complex issue, and several factors should be considered in the determination of whether or not an invasive plant should be, or can be, controlled.

How long has the species been in the United States, how far has it spread, and will it continue to expand its range?

Cheatgrass (see Figure 18.1) was introduced to the United States in the mid-1800s. Abundant seed production and broad environmental tolerances enabled it to expand its range and occupy ecosystems throughout the United States, including Alaska and Hawai'i. It would be costly and impossible to totally eradicate it from landscapes where it has become naturalized. Kudzu (see Figure 18.2), limited primarily to the warmer and rainier southeastern states, was brought to the United States as an ornamental in the late 1800s. It was widely promoted by the federal government in the 1930s for use in erosion control. Its ability to thrive under a wide range of environmental conditions, combined with rapid growth of the vine and spread by vegetative means, allows kudzu to quickly dominate the landscape. Control is intensive and expensive. More recently arrived species, such as giant hogweed (see Figure 18.3) (1917) and mile-a-minute vine (1930s) have more limited distributions, concentrated on the Eastern Seaboard where they were introduced. Plants with seeds that are normally transported by birds, water, or wind, for example, have no means of extremely long-distance dispersal other than by humans. Kudzu would not be able to spread in a continuous pattern to the mild climates of the northwest coast because it cannot tolerate the mountainous and desert western states. Disjunct occurrences in the mild northwestern states, widely separated from the main populations, may be explained by sales as an ornamental or by seed contamination in soil or crop seeds. Such plants may be more feasible to contain or eradicate.

What is the impact? Does the plant alter the natural landscape, adversely affect recreational activities, cause economic losses, provide a host for agricultural pests, or threaten human or animal health?

Because cheatgrass is an annual, the accumulation of dried, dead plant material each year is a serious fire hazard, which in turn destroys shrub growth, altering the ecosystem, causing soil deterioration, and reducing biodiversity. The change in the ecosystem has allowed cheatgrass to replace nutritious native forage grasses, negatively affecting both native grazers and the livestock industry. The stiff, dry awns harm grazing animals, and the seeds create a major weed problem in crops. Although common mullein has been an alien species in a variety of environments throughout the United States since the mid-1700s, it appears to be fairly innocuous. Primarily growing on disturbed sites, it is easily outcompeted by native plants in natural areas and cannot perpetuate itself in the shade. It does, however, threaten alpine areas in Hawai'i and is a host for insect pests that attack apples and pears in the eastern states. Waterhyacinth (see Figure 18.4), which dominates many water bodies in the warm southern states and in the mild-temperature regions of the West Coast, grows so rapidly that it degrades recreational sites, clogs waterways, and disrupts hydrological systems. Giant hogweed, currently with limited distribution in New England, the Upper Midwest, and Pacific Northwest, poses a serious threat to human health. Contact with the plant's sap causes skin to become more sensitive to ultraviolet radiation, resulting in severe sunburns that may take months to heal. Japanese dodder is a parasite with the potential to devastate American agriculture. The extensive vines of both kudzu and mile-a-minute primarily affect natural areas by smothering native vegetation, but the plants can also cause economic damage by overtopping orchards and crops. The weight of kudzu can topple trees, utility lines, and even buildings.

DOES THE PLANT OFFER ANY BENEFITS?

Although many invasive plants seem to have no redeeming qualities, some can be useful in certain situations. Cheatgrass grows earlier in spring than native grass species, providing needed early-season forage for livestock, and may be the

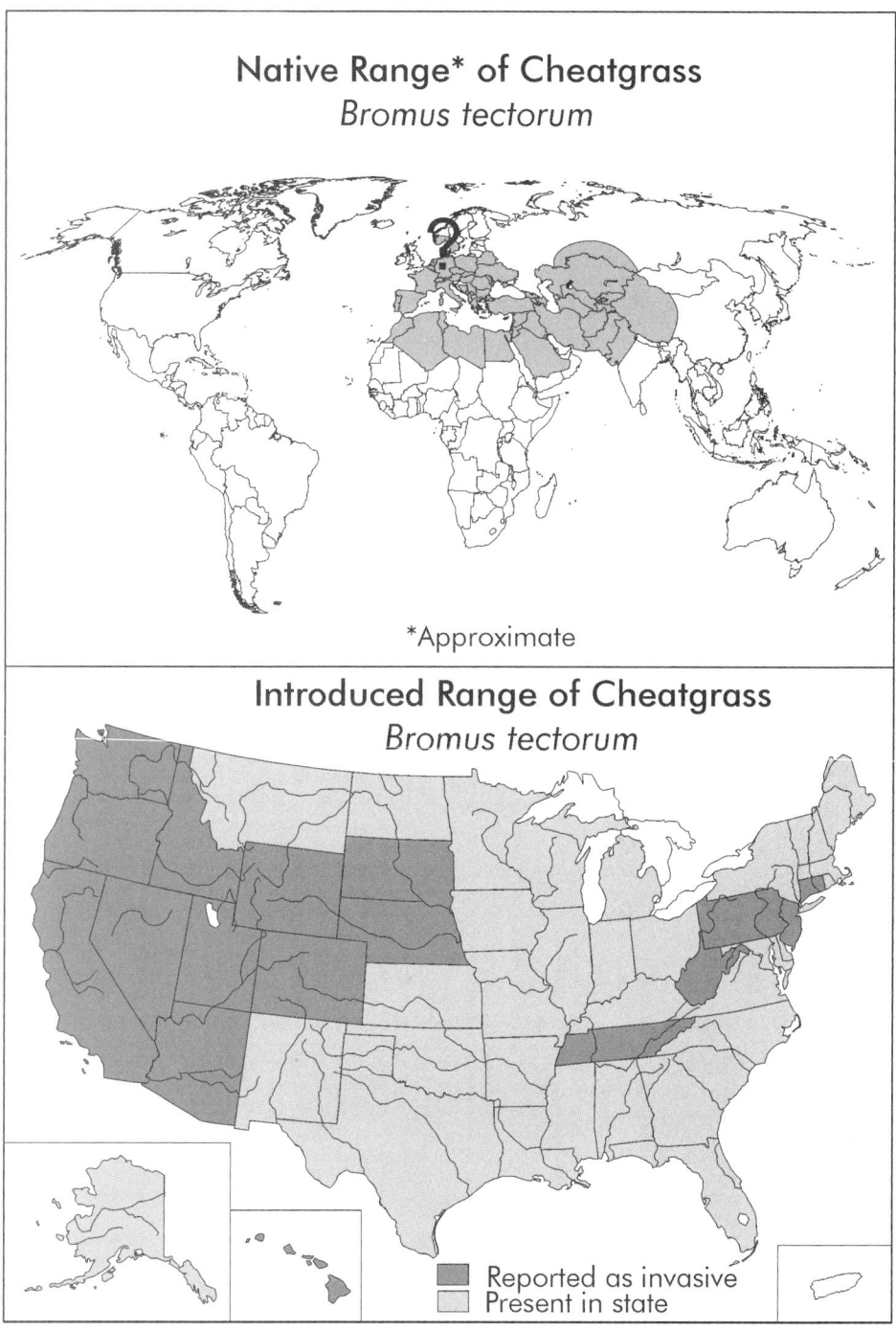

Cheatgrass (Native range adapted from USDA GRIN and selected references. Introduced range adapted from USDA PLANTS Database, Invasive Plant Atlas of the United States, and selected references.)

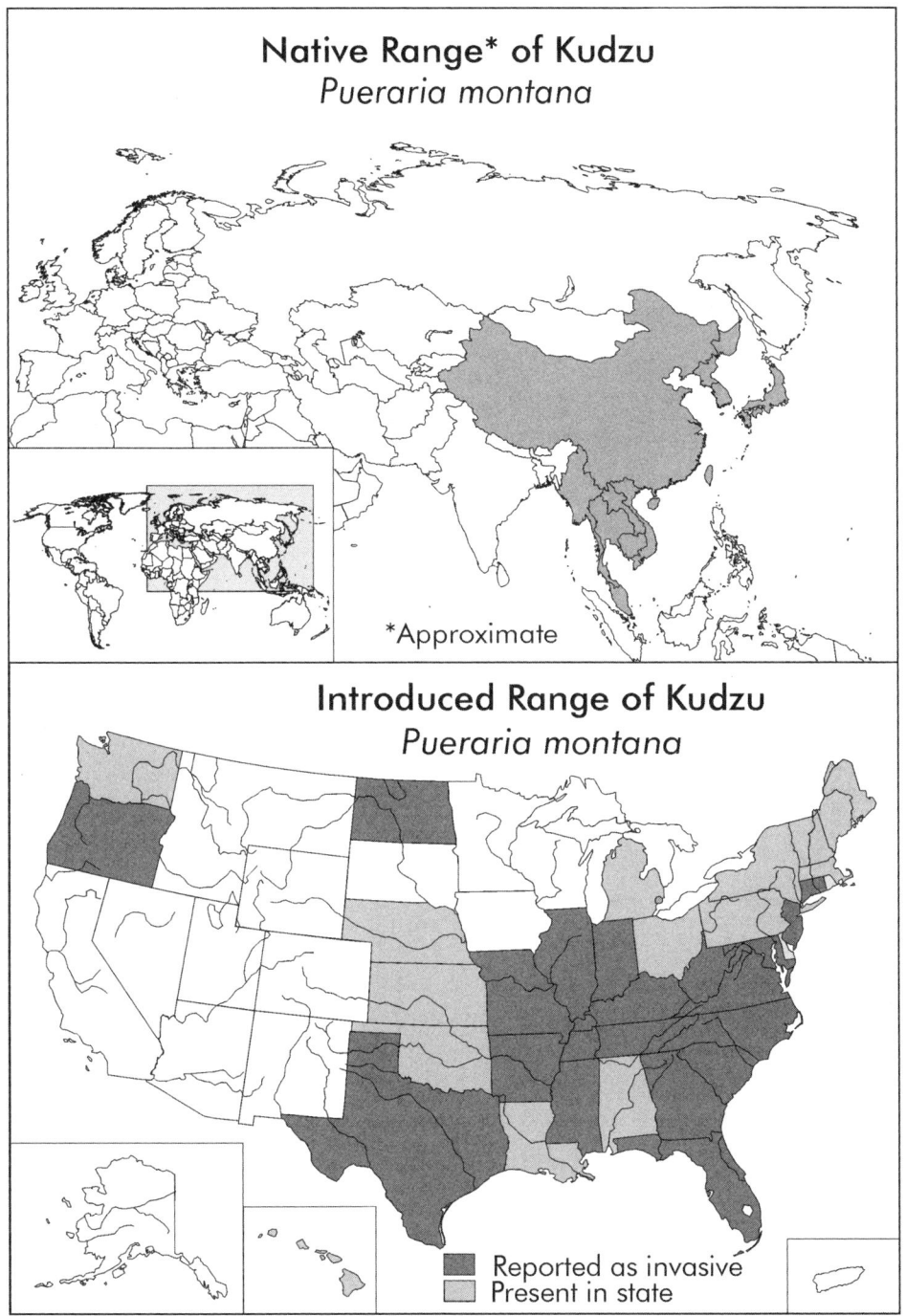

Kudzu (Native range adapted from USDA GRIN and selected references. Introduced range adapted from USDA PLANTS Database, Invasive Plant Atlas of the United States, and selected references.)

only forage available where the native grasses have been displaced. Waterhyacinth roots can filter sewage water or provide food for pond fish. Princess tree is touted as a good source of lumber in the southeastern states. Some Hawaiians are opposed to eradication of strawberry guava because they harvest the wild fruit. Exotic bush honeysuckles may reduce the biodiversity and populations of insect-eating birds while increasing populations of fruit-eating species. Beneficial uses of invasive plants complicate issues of control or eradication.

DOES ONE MANAGEMENT GOAL FIT ALL SITUATIONS?

Eradication of common mullein is necessary to preserve native Hawaiian alpine ecosystems, and its control may be economically worthwhile to protect adjacent orchards in the eastern United States that are negatively affected. While waterhyacinth is a serious problem in warmer southern states, plants cannot regenerate after severe freezing temperatures and are not a recurrent problem in the northern states. Control of waterhyacinth where it disrupts or totally blocks navigation in southern waterways, however, is necessary and worth the millions of dollars spent every year. Cheatgrass is primarily a problem in the native grasslands of the arid western states. Because the grass more easily invades disturbed ground, eradication or control of its spread is feasible and cost-effective where the land has not been totally degraded. Given a chance to grow deeper roots, native grasses can outcompete and replace the shallow-rooted cheatgrass. Both giant hogweed and Japanese dodder, because of limited distribution and potential harm, should be eradicated at all costs.

SHOULD PLANT SALES BE REGULATED? DO AGRICULTURAL INSPECTIONS DO ANY GOOD?

Many alien invasive plants, including waterhyacinth, wisteria, brooms, lantana, English ivy, carrotwood, ice plant, Pampas grass, Chinaberry, and others, continue to be sold in the horticultural trade. While sales in one part of the country may be harmless, sales in other areas could have disastrous results. Kudzu and wisteria are not vigorous growers in the arid or mountainous West and would cause no problems in those regions. Several plants, such as Pampas grass and ice plant, are sensitive to frost and limited to warm regions, while others require cold temperatures to bloom or set seed. Several invasive species are limited to the tropical or subtropical climates in Hawai'i or Florida. Agricultural inspections of goods at United States ports of entry may limit wholesale entry of invasive plants, but it may take only a few stray seeds in a shipment of grain to introduce a new alien plant species. The effectiveness of agricultural inspections at state lines, such as in California, depends on the honesty of the motorists and their awareness of the concept of invasive species and their potential problems.

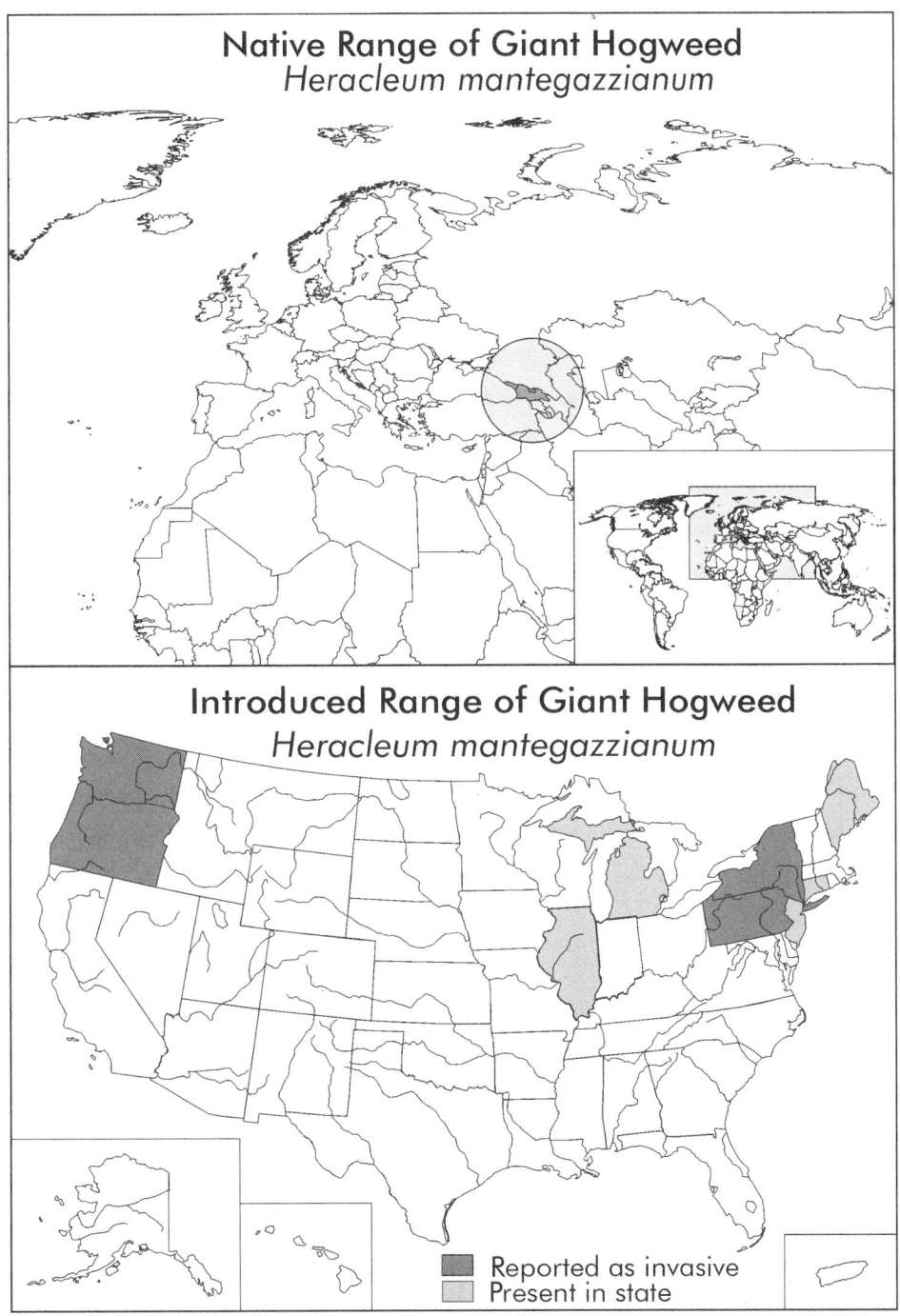

Giant Hogweed (Native range adapted from USDA GRIN and selected references. Introduced range adapted from USDA PLANTS Database, Invasive Plant Atlas of the United States, and selected references.)

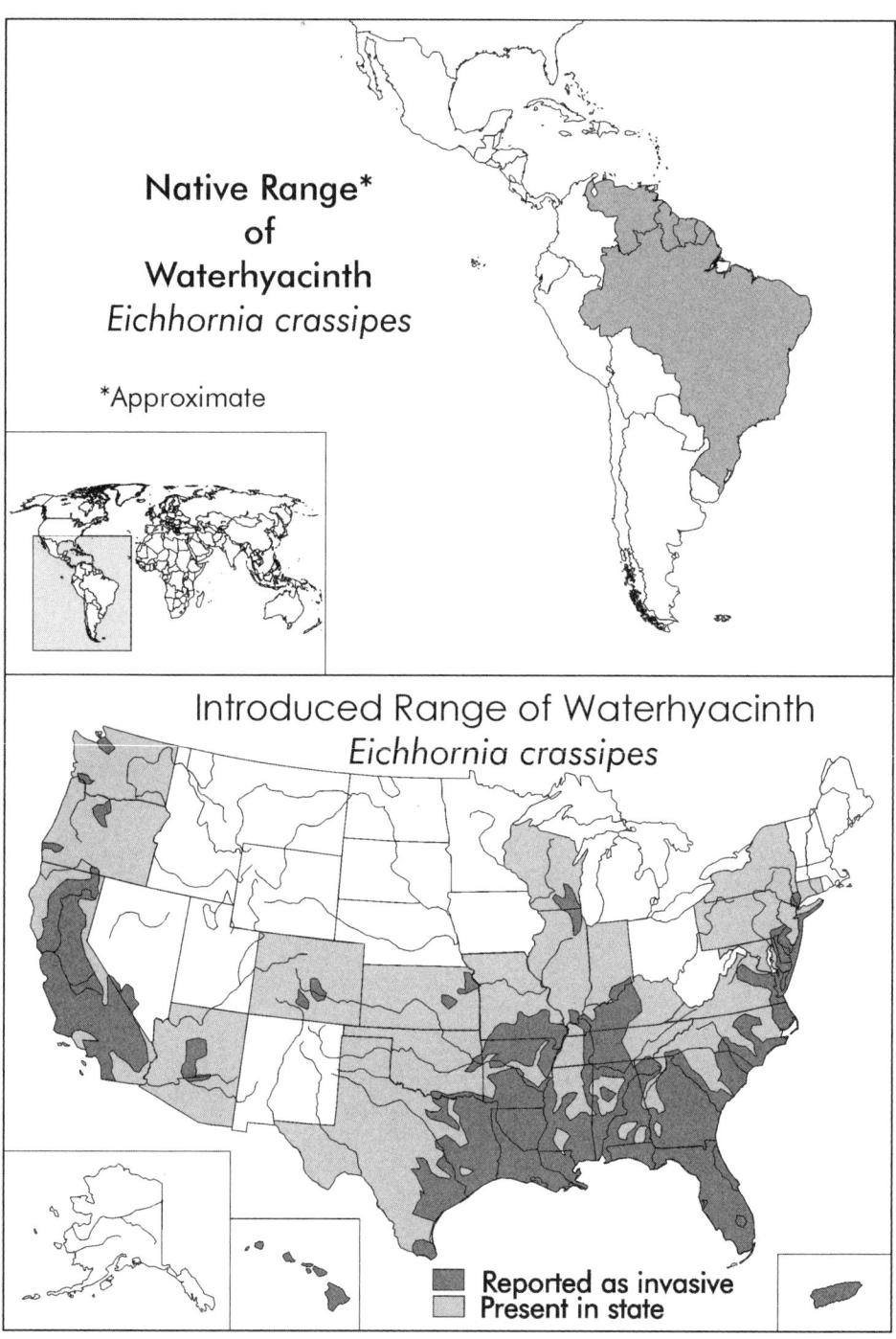

Waterhyacinth (Native range adapted from USDA GRIN and selected references. Introduced range adapted from USGS Nonindigenous Aquatic Species Database and selected references.)

There are no easy answers, only more questions. Does the regulation of plant sales infringe on individual rights? What about Internet sales? How would you deal with a situation where your neighbor wants to grow an invasive species in her yard, but you don't want the excess seeds or sprouts in your own? Should a plant that is invasive in southeastern United States be banned from sale in California or North Dakota? Are all native species considered equal, or are some more worthy of protection from invasive species? Should plants that threaten economic activities be treated more severely than those that alter ecosystems? How much damage, either economically or ecologically, is too much? Should public funds be spent where the control or eradication of invasive species would benefit individuals such as farmers, ranchers, or recreationalists? The many aspects of the control or eradication of invasive plants make it a very complex issue.

PREVENTION, ERADICATION, AND EDUCATION
Susan L. Woodward

The best chance of controlling an invasive species occurs before a population becomes established. This means preventing the entry of new species or eradicating the first pioneers. This essay only discusses organisms found in Volume 1 of the *Encyclopedia of Invasive Species* (Greenwood, 2011). As numerous accounts attest, once an alien animal, fungus, or microorganism becomes established and enters the invasive stage, it is often impossible and/or too difficult and expensive to eradicate it or control the expansion of its introduced range. Furthermore, for some long-established immigrant species, native ecosystems—natural or human-modified—have either accommodated the nonnative (e.g., house finch) or been so drastically changed by its presence (e.g., common periwinkle) that removal would itself be damaging. Thus it seems more reasonable to direct resources toward preventing the introduction of other exotic species into the United States through regulation, inspection, and quarantine at points of entry to the country than to undertake major efforts toward eliminating existing introduced species.

The spread of invasive species into new territory, however, also occurs from points of origin within the country. Commonly, in a process biogeographers refer to as long-distance dispersal, dispersing individuals leapfrog well beyond the range limits of a species and begin new populations in areas distant from the main distribution area. These new colonies appear as "spots" on a map and suggest that opportunities for detection, interception, and eradication of incipient populations of rapidly spreading species may still exist. Preventing the establishment of additional colonies of a nonnative, especially one that has demonstrated its ability to cause damage, is likely the most economical and potentially successful way to slow or halt the spread of many invasive species.

Examine the range maps of actively invading species and you will see this spotty pattern repeated over and over. Bat white-nose syndrome (see Figure 18.5) is a case in point. Only very recently has its cause been confirmed to be the fungus *Geomyces destructans*, which since the writing of the encyclopedia entry has been discovered to be widespread—and not particularly harmful—in Europe and spread by bat-to-bat contact. Numerous isolated populations might be expected, since the winter roosts of affected bats are caves and abandoned mines, themselves disjunct habitats. However, not all caves in a region host the fungus, and sometimes vast distances separate infected hibernacula. Such a deadly disease with major ecological ramifications due to the potential loss of a major predator of flying insects warrants efforts to halt the spread of the fungus. Since it is likely that cavers as well as migrating bats inadvertently spread the organism, slowing its progress might be achieved by barring human entry to caves where infected bats occur and impressing upon everyone who enters any open cave, whether for recreation or scientific study, the need to decontaminate all clothing and gear after the visit.

A similar pattern occurs in the introduced range of the emerald ash borer (see Figure 18.5), an insect first identified in the United States in 2002. The beetle's larvae kill all the trees they infest; and, should the spread continue, widespread and devastating ecological impacts will occur in forests throughout the eastern and central United States. The management goal to contain or at least slow the spread is practical and appropriate in this case. It may be achieved by quarantining affected areas and restricting the movement of materials such as firewood, green lumber, and tree debris that larvae inhabit. Monitoring for the emerald ash borer outside the known distribution area is also important, not only to evaluate the success of quarantines but perhaps to nip in the bud the establishment of a new breeding population. The hope is that slowing the dispersal process will allow time for the development of a sustainable control mechanism, either a suitable parasite or hybridization between native ash trees and resistant European relatives. The latter has been achieved to some degree with American chestnuts and elms, offering a defense against the invasive diseases that threatened them, Chestnut blight and Dutch elm disease, respectively.

The feral pig (see Figure 18.6) also shows the spatial pattern developed from long-distance dispersal. This animal was introduced by European explorers and settlers as early as the 1500s, and was kept as free-range livestock in the Southeast by both Native Americans and immigrant peoples. Until the 1990s, the distribution area was pretty much restricted to southeastern states and Hawaii, but

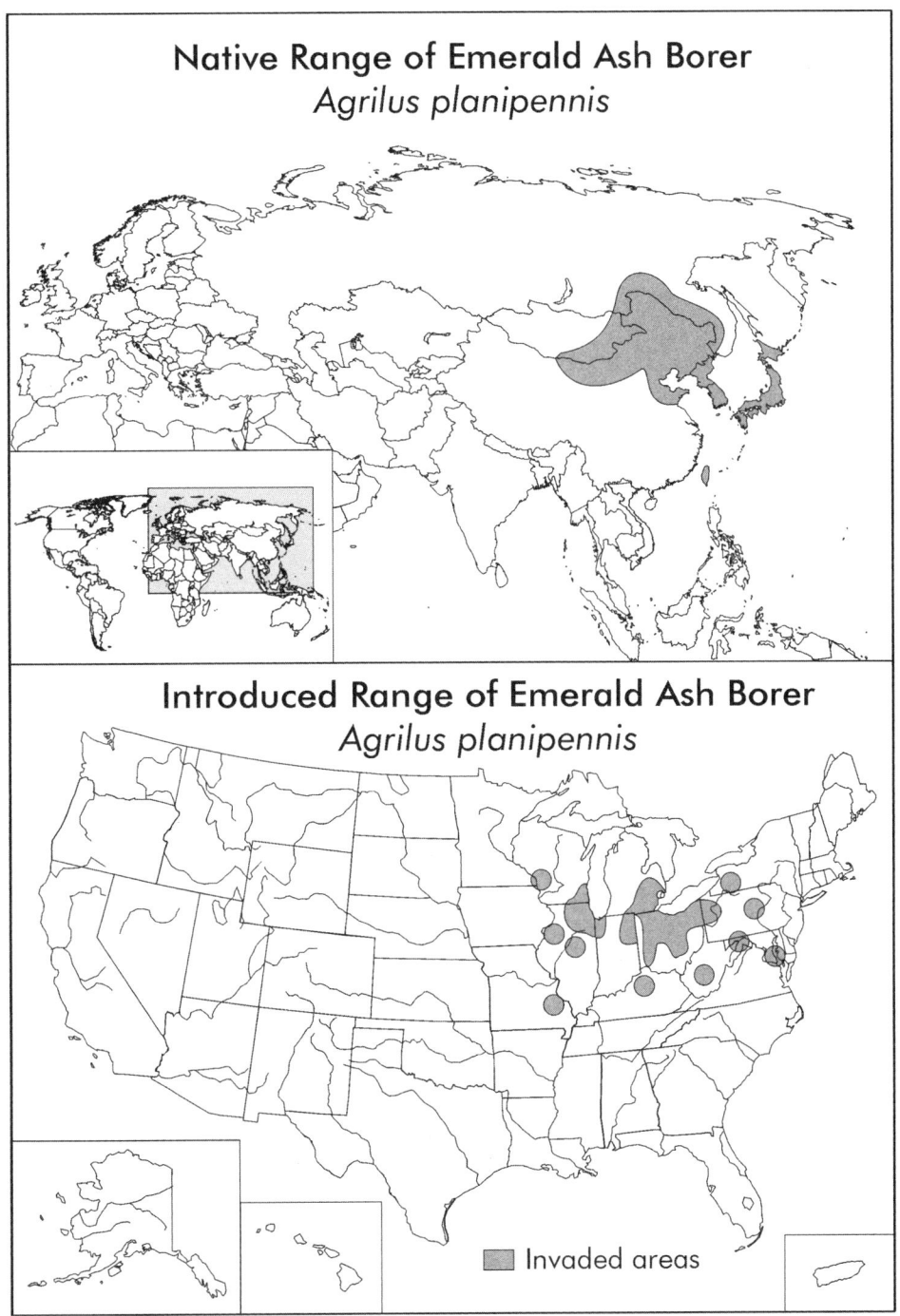

Emerald Ash Borer (Adapted from map by Cooperative Ash Borer Project, USDA Forest Service, 2010. http://www.emeraldashborer.info/Files/Multi-State_EABpos.pdf.)

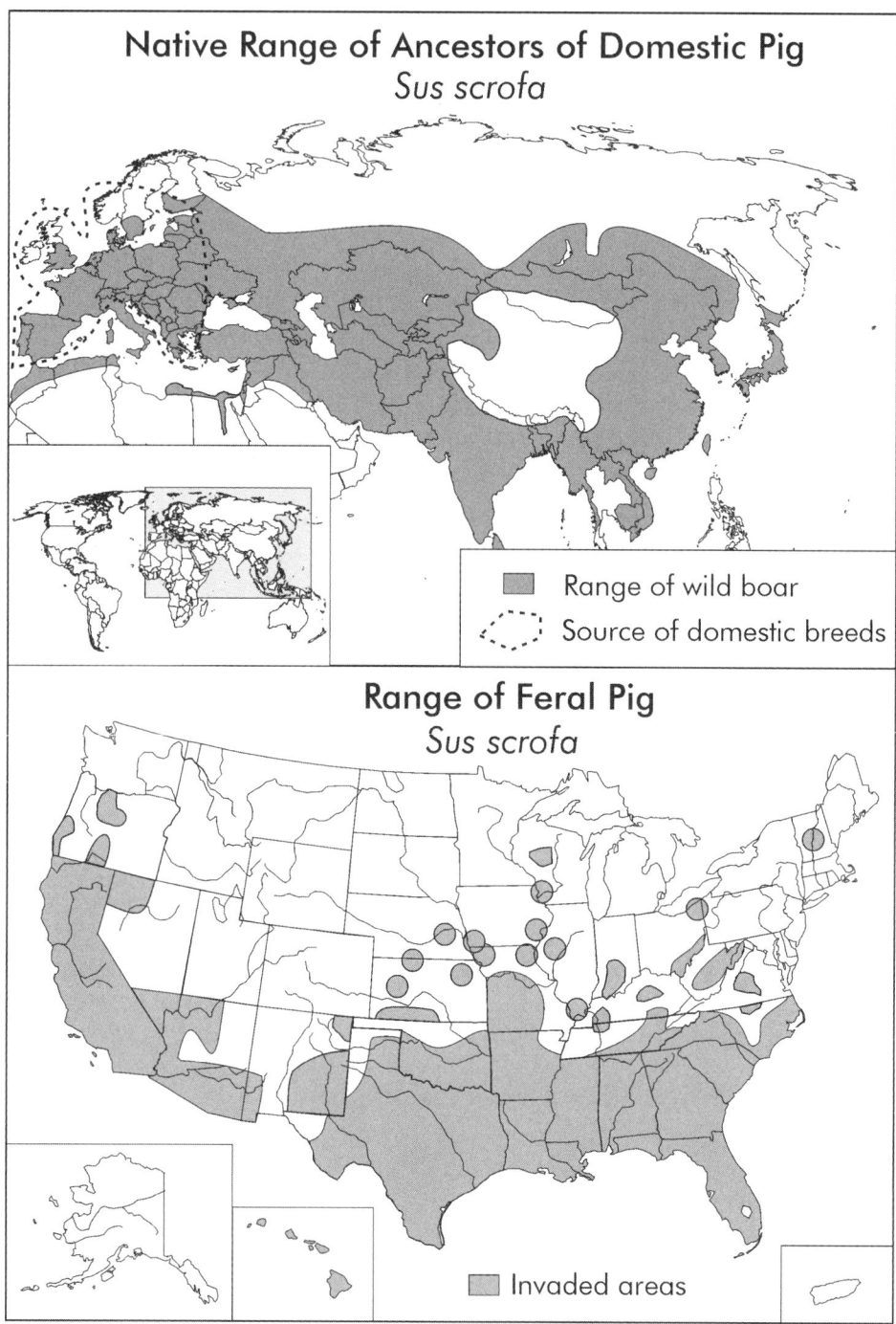

Feral pig (Adapted from "Feral/Wild Pigs: Potential Problems for Farmers and Hunters." USDA Agricultural Bulletin No. 799, 2005.)

since then it has expanded northward in the fashion of many invading species, with populations appearing at some distance from the main distribution area. In these locations, pigs were deliberately introduced for sport hunting. They are highly mobile and prolific, and animals released as game formed the nuclei for ever-expanding populations. The animal's rooting in and trampling of soil are highly destructive, it carries diseases that affect domestic hogs, and it damages various commercial crops; yet, control is controversial and hence difficult. The problem is one of conflicting values, and debate pits conservationists and farmers against hunters. Such problems are often encountered in the management of invasive species, especially if the species in question is "cuddly" (e.g., feral cat), colorful, and entertaining (e.g., Monk Parakeet), or useful (e.g., European earthworms). Solutions require education, societal consensus on what is most desirable, and formation of pragmatic programs to slow the population growth or spread of nonnative species known to harm natural and manmade environments.

Aquatic organisms have different distribution patterns since they, not unexpectedly, spread along waterways. The zebra mussel (see Figure 18.7) provides a good example. Its range map indicates dispersal throughout the Mississippi River drainage system. However, land barriers have been overcome and disjunct populations thrive. Mussels are transported between geographically isolated bodies of water by recreational boaters who fail to decontaminate boat trailers and the hulls, livewells, and engines of their boats when they leave an infested lake or river.

The rusty crayfish (see Figure 18.8) has also been spread to distant water bodies by people, but more deliberately. This crustacean is native to the United States and was preferred bait among fishermen in its native range. When fishermen visited lakes and streams outside the native range of the rusty crayfish, they carried along as live bait and discarded any leftover crayfish into the water when the outing ended. New, invasive populations took hold. A similar cause, but different spatial pattern exists for European earthworms, since they are terrestrial species. The map pattern is somewhat misleading, however; worms are not evenly distributed across their introduced range, but remain concentrated near release points along roads and near recreation areas.

Controlling the spread of invasive animals is warranted when the organism is in the establishment phase of invasion, is demonstrably harmful ecologically and/or economically, and when there is some likelihood of success. Supporting government initiatives on the national scale is important. But much can be accomplished through education and self-policing by local residents. Time and again it is through human activities that accidental or deliberate transport of invasive organisms occurs. Staying informed; not importing nonnative species, plant or animal; accepting inspections; adhering to quarantines; sealing points of entry for, say, multicolored Asian lady beetles, brown marmorated stink bug, or house mice;

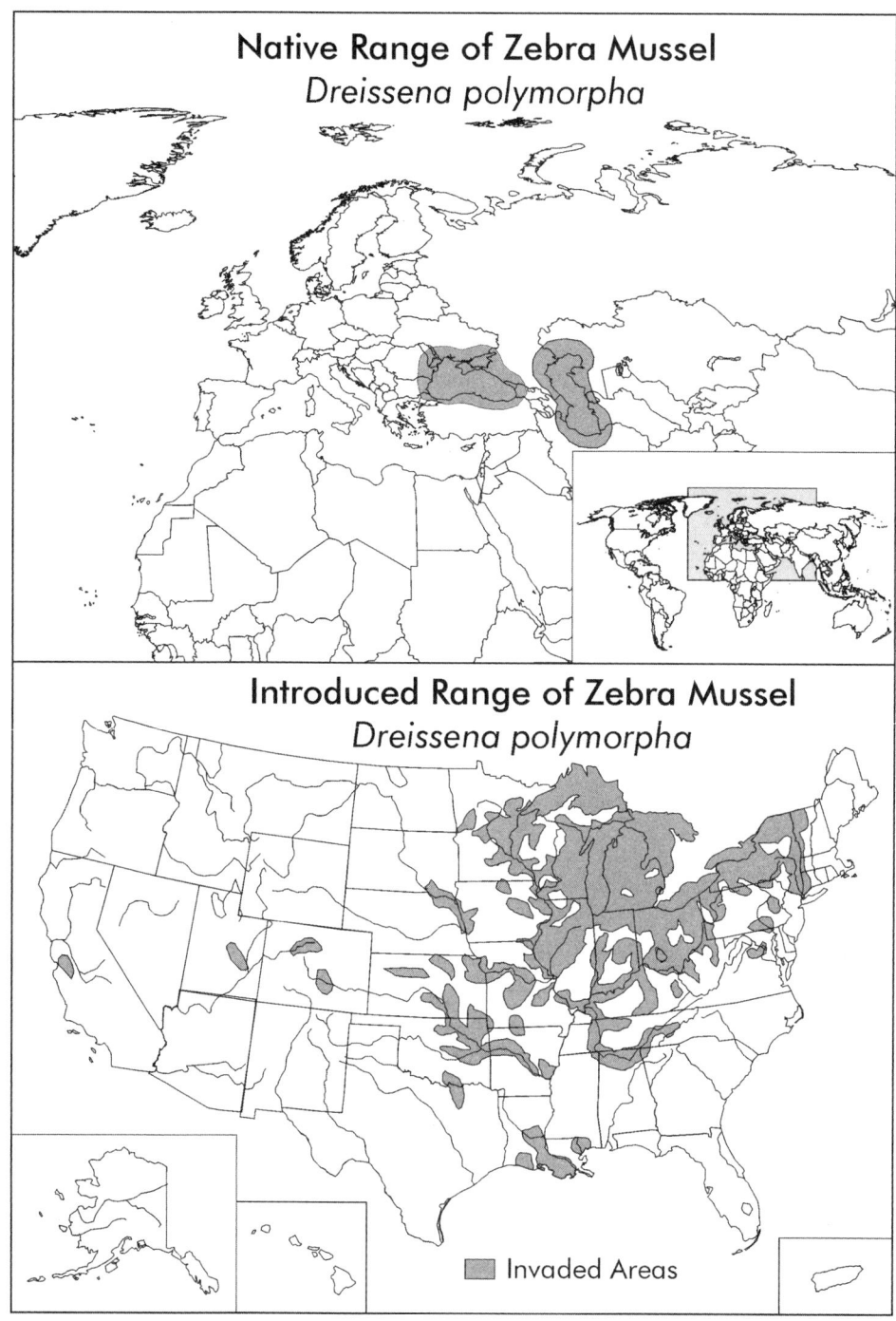

Zebra mussel (Adapted from Benson and Raikow, 2009.)

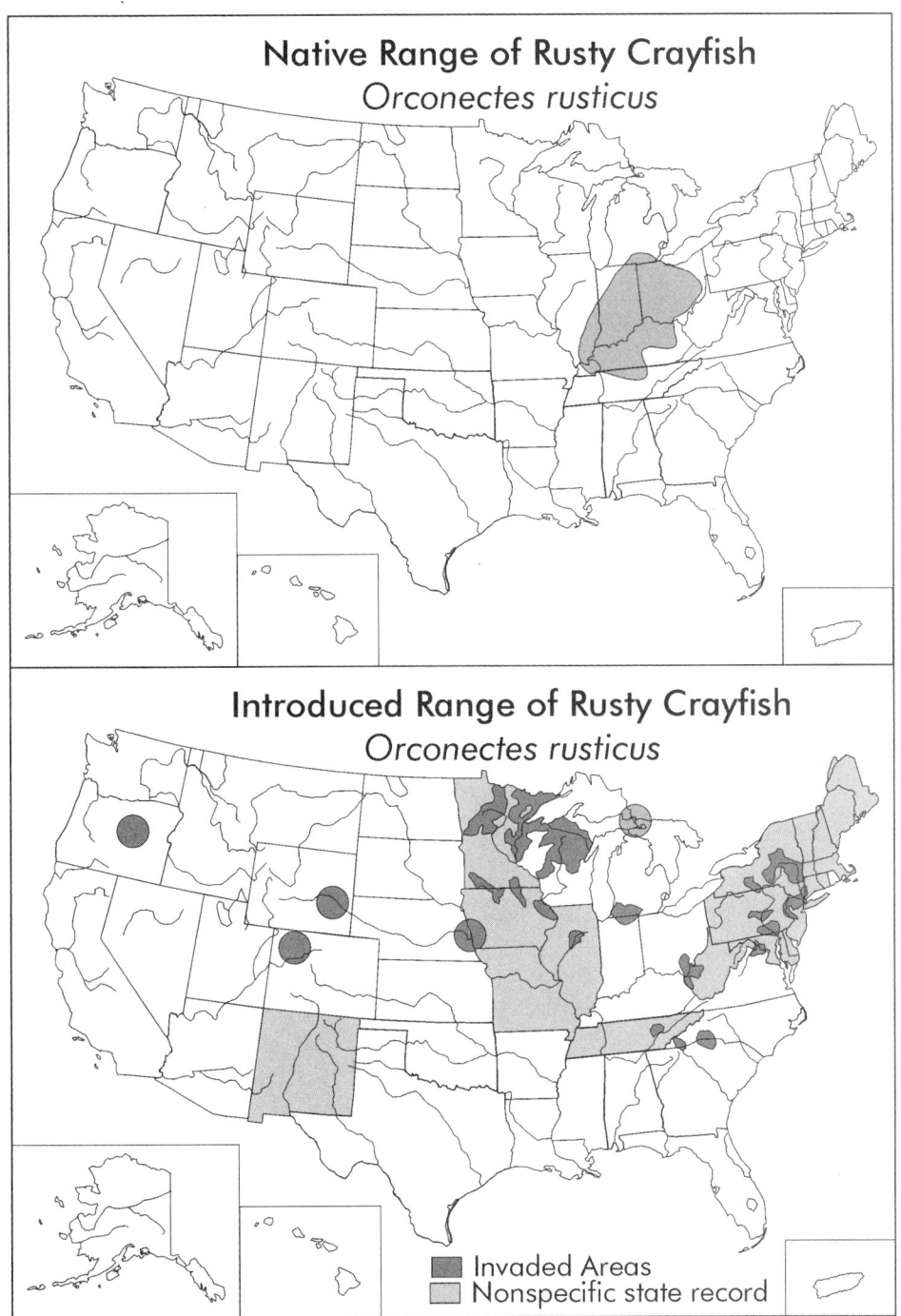

Rusty crayfish (Both maps adapted from USGS, 2008.)

removing landscape plants and debris that invite coquis, Formosan subterranean termites, rats or other pests; not releasing live bait or abandoning unwanted pets; decontaminating gear after exposure to infested habitats—these are things everyone can and should do to reduce the spread as well as the impacts of biological invaders.

19

How Does the Loss of Biodiversity Promote Conflict?

OVERVIEW

M. Troy Burnett

"We should preserve every scrap of biodiversity as priceless while we learn to use it and come to understand what it means to humanity."

—E. O. Wilson

The world is in the midst of a biodiversity crisis. The present rate of extinction equals that experienced during the end of the Cretaceous Period, 65 million years ago, wherein the majority of the species of dinosaurs went extinct. There are five persistent and intensifying factors that have led to the current crisis, each of which directly involves humans: (1) habitat loss and degradation, (2) rapid climate change, (3) pollution; (4) over-use, and (5) introduced and invasive species. With the creation of the UN-sponsored Convention on Biological Diversity in 1992 the world's governing institutions began to acknowledge and address the human-induced aspects of the crisis and develop conservation strategies to mitigate the rapid decline. Presently, 192 countries, including the EU, are parties to the convention. Further, numerous environmental non-governmental organizations (ENGOs) such as the International Union for the Conservation of Nature (IUCN), have emerged to address the loss of biodiversity. In particular, the IUCN maintains a "red list" to evaluate species risk and the conservation status of the most threatened. Unfortunately, despite these efforts and growing concern, the reality is that the loss of biodiversity is dramatically outpacing conservation efforts. The problem is exacerbated as conflicts arise between the differing forces of ecosystem preservation on one side and advocates for natural resource exploitation on the other. Economic development and sustenance inevitably clash with efforts to maintain species- and ecosystem-level biodiversity.

BACKGROUND

There are numerous levels and dimensions to conflicts involving biodiversity. First, there is the material and economic loss when components of biodiversity come in direct contact with human interests. Examples include crop destruction by birds, herbivores, and in some cases primates. There are cases of predatory (carnivore) attacks on livestock, game, and pets; vehicle collisions; disease transfer from wild species to domestic; and direct loss to human life from large animals, venomous reptiles, and zoonosis (the transfer of diseases to humans). Second, there are a host of social conflicts that arise within and near biodiversity conservation areas. Fear, safety, and personal loss are stark realities to those who live in ecosystems that are considered wild and biodiverse. The culture and ways of life of communities within or adjacent to protected areas often feel directly threatened by conservation activities. The 1990s battle in the Pacific Northwest of the United States over the northern spotted owl, its habitat (old growth evergreen forests), and the logging communities provide such an example. One of the criticisms by the loggers was that the preservationists were misanthropes more concerned about saving owls than the locals' livelihoods. Such conflicts between rural people and preservationists often lead to wanton habitat degradation, poaching, anti-logging tactics such as tree spiking, and all kinds of efforts to undermine and demonize the "other side." In other words, biodiversity and conservation goals get subsumed in the mire of a broader culture and economic war. Third, opportunity costs and trade-offs are inevitably involved in biodiversity conservation. Doubtless, conserving intact ecosystems is a necessary goal to maintain global biodiversity in the long term, yet the associated developmental constraints often cause significant economic loss to the local people.

In the first essay, I show how the Maasai people, nomadic herders of Kenya, who have long co-existed with wildlife, found that with the creation of the Kenyan biosphere game reserve and park system their entire way of life began to be compromised. The new land regulatory system prioritizes conservation and tourism over the needs of the people who live in the protected areas. The Maasai, who have been poorly compensated for the dramatic shift in their livelihoods, have thus resisted the government's efforts to preserve biodiversity.

In the second contribution, the author examines the issue in the context of "exploitation for profit" and how international law attempts to address the loss of biodiversity and minimize social conflict. One of the author's cases looks at conflicts emerging from corporate sponsored bio-prospecting in the developing world and the other examines the African elephant and the armed conflict promoted by the illegal ivory trade.

Ecologists and the majority of the general public are convinced that maintaining species richness and ecosystem biodiversity are global imperatives. Yet, efforts to do so, at a variety of scales from the local to the global, have resulted in disagreement, struggle, and conflict. Doubtless, as extinction rates continue to rise, tensions will also mount.

FURTHER READING

Bullock, James M., James Aronson, Adrian C. Newton, Richard F. Pywell, and Jose M. Rey-Benayas. (2011). "Restoration of ecosystem services and biodiversity: conflicts and opportunities," *Trends in Ecology & Evolution 26*(10), 541–549.

Young, Juliette C., Mariella Marzano, Rehema M. White, David I. McCracken, et al. (2010). "The emergence of biodiversity conflicts from biodiversity impacts: characteristics and management strategies," *Biodiversity and Conservation 19*(14), 3973–3990.

BIODIVERSITY AND CONFLICT: ISSUES AND RESOLUTIONS
Jason Macleod

Maintaining the health of our ecosystems requires balancing the demands of human existence and biodiversity. Human activity reduces biodiversity in several key ways: habitat destruction and degradation, introduction of non-native species, pollution, and over-exploitation. In this essay, I will examine the issue in the context of exploitation for profit and how international law attempts to address the loss of biodiversity and minimize social conflict. The first example looks at conflicts emerging from corporate sponsored bio-prospecting in the developing world. The second example examines the African elephant and the armed conflict promoted by the illegal ivory trade.

Wild plants are key to many technological and pharmaceutical innovations. For over a hundred years, corporations have sent scientists around the world to search for plants with exploitable qualities for use in pharmaceuticals and other profitable industries. Many scientists and bio-prospectors have travelled to countries like Brazil—renowned for its biodiversity, with an estimated 11,200 tree species and over 40,000 plant species (Hoorn, 2010). Researchers often consult indigenous herbalists and shamans on what plants they use and take samples back to the lab for further study. Conflicts arise as developed world corporations and their subsidiaries patent a plant's genetic material, thereby conferring the corporation's legal right to commodify and commercialize the resource. Often, the interests of the indigenous peoples, local communities, and the nation-state are ignored. This all too common process of resource exploitation is called biopiracy.

In some cases, large quantities of a particular species are needed for production, leading to unsustainable practices. For instance, the production of one kilogram of taxol (an anti-cancer drug) requires 10,000 kg of Pacific Yew tree bark; each treatment requires the raw material of eight 60-year-old yew trees (Malik, 2011). Likewise, for a drug used in child leukemia and Hodgkins disease, production requires several tons of rosy periwinkles for one ounce of the active alkaloid, leading to significant biodiversity loss in several countries (Fairhead, 2013).

In response to the widespread unsustainable use of the world's biodiversity and the uneven sharing of benefits, the Convention on Biological Diversity (CBD) was structured with 193 countries currently participating. The CBD is the first international legal agreement that explicitly addresses biodiversity conservation, sustainable development, and the fair and equitable sharing of the benefits of genetic resources. Unfortunately, though well intended, the CBD lacks an enforcement mechanism to ensure compliance. The convention does require countries to submit National Reports (Article 26) and a National Biodiversity Strategy and Action Plan (Article 6) to provide information on measures taken to implement the convention on the national level. Moreover, the CBD promotes international cooperation through information sharing and financial support. Concerning indigenous knowledge, Article 8(j) of the convention employs a working group to refine and develop indigenous interests. Despite the convention, exploitation of the world's biodiversity continues to increase resulting in more conflicts between biodiversity-rich nations, indigenous peoples, conservationists, and economic actors.

The case of the African elephant and the illegal ivory trade provides a valuable example of biodiversity and conflict. In 1979, there were an estimated 1.3 million African elephants, but today there are 420,000 to 650,000 with many estimating even lower numbers (UNEP, 2013). The loss of nearly one million elephants is primarily due to killing for ivory. The second factor is loss of habitat due to development, agriculture expansion, and fencing. The ivory trade is estimated to be worth $7 billion annually with ivory catching $1,000 a pound on the streets of Beijing (IFAW, 2013). Illegal trade routes hit upon Africa, the United States, Europe, and Asia, with China and the United States being the largest consumers (CITES, 2013). According to a report published by the Convention on International Trade in Endangered Species of Wild Fauna and Flora (CITES)—which aims to conserve species through regulating international trade—poverty and weak governance along with the demand for ivory are the primary sources of illegal poaching (CITES, 2013). As a result, conflicts have resulted between preservationists and those trying to make a livelihood and their customers.

Of the many challenges concerning the African elephant, armed conflict has increased recently with the militarization of the ivory trade. The CITES report reveals that armed militias such as the Lord's Resistance Army, Sudan's janjaweed, Somali militias, and the Ugandan and Congolese armies have all been implicated in the illegal ivory trade—using the proceeds from poaching to buy weapons and ammunition (UNEP, 2013). A report to the African Elephant Summit estimates that in 2012 some 15,000 elephants were illegally killed at 42 sites across 27 African countries participating in Monitoring the Illegal Killing of Elephants, a CITES program (CITES, 2013). This is an alarmingly unsustainable rate as this number represents 7.4 percent of total elephant population while elephant population growth rate is only 5 percent (CITES, 2013). The involvement of organized crime and trained military or militia groups has made park rangers' jobs very dangerous. Some members of the international community and African nations recommend increasing tactical and military training for park rangers.

As stated, the Convention on International Trade in Endangered Species of Wild Fauna and Flora (CITES), ratified by 177 countries, aims to ensure that international trade in specimens of wild fauna and flora does not threaten the survival of the species. Each party to the convention must administer a licensing system that tracks the import and export of the close to 35,000 species listed in the convention. Within the CITES framework, species are listed as follows: in Appendix 1 (those threatened with extinction), Appendix 2 (those not threatened with extinction but must be controlled), or Appendix 3 (those species that are protected in at least one country and that country seeks international assistance in controlling trade). The African elephant was added to Appendix 1 in 1989. Those species in Appendix 1 can only be traded in exceptional circumstances. However, any party to the convention can make a reservation to not be bound by any provisions relating to trade with a specific species. Despite the convention, illegal poaching and trade continues to occur.

In short, the existence of profitable biomaterials promotes conflict between those who wish to exploit the resource and those who wish to conserve it. International law plays an important role in protecting biodiversity, but despite its intentions, many countries, economic actors, and armed militias seeking economic or political advantage, violate, and/or ignore the treaties. The lack of enforcement mechanisms in ecosystem preserving conventions such as the CBD and CITES reveals their ineffectiveness against countries that are unable or unwilling to conserve their biodiversity resources.

REFERENCES

Convention on International Trade in Endangered Species of Wild Fauna and Flora (CITES). (2013). "Status of African Elephant Populations and Levels of Illegal Killing and the Illegal Trade in Ivory: A Report to the African Elephant Summit," 7–16. Accessed March 5, 2016, at https://cmsdata.iucn.org/downloads/african_elephant_summit_background_document_2013_en.pdf.

Fairhead, James, Melissa Leach, and Ian Scoones. (2013). *Green Grabbing: A New Appropriation of Nature*. London: Routledge.

Hoorn, Carina, and Frank Wesselingh. (2010). *Amazonia: Landscape and Species Evolution. A Look into the Past*. Oxford, UK: Wiley-Blackwell, 1.

International Fund for Animal Welfare (IFAW). (2013, June). "Criminal Nature: The Global Security Implications of the Illegal Wildlife Trade." Accessed March 2, 2016, at https://d2mlnkprj9wd81.cloudfront.net/sites/default/files/ifaw-criminal-nature-2013-low-res_0.pdf.

Malik, Sonia, Rosa M. Cusidó, Mohammad Hossein Mirjalili, Elisabeth Moyano, et al. (2011). "Production of the anticancer drug taxol in Taxus baccata suspension cultures: a review," *Process Biochemistry Process Biochemistry 46*(1), 23–34.

United Nations Environmental Program (UNEP). (2013). "Elephants in the Dust: The African Elephant Crisis: A Rapid Response Assessment." Accessed March 2, 2016, at http://www.unep.org/pdf/RRAivory_draft7.pdf.

CONFLICT IN KENYA—THE UNINTENDED CONSEQUENCES OF BIODIVERSITY CONSERVATION

M. Troy Burnett

Geologists have recently proposed a new epoch—the Anthropocene. To outsiders this may seem like much ado about nothing, but for a geologist to suggest the end of one epoch and the beginning of another, something "Earth-changing" must have occurred. Indeed, humanity's environmental impact is global with the result being dramatic effects on the Earth's biosystems. Among other things, this impact involves mass extinction. Attempts to stem the loss by protecting habitat in the form of national parks and reserves have invariably resulted in social conflict between ecologists, indigenous groups, and various business factions. This risk of conflict is magnified in underdeveloped regions where there are high levels of species and ecosystem diversity but also communities of people who have longed lived in these areas and are often just trying to survive.

For this essay, I will focus on Kenya, a developing country as well as a biodiversity hotspot with a high level of endemism. The situation in Kenya between the government, conservationists, and the local Maasai highlights the contentious nature of this issue and provides a simple and universal truism: if local peoples living in/near conservation areas and biodiversity hotpots are ignored, perceive that they do not benefit from conservation efforts, or are not compensated for their altered lifestyle, they will not support the conservation of biodiversity and may even accelerate the demise of species.

Located on the horn of Africa, Kenya, home to 45 million people, is attempting to balance economic development with the loss of its rich biodiversity. Wild areas

An elephant strolling through the dusty Tsavo East National Park. Elephant hunting and elephant poaching and exploitation of the ivory trade are illegal in Kenya. (Karel Prinsloo/AP Photo)

have either disappeared or been degraded in the face of land use changes that favor agriculture and urban development. Extinctions rates have accelerated as the remaining wilderness areas, ecological corridors, buffer zones, and dispersal areas are threatened by further encroachment and illegal poaching of high-value species for commercial and subsistence purposes. Conservationists and the Kenyan government are not blind to the loss and have long endeavored to preserve their natural heritage. Indeed, Kenya has more than 35 national parks and reserves, including the famed Amboseli National Park anchored by majestic Mount Kilimanjaro. While this has served to reduce the pace of extinction and provide some economic benefit via ecotourism, it has also increased human-wildlife contact and led to the removal from protected lands of indigenous groups, including the historically nomadic, pastoral Maasai people. Inevitably, where wildlife-induced damages to property and life are neither controlled nor compensated, negative local attitudes towards conservation and wildlife resources become entrenched (Okello and Wishitemi, 2006). The conflict intensifies when local communities, despite living on the doorstep of conservation zones, receive little benefit from wildlife protection but rather feel alienated from the wildlife related economic activities of the ecotourism industry. According to Roselyne Okech, "When local communities feel that both governments and conservation stakeholders value wildlife more than their lives, livelihoods or their aspirations, retaliation and opposition to conservation initiatives can be swift and uncompromising" (Okech, 2010).

The Maasai have co-existed with wildlife for centuries, living a pastoral life in balance with the wildlife. With the governmental drive to protect biodiversity at all costs, the Maasai have seemingly become victims of the process. Pastoralists in general have been marginalized by efforts to both modernize societies and protect biodiversity. Conflict is seemingly inevitable as these groups and their historical traditions confront deepening economic insecurity, political marginalization, weakened traditional governance practices, inadequate land tenure policies, and even cattle rustling in the case of the Maasai. Pastoralist communities also tend to be the most vulnerable to global warming and climate change. Wildlife such as the lions and elephants of Amboseli National Park may provide photo-ops for ecotourists, but for the Maasai, they are competition, severing the long history of harmonious co-existence. Close to 70 percent of Kenya's wildlife regularly venture outside park boundaries coming into direct, often dangerous, conflict with people and their livestock. Further, it has been found that wildlife contact spreads diseases including malignant catarrh fever, foot and mouth disease, and east coast fever (a protozoan spread by the ubiquitous African buffalo). Observers have noted that the rise in human-wildlife conflict could evolve into a major crisis if a solution is not immediately found, begging the question "should locals be expected to appreciate the significance of animals even when their interests are not being addressed?" (Ogodo, 2003). The simple fact is, indigenous communities often lose pastoral or agricultural resources due to the segmenting of land for national parks and reserves.

The way forward in Kenya or other biodiversity hotspots were conservation and culture collide is complex and convoluted. The preservation of ecosystem and species biodiversity is clearly a global necessity. Yet this need must be balanced with the interests of the people most closely associated with those species and areas designated as sites of interests. In the case of Kenya, conservation areas cannot sustainably support viable wildlife without functioning dispersal zones, which also happen to be the home of the ancestral Maasai people, who have at best been lukewarm towards the conservation policies of the government. Indeed, many of Africa's pastoral communities occupy such zones and have similar stories of marginalization and conflict. Continuing to genuinely involve these peoples and their concerns in sustainable natural resource usage and conservation must be encouraged and facilitated. National land use practices and plans must be compatible with the socio-economic needs, natural endowment, and climatic constraints of the different bioregions. Stable demographic patterns, improved livelihoods, poverty reduction, economic compensation, and equitable distribution of the wealth from tourism along with policies to enhance the viability of pastoralism can also help minimize human impacts and reduce conflict between the competing groups.

The biodiversity crisis is real and accelerating as the human population surges past 7 billion and the capitalist world economy expands its system of mass production and mass consumption. Habitat preservation in the form of national parks and reserves is one solution to the crisis. Yet, sites and species are often selected for ecological or non-local economic reasons alone, regardless of the people who may live in such areas and are most impacted by the change in land use. The ensuing conflicts can only be resolved or avoided if these people are given legitimate seats and voices at the planning tables.

REFERENCES

Ogodo, Ochieng. (2003, July 7). "Resolving the conflict calls for a tight balancing act-legislator," *East African Standard Newspaper*, The Standard Limited.

Okech, Roselyne N. (2010). "Wildlife-community conflicts in conservation areas in Kenya," *African Journal on Conflict Resolution 10(2)*, 68.

Okello, Moses Makonjio, and B. E. Wishitemi. (2006). "Principles for the establishment of community wildlife sanctuaries for ecotourism: lessons from Maasai group ranches, Kenya," *African Journal of Business and Economics 1(1)*, 90–109.

20

ARE DEBT-FOR-NATURE SWAPS A VIABLE MEANS TO PROMOTE STABILITY IN THE DEVELOPING WORLD?

OVERVIEW
M. Troy Burnett

Since 1984 the World Wildlife Fund (WWF) has worked with creditor nations like the United States, France, and Germany to provide debt forgiveness to the developing world in what has become known as debt-for-nature swaps. These transactions allow debtor nations the option to exchange a portion of their foreign debt for investment into local environmental conservation initiatives (World Wildlife Fund, 2014). Although these agreements have been described as a win-win scenario for both debtors and creditors, the program has been criticized for its inability to provide meaningful debt reduction amongst third-world nations.

BACKGROUND

The idea for debt-for-nature exchanges emerged in the 1980s as a response to the decrease in conservation efforts following the Latin American economic downturn. By 1982, Latin American governments owed the nine largest U.S. money centers a debt accounting for a stunning 176 percent of their capital (Sims and

Romero, 2006). Regional environmental conservation deteriorated as a result. Desperate for economic growth, indebted governments scaled back on conservation spending and implemented destructive environmental policies that included large-scale deforestation and overuse of farmland. For instance, during this time Brazil had a deforestation rate of 50,000 square kilometers per year (Foley, 2013).

In 1984, WWF Vice President Dr. Thomas Lovejoy, with the support of South American NGOs such as the Association for the Conservation of Amazonian Wildlife, proposed debt-for-nature exchanges as a new initiative designed to combat the destruction of these biologically diverse regions of Latin America. These transactions would not only provide nations with the means to reduce foreign debt, but provide local governments much needed funding for conservation efforts. According to the WWF, these exchanges would work as such: creditor entities would agree to "purchase" a portion of foreign debt from a debtor nation at a discounted rate. The proceeds from these transactions would then be converted into local currency used to fund local conservation initiatives (Resor, 1997). The success of the system depended heavily on the willingness of commercial banks (or governments) to sell debt at less than the full value of the original loan (Resor, 1997). Though it may seem counterintuitive to suggest that a bank would be willing to part with a promissory note at a discounted rate, it is important to consider that many of these indebted nations may never be able to fulfill their economic obligations. Therefore, some creditors may prefer to liquidate these debts at a discounted rate rather than gamble on uncertain future payments (Resor, 1997).

Outside of the obvious financial benefits, proponents of debt-for-nature swaps argue these transactions are ideal for both creditors and investors. By forgiving a portion of a developing nation's debt, banks are able to maintain a positive public image while debtor governments are able to increase environmental spending. In theory, these new environmental initiatives would also help pave the way for future economic development projects and conservation efforts between first-world and third-world nations (Resor, 1997).

Because the impact of environmental degradation is not necessarily localized to an individual region, the impact can be transnational, meaning some of the damage to the environment caused by one country's production is felt outside of where it is done (Kessel, 2006). In addition, economists and environmentalist agree that debt-for-nature swaps are a practical means for indebted nations to improve their future financial standing.

The first debt-for-nature swap occurred in 1987 when the Bolivian government reached an agreement with the NGO Conservation International. This agreement allowed Conservation International to purchase over $600,000 worth of Bolivian foreign debt at the reduced price of $100,000. As a condition of this transaction, the Bolivian government pledged to establish the Beni Biosphere Reserve as a region with maximum legal protection, along with the creation of new protected areas and a conservation fund worth 250,000 bolivianos. Furthermore, media exposure of the swap helped raise the conversation surrounding conservation into the public arena (Resor, 1997).

As with the Bolivian Beni Reserve, the amount of debt that is actually exchanged through a debt-for-nature exchange is typically a minimal amount. This has led critics to condemn the program for "politicizing the environment" and turning the real needs of conservation and economic development into a publicity stunt. Further, due to the often-unstable economic and political situations within the developing world, allocation of conservation resources tends to favor the interests of certain groups (such as ruling elites) more than others (Global Issues, n.d.). This raises concerns over the efficacy of conservation efforts when decisions are made in a context of social inequality.

Another criticism is that debt-for-nature swaps often fail to address the concerns of indigenous groups. Because the creation of these wildlife reserves is often done without carefully considering what the impact on the local population will be, natives often find themselves in a position where their livelihood is negatively affected.

Because the value of these debts often exceeds 100 percent of a nation's GDP, financial critics often raise questions regarding the effectiveness of these buyback programs. For example, when Bolivia purchased $308 million worth of debt for $34 million, the market value of the outstanding debt declined from $40.2 to $39.8 million (Kessel, 2006). These marginal decreases in debt are in no way detrimental to indebted nations nor does this data suggesting that the debt-for-nature system should be entirely abandoned; however, these slight reductions still raise questions over whether these exchanges are a sustainable means for creditors to collect a portion of outstanding foreign debt.

As I argue in this section, criticism aside, the fact remains that debt-for-nature swaps have helped alleviate over $1 billion worth of foreign debt in the developing world. Certain nations (like Costa Rica and the Philippines) have not only used these transactions as a way to manage debt, but have profited from the resulting ecotourism industry. Although there are definite questions surrounding the effectiveness of the debt-for-nature swap system, these transactions still provide obvious benefits. Thus it can be concluded that if implemented effectively, debt-for-nature swaps are a viable means of providing both economic and environmental aid to the third world.

REFERENCES

Foley, James A. (2013, November 16). "Deforestation in Brazil up 28 percent on the year," *Nature World News*. Accessed March 4, 2014, at http://www.natureworldnews.com/articles/4942/20131116/deforestation-brazil-up-28-percent-year.htm.

Global Issues. (n.d.). "The Impact of the Debt Crisis on All of Us." Accessed March 4, 2014, at http://www.globalissues.org/article/226/the-impact-of-the-debt-crisis-on-all-of-us.

Kessel, Andrew. (2006). "Debt-for-Nature Swaps: A Critical Approach." Comparative Environment and Development Studies: A Seminar in Cultural and Political Ecology. Accessed March 2, 2016, at http://www.macalester.edu/academics/geography/courses/coursepages/kessel.pdf, p. 13–16.

Resor, James P. (1997). "Debt-for-nature swaps: a decade of experience and new directions for the future," *Unasylva* 1(188), 1–74. Accessed March 2, 2016, at http://www.fao.org/docrep/w3247e/w3247e06.htm#TopOfPage.

Sims, Jocelyn, and Jesse Romero. (2013, November 22). "Latin American Debt Crisis of 1980s—A Detailed Essay on an Important Event in the History of the Federal Reserve." Federal Reserve History. Accessed March 4, 2014, at http://www.federalreservehistory.org/Events/DetailView/46.

FURTHER READING

Hassoun, Nicole. (2012). "The problem of debt-for-nature swaps from a human rights perspective," *Journal of Applied Philosophy* 29(4), 359–377.

Polan, Magdalena, Parmeshwar Ramlogan, and Carlos I. Medeiros. (2007). *A Primer on Sovereign Debt Buybacks and Swaps*. Washington, DC: International Monetary Fund.

Thapa, Brijesh. (2000). "The relationship between debt-for-nature swaps and protected area tourism: a plausible strategy for developing countries," *Forest Service Proceedings*, 15.

World Wildlife Fund (WWF). (2014). "Conservation Finance, Initiatives." Accessed March 4, 2014, at https://worldwildlife.org/initiatives/conservation-finance.

World Wildlife Fund (WWF). (2014). "Debt-for-Nature Swaps." Accessed February 24, 2014, at https://worldwildlife.org/initiatives/conservation-finance.

A CRITICAL VIEW OF DEBT-FOR-NATURE SWAPS
Mia Bennett

Debt-for-nature swaps were first launched in the early 1990s, with advocates promoting them as a sort of win-win solution for both indebted countries and the environment. These mechanisms, largely targeted at developing countries, essentially reduce a country's foreign debt in exchange for legal guarantees that they will protect, in some way, a part of their natural environment. Debt-for-nature swaps were proposed in part to lessen the debt crises that had taken hold of developing countries in places like Latin America, Asia, and Africa in the 1970s and 1980s. Poor lending and borrowing decisions, high interest rates, and unfavorable terms of trade for their main exports led these countries to accumulate debilitating levels of debt to such creditors as developed countries, commercial banks, and multilateral organizations like the World Bank (Alagiri, 1991).

BACKGROUND

It quickly became clear that something would need to be done to help alleviate developing countries' massive foreign debt. One solution tried by certain developing countries was to "borrow" from their often-ample natural resources and export them as products like timber, minerals, and oil and gas. Yet this attempted mechanism to reduce their foreign debt loads exacerbated problems like deforestation in Brazil's Amazon rainforest. Ruination of the environment and depletion of natural resources could theoretically render developing countries even more unstable and more dependent on the export of primary products, whose prices are subject to fluctuations determined by global commodities markets. Thus, another solution, this time suggested by a conservation-minded scientist from a developed country, was floated. In 1984, an American, Dr. Thomas Lovejoy, then director of the conservation program at the World Wildlife Fund (WWF) in the United States, proposed debt-for-nature swaps. This alternative solution would theoretically improve developing countries' balance sheets while curtailing environmental destruction. This was deemed especially important, as some of the countries with the highest amounts of foreign debt also hold some of the planet's most important tropical forests.

Debt-for-nature swaps take two main forms. In the first, called a three-party swap, an environmental non-governmental organization (NGO) like The Nature Conservancy purchases a portion of the developing country's debt owed to a commercial bank on the secondary market. In exchange, the NGO sells back the debt to the developing country at a price lower than what it sold for on the secondary market, but higher than what it paid, so that the NGO, too, makes a small profit. The revenues the debtor country receives thanks to its lowered debt and interest payments then go into a conservation fund. The second type of debt-for-nature swap, called a bilateral or multilateral debt-for-nature swap, involves one or more creditor nations who agree to restructure a developing country's debt. The savings then similarly go into a fund for environmental conservation. While most of the actual debt bought back is small, the savings on interest payments can be substantial. In Ecuador, for instance, in 1987, the WWF purchased $1 million face value of Ecuadoran debt for $355,000 on the secondary market. The $355,000 was then turned into a $1 million bond for environmental conservation, denominated in local currency. In other words, "for every dollar that was donated to WWF for the debt-for-nature swap, $3 worth of local bonds, paying 31 percent interest, were purchased for the conservation effort in Ecuador" (Visser and Mendoza, 1994).

Given their apparent financial and environmental benefits, debt-for-nature swaps enjoyed early popularity. The first agreement took place in 1987 in the form of a three-party debt-for-nature swap. Conservation International, an NGO, alleviated some of Bolivia's debt in exchange for protection of its Beni Biosphere Reserve and environs (Thapa, 1998). Other countries like Jamaica, the Dominican Republic, Ghana, and Poland signed debt-for-nature swaps in the late 1980s and early 1990s. In 1995, a study by Kahn and McDonald in *Ecological Economics* determined that debt played an important role in driving deforestation in tropical countries. Importantly, their study found that debt-for-nature swaps had two positive effects on deforestation: one, by contractually obligating countries to protect their forests, the rate of deforestation slowed. Two, by reducing debt, pressures to fell trees in the first place declined, too, although this effect was somewhat weaker (Kahn and McDonald, 1995). A more recent study in 2011 similarly found that developing countries that did implement debt-for-nature swaps tended to have lower rates of deforestation than those that did not.

Yet as early as 1993, the number of debt-for-nature swaps began to decline (Sheikh, 2009). Several criticisms were lodged. One was that they were "effective but not enforceable" (Hrynik, 1990), with little transparency or oversight over the funds meant to conserve the debtor nation's environment. Three-party debt swaps were considered more vulnerable than bilateral debt swaps, in which the creditor nation could ensure greater safeguards that the funds would be used properly. Other critics noted that they failed to address the root of the problem: unfair first-world lending practices that continue to put developing nations at a global financial disadvantage.

Despite the criticisms, debt-for-nature swaps still exist. In 2008, Madagascar, an island nation with a substantial number of endemic species, signed the largest debt-for-nature swap in its history. France agreed to forgive $20 million of Madagascar's debt in exchange for the same amount of money being put into an endowment administered by the government of Madagascar, the WWF, and Conservation International (World Wildlife Fund, 2008). Additionally, in 2010, the United States agreed to convert $21 million of Brazil's debt into a fund to conserve its Atlantic coastal rainforest and Cerrado and Caatinga ecosystems. Thus, while perhaps less popular than before, debt-for-nature swaps are still seen as a viable means of reducing debt and conserving nature at the same time. As such, one could argue that they help to promote both financial and environmental stability in the developing world. At the same time, however, they also manage to keep stable one other feature of the 21st-century global economic system: the dominance of first-world countries and their associated organizations over those of developing countries.

REFERENCES

Alagiri, Priya. (1991). "Give us sovereignty or give us debt: debtor countries' perspective on debt-for-nature swaps," *American Law Review 41*, 485.

Hrynik, Tamara J. (1990). "Debt-for-nature swaps: effective but not enforceable," *Case Western University Journal of International Law 22*, 141.

Kahn, James R., and Judith A. McDonald. (1995). "Third-world debt and tropical deforestation," *Ecological Economics* 12(2), 107–123.

Sheikh, Prevaze A. (2009). "Debt-for-nature initiatives and the Tropical Forest Conservation Act: status and implementation," Congressional Research Service, Library of Congress.

Thapa, Bnjesh. (1998). "Debt-for-nature swaps: an overview," *The International Journal of Sustainable Development & World Ecology*, 5(4), 249–262.

Visser, Dana R., and Guillermo A. Mendoza. (1994). "Debt-for-nature swaps in Latin America [Canje de deuda externa por naturaleza en Latinoamérica]," *Journal of Forestry* 92(6), 14.

World Wildlife Fund (WWF). (2008, June 11). "Monumental Debt-for-Nature Swap Provides $20 Million to Protect Biodiversity in Madagascar, WWF Announces." Accessed March 2, 2016, at http://www.worldwildlife.org/press-releases/monumental-debt-for-nature-swap-provides-20-million-to-protect-biodiversity-in-madagascar-wwf-announces.

THOUGH FAR FROM IDEAL, DEBT-FOR-NATURE SWAPS PROVIDE ONE CREATIVE SOLUTION TO THE DEBT-HABITAT DESTRUCTION PROBLEM

M. Troy Burnett

In the mid 1970s, developing countries began an era of economic growth, focused on agricultural and industrial modernization. To facilitate this ambitious growth these countries, especially those in South America, began to borrow heavily from foreign creditors. The result has been modest growth coupled with spiraling debt that requires decades of exorbitant interest payments. Further, economic stagflation in the West during the 1980s led to a steep decline in foreign exchange earnings due to lack of demand for developing country's goods. Intertwined with industrial-led, export-focused economic growth and the debt crisis is rampant environmental degradation—namely deforestation. To raise the necessary capital to both "modernize" and pay back the debt, countries have aggressively exploited their natural resource base. This has come at a steep price, as pristine wilderness habitats have been altered and destroyed.

To alleviate the pressure created by the interdependent relationship between the debt crisis and environmental degradation, a debt-for-nature swap, based on debt-for-equity transactions, was proposed in 1984. Quite simply, the debt-for-nature swap process involves exchanging a certain quantity of debtor's foreign debt in return for local currency being invested in domestic environmental projects. These projects include land conservation, natural resource management, habitat restoration, ecotourism development, environmental education, and implementation of various training programs for park personnel. Admittedly, debt-for-nature swaps cannot solve foreign debt accumulation. The size and value of the debt is too high. They do, however, provide an imaginative means to promote conservation and sustainable resource development.

In financial terms, debt-for-nature swaps have been projected to reduce foreign debt by 200 million dollars annually if properly structured and implemented. Though just a drop in the bucket, this debt restructuring acts as a catalyst for overall prosperity and forward thinking. Considering that debt-for-nature swap funds are allocated for use in environmental projects, a change in cognitive framework has taken hold in these regions. The once dominant attitude, acquired via colonialism and western modernism, of frontier expansion and resource exploitation, has now begun to shift towards environmental stewardship and sustainable development. With the creation of new parks and various conservation initiatives, the local people have started to take pride in their environmental endowment and have been able to envision alternative economic opportunities. Emerging employment fields such as ecotourism have been established in an attempt to transition from reliance on resource exploitation and the export of raw materials, to wilderness conservation and the import of environmental enthusiasts and naturalists. Furthermore, with more land designated for protection, an increase in tourism has created a niche for GDP growth. In fact, several of the countries involved in nature-for-debt swaps rely heavily upon tourism for revenue, with more than 6 percent of GDP being generated by tourism alone. Moreover, nature-based tourism has increased anywhere between 10 to 30 percent, which is 2 to 5 times the average increase of tourism in general (Thapa, 2000).

Though each debt-for-nature case is unique and offers challenges, the most successful example can be found in Costa Rica. Between 1988 and 1990, 5 percent of the overall debt burden was reduced, with the income gains directed towards environmental protection and alternative economic development. Arguably, this was the catalyst that has since shifted Costa Rica's economic reality from resource exploitation (deforestation) to land conservation. The country is the regional leader in these efforts, serving as the model for a successful debt-for-nature program, with more than 12 percent of the country's land set aside for protection (Thapa, 2000).

Additionally, debt-for-nature swaps increase funds for environmental organizations. In Ecuador, for example, a debt swap facilitated by the World Wildlife

Fund led to a doubling of the country's parks and reserves budget (Thapa, 2000). Consequently, every dollar of acquired debt resulted in more than eight dollars worth of Ecuadorian currency being used towards conservation. Presently, over 1.5 billion dollars in funds have been designated toward nature-for-debt swaps, with over 19 countries participating in the program.

Earlier attempts to combat the increasing debt load accumulating in developing countries have been deemed largely unsuccessful. Furthermore, some cases of debt alleviation measures lead to added pressures upon the debt-bearing nations. In the 1980s, the United States implemented the Baker plan, the Brady plan, and the Enterprise for the Americas Initiative to stimulate economies in developing countries (Thapa, 2000). These plans hoped to negotiate some form of debt relief in an attempt to rejuvenate economic progress, while in turn encouraging and implementing new, stricter lending practices. Though considered partly successful, these and other debt abatement strategies led to harsh governmental austerity measures. The austerity measures, under the rubric provided by the neoliberal-open market agenda, included the "monocropping" of agriculture for export, devaluation of local currencies, decreasing government spending, subsidy elimination, and increase in exports of cash crops such as coffee or soybeans. Monocropping in particular, often leads to a reduction of food production for the local population, resulting in food shortages and the reliance on imported food.

Debt-for-nature swaps may not represent a comprehensive solution to debt reduction to foreign creditors in developing countries, but they do aid in progress and stability in these regions. With concerns of global warming, wildlife habitat destruction, and the loss of biodiversity becoming more prevalent, countries where environmental degradation is increasing need social and economic incentives to encourage conservation. Debt-for-nature swaps can be a useful tool because they have the potential to create new, more sustainable economic opportunities. They also encourage and empower people and their governments to preserve and protect their natural heritages. Other solutions have turned out to be, in many cases, more harmful than good, with poverty, and further economic exploitation prevailing over prosperity. Stability, economic growth, and environmental stewardship, can be viewed as the ability to look beyond the economic burdens of past mistakes in an attempt to prevent future abuse of our natural world. In that case, debt-for-nature swaps not only promote stability, but represent it.

REFERENCE

Thapa, Brijesh. (2000). "The relationship between debt-for-nature swaps and protected area tourism: a plausible strategy for developing countries," *Forest Service Proceedings*, 15.

FURTHER READING

Alagiri, Priya. (1991). "Give us sovereignty or give us debt: debtor countries' perspective on debt-for-nature swaps," *American Law Review 41*, 485.

Gockel, Catherine Kilbane, and Leslie C. Gray. (2011). "Debt-for-nature swaps in action: two case studies in Peru," *Ecology and Society 16*(3), 13.

Kahn, James R., and Judith A. McDonald. (1995). "Third-world debt and tropical deforestation," *Ecological Economics 12*(2), 107–123.

Part II
Africa

21

WAS THE RWANDAN GENOCIDE OF 1994 A RESULT OF CONFLICT OVER NATURAL RESOURCES?

OVERVIEW
William von Lopik

If it was not for the events that transpired during the first half of 1994, it is doubtful whether most people in the United States would be able to find the country of Rwanda on a world map. The genocide of 1 million Tutsi by their Hutu neighbors shocked the world and seemed to have come out of nowhere with little provocation. However, as with any critical analysis it is important to understand the context of this horrific event. In this case some geographical perspective of Rwanda is helpful in gathering a more comprehensive understanding of why this happened.

BACKGROUND

The land area of Rwanda is smaller than the state of Maryland; it is landlocked without access to any ocean and dwarfed by its more famous western neighbor, the Democratic Republic of the Congo. It is an economy in which 80 percent of the 11.5 million people who live in the country rely on some form of subsistence agriculture. Agriculture accounts for one-third of the total gross domestic product (GDP) of the country. According to the Rwanda Development Board, this sector supports 90 percent of national food needs and generates more than 70 percent of the country's export revenues, mostly through tea and coffee. The population of Rwanda is growing very fast with an annual increase of 2.7 percent. At this rate, the total population will double in 26 years. More than half of the population of the country was born after the 1994 genocide and therefore did not directly live through it. It is the most densely populated country in all of Africa and an astonishing 80 percent of the people live in rural areas, not in urban areas. Despite lying almost directly on the equator, Rwanda's agriculture has flourished because of its temperate, mountainous highlands and rich volcanic soils. Most subsistence farming takes place on steep hillsides that are highly susceptible to soil erosion if not sustainably cared for.

The anonymity of Rwanda to the outside world was completely broken after the events that transpired on April 1994. This atrocity sealed the fate of Rwanda in the annals of other historic genocidal massacres that have shaken the moral consciousness of our world. The brutal slaughter of innocent Tutsi men, women, and children as well as animals over the course of 90 days caught the world by surprise, not only in the enormity of the genocide but also in the shear brutality of it. A seemingly peaceful country was thrust overnight into terror and anarchy with neighbors slaughtering neighbors for the simple fact that they were perceived to be ethnically different.

The ethnic diversity of the country breaks down to Hutus making up 84 percent of the population with Tutsis accounting for 15 percent and Twas the remaining 1percent. Tensions between the Hutus and Tutsis had been simmering for many years since the German and Belgian colonial powers exacerbated the ethnic cleavages in the late 1800s and early 1900s as they gave special privileges to the Tutsi leaders and kings. No doubt it was a contrived strategy undertaken by the colonists to "divide and conquer" the people of Rwanda who totally outnumbered them. They used the elitist positions of the Tutsi to subjugate the majority Hutus. This low-grade form of suppression came to a head in 1959 when the Hutus rebelled against the Belgian colonists and the Tutsi elite. Many Tutsi were killed during this time and others fled to neighboring countries where they began to organize the Rwandan Patriotic Front (RPF). This exiled rebel army gained strength over the next few decades and Hutus became increasingly wary of its potential. It can be speculated that the genocide of 1994 was an attempt to wipe out all Tutsis from Rwanda so that the RPF would have nothing to return to when they decided to regain control of the country.

Most of the analysis during the 21 years since the genocidal anarchy of 1994 has focused on the ethnic tensions that existed in the country. Certainly a strong case can be made that it was the culmination of many years of animosity, frustration, fear, and jealousy that was made worse by policies of colonization. However it is important to point out that the country was growing fast, had a dense population that relied on a finite land base and with limited natural resources to support the population. Certainly one has to consider the fact that environmental and population pressures can produce social stress, which in turn can result in violent conflict. This scenario has been repeated throughout the world with conflicts in El Salvador, Haiti, Peru, Chiapas, and the West Bank. The case of Rwanda undoubtedly warrants a closer examination on whether the genocide was a result of conflict over natural resources.

By many accounts the situation in Rwanda has improved dramatically since 1994. Many of the exiled Tutsi and Hutu refugees who had been living in neighboring countries are now being repatriated either by choice or by force. The economy is considered to be one of the fastest growing in the world with an annual GDP growth rate of around 8 percent. Although, if you consider from where it started this might be a bit of an aberration. Paul Kagame, former leader of the RPF, has been president of the country since 2000 and seems to have brought some stability and accountability to the country. However, we would be naïve if we did not keep attention focused on Rwanda. After all, the outside world also thought that the country was progressing nicely prior to 1994. Population and land pressures have not gone away. Soil erosion and deforestation are ongoing problems. The variability that climate change presents to the consistency of annual rainfall amounts adds another layer of concern to an economy so dependent on agriculture. It is important to stay vigilant to what is occurring in highly vulnerable countries like Rwanda. The end result of a slow-onset disaster can be just as devastating as a sudden catastrophic event.

FURTHER READING

Hintjens, Helen M. (1999). "Explaining the 1994 genocide in Rwanda," *The Journal of Modern African Studies* 37(02), 241–286.

Percival, Val, and Thomas Homer-Dixon. (1996, September). "Environmental scarcity and violent conflict: the case of Rwanda," *Journal of Environment and Development* 5(3), 270–291.

Reyntjens, Filip. (1996). "Rwanda: genocide and beyond," *Journal of Refugee Studies* 9(3), 240–251.

THE RWANDAN GENOCIDE: A COMPLEX CONFLUENCE OF CAUSAL FACTORS
M. Troy Burnett

On April 6, 1994, one day before the Rwandan genocide began, an airplane carrying both Rwandan President Juvenal Habyarimana and Burundian President Cyprien Ntaryamira, both Hutus, was shot down on approach to Kigali airport, killing all those on board. Arguably, this was the catalyst for the horrific events that were to follow. Hours after the presidents' deaths, Rwandan government and military leaders gathered to announce the "assassination" of the president, focusing blame upon the members of the primary rival group, the Rwandan Patriotic Front (RPF). At the time, the RPF consisted mainly of Tutsi refugees from Uganda, who had migrated to Rwanda in the mid-1980s. Within days, countless Tutsi bodies lined the streets as the Hutu people hunted them down in their own homes. Close to 70 percent of the Tutsis living in Rwanda were slaughtered during this period in one of the bloodiest examples of genocide in the 20th century.

When reviewing the events, one discovers a multitude of factors—natural resource stress being one among many. Though the 100-day massacre of Hutu against Tutsi occurred within the context of the Rwandan Civil War (1990–1994), precipitated by the death of Habyarimana, the tensions between the two ethnic groups had long historical roots. Prior to the civil war, tensions and mistrust had been mounting between the Tutsi and Hutu peoples primarily as a result of difficult economic times and the perception of historically entrenched unequal development and cultural favoritism. Specifically, in the 1980s, coffee bean prices, a staple of the Rwandan economy, began to plummet, causing a series of recessions. Both the Tutsis and Hutus began to scapegoat each other as their leaders stoked the fires with populist extremism and cries of "it's their fault!" Yet, even during the civil war, Tutsis and Hutus continued to co-exist. Most citizens perceived the conflict as a political struggle between Habyarimana's government forces and the RPF. How was it, many have asked, that the struggle between political rivals devolved into a genocidal massacre?

There have been many accounts of the causes, framed within three broad types of explanations: (1) colonial and post-colonial influences, (2) domestic factors—ethnic tensions and overpopulation, and (3) the psychosocial perspective that presumes embedded traits of social conformity and obedience in Rwandan identity (Hintjens, 1998). Along with these standard interpretations, there are also the central roles played by economic reality, Rwanda's post-political regime and its power politics, and the nature of the Rwandan state and the means by which national identity was being shaped. As Hintjens starkly observes: "A redefinition of national identity along exclusively racial or ethnic lines became the prelude for later implementation of genocide" (Hintjens, 1999).

Arguably, Rwanda's experience with colonialism and neocolonialism were significant in planting the seeds of group mistrust and hatred. According to Hintjens, Rwanda, of all African countries, was particularly vulnerable to colonial and neocolonial manipulation (Hintjens, 1998). When Europeans first encountered and began to exploit the area, the indigenous peoples were forcibly categorized into three racially distinct groups: the Tutsis, Hutus, and Twa. Prior to European involvement, these ethnic labels did not exist, and once invented and established they clearly contradicted the complex ways identity had been shaped in the African Great Lakes region for centuries. This created deep levels of confusion and insecurity. Not that the colonials cared—"divide and conquer" had long been the favored policy. By creating such groups, the colonials could play one off the other in order to better control and exploit the region. Further, the Germans, who, along with the Belgians, were the dominant colonial power in Rwanda, actively promoted Tutsi dominance, feeling that they were more Caucasian, and thus racially superior and better able to serve in administrative positions. The Hutus and Twa quickly began to resent the Tutsis and their more privileged position.

Research has also shown that prior to the 100-day genocide, a core group within the Rwandan leadership, centered in the military, covertly strategized schemes for ethnic cleansing and power consolidation. This Hutu faction, known as the Akazu, and its supporters in the military were skeptical of the peace accords with the RPF and the power-sharing plans of the Arusha Accords, and feared for their and their extreme ideology's survival. At the time, they were not willing to give power up without a fight and fomented their position by spreading propaganda that the RPF was an alien force intent on reinstating Tutsi monarchal dominance and Hutu enslavement. As Hintjens notes, "this provides us with the beginnings of an explanation of the 1994 genocide: as a state organized incitement to violence, imposed through terror and ideology, and directed against the minority Tutsi" (Hintjens, 1999). Quite simply, extreme Hutu leaders wanted to completely remove once and for all the Tutsis from their territory and were willing to use the instability and climate of fear induced by the civil war and the alleged assassination of the president to justify this "cleansing."

In short, there is no single, simple explanation of the 1994 Rwandan genocide. Causes do include environmental factors and resource shortages, but more so the colonial ideology of racial division, the economic and political instability of the 1980s and early 1990s, the historically structured class hierarchy of Rwandan society, and the political extremism of both Hutu and Tutsi ethno-national propagandists.

Today, Rwandan society has stabilized, with clear signs of healing and forgiveness. The country has two public holidays commemorating the genocide—Genocide Memorial Day on April 7 and Liberation Day on July 4. The entire week following April 7 is designated an official week of mourning. The massacre in Rwanda also inspired the creation of the International Criminal Court and its mandate to prosecute anyone accused of genocide, crimes against humanity, or war crimes. The tragic event in Rwanda now continues to serve as a reminder of how quickly conflicts, whatever their causes, can turn into genocide.

REFERENCE

Hintjens, Helen M. (1999). "Explaining the 1994 genocide in Rwanda," *The Journal of Modern African Studies* 37(02), 241–286.

FURTHER READING

Reyntjens, Filip. (1996). "Rwanda: genocide and beyond," *Journal of Refugee Studies* 9(3), 240–251.

Yanagizawa-Drott, D. (2010). "Propaganda and conflict: theory and evidence from the Rwandan genocide," in *The Ghost of Causation in International Speech Crime Cases*, 267. Draft on file with author.

THE ROLE OF ENVIRONMENTAL FACTORS IN THE RWANDAN GENOCIDE
William Van Lopik

The Rwandan genocide of 1994 tends to be commonly viewed as an ethnic conflict between the Hutu and Tutsi ethnic groups. Historical antagonism existed between the two groups even prior to the colonization of Rwanda by the Germans and later the Belgians. In the 1920s, Belgian ethnologists analyzed the skulls of Tutsis and Hutus and declared the Tutsi people to be the superior tribe. This set up a hierarchical division in the country that exacerbated tensions and established what some term "race science" (Gourevitch, 1998). The German and Belgian colonists used this rationale to create divisions and prejudices in the country, thus making

Refugees wait for water at a water distribution center, on their way back to Rwanda after the Rwandan Genocide in 1994. (U.S. Department of Defense)

the country easier to subdue and colonize. Resentment and discrimination started to form between the tribes as the Tutsis considered themselves as superior. Even though they spoke the same language, shared in the same religions, and intermarried, sharp divisions started to form between the two groups. The Belgians imposed their authority over the Hutus and elevated the Tutsi people, causing Rwandans to become a divided people. The colonists knew a divided country could not stand, and knew this strategy would eventually destroy whatever unity existed in the people of Rwanda. The colonial dogma never left the minds of Rwandans for generations, and was a root cause of the 1994 genocide (Irivuzumugabe, 2009). However, it would be a gross injustice to the 800,000 people who died if one simply described it as "tribal warfare."

Closer examination of the events that led up to those horrific months in 1994 reveal a very complex web of causal factors. The purpose of this essay is to discuss what role environmental degradation and scarcity played in the genocide. There are certainly many precedents throughout the world where the inequitable access to land and resources has been the overriding reason for the onset of civil unrest (Weinberg, 1991; Prosterman and Riedinger, 1987). Peter Uvin suggests that there are three alternative perspectives one could take when looking at the Rwandan case: (1) overpopulation and the ensuing scramble for limited land directly led to unavoidable social conflict; (2) environmental scarcity was more of a catalyst to the genocide than its fundamental cause; and (3) there was no correlation at all between conflict and the environment, rather the violence and ensuing genocide were precipitated by social factors (Uvin, 1998).

Rwanda was suffering under intense environmental pressures leading up to the genocide. The country's rapid population growth was causing a dramatic reduction in the size of family farm holdings. Farmers had to subsist on smaller plots of land. This meant that they could not let their land rest and lie fallow at any time and had to intensively farm it. This resulted in the exhaustion of soil nutrients and overall fertility. Scarcity led to local conflicts over land with the more powerful elites of the country, who imposed their will and dominance. The result was a stark imbalance in who controlled valuable natural resources. As a result of population pressures and the short supply of arable land, farmers were left to till marginal, hilly plots resulting in higher rates of soil salinization and erosion. Deforestation also contributed to erosion because of a population base that relied almost exclusively on fuel-wood for cooking. As soil fertility decreased food production declined and cycles of famine and malnutrition increased in the mid-1980s (Gasana, 2002). Additionally, the country was beset by a persistent drought in 1994 that exacerbated the crisis (Percival and Homer-Dixon, 1996). The degradation of the environmental fabric of the country did not just occur in 1994, but rather it was a gradual, structural process that had begun with the colonial era and its economic system of resource exploitation. Whether this deteriorating environment was an aggravating factor or the main cause of the genocide is a point to be debated.

Val Percival and Thomas Homer-Dixon point out that environmental scarcity has four specific social effects: decreased agricultural potential, regional economic decline, population displacement, and the disruption of legitimized and authoritative institutions and social relations (Percival and Homer-Dixon, 1996). All of these factors were evident in Rwanda leading up to the genocide. Certainly each one or a combination of all could facilitate the conflict between the Hutu and Tutsi.

Finding a response to what role natural resource conflict had in causing the genocide is not an easy one to answer. To the outside world Rwanda was a shining model of development in Africa. International aid agencies were pouring money into the country. They seemed oblivious to the downward spiral of Rwandan society. Peter Uvin writes that "where development aid provides a large share of the financial and moral resources of government and civil society, development aid cannot help but play a crucial role in shaping the processes that lead to violence" (Uvin, 1998). The causes of the genocide are difficult to decipher and it may be impossible to pinpoint on a specific cause, but doubtless the degraded environment and inequitable distribution of natural resources played critical roles.

REFERENCES

Gasana, J. (2002, September/October). "Remember Rwanda," *Worldwatch Magazine* 15(5).

Gourevitch, Philip. (1998). *We Wish to Inform You That Tomorrow We Will Be Killed with Our Families*. New York: Picador USA, 50.

Irivuzumugabe, Eric. (2009). *My Father, Maker of the Trees*. Grand Rapids, MI: Baker Books.

Percival, Val, and Thomas Homer-Dixon. (1996, September). "Environmental scarcity and violent conflict: The case of Rwanda," *Journal of Environment and Development* 5(3), 270–291.

Prosterman, Roy, and Jeffrey Riedinger. (1987). *Land Reform and Democratic Development*. Baltimore, MD: Johns Hopkins University Press.

Uvin, Peter. (1998). *Aiding Violence: The Development Enterprise in Rwanda*. West Hartford, CT: Kumarian Press.

Weinberg, Bill. (1991). *War on the Land: Ecology and Politics in Central America*. London: Zed Books Ltd.

22

WHAT ROLE HAVE NATURAL RESOURCES PLAYED IN THE SUDANESE CIVIL WAR?

OVERVIEW
M. Troy Burnett

Images of war, famine, drought, and suffering unfortunately come to mind when one mentions Sudan. The tragedy of the "lost boys"[1] has indelibly left its mark on the modern era. The sad fact is that since gaining independence from Britain in 1956, Sudan has been plagued by an intractable and endless civil war. It ranks as the longest conflict in African history, claiming the lives of more than 2 million people and displacing millions more. Despite a Comprehensive Peace Agreement (CPA) in 2005 between the government of Sudan and the Sudan People's Liberation Movement (SPLM) that effectively created the state of South Sudan, the unrest and conflict continue—namely in the Darfur region and Western Sudan.

With an area covering 2.5 million square kilometers, Sudan is the largest country in Africa. Its population is close to 40 million people. Its most notable geographic feature is the Nile River, along which the majority of the 40 million people

---

[1] Beginning in the late 1980s, roughly 26,000 Sudanese boys, mostly from the Dinka and Nuer tribes and predominately Christian, were forced from their villages. Snaking their way through Sudan, hordes of boys aged 5 through approximately 13 gathered in a massive confluence in the hope of finding safety. The "lost boys" (so dubbed by aid workers after Peter Pan's cadre of orphans) fled their homeland by foot across 1,000 miles of rugged and dangerous terrain to a refugee camp in Ethiopia. The trek through the sub-Saharan heat and wilderness took two months.

live. Historically, the Blue and White Nile river basins have acted as pathways for invasion and exploitation by northern invaders—the Egyptian pharaohs, the Mameluks, the Ottomans, and, in the 19th century, the British. The latter in particular were keen on creating and maintaining separate political and cultural systems between the north and south.

BACKGROUND

By the time large-scale fighting broke out in 1983, the SPLM called for the overthrow of all Islamic leaders from national power. Influenced by communist theories of social and economic reform, the movement's leaders emphasized a Sudan based on equality rather than factors of race, ethnicity, religious persuasion, gender, or cultural beliefs. In response, an Islamic fundamentalist movement grew in northern Sudan. Islamic clerics took over control of the government on June 30, 1989, and began to rule the country through the military and the Sharia (Islamic) law.

Fighting had severely affected the entire nation and had even led to starvation and bloodshed in neighboring nations, a development that threatened to widen the war beyond Sudan. In 1992 and 1993, a peace agreement was reached through the auspices of the Inter-Governmental Authority on Drought and Desertification. The organization offered a secularization plan to separate religion from the state in order to reduce the ethnic and religious tensions fueling the conflict. Although the Islamic government rejected the plan for religious reasons in late 1993, they reached a peace agreement with rebel groups four years later. The government, however, still adamantly refused to remove Islamic values from the functions of the state, which has prompted rebel factions to reject the government's recent call for "peace and unity." A cease-fire agreement was never established and fighting resumed.

After another decade of intermittent fighting, on January 19, 2002, a cease-fire agreement was brokered by the United States and Switzerland in the hope of ending the civil war. The agreement called for a cessation of fighting in the Nuba Mountain region, a key stronghold for southern forces, a halt to the aerial bombardment of civilians, and the establishment of "tranquility zones" to allow humanitarian aide to resume unfettered. Further negotiations on power- and revenue-sharing between the north and south eventually led to the signing of the CPA in January 2005, formally ending the two-decade second phase of the war, which is estimated to have killed more than 2 million people and internally displaced more than 4.5 million others from their homes due to fighting or war-related famine.

The CPA established a semi-autonomous region for 10 states in the south of Sudan and called for a referendum in 2011 in which southerners could elect to secede and form an independent country. In the South Sudanese referendum, held in January 2011, more than 98 percent of southern voters opted to secede. The Republic of South Sudan was formally declared on July 9, 2011; however, hostilities along border areas and in the disputed region of Abyei have continued.

The seemingly intractable war has often been characterized as a conflict between the Arab Muslim north and the African Christian south, in other words an ethno-religious–motivated conflict. Indeed, along with the religious differences, Sudan comprises more than 700 tribes speaking up to 300 languages and dialects. Similar to most African countries, Sudan was a colonial-territorial entity that amalgamated and manipulated many different ethno-linguistic groups. And like most post-colonial African states, conflict was seemingly inevitable. For instance, in this section Meredith Deboom argues that while oil and other natural resources have certainly complicated Sudan's history of conflict the roots are much deeper, involving the lasting effects of colonialism and the long history of cultural differences and unsettled grievances between the north and south. She writes, "rather than acting as the root cause of Sudan's civil wars, oil has served as a conflict multiplier, reinforcing and deepening previously-existing disagreements and grievances, including identity-based differences and historical inequalities between northern and southern Sudan rooted in colonialism."

On the other hand, as I argue in an essay on Darfur, political-cultural reasons are just part of the story; rather, one has to assess the influence of natural resources and the way they are managed, controlled, and distributed across various sectors of society. The quality of the natural resource base, namely water and land, often plays the key role in triggering and perpetuating conflicts; especially, if one group perceives another as exploiting and benefiting disproportionately. As Suliman notes, "Few wars are ever fought in the name of their real cause" (Suliman 1994).

Although the Sudan is a vast country with a relatively small population, the natural resources are physically and socially unevenly distributed. For example, the discovery of vast reserves of oil in 1976 in Bentiu in southern Sudan arguably continues to fuel lingering tensions between the countries. North American and European oil companies have poured millions of dollars into the region. Unfortunately, it has been widely reported that the revenue has greatly assisted the governments in the purchase of weaponry and inadvertently sanctioned repressive policies. For instance, Amnesty International, in a report entitled "The Human Price of Oil in Sudan," observed the displacement of thousands of Dinka and Nuer people by the government who felt it necessary to open up oil fields. Further, an armed conflict between Sudan and South Sudan took place in 2012. Called the Heglig Crisis, the fight between the two countries was over the oil fields between the South Sudan's Unity and Sudan's South Kordofan regions. South Sudan invaded and briefly occupied the small border town of Heglig before being pushed back by the Sudanese army.

Whatever the causes, social or environmental/ecological, the situation between and within Sudan and South Sudan is fragile, with armed conflict lurking beneath the surface.

REFERENCE

Suliman, Mohamed. (1994). *Civil War in Sudan: The Impact of Ecological Degradation.* Zurich, Centre for Security Studies and Conflict Research, and Bern, Swiss Peace Foundation, Environment and Conflicts Project, p. 8.

FURTHER READING

Johnson, Douglas H. (2003). "The root causes of Sudan's civil wars," *African Security Review 12*(2), 115–115.
Ross, Michael. (2002). "Natural Resources and Civil War: An Overview with Some Policy Options." Draft report prepared for conference on The Governance of Natural Resources Revenues, World Bank and Agence Française de Développement, Paris, December 9–10.
Ross, Michael L. (2004). "What do we know about natural resources and civil war?," *Journal of Peace Research 41*(3), 337–356.
Salih, Kamal Osman. (1990). "British policy and the accentuation of inter-ethnic divisions: the case of the Nuba Mountains region of Sudan, 1920–1940," *African Affairs*, 417–436.

OIL IN THE SUDAN: A CONFLICT MULTIPLIER, NOT THE SOLE CAUSE
Meredith DeBoom

Even before its 1956 independence, Sudan had been plagued by conflict, both internal and external. Violence peaked in two civil wars (1955–1972 and 1983–2005), both of which were rooted in disagreements between northern and southern Sudan. Oil has certainly complicated Sudan's history of conflict, including making more difficult the implementation of the 2005 Comprehensive Peace that paved the way for South Sudan's 2011 independence, and some analysts have cited oil as the primary catalyst of violence in Sudan. Yet, a careful examination of the timing of Sudan's conflicts, the lasting effects of colonialism, and the long history of differences and grievances between northern and southern Sudan demonstrates that oil has been far from the only catalyst of violence. Rather than acting as the root cause of Sudan's civil wars, oil has served as a conflict multiplier, reinforcing and deepening previously existing disagreements and grievances, including identity-based differences and historical inequalities between northern and southern Sudan rooted in colonialism.

The argument that oil caused the Sudanese civil wars draws on the "greed" explanation for conflict. This explanation, along with its "grievance" counterpart, is based in the research of Dr. Paul Collier, professor of economics and public policy at the University of Oxford, and Dr. Anke Hoeffler, an economist at the University of Oxford's Centre for the Study of African Economies. According to Drs. Collier and Hoeffler, most conflicts can be understood as motivated by greed, grievance, or both of these factors. Actors motivated by greed join rebellions primarily for economic reasons (i.e., by determining that the potential benefits of participating in the conflict are greater than the potential costs). The potential to access revenues from resources such as oil is one example of a conflict participation benefit. According to this theory, even though commercial-scale oil extraction did not begin in Sudan until 1999, it is possible that conflict actors in the second civil war were motivated by the opportunity to gain control over potential future oil revenues.

However, by framing the second Sudanese civil war as greed motivated, analysts risk overlooking persistent grievances that have contributed even more directly to Sudan's violent history. Grievances, according to Collier and Hoeffler, refer to identity and exploitation-based motivations for conflict. In the case of Sudan, these grievances include persistent inequalities between northern and southern Sudan and related identity-based grievances tied to religion, race, and language, among other factors, that are rooted in Sudan's colonial history.

From 1899 until 1955, Sudan was a British colony governed in cooperation with Egypt. Until 1946, the British administered northern and southern Sudan as separate regions. Trade between the two regions was discouraged, and southern Sudan was largely ignored by the British. In 1946, however, the British integrated northern and southern Sudan. Because Arabic was named the official language of governance and British-administered education in northern Sudan was far more comprehensive than education in the south, northern elites dominated this unified governance structure. When the British awarded independence to the northern-dominated government in 1955, southern members of the Sudan Defense Force mutinied, instigating the first civil war between the north and south.

The Addis Ababa Agreement ended the first civil war in 1972 by establishing a Southern Sudan Autonomous Region, but it did not address the underlying inequalities. Furthermore, the agreement was quickly violated by the national government, which declared northern ownership of cross-border oil fields under exploration in the late 1970s and proclaimed Sudan to be an Islamic state in 1983. Southern leaders interpreted this latter declaration as an indication of the national government's lack of respect for Sudan's religious and cultural diversity. In protest, they formed the Sudan People's Liberation Movement (SPLM), setting off the second Sudanese civil war in 1983. While the SPLM is often portrayed as a pro-south organization, it initially framed itself as pro-Sudanese unity and as an advocate for all Sudanese citizens, not just southerners, who were being oppressed by the national government. While the northern seizure of cross-border oilfields provided one incentive for the SPLM to take action, it was far from the only reason. The declaration of Sudan as an Islamic state, the expropriation of land by national government-affiliated commercial agricultural actors, persistent conflicts between Arab herders and southern farmers, and, most importantly, the continued dominance of northern elites in national politics, were equally, if not more, important catalysts for the second civil war.

In addition to generating significant inequality, the separate governance of northern and southern Sudan under British colonialism also strengthened identity-based differences between the two regions. Many of these differences existed before British colonialism and the Turko-Egyptian colonialism (1820–1885) that preceded it, but colonialism institutionalized and politicized them. While the British treated northern Sudan as a Middle Eastern entity, they characterized southern Sudan as most similar to British colonies in East Africa. Through this separate governance, northern Sudanese culture became increasingly Arabic in terms of trade and Islamic in terms of religion and culture, while British missionaries promoted Christianity in the south. Northern elites were trained in Arabic and enjoyed substantial support for education, while southern elites were trained in English and British-provided education was minimal. These policies made it difficult for southern Sudanese to take leadership roles in the unified Sudanese government after 1946. Even more importantly, they politicized differences between northern and southern Sudan by administering the two regions in a hierarchical manner that privileged the north, promoting inequalities that continue to drive conflict in the region today.

While oil has complicated Sudan's history, Sudan's civil wars are more directly based in historical grievances that began long before the discovery of oil. By framing the Sudanese civil wars as caused solely by oil, we risk over-simplifying an incredibly complex conflict that has its roots not only in economic motivations but also in long-standing grievances between what is now Sudan and South Sudan, including a history of inequality rooted in colonialism and identity-based grievances tied to race, language, and religion. Oil has served as a conflict multiplier in Sudan's violent history, complicating and reinforcing these grievances, but it has been far from the only conflict catalyst in the Sudanese civil wars.

FURTHER READING

BBC World News. (2011, July 5). "South Sudan Profile." Accessed April 15, 2014, at http://www.bbc.com/news/world-africa-14069082.

BBC World News. (2015, December 7). "Sudan Profile." Accessed April 15, 2014, at http://www.bbc.com/news/world-africa-14094995.

Collier, Paul. (2009). *War, Guns, and Votes: Democracy in Dangerous Places.* New York: Harper/HarperCollins Publishers.
Collier, Paul, and Anke Hoeffler. (2004). "Greed and grievance in civil war," *Oxford Economic Papers 56*(4), 563–595.
Collins, Robert O. (2008). *A History of Modern Sudan.* Cambridge, UK: Cambridge University Press.
Deng, Francis. (1995). *War of Visions: Conflict of Identities in the Sudan.* Washington, DC: Brookings Institution.
Johnson, Douglas H. (2011). *The Root Causes of Sudan's Civil Wars: Peace or Truce,* revised edition. Martlesham, UK: James Currey.
University of California, Berkeley. (2011). "Understanding Sudan: A Teaching and Learning Resource." International and Area Studies. Accessed April 20, 2014, at http://understandingsudan.org/index.html.

CONFLICT IN DARFUR—THE RESOURCE PERSPECTIVE

M. Troy Burnett

The ongoing conflicts in Darfur in particular and the Sudan in general are both the result of disputes over natural resources and the cause of further environmental and resource degradation. It's a vicious cycle wherein war and instability further undermines the subsistence livelihoods of the people who are forced to seek desperate, often further violent, solutions. Without a multi-level strategy that involves stable and facilitative governance and natural resource management, conflict will ever linger near the surface in this region.

Geographically, the Sudan and Darfur are situated on the edge of a harsh desert in an area that chronically suffers from an overall lack of natural resources. The vulnerability of livelihoods in the region is typical of the rest of the Sahel, which also suffers from many of the same issues: environmental degradation, population growth, poor governance, conflict, climate change, under-investment, dependency on natural resources, and lack of opportunities. While resource scarcity and competition is not solely responsible for conflict—indeed there are many cases where scarcity promotes peace and cooperation—it is a major driver, and must be seen in the wider political and economic context.

Being predominantly in the sub-tropical high-pressure zone, Darfur has low and variable rainfall with marked wet (summer) and dry (winter) seasons as the inter-tropical convergence zone shifts north and south. The variability in water supply is exacerbated by the region's limited storage capacity. The complex geology minimizes groundwater storage and the hot-dry air maximizes evaporation rates. As moisture is the primary determinant of the amount and distribution of

People try to earn some money by selling peanuts and sugar outside of their shelters in East Darfur, Sudan. (David Snyder/Dreamstime.com)

vegetation, the variability and poor storage is reflected in the high spatial and temporal variability of vegetation. More significantly, droughts have become more frequent; 16 of the 20 driest years recorded have occurred since 1972. Climate change models also predict a reduction in the length of the growing period and increase in the processes of desertification. This will have a considerable impact on subsistence livelihoods and resource security.

Nevertheless, scarcity and variability are nothing new to the people of the region who have over time, even in the era of colonization, developed a high level of localized management and resource-sharing strategies. During the dry season, livestock migrates off the rangeland to the wadi areas for shade and to feed on crop detritus. A variety of longer-distance migrations also take place, including from the wet-season pasturelands in the north to the less-arid south for the dry season. This system requires a high degree of cooperation between pastoralist and farming communities to determine access for herders and to safeguard farmers' crops from grazing animals. A wide range of traditional rules for the management of long-distance routes, access-to-water sources, and dispute resolution evolved and were maintained over time.

Unfortunately, in the past few decades traditional, long-standing tribal-level governance has been weakened and replaced with the modern top-down, centralized state system. The tribal system effectively lost its legal authority with the abolishment of the Native Administration System in 1971. Profound political and social changes resulted, including the redrawing of state boundaries that cut across tribal affiliations and territories. In terms of environmental and natural resource management, the state model has proved inconsistent, unreliable, and corrupt in its management of resources.

The abolition of the Native Administration System in 1971 preceded the 1972–1973 drought, which meant that there was reduced governance capacity to address the problems of migration and resource tensions that resulted. The most severe drought, in 1984, triggered major migrations and changes in livelihoods, again in the absence of tribal governance. While cooperation, coordination, and trust decreased, the number of weapons increased to go along with an increase in ethnic and religious scapegoating. One result was the first significant conflict between Fur and Arab tribes from 1987 to 1989. As noted in a United Nations Environmental Program (UNEP) report, the conflict was the result of both natural resources stresses and political failure (UNEP, 2004). UN observers highlighted the weak governance at the time and the fact that the conflict was not an isolated event: since 1975 environment and resources have been key components in 27 separate conflicts in Darfur (UNEP, 2004).

As economic and political power became concentrated in the capital, Khartoum, Darfur suffered from under-investment in infrastructure and services. Lack of education and health services as well as constrained access to markets restricted opportunities, making it more difficult to adapt to the deteriorating environmental conditions.

Even with the resource stresses and tensions, Darfur experienced significant growth in population—from just over 1 million people in the mid-1950s to around 6.5 million in the early 2000s. Lacking diversified economic opportunities and technological support, this increase put pressure on both farmer and pastoral livelihoods. The UN-sponsored conference "Environmental Degradation as a Cause of Conflict in Darfur," held in Khartoum in December 2004, noted the following links between population, environment, and conflict: (1) an increase in population density intensified cropping and grazing; (2) subsequently shorter fallow periods for fields and overgrazed rangeland; (3) a deterioration in yields and carrying capacities caused by both previous factors; (4) larger areas needed to support the same yields and herds while demands and herds increased; and (5) herders and farmers aggressively competing for access to resources, which led to escalating tensions and violent conflict.

These population stresses also resulted in rapid degradation of forested lands. Again, UNEP's Post Conflict Environmental Assessment of Sudan estimated that deforestation in Darfur was in excess of 1 percent per annum. Forestry is key to the region's stability, not just because of its value for timber and fuel but also because of its role in protecting land quality. UNEP estimates that within 5 to 10 years the northern states will be dependent on the south and Darfur for charcoal, exacerbating local conflict over control of dwindling natural resources.

The chronic processes of environmental degradation and the loss of traditional environmental governance have been greatly magnified during the more recent crisis, both by the effects of massive displacement and by the fighting itself. The high concentrations of desperate people in Darfur are causing local resource depletion. In Abu Shouk and Al Salaam camps, 12 to 15 boreholes of the 66 drilled have run dry. IDP camps are generally located on the outskirts of market towns, resulting in the destruction of shelterbelts, forestry, and farmland. In addition to displacement, the following processes are causing severe environmental degradation:

1. Uncontrolled deforestation is taking place, in the context of a breakdown of governance, driven by the role of timber and fuel wood in the war and crisis economy.
2. Natural and physical assets are being destroyed as a feature of the war (e.g., farmers' crops are grazed by pastoralists' livestock, rangeland is burnt to prevent grazing, hand pumps are destroyed).
3. Crisis livelihood strategies have short-term horizons, undermining the natural resource base.
4. Migration routes are blocked, leading to overgrazing in areas where livestock are concentrated. (Bromwich 2008)

The solution to the problems in Sudan and Darfur is complex, though the recent separation of the country into two independent units offers hope for greater stability. Because Darfur's economy, like most regional economies in Sudan and South Sudan, are founded on natural resources, equitable and sustainable environmental governance at village and tribal level needs to be restored as a foundation for development and conflict management. This will allow communities to better address and minimize the impacts of recurring droughts, vegetative inconsistencies, and crop failure. Local, tribal groups have long survived in this region utilizing placed-based experiences, knowledge, and cooperation. Within the context of a facilitative centralized state and international donor community, the more local communities are empowered to control their own livelihoods as they have done for millennia, the more likely violent conflicts will cease to be the only option.

REFERENCES

Bromwich, Brendan. (2008). "Environmental Degradation and Conflict in Darfur: Implications for Peace and Recovery," *Humanitarian Exchange, 39.*

United Nations Environmental Program (UNEP). (2004). "Environmental Degradation as a Cause of Conflict in Darfur." Conference proceedings, University for Peace, Khartoum. Accessed March 2, 2016, at http://cms.unige.ch/isdd/IMG/pdf/darfur_unpeace.pdf.

FURTHER READING

Tearfund. (2007). "Darfur: Relief in a Vulnerable Environment." Accessed March 2, 2016, http://www.tearfund.org/webdocs/website/Campaigning/Policy%20and%20research/Relief%20in%20a%20vulnerable%20envirionment%20final.pdf.

Tearfund. (2007). "Darfur: Water Supply in a Vulnerable Environment." Accessed March 2, 2016, at http://www.unep.org/disastersandconflicts/portals/155/countries/Sudan/pdf/dafur_water/Darfur%20Water%20Resources%20TF.pdf.

Thornton, P. K., P. G. Jones, T. Owiyo, R. L. Kruska, et al. (2006). "Mapping Climate Vulnerability and Poverty in Africa." International Livestock Research Institute, Energy and Resources Institute and Africa Centre for Technology Studies. Accessed March 2, 2016, at www.napa-pana.org/extranapa/UserFiles/File/Mapping_Vuln_Africa.pdf.

23

Do Diamonds Have a Negative Influence on Development in Africa?

OVERVIEW
Laura Kerrigan and Jacob C. Brenner

Many people are aware of the controversial diamond industry in Africa thanks to the 2006 Hollywood film *Blood Diamond*. In this portrayal of the scramble to control the diamond mines in Sierra Leone, the film depicts a society torn apart by the 11-year civil war between government loyalists and rebel factions such as the Revolutionary United Front. The film depicts local people who were enslaved to harvest diamonds, which in turn funded the insurgents' increasingly successful war effort. While the film raised public awareness of the controversial nature of diamond mining in parts of Africa and drew attention to some of the key issues, it only scratched the surface of this extremely complicated development conundrum.

BACKGROUND

For a more complete understanding we must consider several facts that are either distorted or not elaborated in the film. For example, although the African continent faces challenges typical of the developing world, the specific places in which diamonds are produced (e.g., South Africa, Botswana, Sierra Leone, to name a few) have very different historical, socioeconomic, cultural, and political circumstances. Generalizations about diamond mining and its relationship with development in Africa are therefore highly problematic.

Nevertheless, Africa stands apart from other world regions in its role in diamond production and trade. Most of the world's gem-quality diamonds are produced in the world's poorest region south of the Sahara desert known as sub-Saharan Africa. The primary African diamond-producing countries are Ivory Coast, Liberia, and Sierra Leone in the west; Angola, Central African Republic, Democratic Republic of Congo, in the center; Tanzania in the east; and Namibia, Botswana and South Africa in the south. Most African countries began mining diamonds around the time of the First World War, but there is significant variability among these countries. For example, diamond extraction began in South Africa as early as 1870, while in Liberia it started much later, in 1950. The fact that Africa's various countries became involved with diamond production at different historical moments makes for a range of experiences in terms of development.

Many sub-Saharan African countries remained European colonies until the mid- to late 20th century. As a result of their very recent independence, these countries tend to struggle with political instability as the social and cultural institutions disrupted by colonial rule re-emerge in new geopolitical circumstances. Transferring a high-stakes industry such as diamond mining from colonial to independent control in a political climate of "ineffective and corrupt government bodies and general lack of judicial systems and oversight" (Sethi, 2011) can be a risky venture. Thus, sub-Saharan Africa struggles to harness the extreme economic potential of a now globalized, relatively decentralized, diamond industry that was controlled for decades through a sort of colonial monopoly.

In the many places in Africa where precious mineral extraction remains unregulated and labor laws are weak or non-existent, there is great potential to control mines through forced labor. Raw material from mines in Africa is typically exported to refineries in Southeast Asia, where it is processed for entry into the global market (Enough Project, 2011). Before leaving Africa, however, diamonds can be stolen or otherwise co-opted by armed militias. Extreme profits from clandestine diamond trading typically go toward buying more weapons to consolidate control over mines, a process that culminates in "systematic mass killings, gross human rights violations, atrocities against women and children, and forced migration" (Sethi, 2011). Clandestine trading also enables these militias to gain political and economic leverage against enemies (including state governments) through bribery and extortion. Diamonds, then, are not only an object of struggle in themselves, but also become fuel for ongoing local and regional conflicts. When political instability, extreme wealth potential, and globalization combine, the stage is set for violence. Hence the "blood" in the recent Hollywood film title and the now commonplace term, blood diamonds.

The global nature of the diamond industry makes it difficult for retailers and consumers to know where the diamonds they buy originated and by what means they appeared on the market. While this obscurity makes it difficult for the international community to promote peace and justice in the diamond industry, there have been significant advances in recent years through the introduction of the Kimberly Process Certification Scheme in 2003 and legislation such as the Dodd-Frank Wall Street Reform Act, signed in 2010. Diamond certification initiatives such as these have led many (including some critics of the industry as a whole) to see hope in diamonds as a just and sustainable development mechanism for countries in sub-Saharan Africa.

The Kimberly Process Certification Scheme (KPCS) was created to control the illegal mining and trade of diamonds from violence-ridden countries in Africa. It relies on the cooperation of national governments, business groups, and non-governmental organizations (NGOs), to regulate their own role in the diamond trade to achieve the mutual goal of peaceful and just development in the diamond industry. The KPCS uses incentives rather than punitive measures to encourage countries to act for the common good as well as their own best interests (Sethi, 2011). The KPCS is regulated through a peer-review process, through which a country can be expelled from the certification scheme or banned from trading, importing, and exporting diamonds (Paes, 2005). The KPCS is designed to be flexible and dynamic, with all parties involved meeting twice a year to improve and refine it (Bone, 2012). While the KPCS has great intentions, many scholars agree that the practicality of this process has many flaws.

Legislation in the United States, such as the Dodd-Frank Wall Street Reform Act, signed in 2010, is another promising attempt to turn blood diamonds into a just and peaceful instrument of economic development. This policy requires U.S.companies to undergo mineral supply chain audits to ensure that the raw materials used in their products are not tied to ongoing conflicts in central Africa (Enough Project, 2011).

Even with these programs in place, development indicators for precious-mineral-rich countries in sub-Saharan Africa remain low. Sierra Leone, for example, has gone under the KPCS, but still has a UN Human Development Index (HDI) value of 0.359 (out of 1.000) (United Nations Development Reports, 2013). Sierra Leone's HDI value has improved since 2000 (during its civil war it was 0.244), but it still ranks low compared to other developing countries worldwide and within Africa. Egypt, by contrast, has a HDI value of 0.662. Thus, certification of the diamond industry is no guarantee of safe and just economic growth.

If conflict is taken out of the diamond-mining equation, it has the potential to be beneficial to poor countries in Africa that rely on minerals and other raw commodities for development revenue. If miners worked in decent conditions and earned a fair living wage, if the trade of diamonds and other lucrative minerals could be regulated, or if the political climate in diamond-producing countries independently became more stable, the precious minerals could provide enormous benefits to poor communities. For now, non-governmental organizations such as

Hope for Congo, the Enough Project, and Amnesty International are stationed within some of sub-Saharan Africa's most stricken communities. There they work toward making mining practices, both good and bad, transparent to the international community.

REFERENCES

Bone, Andrew. (2012). "The Kimberly Process Certification Scheme: the primary safeguard for the diamond industry," in Päiva Lujala and Siri Aas Rustad (eds.), *High-Value Natural Resources and Post-Conflict Peacebuilding*. New York: Earthscan, 189–194.

Enough Project. (2011). "Understanding Conflict Minerals Provisions." Accessed March 2, 2016, at http://www.enoughproject.org/special-topics/understanding-conflict-minerals-provisions.

Paes, W. C. (2005). "'Conflict diamonds' to 'clean diamonds': the development of the Kimberley Process Certification Scheme," in Matthias Basedau and Andreas Mehler (eds.), *Resource Politics in Sub-Saharan Africa*. Hamburg, Germany: Institut fur Afrika-Kunde, 305–323.

Sethi, S. Prakash. (2011). *Globalization and Self-Regulation: The Crucial Role That Corporate Codes of Conduct Play in Global Business*. New York: Palgrave Macmillan, 213–214.

United Nations Development Reports. (2013). "International Human Development Indicators." Accessed March 2, 2016, at http://hdr.undp.org/en/countries.

FURTHER READING

Campbell, Greg. (2004). *Blood Diamonds: Tracing the Deadly Path of the World's Most Precious Stones*, revised and expanded edition. New York: Basic Books.

Prendergast, John, and Sasha Lezhnev. (2009, November 10). "From mine to mobile phone: the conflict minerals supply chain," Enough, the Project to End Genocide and Crimes against Humanity. Accessed March 8, 2016, at http://www.enoughproject.org/publications/mine-mobile-phone.

DIAMOND MINING AND VIOLENCE ON THE AFRICAN CONTINENT

Laura Kerrigan and Jacob C. Brenner

In many sub-Saharan countries, such as Angola, Democratic Republic of Congo, Liberia, and Sierra Leone, armed conflict fueled by precious mineral extraction has had detrimental social and economic outcomes. Although protocols such as the Kimberly Process have begun to shift the way that diamond extraction affects African nations, there are still many hurdles to human development that still need

Soldiers from the Revolutionary United Front (RUF) ride in a truck at their base in the outskirts of Freetown, Sierra Leone, in 1997. Through the exploitation of Sierra Leone's diamond trade, the RUF earned an estimated $25 million per year during the 1990s. (AP/Wide World Photos)

to be addressed. Additionally, several other precious minerals, including tin, tungsten, tantalum, and gold, are not regulated in the same way that diamonds are and still fuel ongoing violent conflict (McHaney and Veit, 2009).

The term "blood diamonds" specifically refers to diamonds that are "extracted and exported from particular regions in sub-Saharan Africa that are still ravaged by vicious armed conflicts" (Orogun, 2004). Warlords and armed militia groups rely on the illegal sale of diamonds in exchange for weapons, which aid in the control of these geographic regions. In the case of Sierra Leone, rebel militias, most notably the Revolutionary United Front (RUF), would force civilians (including children) into slave conditions in order to harvest diamonds or assist in the armed conflict. Sierra Leone is just one case of several that have the same story. In fact, the leader and founder of RUF was backed by the notorious Liberian warlord Charles Taylor, who also used child soldiers and forced civilian labor to continue the civil war and diamond extraction in Liberia.

The conflicts in Liberia and Sierra Leone, which were inextricably bound to the diamond trade, had atrocious results, which have severely slowed the development in these nations. According to Global Witness, a non-governmental organization (NGO) that focuses on natural resource related conflict and corruption, the human cost of these conflicts was staggering, with estimates of close to 200,000 people killed, 2 million displaced, and half of Sierra Leone's female population subjected to sexual violence including rape, torture, and sexual slavery. Even though the Kimberly Process went into effect in 2004, the losses that occurred in these resource rich countries have not been remediated. These losses cannot be ignored when thinking about development, as they are tied to the financial and social progress of these nations. Looking at the World Bank data addressing poverty, the percentage of citizens in Sierra Leone living on less than two U.S. dollars a day was 79.6 percent in 2011.

The Kimberley Process Certification Scheme (KPCS) was put in place to try to end the atrocities that were continuously occurring within diamond-rich countries in Africa. The peer-review mechanism that expels countries from the KPCS is problematic. For example, when the Democratic Republic of Congo and the Republic of Congo (neighboring central African nations) agreed to sign on to the Kimberley Process, they agreed to stop the flow of conflict-ridden diamonds through their countries. When the Republic of Congo was expelled from the Kimberley Process in July of 2004, the movement of conflict minerals out of the Democratic Republic of Congo into the Republic of Congo increased, which escalated violence throughout the region.

Additionally, the Kimberley Process is unique in that it was born out of action taken by impacted national governments, the diamond industry, and NGOs. The Kimberley Process was not created by the United Nations or any other transnational governing body, and has limited influence over the practical application and enforcement mechanisms in the affected regions. While there is potential for strength within the Kimberley Process to regulate the flow of diamonds throughout Africa, it relies on the state-led border controls. These border controls, however, are unreliable due to weak national governments (Haufler, 2009).

The reason why the process relies so heavily on state border control is because illegal trafficking of diamonds and other precious minerals is a crucial part of this conflict-ridden process. The illegal trade of precious minerals out of the Democratic Republic of Congo, for example, is an important case study to look at when deconstructing the complex nature of these issues. While this case study does not focus on diamonds, it looks at minerals that are just as precious and used in electronics all around the world.

The minerals trade has been fueling the ongoing violent conflict in the eastern Democratic Republic of Congo since 1998. Since that time it is estimated that more than 5.4 million civilians have been killed by this conflict over minerals. Armed groups, including the Democratic Forces for the Liberation of Rwanda, local militias, Congolese rebel groups, and units of the Congolese army, largely control the mines (Prendergast and Lezhnev, 2009). The domination of the minerals trade by different armed groups is carried out in various ways. Armed groups coerce miners into working in desperate and dangerous conditions. Mass rape is used as an intimidation strategy to control communities and has led to the spread of sexually transmitted diseases such as HIV/AIDS. Through violent manipulation, armed groups are able to profit from the illicit trade of conflict minerals—tin, tungsten, tantalum, and gold.

These raw minerals follow smuggling routes through neighboring sub-Saharan African nations (namely Rwanda and Uganda), with the raw materials being exchanged for weapons and funds to support armed groups. These smuggling routes are key to the success of the various militia groups that control the mines.

In addition to the practical shortcomings of the Kimberley Process, the United Nations Development Program suggests that diamond-rich countries in Africa have not benefited developmentally since the Kimberley Process was enacted in 2004. Sierra Leone, for example, has gone under the KPCS, but still has a Human Development Index value of 0.359 (out of 1.000) (United Nations Development Reports, 2013). This is certainly an improvement from the HDI value of 0.244 it had in 2000 during the civil war. However, Libya by contrast has a Human Development Index of 0.769 and in 2000 had an HDI value of 0.704, which suggests that diamonds do not positively influence development.

While it is difficult to advocate whether the presence of diamonds in Africa is good or bad due to the vastly diverse nature of the continent, the historically ubiquitous conflicts surrounding diamond mining suggests the harmful nature of the precious mineral industry in Africa. If a new set of regulations were introduced in addition to the Kimberley Process, it is possible that diamonds could benefit the development of many mineral-rich African nations. However, without a current process that functions well within these weak state governments, natural resource extraction is still fueling many conflicts within the continent of Africa, stagnating development in these regions.

REFERENCES

Haufler, Virginia. (2009). "The Kimberley Process Certification scheme: an innovation in global governance and conflict prevention," *Journal of Business Ethics* 89(4).

Orogun, Paul. (2004). "'Blood diamonds' and Africa's armed conflicts in the post–Cold War era," *World Affairs* 166(3), 151–161.

Prendergast, John, and Sasha Lezhnev. (2009, November 10). "From Mine to Mobile Phone: The Conflict Minerals Supply Chain." Enough, the Project to End Genocide and Crimes against Humanity. Accessed March 8, 2016, at http://www.enoughproject.org/publications/mine-mobile-phone.

United Nations Development Reports. (2013). International Human Development Indicators. Accessed March 21, 2016, at http://hdr.undp.org/en/countries.

DIAMOND MINING: A POSITIVE VIEW
M. Troy Burnett

Diamond mining on the African continent has a bad reputation, and to a certain degree, justifiably so. Movies such as the melodramatic *Blood Diamond* (2006), starring Leonardo DiCaprio, portray heartless insurgents using diamonds to fund violence, slavery, and the kidnapping of children to be used as soldiers while corrupt government officials are either complicit or powerless. Civil war is omnipresent and fed by the money diamond smuggling provides. Greedy mining corporations, engaged in neo-colonial exploitation and the search for a more profitable bottom line, turn a blind eye to both the social and environmental damage. Or so the story goes.

Diamonds, and other resources, have doubtless been used by various military factions to fund their bloody operations. The brutal civil war in Sierra Leone in the late 1990s was the poster child of this situation, giving rise to the world's concern with diamond production while introducing into the lexicon the term "conflict diamonds." It was estimated that roughly 4 percent of the global diamond trade was being used to support violence in Africa, in places such as Angola, Liberia, Ivory Coast, and the Congo River basin. As a result, by July of 2000 the global diamond industry, both its production and distribution businesses, began promoting a zero-tolerance policy towards these conflict diamonds. In conjunction with the United Nations the result was the Kimberley Process Certification System (KPCS). However flawed the certification system has been, presently, almost 100 percent of the diamond industry, including the largest, De Beers, and more than 70 governments are signatories to the certification system, to the degree that the system oversees 99 percent of the trade in conflict-free diamonds.

The fact is, the vast majority of African diamond mining is done in countries at peace— South Africa, Botswana, and Namibia are prime examples—and the revenues are used to support economic and social development, infrastructure and the expansion of trade. Like the mining and usage of any natural resource (e.g., oil, minerals, forestry) there are inherent costs and impacts, but the reality for many African countries, struggling to develop in the post-Cold War, post-colonial world, is that diamond mining creates a livelihood for millions of people, increasing the standard of living and in many cases is used to fund essential government services, including health care, education, and old-age pensions.

Diamond mining in Africa accounts for 65 percent of global production and injects close to $8.5 billion per year into African economies. The majority of this wealth is used in positive ways to promote development. Two cases in particular affirm this—South Africa and Botswana. Nelson Mandela, former esteemed president of post-Apartheid South Africa, understood the value and stated in 1999 that "the diamond industry is vital to the southern African economy" (World Diamond

Council, 2014). His successor Thabo Mbeki agreed, stating: "we know that diamonds are a valued source of employment, foreign exchange, tax revenue, new investments and play a positive role in enhancing the overall economic well being of countries and local communities" (World Diamond Council, 2014). South Africa produces approximately $1.5 billion worth of diamonds a year. The diamond mine in Kimberley, considered to be one of the largest hand-dug mines in the world, has recently been converted into a museum and popular tourist attraction. Millions of dollars are donated from South Africa's diamond industry to sponsor social programs, including HIV/AIDS treatment services, the Soul City Institute for Health and Development Communication, the development and operation of rural schools in the Limpopo province, and the formation of Namaqualand Diamond Fund Trust, which promotes community development, sustainable development, and gender empowerment.

Along with the positive impact in South Africa, the diamond industry in Botswana is viewed as a success story. Since independence, the economy of Botswana has thrived, making it one of Africa's fastest growing—an average of 7 percent per year. With the discovery of diamonds in 1966, mining has been a key factor in this growth. Currently, 80 percent of export profits, 45 percent of government revenue, and 33 percent of the gross domestic product (approximately $3.3 billion) are directly associated with mining, processing, and distribution. The leading company, Debswana, is the first mining company in the world to offer free HIV treatment to its employees and families as part of its comprehensive health-and-disease–management program. The company employs more than 6,500 people, 96 percent of whom are native Botswanans. Indeed, 25 percent of employment in Botswana is directly or indirectly linked to diamonds. In 1966, before independence and before the discovery of diamonds and other natural resources, there were only three secondary schools in Botswana, today there are more than 300. As a result of the economic growth associated with diamonds, every child in Botswana receives free schooling up to the age of 13, after which the government funds 95 percent. According to President Mogae of Botswana, "it is thanks to diamonds that we have seen our country transform from one of the poorest in the world at independence, to the middle income status that is has now attained" (World Diamond Council, 2014). The stable and positive economic growth in Botswana has also allowed the country to protect vast areas of land, turning them into wildlife refuges and national parks.

While not every case of diamond mining in Africa is as positive as Botswana or South Africa, and assuredly there are still environmental costs with mining that need to be addressed, it has and does provide a positive developmental model that other countries in Africa are trying to emulate. Like any resource extraction industry, the revenues can be used for positive economic growth and development or thievery, exploitation, and war. Doubtless, political stability, corporate accountability, a functioning and reliable legal system, and minimal corruption need to be in place so that an industry like diamond mining can be a positive influence.

REFERENCE

World Diamond Council. (2014). "Diamonds and Their Benefits to Africa Fact Sheet." Accessed May 1, 2016, at http://www.diamondfacts.org/pdfs/media/media_resources/fact_sheets/Diamonds_and_Their_Benefits_to_Africa_Fact_Sheet.pdf, 1.

24

WILL THE MINING OF COLTAN IN THE CONGO FURTHER DESTABILIZE THE REGION?

OVERVIEW
M. Troy Burnett

Mobile phones have become a vital part of our lives; as such, the usual afternoon gatherings have transformed into glowing faces lit up by their personal devices and voices have become quiet. Cell phones, like many other electronic devices, require sophisticated parts comprised of expensive rare minerals. One such rare-earth element is coltan. Comprising two parts, columbite and tantalite, coltan ore is refined to extract the valuable tantalum. The refined tantalum is then used in capacitors from everything from cell phones to computers. Yet, often those who use electronic devices are unaware of the social and environmental issues associated with their production. In the case of coltan, labor disputes, social violence, and environmental destruction are an unfortunate part of the process.

An emerging supplier of coltan ore is the Democratic Republic of Congo (DRC)—a post-colonial region historically fraught with authoritarian governance, corruption, and civil instability. The DRC is "blessed" with an abundance of natural resources, yet the trade in valuable minerals such as diamonds, copper, gold, timber, and cobalt has helped finance government atrocities and rebel insurgents.

Coltan can now be added to the list of minerals of what some scholars call the "resource curse." Without proper management and corporate responsibility, the mining of coltan looks to further destabilize the region and continue the rampant cruelty faced by the Congolese.

BACKGROUND

Since the beginning of the 2001, the increasing popularity of cellular devices has fueled the coltan explosion as the need for cellular capacitors has grown exponentially. In 2001, total global production of tantalum reached 2,000 tons, with much of the demand placed upon economically stable countries such as Australia and Canada. However, the global recession of 2008 forced several mines in these countries to shut down, allowing the DRC to emerge as a potential player in the coltan market. The increase in demand allowed for rebels to exploit this new economic source, with much of the local population facing brutalities and injustices on a wide scale. Farmers in local villages in some instances have been forced into mining as their farms have been raided by both rebels and the Congolese army. These former farmers are now reliant on as little as a one dollar a day to survive as the rebel factions control the movement of coltan from the mines to the suppliers. Furthermore, these mines have become a concentration area of prostitution as women are kidnapped and forced into the sex trade. This furthers the spread of diseases including the rampant HIV virus that plagues many African countries. Children have also been forced into the coltan mining trade in an attempt to help provide income for their struggling family. Some estimates place 30 percent of Congolese school children leaving school to work in the mines (Essick, 2001). Moreover, these children are placed at risk to harmful levels of naturally occurring radioactive material that is found in coltan ore. Radon, uranium, thorium, and potassium radionuclides are naturally present in the mines (Baena et al., 2014). Beyond the human risk, the extraction of coltan has created an ecological disaster.

With the movement of workers from larger urban areas to the remote mining camps, came the need for a consistent food source. This has placed pressure on the local ecosystems as many animals have been hunted to extirpation. In particular, the Grauer's gorilla population is now facing extinction as miners have either massacred or driven the local gorilla population from their natural range. The exploitation of animal resources has reached unstable levels, with one study showing that from 1999 to 2001 the local population had gone from eating large game such as buffalo, antelope, and elephant to much smaller prey such as small birds, rodents, and tortoises in order to find adequate sustenance (Baena et al., 2014). Moreover, the artisanal open-pit mining technique used in the coltan operations pollutes groundwater and cause devastating soil erosion. Laborers dig straight down into the earth using shovels and pickaxes in order to extract the precious ore by hand. Radioactive waste is often released into these open pits, leaching into the groundwater and adversely affecting the local ecosystem. In many cases, agricultural lands have grown sterile because of the pollutants left in open-pit operations (Baena et al., 2014). Thus, arable land becomes unusable forcing more farmers to become miners in order to provide for their families. With this, more workers can be extorted and brutalized by various armies throughout the DRC.

Though electronic devices have become a staple in everyday life, they often come at an unseen cost. Behind hidden doors the Congolese people have become an unwilling participant in the drive for technological advancements. The precious coltan ore required in our everyday electronics is now mined feverously by miners in the DRC, many of whom are at the mercy of rebel forces. Trapped within a so called "resource curse," the DRC is being further destabilized from the addition of another precious natural commodity found within its borders. Gold, diamonds, and timber have all added strife upon an already fragile state, and the addition of coltan ore being exploited has only exacerbated the situation. Other countries that could handle excavation of the rare earth material have taken a back seat to the eagerness offered within the DRC. This has lead to corruption throughout the borders of the DRC as rebels and the Congolese armies take advantage of the current economic upswing caused by the coltan boom. Checks and balances have been attempted by suppliers of coltan to manufactures; however, most efforts are in vain. Thus, atrocities, barbarism, and genocide continue to be present throughout this war-torn nation. Without changing the current structure of the coltan ore industry, the DRC is set to become more unstable and the resource curse will continue its reign throughout this volatile African country.

REFERENCES

Baena, Benjamin, Amy Bronson, Tobias Jones, and Lindsey Champaigne. (2014). "Applying and assessing free market environmentalism to the Democratic Republic of Congo's coltan resources: Challenges and possibilities," *Studies by Undergraduate Researchers at Guelph* 7(1), 5–16.

Essick, Kristi. (2001, June 11). "Guns, money and cell phones," *The Industry Standard Magazine*. Accessed March 2, 2016 at http://www.globalissues.org/article/442/guns-money-and-cell-phones.

FURTHER READING

Montague, Dena. (2002). "Stolen goods: Coltan and conflict in the Democratic Republic of Congo," *Sais Review* 22(1), 103–118.

THE MINING OF COLTAN IN THE DRC: THE SAME SAD STORY OF EXPLOITATION AND CONFLICT
Joseph Oppong and M. Troy Burnett

Despite vast mineral wealth, agricultural resources, and energy potential, the Democratic Republic of Congo (DRC) is one of the poorest countries in Africa; an estimated 71 percent of the population lives in poverty. Crippled by years of corruption, mismanagement, and war, its economy has for years teetered on the brink of collapse. In 2001, the United Nations blamed the various factions that fought a brutal five-year war in the DRC for deliberately extending the conflict in order to plunder the country's extensive supplies of gold, diamonds, and timber and columbite-tantalite. Columbite-tantalite, also known as coltan, is a metallic ore that the high-tech boom has made enormously valuable, because it is used

Leopold II was king of Belgium from 1865 until his death in 1909. Largely remembered for his expansion of Belgian power onto the African continent that came to be known as the Belgian Congo, Leopold II terrorized the indigenous people of the region with atrocities such as mass killings and maimings in order to procure slave labor in the rubber industry. (Library of Congress)

in circuit boards in cellphones, laptops, and other electronic devices. The DRC's other abundant mineral resources include copper, cobalt, zinc, and diamonds. Key crops include coffee, cocoa, sugar, tea, palm oil, cotton, and rubber.

Developing countries that have such massive natural resources should be rich from the profits of such resource exploitation, yet exactly the opposite seems to be the case. Instead of economic development and prosperity, such valuable resources fuel and sustain devastating local conflicts that could not be sustained otherwise. Rebel movements target and occupy the resource area, exploit the resource, and use the proceeds to fund weapons purchases and combat training. Activities of opposing sides in such conflicts—including amputations, mass executions, rape, and even more unimaginable atrocities—are designed to force the native residents to leave the area and permit unhindered resource exploitation. Such events are so commonplace that researchers have coined a phrase for it—the "resource curse."

Political instability tends to be the norm. Minor local conflicts quickly escalate into massive regional or even international conflicts because of global interests in particular resources. Developed countries that benefit from such resources usually ignore the human rights abuses and other detrimental consequences of such resource exploitation. In fact, sometimes, the major developed countries support opposing factions in the war, as was the case in Angola and Mozambique, where the United States and the Soviet Union were on opposing sides of devastating conflicts. For nearly three decades, the Angolan people saw nothing but conflict and devastation. Jonas Savimbi, the rebel leader of the National Union for the Total Independence of Angola (UNITA), admitted to funding the war primarily from diamond sales. UNITA took up armed insurrection against the ruling Popular Movement for the Liberation of Angola-Labor Party in 1975 after its joint rival government with the National Front for the Liberation of Angola failed. The civil war ended in April 2002, when UNITA signed a peace deal with the ruling government, and many former UNITA rebels now have entered politics or joined the Angolan Army. UNITA is no longer a rebel movement but a legitimate political party.

Unfortunately, diamonds are not the only resource that attracts conflict or devastating human atrocities. One of the earliest and perhaps most notorious examples is the activity of Belgium's King Leopold II in what was then known as Belgian Congo, currently the DRC. Craving the naturally occurring rubber in the Congo forest, Leopold II imposed forced labor on the citizens, requiring them to produce set quotas or have their hands amputated. Wives and children would be kept hostage until the men returned with the required quota of rubber. This terror campaign created soaring profits for the king while the Congolese were brutalized. Historians estimate that 8 million to 10 million people died from the consequences of violence, forced labor, starvation, and diseases during the period of 1885–1908 under Leopold II. Sadly, this model of production has continued with Congo's other valuable minerals like diamonds and coltan.

Sometimes the scramble for the resource involves local neighbors, not necessarily foreigners. This was the situation in the DRC, where seven African nations engaged in "Africa's World War," a devastating conflict centered on the eastern part of the country, the source of large quantities of gold, diamonds, coltan/tantalum, and other scarce minerals. During the war, Rwanda and Uganda began to see rapid economic growth as the DRC descended into chaos, killing an estimated 30,000 people each month. According to the UN Security Council, global demand for coltan, a vital element used in cell phones, laptops, pagers, and other electronics that abounds in massive quantities in the eastern areas of Congo, is one reason for the ongoing war in the DRC. Military forces from neighboring Rwanda, Uganda, and Burundi smuggle coltan from the DRC and use the revenues to support their efforts in the war. The armies provide protection and security to the individuals and companies extracting the mineral. According to the UN, the Rwandan army was exporting at least 100 tons of coltan per month, making about $20 million per month in coltan sales alone and an estimated $250 million over a period of 18 months, even though no coltan is mined in Rwanda. Will the global demand for cell phones keep the DRC and its people in eternal war and misery? The next time your cell phone rings, will you hear the cries of the Congolese children?

The trade in African blood minerals bears a striking resemblance to the notorious historical trade in another African resource: slave labor. Slaves, captured as prisoners of war, were shipped from Africa to feed the demand for labor on New World plantations. Surplus wealth and capital accumulated in Europe while Africans were stuck with profound social and economic upheaval and increased warfare. Capital generated in Europe procured still more slaves from Africa by delivering European weapons to the continent to fuel local conflicts and produce more prisoners of war. In striking similarity, illicit minerals from Africa feed demand from the developed world; wealth from mineral sales accumulates in Europe, the hub of mineral processing, and finally, light-automatic weapons such as Kalashnikov rifles and grenade launchers, primarily from European and former Eastern Bloc countries, are sent to African conflict zones, thus maintaining the violence in mineral producing areas and producing an unstable local political climate ideal for the extraction and smuggling of more resources.

When put into the context of the resource curse, a popular film like *Blood Diamond* (2006) can provide us with the opportunity to consider the consequences of natural resource exploitation. How much is the world willing to tolerate in order to maintain the flow of such mineral resources? Such an exercise has the potential to stimulate us to ask good questions about the victims, ensure fairer resource exploitation, and think critically about the global distribution of conflict and wealth.

WITH ATTENTION AND GUIDANCE, COLTAN MINING CAN BENEFIT THE DRC
Olga Govdyak and Edward Jackiewicz

The Democratic Republic of Congo (DRC) is a nation historically torn by civil war and perpetual leadership crises. It is also a county that is believed to possess an estimated 64 percent of the global coltan reserves. Due to its high-charge conductor content, coltan is a highly valued mineral that has the potential to bring long-sought economic growth and development to the DRC. However, much of the profits from its extraction and sale have been used as sources of funding for rebel factions, earning it the inglorious title of the "blood diamond of the digital age" (Montague, 2002). As a result, many have argued that the mining and trading of coltan in the DRC should be discouraged. However, I argue that beyond the melodramatic rhetoric, mining operations in the DRC in general and coltan in particular have the potential to stabilize the economy and lift the long struggling country out of poverty and perpetual cycles of underdevelopment.

The rapid acceleration of our digital age is concomitant with the new millennium. The year 2000 saw rapid technological advancement and exponential demand for new varieties of electronic products, which in turn triggered increased demand for coltan. Also referred to as tantalum, coltan is a sturdy metal with exceptional density, double to that of steel, allowing it to withstand extreme levels of heat and corrosion. It is also able to cache and release an electrical charge, thus making it highly suitable for built-in components of portable electronics, including mobile phones, video recorders, pagers, and video game units such as the Playstation (Hayes, 2002). Indeed, without this valuable metal, many of the products of the digital age would not be possible.

Production efforts in Australia (41 percent) and Brazil (21 percent) currently comprise a majority of the global production of coltan, while the DRC currently accounts for a modest 4 percent of the global production in spite of having greater reserves. Unfortunately, much of the DRC's coltan deposits are found in either national parks or politically unstable and contested territory. The eastern regions specifically are home to many of the civil conflicts in the fledgling country and, not surprisingly, the rebel factions have seized control of the mines and used the illegally traded proceeds to buy weapons and support for their struggle. The legitimate, government-supported coltan industry has had to search elsewhere for the resource—tropical rainforests, national parks, and other ecological valuable habitats. On the surface, for global purchasers of coltan from the Congo it appears that the options are either to support the denudation of fragile ecosystems or civil war.

The response by the international community has been two sided. The first and rather extreme option has been to place a global ban on the trade of coltan with the DRC. The second and considerably more viable option proposes an expansion of regulation guidelines pertaining to the mining and export of coltan (Hayes, 2002). While the first option might help to alleviate global pressures of coltan attained through conflict and destructive ecological practices, it does not offer alternatives that would work towards the enhancement of social stability nor does it support a regeneration of the local economy or restoration of the degraded landscapes. The second option is better suited to combat exploitation and violence associated with mining operations, with the primary reason being that it acts to legitimate the current production and trading system rather than drive it further underground and into the hands of nefarious actors.

Doubtless, the situation first calls for greater dialogue and collaboration among internal and external players in the coltan industry. Globally prominent mining companies in Australia and Brazil carry significant influence over the direction of the market, making them ideal partners and motivators for the development of a sustainable and ethical industry in the DRC. Collaborative efforts across the spectrum of the coltan chain would provide a model and forum for companies to consistently pay fair market prices for more ethically sourced products. In consideration of the idea that modern conflicts surrounding the production and distribution of coltan stem from the basis of predictions of economic turnover, collaboration among players would stimulate gravitation toward an equilibrium where players build on the efforts of one another to create a mutually satisfying relationship. The mission for companies to achieve balance would in-turn stimulate the peace process in the region because it requires untangling and legitimizing the complexity of doing business in what is otherwise regarded as a war zone (Hayes, 2002).

Generally, the idea of increased transparency creates a platform from which improvements can be made, and integrating this idea in a way that is meaningful for the coltan industry would set the standard for corporate responsibility. As full compliance by corporations is required for successful implementation of regulations and mitigation of detrimental effects on local conditions in the DRC, the shift is likely to spark enhanced efforts for sustainable development. If coltan mining in the DRC is elevated on the global stage and thrust into public consciousness, then much like the diamond industry and its experience with "conflict diamonds," the industry and valuable resource can be better managed and controlled to promote growth and stability.

REFERENCES

Hayes, Karen. (2002). *Coltan Mining in the Democratic Republic of Congo: The Implications and Opportunities for the Telecommunications Industry*. Cambridge, UK: Fauna and Flora International.

Montague, Dena. (2002). "Stolen goods: Coltan and conflict in the Democratic Republic of Congo," *SAIS Review 22*, 103–118.

25

How Will the Grand Ethiopian Renaissance Dam Affect Peace in the Region?

OVERVIEW
Jennifer C. Veilleux and M. Troy Burnett

The Grand Ethiopian Renaissance Dam (GERD), formerly known as the Millennium Dam and sometimes referred to as Hidase Dam, is a gravity dam on the Blue Nile River in Ethiopia. As the project moves forward and nears completion, it has sparked a series of conflicts and intense diplomatic maneuvering, with some in Egypt threatening to sabotage it. Frustrated with the process, the Ethiopian government has more or less made the unilateral decision to build and operate the Dam "no matter what," though in public they state that they are cognizant of the downstream impacts, and are willing to remain open to discussion and will consider modifying the design if there are significant impacts. As the two essays in this section will show, there are arguments suggesting that the project promotes stability in the region as well as arguments that emphasize how it has destabilized political relations in an already unstable region.

BACKGROUND

The Nile River, found in North and East Africa, is said to be the longest river in the world, with a length exceeding 6,850 kilometers (4,255 miles). The river cuts a path through many different cultures, climates, and landscapes before it empties into the Mediterranean Sea. Though the Nile basin spans 11 countries, only Egypt and Sudan have extensively developed the river's water resources for human use for food and electricity. The other basin countries (Burundi, Democratic Republic of the Congo, Eritrea, Ethiopia, Kenya, Rwanda, South Sudan, Tanzania, and Uganda) are only marginally involved with Nile politics. With the exception of Egypt and Kenya, most of the countries are considered the world's least developed. Until recently, economic poverty and/or political instability have prevented significant development projects on the river, but this is changing. The GERD being constructed in the Nile basin is the largest hydroelectric project under construction on the African continent. The dam has become a potent symbol of African modernization and development, and as such, is a lightening rod of conflict and negotiation—primarily involving Egypt, Ethiopia, and the Sudan.

Water resources are problematic in North and East Africa as water is scarce and unavailable for much of the year due to the arid climate and highly variable precipitation patterns. The Nile basin includes many tributaries and two main rivers sections: the Blue Nile and the White Nile. The Blue Nile is where the GERD is being constructed. The dam will be over 145 meters (475 feet) high, 1,780 meters (5,840 feet) wide, and hold back approximately 63 billion cubic meters of water. That the Blue Nile accounts for over 80 percent of the water flow in the Nile River is an issue of concern for the downstream countries of Egypt and Sudan. The Blue Nile water primarily comes from precipitation that falls in the Ethiopian highlands during the summer monsoon. There is already a hydropower dam on the Blue Nile (the Roseires) located in Sudan near the Ethiopian border. Otherwise, the river remains largely undeveloped and wild, subject to intense flooding in the monsoon summer rainy season and conversely bouts of minimal flow in the dry winter season.

The GERD has a planned potential generating capacity of 6,000 megawatts. The dam's current design is for 16 turbines with 375-megawatts installed capacity. For comparison, the Hoover Dam has an installed generating capacity of 2,080 megawatts and the city of Toronto on an average Saturday consumes 3,000 megawatts. Ethiopia currently has less than 2,000 megawatts in the grid from its existing power plants. The potential energy increase for Ethiopia and neighboring countries gives an unprecedented opportunity for economic development based on electricity availability. Given information provided by a U.S. Bureau of Reclamation survey conducted in the 1950s, the Blue Nile has the potential to provide about 10,000 megawatts of hydropower generation. Construction of the GERD began in 2011 and it is planned to be completed by 2017. The cost exceeds $4 billion U.S. dollars and as of 2015, the money has largely come from contributions and purchases of bonds by the Ethiopian people both living in Ethiopia and living in other countries.

That the GERD is the first major development project on the Nile River to occur outside Sudan and Egypt is significant both politically and economically. The existing international treaty that regulates water rights on the Nile River stipulates that Egypt and Sudan have exclusive rights to develop and use Nile water resources, at the exclusion of the other upstream basin countries. Today, the treaty's validity is questioned because it was drafted before many of the countries in the Nile basin were independent and because of this regional people feel the treaty does not give fair representation of their rights. The treaty was modified once to change water allocations in Egypt and Sudan in 1954, following the construction of the High Aswan Dam in Egypt. Today, the nine other countries in the Nile River basin have sought to amend or even complete abolish the existing treaty. Through diplomatic negotiations, the countries have endeavored to develop new terms for a treaty that would allow water rights for development outside the core countries. The Nile treaty itself is controversial for most, as it was created during the colonial era.

The dam will displace approximately 20,000 local people who subsist on the river and surrounding natural resources. The dam site is located in a remote location in Ethiopia 730 kilometers from Addis Ababa and 17 kilometers from the Sudan border in the Benishangul-Gumuz State. The Benishangul-Gumuz State borders Sudan, is considered remote, experiences food insecurity, is sparsely populated, and is one of the most impoverished states in Ethiopia. The local people, mostly from an ethnic minority group collectively called the Gumuz, subsist from the river, and do not have access to electricity or basic services. The Gumuz people pan for gold, practice flood-recession agriculture, and fish in the river. Due to the reservoir that will result from the GERD, this population will no longer have access to the river resources listed above. What potential access to the water resources these 20,000 displaced will have in the future will be modified from how they use the river today. Historically, the Gumuz do not have good relations with other ethnic groups, particularly the highland Amhara, and are considered still today to be violent and hostile people.However, the Gumuz communities living in the shadow of the GERD have not expressed any action or words to be interpreted as resistant to the project.

The Ethiopian national agenda is to improve the national economy and alleviate poverty. The country's population doubled from 40 million to 80 million between 1990 and 2010. The Blue Nile accounts for close to 50 percent of all surface freshwater resources within Ethiopia. The Ethiopian Electric Power Corporation has already signed agreements for the electricity expected to generate from several hydropower projects across the country, including most significantly the Grand Ethiopian Renaissance Dam. The countries that have signed some level of agreement to buy electricity from Ethiopia are Kenya, Sudan, Djibouti, and potentially South Sudan, before the civil war erupted. The Ethiopian government has a plan to take the revenue and apply it to further development projects throughout the country.

FURTHER READING

Abdelhady, Dalia, Karin Aggestam, Dan-Erik Andersson, and Olof Beckman, et al. (2015). "The Nile and the Grand Ethiopian Renaissance Dam: Is there a meeting point between nationalism and hydrosolidarity?," *Journal of Contemporary Water Research & Education*, 155(1), 73–82.

Gebreluel, Goitom. (2014). "Ethiopia's Grand Renaissance Dam: Ending Africa's oldest geopolitical rivalry?," *The Washington Quarterly*, 37(2), 25–37.

Tvedt, Terje. (2010). *The River Nile in the Post-Colonial Age: Conflict and Cooperation among the Nile Basin Countries*. London: I. B. Tauris.

Veilleux, Jennifer C. (2013). "The human security dimensions of dam development: the Grand Ethiopian Renaissance Dam," *Global Dialogue* 15(2), 42.

THE CONTENTIOUS GERD: A THORN IN THE SIDE OF NILE BASIN POLITICS
M. Troy Burnett

Despite its promise, the Grand Ethiopian Renaissance Dam (GERD) has unsettled efforts at regional stability, economic cooperation, and peace. The lack of transparency with the project and political intransigency of the Ethiopian and Egyptian governments continues to heighten tensions in the region as the stakeholders bicker over current and evolving Nile basin treaties, compacts, and agreements.

The ambitious Renaissance Dam is Ethiopia's largest-ever engineering project. The expected energy output of 6,000 megawatts is triple the capacity of the country's second largest dam, the Gilgel Gibe IV. Along with being viewed as vital to the country's economic development and future prosperity, the GERD has become a potent symbol of national pride and hope. Conversely, the dam has many critics—environmental and political—with the most vocal found in Egypt. As the last of the downriver countries, Egypt fears a serious disruption to the quantity and quality of water from the river. The reservoir will contain an amount equal to 1.3 times the annual flow of the Blue Nile. A diplomatic row has ensued with factions in Egypt going so far as to threaten to sabotage the project. For their part, Ethiopians respond by accusing their neighbors of living in the past and being unwilling to accept Ethiopia's economic and political development. Outside observers and critics, such as the non-governmental organization (NGO) International Rivers, note that from its inception the project has been veiled in secrecy. The government of Ethiopia and the Ethiopian Electric Power Corporation have

Ethiopia, Kuch, Blue Nile river valley. (Andrew Holt/Getty Images)

been accused, not just by their harshest critic Egypt, of suppressing internal discussion and criticism. It doesn't help Ethiopia's position that it has yet to produce an environmental or social impact assessment and failed to consult downstream nations prior to construction. Indeed, very little is known about the ecological or hydrological impacts.

An independent field report commissioned by International Rivers has help to shed light on some of the most important social and environmental issues (International Rivers, 2012). The report, undertaken without consent of the Ethiopian government, confirmed many of the concerns of the downriver countries and international observers. According to the report, between 5,000 and 20,000 people will be forced to resettle as villages in the flooded area will be completely inundated. This directly contradicts the government's estimate of only 800 people. As the report notes, none of the affected people were consulted about the dam and their fate. Indeed, the political climate in the country continues to make it risky for civil society and conservationists to question the government's plans. There are legitimate fears of government persecution. For example, in June 2011, Ethiopian journalist Reeyot Alemu was imprisoned after she raised questions about the project. During their efforts to assess the impacts of the dam, International Rivers staff members received anonymous death threats (Pottinger, 2013). Matters were made more tense when, at a 2011 conference of the International Hydropower Association in Addis Ababa, the then Prime Minister Meles Zenawi called critics of the project "hydropower extremists bordering on the criminal" (Bosshard, 2011).

Along with the social impacts and continued lack of transparency and discussion with the project, there is a long list of environmental impacts that the Ethiopian government continues to deny or dismiss. Geomorphologically, the Ethiopian highlands have been heavily deforested and subsequently are highly sensitive and prone to mass erosion. Sedimentation, a common problem for all dams and reservoirs, is a major risk for the GERD. There have been no studies to quantify the sedimentation risk, or the impact it would have on the dam's power output, maintenance, and lifespan. Further, a soil conservation plan for the watershed is nonexistent. The Benishangul-Gumuz region, where the GERD and its reservoir are being constructed, is one of the few places in the country that is still forested. The community, which has long lived with and depended on the resources of this forest system, will see, seemingly by government fiat, 90 percent of this forest flooded. Scientific studies have documented more than 150 endemic freshwater fish species in Ethiopia's portion of the Blue Nile (Pottinger, 2013). The fish are a staple for many who live along the banks of the river. Yet again, there have been no significant efforts to document the affects that the dam is expected to have on fish habitat—a lake is a very different place to live for fish that have evolved in a riparian environment. Doubtless those locals directly affected by these impacts, without adequate compensation, will have a hard time sitting back idly and watching their livelihoods destroyed despite appeals to their sense of national pride.

Though President Omar al-Bashir of Sudan said in 2012 that he supported the building of the dam, Egypt continues to be unsettled by the project and demands to be allowed full inspection and consultation on the design and implementation. Ethiopia vehemently denounces Egyptian involvement unless Egypt relinquishes its veto on water allocation as stipulated in the 1959 Nile Waters Agreement—an agreement, administered by former colonial power Great Britain, which clearly favored Egypt and Sudan by granting them exclusive rights to the waters of the Nile. Tensions have escalated as Egypt holds fast to the parameters of the 1959 treaty, whereas Ethiopia and other upper basin countries proceed under the 2010 Nile Basin Initiative and the Cooperative Framework Agreement.

In an effort to diffuse tensions, Egypt, Ethiopian, and Sudan established an International Panel of Experts to review and assess the project. However, diplomatic efforts were dealt a serious blow when Egyptian President Mohammed Morsi—in an unknowingly televised discussion with the panel on June 3, 2013—suggested methods to destroy the dam, including support for anti-government rebel factions in Ethiopia. The Morsi government subsequently apologized for the comment, though the gaffe clearly destabilized relations and reinforced Ethiopia's mistrust of its northern neighbor. Indeed, the Morsi government confirmed in 2013 that "Egypt's water security cannot be violated at all" or "endangered" and that "all options are open" (BBC News, 2013).

Despite the criticism and concern, Ethiopia continues to move forward with the GERD. With a scheduled opening date sometime in 2017, observers can only hope that the harsh political rhetoric will abate and a workable framework can be crafted where all members of the Nile Basin feel part of the process. The future demands it, for Ethiopia has plans to build a host of dams and reservoirs along its portion of the Blue Nile and doubtless, Egypt will not willingly let them continue to act so arbitrarily.

REFERENCES

BBC. (2013, June 10). "Egyptian Warning over Ethiopia Nile Dam." BBC News: Africa. Accessed March 3, 2016, at http://www.bbc.com/news/world-africa-22850124.

Bosshard, Peter. (2011). "Sustainable Hydropower—Ethiopian Style." International Rivers. Accessed March 20, 2015, at http://www.internationalrivers.org/blogs/227/sustainable-hydropower-%E2%80%93-ethiopian-style.

International Rivers. (2012). "Field Visit Report." GERD Project. Accessed March 2, 2016, at http://www.internationalrivers.org/files/attached-files/grandren_ethiopia_2013.pdf.

Pottinger, Lori. (2013). "Field Visit Report on the Grand Ethiopian Renaissance Dam." International Rivers. Accessed March 20, 2016, http://www.internationalrivers.org/resources/field-visit-report-on-the-grand-ethiopian-renaissance-dam-7815.

THE RENAISSANCE DAM—A PLATFORM FOR PEACE

Jennifer C. Veilleux

The Grand Ethiopian Renaissance Dam (GERD) represents a new dynamic and new discourse in the regional history of the Nile basin. Examination of the amount of news events related to the basin in the years since construction began shows significant discussion about water rights, historic claims, economic development and cooperation, national interest, and even the greater good. Though dramatic headlines about the dam—such as the March 20, 2013, article titled "Egypt, Ethiopia Headed for War over Water" in *Al-Safir Al-Monitor*, Lebanon's leading newspaper—suggest that Egypt and Ethiopia are at risk for water-based conflict, the reality is that the governments of Egypt, Ethiopia, and Sudan are engaged in ongoing, civil dialogue about dam feasibility and regional institutions of cooperation. The Renaissance Dam decision, although taken unilaterally by Ethiopia in 2011, is inspiring an unprecedented level of diplomacy between the three Blue Nile basin countries and offering a resources-based platform for dialogue that has the potential to lead to regional peace and stability. This essay considers the aspects of the Renaissance dam that lend themselves to promotion of peace and cooperation between Nile basin countries.

Doubtless, this new era of cooperative dialogue in North and East Africa still suffers from many of the same, historical antagonisms—political instability, weak economies, cultural conflict, and natural disasters. For instance, the regional economies do not have strong international trade agreements with neighboring countries. Nine of the eleven basin countries are on the United Nation's Least Developed Countries List, a list that maintains information on about 50 of the world's lowest economies. Populations are expanding but reliant on the same amount of resources. Egypt's High Aswan Dam on the Nile generates a large percentage of that country's energy. Sudan's Merowe and Roseries dams account for 75 percent of generated domestic electricity supplies. Regardless, there are several motivations for the three basin countries to put these familiar challenges aside and move ahead with diplomatic discussion over the dam. The fact is, the Renaissance Dam will impact downstream flows of water and sediment to Egypt and Sudan, will generate 6,000 megawatts of electricity for domestic and export use, represents a political power shift in the basin in relation to the Nile Treaty, and marks a new era of social development for upstream countries.

The Nile Treaty was originally drafted and signed in 1929 by Britain and revised in 1959 by Egypt and Sudan, just before sweeping independence for African countries from colonial powers. This treaty was developed to allocate Nile River waters to both Egypt and Sudan only. The original treaty is a product of the colonial era with Britain signing on behalf of the basin countries. Today, it is not considered fair or legitimate by many of the upstream countries. In fact, colonial-era treaties in general in Africa are fraught with cultural feelings of illegitimate rule from colonial interests and powers to exploit African nations. The GERD opens the conversation beyond theoretical ideas of national development because it violates Egypt and Sudan's exclusive water rights. Egypt and Sudan are in a situation where they are being asked to engage with their upstream neighbors outside the terms of the original treaty, and positively, they are complying. These two countries are extremely arid, and have little water resources alternative to the Nile River. While open conflict is an option to promote their interests, they clearly stand to benefit more from engaging diplomatically with each other. This cooperation could then set a precedent for future cooperation and collaboration. Further, each of the basin countries has Nile development plans of their own that will require a cooperative mood to come to fruition.

Arguably, the Renaissance Dam offers direct benefits to the downstream countries. If the Blue Nile River is managed cooperatively, there is an opportunity to enhance these benefits. Egypt's Lake Nasser, which has incredibly high evaporation rates, may not be the best place to store water, whereas the reservoir behind Renaissance may offer storage with lower evaporation rates, enhanced flood and sediment control systems, and expansion of available hydro-electric energy. The region currently experiences frequent energy shortages. Sudan, recognizing the potential, has already signed a contract with the Ethiopian Electric Power Corporation to import electricity. Available and reliable energy is a precursor to sustained, economic growth. Further, available and reliable freshwater resources are also vital to growth and political stability. Most assuredly, the Renaissance Dam will increase energy and water availability in the region.

From a social perspective, the Renaissance Dam provides a salient example of development divorced from colonial influences, especially in the context of the Nile basin treaty. The shift has provided upstream Nile basin countries a voice in discussions. The discussions began with the Nile Basin Initiative. A working group of basin country representatives drafted new language and amendments to the original, colonial-devised treaty. Included in the new treaty is the establishment of an international riparian commission to help steer development and cooperation in the basin. The initiative further includes a component known as the Tripartite Talks—a forum for ongoing diplomatic discussions between Egypt, Ethiopia, and Sudan.

Given that the Grand Ethiopian Renaissance Dam has already resulted in more than one year of structured and peaceful negotiations and diplomatic relations between the Blue Nile basin countries, the dam arguably has the capacity to serve as a platform for peace. As highlighted, there are many potential benefits that this project brings: politically, in empowering upstream countries previously denied via British imperialism; economically, in sharing benefits of energy generation and helping to elevate the Ethiopian population out of poverty; environmentally, in allowing for scientific investigation and cooperative mitigation of impacts; and socio-culturally, by igniting cross-cultural dialogue between basin countries that for too long have not had or made opportunities to engage on joint development efforts.

Seizing upon the experience with the Renaissance Dam, one can only hope that this era of cooperation between the Nile basin countries will spill over into other social and political arenas.

26

Does the Kimberley Process Work?

OVERVIEW
M. Troy Burnett

Throughout malls in Canada and the United States are jewelry stores vying for your attention and your money. Giant banners with slogans of diamond quality and why their diamonds are better than the competition are plastered along the hallways. However, beyond the marketing hyperbole and dreams of marriage proposals, anniversaries, and graduations, most people do not think of the true origins of the beautiful stone. Indeed, until recently, close to 15 percent were considered "conflict diamonds," originating from areas controlled by forces or factions opposed to legitimate and internationally recognized governments. As the name implies, the proceeds of sales from these diamonds have been used to fund military action in opposition to those governments. An estimated 3.7 million people have lost their lives because of diamond-financed conflicts, with more than 6.5 million being displaced. These precious, desirable stones were proven to be brought to consumers via a network of conflict and violence.

BACKGROUND

In May of 2000, African diamond-producing countries came together in Kimberley, South Africa, to institutionalize a solution. In July of that same year, the International Diamond Manufacturers' Association and the World Federation of Diamond Bourses issued a zero-tolerance resolution on conflict diamonds in an attempt to eliminate these diamonds from circulation. This resolution became known as the Kimberley Process, in which various checks and balances were implemented to prevent the solicitation of conflict diamonds worldwide. Over the past several years, numerous successes have been cited from the organizers of the group in the battle to remove conflict diamonds from the diamond trade. However, others have criticized the Kimberley Process for its lack of accountability in providing useful discouragement in the sale of conflict diamonds.

The Kimberley Process relies on a certification scheme that requires all shipments of rough diamonds that are exported internationally from their source to have a tamper-resistant container with an enclosed Kimberley Process Certificate validated by the government (Wallis, 2005). A shipment may only be exported to another Kimberley Process–participating country, and no uncertified shipments may enter participating countries. All participants in the Kimberley Process are expected to maintain records of warranties that were received and issued or face expulsion from the global diamond industry if they fail to comply with the standards. Although this proposal at the surface seems to avoid contamination of conflict diamonds entering into a participating country, diamonds from multiple shipments may be mixed together. In such a case, the actual Kimberley certificate is not required to follow the shipment (Wallis, 2005). Moreover, front-end retailers are not required to provide the Kimberley certificate to the consumers before a purchase is made. Retailers only need to inform the suppliers that they require a Kimberley certificate, to which they must keep for at least five years (Wallis, 2005). In Canada and the United States, data from Kimberley Process certificates are not recorded because other trade data recording procedures are in place. This renders it impossible to make cross comparisons with other participants in the process, allowing flaws in the system to trickle down to the consumer. Furthermore, several other countries statistical data submissions are delayed or found to be statistically inaccurate due to different reporting methods and claims of corruption (Willis, 2005). In cases of countries submitting their statistics late or not at all, no penalty will be placed upon them, despite the fact that the process hinders directly on the use of data collected.

According to some observers, the fact that the Kimberley Process exists at all is viewed as a great success. Created in the wake of national attention being drawn upon the industry for the brutal inhumanities caused by the diamond trade in war-torn countries, large diamond distributors in good faith came together to craft a solution. Not often do non-governmental organizations create processes that cause a hindrance to profiteering, yet in the case of the Kimberley Process that was the case. Coupled with this is the fact that conflict diamonds are believed to represent only 15 percent of the global diamond trade (Willis, 2005). With such a small representation, one could assume that removal of these diamonds would pose little risk of significant loss of revenues to any participant in the process without the constraints of the Kimberley Process. Yet, the process was implemented in an attempt to permanently remove conflict diamonds. Self-governance is viewed by many as the biggest flaw with the process. A lack of accountability means that many aspects are completely ignored. In February 2002, the director of international affairs and trade of the UN's General Account Office, stated that without effective accountability, the certification scheme may provide the appearance of control while still allowing conflict diamonds to enter the legitimate diamond trade and, as a result, continue to fuel conflict (Wallis, 2005). Furthermore, monitoring within the process is based on requests that one participant be reviewed by another. There are no guidelines for self-assessment, nor are the procedures for external auditing. This renders the Kimberley Process vulnerable to inconsistencies, inaccuracies, and corruption.

The two essays highlight the successes and failures of the process. Meredith DeBoom argues that since its inception the Kimberley Process Certification Scheme has been plagued by poor implementation, a lack of accountability, and a failure to expand its scope to address all types of diamond-related violence and is an inadequate long-term solution, whereas I explain that, while broken, with the right motivation and leadership the process can be fixed.

REFERENCE

Wallis, Annie. (2005). "Data mining: lessons from the Kimberley Process for the United Nations' development of human rights norms for transnational corporations," *Northwestern Journal of International Human Rights* 4(2), 388.

FURTHER READING

Bieri, Franziska. (2013). *From Blood Diamonds to the Kimberley Process: How NGOs Cleaned Up the Global Diamond Industry*. Burlington, VT: Ashgate Publishing Company.

Grant, J. Andrew. (2013). "Consensus dynamics and global governance frameworks: Insights from the Kimberley Process on conflict diamonds," *Canadian Foreign Policy* 19(3), 323.

Smillie, I. (2005). "What lessons from the Kimberley Process Certification Scheme?," in Karen Ballentine and Heiko Nitzschke (eds.), *Profiting from Peace: Managing the Resource Dimensions of Civil War*. Boulder, CO: Lynne Rienner Publishers.

THE KIMBERLEY PROCESS IS BROKEN
Meredith DeBoom

Upon its establishment in 2003, the Kimberley Process Certification Scheme (KPCS) represented a much-needed first step in stemming the global flow of conflict diamonds. Unfortunately, in the years since its establishment, the KPCS has been plagued by poor implementation, a lack of accountability, and a failure to expand its scope to address all types of diamond-related violence. While the use of diamonds to fund violence remains an issue of global importance, the KPCS is not a long-term solution to the complex and persistent problems associated with diamond mining.

The legitimacy of the KPCS as a certification standard has been fatally injured by its failure to hold its member states accountable for successfully implementing KPCS requirements. This failure is due both to the leadership structure of the KPCS itself and to its lack of credible enforcement mechanisms. Under the KPCS Core Document, which lays out the responsibilities of the Kimberley Process's 54 member states, all KPCS decisions must be made by consensus. As a result, it only takes one member state to block changes to regulations, including changes that would strengthen certification requirements or amend the KPCS leadership structure to make it more accountable.

With the exception of a few cases in which member states have been expelled for blatantly ignoring KPCS requirements, the KPCS's consensus-based structure has made it nearly impossible for it to effectively respond to violations of its regulations by member states. While the KPCS offers an appealing "carrot" to its member states in the form of a certification that their diamonds are conflict-free, there are no "sticks" to punish member states that violate the KPCS agreement. The KPCS has no institutional body, for example, to monitor whether member states are appropriately implementing its regulations. As a result, there are few resources to investigate abuses by member states or to ensure that member states follow through with the recommendations of KPCS compliance reports when there are problems. This is particularly problematic when we consider the ease with which illegally mined and smuggled diamonds can be mixed with diamonds mined according to the KPCS regulations. Because there are no institutional resources to investigate whether member states are taking appropriate measures to prevent the mixing of legitimately mined and smuggled diamonds, there is no way of verifying that smuggled diamonds, which may be used to fund conflicts, are not being inaccurately certified as conflict free. While the KPCS may make it more difficult to use diamonds to fund conflicts on paper, it does little to guarantee this in practice. In the meantime, violator countries continue to benefit from their certification as producers of conflict-free diamonds.

Zimbabwe has become a prominent example of the Kimberley Process's failure to hold its member states accountable. In June 2009, diamond exports from Zimbabwe's Marange diamond fields were banned internationally in response to mounting evidence that members of Zimbabwe's state security agencies were killing and beating miners and compelling some miners to work under conditions of forced labor. There was also evidence that diamond exports were being used to fund violence against civilians by Zimbabwe's Zanu-PF party, led by President Robert

Mugabe. In November 2009, the KPCS and Zimbabwe's government agreed on a plan to address these problems, which included a pledge from Zimbabwe to withdraw all security forces from the Marange as well as the implementation of a monitoring process to ensure that all diamonds produced at Marange met KPCS standards. After over a year of deadlock among KPCS member states, and despite a lack of evidence that Zimbabwe had followed through on its agreement with the KPCS, the KPCS chairman, Mathieu Yamba, announced in June 2011 that diamond exports from Zimbabwe could resume. In response to this decision, several prominent human rights organizations, including Global Witness, withdrew their support for the Kimberley Process. The Zimbabwean case thus speaks both to the failure of the KPCS to hold its member states accountable and to the detrimental impact that this failure has had on the international legitimacy of the KPCS.

Beyond these problems with its structure and implementation, the KPCS has also failed in its mission of preventing the use of diamonds to fund conflict by limiting its scope to rebel movements. The KPCS currently defines conflict diamonds as "rough diamonds used by rebel movements or their allies to finance conflict aimed at undermining legitimate governments" (KPCS, 2003). This limited definition reflects the context of the founding of the KPCS, when there were rising global concerns regarding violence committed by rebels in countries such as Liberia, Sierra Leone, and the Democratic Republic of the Congo. Unfortunately, however, the focus of the KPCS on only rebel-sponsored violence has made it seemingly blind to other forms of diamond-supported violence that are much more widespread than rebel-related violence today, including human rights violations (such as the use of child labor and forced labor), environmental injustices, corruption, and violence against citizens by governments in the states where mining occurs.

The KPCS's failure to address structural and direct violence committed by governments using diamond revenues is particularly problematic. In contexts ranging from Zimbabwe to the Central African Republic, Kimberley-certified diamond exports have funded the repression of citizens through violent and non-violent means and have fueled corruption that reduces the quality of life of citizens of these states. When consumers see the label "conflict-free," they assume that this certification refers to *all* types of conflict, not just conflict perpetrated by rebels. The failure of the Kimberley Process to address violence committed by non-rebel actors such as states gives consumers false confidence that the diamonds they are purchasing have not contributed to violence. It may be accurate to certify diamonds produced according to the KPCS as "free of rebel involvement," but it is inaccurate and misleading to certify them as "conflict free." Furthermore, given the consensus-based structure of the KPCS, it is doubtful that the definition of conflict diamonds will ever be expanded to include all of the forms of violence that diamond-based conflicts can take.

Finally, by focusing primarily on states, the KPCS shifts the burden of responsibility for a global problem, in which consumers, traders, and producers are also implicated, onto states. This is particularly troublesome because many diamond-producing states are located in the Global South and may lack the resources and infrastructure needed to verify the locations of origin of rough diamonds or to ensure that smuggled diamonds have not been comingled with diamonds produced according to KPCS requirements. Non-governmental organizations (NGOs), companies, and other industry stakeholders participate in the KPCS, but, unlike states, they participate as self-regulating entities. Thus, the burden for preventing the sale of conflict diamonds is placed almost entirely on states rather than on the diamond industry itself, which arguably benefits the most from the KPCS through its ability to sell diamonds certified as conflict-free.

In conclusion, the Kimberley Process is broken, likely beyond repair. Its failure to hold member states accountable and lack of monitoring and enforcement capabilities have irreparably weakened its legitimacy in international politics, while its narrow focus on rebel-based conflict and on states have rendered it incapable of addressing the complexity of diamond-related violence. Rather than trying to fix a broken system, it is time for international leaders to learn from where the KPCS went wrong and to establish a new, stronger international regulatory mechanism for diamond mining that holds both diamond-producing states and the diamond industry itself accountable.

REFERENCE

Kimberley Process Certification Scheme. (2003). "Core Document." Accessed March 8, 2014, at http://www.kimberleyprocess.com/en/kpcs-core-document.

FURTHER READING

Global Witness. (2014). "The Kimberley Process." Accessed March 10, 2014, at http://www.globalwitness.org/campaigns/conflict/conflict-diamonds/kimberley-process.

Grant, J. Andrew, and Ian Taylor. (2004). "Global governance and conflict diamonds: The Kimberley Process and the quest for clean gems," *The Round Table: The Commonwealth Journal of International Affairs* 93(375), 385–401.

Murphy, Shannon K. (2010). "Clouded diamonds: Without binding arbitration and more sophisticated dispute resolution mechanisms, the Kimberley Process will ultimately fail in ending conflicts fueled by blood diamonds," *Pepperdine Dispute Resolution Law Journal*, 11, 207–228.

Nichols, Julie E. (2012). "A conflict of diamonds: The Kimberley Process and Zimbabwe's Marange diamond fields," *Denver Journal of International Law & Policy*, 40(4), 648–685.

Sharife, Khadija, and John Grobler. (2013/2014, winter). "Kimberley's illicit process," *World Policy Journal*.

Smillie, I. (2005). "What lessons from the Kimberley Process certification scheme?," in Karen Ballentine and Heiko Nitzschke (eds.), *Profiting from Peace: Managing the Resource Dimensions of Civil War.* Boulder, CO: Lynne Rienner Publishers.

Winetroub, Andrew H. (2013). "A diamond scheme is forever lost: The Kimberley Process's deteriorating tripartite structure and its consequences for the scheme's survival," *Indiana Journal of Global Legal Studies,* 1425, 20.

IN DEFENSE OF THE KIMBERLEY PROCESS
M. Troy Burnett

As a direct result of the work of non-government organizations (NGOs) such as Global Witness and Partnership Africa Canada, by the late 1990s the world became aware of "conflict diamonds" and the social and moral ramifications of purchasing these precious stones. It was realized that the profits from diamond mining in particular African regions were being used by governments and anti-government forces to directly fund armed conflict against each other and their peoples. The simple facts were that war, massive death, violent atrocities, and refugee crises in African nations such as Sierra Leone, Liberia, Ivory Coast, and Angola were being sustained by the diamond trade. Without a mechanism to know exactly where and how a diamond was mined, a crisis of conscience took root in the minds of consumers and the legitimate industry. Something had to be done.

The Kimberley Process (KP), ratified in 2003, was designed to curtail the trade in blood diamonds. Presently, 81 countries are party to the agreement, including all the major diamond-mining nations. According to the agreement, members must establish a system of internal controls designed to eliminate the presence of conflict diamonds from shipments of rough diamonds imported into and exported from its territory, and amend or enact appropriate laws or regulations to implement and enforce the certification scheme and to maintain dissuasive and proportional penalties for transgressions. In the first decade of the process, enforcement has relied on self-monitoring and self-policing between participating governments and diamond producers. The agreement is unique in that first, it is a voluntary certification process outside the boundaries of traditional international law; second, it involves a tri-partite arrangement of states, NGOs, and the diamond industry; and third, is a monumental accord that responded to a clear industry failure and was negotiated in record speed.

Before the KP, estimates of the global trade in conflict diamonds ran as high as 15 percent. Today, that number is less then 1 percent. Expectations of corporate responsibility and conflict-free business practices are now standard. The diamond-funded civil wars in Angola and Sierra Leone, dramatically portrayed in the film *Blood Diamond* (2006), starring Leonardo DiCaprio, have ended. The KP has been credited for facilitating and increasing the market share of legitimate, certified production, and significantly boosting the tax revenues in Botswana, as well as those countries ravaged by civil war. The accord also has served as a model for other tripartite agreements between industry, civil society, and state governments on a host of global social-economic issues. Yet, there are legitimate criticisms of the Kimberley Process; namely of the inability or unwillingness of its members to ramp up its monitoring efforts and respond to overt violations.

As Franziska Bieri observes in his seminal work on the subject, *From Blood Diamonds to the Kimberley Process: How NGOs Cleaned Up the Global Diamond Industry* (2010), there are several instances where the KP has failed to fully deliver on its promise. Unchecked and unsanctioned diamond smuggling continues to occur in places such as Ivory Coast, Guinea, and the border area between Zimbabwe and Mozambique. Diamonds that are traded to specifically fund conflict can readily be mixed with certified diamonds via transshipment hubs in Brazil, Guyana, and Lebanon. Sadly, as consumer attention has ebbed, many of the participating governments and large diamond-mining corporations such as De Beers have lost the will to aggressively monitor and police the trade.

There are also the structural shortcomings of the Kimberley Process itself. Ineffective responses to non-compliance and week monitoring, rooted in the bureaucratic structure of unanimous decision-making and the absence of a permanent secretariat, are two key weaknesses of the KP. Moving decision-making to a member voting system from the existing vetoing system would help to minimize gridlock. Arguably, consensus-building that worked very well in the initial stages of the KP has proven to be a major stumbling block to effective implementation. One or two members with vested political or commercial interests can delay needed reforms. Further, a centralized leadership structure with a permanent annual budget is needed to better coordinate activities and manage the certification mechanism. A KP secretariat would be better positioned to facilitate effective and timely monitoring, coordinate research and data collection, address concerns of unequal burden sharing, serve as the clear link between public demands and the industry, and provide greater transparency. Critics also call for regular, independent auditing of KP reports and trade statistics. NGOs, such as Global Witness, do not fully trust the profit-seeking global diamond industry to continue its present mood of corporate responsibility in the absence of consumer and public-relations pressure.

The Kimberley Process is a dynamic process that while needing to be reformed should not be abandoned. Without its inspiring efforts and global campaign the trade in conflict diamonds would have continued unabated. Doubtless, the KP can and should evolve into a more permanent institution. The definition of conflict diamonds and the illicit profits derived from trade should expand to include all forms of conflict as well as political oppression. Countries that don't actually mine diamonds, the so-called transshipment hubs, should not be allowed to issue KP certification. The process needs to more aggressively sanction those dictatorial regimes and greedy corporations that refuse to play by all the rules. Despite the flaws, the worst thing for the diamond industry (producers and consumers) is to abandon the KP, as unfortunately the NGO Global Witness did in 2011. Conflict diamonds still exist and need to be regulated as many of the peace agreements in former civil war zones hang precariously in the balance. As The Partnership Africa Canada bluntly suggests: "the cost of a Kimberley Process collapse would be disastrous for an industry that benefits so many countries, and for the millions of people in poor countries who depend, directly and indirectly on it . . . a criminalized diamond economy would undoubtedly re-emerge and conflict diamonds could soon follow . . . the KP is too important to fail" (Bieri, 2010). It's difficult not to agree with this sentiment.

REFERENCE

Bieri, Franziska. (2010). *From Blood Diamonds to the Kimberley Process: How NGOs Cleaned Up the Global Diamond Industry.* Burlington, VT: Ashgate Publishing Company

FURTHER READING

Haufler, Virginia. (2009). "The Kimberley Process Certification Scheme: an innovation in global governance and conflict prevention," *Journal of Business Ethics 89*(4).
Sharife, K., and J. Grobler. (2013, December). "Kimberley's illicit process," *World Policy Journal, 30*(4), 65–77.

27

How Does China's Increasing Demand for Natural Resources Affect Stability in Africa?

OVERVIEW
Mia Bennett

China's rapid industrialization over the past couple decades has been powered by massive amounts of natural resources drawn both from its own territory and imported from continents as far away as Africa. The east Asian nation is vast and has many natural resource deposits of its own, including coal, iron, and minerals. It even controls 90 percent of the world's rare earth mineral supplies (Reuters, 2014), which are critical for the components inside many of the high-tech gadgets we have come to rely on such as computers and cell phones. China's rapid growth has led the country to look beyond its borders for resources, too. While Chinese government officials and businessmen have fostered ties with countries around the world that hold precious deposits of natural resources in places like Myanmar, Canada, Russia, and Brazil, their dealings with African countries have drawn some of the most scrutiny.

BACKGROUND

China's relationships with African countries actually span several centuries, although they have intensified since the Cold War in line with the country's industrialization and search for natural resources. In 1415, the famed Chinese mariner Zheng He reputedly docked in Tanzania after sailing across the Indian Ocean (Guangqi, 1992). Chinese officials promote He's voyages as a symbol of China's "peaceful rising" (*heping jeuqi*) (Callahan, 2009), even though they also mark the beginning of China's entry into the continent, for better or for worse. On a continent-wide scale, the United States and Europe still dominate African foreign aid and investment, but China's proportion is increasing. In 2012, Chinese outward foreign direct investment (OFDI) in Africa totaled $2.52 billion—up from just $317 million in 2004 (Leung and Zhou, 2014).

Chinese funds have helped make possible the construction of many infrastructure and transportation projects in Africa, from railways to power plants. Five hundred and fifty years after He landed in Tanzania, the Chinese helped build the Tanzania-Zambia (Tan-Zam) Railway, which connected Zambia to the port of Dar-Es-Salaam in Tanzania, on the Indian Ocean (Gleave, 1992). Together with Tanzania and Zambia, China financed the construction of the railway in its largest-ever foreign aid project. It gave an interest-free $500 million loan to the project, a remarkable sum for the Asian nation, which was then still poor. Built in the 1970s during the Cold War, the Tan-Zam Railway was important for two main reasons: first, it gave landlocked Zambia a means to access an outlet to the sea without having to depend on white-dominated South Africa and Rhodesia (now Zimbabwe). Second, it opened up access to Zambia's enormous copper reserves, the so-called Copperbelt. The railway was nicknamed the "Great Uhuru Railway"—Swahili for freedom. Zambia's economy benefited from new transportation infrastructure through more friendly territory coupled with maritime access, while China gained new friends in Africa and new sources of copper. Still today, it is the largest importer of the Zambia commodity (Simoes, 2014).

The Tanzania-Zambia Railway may stand out as a positive example of what Chinese demand for resources can do for Africa. Some argue that the Asian country has helped energize African economies, making them more business-oriented and less dependent on flows of foreign aid (Hsu, 2014). In Zimbabwe, for instance, Shanghai Electric Group is leading a consortium of three Chinese companies that are considering building a thermal power station, which would both bring much-needed electricity to businesses and households alike. Unsurprisingly, it would also help power a coal mine that is being developed—China rarely invests in Africa out of charity, but rather does so strategically in line with its search for natural resources.

There is a darker side to China's demands for natural resources. The bulk of Chinese OFDI in Africa is issued by the state-run Export-Import Bank of China, which specializes in loans for mining, oil, gas, and infrastructure projects. A full 31 percent of China's OFDI in the continent goes to the energy, industrial, and minerals sectors (People's Republic of China, 2013), whose revenues rarely trickle down to the average African citizen due to endemic corruption.

The situation in Angola exemplifies this problem. China and Angola first signed a bilateral trade agreement in 1984 (Zhao, 2011), and today, the former Portuguese colony is China's largest African supplier of oil and largest overall African trade partner. One observer characterized the relationship between China and Angola as an "oil for infrastructure" arrangement (Zhao, 2011). Each country gets something out of the relationship, but the problem is that in the southwest African nation, the benefits from infrastructure are far from equally distributed amongst the people. The country is a textbook example of the "resource curse": the big profits to be earned from natural resource development leads to rent-seeking, corruption, and the overall decline of state institutions, while economically, the country becomes susceptible to volatility due to globally traded commodity prices (Sala-i-Martin and Subramanian, 2003). The resource curse is hypothesized to be more severe when a resource boom takes hold before the institutional framework of a democracy solidifies. In Africa, Freedom House, a think tank, classifies only one African country (Mauritius) as a full democracy; the rest are either "flawed states" at best or "failed states" at worst (Puddington, 2013). This state of affairs does not bode well for increased Chinese investment into African countries, especially when upwards of 33 percent of foreign investment is devoted to natural resource extraction.

In 2008, the Chinese Olympic Torch relay passed through only one location in Africa: Dar-Es-Salaam, Tanzania—the terminus of the Tan-Zam Railway. Even as profits on the railway fall and copper prices slump, the port city remains a symbol and material example of the positive benefits of Chinese aid, investment, and demand for natural resources. The torch that blazed through the streets of Dar-Es-Salaam, however, stole the spotlight from the myriad problems that have come with Chinese demand for resources and subsequent investment in Africa, including heightened inequality, political instability, and the resource curse. As the next two essays explore in more detail, for Africa, Chinese demand for natural resources is both a blessing and a curse.

REFERENCES

Callahan, William A. (2009). *China: The Pessoptimist Nation*. Oxford, UK: Oxford University Press, 33.

Gleave, M. B. (1992). "The Dar es Salaam transport corridor: An appraisal," *African Affairs*, 249–267.

Guangqi, Sun. (1992). "Zheng He's expeditions to the western ocean and his navigation technology," *Journal of Navigation*, 45(03), 329–343.

Hsu, Sara. (2014, August 14). "China's model for Africa," *The Diplomat*. Accessed November 12, 2014, at http://thediplomat.com/2014/08/chinas-model-for-africa/.

Leung, Denise, and Lihoun Zhou. (2014). "Where are Chinese investments in Africa headed?," *World Resources Institute*. Accessed November 12, 2014, at http://www.wri.org/blog/2014/05/where-are-chinese-investments-africa-headed.

People's Republic of China, Information Office of the State Council. (2013). "China-Africa Economic and Trade Cooperation." White paper. Accessed March 3, 2016, at http://english.gov.cn/archive/white_paper/2014/08/23/content_281474982986536.htm.

Puddington, Arch. (2013). *Freedom in the World 2013: Democratic Breakthroughs in the Balance*. Washington, DC: Freedom House.

Reuters (eds.). (2014, August 7). "China loses appeal of WTO ruling on rare earth exports." Accessed on November 14, 2014, at http://www.reuters.com/article/2014/08/07/china-wto-rareearths-idUSL6N0QD5T820140807.

Sala-i-Martin, Xavier, and Arvind Subramanian. (2003). "Addressing the Natural Resource Curse: An Illustration from Nigeria." Working Paper No. w9804, National Bureau of Economic Research.

Simoes, Alexander. (n.d.). "Country Profile: Zambia." Observatory of Economic Complexity. Accessed November 12, 2014, at http://atlas.media.mit.edu/profile/country/zmb/.

Zhao, Shelly. (2011, May). "The China-Angola partnership: A case study of China's oil relations in Africa," *China Briefing*. Accessed March 8, 2016, at http://www.china-briefing.com/news/2011/05/25/the-china-angola-partnership-a-case-study-of-chinas-oil-relationships-with-african-nations.html.

FURTHER READING

Dijk, Meine Pieter van. (2009). *The New Presence of China in Africa*. Amsterdam, Netherlands: Amsterdam University Press.

Girouard, Étienne. (2008). "China in Africa: Neo-Colonialism or a New Avenue for South-South Cooperation? A Review of Perspectives." Canadian Coalition to End Global Poverty.

Rotberg, Robert I. (2009). *China into Africa: Trade, Aid, and Influence*, illustrated edition. Washington, DC: Brookings Institution Press.

CHINA'S APPETITE FOR RESOURCES PROMOTES INSTABILITY IN AFRICA
Mia Bennett

China's voracious appetite for natural resources indirectly and directly engenders political instability in African countries, especially in those countries overly reliant on primary resource exports. China's increasing demand for commodities from oil and gas to coal to minerals is helping to further entrench the dreaded "resource curse." This affliction is particularly apparent in states without stable democratic institutions and respect for the rule of law. Further, China has even sold weapons to insurgents in places like Sudan, in some cases to those who directly are seeking to control Sudan's oil production. In these situations, the combination of Chinese demand for oil plus Chinese arms makes it especially difficult to encourage political stability and peace.

On a global scale, China is pushing countries to intensify development of their natural resource deposits. In the rush to take advantage of commodity cycles and China's demand before it drops or before the country goes full steam ahead into transitioning to renewable energy, countries from Australia to Zimbabwe are plundering their earths for oil, gas, and minerals to send to the Far East. Sinopec, a state-owned Chinese oil company, either invests or is directly engaged in operations in 15 countries across Africa (Du, 2012). China's demand may help to fill the coffers of a nation's treasury, but it can also lead to political instability, corruption, and economic exploitation. While countries like Australia already export a significant amount of natural resources to China, they have strong and relatively transparent governments and highly developed tertiary sectors to complement their primary exports. In contrast, the countries without diversified economies and with weak governments are most vulnerable to instability—an all-too-common feature of African economies.

China finances the primary sector in countries even when it clearly leads to political instability and outright war in order to ensure a steady flow of natural resources from certain countries. Angola is one such country where China's economic and political policies have helped to weaken the former Portuguese colony even further. Similarly, resource-rich albeit authoritarian Sudan is an ally and active trading partner with China, despite the admonishments of the European Union and United States. Indeed, China is the biggest provider of foreign aid to Sudan, with most of the $6 billion earmarked to modernize the oil sector. China's moral indifference has paid off, for Sudan provides 8 percent of China's energy imports. In turn, China sold $83 million worth of arms and munitions to Sudan in 2005 and through its seat on the UN Security Council continues to veto U.S. and European efforts at trade and arms embargoes (Fatal Transactions, 2008). These policies are clearly the result of China's primary interest in ensuring the stability of oil supplies.

China is now trying to improve its relationship with South Sudan perhaps because it, too, has oil resources, but things have not gone so smoothly. In fact, South Sudan recently kicked out Chinese officials. In February 2012, the South Sudanese government in Juba expelled Liu Yingcai, an executive at the local branch of Chinese-Malaysian oil company Petrodar. The government accused him of stealing $815 million worth of South Sudanese oil by failing to pay transit fees (BBC, 2012). South Sudan's oil must travel through Sudan in order to reach port. Reprehensible business practices such as these could generate additional adverse effects on relations between the two warring countries, revealing that China's demand for resources affects more than just political instability within one country.

China's demand for natural resources, of course, is not alone in fomenting instability in Africa. Other countries, like the United States, United Kingdom, and France all import natural resources like Angolan oil and Congolese coltan without always attaching demands for good governance or transparency. Yet, as the country that holds a number of superlatives—from being the largest carbon emitter on Earth to the planet's top coal consumer. China has an outsize responsibility to try to bring some stability to the African nations that are supplying it with much-needed natural resources.

Already, China has made strides in combating climate change, which should help decrease its demand for some of the natural resources it currently imports from Africa. In November 2014, it signed a landmark bilateral deal with the United States in which both sides agreed to lower carbon emissions and invest in green technologies. This will ultimately lower China's need to import commodities like coal and oil and will send an encouraging sign to countries that depend on its exports to consider diversifying their economies. Yet in many respects, China is in a much better position to tackle climate change than instability in Africa even though both issues are related in part to its natural resource consumption. Since China follows a policy of non-interference with respect to other governments and their sovereign territory (Large, 2008), it is unlikely to make demands of African leaders—especially when Beijing is accused of many human-rights violations back home. Its hands-off approach coupled with its significant investments in African natural resource development projects and infrastructure is in many ways helping to prop up corrupt regimes in Africa made rich by siphoning revenues from these very projects.

China is upstaging the model that the United States and Europe have for years fostered in Africa, which involves providing foreign aid in exchange for measurable progress towards good governance. This model has clearly not generated many success stories, but the Chinese model will not, either. The country's no-questions-asked policy and its "oil for infrastructure" deals are admittedly bringing much-needed capital investments into Africa, potentially aiding the climate for economic development. But more often than not, China's policies are also leading to unstable political situations and volatile economic cycles in Africa. The ball is in Beijing's court. If ceasing demand for natural resources and slowing down industrial growth is not an option, then decisions about where and in what projects to fund should be made more carefully before bringing about another lost century to the African continent.

REFERENCES

BBC. (2012, February 22). "South Sudan Expels Chinese Oil Firm Boss." BBC News: Africa. Accessed November 12, 2014, at http://www.bbc.co.uk/news/world-africa-17126340.

Fatal Transactions and European Coalition on Oil in Sudan. (2008, April). "Sudan: Whose Oil? Sudan's Oil Industry: Facts and Analysis." Accessed November 13, 2014 at https://www.globalpolicy.org/images/pdfs/042008sudanoil.pdf.

Juan, Du. (2012, December 10). "Sinopec drills deep into Africa," *China Daily.* Accessed November 12, 2014, at http://usa.chinadaily.com.cn/epaper/2013-12/10/content_17164264.htm.

Large, Daniel. (2008). "China & the contradictions of 'non-interference' in Sudan," *Review of African Political Economy* 35(115), 93–106.

THE CHINESE IN AFRICA—ALTRUISTIC, NO! BUT BENIGN AND POTENTIALLY STABILIZING

M. Troy Burnett

As the 21st century progresses, China's emergence as a distinct, global economic and political superpower continues. Needless to say, this rankles those in Europe and the United States who firmly believe that Western civilization and its notions of democracy and liberalism are the best means to social progress. One such arena where these conflicting ideologies are being played out is Africa. Long the colonial plaything of American slavers and European powers, the resource-rich continent has emerged onto the Chinese international development agenda. Critics suggest that China's expanded investment and involvement on the continent is solely motivated by resource greed and self-interest, is just another form of colonial exploitation, and will invariably destabilize the region, sabotage international efforts to spread democracy, and promote conflict.

Admittedly, China's interest in the continent is not altruistic. While there is genuine human concern within China for Africa and the difficulties it faces, just as there is shared sympathy for any place believed to have been subjugated and dominated by Western powers, China would not be investing so heavily if it had nothing to gain—quid pro quo, as the saying goes. Unlike the West, which it views as unforthright and hypocritical, China has long been straightforward and honest with its foreign relations and emphasis that any bilateral relationship has to be mutually beneficial. And China's involvement in Africa has indeed been politically and economically productive. Economically, the country has gained access to and a ready supply of natural resources, access to local markets, migration and employment opportunities for Chinese citizens, and long-term infrastructure contracts for its companies. On the political side, China has garnered a modicum of respect from the international community for its willingness to send aid to the most beleaguered countries and, concurrently, China has effectively recruited a host of supporters to its brand of international diplomacy—dubbed the "don't meddle in others affairs" approach.

With its considerable capacity and willingness to provide financing, many agree that China's economic involvement has created noticeable benefits. During a trip in 2013, President Xi Jinping pledged to provide another $20 billion dollars towards African infrastructural development. Prior to this, $5 billion alone had been earmarked for the Congo that, as Howard French noted, resulted in a "great leap forward for Congo" (French, 2007). Throughout the 20th century, the former Belgian-controlled Congo with its CIA-backed despot Mobutu Sese Seko had been a war-torn, illiberal mess. With Chinese financial assistance, over 6,400 kilometers of new rail lines and roads were built, as were 31 hospitals, 145 health centers, 2 universities, and 5,000 housing units.

China's involvement in Africa dates back to the late 1960s with its financial and logistical support of Tanzania's "Tan-Zam" railway. The 1,161-mile–long railway provided an alternative route for Tanzania, Zambia, and others, allowing them to transport goods away from the high tariff ports in those African countries dominated by white, European minority governments. At the time, the project was China's largest foreign venture and still remains a potent symbol of non-capitalist inspired development. To commemorate this project and China's supportive involvement in Africa, one of the routes of the torch relay for the 2008 Beijing Olympics began and ended at the main terminal of the TanZam in Dar es Salaam, Tanzania.

As the Tan-Zam project shows, China has long been a regional actor on the African continent. What has changed is the scope and the scale of its involvement. The notion that its increasing appetite for natural resources will lead it to wantonly exploit Africa is unsubstantiated. The fact is, China's intentions in Africa are benign. It has no desire to colonize the continent, dictate the economy or politics, or deprive the continent of development opportunities. Rather, through its actions, it has sought an infrastructure development approach that is inherently different from than the West, one that patently avoids the meddling with the internal affairs of African countries through conditional aid (Sun, 2013). Critics are correct in pointing out that China's approach under-emphasizes good governance, but this is a reflection of China's philosophy that economic development will bring political stability and progress, not vice versa. As Sun notes,

> Many Chinese officials, analysts and businessmen find the West's overwhelming emphasis on democracy, governance, transparency in Africa amusing . . . to the West, they would ask an innocent but critical question: for people who do not have food on the table, what's the point of having democracy? . . . Using its own experience of subjugating political liberalization to the higher cause of economic development, China finds its approach to Africa as one that prioritizes the provision of basic elements of development, completely legitimate and fully justified. (Sun, 2013)

In short, over the last several years, China's involvement in Africa has been mutually beneficial and stabilizing—the former gaining another supply of much-needed natural resources, the latter gaining an alternative development model and partner who as yet, comes with so much historical baggage.

REFERENCES

Brautigam, Deborah. (2009). "Zhu Rongji and the TanZam Railway Redux," in *The Dragon's Gift the Real Story of China in Africa*. Oxford, UK: Oxford University Press, 40–41.

French, Howard. (2007, September 7). "The Chinese and Congo take a giant leap of faith," *New York Times*. Accessed May 1, 2016, at http://www.nytimes.com/2007/09/21/world/asia/21iht-letter.1.7595719.html.

Sun, Yun. (2013, April 5). "China's Increasing Interest in Africa: Benign but Hardly Altruistic." The Brookings Institution. Accessed March 30, 2015, at http://www.brookings.edu/blogs/up-front/posts/2013/04/05-china-africa-sun.

28

HOW HAVE LARGE-SCALE CONSERVATION EFFORTS PROMOTED CONFLICT IN SUB-SAHARAN AFRICA?

OVERVIEW
M. Troy Burnett and Gregory Maddox

One of the most abiding images of Africa in non-African perception remains that of wild Africa, teeming with wildlife. The image dates back to antiquity with the use of African animals in Roman circuses and Hannibal's use of elephants in his attack on ancient Rome. It stretches across the globe through the Muslim world and on to China. In the 19th century, Europeans avidly read the works of explorers like David Livingstone and Henry Stanley and of hunters like F. C. Selous and R. G. G. Cumming. In the 20th century, Theodore Roosevelt's African safari in Kenya and German East Africa in 1909 sparked interest in an imaginative genre of literature that included the literary works of Ryder Haggard and Edgar Rice Burroughs. From Tarzan to Disney's animated feature and television series *The Lion King*, the image of wild Africa has struck a responsive cord in non-Africans.

BACKGROUND

In the last several decades, the image of Africa as a hunting ground has declined in favor of an image of wild Africa at risk. While conservation efforts in parts of

Africa date to the late 19th century, in the 1950s, concern over the threat to wildlife in Africa became an international movement. The 1959 film, *Serengeti Must Not Die*, made by the head of the Frankfurt Zoo, Dr. Bernhard Grzimek, made wildlife conservation a part of the growing environmental movement in the West just as much of Africa became independent. Since then, a string of popular entertainment works, drawing in some cases on the work of widely renowned scientists such as Dian Fossey and Jane Goodall, have fronted a concentrated effort by nongovernmental organizations to promote wildlife conservation. The pressures these groups have brought to bear, and the money they have raised and that raised from tourism, have convinced many African governments to continue to expand colonial-era efforts at conservation.

The results have been spectacular in some areas. Several African nations have set large amounts of their territory off-limits to economic activities outside of tourism. Tanzania, Kenya, Togo, South Africa, Zimbabwe, Zambia, Botswana, and several other countries all have allocated over 10 percent of their total area to national parks or reserves. In parts of eastern and especially southern Africa, wildlife populations of many species are larger and more stable than they were 100 or 50 years ago. The growth of population and the spread of cultivation to feed that population has restricted range in some areas and created what some scholars call "fortress conservation," which uses military-style force to protect wildlife. On the negative side, some species, especially rhinoceroses and in some areas elephants, subject to hunting for their horns and tusks, have come under threat. In Central and West Africa, animal populations face increasing stress as a result of forest clearance for agriculture and hunting. "Bush meat," especially in forested regions, has become a major commodity available in markets. In general, however, conservation is an established practice, and the amount of land in reserves of various kinds is expanding.

Even so, conservation remains a contested idea within African nations. In such times of crisis as the recurrent civil wars in the Democratic Republic of Congo (formerly Zaire) or in Uganda before 1987, conservation generally becomes one of the first casualties of war. Part of the reason is that in many cases local populations view wildlife conservation in the same way that they saw colonial rule: as an oppressive denial of resources, rights, and heritage. The total segregation between people and wilderness imposed by modern conservation denies local people access to land and to important religious and historical sites. The beneficiaries are seen to be governments and their officials as well as the foreigners who visit the parks. The roots of this conflict lie in the origins of the colonial era's conservation efforts.

Before the 20th century, African societies lived side by side with game. Disease, especially trypanosomiasis (carried from wild animals to humans and livestock by the tsetse fly), had helped limit the areas available to dense human settlement and had given Africa the largest population of big game animals in the world. Human societies lived in a patchwork with areas infested by tsetse and harboring large animal populations. The animals could make forays into areas free of tsetse as humans could go into tsetse areas to hunt. Humans could and did push back this frontier through intensive clearing, burning, and grazing of domestic animals. The boundaries changed as human societies expanded or diminished the area they could manage to keep clear.

Two factors in the 19th century served to upset this "mobile environmental equilibrium." First, extensive hunting driven by European settlement in southern Africa cleared large areas of the southern part of the continent of its animal populations. Second, at the end of the 19th century, the great rinderpest epidemic that killed a substantial proportion of cattle in the continent forced the abandonment of large areas by herders and farmers and the rapid generation of tsetse-bearing bush. This expansion of tsetse-bearing bush coming at the beginning of the colonial era then allowed colonial regimes to develop the idea of segregated game reserves that contained no permanent human population.

Indeed, sub-Saharan countries today face many environmental problems, such as loss of wildlife, desertification, deforestation, water pollution, and water scarcity. In addition to the severity these problems pose for human populations, often they are also triggers for conflict among tribal groups or nations. That in turn can complicate environmental protection and remediation efforts because they are often among the first casualties in times of conflict. In addition, current environmental protection and wildlife preservation efforts in sub-Saharan Africa are sometimes controversial in ways that have roots in the first conservation measures undertaken in colonial times.

In the first essay on this question, the author describes the colonial governments' post-World War II emphasis on further imposing environmental policies, often in ways that intruded on the lives of African farmers and villagers. These policies also sought to increase agricultural output and mining activities in part to provide European governments with more revenue to help their domestic postwar rebuilding efforts. The postwar era was also a time of rising African population expansion, urbanization, and anticolonial activism. In this era many of the seeds of controversy were planted.

In the second essay, the author discusses the development of environmental policies among independent African governments in the post-colonial era beginning in the 1960s. It was during this period that new environmental problems erupted, such as oil pollution in the Niger River Delta and a proliferation of wild game poachers.

FURTHER READING

Davies, Jonathan. (2012). *Conservation and Sustainable Development: Linking Practice and Policy in Eastern Africa*. New York: Routledge.

Fabricius, Christo, Eddie Koch, Hector Magome, and Stephen Turner. (2013). *Rights, Resources and Rural Development: Community-Based Natural Resource Management in Southern Africa*. London: Earthscan.

Ramutsindela, Maano. (2007). *Transfrontier Conservation in Africa: At the Confluence of Capital, Politics, and Nature*. Cambridge, MA: CAB International.

CONSERVATION DEVELOPMENT HAS DESTABILIZED AFRICA
Gregory Maddux

The end of World War II heralded a "second colonial occupation," in the words of prominent Africanist scholar John Iliffe, just as African peoples learned to organize themselves to fight against colonial rule. Much of the new energy that Britain and France in particular brought to their colonial empires took the form of efforts to create an environmental policy. Efforts to protect natural resources, to expand production, to promote soil conservation, and to control disease all intensified with new investment from the British, French, Belgians, Portuguese, and even in

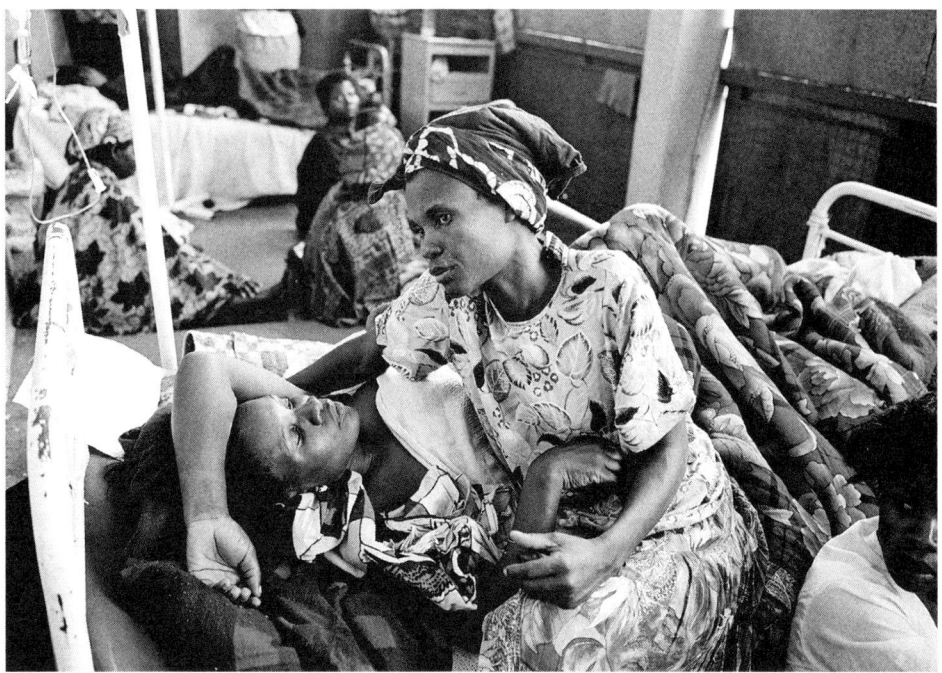

A woman comforts her sister who has malaria in the female general medical ward of Kamazu Central Hospital, the second largest in Malawi. Many of the patients here have typical diseases associated with AIDS. (Gideon Mendel/Action Aid/Corbis)

settler-dominated South Africa. In the immediate aftermath of the war, the colonial regimes also needed to increase production to help support the costs of domestic reconstruction. Many colonial economies grew rapidly in the two decades after the war as demand for their agricultural and mineral production remained strong. Yet the colonial governments' increased interference in the day-to-day life of Africans became the immediate cause for the rejection of colonial rule. Whether in the creation of Apartheid in South Africa with its more oppressive segregation, or new rules requiring farmers to build conservation works in their fields, or the expulsion of herders or farmers from an area newly declared a game reserve, all helped fuel anticolonial nationalism.

The dramatic rise in demand for African commodities, whether mineral or agricultural, in the aftermath of World War II provided the background to the development programs of the late empire. Prices for many commodities rose sharply. African producers responded by increasing production of crops like coffee, tea, cocoa, cotton, and tobacco. In West Africa, African farmers expanded their production. In Kenya, Rhodesia, Nyasaland, Mozambique, and Angola, European immigrants took up newly alienated land to convert to highly capitalized farming. The rapid growth in the production of copper in the Belgian Congo and Northern Rhodesia, and eventually oil in Nigeria, Angola, and Gabon, meant increasing urbanization and greater demands for food. As this increased production occurred, concern over the sustainability of the increase in production grew.

By the 1950s, almost every region in Africa saw some level of government effort to promote soil conservation. Most British colonies appointed a "soil conservation officer" to oversee the development of conservation plans and their implementation by district officials, agricultural officers, and "native authority" chiefs. These efforts included the promotion of terraces of various sorts on sloped land, extension of forest reservations on hilltops, rotational cropping and grazing schemes, and in many areas, resettlement out of overcrowded areas into less densely populated areas. These efforts resulted from a perceived decline in forest cover, soil productivity, and grazing facing African rural communities. In many cases, they represented a strikingly myopic vision by colonial observers. Observers projected an "Edenic" past onto the landscape and ignored evidence of landscape manipulation by local populations that were of long standing. Colonial officials, officials of the technical services, and colonial scientists repeated this reasoning across the continent.

The colonial state's authoritative and top-down approach for the most part failed miserably. However, throughout the continent, African farmers and herders adopted a huge number of new crops and techniques throughout the colonial era—sometimes with the assistance of colonial agents and sometimes totally outside the sight of those agents. Perhaps the most intensively developed case study of these efforts comes from Malawi (colonial Nyasaland). In that colony, farmers practiced a form of burning for cultivation called citimene in the southern Shire Valley and visoso in the north. Farmers cut bush and made piles in the fields just before the rains began. They burned the dried piles of brush, and the rains washed nutrients back into the mounds left by the brush. Colonial officials saw these practices as leading to deforestation and desertification and sought to ban or limit them. They also tried to impose "strip" cultivation where farmers planted in alternate strips of land every year. The British required that the strips be marked by rows of grass. A number of tests carried out by local officials showed that these methods led to less production and much more labor. Yet the colonial government continued to enforce them in the name of conserving trees and soil. They used the local courts to impose fines, require supervised labor on the workers, and even jail resisters. By the 1950s, opposition to these rules had spread throughout the country, and the nationalist movement led by Dr. Hastings Banda used this discontent as a major organizing tool in the struggle for independence.

Such resistance occurred throughout Africa. During the Mau Mau uprising in colonial Kenya in the early 1950s, conservation rules requiring the building of terraces in the increasingly overcrowded "Kikuyu reserves" helped build support for the uprising. In Buganda in Uganda, soil conservation rules also sparked resistance. Throughout the West African forests, efforts to prevent people from cutting wood drove them to increasingly ignore local African authorities and spurred corruption.

Perhaps no set of colonial conservation policies created more resistance than those designed to protect grazing lands. From South Africa to West Africa, colonial officials contended that African herders kept too many cattle and caused degradation and desertification through overgrazing. As happened with so many colonial concerns, the issue first surfaced in South Africa. In the aftermath of the rinderpest outbreak of the 1890s, both colonial officials and African herders had sought to rebuild herds rapidly. In areas that kept stock, colonial governments sought to provide veterinary services to prevent diseases. Colonial officials, however, viewed these herds as potential sources of cash for their owners and revenue for the colonial state. Herders often looked at them very differently; for them, herds represented subsistence. Herders sought to hold as many cattle as possible and to share the risk in cattle keeping from disease and drought by reciprocal cattle pawning. Herders generally took advantage of markets for both stock and for hides when they needed cash, but they did not raise cattle as a commodity to be sold every year. Hence, colonial officials saw overgrazed land and too many head of livestock as one of the great causes of degradation in the drylands of Africa.

Rapid population growth has led to tremendous changes in African landscapes since the 1940s. Africans have put more land under cultivation in one way or another than ever before. They have found ways to increase production and productivity in agriculture that have generally kept pace with population growth, despite the reduction in fallow times for land under cultivation. Observers and officials both noted with alarm the increasing "deforestation" of Africa throughout the continent by the 1950s. It led to increasing efforts to promote nature or wildlife conservation through the total segregation of populations from reserves just as in much of Africa colonial powers were reluctantly ceding political power to African leaders. The creation of "fortress conservation," in Daniel Brockington's phrase, at the very end of the colonial era symbolized the continuing dependence of the newly independent African states on the wealthy nations of the world.

THE PROMISE AND THE POTENTIAL OF CONSERVATION IN AFRICA
Gregory Maddux

Julius Nyerere, the leader of the struggle for independence in Tanganyika and longtime president of Tanzania (created by the union of Tanganyika with Zanzibar in 1963), announced at the independence celebrations for Tanganyika that in combating a food shortage in many parts of the country at the time, the new nation was now fighting "not man but nature." The image of fighting nature, of trying to ensure survival for African peoples, captures the perception of many people in Africa in facing the string of disasters that have befallen parts of the continent since the 1960s. Famine has reappeared at times in several parts of the continent. Malarial parasites acquired resistance to the most commonly used (and least expensive) form of treatment for the disease. In some parts of the continent, the expansion of reserves seemed to indicate that the world placed a greater value on nature than on the people who depended on African environments for their survival. Droughts, storms, and floods wreaked havoc on communities and infrastructure alike as climate change made the weather even less predictable. HIV/AIDS became an epidemic and reduced life expectancy across the continent. It is understandable why many Africans like Nyerere saw their relationship with nature as a war.

At the same time, Nyerere's comment proved optimistic. Human activity continued to cause many of the problems perceived as environmental in Africa. While drought, floods, and crop failures continued at about the same pace as before 1960, famines occurred not just because of crop failure, but because of human action. Famine became associated with war. In Nigeria, the civil war of 1967–1970 caused a famine in Biafra, the southeastern region of that country that sought independence. In Ethiopia in the late 1970s, in Sudan in the 1980s, and again in Ethiopia in the early 1990s, famine resulted when civil strife combined with a climatic event.

Newly independent African nations tended to maintain similar policies toward environmental resources as colonial governments, despite the occasional populist action in loosening some conservation regulations. This continuity occurred for several reasons. First, the newly independent governments were made up of people who were both trained under colonial rule and accepted the generalized development paradigm that had taken hold in the late colonial period. They believed that the way for Africa to "catch up" was to practice scientific management of resources. Second, large-scale development projects legitimized the new governments in their own eyes and in the eyes of the people. They gave the new rulers patronage to pass around. Third, international aid agencies generally all followed the same scientific orthodoxy. Whether multilateral like the World Bank or United Nations, or bilateral, whether Western or Soviet bloc in the period up to 1989, most promoted the same general policies.

Many regions of Africa faced food shortages throughout the post-independence period without widespread increase in mortality. The transportation and marketing systems developed during the colonial era continued to be able to bring food into food-shortage regions. The most well-studied drought of the post-colonial era, the mid-1970s drought in the Sahel (as well as in eastern and southern Africa), caused relatively little increased mortality. A series of years with rainfall below the century-long norms brought crop failure, the reduction of cattle herds, and the spread southward of desert conditions throughout the Sahel. It also brought crop failures to many other countries in the continent. Yet it only coincided with famine in those countries undergoing civil conflict.

Nigeria became the first major oil-exporting nation in sub-Saharan Africa. As oil prices rose throughout the period after 1973, multinational oil firms signed agreements to explore for oil and gas deposits throughout the continent, especially in offshore areas. By the 1990s, major producers included Angola, Gabon, and Equatorial Guinea. Oil revenues were siphoned off into the military, wasteful public spending, and corruption. Oil money (along with proceeds from illicit diamond sales) helped fuel a two-decade-long civil war in Angola and propped up repressive governments in Nigeria and Equatorial Guinea. In addition, oil companies stood accused of causing severe environmental damage in parts of Africa. They generally sought to ensure that environmental protection regulations were weak and that enforcement was minimal. In Nigeria, environmental destruction in the Niger Delta region became one of the major issues surrounding protests against the then-military dictatorship led by General Sani Abacha.

The economic crisis of the 1970s and 1980s led to resource mining of sorts in Africa by people and governments desperate to get cash. The poaching of wildlife, especially elephants and rhinoceroses, presents perhaps the most extreme version of resource mining. Rhinoceroses have almost totally disappeared from the wild, and for a period in the 1980s, some thought elephants would face the same fate. Poachers used automatic weapons readily available in eastern and southern Africa to decimate herds. The international ban on ivory sale did much to reduce the demand for tusks, although the protection may have come too late for rhinoceroses. Elephant populations, as in the early 20th century, recovered fairly rapidly, and by the late 1990s, southern African nations were again complaining about having an overpopulation of elephants.

An added crisis was the outbreak of the HIV/AIDS epidemic in the early 1980s. By the time the disease had been identified in Europe and the United States, it had already become an epidemic in Africa. Infection rates seem to have spiked first in Uganda, fueled by a decade of war after the fall of dictator Idi Amin. High rates of infection then came to be recognized in the rest of East and Central Africa. The highest rates of infection have been recorded in southern Africa. Botswana had an estimated infection rate of 38.8 percent. Between one-third and one-quarter of all adults are infected in Lesotho, Swaziland, Zimbabwe, and South Africa (which has the largest number of HIV positive individuals in the world). Kenya, Namibia, and Zambia all have infection rates of between 15 percent and 20 percent. The result has been dramatic, with life expectancy falling in most African countries. Of the 28 million AIDS deaths up to 2003, 26 million were in Africa. Five countries may even see population decline as a result of the epidemic. Although these figures do not mean that Africa will become depopulated, they do mean that the continent will be poorer and people will suffer more. The resources necessary to create sustainable development for African countries will be harder to come by because so much will be taken up in combating the spread of the disease. Resource mining to cover the costs of the epidemic will increase. This includes the exploitation of minerals, petroleum, and timber as well as, for example, the expansion of the "bush meat" market in Central Africa.

In 2004, Wangari Muta Maathai received the Nobel Peace Prize for her work as an environmental activist and political dissident in Kenya. Dr. Maathai, the first woman in Kenya to earn a PhD (in veterinary medicine), rose to become a dean at the University of Nairobi. In the 1970s, she became active in the Green Belt movement in Kenya, which promoted tree planting as a means of combating soil erosion around Kenya. Maathai argued that planting trees improved the life of rural and poor women because they could then have easier and more secure access to firewood. This benefit came on top of the struggle to combat deforestation. Her grassroots environmental activism reached a peak in 1989 when she led the movement to save Nairobi's Uhuru Park from a plan supported by the government of Daniel Arap Moi to build a large office building on it. From this point she became active in pro-democracy politics and was arrested several times; she received serious injuries in 1999 when she was beaten by police as she led a group trying to plant trees in a national forest to protest continuing deforestation. After running briefly in the 1997 presidential election, she was elected to the Kenyan Parliament in

2003 as the leader of the small Mazingira Green Party and became assistant minister in the Ministry of Environment, Natural Resources, and Wildlife in the new government that had defeated the candidate of the previous regime. She had won several major prizes for her work before being named a Nobel laureate in 2004.

Dr. Maathai's long struggle illustrates the promise for Africa's environments. Her fame and even her effectiveness derived in part from her position in post-colonial Kenyan society. As a member of the post-colonial elite, albeit a path-breaking one as the first female holder of the doctorate and head of a university department, her voice carried weight when she decided to speak. Yet her success in creating a movement that has planted more than 30 million trees over two decades in Kenya came not because of her degrees, but because of her understanding of the costs of environmental degradation for poor people in Kenya. It is in such action that the hope for Africa's future lies.

Part III

Asia and the Pacific

29

Can It Be Argued That the Wealth Generated from Oil Is a Primary Cause of the Disempowerment of Women in the Middle East?

OVERVIEW

M. Troy Burnett

The global trend in the 21st century shows that as development progresses women have become more empowered—ideologically, economically, and politically. This is not the case in the Middle East, however, where there are fewer women in the labor force and government and their primary responsibilities in life remain tied to the domestic sphere (Ross, 2012). As a 2004 World Bank study found, 14 of the region's 17 countries have legal restrictions on the types of jobs women can have and the number of hours and time of day they can work. Six of the 17, including oil powerhouse Saudi Arabia, also have laws restricting women from traveling without permission or male guardianship. These restrictions, when combined with cultural expectations, make it extremely difficult for women to work outside the home, in any economic sector. The result is disempowerment and subjugation. The standard explanations hold that both Arabic cultural traditions and the Islamic religion are to blame. The question under discussion here is whether the wealth generated from oil and gas specifically and directly blocks the path toward greater gender rights and empowerment for women in the Middle East.

Social theorists going as far back as Karl Marx and Friedrich Engels in the middle of the 19th century have shown that entering the labor force has a profound and transformative effect on women and their societies. More women go to and stay in school, and, upon finishing school are drawn toward applying what they've learned in a "wage earning" career. As a result of going to school and working, women will delay marriage and childbirth. Earning a wage, as opposed to being an unpaid domestic servant dependent on a man's income, enables women to make economic decisions and acquire more influence over family decisions. Working helps women, especially young women, gain self-confidence, pride, and independence as they are exposed to new social networks and gain exposure to new information. Ultimately, as a result of being in the labor force women start to demand and gain political recognition and rights. Opportunities beyond the domestic sphere also force women and men to come face-to-face with cultural norms of gender discrimination. The transformations can be profound: many of the most modern, developed countries, including the United States and Britain, were once staunch patriarchies.

The fact is, women clearly gain economic and political power when they have the opportunity to enter the labor force and do not when they remain in the home. The pattern in countries where oil dominates is such that women are either encouraged to remain home or unable to join the "oil-based" workforce, whereas economic development based on agricultural modernization and industrialization tends to increase economic opportunities for women. According to Michael Ross in his book *The Oil Curse* there are two specific effects oil income can have on female labor opportunities: (1) the scale of oil revenues both for industry and the government is such that families do not need a second income, which discourages women from seeking work outside the home; and (2) oil wealth often leads to what's known as the "Dutch Disease," an economic development model that results in a decrease in export-oriented manufacturing, a sector dominated by female workers. Ross baldly states that "more oil leads to fewer paychecks for women" (Ross, 2012, p. 118). The question is whether fewer paychecks mean less opportunity and more disempowerment.

Echoing Ross, Kirsten Von Meter argues in her essay in this section that the great wealth generated by the oil industry when combined with the cultural traditions of the Middle East exacerbates the long history of female disempowerment in the region. The simple fact is that the dominant interpretation of Islam based on "Sharia law" quite blatantly allows the religious authorities in particular and men in general to have absolute control over many aspects of female behavior including work, public life, and marriage. Regardless of the economic development model, women's lives are considered secondary and supportive to men's. Von Meter writes, "Oil brings in a great amount of wealth but wealth that is filtered through the religious and cultural characteristics that define these societies and, as such, has not benefitted women nearly to the same extent it has men. The wealth gains from the oil industry in conjunction with Islamic tradition has further entrenched the cultural tradition of patriarchal power."

For Natalie Koch the answer to the question is more nuanced. The Middle East is both spatially and temporally diverse, and a one-size-fits-all explanation for female disempowerment is inherently flawed. Further, as a result of globalization and Western involvement, in some Middle Eastern petro-states women's opportunities, namely in education at U.S.-sponsored universities, have expanded. As technological connections spread throughout the region, women will continue to be exposed to different ideologies and cultures. The result will be a more critical understanding of themselves, their culture, and their roles in society. Inevitably, at least at the ideological level, this will help empower them. There is also the general view that while oil booms tend to inhibit the development of a manufacturing sector (the "Dutch Disease"), they do create jobs in the service sector. Clearly, not all oil-rich countries are susceptible to resource curses and gender disempowerment issues. In lower-middle income countries such as Mexico, Colombia, and Malaysia (which is Islamic) many women work in government and the service sector, and are not negatively affected by their country's oil wealth. If Middle Eastern women can continue to find jobs in the service sector, despite the Islamic restrictions, then they will inevitably be on the path towards empowerment.

REFERENCE

Ross, Michael. (2012). *The Oil Curse: How Petroleum Wealth Shapes the Development of Nations*. Princeton, NJ: Princeton University Press.

FURTHER READING

Tripp, Aili. (2009). "Debate: oil, Islam, and women debate: does oil wealth hurt women?," *Politics & Gender* 5(4), 545–546.

OIL, RELIGION, ISLAMIC KINSHIP AND THE DISEMPOWERMENT OF MIDDLE EASTERN WOMEN
Kirsten Von Meter

While there is an ongoing struggle for women's rights in the Middle East, connecting disempowerment to oil is not always evident. The question in this context is does an oil-based economy with exceedingly high wealth gains hurt women?

Associated with this question is the role played by a patriarchal social structure rooted in an Islamic kinship network.

With wealth comes power and influence. It is well understood that the discovery and development of oil has brought great wealth to the Middle East, albeit wealth that is not spread equitably. For Middle Eastern nations, the increasing power that has come from oil wealth mixes with religious ideologies that are rooted in divinely inspired patriarchy. The social norm, as dictated by religious doctrines, is such that women are discouraged from entering the labor force. Indeed, women typically hold inferior social status to the men of the region. As a result, it is exceptionally rare, though not unheard of, for women to be in positions of power in the Middle East.

The Middle East is a region that includes the Arab countries of North Africa and the eastern Mediterranean, plus Iran, Turkey, Israel and, at times, Afghanistan and Cyprus. Even though many of these places do not share the same religion, culture, language, or level of economic development, it has become historically clear that oil has contributed to the vast wealth gains and resultant disparities between and within countries. Oil has also acted as source of conflict and threat multiplier in the region. Its influence in the region cannot be overestimated as it directly or indirectly influences all aspects of life, including gender relations. Such is the central argument in Michael Ross's 2008 article, "Oil, Islam, and Women." According to Ross, the wealth generated from oil is the key to keeping women out of the labor force and, consequently, key to their political disenfranchisement (Ross, 2008). His premise is based on the comparative fact that women in lower-middle income, resource poor countries often enter the labor force either in the service sector or manufacturing. By doing so, they are able to garner a modicum of economic independence and social power. Conversely, those countries with wealth derived from petroleum extraction and export typically lack these types of jobs because with the gains from oil there has been little incentive to diversify the economy. Thus it can be argued that petroleum wealth, or wealth from any type of primary resource, tends to discourage economic diversification and by default important routes towards gender equality (Ross 2008). By not having many options, women are less likely to take wage earning work but rather fully immerse themselves into the domestic, unpaid, sphere. This situation tends to be exacerbated when women are denied educational opportunities.

Such factors can give the outward appearance that an oil economy is valued more than gender equality and female empowerment. Ross' argument in the context of the Middle East becomes more salient when coupled with the region's Islamic traditions.

The culture of the Middle East has been profoundly shaped by Islam—a tradition that overtly eschews equal rights for women. A primary aspect of the Islamic faith is the command to follow Sharia Law, which, as Friedland notes, is often degrading to women, yet clearly enables men to be more powerful and have more freedoms (Friedland 2014, p. 1). Sharia Law allows the religious authorities in particular and men in general to have absolute control over many aspects of female behavior; including work, public life, and marriage. Women's lives are considered secondary and supportive to men's. Across much of the Islamic region, patriarchy is rooted in kin-based networks, which may help explain the Middle East effect—a complex set of variables that are poorly understood creating a facile generalization about women's movements in the region and how they lack any real empowerment objectives or are clearly shown to originate in the male dominated government and religious initiatives (Ross, 2008).

When trying to understand the disempowerment of women in Middle Eastern countries, it is important to examine the intersection of oil, religion and culture. Oil brings in a great amount of wealth but is filtered through the religious and cultural characteristics that define these societies and, as such, has not benefitted women nearly to the same extent as it has men. The wealth gains from the oil industry in conjunction with Islamic tradition has further entrenched the cultural tradition of patriarchal power. Sadly, it doesn't look like it is going to change anytime soon.

REFERENCES

BBC. (2014). "Religions: Islam." *BBC News: Religions.* Accessed March 5, 2015, at http://www.bbc.co.uk/religion/religions/islam/.

Friedland, Elliot. (2014, February 19). "Women's rights under Sharia." Understanding Islamism. *The Clarion Project.* Accessed March 5, 2015, at http://www.clarionproject.org/understanding-islamism/womens-rights-under-sharia.

Joseph, Suad. (1996). "Gender and citizenship in Middle Eastern states," *Middle East Research and Information Project 26,* Spring. Accessed March 5, 2015, at http://www.merip.org/mer/mer198/gender-citizenship-middle-eastern-states.

Ross, Michael L. (2008.). "Oil, Islam, and women," *American Political Science Review 102*(1), 107.

Ross, Michael L. (2009). "Does oil wealth hurt women? A reply to Caraway, Charrad, Kang, and Norris," *Politics & Gender 5*(4), 575.

OIL WEALTH EXPANDS OPPORTUNITIES FOR WOMEN IN THE MIDDLE EAST
Natalie Koch

The Middle East is one of the most diverse regions in the world—so much so that few scholars, experts, and locals agree on its boundaries (Bonine et al., 2012). The countries that are generally understood to be part of the "Middle East" vary

A Saudi Arabian woman holds an application as she heads to register to vote in the port city of Jeddah on August 30, 2015. In a country where women face a host of restrictions including a driving ban, the move to allow women to vote was welcomed as an important step forward. (STR/AFP/Getty Images)

tremendously in terms of their economic, political, cultural, religious, and ethnic compositions. This means that the political position of women in the Middle East varies from country to country. Even in states where women have a high degree of "empowerment," or political rights and activity in the public sphere, there can be significant variations within a country. For instance, women are often more empowered in cities than in the rural areas. But even within these different places, some families may hold a stronger commitment to women's empowerment than others. For example, a family in a rural village might believe strongly in women's education, whereas a family in the city might not.

This diversity is ultimately the result of many forces: politics, culture, economics, geographic awareness, and ideological exposure of different people. Consequently, when considering the impact of wealth generated from oil on women's empowerment, it is necessary to consider it as only one dimension of a much larger story. Generally speaking, however, Middle Eastern countries with significant oil wealth have been characterized by increasing empowerment of women in recent years. Thus, it cannot be argued that the wealth generated from oil is a primary cause of the disempowerment of women in the Middle East.

There are two main developments that help to explain why, when oil wealth enters the equation in the Middle East, women's empowerment appears to be expanding. The first development is connected to geopolitics. With the end of formal colonialism after World War II, European forces left the region en masse and many new states gained independence. Notably, this exodus took place during the Cold War, which was a cause of great concern for many decision makers in the U.S. government who feared that the post-colonial vacuum would be filled by the Soviet Union and communist movements (Little, 2008). This fear resulted in a series of U.S. interventions (both overt and covert) in the region, with the aim of promoting pro-American governments in the new states. Many believe that U.S. involvement is connected to its commercial and strategic interests in the region's oil wealth.

Regardless of the real drivers behind Western involvement, it has significantly raised awareness about the disempowerment of women in many parts of the Middle East. This has resulted in a wide range of programs, implemented by U.S. government agencies, local governments, and non-profit organizations, to empower women through promoting their education and increasing their participation in (re)development projects and the political process. So even if the West is mainly interested in oil wealth, the improved status of women has been treated as a benchmark for evaluating the effectiveness of its efforts to spread its democratic ideals in the Middle East. In brief, it appears that the increased empowerment of Middle Eastern women has been one side effect of this policy agenda.

Increasing globalization—the economic and cultural global integration of the Middle East—is the second development that helps explain the expansion of women's empowerment. This is most visible in the globalization of higher education in the resource-rich monarchies of the Arabian Peninsula that make up the Gulf Cooperation Council (GCC): Bahrain, Kuwait, Oman, Qatar, Saudi Arabia, and the United Arab Emirates. In recent years, these governments have used their tremendous oil wealth, much to the disparagement of Islamic extremists, to expand their education sectors, and especially higher education. Until the late 1970s, there were very few universities in the GCC and students mostly went abroad to study. However, because of religious and cultural norms, women were far less likely to travel abroad for an education. Yet over the past 40 years, the number of universities in Arab Gulf countries has exploded from a dozen to hundreds of institutions. Notably, women are enrolling in university in record numbers and matriculating from these campuses at rates that vastly outnumber their male counterparts (Al Khaldi, 2007). This vastly expanded access to higher education has been paralleled by increasing female participation in the labor force (Willoughby, 2008).

Furthermore, most of the GCC states (with the exception of Saudi Arabia) have focused on a "branch campus" model, whereby Western universities set up a branch in their country. This access to American-style education raises numerous questions about what the students are learning in the classes, most of which are taught by Western expatriates who introduce their own cultural norms about women's empowerment in the classroom. Research on this topic is ongoing, but dramatic advances in female participation in work outside the home and involvement in politics suggests that the globalization of higher education—made possible by oil wealth—is significantly altering gender norms and leading to increased female empowerment in the region.

Just as the Middle East is spatially diverse so too is it temporally diverse—that is, the region is constantly changing over time, the status of women changing with it. Historically, women in the Middle East have been subjugated and disempowered, but on the basis of numerous forces related to geopolitics and globalization, this situation is rapidly evolving today. Accordingly, the trend, however slow, is that the wealth generated from oil helps in the political, economic, and social empowerment of women.

REFERENCES

Al-Khaldi, Salem. (2007). "Education policies in the GCC states." Dubai, UAE: Gulf Research Center.

Bonine, Michael E., Abbas Amanat, and Michael Ezekiel Gasper. (2012). *Is There a Middle East?: The Evolution of a Geopolitical Concept*. Stanford, CA: Stanford University Press.

Little, Douglas. (2008). *American Orientalism: The United States and the Middle East Since 1945*. Chapel Hill, NC: University of North Carolina Press.

Willoughby, John. (2008). "Segmented feminization and the decline of neopatriarchy in GCC countries of the Persian Gulf," *Comparative Studies of South Asia, Africa and the Middle East* 28(1), 184–199.

30

Is the Jordan River a Source of Regional Conflict or Stability?

OVERVIEW

M. Troy Burnett

The Jordan River runs 200 miles from northern Israel to the Dead Sea. The longest and most important waterway of Palestine, the river rises at the foot of Mount Herman in the three springs near Tel Dan, Banias, and Hasbani. It then descends rapidly to the Huleh Valley, a shallow lake until recent times. From this point the river, now properly called the Jordan, plunges through a gorge to the Sea of Galilee at an elevation of 696 feet below sea level. This rapid drop continues south along the main course of the river on the way to the Dead Sea (called the Salt Sea in ancient times), which lies at the lowest point in the valley, at an elevation of 1,292 feet below sea level. This rapid drop probably explains the river's name (from the Hebrew "to go down").

The middle and lower courses of the Jordan are sluggish, even as it receives its major tributaries from the east: the Yarmuk and the Jabbok. Below the Sea of Galilee the river takes on a character very different from that of the upper river. It meanders widely across the soft alluvium of its lower level, with a length of some 200 miles between the south end of the Sea of Galilee and the north end of the Dead Sea. The distinctive lower level of the Jordan, known as the Zhor, is covered with a dense thicket of tamarisk, willows, papyrus, and thornbushes that in the past harbored an assortment of wild animals, reputedly including lions. This virtually impenetrable jungle of vegetation resembles that of tropical locations farther to the south. The Zhor varies in width between 200 yards and 1 mile and is separated from the higher level of the Ghor region, a 150-foot step above the river bottom suitable for cropland and pasturage, by highly eroded marl badlands.

The Jordan Valley is part of the Great Rift System, which extends from the Bekáa Valley in Lebanon southward through the Jordan Valley, the Red Sea, and the East African lake country. It is a conspicuous north-south trending trough lying between the ranges of Galilee and Samaria to the west and Gilead to the east. Although the Jordan receives a considerable volume of water, its low gradient (in the lower course), crumbling river bluffs, extremely high temperatures (especially in the summer), and lack of navigability have made the region less desirable as a focus for settlement than the adjacent highlands. In ancient times the sluggish, mud-colored Jordan was often compared unfavorably to clear, fast-flowing rivers nearby such as the Euphrates.

Today the waters of the Jordan are as much a source of contention between rival powers of the region as the surrounding land. In the 1960s Israel first began to tap the reservoir of the Sea of Galilee, channeling water as far away as the Negev Desert, with the inevitable reduction in water along the lower Jordan River. The Hashemite kingdom of Jordan was late in bringing its water projects on line, and it was not until the 1970s that the East Ghor (King Abdullah) Canal was extended from the Yarmuk River south along the Jordan. This canal provides irrigation water for Jordanian farmers, who returned to the East Bank, which had been left vacant since the shelling of the 1967 war. Joint Jordanian-Syrian efforts to dam the Yarmuk (it defines part of their political border) have been hampered by warfare and a diplomatic impasse. Although groundwater pumping, desalination plants, and more efficient use of drip irrigation, especially by the Arabs, would go far to extend the resource, the surface waters of the Jordan will continue to be important in the economic and political geography of Palestine.

Although water is not the greatest issue dividing the people of this region, its significance should not be underestimated. In 1951, when Jordan first announced a plan to tap the Yarmuk River for irrigation, Israel responded by closing the gates of an existing dam and draining the Huleh swamps. The swamps lay within a demilitarized zone with Syria, and Israel's action led to border skirmishes between Israel and Syria. Israel's construction of its National Water Carrier led to Syrian attacks and protests to the United Nations. Water disputes also figured in the 1967 Six-Day War between Israel and Arab nations. Control of the Golan Heights gave Israel control of the Jordan River headwaters.

To highlight the contentious situation in the Jordan River basin, Amy Blackwell argues that water rights and resources lie at the heart of the Arab-Israeli conflict. In a land of limited resources and inequitable distribution, water is nearly as powerful a polarizing force as religion. Israel has controlled the lion's share of water since 1948, and since that time both Jews and Arabs have argued over who owns which resources and who is using them irresponsibly. The main problem facing the human population in the area is one of uneven water distribution. Though experts insist that there is enough water for all current inhabitants, Israel has controlled most of the water resources available to the Palestinians since 1967, and Palestinians claim that Israel has routinely denied them access to their fair share of the precious resource.

On the other hand, Chris Hrynkow argues that while contentious, the states and actors in the Jordan basin often put aside their differences to ensure the best possible management strategies. In his view, the Jordan basin is a historic jewel with socio-economic, theological, and ecological value. As recent technology-based initiatives by the Israeli government signify, this means that regional actors cannot let the river basin wither and die. The cost would simply be too high on too many levels. Thus, we arrive at a situation where mutual interest in the vitality of the river creates a realm of shared fate that is marked by a situation of freshwater interdependence in the Jordan basin. In political science terms, the health of the Jordan cannot be a zero-sum game, where one side wins at the expense of the other. Ways must be found for all stakeholders to participate and benefit from that cooperation accordingly or the result will be what conflict theorists call a "lose-lose" outcome.

FURTHER READING

Advanced Research Workshop on Water Resources, NATO. (2009). *The Jordan River and Dead Sea Basin: Cooperation amid Conflict.* Dordrecht, Netherlands: Springer.
Sosland, Jeffrey K. (2007). *Cooperating Rivals: The Riparian Politics of the Jordan River Basin.* Albany: State University of New York Press.
Zeitoun, Mark. (2008). *Power and Water in the Middle East: The Hidden Politics of the Palestinian-Israeli water conflict.* New York: I. B. Tauris.

THE JORDAN RIVER: A SOURCE OF CONFLICT
Amy Hackney Blackwell

Water rights and resources lie at the heart of the Arab-Israeli conflict. In a land of limited resources and inequitable distribution, water is nearly as powerful a polarizing force as religion. Israel has controlled the lion's share of water since 1948, and since that time both Jews and Arabs have argued over who owns which resources and who is using them irresponsibly. The main problem facing the human population in the area is one of uneven water distribution. Though experts insist that there is enough water for all current inhabitants, Israel has controlled most of the water resources available to the Palestinians since 1967, and Palestinians claim that Israel has routinely denied them access to their fair share of the precious resource.

Israel, the Palestinian Autonomous Region, and Jordan all have very limited water resources. Water is naturally scarce in the region due to the arid climate and available resources cannot accommodate all proposed uses. The main water source for Israel is the Jordan River drainage basin, which includes the Sea of Galilee. The Jordan originates in headwaters in northern Israel, in Golan Heights, and in southern Lebanon. These waters feed Lake Tiberias. Runoff from the West Bank, Syria, and Jordan adds water to the lower Jordan. Israel uses all of the water from the Jordan River—Palestine does not receive any of it, though geographically the Palestinians are riparian. In fact, only 30 percent of the water in Palestine comes from surface sources, the rest from underground aquifers. The Mountain or West Bank Aquifer system supplies most of the water to the West Bank, while the water in Gaza comes from the Gaza Strip Aquifer, part of the Coastal Aquifer. Because the Gaza Strip Aquifer has been over-pumped for many years to supply the needs of the large population of Gaza and of Israel, the water table can no longer recharge. The water has been contaminated with enough seawater that it is no longer drinkable, representing a major water crisis for the area.

In 1953, Israel's foreign minister Moshe Sharett insisted on Israel's right to use the waters from the Jordan as it wished, for hydroelectric power, agriculture, and other needs. He claimed that Israel was willing to engage in negotiations with Jordan, Syria, and Lebanon to come up with a just apportionment of regional resources, but that the neighboring countries had refused to convene with Israel. Israel therefore felt justified in treating the waters of the Jordan as its own and in using these waters for development in the north and elsewhere. Between 1953 and 1965, U.S. ambassador Eric Johnston traveled between Israel and neighboring Arab states attempting to divide water rights equitably. Experts from the affected nations agreed on a plan to divide and exploit existing resources, but the Arab League rejected the plan because it did not want to imply recognition of Israel. If the agreement had taken effect, Jordan would have been required to supply the West Bank with a large amount of water. It has never done so, and Israel claims that it has been forced to supply the West Bank from its own resources.

Palestinians and others accuse Israel of mismanaging the region's water, in part because many Israelis live a consumer-oriented lifestyle that depends on ample water. Green lawns and swimming pools are common, and Israelis have continuously developed the land, building homes, kibbutzim, and farms. The government subsidizes water for Israelis, which discourages conservation. In 1995 the Ministry

of Agriculture recommended ending subsidies to agriculture, but the Water Commissioner's office rejected this idea.

Almost half of the land in Israel is irrigated for agricultural purposes, and agriculture uses 75 percent of the nation's water resources. In the 1960s, Israel was on the forefront of research into drip irrigation, which greatly reduces the amount of water needed to grow crops, but most of this experimentation ended after Israel took control of more water resources in 1967. Neighboring countries use much less water for agriculture than Israel does; less than 10 percent of cultivated fields in Palestine are irrigated and only about 8 percent of Jordan's farmland receives irrigation. Critics note that agriculture supplies only 6 percent of Israel's gross domestic product and suggest that the scarce water resources might be better used to nourish non-irrigated traditional crops.

In spite of Israel's position, Palestinians living in Israel lack ready access to water. Since 1967 Palestinians living in the West Bank have been prevented from digging new wells while Israelis have been exploiting the water resources underlying land inhabited by Arabs. Palestinians pay between three and eight times more for water than Israelis. Each Israeli uses more than 3.5 times the amount of water used by each Palestinian. Palestinians living in the Occupied Territories receive on average less than 100 liters of water per day, less than the 150 liters daily water allotment recommended by the World Health Organization.

Palestinians have learned to conserve water, saving rainwater in rooftop cisterns and recycling water used for cooking and cleaning. Under international law, the water resources should be shared equitably, but inequity has been the rule since the state of Israel was established. Palestinians argue in particular that Israel's taking control of the West Bank in 1967 has also given Israel those water resources. Israel has countered that argument with the claim that international law gives priority to past and existing uses of water at the expense of potential uses, and that because it has been using that water for years, it has the right to continue to use it.

The Sea of Galilee and the Coastal Aquifer are both entirely within Israel's pre-1967 borders, and Israel claims these completely. Israel also notes that most of the water from the Western Aquifer emerges from springs in Israel, and that it has used the Western Aquifer's water since the early 1950s. Israelis argue that Palestinians are in fact benefiting from Israel's water, because Palestinian settlements in the West Bank use water sources developed by Israel. Israeli water also goes to settlements in Gaza, Jordan, and south Lebanon. Under the 1994 peace agreement between Israel and Jordan, Israel and Jordan agreed to share the Jordan River, and Israel agreed to supply a large amount of water to Jordan.

Israel has been investigating the use of desalinization plants to purify saltwater. Population experts fear that if the population of the region continues to grow at current rates, there will soon be a severe water shortage even if distribution problems are resolved, making further conflict seemingly inevitable.

THE JORDAN RIVER AS A NEXUS FOR PEACEFUL COOPERATION

Chris Hrynkow

At first glance, the Jordan River, with its arid location and international drainage basin reaching into the territories of Syria, Lebanon, Jordan, Israel, Egypt, and the Palestinian Authority, may seem to be a conflict stressor; a scarce source of water in a hostile geopolitical environment. However, I argue that the Jordan River is too important a social, economic, religious, and ecological resource to be anything other than a nexus for regional cooperation.

The Jordan River, its drainage basin and the underlying aquifers, represents valuable fresh water in a dry land. The Middle East as a whole may be said to have effectively run out of the fresh water necessary for its population in the 1970s. The problem is so acute that it takes nation-centric water security off the table for many of the actors involved. Indeed, even if the Palestinian Authority, Israel, or Jordan were able to control and use all of the water in the Jordan River basin, they would still not, according to the World Bank standards, be able to meet the freshwater needs of their populations without international cooperation. Nonetheless, today the Jordan River basin helps quench the thirst, water the crops, and drive the industry of citizens of Egypt, Syria, Lebanon, and, in particular, Jordan, Israel, and the Palestinian Authority.

The quantitative division of the fresh water in the Jordan basin is not the only issue, quality is also a concern. If the water becomes too polluted or too salinated, then its socio-economic utility declines drastically. Additionally, the ecosystem the Jordan supports, already noticeably degraded, especially in the lower section of the river, would be irreparably damaged if pollution levels became unmanageable or flow levels become negligible. Because of its connection to Jewish, Christian, and Muslim history, the Jordan River and the Sea of Galilee (Lake Kinneret/Tiberius), which forms part of the river's course, are major sources of tourism, including for Christians seeking to be baptized through immersion in the river. Too degraded and polluted, these bodies of water would not hold the same attraction. The dangers of further degradation and collapse of the river system as a whole are real. Currently, the flow of the river into the Dead Sea is at a fraction of its historic levels. As a result, the Dead Sea itself is shrinking, which has already negatively affected tourism. This dire situation motivated Jewish, Christian, and Muslim leaders to jointly craft a "Covenant for the Jordan River" in November 2013, calling on governmental actors to work swiftly for the rehabilitation of the lower river. That the document grew from an EcoPeace initiative of Friends of the Earth Middle East and its language of covenant, with rights and responsibilities shared amongst the signatories, further reveals the Jordan's potential as nexus for nonviolent conflict transformation. The religious leaders noted the sacred, contemporary, and historical significance of the river as indicative of a need for cooperation, posing the cogent question about the Jordan ecosystem's integrity: "if we cannot protect a place of such exceptional value, what part of the earth will we hand on intact to our children?"

In short, the Jordan basin is a historic jewel with socio-economic, theological, and ecological value. As recent technology-based initiatives by the Israeli government signify, this means that regional actors cannot let the river basin wither and die. The cost would simply be too high on too many levels. Thus, we arrive at a situation where mutual interest in the vitality of the river creates a realm of shared fate that is marked by a situation of freshwater interdependence in the Jordan basin. In political science terms, the health of the Jordan cannot be a zero-sum game, where one side wins at the expense of the other. Ways must be found for all stakeholders to participate and benefit from that cooperation accordingly or the result will be what conflict theorists call a "lose-lose" outcome.

The population of the Middle East is set to double by mid-century so that Israel, Jordan, and the Palestinian Territories alone will have a combined population of 36 million people, creating additional requirements for creative water relationships in the region. This is yet another factor supporting the conclusion that international cooperation is necessary to maintain the Jordan River's health and increase its flow levels. There are several ways that these goals can be accomplished. The first centers on the structure of the regional economy. In this regard, Israel, Jordan, and the Palestinian Authority have a common interest in developing an economy that moves away from water-intensive agriculture, allowing more of the region's water to be directed to ecological stability, human health, and other sustainable uses. Hence, the value of tourism and other service-based features of the economy that can generate the wealth to allow for "virtual water" imports in the form of commodities like wheat. Also important to the Jordan's health is that water-conserving technology be accessible to all three constituencies so that the remaining agricultural producers, industry, and growing urban areas use water as effectively as possible. Stability in the region could be enhanced through economic cooperation and sharing technologies for reduced freshwater use amongst all the stakeholders. Because agricultural runoff is also major pollutant and cause of salination, this scenario would reduce per capita demand, allowing more volume and better quality water to flow through the Jordan.

Another option, though less sustainable, would be to add volume to the system by diverting water into the Jordan basin from Syria. This could be accomplished in a number of ways, which might include dovetailing infrastructure bringing much-needed additional fresh water to Damascus. This option could be brought to fruition by including multi-actor deals to allocate more of the Jordan basin water to Lebanon and selling a percentage of the water not only to Israel but also to Jordan and the Palestinian Authority. In this manner, five actors could be bound together in a mutual-enhancing agreement. Alternatively, an undersea pipeline could be constructed to feed the Jordan basin and Damascus from Turkey. This pipeline could be routed through Syria or across the Mediterranean Sea by enhancing the capacity of an ongoing project to Cyprus. The latter strategy would have the advantage of using fresh water as a tool for peacebuilding in three areas of potential conflict (Israel and its neighbors; Greek and Turkish Cypriots; and Syria and Turkey).

However, fresh water's characteristic as a tool for peacebuilding does not just exist on the level of possibilities in the Jordan basin. Already, fresh water has shown its ability to start conversations among belligerents and enhance peace processes in the region. Notably, even when officially in a state of broken diplomatic relations, the Israeli and Jordanian governments met on several occasions between 1948 and 1994 to broker deals about the use of water in the Jordan River basin. Further, the 1994 peace treaty between the countries included the establishment of a Joint Water Commission. Since implementation of the 1995 Olso II Accord, the Palestinian and Israeli governments have also had a Joint Water Commission, which continued to meet even during the height of the 2001 *Intifada*. To compliment such bilateral arrangements, in December 2013 the Palestinian Authority, Israel, and Jordan signed a tri-party memorandum of understanding for three water-sharing projects in the region, seeking to combine the stakeholders' relative geographical advantages. This document is indicative of a broader trend of fostering a cooperative peace, and of de-nationalizing and de-securitizing water to the mutual benefit of the peoples of the region.

In short, the health of the Jordan basin is directly linked to peace and stability in the region. The river and its sources can be seen as a barometer. Doubtless, a healthy Jordan River will be indicative of a healthy geopolitical situation in the region. In this manner the Jordan basin is not only a natural treasure from which cooperation can by necessity emerge, its general health and ecological integrity can further serve as a mutually agreeable focal point for cooperative arrangements amongst the regional stakeholders.

REFERENCES

Aggestam, Karin, and Anna Sundell-Elkund. (2014). "Situating water in peacebuilding: revisiting the Middle East peace process," *Water International* 39(1), 10–22.

Allan, John A. (2002). "Hydro-peace in the Middle East: why no water wars?: A case study of the Jordan River basin," *SAIS Review* 22(2), 255–272.

Friends of the Earth Middle East. (2013, November 12). "Covenant for the Jordan River." Save the Jordan. Accessed February 25, 2014, at http://foeme.org/uploads/13832213651~%5E$%5E~JR_Covenant.pdf.

Harris, Leila M., and Samer Alatout. (2010). "Negotiating hydro-scales, forging state: comparison of the upper Tigris/Euphrates and the Jordan River basins," *Political Geography* 29, 148–156.

Jägerskog, Anders. (2003). *Why States Cooperate over Shared Water: The Water Negotiation in the Jordan River Basin*. Unitruck, Sweden: Linköping University Press.

Udasin, Sharon. (2013, May 26). "Water flows from Lake Kinneret to Jordan River," *Jerusalem Post*. Accessed February 19, 2014, at http://www.jpost.com/Enviro-Tech/Water-flows-from-Lake-Kinneret-to-Jordan-River-314442.

Wolf, Aaron, Annika Kramer, Alexander Carius, and Geoffrey D. Dabelko. (2006). "Water can be a pathway to peace, not war," *Navigating Peace* 1, 1–6.

World Bank. (2013, December 9). "Senior Israeli, Jordanian and Palestinian representatives sign milestone water sharing agreement." Accessed February 19, 2014, at http://www.worldbank.org/en/news/press-release/2013/12/09/senior-israel-jordanian-palestinian-representatives-water-sharing-agreement.

31

WHAT IMPACT DOES CONTROL OF VALUABLE RESOURCES HAVE ON POLITICS IN THE MIDDLE EAST?

OVERVIEW
Larry Simpson and M. Troy Burnett

Oil and water are two resources that have played an important role in the history of the Middle East. The discovery of vast amounts of oil in the Middle East in the early 20th century caused the world to view the region in a new light. Although at first control of this oil was largely in the hands of countries outside of the region, before long many Middle Eastern nations had asserted their control over this valuable resource. The Middle East began to take center stage in the foreign policies of industrialized nations wishing to maintain a steady flow of oil from the region. Water issues, such as the diversion of the Jordan River and the controversy it caused between Israel and several neighboring Arab countries, continues to be a divisive issue in the Middle East.

Spencer C. Tucker examines two facets of the Arab-Israeli conflict—economics and international influence. On the surface, these topics seem markedly different.

The first has had a very real impact on the conflict, while the second has come to prominence only through the perceptions and cultural biases of others. Yet these defining moments share an important similarity: they both illustrate how the Arab-Israeli conflict has shaped and been shaped by the larger international community and its fixation on both the resources of the region and the culture. Oil, for instance, has focused worldwide attention on the Middle East, but it has also been used by Arab states in an attempt to alter other nations' Middle Eastern policies.

Larry Simpson takes a closer look at these two important issues regarding resources in the Middle East. In the first, he focuses on the waters of the Jordan River Basin. The Jordan River provides water for irrigation to a number of countries. When Israel sought to divert part of the river in order to irrigate the Negev Desert, this action caused great resentment among Syria, Jordan, and Lebanon. The conflict would eventually escalate into the June 1967 Six-Day War. In the second defining moment, Simpson explores the 1973 Arab oil embargo and the worldwide effects of price hikes. Territory that Israel had gained in 1967 was still in dispute, and the Organization of Petroleum Exporting Countries (OPEC) called for a 5-percent cut in production until Israel returned the disputed land and the world recognized the rights of the Palestinian people. With the United States on the verge of sending an aid package to Israel, OPEC launched an embargo against any nation supporting Israel. This event had devastating worldwide economic effects.

BACKGROUND

Some say that oil and water do not mix, but the two have certainly combined to influence the course of the Arab-Israeli dispute. The former is a fast-diminishing resource for most of the world, yet it can be found in abundance in many parts of the Middle East. Although there is no problem obtaining the latter in many parts of the globe, there is a dearth of water in much of the region and conflicts over water rights there have contributed to war. To understand the Arab-Israeli conflict, one must consider both of these economic resources at further length.

The history of Middle Eastern oil began in 1901 when the Englishman William Knox D'Arcy managed to obtain an oil concession from the Persian shah, Muzzaffar al-Din. Seven years later, drillers struck oil in southwest Persia. From these roots arose the Anglo-Persian (later Iranian) Oil Company. During the 1920s and 1930s, prospectors found oil elsewhere in the Persian Gulf region. An international consortium, which later became the Iraq Petroleum Company, hit oil at Kirkuk in Kurdistan in 1927, just two years after the Iraqi government granted it rights to search for the precious commodity. Elsewhere, in Bahrain, Standard Oil of California (Socal) set up a Canadian subsidiary called the Bahrain Petroleum Company that discovered oil in 1932. Six years later, the Anglo-Persian Oil Company and William Mellon's Gulf Oil found oil in the tiny emirate of Kuwait.

It was also in 1938 that drillers made their greatest find in Saudi Arabia. Socal, later joined by Texaco, had persuaded the debt-ridden king, Ibn Saud, to grant the companies a concession in exchange for a $28,000 loan and the payment of $7000 for a lease. The joint company they created, which took the name Arabian American Oil Company (Aramco) in 1944, had come upon a huge, underground petroleum lake with an estimated reserve of 206 billion barrels—a number equivalent to proven U.S. reserves at the time. Yet, to put things in perspective, these Middle Eastern oil fields were just coming on line when World War II began. At the time of World War II, the United States still produced 60 percent of the world's oil. Only a trickle came from the Persian Gulf region, with Iran then producing 4 percent of global output, Iraq 2 percent, and Saudi Arabia less than 1 percent.

World War II would demonstrate the importance of oil for the world economy. Adolf Hitler's bid to conquer the Soviet Union failed as he drove south to capture oil fields in the Caucasus region. Likewise, Japan's drive to obtain the oil of the Dutch East Indies led it into confrontation with the United States. Nonetheless, the strategic importance of the commodity was not so obvious to policy makers, as the period from the end of World War II through the 1960s was a time of plenty with low gasoline prices for motorists at the pump. Looking deeper, however, it becomes obvious that this would inevitably change. The same years witnessed the massive growth of the European and Japanese economies as well as the mass production of automobiles in the American economy. Moreover, oil was not used simply for transportation, but also increasingly in the far-reaching petrochemical industry.

The 1970s were a watershed period in the history of oil. By that time, demand had reached the point that oil companies were producing at full capacity. The government of Libya, where Esso first discovered oil in 1957, was the first to take advantage of this by raising prices and demanding a larger share of oil company profits. Other countries that were part of OPEC, an international cartel, soon followed and prices began to skyrocket. Then, Arab countries used oil as a weapon during the 1973 Yom Kippur War between Israel and the Arab nations of Egypt and Syria. Following Saudi Arabia's lead, they imposed an embargo on any country that supported the Jewish state. The price hikes and embargo led to panic in world markets and prices reached unprecedented levels before the situation stabilized. Meanwhile, the global economy experienced high inflation and serious unemployment. A second wave of price hikes at the end of the 1970s only exacerbated the problem. The West responded by seeking new energy sources, more aggressively exploring for and exploiting domestic sources of oil whenever possible, and adopting conservation measures. On the other hand, energy dependency on the Middle East remains a fundamental issue. By 2005, for example, the United States was importing 61 percent of its oil and Saudi Arabia remained the largest source of its crude oil imports.

Finally, no discussion of Middle East economic issues would be complete without some mention of water rights. Israel has long disputed its access to water from the Jordan River with Jordan, Syria, and Lebanon. When Israel began to take water from Lake Tiberias and use it for agriculture in the Negev Desert in 1964, its actions led to Arab protests followed by a Syrian scheme to divert the headwaters of the Jordan River and deny the valuable resource to the Israelis. A cycle of violence followed that culminated in the June 1967 Six-Day War. Today, conflict over water persists in the region. Competing claims between the Israelis and Palestinians over access to water have been part of the ongoing interrupted peace process from the time of the 1993 Oslo Accords. Likewise, Syria and Turkey have had a long-simmering dispute over the latter's damming of the Euphrates River and offtake of waters that otherwise would have flowed into Syria.

FURTHER READING

Allan, Tony. (2002). *The Middle East Water Question: Hydropolitics and the Global Economy.* London and New York: I. B. Tauris.

Diop, Ndiame, Daniela Marotta, and Jaime de Melo. (2012). *Natural Resource Abundance, Growth, and Diversification in the Middle East and North Africa: The Effects of Natural Resources and the Role of Policies.* Washington, DC: World Bank Publications.

IT'S NOT JUST ABOUT RELIGION, BUT ECONOMICS AS WELL
Spencer Tucker

Although the Arab-Israeli conflict is often attributed solely to deep-seated religious and political tensions between Arabs and Jews, a number of other factors have contributed to the violence that continues to plague the Middle East. These issues further convolute a situation already characterized by complexity, making a final and mutually satisfactory solution all the more difficult to find.

Economics is perhaps the most significant of these issues, as it has always been intricately intertwined with the politics of the region. Agriculture has been an important facet of Zionism since the late 19th century. Before the declaration of the State of Israel, farming allowed Jewish immigrants to make tangible territorial claims in Palestine and provided sustenance and security for the growing Jewish population. The spread of Jewish farming collectives (kibbutzim) often meant the dispossession of native Palestinians, however. These kibbutzim have also served as military outposts during Israel's many wars, further conflating the issues of economics and national security in the minds of both Israelis and Arabs. Threats to economic security have also provided the impetus for military conflict, as was the case in 1956 when Egypt closed the Straits of Tiran to Israeli shipping.

316 Asia and the Pacific

The rise of the Zionist movement in the late 19th century was influenced by nationalist currents in Europe, as well as by the secularization of Jewish life in Eastern Europe, which led many assimilated Jewish intellectuals, such as Theodor Herzl, to seek a new, non-European basis for a Jewish national life. (Library of Congress)

The economies of the Middle East are largely dictated by the presence (or absence) of two important resources—water and oil. Water resources are often prime targets of military and terrorist sabotage. The poisoning of wells, for instance, has been perpetrated by both Arabs and Israelis in wartime. During the 1960s, the new Israeli National Water Carrier (NWC) and its counterpart irrigation systems in various Arab nations were attacked because they were seen as extensions of national aggression. In January 1965, Fatah's first terrorist act targeted the NWC.

The 1967 Six-Day War vastly increased Israel's access to water, to the detriment of its Arab opponents. By occupying the West Bank, Israel denied Jordan about half of its agricultural land. In 1982, many viewed the Israeli invasion of Lebanon as a ploy to secure the Litani River. Although eventually compelled to withdraw from Lebanon, the Israelis were able to establish a security zone that allowed them to siphon off some of the Litani's waters. Today, approximately 55 percent of Israel's water comes from the Occupied Territories.

Oil is also an important economic factor because it has widened the Arab-Israeli conflict into an international issue. Oil has been used as a diplomatic weapon, as was the case in 1973 when the Arab members of the Organization of Petroleum Exporting Countries (OPEC) instituted an embargo against all nations supporting Israel during the Yom Kippur War. Although vast oil reserves have given a number of Arab nations global clout, industrialized nations' need for petroleum is, in fact, largely responsible for the genesis of the Arab-Israeli conflict. Economic interest in the Middle East after World War I, coupled with the strategic importance of the Suez Canal, led to the domination of the region by the United Kingdom and France under the League of Nations mandate system. Territorial and, later, national boundaries were drawn arbitrarily by the European powers and did not take into account the long history and ethno-religious makeup of the area. The region of Palestine proved particularly problematic, as Britain had made promises of statehood to both the Arab and Jewish populations in the area in order to secure their assistance during the war.

International influence in the Middle East did not end with the creation of sovereign Middle Eastern nations. In fact, as World War II ended and the Cold War dawned, the region became the pawn in a new international power play—this time between the United States and the Soviet Union. The superpowers sought to extend their influence by funneling aid and arms into their client states, which in turn gave both the Arabs and the Israelis the means they needed to perpetuate the conflict. A strong sense of Arab nationalism emerged as a backlash against this continued and often meddlesome foreign presence in the Middle East that, when combined with Israel's aggressive program of territorial acquisition, only fanned the flames of war. Given this troubled history with foreign intervention, it is not surprising that the United States and other countries and international organizations have had difficulty in brokering a lasting peace. Indeed, many cite the United States' dual interests in the region—its dependence on Arab oil and its continued economic and military support of Israel—as a direct impediment to the peace process.

Although perhaps not innately integral to the Arab-Israeli conflict, many nations in the West—particularly the United States—have cast the fighting in the Middle East in cultural terms. Many Westerners view the conflict as a clash between an industrialized, democratic Israel and a collection of primitive, repressive Arab nations. Although grossly inaccurate and overly simplistic, this viewpoint has nevertheless shaped both foreign policy and public opinion regarding the conflict. Women's rights, the openness of the electoral process, and access to education and social services have become hot topics in the international community, even if they are not points of contention between Arabs and Israelis.

The multidimensional nature of the Arab-Israeli conflict has made achieving resolution particularly difficult. While its international scope has only complicated matters, the interests and involvement of the wider global community have made such a resolution all the more important.

OIL AND WATER—THE RESOURCE DISPUTES THAT CONTRIBUTE TO CONFLICTS IN THE MIDDLE EAST
Larry Simpson

During the second week of the 1973 Yom Kippur War, Arab members of the Organization of Petroleum Exporting Countries (OPEC), led by Saudi Arabia, announced a 5-percent cut in production until Israel withdrew from territory it occupied in 1967 and the world recognized the rights of the Palestinian people. The stunning event followed a prior agreement between Egyptian president Anwar Sadat and the Saudis and was Riyadh's way of expressing solidarity with the Arab cause. When U.S. President Richard Nixon turned to the U.S. Congress to send emergency aid to Israel, the Arab OPEC members imposed a complete embargo on the United States and any other country they deemed guilty of supporting the Jewish state.

The idea of using oil as a weapon in the dispute over Palestine was not new, as the Arab League had considered doing so as early as 1946. At that time, however, there was an oil glut, and this continued throughout the 1950s and into the 1960s. Likewise, the petroleum-producing countries were not united and it was not until 1960 that several of them formed OPEC. In the meantime, demand for oil continued to grow in the United States as well as in Europe and Japan. By 1970, the oil industry was running at full capacity so that suppliers were in a unique position. Beginning that year, the radical Libyan leader Muammar Qaddafi would initiate a cycle of price hikes by coercing Occidental Petroleum into accepting a number of concessions, including a 30-cent price hike on a barrel of oil and a 5-percent increase of Libya's share of profits. The shah of Iran soon followed suit, as did Venezuela. A game of leapfrog ensued with OPEC countries joining together to demand better terms from the oil companies and with the latter unable to unite in the face of the pressure. The cost of a barrel of oil would soar from $1.80 in 1970 to reach $11.65 in late 1974.

The Arab boycott was just one element that contributed to spiraling petroleum prices. Iraq's nationalization of oil in 1973 also was a major factor in spreading fear on world markets. Indeed, prices continued to rise even after the Arab OPEC members lifted the embargo after March 1974 at the urging of Sadat. Moreover, it was not only Arab countries that jacked up prices. Other major petroleum

View of the Sea of Galilee at Tiberias, Israel. (Gilad Levy)

producers such as Iran and Venezuela saw a golden opportunity for an economic windfall with the price raises.

The response to this revolution in world economics was near panic. Long gas lines suddenly sprang up and there were fuel shortages and rationing. As petroleum has a wide variety of uses in modern industrial economies beyond transportation, such as in the production of plastics and fertilizers, the effects rippled through Western economies and had a kind of negative multiplier effect. While oil-producing countries reaped windfall profits, the global economy suffered from high inflation and unemployment, and developing countries were hit particularly hard. The 1970s was a decade of economic challenges, and a subsequent wave of petroleum price increases would leave the price of oil at $40 per barrel. There were also political consequences. Although the United States continued to support Israel, the European countries began to take a more pro-Arab view of the Arab-Israeli dispute. Developing nations, particularly those in Africa, went even further and broke relations with Tel Aviv. Likewise, there were unintended consequences for the "winners" as well. The socioeconomic changes helped to destabilize traditional political systems, as the revolution in Iran well illustrates.

WATER

An often-neglected aspect of the Arab-Israeli conflict concerns the dispute over the control of water resources. In 1953, the Israelis began the construction of a National Water Carrier to transport water from the Jordan River to the Negev and "make the desert bloom." As the Arabs vehemently objected to this diversion of the scarce resource, the United States tried to find a compromise on the issue. Between 1953 and 1955, American officials came up with the Johnson Plan for an equitable division of water. Neither side, however, would agree to the proposal and tensions continued over the issue. When the Israelis unilaterally began in 1964 to pump water from Lake Tiberias and dam its southern outlet, this act added to the growing strains that ultimately culminated in the Six-Day War of June 1967. The Arabs objected not only on account of the fact that Israel's offtake of water would deny the same to thousands of Jordanian farmers farther south in the Jordan River Valley, but also because they claimed Israel's access to more resources would allow greater immigration and thus tighten its hold on Palestine and increase the threat of Zionist expansionism.

In response, an Arab Summit approved $17.5 million in funds for diverting the headwaters of the Jordan River farther north in Lebanon and Syria. It was the Syrians who actually began a project to divert water in November 1964 and began building the Mukeiba Dam. As this threatened to deprive Israel of 35 percent of the water resources from the upper Jordan, Israeli Prime Minister Levi Eshkol considered the Syrian action a *casus belli* and began to take preemptive military actions to ensure the continued flow of what he called "Israel's life-blood." Following this logic, Israeli tanks destroyed Syrian bulldozers that were within range on the other side of the border. When the Syrians persisted with the project beyond where Israeli shells could reach and when border incidents were followed by Syrian artillery bombardments of Israeli settlements, Tel Aviv did Damascus one better and escalated the conflict. The Israelis employed the Israeli Air Force (IAF) to silence the Syrian guns and halt the construction of the diversionary project.

Thus, the issue of water was one of the central points of contention between the Arabs, particularly the Syrians, and the Israelis. Unable to defeat the Israelis by conventional methods, Syrian leaders increasingly turned to support of fedayeen, or guerrilla, raids into Israel. The number of such attacks continued to rise—especially after a February 1966 coup brought General Salal al-Jadid into power in Syria—and there were some 93 border incidents that year. Realizing that they needed a counter to the IAF, Syrian leaders purchased MiG-21s from the Soviet Union. Nevertheless, the Syrian Air Force proved no match for the IAF. In two aerial encounters in July and August 1966, for instance, the IAF shot down a total of three MiGs. All of this was part of the escalation that culminated in the Six-Day War in 1967. The Israeli capture of the Golan Heights eliminated the threat posed by the Syrian water diversion program, but it in no way ended the bitter dispute between the Arabs and Jews over water rights regarding the Jordan River.

32

IS CHINA'S GREEN GREAT WALL AN ADEQUATE SOLUTION TO DESERTIFICATION?

OVERVIEW
Bruce E. Johansen

China has a long history of deforestation, felling its forests for at least 2,000 years. The Yellow River got its color from eroded soil laid bare by this practice. After World War II, much of China's old growth was stripped to grow food, supply fuel for steel mills, and other reasons. Until the 1970s, the countryside was being stripped, as sandstorms, called "yellow dragons" raked Beijing. In 1978, however, China decided to reverse this long practice via, among other things, a massive replanting scheme colloquially known as the "Great Green Wall." In 1981, the National People's Congress mandated by law that each citizen more than 11 years of age plant at least three poplar, larch, or eucalyptus saplings each year. The numbers have been astounding: roughly 56 billion trees have been planted between 1999 and 2009. Today, however, this grand reforestation project is threatened by climate change, poor management, and ever-increasing desertification. The question is, has the project been worth it?

BACKGROUND

The official name of the massive project is the Three-North Shelter Forest Program. Three-north is a reference to the three regions of China involved in the program: Northeast, North, and Northwest. By 2050, this artificial forest is planned to stretch over 400 million hectares, making it the largest ecological restoration project in human history. By 2010, China's Communist Party announced with considerable fanfare that the country already had the largest human-made forest in the world, more than 500,000 square kilometers, providing China with roughly 20-percent forest cover. By 2050, government planners foresee an arc of greenery 4,480 kilometers (or about 2,800 miles) long, from Xinjiang province in China's far west to Heilongjiang in the east.

China faces a tall order, as deserts expand over many areas in its north and west. In Inner Mongolia's Kubuqi Desert, which adjoins the Gobi Desert, reaching close to Beijing, "We are on the front line of a huge Chinese dust bowl advancing east," said Byong Hyon Kwon, once a South Korean ambassador to China who has become an advocate of the Green Great Wall (Trafford, 2014). China has been losing roughly 3,600 square kilometers (1,400 square miles) a year to the Gobi Desert. Dust storms, which have been increasing in severity, blow away topsoil across the northern provinces. The storms also have affected agriculture in North and South Korea as well as Japan, and traces of them have reached the West Coast of the United States.

Aerial seeding has been used in areas with enough precipitation to, at least in theory, allow the trees to take root on their own. In drier areas, farmers are given cash incentives to plant trees and shrubs. Sand-tolerant vegetation is also used to stabilize advancing sand dunes, with varying rates of success. Some of the forests are planted quite carefully: "1.5-metre-square frames are set in the sand and wired together to make a grid that is heavy enough not to blow away. Trees are then planted inside the squares. Poplars are chosen in part because their roots, which grow like spider webs, can sprout more baby trees. If the tree survives, it should reach a man's height in about four years. The volunteers also plant salix, a shrub that grows in sandy soil" (Trafford, 2014).∆

Tree planting has become a mass spectacle. Each spring, as many as 3 million Communist Party members, civil servants, and others plant trees as part of a nation-wide campaign to showcase China's environmental consciousness. Former U.S. vice president, Nobel Prize-winner, and best-selling author Al Gore was impressed, declaring that China had planted two and a half times as many trees per year as the rest of the world combined: "The largest tree-planting program the world has ever seen" (Moxley, 2010). China's official goal is to have 42 percent of its land covered with forests by 2050 (Land, 2014).

While Gore was dutifully impressed, some scientists in China continue to express concerns about the massive project. According to an account in the U.K.

Guardian, Jiang Gaoming, professor at the Chinese Academy of Sciences' Institute of Botany and vice secretary-general of the China Society of Biological Conservation, said the Great Green Wall has, in some places, "accelerated ecological degeneration by putting pressure on precious water resources in arid and semi-arid regions." Jiang also said that trees planted during the Great Green Wall project are non-native are require vast amounts of resources to maintain, whereas forest scientists have long known that native trees actually play a much bigger role in preventing desertification (Moxley, 2010). In addition, recently planted forests are less efficient than older/complex systems at removing greenhouse gases from the atmosphere. Critics also note that to grasslands are better suited to mitigate desertification and also can sequester more carbon dioxide and methane than young forests. In short, the long-term viability of the project is not guaranteed (Luoma, 2012).

Yet, as M. Troy Burnett argues in this section, the Herculean efforts of the Chinese people to address its desertification crisis, has brought some benefits and has not been completely in vain. Along with the general increase in public awareness as to the scale of the problem and the government's willingness to actually do something about it, the project has provided a modicum of farmland protection, soil and water conservation, wind reduction, and sand dune stabilization. The rate of soil erosion and desertification, while not reversed, has lessened since the project began. Further, the amount of sand and sediment entering the Yellow River has been reduced. There has also been an uptick in development of the semi-arid region as the curious, the opportunist, and the tourist descend on the area.

REFERENCES

Land, Graham. (2014, February 3). "The Great Green Wall: reforesting China," *Asian Correspondent*. Accessed March 3, 2016, at http://asiancorrespondent.com/119175/reforesting-china/.

Luoma, Jon R. (2012, January 17). "China's reforestation programs: big success or just an illusion?," *Environment 360: Opinion, Analysis, Reporting and Debate*, Yale University. Accessed March 3, 2016, at http://e360.yale.edu/feature/chinas_reforestation_programs_big_success_or_just_an_illusion/2484/.

Moxley, Mitch. (2010, September 23). "China's Great Green Wall grows in climate fight," *The Guardian*. Accessed March 3, 2016, at http://www.theguardian.com/environment/2010/sep/23/china-great-green-wall-climate.

Trafford, Abigail. (2014, February 1). "Can China's great, green wall stop its creeping deserts?," *Toronto Star* (republished from the *Washington Post*). Accessed March 3, 2016, at http://www.thestar.com/news/world/2014/02/01/can_chinas_great_green_wall_stop_its_creeping_deserts.html.

FURTHER READING

Bawany, Bilal. (2013, November 1). "The Green Wall of China: enough to keep the Yellow Dragon at bay?" University of Texas. Accessed March 3, 2013, at https://sites.utexas.edu/mecc/2013/11/01/the-green-wall-of-china-enough-to-keep-the-yellow-dragon-at-bay/.

Heshmati, G. Ali, and Victor R. Squires. (2013). *Combating Desertification in Asia, Africa and the Middle East: Proven Practices*. Dordrecht, Netherlands, and New York: Springer.

THE GREAT GREEN WALL AND ITS MANY CRACKS
Bruce E. Johansen

China's Green Great Wall will not adequately address desertification because it deals only with desertification's surface manifestations. The roots of spreading deserts lie in global warming, including worldwide changes in atmospheric circulation patterns, which require long-term global-scale solutions. The Green Great Wall may stall the advance of deserts in China, but it is not a cure. Jiang Fengguo, director at the Soil and Water Conservation Supervision Station in Hexigtan Banner, Inner Mongolia Autonomous Region, said that the Green Great Wall may stall desertification for a time, but probably will not reverse it: "There will still be problems. Desertification still exists, and the continuing deterioration of the environment has not been reversed" (Moxley, 2010).

This "solution" has several problems, despite its overblown claims. The numbers are indeed impressive (roughly 56 billion trees planted between 1999 and 2009, comprising 5.88 million hectares of forest) until one delves under the public-relations gloss. A substantial number of these trees were "planted" by airplanes, and subsequently died. Others were planted by hand with a great deal of care in planned shelterbelts, but were unsuited to their surroundings, and sucked up groundwater at rates that were not sustainable in a dry climate that shows every sign of further drought. Some of the forests that did take root are biologically relatively sterile monocultures.

The "yellow dragons," Beijing's dust storms, have persisted even after more than 30 years of tree planting, as they "thicken the skies over Beijing with dust and send people with asthmatic lungs and weak hearts to the hospital," aggravating air pollution from coal-fired power plants that gives that city and others in China the dirtiest air on Earth (Land, 2014).

Some of China's enduring drought stems from changes in worldwide atmospheric circulation compelled by worldwide climate change. Even though warmer air generally holds more moisture, not everyone will see more precipitation in a globally warmed world. Many deserts already are expanding, in a worldwide pattern influenced by atmospheric circulation patterns that meteorologists call "Hadley cells."

Near the equator, warm, moist air rises, cools, and unleashes downpours. In the upper troposphere, the air spreads north and southward toward both poles, descending at about 30 degrees north and south latitude, creating deserts. As temperatures rise, the Hadley cells reach further north and south of the equator. While precipitation patterns are also influenced by other factors (e.g., ready access, or lack thereof, to ocean-borne moisture), rainfall is strongly influenced by Hadley cells. Rising air portends instability, low pressure, and storminess, whereas descending air generally produces high pressure and clear skies. In a warmer world, Hadley cells expand, which causes deserts to expand, a process that is already evident from news reports around the world.

Droughts in regions where Hadley cells favor descending air now span the globe, from Australia, to Spain, Iraq, Afghanistan, parts of China, the Murray-Darling Basin of Australia,and the United States Southwest, including California, Nevada, New Mexico, Arizona, and Texas. In China, the Gobi desert, also within the northern reaches of Hadley cell range, has been expanding. In Iran, Lake Urmia, once plied by cruise ships, has lost nearly all of its water, and water rationing has been proposed for Tehran.

Even as it seeded billions of trees, in a 2006 report China told the United Nations Convention to Combat Desertification that 2.63 million square kilometers (a quarter of its land mass) was covered with desert, compared with 18 percent in 1994. Between the early 1980s, when mass tree planting began, and 1994, even the Chinese government admitted that its grasslands shrunk by about 15,000 square kilometers annually. Every year, 30 percent of the newly planted trees die and have to be replaced. In 2009, one-quarter of 53,000 hectares planted died, some due to drought, others because of severe winter storms.

Major stands of thirsty trees can be counterproductive in the long run. For example, in Mingin, a relatively arid area in Northwestern China, planting large numbers of non-native trees with high water demands played a role in a groundwater decline of 12 to 19 meters. Land erosion, over-farming, and pollution also have played a role in making soils in some areas unsuitable for intense planting of trees. Lack of diversiry also makes the new forersts more prone to diseases.

Jiang Gaoming, an ecologist at the Chinese Academy of Sciences, has characterized this grand design as "a fairy tale" (Luoma, 2013). In an analysis in *Earth Science Reviews*, Beijing Forestry University scientist Shixiong Cao and five co-authors said that on-the-ground surveys have shown that, over time, as many as 85 percent of the plantings will fail (Luoma, 2013). David Shankman, a geographer at the University of Alabama, said that "over years or decades the plantings have tended to eventually deplete local soil moisture and die *en masse* simply because the planted species are not native to the region, and don't tolerate local conditions" (Luoma, 2013).

Writing in *Nature* in September, Jianchu Xu, a senior scientist at the World Agroforestry Centre and a professor at the Kunming Institute of Botany, Chinese Academy of Science, said that that native perennial grasses, "with their extensive root systems would be better protectors of topsoil" (Luoma, 2013).

"In what could be a hopeful turn, China's State Forestry Administration has indicated that it has gotten the message," Jon R. Luoma wrote in Yale University's *Environment 360*, "The nation's lead forestry agency has begun collaborating on projects aimed specifically at restoring native species. The agency is working with the Climate Community and Biodiversity Alliance (CCBA), whose members include Conservation International, the Nature Conservancy, and the Rainforest Alliance."

The hope is that the Chinese authorities can learn from the experience of the Great Green Wall and while continuing in its spirit, implement a program that, base on native grass species, will actually do the job of slowing desertification.

REFERENCES

Land, Graham. (2014, February 3). "The Great Green Wall: reforesting China," *Asian Correspondent*. Accessed March 3, 2016, at http://asiancorrespondent.com/119175/reforesting-china/.

Luoma, Jon R. (2012, January 17). "China's reforestation programs: big success or just an illusion?" *Environment 360: Opinion, Analysis, Reporting & Debate*, Yale University. Accessed March 13, 2016, at http://e360.yale.edu/feature/chinas_reforestation_programs_big_success_or_just_an_illusion/2484/.

Moxley, Mitch. (2010, September 23). "China's Great Green Wall grows in climate fight," *The Guardian*. Accessed March 3, 2016, at http://www.theguardian.com/environment/2010/sep/23/china-great-green-wall-climate.

THE GREAT GREEN WALL—A HERCULEAN EFFORT

M. Troy Burnett

The Three-North Shelter Forest Program, colloquially known as the "Great Green Wall," is one of the most ambitious, and arguably desperate, ecological programs of the modern era. Not surprisingly, it has drawn considerable global attention, most of it negative. Yet the Herculean efforts of the Chinese people to address the

Chinese women wear plastic bags to protect their hair and faces during a severe dust storm in Beijing on March 20, 2002. Sulfur (an acid rain component), soot, ash, carbon monoxide, and other toxic pollutants including heavy metals and other carcinogens often accompany the dust storms, as well as viruses, bacteria, fungi, and pesticides. (AP/Wide World Photos)

desertification crisis has brought some benefits and has not been completely in vain. Along with the general increase in public awareness as to the scale of the problem and the government's willingness to actually do something about it, the project has provided a modicum of farmland protection, soil and water conservation, wind reduction, and sand dune stabilization. The rate of soil erosion and desertification, while not reversed, has lessened since the project began. Further, the amount of sand and sediment entering the Yellow River has been reduced. There has also been an uptick in development of the semi-arid region as the curious, the opportunist, and the tourist descend on the area. However, it is clear after more than 30 years that, from the scientific and ecological perspectives, the project has flaws and a large number of challenges exist. In a project of such grand scale there are inevitable failures, but as the old adage goes, it's not necessary to throw the baby out with the bathwater.

Each year, the infamous dust storms known as the Yellow Dragon torment Beijing and other major East Asian cities. The skies turn yellow-orange and the pollution level reaches its maximum of five—unhealthy for everyone. The root of the problem has been clear to the Chinese people and government for some time—desertification. To address the growing threat of expanding deserts, in 1978 the country embarked on the largest reforestation program in the world, dubbed the Three-North Shelter Forest Program. The idea behind the program is as simple as its scale is large. The country's rapid economic development has initiated an environmental decline. Large forests that have longed acted as protection against erosion have disappeared. Intensive agricultural practices, deforestation, and land degradation have all led to rapid desertification with the Gobi expanding an average of 1600 square kilometers every year, affecting 400 million people, and costing $6.5 billion.

The primary goal was to plant up to 90 million acres of new, fast-growing, carbon-capturing trees along a band reaching more than 2,800 miles across northwest China. The hope was to both provide the requisite ecological benefits of reduced land erosion and increased forest cover as well as the economic benefits associated with forest resource extraction, local jobs and development, and a decrease in the costs associated with the dust storms. It was also an obvious propaganda tool for the Chinese Communist government's efforts to be viewed, domestically and globally, as active in environmental stewardship.

In terms of straight reforestation, the effort saw the annual cover increase by 11,000 square miles between 2000 and 2010 alone. Indeed, according to the reports of the Chinese State Forestry Administration, total forest cover has risen from 12 percent to 18 percent—the overall goal being 42 percent by 2050. However, scientists and environmental groups, both outside and within China, skeptical of the government's reports, argue that the project has been on the wrong path, calling it counterproductive and even ecologically destructive. The Chinese government and bureaucracy, for their part, are open to the criticisms and are endeavoring to address and mitigate the concerns. The mood in the governmental environmental ministries is clear: do the right thing.

A major concern of officials, scientists, and conservation groups is the long-term sustainability of the project. Biodiversity has been sacrificed as non-native, quick-growing trees are planted. Trees such as poplars and eucalyptus, with root systems that run deep and draw large quantities of water from the ground, have been planted in favor of endemic shrubs and grasses. Rubber and pulpwood have also been given preference due to their commercial demands. The concern is that these non-native species will not just reduce regional biodiversity but may actually increase the problem they've been planted to address—desertification. Further, techniques used to "build" the Great Green Wall, such as dropping seeds in capsules from the air, have resulted in a growth failure rate of almost 85 percent, suggesting a high level of wasted time, effort, and money.

To complicate the situation, the Chinese government has never been a model of transparency and cooperation. Bureaucratic infighting, corruption, and false reporting of results have blighted the initiative from the start. Outside scientific groups and foreign governments are skeptical of China's claims of success and the projects overall viability. Infighting between the two primary project bureaucracies, the State Forestry Administration and the Three-North Shelter Forest Program Office, is rampant. Operational factors that affect design, management, and facilitation have been muddied by the infighting, making progress very slow.

Despite the justified criticism and concerns, the Chinese government is showing legitimate concern to address the scientific and administrative challenges. There are models of successful reforestation in China to emulate. For instance the Tengchong restoration project has proven to have reduced erosion, promoted ecological stability, and encouraged local commitment and development. With its emphasis on endemic species and local empowerment, the State Forestry Administration and Three-North Shelter Forest Program Office are attempting to adopt the Tengchong model into the Great Green Wall initiative. Though many are skeptical, historically the Chinese government prefers top-down mega-projects to address problems rather than bottom up, grassroots solutions.

In another case, the Horqin Sandy Land of Northeast China, the reforestation program has proven to have directly reduced desertification. Again, the concern in this part of the "Wall," like many other places, is its long-term viability. First, suitable tree species and planting densities will need to be monitored and controlled in accordance with local precipitation patterns, groundwater levels, and the dynamic geomorphologic conditions. Second, the newly forested landscape will need to be regularly tended (i.e., thinned, trimmed, maintained with pest removal) to ensure the subtle balance between growth rates, leaf density, and water requirements. The model of a successful reforestation program exists; what remains to be seen is the will to apply it throughout.

In short, desertification and dust storms have long plagued northwestern Chinese famers and city dwellers alike. Unsustainable, industrial agricultural practices and land management coupled with the observed soil desiccation caused by late 20th-century global warming have exacerbated the problem. The Chinese government and people have attempted, dramatically to say the least, to build a long, natural line of defense against this threat. Many feel it is not an adequate solution to the crisis, both in theory as well as in practice. With the initial phase of this multi-decade reforestation project coming to an end, it's hard not to agree with the critics. Yet, the project has had some small measure of success. At a minimum, it has inspired the Chinese government and people to action. In recognition of its grand efforts, the United Nations Environmental Program awarded the project a Global 500 award in 1994.

For the project to ultimately be an adequate solution to China's desertification crisis, it must continue to address the ecological and scientific failures of the first stage, while making the entire process as transparent and cooperative as possible. If not, this green wall will be anything but great.

FURTHER READING

Wang, X. M., C. X. Zhang, E. Hasi, and Z. B. Dong. (2010). "Has the Three Norths Forest Shelterbelt Program solved the desertification and dust storm problems in arid and semiarid China?," *Journal of Arid Environments*, 74(1), 13–22.

33

WHAT CONFLICTS HAVE ARISEN AS A RESULT OF CHINA'S BUILDING OF THE THREE GORGES DAM?

OVERVIEW
Allen Raichelle

The 1992 decision to begin construction of the Three Gorges Dam sparked worldwide debate and controversy from the outset. On one side, activists and environmentalists shared growing concerns for the wildlife whose habitat lay in the Yangtze River Valley, fauna that many environmentalists feared would become extinct. Critics also worried about the damage to and eventual loss of some of China's most fertile farmland. More than a million citizens, mostly farmers, had to be relocated from the area prior to the flooding of the Yangtze River Valley, which created the dam's reservoir. Historical artifacts would also be lost when the valley was flooded. On the other side, the dam's proponents pointed to the large amount of hydroelectric power that the dam has begun generating, significantly reducing the amount of high-polluting coal used throughout China. Supporters also pointed to the plan to extend the range of heavy barges and freighters, so that these ships can travel much farther inland. In addition, the dam will allow for much greater control over the catastrophic floods that devastate the Yangtze River almost every year.

In this chapter's first essay, Elizabeth J. Leppman writes from the viewpoint that the costs of the Three Gorges Dam far outweigh the benefits and the project will long be a source of tension both within and outside China. Leppman argues that the dam project is dangerous to China's ecosystem, has displaced hundreds of thousands of Chinese citizens, and in general is susceptible to failure. In contrast, in the second essay, Charles Fuller takes the position that the benefits resulting from the project—namely hydroelectric power and flood control along the Yangtze River—make the Three Gorges Dam worthwhile as a means of improving the quality of life for millions of Chinese citizens. In the long run, the controversies will subside and the locals will view the dam as a source of pride.

BACKGROUND

The Three Gorges region (named for the Qutang, Wu, and Xiling gorges) may have served as the southern cradle of Chinese civilization, according to archaeologists excavating sites in the region dating back to 2000 BCE. The spectacular Three Gorges were known for their high peaks rising along the banks of the Yangtze River, overhanging rock towers, steep cliffs, misty waterfalls, and seething torrents. And at the center of all this activity was the 3,937-mile-long Yangtze, the world's third-longest river after the Nile and the Amazon.

Over the course of China's 4,000-year recorded history, the Yangtze became infamous for its devastating floods, which have taken more than 1 million lives during the past 100 years. Sun Yat-sen, the father of modern China, first proposed the idea of a hydroelectric dam at Three Gorges in 1919. Then, during the 1950s, China's leader Mao Zedong ordered studies performed on the feasibility of damming the Yangtze. Although the government considered building the Three Gorges Dam during the 1960s, economic resources were limited and Chinese leaders decided to first build the Gezhouba Dam, 24 miles downriver from the Three Gorges Dam. Although much smaller than the Three Gorges Dam, the Gezhouba Dam took 18 years to build (1970–1988). Once the Gezhouba Dam was completed, government officials began planning the massive Three Gorges project.

When it was first proposed in 1992, the new dam triggered what has been described as the biggest-ever political debate in the history of Communist China. The dispute sent shock waves through the National People's Congress. Nearly one-third of the delegates abstained or voted against the dam—an unprecedented figure in a one-party legislature. However, then-Prime Minister Li Peng abruptly declared debate over and government leaders granted final approval. Dam construction began in 1994.

The Three Gorges Dam—dubbed the "Great Wall of the Yangtze"—was completed in 2008 and became fully functional in 2012. Heralded as the world's biggest hydroelectric dam, the Three Gorges Dam is more than 600 feet high and stretches almost one-and-a-half miles across the Yangtze. The main wall was completed in 2006, creating a 410-mile-long reservoir that is nearly 600 feet deep and about 3,600 feet wide, which permanently flooded the Three Gorges from which the dam takes its name. The dam also created a waterway wide enough for oceangoing ships to travel 1,500 miles into China's interior, making it possible for freighters to reach Wuhan, a major industrial city.

Since the project's inception, China has promoted it as a solution to the Yangtze's disastrous flooding because the dam will allow the regulation of water flow downstream. Over the years, increasingly higher levees have been required to restrain the surging waters—levees that will no longer be needed with the completion of the massive dam. The project's managers say the level of water stored in the Three Gorges Reservoir will be kept below 490 feet during the summer flood season. However, if an emergency occurs, the reservoir's water level can be raised to control the Yangtze's flow and to alleviate pressure on the middle and lower courses of the river.

According to officials, the dam's 32 generators produce more than 22,000 megawatts of hydroelectric power, enough to supply more than 3 percent of the country's total energy needs by means other than coal-burning power plants. The Three Gorges Dam is the world's largest supplier of hydroelectric power; the facility with the next-largest generating capacity is Brazil's Itaipú dam at 12,600 megawatts. From an environmental standpoint, supporters claim that the Three Gorges Dam supplies clean energy, as it replaces the combustion of 50 million tons of coal every year. According to the government's calculations, because the dam replaces many coal-burning plants, it will drastically reduce the emission into the atmosphere of 100 million tons of carbon dioxide, 2 million tons of sulphur dioxide, 10,000 tons of carbon monoxide, and large amounts of soot and dust. The Chinese government has set a goal of providing 15 percent of its energy from nonrenewable sources by 2020, and achieving that goal will involve the completion of further hydroelectric dam projects in the country by then.

However, the dam's construction has failed to hold back a flood of questions about its effect on the Yangtze River Valley and its inhabitants—especially the approximately 1.4 million people who were displaced by the dam. Although the Chinese government offered financial assistance to relocated residents, some families are having difficulty adjusting to their new villages and farmlands. The government itself has admitted in fact that relocation compensation has been inadequate. Environmental critics have argued that the dam's ability to prevent floods will be short-lived, as they say the Yangtze's high silt content will clog the dam and raise the reservoir's floor, leading to worse floods. In addition, some fear that pollution from nearby industries will build up in the reservoir. According to the International Rivers Network (IRN), a watershed protection nonprofit based in Berkeley, California, the submergence of hundreds of factories, mines, and toxic dumps is already polluting the reservoir and the Yangtze's tributaries. The IRN says that for the five months each year when the river's water levels are lowered to control summer flooding, a marsh consisting of sewage, silt, industrial pollutants, and garbage will remain in the previously submerged areas.

Environmentalists also point to an endangered species of river dolphin, the baiji, now believed to be extinct due to the damming of the Yangtze, which has dramatically altered the river and thereby eliminated much of the baiji's flowing habitat. The baiji population has been drastically reduced in recent years by the damming of tributaries, drainage for land reclamation, overfishing of the baiji's food, and noise and congestion caused by ship traffic in the Yangtze. Although efforts were made to conserve the species, a 2006 expedition failed to locate a single baiji in the river.

Another controversy involves the dam's impact on China's cultural treasures. Before the dam's construction, the Three Gorges contained structures and artifacts that were thousands of years old—including ancestral burial grounds, temples, and fossils—with some sites dating back to the Paleolithic Age. Archaeologists argued that the artifacts are irreplaceable links to China's history and too valuable to lose. Although the government earmarked $135 million to preserve more than 8,000 historical artifacts, the submerging of the Three Gorges proceeded too rapidly for many of these treasures to be saved.

Throughout its long history, China has never been a stranger to controversy or to upheaval, and the Three Gorges Dam project is another example. Even with the dam's completion, the controversy continues.

FURTHER READING

The Economist (eds.). (2006). "A terrible beauty is born; the Three Gorges Dam," *The Economist* 379(8479), 39.

Li, Kaifeng, Cheng Zhu, Li Wu, and Linyan Huang. (2013). "Problems caused by the Three Gorges Dam construction in the Yangtze River basin: a review," *Environmental Reviews* 21(3), 127–35.

Tortajada, Cecilia, Doğan Altınbilek, and Asit K. Biswas. (2012). *Impacts of Large Dams: A Global Assessment*. Berlin, Germany: Springer.

THE ENVIRONMENTAL CONFLICT OVER THE THREE GORGES
Elizabeth J. Leppman

China's Three Gorges Dam—known as the "Great Wall across the Yangtze (Chang Jiang) River"—is a monumental project. The dam is supposed to solve problems of navigation, irrigation, flooding, and electricity supply for China. However, because

A farmer ploughs his new land high above the banks of the Yangtze River in Fongjie, Sichuan Province, where people are being relocated as construction of the Three Gorges Dam continues. (AFP/Getty Images)

the massive dam is vulnerable to failure, upsets the ecology of the entire river valley, and drowns people's homes and historical sites, the costs and conflicts are much greater than the benefits.

The site of the Three Gorges Dam is a region that is subject to earthquakes. A massive earthquake could literally shake the dam apart. In 2003, cracks appeared in an old landslide, and soon thereafter more than 31 million cubic yards of earth crashed into the nearby Qinggan River. The dam is supposed to control flooding that has long plagued the Yangtze Valley. However, if it fails, the resulting flood could be worse than anything the country has ever seen because all the accumulated water in the reservoir would rush downstream at once. Even if there are no earthquakes, dams are subject to enormous forces of water pressure and weather, and they wear out. At best, the Three Gorges Dam's expected life span is only about 50 to 75 years. In addition, in a 2001 report for CNN, Bruce Kennedy cited problems of shoddy construction in China.

In those years, the dam will have enormous impact on the ecology of the entire Yangtze River. As it has flowed naturally, the river has scoured out its valley and transported silt downstream. The dam will trap the silt and reduce the river's flow. Silt will no longer accumulate at the mouth of the river near Shanghai to build up land in the delta. Ocean currents will erode land that is there, reducing the amount of land in that rich farming region. The city of Shanghai is built on silt from the Yangtze. Reducing the amount of silt reaching the river's mouth could lead to the sinking of Shanghai.

These ecological changes also threaten one of the world's biggest fisheries, in the East China Sea, 1,243 miles away. Because less freshwater is reaching the sea, the amount of phytoplankton in the seawater is reduced. Phytoplankton forms the base of the sea's food chain because it manufactures food from sunlight and minerals and fish then eat it. Phytoplankton need carbon dioxide to perform this chemical reaction. Almost immediately after the dam was built and the flow of the river reduced, the amount of carbon dioxide began to decline, meaning that fewer phytoplankton and therefore fewer fish could be supported in the sea. Although the Chinese government promised that the amount of freshwater would remain the same after the dam's construction, much of the available water is used for irrigation and does not reach the sea. Phytoplankton depend on the high flow of water in the summer flood season to survive. However, flood control is one of the purposes of the dam. Instead, the silt will accumulate in the reservoir behind the dam, which can clog the intakes for the electricity-generating turbines. If enough silt clogs these channels, the turbines will no longer work, hindering the dam's ability to meet another goal of its construction: the generation of electricity. Silt in the reservoir will also pose a threat to the port of Chongqing, reducing the improvements in navigation that the dam is supposed to provide.

The huge reservoir created by the Three Gorges Dam is an environmental hazard. First, the methane produced by the living organisms in such a large body of water is a greenhouse gas, adding to global warming. As the dam slows down the river's speed, the river will be unable to generate as much oxygen. Second, as both Jessica Marshall, in *New Scientist* magazine, and Bruce Kennedy have pointed out, because the reservoir has flooded so many industrial plants, cities, and other waste producers, it contains huge amounts of pollutants.

The reservoir is 400 miles long, submerging farmland and more than 100 towns. Some 1.4 million people were relocated. The government says that land is being provided for 300,000 farmers, but some observers estimate that land may be needed for 700,000 more than that. If they cannot receive land, they will have no work and no future. Furthermore, the land that is flooded is some of the most fertile in China, and the land that farmers are receiving is not as good. Clifford Coonan of the British newspaper *The Independent* noted in a March 2006 article that although the displaced people are supposed to be provided with homes, those who have been relocated complain that they have not received compensation for the homes they lost.

The Three Gorges reservoir has also submerged an estimated 1,300 historical and cultural sites. Some of the artifacts have been moved and preserved, but others cannot be because of their size or location. This part of the Yangtze River

Valley was home to the Ba people who settled there about 4,000 years ago, and the region remains the best place to study their culture. The Ba buried their dead in coffins placed in caves high on a cliff. Some of these sites will be flooded. In all, 8,000 areas of social and historical interests that scholars had catalogued have already been flooded.

In today's world of terrorist threats, a further human concern is that the dam could be a very attractive target, as the U.S. Department of Defense reported in its Annual Report on China in 2007. Destruction of the dam by outside forces would bring havoc, death, and destruction to a vast part of China's heartland and millions of people.

The Three Gorges Dam is not only a very expensive undertaking financially, but is also costly in damage to the ecology and to people's lives. It is not worth these costs.

FURTHER READING

Coonan, Clifford. (2006, March 17). "The dammed: environmentalists watch and wait for opening of world's largest dam," *The Independent*. Accessed July 8, 2007, at http://www.independent.co.uk/news/world/asia/the-dammed-environmentalists-watch-and-wait-for-opening-of-worlds-largest-dam-5545071.html.

Kennedy, Bruce. (2001). "China's Three Gorges Dam." CNN. Accessed March 3, 2016, at http://www.cnn.com/SPECIALS/1999/china.50/asian.superpower/three.gorges.

Marshall, Jessica. (2006, February 25). "Three Gorges Dam threatens vast fishery," *New Scientist*. Accessed July 8, 2007, at http://www.newscientist.com/channel/earth/energy-fuels/mg18925404.800.html.

U.S. Department of Defense. (2015). "Annual Report on the Military Power of the People's Republic of China." Accessed January 28, 2007, at http://www.defense.gov/Portals/1/Documents/pubs/2015_China_Military_Power_Report.pdf.

THOUGH CONTROVERSIAL AND THE SOURCE OF EXTERNAL AND INTERNAL CONFLICTS, BUILDING THE DAM WAS NECESSARY!

Charles Fuller

Despite the national and international controversy and it being a source of ongoing tensions, the benefits of China's Three Gorges Dam will ultimately prove to be a stabilizing factor that helps promote development. The dam's flood control and power generation will improve the quality of life for millions of Chinese citizens. Floods along the Yangtze River have killed hundreds of thousands of people over

This photo taken on June 13, 2003, shows a bird's-eye view of the Three Gorges Dam on the Yangtze River in central China's Hubei Province. (Xinhua, Du Huaju/AP Photo)

the last century alone, and China needs the electricity to promote social and economic growth and development.

Consider the awesome power of the Yangtze River. At 3,964 miles, it is the third-longest river in the world. The discharge at its mouth is roughly 46,000 cubic yards per second—also third among the world's great rivers. From its glacial source in the Dangla Mountains, the Yangtze traverses lofty mountains, broad plains, scenic gorges, rolling hills, and coastal lowlands. While it has inspired poets, painters, and modern camera-toting tourists, the Yangtze has also engendered great fear. In the 20th century alone, at least 300,000 people perished in the Yangtze's floodwaters, with some estimates as high as 1 million deaths. As a result of these floods, tens of millions of people have been made homeless, billions of dollars of property has been destroyed, enormous areas of fertile farmland have been rendered unusable, and vital transportation networks have been knocked out for extended periods. Therefore, it should not be surprising that taming the Yangtze River has long been the goal of successive Chinese governments. If flood-control projects can simultaneously generate enormous amounts of hydroelectricity for a booming but energy-deficient economy; reduce dependency on poor-quality, highly polluting coal; extend the range of heavy barges and 10,000-ton freighters deep into the country's interior; provide water for irrigation; attract tourists to an engineering marvel; and serve as a powerful reminder of China's reemergence as a world power, then what is there not to like about the Three Gorges Dam project?

The dam has been controversial from its conception. Even before construction began in 1994, officials knew there would be consequential trade-offs: the relocation of at least 1.2 million people and the resulting need to find new land for 300,000 farmers, the razing and drowning of 100 towns, and the loss of more than 1,000 significant historical and archeological sites. Critics of the dam have added a long list of other calculable and credible disasters, including landslides and local tsunamis in the gorges themselves as water levels rise and lubricate geological bedding planes, silt accumulation behind the dam affecting the power-generating turbines, possible dam collapse in this seismically active region, accumulation of anthropogenic toxins in the reservoir, and the dam's questionable value for flood prevention given the hundreds of significant streams that feed the middle and lower Yangtze River downstream. China's engineers, geologists, and politicians were well aware of these possibilities. The decision ultimately came down to cost-benefit analysis: Chinese leaders decided that the dam's nearly immediate benefits outweighed speculation about what might happen.

What, then, is the economic and social justification for the proposed project? If the predictions of the dam's critics come true, the loss of life and property would be incalculable. Could the benefits of the dam indeed be worth the risk? Consider the actual gains that weigh against the possible losses. The Three Gorges Dam is expected to greatly reduce the amount of flooding that occurs downstream of the dam as a result of excessive rainfall in the upper reaches of the Yangtze. Minor flooding could still take place, but the dam should be able to prevent all but 100-year floods—that is, floods of such severity that there is only a 1-percent probability of one occurring in any given year. The dam's height is 574 feet, but during the rainy season the stored water will be kept below 492 feet; over the length and volume of the reservoir, that is, a flood-storage capacity of about 26.1 billion cubic yards. According to the Yangtze River Water Resources Committee, the Three Gorges project is expected to spare from inundation an average of 90 square miles of farmland each year. Cost-benefit calculations in 1992, the year the project was finally approved, suggest that $250 million of other economic losses could be prevented annually—a number no doubt significantly higher give the region's development over the past 15 years.

For less-developed countries, perhaps the biggest obstacle to development is access to energy. Until now, China's economic growth has depended on its ample coal reserves and its limited, quickly depleting petroleum resources. China has already passed Japan to become the second-largest consumer of petroleum after the United States. Being thus increasingly dependent on imported oil, China finds itself uncomfortably vulnerable to the fickle global petroleum market. As it has become fully operational as a hydropower station, the dam's 32 generators (each with 700,000-kilowatt capacity) are meeting the expected capacity of 22 gigawatts with a planned annual power generation of 85 billion kilowatt hours.

Not only will the Three Gorges Dam reduce China's dependence on imported petroleum, it will replace the burning of 40 million to 50 million tons of coal annually—the majority of which is bituminous, a medium-grade coal that contributes to China's well-documented poor air quality. The ramifications of increased hydropower include less air pollution and acid rain, less stress on the railway system that transports the coal, and improved public health. Transmission lines will carry electricity throughout the western region and all the way to Shanghai, thus sustaining China's role as the world's factory. Finally, income from the sale of electricity is expected to pay for the dam's construction costs of in less than 10 years.

Flood control and power generation are clearly the most important motives for building the Three Gorges Dam and its ancillary projects. Other significant benefits, mentioned above, include improved river navigation, water for irrigation, and tourism. Yes, there are well-known actual and potential trade-offs, some quite significant and immediate. While the government does not tolerate political opposition to the Three Gorges Dam, it does abide considerable public discussion of those trade-offs when based on objective scientific study and reasoning. When we question whether or not the sacrifices China has made to build the Three Gorges Dam are justified, we might ask the same question of the dam's ideological "hero": the Tennessee Valley Authority (TVA).

This expensive, comprehensive U.S. power-generation and water-conservation project addressed the same issues as the Three Gorges Dam: navigation, flood control, electricity generation, and economic development. It too had its critics, and some of the unintended, negative consequences in the Tennessee Valley are being addressed today. Yet a good wager would be that the social and economic benefits from TVA projects over time have far outweighed past and present costs. The TVA is an undisputed success as an integrated set of projects, built with 1930s civil engineering and technology. The Three Gorges Dam's engineers have the benefit of five additional decades of technological growth. They have had the opportunity to learn from dozens of major hydroelectric projects around the world—those that worked and those that failed spectacularly—domestically and abroad. With such a clear vision of the consequences of failure and the rewards of success, we must conclude that over time the Three Gorges Dam will prove itself a worthy successor to the TVA as a source of energy, flood control, and national pride.

FURTHER READING

China View. (2007, July 15). "Three Gorges Project." Accessed March 3, 2016, at http://news.xinhuanet.com/english/2006-05/13/content_4540727.htm.

Jones, William C., and Marsha Freeman. (2005). "Three Gorges Dam: the TVA on the Yangtze River," *21st Century: Science and Technology Magazine*. Accessed March 7, 2016, at http://www.21stcenturysciencetech.com/articles/Three_Gorges.html.

34

How Can Conflicts Be Avoided with Japan's Fishing Industry?

OVERVIEW
Tracy Dobson and M. Troy Burnett

Fish and other aquatic living resources hold a critical position in human nutrition, livelihoods, local and national economies, and ecosystem health. Key fish stocks have been in precipitous decline in many fisheries. Recent studies of fisheries abundance indicate that this is a global and not merely a local issue. Indeed, many marine species are now considered threatened. As one species is fished beyond commercial viability, another takes its place, only to be similarly depleted.

Fisheries scientists have published and written extensively on the grim state of fish and fishing around the world. Constant and systematic overharvesting is driven primarily by too many boats chasing a diminishing stock of fish. The International Commission for the Conservation of Atlantic Tunas estimates that western North Atlantic bluefin tuna populations, for example, have been reduced by nearly 97 percent since 1960 (and the size and age of those caught has concomitantly reduced), much of it by Japanese long-line fishing.

BACKGROUND

Along with overcapitalization, many modern fishing methods that in effect scour the ocean, lake, river, or pond clean of fish have contributed to the fisheries crisis.

Most significant in this category are the enormous factory ships that can catch and process tons of fish while at sea, but even at the artisanal fishing level, small mesh nets that drag the bottom leave no room for fish to escape and also degrade the benthic (bottom of a body of water) habitat. The relentless quest for more and more fish is motivated by desires and needs for food and profit, and it ignores the long-term consequences of this behavior.

Overwhelming fishing pressure and habitat degradation ultimately result in smaller and fewer fish to feed humans, shrinking biological diversity, and reduced ecosystem vitality and resilience. This is true in the fishing communities of the eastern United States as well as the lakeshores of Malawi, where fish historically accounted for 70 percent of dietary animal protein. That percentage diminished to 30 percent in 2005.

Seventy-five percent of fish harvested are used for food, and 25 percent for other purposes. Generalizing, fish provide about 20 percent of per-capita dietary protein, highlighting their significance for human subsistence around the globe. In contrast to a trend of increasing fish consumption in many countries, however, the amount has shrunk significantly in some developing countries in sub-Saharan Africa, from 9.9 kilograms per capita in 1982 to an estimated 7.6 kilograms in 2006.

Fisheries are a significant source of employment. Forty-one million people (13 million in China) work in the capture and aquaculture industries. This number includes those engaged in fishing, fish processing, gear manufacture, fish trade, and other support areas. It does not take into account the less-well-documented number of people engaged in subsistence fishing. In 1994 in Malawi, a government report estimated this number to be 42,000, suggesting that it is likely a significant sector, especially in developing nations. Although this important source of employment is shrinking where fisheries have collapsed (e.g., the U.S. Atlantic cod fishery, which closed in the late 1970s and again in 1994, and then reopened in 2001), it is expanding in aquaculture, so that fishing and fish product production remain significant livelihood activities.

The seemingly never-ending bounty of the seas led to the expansion of fishing fleets of many nations after World War II, to levels that the fisheries ultimately could not support. In the end, they reached a state of "overcapitalization," and many countries instituted regulations on fleet growth. Such restrictions may have led to a reduction in the number of vessels. However, this restriction pushed producers to employ fewer but larger ships, resulting in no reduction in fish catches. Recent fuel price increases may help control fishing efforts. Even as more energy-efficient ships are built, skyrocketing petroleum costs could dampen fishing activity.

In addition to their ecological significance, fisheries provide critical food resources to humans. Currently, capture fisheries everywhere are in peril. The threats to fisheries are widely recognized by governments, scientists, and environmental non-governmental organizations, but wider citizen support will be necessary to overcome the political might of industrial fishing operations.

Nowhere is the issue as grave as in Japanese waters. The country's insatiable appetite for seafood makes it the world's largest consumer of fish. In fact, the country consumes 7.5 billion tons of fish every year, which is about 10 percent of the world's catch.

Japan is also the world's largest fish harvester—a $14 billion national industry. In the last 20 years however, Japan has seen dramatically lower catch numbers. In 2010, there were just 20,000 tons of horse mackerel caught in Japanese waters, compared to 70,000 tons in 1991. The going price for Pacific Saury is now $8 a fish, which is eight times the price it was just a few years ago. The country is becoming more dependent on fish imports and the higher prices are forcing restaurants out of business. After World War II, the Japanese government pushed fishermen to catch as many fish as they could because there was a high need for protein. Although fishing numbers peaked in the 1960s and 1970s, current policies continue to support the fishing industry rather than regulate it even though scientists are pointing to overfishing as one of the primary culprits of declining catch numbers. So how can Japan mitigate the conflicts associated with its unsustainable fishing industry while balancing its appetite for fish and supporting its lucrative seafood industry?

FURTHER READING

Katsukawa, Toshio, Hisao Iwasaki, and Mitsutaku Makino. (2010). "Perspective of Japanese future fisheries II—management and sustainable utilization of fisheries stocks," *Nippon Suisan Gakkaishi (Japanese Edition)* 76(2), 216–48.

Vidas, Davor, and Peter Johan Schei. (2011). *The World Ocean in Globalisation: Climate Change, Sustainable Fisheries, Biodiversity, Shipping, Regional Issues*. Leiden, Netherlands, and Boston: Martinus Nijhoff Publishers.

Yeh, Yun-Hu, Huan-Sheng Tseng, Dong-Taur Su, and Ching-Hsiewn Ou. (2015). "Taiwan and Japan: a complex fisheries relationship," *Marine Policy 51*, 293–301.

THINKING OUTSIDE THE SEA: HOW TO REDUCE CONFLICT WITH JAPANESE SEAFOOD

Lynn Galvin

Japan can meet its demand for seafood by learning "to think outside the sea." The powers of education, aquaculture, and societal and world trends combine to assist Japan in finding adequate sources for its population's seafood demand. Sociological and cultural developments in Japan further impact the situation, including aging population issues, declining birthrate, shrinking work force, and national debt complications.

Japan is not alone, however, in its search for resources from the open seas. Maintaining sustainable fisheries cannot be accomplished only by Japan, as problem-solving strategies are dependent on world interactions and ocean sharing. Japan, as the highest national importer at a 6-percent share of the world sea market, impacts seafood demand and supply beyond its own fisheries. It is a complicated circle of world demand, supply, fishing policies, needs, and cooperation.

The Japanese people have one of the highest (fifth in the world) per-capita levels of fish consumption at about 60 kilograms (132 lbs.) of fish annually. Scientists and food producers are aware of the declining seafood resources, and many programs already exist to protect Japan's sustainable fisheries. An interesting statistic is that the fish products consumed by Japan include about one-third aqua-farmed seafood, an industry that has become more popular around the planet, although limited in growth scope by similar factors that affect wild fisheries.

Interestingly, it is reported that the Japanese government and fishing industry are currently working at increasing efforts to stop a decline in seafood consumption, at least partially a result of a two-decade trend for meat consumption. Since 2008, meat has actually overtaken fish consumption in Japan. The government is concerned about the impact of a continuing decline on coastal populations that have dedicated their living to the production of seafood produce.

At a time when the world population has now surpassed 7 billion, the Japanese population is in decline. Japan currently has the world's oldest population with a life expectancy for women of 86 and for men 79. Its aging populace is predicted to shrink by one-third in the next 50 years, resulting in a decreased labor pool and reduced consumer base. At the same time, Japanese people are refraining from marriage and child bearing, partially due to economic considerations. Government tax increases have assisted the support of social programs, but have also expanded an already heavy debt burden. Japan's population of 126.6 million today is projected to decline to 105 million by 2050. Thus, while the world cries for more fish, one assessment is that there will be a lesser demand in Japan for seafood in a future that has one-third less the number of people.

Culturally, Japan, as an island nation with four main islands and 6,800 small ones, has a long and fruitful association with all things that come from the sea: food, designs, patterns, and shapes used in textiles and art, bones and fishmeal used in everything from fertilizer to animal feed to aquaculture. The mark of the sea and its importance in Japan is everywhere in the culture. In fact, as salt and pepper are to the United States, fish flakes are to Japan. No meal seems to be complete without them. Still, helping its citizens reframe their cultural understanding and relationship to the sea is the kind of project for which the Japanese are well-suited. Japan has long been recognized for its exceptionally cooperative population, believed to be partially rooted in the early cultivation of rice, a food source whose production requires the dedicated attention of multiples of people. A public cooperative spirit and the will to combine strengths for achieving success are national characteristics that Japan can depend upon when major projects are planned.

Of course, the problem of over-fishing has not gone unaddressed. The World Health Organization reports that world fisheries production leveled off in the 1970s. Numerous other world organizations, including Greenpeace, the World Wildlife Fund, and the Marine Stewardship Council, reward sustainable fishing practices through eco-labeling and certification, public education, and international agreement, and include the Japanese in their supporters and participants. Annual international Seafood Summits have met since 2000 with leaders and stakeholders from the seafood industry, the conservation community, academia, government, and the media to share information and network around the issues of sustainable seafood.

Japan (and the world) wants seafood. Marketing studies presented at the 2012 International Seafood Summit show that present awareness of the problems in maintaining seafood sustainability are low on consumer purchasing choices (ranked 10 of 12 factors in one 2009 study); and price, species choice, and family preference outweighing sustainability and origin factors in studies in 2010 and 2012. Consumer education in regard to sustainable fishery practices, eco-labeling, certification, and alternative food choices, are paramount, and must be incorporated into protecting the produce of the world's seas now and for the future.

Capture fisheries have reached their limit and "sustainable fishery" is not sustainable. But alternatives exist. Japan has legislated nationally to regulate its own fishery industry. It is well represented in the growing eco-labeling and certification programs, which account for 10 percent of the world's seafood products. It is actively involved on all levels with world organizations dealing with the issues of fisheries sustainability, including public awareness and education. Even with changing social demographics, Japan is a fish-loving place. Sustainability will be maintained, perhaps at a different percentage level, in a future that may fish more from land than sea—even as fish flakes continue to spice Japan's palate.

FURTHER READING

Fujita, Akiko. (2012, January 30). "Japan's Population to Shrink Nearly a Third by 2060." ABC News. Accessed February 19, 2014, at http://abcnews.go.com/blogs/headlines/2012/01/japans-population-to-shrink-nearly-a-third-by-2060/.

SeaWeb. (2012). "About the 10th International Seafood Summit in Hong Kong." 10th International Seafood Summit. Accessed February 19, 2014, at http://www.seafoodsummit2012.org/.

White, Kathryn, Brendan O'Neill, and Zdravka Tzankova. (2004). "At a Crossroads: Will Aquaculture Fulfill the Promise of a Blue Revolution?" SeaWeb Aquaculture Clearinghouse report. Accessed February 19, 2014, at http://www.seaweb.org/resources/documents/reports_crossroads.pdf.

BETTER MANAGEMENT IS NEEDED TO SUSTAIN JAPANESE FISHERIES
Riley Walters

Japanese fisheries have the ability to meet and sustain Japan's demand for fish. Through a change in management procedures and industry policies, fisheries can help keep catch quotas stable, customers happy, and the seas from being depleted of their natural wildlife.

Anyone who has spent time in Japan knows fish is the chicken of the Japanese diet. Menus hold a wide assortment of aquatic life ranging from the bluefin tuna, which are made luxury items with fish markets selling them for as much as $1.8 million, to the native eel, popular during the summer for its stamina-giving properties. Demand for fish remains at a constant high in Japan, but the total amount of fish being caught just isn't what it used to be.

Comprising a chain of islands roughly equaling the size of California, Japan is already associated with a limited supply of natural resources. And after joining the Law of the Sea Treaty, an international treaty limiting maritime territory, Japan reduced its area allotted to fishing without international scrutiny to within 200 nautical miles of land.

Japanese fisheries currently work under a communal system called Territorial Use Rights Fisheries (TURFs), which is managed by local groups called Fishery Cooperative Associations (FCAs). This system attempts to allocate specific zones for fisheries to work within. This system doesn't specifically address who owns what but addresses which fisheries have access to TURF and to what degree they have access. This becomes a bigger issue when addressing the issue of migratory fish species that are not part of just one TURF.

Every year the number of Japanese fisheries decreases, along with the total amount of fish caught. Since 1982, Japanese fisheries have seen a 60 percent decrease in their total amount of fish caught, declining from roughly 11 million tons to 4 million tons of fish. Simultaneously, the total number of fisheries have

Table 34.1 Japanese Marine Fisheries (not including aquaculture)

	Quantity Caught by Fisheries (thousands of tons)	Value of Catch (billions, ¥)	Number of Fisheries (thousands)	Japan Total Population (millions)
1992	7,770	1,827	350	125
2002	4,430	1,136	240	127
2010	4,121	1,400	202	128

Source: Japan Ministry of Agriculture, Forestry and Fisheries: Fishery Census.

nearly halved over the past 20 years. This can mostly be attributed to inefficient fishing practices and overfishing, as well as an aging population, with the average Japanese fisherman age 65.

Like most other countries, Japan has set total amounts, or Total Allowable Catch (TAC), of fish allowed to be caught each year. A country's TAC is what experts have determined necessary to balance both fishing demands while allowing for aquatic life to sustain and replenish their numbers. Quotas are usually determined by the government or through international cooperation, such as the Commission for the Conservation of Southern Bluefin Tuna (CCSBT). In 2012, Japan had just a 2,500-ton TAC on bluefin tuna set through the CCSBT compared to a 6,000-ton TAC in 2006.

Japan's current system incentivizes fisheries to be the first to fish as much as they can before fishing quotas are met. For example, if the entirety of Japan has a TAC of 1,000 tons of sardines for the year 2013, each fishery will try to catch as many sardines as it can before the 1,000-ton limit is met. This can often lead to destructive methods of fishing that can be harmful to other aquatic life.

The seas have long been called a "tragedy of the commons." This is the concept that something so vast and accessible to everyone is owned, and therefore cared for, by no one. This leads to an inefficient use of the ocean's resources. Only defining property rights (i.e., who owns what) helps solve this issue. That's why it is important to clearly define and uphold the individual amount each fishery is allowed to catch each year. One possible solution is through a program called Individual Interchangeable Quotas (ITQ).

The ITQ system of fishing allows fisheries access to a percentage of the TAC, instead of the current first-come, first-catch system. Meaning, for example, instead of a free-for-all access to the 1,000 tons of sardines, each fishery would get access to 5 percent of the 1000-ton limit. The percentage would vary per fishery, and ITQs could be exchangeable if some fisheries wanted a larger (or smaller) percentage.

This system of ITQs takes the rush out of catching fish as soon as possible, allowing fisheries to use safer and more efficient methods. It would also incentivize fisheries to keep an eye on competing fisheries as to whether they're over fishing their percent of the quota or not. A fishery taking more than its percent (overfishing) could negatively affect the following year's TAC, hurting all fisheries. ITQs would also entice fisheries to explore methods to increase their total population of fish available, increasing the number of fish available to catch. The ITQ system has already been successful in countries like Iceland and New Zealand.

For Japan to meet its demand of fish, it is up to designating clearer property rights by assigning fisheries more responsibility in their catching methods and incentivizing them not to overfish to the point of extinction. Japan doesn't need to see a complete eradication of its current system of fisheries organizing under FCAs, but Japan's style of fishing may need to see a change from its communal access to the TURFs system to an individually responsible ITQ system.

35

Is the Crisis in Australia's Murray-Darling Basin the Result of Climate Change or the Decisions and Actions of Humans?

OVERVIEW

Bruce E. Johansen

The Murray-Darling Basin, which includes the drainage of two rivers by those names, spans most of New South Wales and Victoria, as well as parts of Queensland and South Australia. It arcs across inland southeastern Australia between Brisbane on the northeast and Melbourne in the south. Like most of temperate-zone Australia, it usually receives little rainfall, and has become the continent's major agricultural area largely though irrigation. In the late 20th and early 21st centuries, this area has been subjected to chronic drought punctuated by torrential rains, a climatic signature characteristic of rising temperatures. Droughts have been linked to El Niño weather patterns, and deluges with La Niña conditions.

BACKGROUND

Global warming was on stage in 2014, during the Australian Open tennis tournament, when temperatures as high as 111°F (44°C) in Melbourne forced officials to invoke an "extreme heat policy" that shut down play on outside courts. The year 2013 turned out to be Australia's hottest year on record, as the calendar year started and ended with record heat across much of the continent. Temperatures reached 120.7°F in Moomba, Queensland, and 118°F at several other locations. The heat wave was accompanied by intense drought and frequent wildfires that included Australia's agricultural heartland in the Murray-Darling river valley. Fires blazed on all sides of Sydney, Australia's largest city.

Australia in April 2007 considered, but chose not to implement, a ban of irrigation in the Murray-Darling Basin, where 40 percent of the country's agricultural produce is grown. The country was then in the midst of its worst drought on record, one that continued in several subsequent years. An irrigation ban could have ruined many farmers who had gone heavily into debt following several dry years.

A four-month heat wave during the Australian summer culminated in January in bush fires that tore through the eastern and southeastern coasts of the country, where most Australians live. Those record-setting temperatures were followed by torrential rains and flooding in the more densely populated states of New South Wales and Queensland that left at least six people dead and caused roughly $2.43 billion in damage along the eastern seaboard (Siegel, 2013). The country's natural cycles of drought and deluge, already extreme compared with much of the world, have become worse as temperatures have risen. Thousands of cattle and sheep died in the fires that whipped through parts of Australia's agricultural heartland, which had expanded and prospered during more tranquil times with irrigation.

With irrigation, cultivation of cotton prospered in Australia's Outback. By 2007, however, production of cotton, with its thirst for water, had fallen sharply. Patrick Barta wrote in the *Wall Street Journal* that in the town of Wee Waa, Australia's self-described "cotton capital," population 2,000, about 250 miles northwest of Sydney: "The Cotton Fields Motel that once was busy with seasonal workers now struggles to fill rooms. Elsewhere in the flat basin [of Australia's largest river system, the Murray-Darling, kangaroos hop along dry levees, and the end of giant water-transport pipes poke out over empty reservoirs" (Barta, 2007).

Australia's cotton production fell by two thirds between 2001 and 2007 (Barta, 2007). Some fields were down to 2 percent of the usual harvest, and reservoirs as large as 240,000 acres had completely dried up. In 2008, the drought in the Murray-Darling Basin continued, following a record-dry June, even after parts of Australia received occasional torrential rains during a strong La Niña that briefly countered some effects of the drought.

During the 1950s and 1960s, Australia built multi-year reservoirs that were supposed to protect its urban areas as well as farming regions against recurring droughts. These gave the country the highest storage capacity per capita in the world. Together with hundreds of miles of irrigation conduits, Australia was said, at the time, to be "drought-proof." However, the post-2000 droughts exceeded the capacity of this system. Melbourne's water storage was 28 percent of capacity by mid-2007, Sydney's 37 percent, and Perth's 15 percent. Inflows behind Sydney's dams in 1991–2006 were 71 percent less than their averages from 1948 to 1990 (Pincock, 2007).

According to government estimates, the Murray-Darling Basin faces a 12–35 percent reduction in average water flow by 2050 as southern regions grow hotter and drier, adding to the pressures on its over-extracted and salt-affected rivers. By 2009, the Murray-Darling Basin was becoming extremely dry, to an extent that hundreds of thousands of river red gum trees, the world's largest such forest, died suddenly. Some former wetlands, now encrusted with cracking dried earth that were once swamps, absent periodic flushing, have been reacting with the atmosphere to form sulfuric acid. These are signs of an epic drought, beyond the cycles that usually affect the area (Draper, 2009).

The question under discussion is the cause of this crisis. Is it a product of global warming and climate change, or rather more the result of the actions of humans?

REFERENCES

Barta, Patrick. (2007, July 11). "Parched outback: in Australia, a drought spurs a radical remedy," *Wall Street Journal*, A1, A12.

Draper, Robert. (2009, April). "Australia's dry ruin," *National Geographic*, 34–59.

Pincock, Steve. (2007, November 15). "Showdown in a sun-burnt country," *Nature 450*, 336–338.

Siegel, Matt. (2013, March 4). "Report blames climate change for extremes in Australia," *New York Times*. Accessed March 3, 2016, at http://www.nytimes.com/2013/03/05/world/asia/australian-government-blames-climate-change-for-angry-summer.html.

FURTHER READING

Connell, Daniel. (2007). *Water Politics in the Murray-Darling Basin*. Annandale, Australia: Federation Press.

Nicholls, Neville. (2004). "The changing nature of Australian droughts," *Climatic Change 63*, 323–336.

Pigram, John. J. (2006). *Australia's Water Resources: From Use to Management*. Clayton, Australia: CSIRO Publishing.

Quiggin, John, Thilak Mallawaarachchi, and Sarah Chambers. (2012). *Water Policy Reform: Lessons in Sustainability from the Murray-Darling Basin*. Cheltenham, UK: John Quiggin.

AUSTRALIA'S DROUGHT AND CHANGING ATMOSPHERIC CIRCULATION PATTERNS
Bruce E. Johansen

Although human actions on site are responsible for some of the enduring drought problems in Australia's Murray-Darling Basin, climate change (due to human actions writ large) is the major factor. "Climate change is potentially the biggest risk to Australian agriculture," said Ben Fargher, chief executive of the National Farmers' Federation in Australia (Bradsher, 2008). The Australian government's Climate Commission in March 2013 found that its scorching summer of 2012–2013 and similar weather patterns for several preceding years had been provoked by human injection of greenhouse gases into the atmosphere and the resultant accelerated warming of the Earth's troposphere.

Some of Australia's enduring drought stems from changes in worldwide atmospheric circulation compelled by worldwide climate change. Even though warmer air generally holds more moisture, not everyone will see more precipitation in a globally warmed world. Many deserts already are expanding, in a worldwide pattern influenced by atmospheric circulation patterns that meteorologists call "Hadley cells." Near the equator, warm, moist air rises, cools, and unleashes downpours.

A huge dust cloud rolls over the Australian town of Griffith, New South Wales, after high winds whipped up topsoil dried from a prolonged drought. (AP/Wide World Photos)

In the upper troposphere, the air spreads north and southward toward both poles, descending at about 30 degrees north and south latitude. The descending adiabatically warmed air results in desert environments at these latitudes. For reasons that are not yet fully understood, as temperatures rise, the Hadley cells reach further north and south of the equator causing deserts to expand—a process that is already evident from news reports around the world.

Droughts in regions where Hadley cells favor descending air now span the globe, from Australia, to Spain, Iraq, Afghanistan, parts of China, and the U.S. Southwest, including California, Nevada, New Mexico, Arizona, and Texas. In China, the Gobi desert, also within the northern reaches of Hadley cell range, has been expanding, sending occasional dust storms into Beijing that aggravates air pollution from coal-fired power plants.

In Iran, Lake Urmia, once plied by cruise ships, has lost nearly all of its water, and water rationing has been implemented in the capital, Tehran. As in the Murray Darling Basin, wasteful irrigation practices and misuse of dams have played a role in the drought, but changing atmospheric circulation also plays a major role in reducing precipitation. Groundwater levels also have declined as increasing numbers of wells tap finite aquifers. Rising temperatures also have accelerated evaporation everywhere.

The city of Las Vegas, Nevada, has been pumping Lake Mead dry with a series of pipes, each one deeper than the last. The lake's level is close to a point at which water will have to be severely rationed in that city. People already are using each others' recycled sewage water. In June 2008, California declared a drought and warned that water rationing might follow. California in 2014 experienced its driest spring in 88 years and as of early 2016 is still in the midst of one of its longest droughts. Los Angeles announced plans to use cleansed sewage water to augment supplies (Reuters, 2008). Drought intensified in the Fertile Crescent region of northern Iraq and eastern Syria during the winter of 2007–2008 as sufficient winter rains and snows failed to arrive in the mountains of Turkey, which have fed rivers in the area since the beginnings of human urban civilization. Lack of moisture also limited irrigation that is crucial for agriculture in the desert. Barcelona, Spain, was so dry by May 2008 that water was being imported, for the first time ever, by ship. A desalinization plant and pipeline from the Ebro River (to the west) was being planned. Parts of southeastern Spain were turning to desert by 2008, even amidst new developments of vacation homes and golf courses. Water has become a valuable commodity and source of conflict. This area has experienced cyclical droughts in the past, but this one may be long lasting. Local aquifers are retreating below the range of pumps as well, as the area's climate comes to resemble that of northern Africa. The Spanish Environment Ministry warns that a third of the country may turn to desert in coming years (Rosenthal, 2008). Barcelona, Spain was so dry by May 2008 that water was being imported, for the first time ever, by ship. A desalinization plant and pipeline from the Ebro River (to the west) were being planned (Wall Street Journal, 2008).

While the drought crisis in the Murray-Darling Basin has partially resulted from misuse of water resources, the root cause is lack of rainfall and a drier, hotter climate. This persistent drought is directly tied to the human-induced warming of the global troposphere. The fact is, as the many examples listed above show, global warming and climate change are dramatically altering the Earth's hydrologic cycle.

REFERENCES

Bradsher, Keith. (2008, April, 17). "A drought in Australia, a global shortage of rice," *New York Times*. Accessed March 3, 2016, at http://www.nytimes.com/2008/04/17/business/worldbusiness/17warm.html.

NASA (eds.). (2008, June 4). "Drought in Iraq." NASA Earth Observatory. Accessed March 3, 2016, at http://earthobservatory.nasa.gov/NaturalHazards/view.php?id=38914.

Reuters (eds.). (2008, June 4). "Hunger, water scarcity displaces thousands of Afghans," *New York Times*. Accessed March 3, 2016, http://www.nytimes.com/reuters/world/international-afghan-displacement.html.

Rosenthal, Elisabeth. (2008, June 3). "Water is new battleground in drying Spain," *New York Times*, A1, A12.

Wall Street Journal (eds.). (2008, May 14). "Drought forces Barcelona to ship in drinking water," *Wall Street Journal*, A13.

HUMAN ACTIONS ARE THE ROOT OF THE CRISIS IN THE MURRAY-DARLING BASIN

Mia Bennett

The dry, dusty, arid landscapes of the Outback and Ayers Rock loom large in the popular imagination about Australia. Yet there are also vital rivers that make life possible for Australia's unique flora and fauna—along with its indigenous Aboriginal inhabitants and the millions of people who have moved to the continent since the first English settlement was established at Botany Bay in 1788. Two of the most important rivers in southeastern Australia are the Murray and the Darling. Together, they form the Murray-Darling Basin, which stretches over one million kilometers from the state of Queensland across New South Wales, Victoria, the Australian Capital Territory, and South Australia, where it drains out to the Southern Ocean.

The Murray-Darling Basin, however, is far from a lush paradise. Its water flow has averaged only 24,000 gigaliters since measurements began in 1885. This is one of the lowest rates for any major river system in the world (Pigram, 2006). While the low availability of water leads to a naturally less-flourishing ecosystem than in the water-saturated basins of rivers like the Amazon, Ganges, and Congo, it has not stopped humans from settling in the basin and exerting an increasing amount of pressure on limited water resources. Two million people now live in the basin, an area that is also of national importance for agriculture. Some 40 percent of Australia's farms and 70 percent of Australia's irrigated land are located there (Murray-Darling Basin Authority, "Irrigated agriculture," n.d.). Much of the food produced in the basin's farms is exported, meaning that the area is being strained to feed people beyond Australia's borders. Already, the basin had little annual rainfall, and the relatively flat topography means that the rivers flow slowly. Unlike powerful rivers in other parts of the world that can regularly flush themselves of contaminants, the meandering rivers of the Murray-Darling Basin easily become clogged with sediments and salt, worsening degradation. As a result, anthropogenic pressures on top of an already fragile system have generated a crisis in the Murray-Darling Basin.

THE ROOTS OF A CRISIS

Australia's Aboriginal people have inhabited the Murray-Darling Basin for 45,000 years. They hunted giant wombats, giant kangaroos, and large flightless birds (Murray-Darling Basin Authority, "Aboriginal culture," n.d.), animals that disappeared from the landscape eons ago. Scientists have debated over whether climate change or human activity brought about the extinction of these megafauna (Wroe, 2013). Yet fast forward to the 21st century and it is easy to discern that the current crisis in the basin has definite anthropogenic roots. These can be traced to the settlement of Europeans in the region via boats sailing upstream from South Australia beginning in the 18th century.

Entrepreneurial farmers and settlers were eager to turn the basin into a productive agricultural zone for Australia's burgeoning British colonies. The Murray's peak flow, however, occurred at the opposite time as the ideal harvesting time. This problem stymied rapid agricultural growth until the development of dam technology in the 19th century. The 1914–1915 River Murray Waters Agreement paved the way to build a network of dams, weirs, locks, and barrages and manage a water-sharing agreement that gave at least some degree of security of supply (Connell, 2007). Now, humans could store the waters of the Murray-Darling Basin until a time they thought appropriate, much like in the western United States. In both regions, however, dams have ironically led to a water crisis. Humans overtaxed the environment through increased settlement and agriculture motivated by the false security of dams and reservoirs. Throughout the 1950s and 1960s, the government continued to strongly support an irrigation-based industry. The capacity of Australia's most important dams surged by 10 times from 1940 to 1990 (Connell, 2007).

True recognition of the scale of the crisis facing the Murray-Darling Basin did not come until late in the game. In 1992, the government released a Natural Resources Management Strategy for the basin, which has since been replaced by newer plans. The 2007 Federal Water Act established the Murray-Darling Basin Authority, an independent statutory agency charged with sustainable management of the area's water resources "in a way that best meets social, economic, and environmental needs of the Basin and its communities" (Murray-Darling Basin Authority, 2014). Yet the agency has been accused of focusing too much on environmental restoration at the cost of local farmers. Additionally, the current iteration of Murray-Darling Basin Plan, which calls for the pumping of 3,200 billion liters of water into the river system via improved dams and channels, has been assailed as yet another technocratic solution that fails to address the root of the problem—unsustainable levels of agriculture and human demand on the basin.

CLIMATE CHANGE?

Climate change has also been blamed for the crisis in the Murray-Darling Basin, an explanation that sometimes shifts blame away from the direct impacts of humans living within the basin. Certainly, hotter temperatures and lower rainfall have exacerbated problems in the area, while severe climatic disturbances such as the Millennium Drought (1995–2009) impacted the basin and the health of the rural economies within it (Murray-Darling Basin Authority, "Sustainable rivers," n.d.). Yet at the end of the day, there is consensus within the scientific community that humans are responsible for driving climate change (Oreskes, 2004). Furthermore, the scale of climate change and its causes are global, but Australia is one of the world's largest emitters per capita of greenhouse gases (The World Bank Group, 2015). As such, it is clear that humans and our activities, particularly in Australia and particularly within the Murray-Darling Basin, are responsible for the bulk of its problems.

Because the decisions and actions of humans are responsible for the current crisis in Australia's Murray-Darling Basin, if the basin is to be returned to a healthy balance between human needs and ecosystem functioning, it is people who will have to provide the solution. We cannot wait for nature to suddenly decide to become generous and unleash copious amounts of rainfall onto a landscape that has been sucked dry and poisoned by salt by generations of unsustainable practices. In order for the crisis to subside, humans must learn to work within the Murray-Darling Basin's limits and accept that geo-engineered solutions may not be enough.

REFERENCES

Connell, Daniel. (2007). *Water Politics in the Murray-Darling Basin*. Annandale, Australia: Federation Press, 15.

Murray-Darling Basin Authority (n.d.). "Irrigated Agriculture in the Basin—Facts and Figures." Australian Government. Accessed April 28, 2015, at http://www.mdba.gov.au/about-basin/irrigated-agriculture-in-the-basin.

Murray-Darling Basin Authority. (2014, December 24). "About MDBA." Australian Government. Accessed April 28, 2015, at http://www.mdba.gov.au/about-mdba.

Murray-Darling Basin Authority. (n.d.). "Aboriginal Culture and Heritage." Australian Government. Accessed April 28, 2015, at http://www.mdba.gov.au/about-basin/basin-people/aboriginal-culture-heritage.

Murray-Darling Basin Authority. (n.d.). "Sustainable Rivers Audit: Interpreting the Results." Australian Government. Accessed April 28, 2015, at http://www.mdba.gov.au/what-we-do/mon-eval-reporting/sustainable-rivers-audit/interpreting-the-results.

Oreskes, Naomi. (2004). "The scientific consensus on climate change," *Science 306*(5702), 1686–1686.

Pigram, John J. (2006). *Australia's Water Resources: From Use to Management*. Clayton, Australia: CSIRO Publishing.

World Bank. (2015). "CO_2 Emissions (Metric Tons per Capita)." Accessed April 28, 2015, at http://data.worldbank.org/indicator/EN.ATM.CO2E.PC?order=wbapi_data_value_2010+wbapi_data_value+wbapi_data_value-first&sort=desc.

Wroe, Stephen. (2013, May 23). "What killed Australia's megafauna?," *Australian Geographic*. Accessed April 28, 2015, at http://www.australiangeographic.com.au/topics/science-environment/2013/05/opinion-what-killed-australias-megafauna/.

36

IS SUSTAINABLE DEVELOPMENT AND CONSERVATION OR FURTHER RESOURCE EXPLOITATION AND CONFLICT THE FUTURE IN BORNEO?

OVERVIEW
M. Troy Burnett

Logging in Borneo reached its peak in the 1980s and 1990s. The island was experiencing its most intense period of deforestation during those decades and it was clear it would soon reach crisis-level. As logging opportunities dwindled in the mid-1990s, interest in lucrative oil palm tree cultivation rose. Because land has to be cleared (by fire) for oil palm, the results from the logging and oil palm industries are the same—depletion of Borneo's rainforest. Burning land for oil palm cultivation has however added another factor detrimental to the environment—the release of massive amounts of carbon into the atmosphere. The fires are so extensive and cause so much pollution that they are responsible for political tensions in the region.

BACKGROUND

In April 2006, China announced an agreement with the government of Indonesia that would allow it to harvest most of the tropical forest remaining on the island of Borneo. The arrangement, for which the Chinese paid more than $7 billion, would provide China with wood badly needed for flooring, furniture, and other domestic uses. The Chinese would also be able to convert the cleared land for use in growing palm trees to supply them with palm oil, essential to their economy. In return, the deal would provide Indonesia with a very large and reliable source of income for many years into the future. The deal sounds like a win-win situation for both parties. It may not be as beneficial to Borneo's environment, which would lose not only its last remaining natural forests, but also untold numbers of other plant and animal species.

The destruction of Borneo's forest reserves is hardly a new story in human history. Few natural resources are taken so much for granted as are forest reserves. Wherever trees occur in abundance, and that includes a large part of the Earth's surface, humans have traditionally felt free to harvest those timber resources without a second thought, believing that forests will eventually regenerate themselves. While we wait for that process to occur, we usually move on to the next stand of trees, taking what we need and leaving behind another area stripped of vegetation. The problem is that forest renewal takes many decades, and human destruction of wooded areas generally occurs much more rapidly than does renewal. As a consequence, some human societies have wiped out their forest reserves essentially forever. Today, broad stretches of Europe, the United States, and other parts of the world that were once covered with trees have been converted to farmland, prairies, or grassland that may still have value, but a value different from that provided by forests. A forest's value consists of the wood itself obtained from trees (used for the construction of homes and furniture, as a fuel for cooking and heating, and as a raw material in many other areas), the protection it provides to other plants and animals (many of whom are not adapted to survival in any other kind of ecosystem), and the protection it provides for soil and water resources.

So far there is little political oversight of deforestation on Borneo or the polluting effects of the oil palm industry because there are few alternatives to these industries that would contribute as much to the economy. Still, there are many international organizations that are stepping in to provide opportunities for sustainable management of the existing industries. Their efforts to turn the momentum of deforestation around are debatable. In the first essay, Bruce E. Johansen argues that sustainable resource management is just a theory "on some academics' lips," but the reality is that Borneo is succumbing to a worldwide market hungry for natural resources making the future quite bleak. In the second essay, Donald Rallis argues that it is possible to reclaim some of Borneo's lost environment and protect its remaining environments through sustainable resource management.

FURTHER READING

Moeliono, Moira, Eva Wollenberg, and Godwin Limberg. (2012). *The Decentralization of Forest Governance: Politics, Economics and the Fight for Control of Forests in Indonesian Borneo.* London and Sterling, VA: Earthscan.

White, Mel. (2008, November). "Borneo's moment of truth," *National Geographic.* Accessed March 7, 2016, at http://ngm.nationalgeographic.com/2008/11/borneo/white-text.

World Wildlife Fund. (2005, June 7). "Borneo: Treasure Island at Risk." Accessed March 3, 2016, at http://wwf.panda.org/wwf_news/?21037%2FReport-Borneo-Treasure-Island-at-Risk.

TENSIONS MOUNT AS DESTRUCTION OF BORNEO CONTINUES
Bruce E. Johansen

Natural resources have long been a source of contention in many places. The question at hand is, can Borneo develop sustainable economic growth without further destroying its environmental resources? For the most part, today, Borneo is serving as a resource plantation for the developed world. The question of sustainable development has been raised, but mainly as an intellectual exercise. Down on the oil palm tree farms, in the gold mines, and across the logged-off forests, it's still mainly "rip and run." As it stands, Borneo's ecosystem is unlikely to become sustainable, with all of us having to live with the consequences.

LOGGING

Indonesia, which exercises jurisdiction over most of Borneo, has banned the export of raw logs. This does not mean that devastation of Borneo's rainforests has stopped. It means that Indonesia has become one of the world's largest exporters of manufactured plywood by developing a large timber-processing industry. Massive logging feeds Asian markets, mainly in China, India, and Japan. Once milled in Japan, wood harvested from what used to be one of the oldest and richest rainforests in the world becomes furniture and packing crates. Much of it becomes construction material, primarily plywood cement forms that are used once or twice and then discarded.

PALM OIL

Palm oil, as a biofuel, is being marketed as carbon-friendly. The problem is that to create its oil palm plantations (and other agriculture), Borneo has been burning enough sub-surface peat to alter the global carbon balance in a negative way. In

Indonesia, layers of peat as thick as 66 feet cover an area of about 112,000 square miles in Borneo, Sumatra, and Papua New Guinea. Susan E. Page and colleagues used satellite images of a 2.5-million-hectare study area in central Borneo from before and after fires in 1997. According to their estimates, about 32 percent of the area had burned, of which peat land accounted for 91.5 percent. An estimated 0.19 to 0.23 gigatons of carbon were released to the atmosphere through peat combustion, with a further 0.05 gigaton released from burning of the overlying vegetation. Extrapolating these estimates to Indonesia as a whole, the researchers estimated that between 0.81 and 2.57 gigatons of carbon were released to the atmosphere in 1997 as a result of burning peat and vegetation in Indonesia. According to the researchers, "This is equivalent to [between] 13 [and] 40 percent of the mean annual global carbon emissions from fossil fuels," which contributed measurably to the largest annual increase in atmospheric CO_2 concentration detected since records began in 1957 (Page et al., 2002; Richardson, 2002).

INDIGENOUS POPULATION

In Sumatra and Borneo, as several million hectares of forests also have been converted to oil palm plantations, many indigenous people have been evicted from their lands as the lands have been deforested by fire to develop these plantations. Traditional peoples in Borneo have survived by accommodating in several ways. Some former headhunters have turned their longhouses into bed-and-breakfasts for Japanese tourists. Of roughly 9,000 Penan people surviving in the rainforests of Sarawek (in northern Borneo), only a few hundred live as nomads, in the traditional way, in a forest laced by rivers. Some Penan have tried to attack loggers with blowpipes, with little success. They also have erected blockades, then been arrested or killed.

Seven indigenous people were killed on October 8, 2000, by the Indonesian Mobile Police Brigade after they erected a blockade of Unocal's Tanjung Santan Oil Refinery that lasted two weeks. They were protesting pervasive air and water pollution in their homelands. In the same area, Rio Tinto's Kelian Gold Mine has produced more than 400,000 troy ounces of gold per year using the cyanide heap-leaching process, producing cyanide-laced tailings. Local people cannot drink or bathe in the water because it causes skin lesions and stomach aches. In addition to logging, homelands of indigenous peoples in Borneo have become sites for several hydroelectric dams.

On several fronts, Borneo, like many other "developing" regions of the world, finds itself caught in a worldwide system that consumes natural resources, turning them into salable products, profits, and waste carbon dioxide. Increases in population and affluence are making these problems worse around the world. Borneo's ecosystem is not likely to become sustainable unless steps toward this goal are taken on a broader scale. In the meantime, Indonesia, including Borneo, has become a case study in just how quickly the resources of the Earth are being consumed by the industrial engines of capitalism. When considering development, one must ask, sustainable for whom? At what price?

REFERENCES

Page, Susan E., Florian Siegert, John O. Rieley, Hans-Dieter V. Boehm, et al. (2002, November 7). "The amount of carbon released from peat and forest fires in Indonesia during 1997," *Nature 420*, 61–65.

Richardson, Michael. (2002, December 13). "Indonesian peat fires stoke rise of pollution," *International Herald-Tribune*, 5.

DEVELOPMENT, STABILITY, AND CONSERVATION ARE POSSIBLE IN BORNEO

Donald Rallis

The tropical island of Borneo is one of the most biologically diverse places on Earth. Its rainforests, rivers, coastlines, and coral reefs are home to tens of thousands of species of plants and animals, with more being identified each year. Over the past few decades however, vast changes have come to Borneo. Tropical hardwoods have been cut down for the valuable timber they provide, and forests have been cleared to make way for profitable plantations, primarily oil palms. In many areas forests may never return and numerous species have already become extinct. It is not too late, however, to save most of the considerable biodiversity that remains. By protecting remaining environments from further destruction, and by promoting managed resource utilization, it is possible not only to preserve those natural environments that remain in Borneo, but promote sustainable development and social stability.

According to the Worldwide Fund for Nature (also known as the World Wildlife Fund, WWF) Borneo is the only part of Southeast Asia where rainforests can still be preserved "on a grand scale." There are three main reasons to be optimistic about the future of sustainable development in Borneo: the island's topography, its sparse and unevenly distributed population, and the recent establishment of the vast and ambitious Heart of Borneo conservation and development project.

TOPOGRAPHY

Most of Borneo's remaining rainforest lies along the mountain spine that runs from the island's northern tip to its central region. Although the mountain range is not particularly high, its steep slopes mean that rivers are not navigable, and roads and rail lines are difficult and expensive to build. As a result, while Borneo's lowland forests have almost given way to palm oil plantations and farms, most of the forest in the upland areas—the "Heart of Borneo"—remains intact, and can continue to survive well into the future if it is protected and managed properly.

POPULATION

By comparison with some of its neighboring islands, Borneo is very sparsely populated. It is home to some 20 million people and has an average population density of about 27 people per square kilometer. This average is misleading, however: the vast majority of Borneo's people live on or near the coasts, leaving the island's highland interior very sparsely populated indeed. Many of the people living in the interior are Dayaks and other indigenous people who know the forests well and have exploited it sustainably for tens of thousands of years. Low population density and an informed local population with an interest in maintaining the forest make sustainable development in Borneo a much more likely prospect that it would be in some of the more densely populated parts of Southeast Asia.

HEART OF BORNEO

Sustainable development plans in Borneo were given a major boost in 2007 when the governments of Brunei, Indonesia, and Malaysia jointly committed to managing sustainably a large transnational area called the "Heart of Borneo." The area was not to be a national park or conservation area; rather, it would be developed in a way that supported a green economy, where forest destruction would be stopped, greenhouse gas emissions would be reduced, and local people supported in making their living in an environmentally sustainable way. The project is a huge undertaking, and its success is far from certain. It does offer hope, however, and it represents an important recognition by the governments that control Borneo that one of the world's most important and diverse ecosystems is under their control, and that they have an obligation to ensure its survival for future generations.

SUSTAINABLE RESOURCE MANAGEMENT

Southeast Asia is a region with an expanding population, and it home to some of the world's most rapidly growing economies. It is also a place where some of Earth's most critically endangered and biologically diverse ecosystems sit atop valuable mineral resources and occupy land ideally suited for the growth of lucrative cash crops like oil palms and rubber trees. Development cannot be stopped, but it can be managed in a way that makes it sustainable and minimizes environmental damage.

Declaring Borneo's rainforests to be off limits to all development may well protect local ecosystems, but it would also deny governments, investors, and local inhabitants the chance to profit from resources they understandably regard as their own. Permitting unrestricted exploitation of resources, however, would certainly mean that they would be lost forever. Sustainable development is a middle path between these two options: it allows exploitation of natural resources for the benefit of inhabitants and investors, but only in ways that would not unduly harm the long-term future of the region's natural environment.

A hundred years ago, the island of Borneo was virtually untouched by all but the members of its small population of indigenous inhabitants. By the beginning of the 21st century, its forests were being destroyed at an unparalleled rate, its indigenous people displaced from their traditional homelands, and the survival of its myriad species of plants and animals imperiled by the disappearance of their natural habitats. Devastating harm has already come to Borneo, and much of it cannot be reversed.

A great deal of Borneo's unique rainforest remains, however, and it can be saved. It will take a concerted effort by local inhabitants, businesses, and governments. Consumers around the world will need to help too, by refusing to buy products manufactured unsustainably using resources from threatened environments. Students can help by making sure that they learn what these products are, and by sharing what they know with others. Sustainable development in Borneo is possible, but it will not be easy, and it will take a global effort to make sure that it succeeds.

37

WAS THE CONFLICT IN EAST TIMOR, INDONESIA, THE DIRECT RESULT OF NATURAL RESOURCES?

OVERVIEW

M. Troy Burnett

Officially the Democratic Republic of Timor-Leste, or East Timor, is a maritime country of Southeast Asia. A smallish country, roughly 5,400 square miles, it comprises the eastern half of the island of Timor, the neighboring islands of Atauro and Jaco, and the non-contiguous, west Timorese territory of Oecusse. Like many former colonies, Timor-Leste's history has been contentious, its people having endured cycles of violence with its former colonial master, Portugal; its former post-colonial state partner, Indonesia; and even with itself. The question to be discussed herein is, what role have natural resources (e.g., timber, minerals, oil) played in the various conflicts?

BACKGROUND

The Portuguese first colonized Timor Leste (or East Timor) in the 17th century. This period of occupation lasted until 1974, when the people declared their independence. Unfortunately, within the year the territory was invaded and occupied by Indonesia. The 24-year period of Indonesian rule was the most contentious and violent. It is estimated that up to 200,000 Timorese died during the conflict, amounting to a staggering percentage of the current population of just over 1.2 million (O'Rourke, 2002; CIA, 2014). In 1999, in the wake of regime change in Indonesia, calls for independence for East Timor grew louder and gained traction, but not before a period of heightened violence. The conflict continued until 2002 when the United Nations was finally able to recognize East Timor's independence. Subsequently, Timor-Leste became the first new sovereign state of the 21st century.

However, peace and stability were short lived as another crisis engulfed the region in 2006. This particular conflict began as an internal dispute between ethnic factions of the East Timor military. Soldiers from the western part of the country (the Loromonu) claimed they were being discriminated against, and that the easterners (Lorosae) were granted special privileges as well as quicker promotions. The dispute, centered in the capital city Dili, expanded to include the police and former members of the Indonesian military. General violence ensued throughout the country and even included and a coup attempt against the elected leadership prompting military intervention by neighboring countries. Eventually, tensions subsided but not before bouts of protest, violence, death, and the resignation of the Prime Minister, Mari Alkatiri. The situation has since stabilized culminating with East Timor being granted "observer status" in the chief regional economic trading bloc—the Association of Southeast Asian Nations (ASEAN). Tensions are still high in the new country, and conflict continues to lurk beneath the surface.

Micah Fisher argues that, within the context of post-colonialism and Indonesian imperialism, control and management of natural resources has played the central role in defining and exacerbating the conflict. In his view, civil unrest in East Timor largely began with the Indonesian military exerting power over the flow of land-based resources by defining and controlling economic activities. Indeed, the regional military leadership, in a policy known as *dwifungsi*, was tasked by the central government to both maintain security as well as generate revenues through the control and exploitation of natural resources, namely timber and oil. Such close military involvement over the flow of resources also allowed the Indonesian state to better control the local population by controlling their economic reality. Such obvious injustice and exploitation fomented deep levels of resentment in the local population. Further, the stakes over East Timor heightened as the oil crisis of the 1970s brought special attention to the petroleum deposits found off the coast. Much of the tension and unfortunately the widespread violence can be attributed to the struggle over these areas. To a large degree, even after independence, decisions over natural resources continue to define the fate of this small and geographically fragmented democracy as the governing elites face tough challenges over the management of the lucrative petroleum deposits. Most assuredly, if policies are perceived to favor the wealthy elites at the expense of the majority of the population, the citizens of East Timor will rise up again.

On the other hand, Keith Bettinger argues that the gruesome and terrible drama that played out in East Timor from 1975 until 2006 was the result of internal and external political and economic circumstances, with the struggle over natural resources playing a minimal role. The exigencies of Cold War geopolitics as well as the obsession of the authoritarian Suharto regime with Indonesian regional power and territorial sovereignty conspired to foment conflict and block East Timor's road to self-determination for a quarter of a century. Furthermore, the recent conflicts are more the growing pains of a new country that contends with economic development, post-colonial dependency, and a multiethnic/multicultural population. Like most nascent multiethnic states, forging a common national identity and united state project are the most difficult and incendiary. Therefore, it's hardly surprising that violence has ensued in this region, and to a certain degree it could have been a lot worse, many scholars expressing opinions that genocide is a distinct possibility.

REFERENCES

Central Intelligence Agency (CIA). (2016). "Timor-Leste." *The World Factbook*. Accessed March 3, 2016, at https://www.cia.gov/library/publications/the-world-factbook/geos/tt.html.

O'Rourke, Kevin. (2002). *Reformasi: The Struggle for Power in Post-Soeharto Indonesia*. Crows Nest, NSW, Australia: Allen & Unwin.

FURTHER READING

Aditjondro, George. J. (1998). *Is Oil Thicker Than Blood? A Study of Oil Companies' Interests and Western Complicity in Indonesia's Annexation of East Timor*. New York: Nova Science Publishers.

Cleary, Paul. (2007). *Shakedown: Australia's Grab for Timor Oil*. Crows Nest, NSW, Australia: Allen & Unwin.

Dunn, James. (2003). *East Timor: A Rough Passage to Independence*. Double Bay, NSW, Australia: Longueville Books.

Fernandes, Clinton. (2011). *The Independence of East Timor: Multi-Dimensional Perspectives—Occupation, Resistance, and International Political Activism*. Eastbourne, UK: Sussex Academic Press.

EAST TIMOR: A CONFLICT ROOTED IN NATURAL RESOURCES

Micah Fisher

Though the decades-long conflict in East Timor has had many factors, control and management of natural resources has played the central role in defining and exacerbating the conflict. Even today, the young nation-state of East Timor continues to face tough challenges over the management of lucrative petroleum deposits in the Timor Sea. Conflict in East Timor largely began with the Indonesian military exerting power over the flow of land-based resources by defining and controlling economic activities. Such close military involvement over the flow of resources also allowed the Indonesian state to better control the local population. The stakes over East Timor heightened, however, as the oil crisis of the 1970s brought special attention to the petroleum deposits found off the coast. Much of the geopolitical tension and unfortunately the widespread violence can be attributed to the struggle over these areas. To a large degree, decisions over this natural resource continue to define the fate of this small and geographically fragmented democracy situated between Indonesia and Australia.

DWIFUNGSI AND LAND-USE CHANGE IN EAST TIMOR

When the conflict began in 1970s the occupying forces of the Indonesian military was encouraged to follow a strategy of dual functionality—known as *dwifungsi*. The intention of dwifungsi was to maintain security while also seeking to generate revenues. East Timor felt the brunt of this policy, as military personnel benefited from regulating the dynamics of the local economy, especially through the management of natural resources. Military officers would insert themselves into extortionist relationships with local communities demanding security payments. Furthermore, officers would also actively pursue larger-scale business ventures, actively financing, implementing, and managing operations. For instance, the Indonesian military took an active role in harvesting valuable timber for short-term gains, namely hardwoods such as sandalwood and teak. This led to pronounced deforestation and soil erosion of the Timorese landscape. Over the duration of the Indonesian military occupation, of the 1.3-million-hectare total forest area, East Timor lost about 200,000 hectares to conversion or burning (Miyazawa, 2013). Such overtly exploitative practices frustrated the local population and served to mobilize sentiment to break from the Indonesian state.

THE PROMISING WINDFALL OF OIL AND GAS IN THE TIMOR SEA

As the involvement of the Indonesian military on both security and economic fronts certainly played an important role in defining conflict in East Timor, the presence of untapped petroleum deposits in the East Timor Sea brought the region into a larger, geopolitical game involving its former colonial master, Portugal, as well as Australia, China, and the United States. The Portuguese led early efforts to explore and exploit oil and gas deposits in the 1960s, but due to Portugal's waning global influence it was forced to abandon these efforts and ultimately to relinquish colonial control. Australia, recognizing the political and economic advantages, was next to take an active interest. Clearly in pursuit of its own interests, Australia supported Indonesia's incorporation of East Timor into the expanding Indonesian state—which subsequently, according to international law, allowed Australia to claim a larger area of the Timor Sea that contained petroleum deposits.

The 1972 Australia-Indonesia Seabed Boundary caused controversy in Indonesia when diplomats learned much later that Australia had strategically and unfairly delineated its claims in accordance with international maritime law. Indonesia thus began to take a much more protective and deliberate interest in controlling East Timor, for regional geopolitical aims as well as economic reasons—both of which were defined by natural resource opportunities.

By the late 1970s Indonesia's role on the global stage had expanded. The country had gained international support from the pragmatic West as a key regional ally during the Cold War and the Vietnam War. The 1970s also saw a large rise in oil prices. Negotiations and treaties concerning the Timor Sea oil reserves involved mutual zones of cooperation and development. By the late 1980s, Indonesia was poised to begin work on jointly developing sites in an area called the Timor Gap, located in the waters between East Timor and Indonesia. By 1999, development and exploitation promised a profit windfall for the foreseeable future. According to George Aditjondros, Indonesia's desire to control these natural resources at all costs trumped the lives of the Timorese people (Aditjondros, 1998). As calls for independence grew louder and conflict heightened in East Timor, Indonesia was increasingly adverse to recognize any claims to sovereignty. The conflict was compounded by the international community's silence and complicity in oil development.

By 2002 however, international support of Indonesia's thuggish and exploitative, albeit geopolitically condoned, behavior towards East Timor had waned. East Timor was subsequently recognized by the United Nations as an independent state. However, conflict over the resources in the Timor Sea has continued. Post-independence negotiations between East Timor and Australia over natural resources have been contentious and remain undecided. To bolster the point, protests and violent riots reminiscent of the years of the bloody civil war erupted in the capital city of Dili in 2006.

In short, the regional conflict in and with East Timor is and has been centered on natural resource control. It has at times been a violent conflict, played out in different ways over resources on land and sea. At the local level, the Indonesian military's ubiquitous presence through the policy of dwifungsi encouraged an exploitative relationship with the Timorese people that resulted in mutual suspicion, bitterness, and resistance as well as massive deforestation. At the regional geopolitical level the petroleum reserves available in the Timor Sea created intense negotiations that erupted into violence among multiple national and corporate interests.

Currently the situation remains tense, dominated by the continuing ambiguity over natural resources and distribution of the wealth generated. Unfortunately, East Timor primarily has a local, subsistence economy rendering the country's conflict-ravaged past into one of the poorest countries in the world today. According to an IMF report, "Timor-Leste stands out as the most oil-dependent economy in the world," and has yet been unable to use these revenues to meaningfully affect per capita earnings (IMF, 2012). While there is optimism for the future, East Timorese remain skeptical that the natural resource base will bring them anything but conflict.

REFERENCES

Aditjondro, George. J. (1998). *Is Oil Thicker Than Blood? A Study of Oil Companies' Interests and Western Complicity in Indonesia's Annexation of East Timor.* New York: Nova Science Publishers.

International Monetary Fund (IMF). (2012, March 8). "IMF Executive Board concludes 2010 Article IV Consultation with the Democratic Republic of Timor-Leste." Public Information Notice (PIN) No. 11/31.

Miyazawa, Naori. (2013). *Role of Customary Law and Communities in Natural Resource Management in Post-Conflict East Timor.* London: Routledge.

FURTHER READING

Central Intelligence Agency (CIA). (2016). "Timor-Leste." *The World Factbook.* Accessed March 3, 2016, at https://www.cia.gov/library/publications/the-world-factbook/geos/tt.html.

Cleary, Paul. (2007). *Shakedown: Australia's Grab for Timor Oil.* Crows Nest, NSW, Australia: Allen & Unwin.

Fernandes, Clinton. (2011). *The Independence of East Timor: Multi-Dimensional Perspectives—Occupation, Resistance, and International Political Activism.* Eastbourne, UK: Sussex Academic Press.

O'Rourke, Kevin. (2002). *Reformasi: The Struggle for Power in Post-Soeharto Indonesia.* Crows Nest, NSW, Australia: Allen & Unwin.

NATIONALISM, GEOPOLITICS, AND THE BLEEDING OF EAST TIMOR
Keith Bettinger

East Timor was wracked by occupation and insurgency for more than a quarter of a century. However, as tempting as it is to attribute the conflict to a desire to control the region's petroleum wealth, the violence had little to do with natural

East Timorese pro-Indonesian militiamen stand guard with their arms during a show of force in front of the provincial governor's office in Dili, about 1,200 miles east of Jakarta, in 1999. More than 3,000 anti-independence militiamen paraded in the provincial capital to show that they were ready to fight separatist rebels that have been struggling for independence since 1975. (Sam Martins/AP Photo)

resources. Rather, the bloody conflict is a sad tale of a people caught in the middle of a convergence of nationalist ambition on the part of Indonesia and Cold War calculation on the part of the United States and its allies.

The roots of the conflict began shortly after the so-called "Carnation Revolution," a military coup that overthrew the long-ruling fascist regime in Portugal, when the Portuguese withdrew from East Timor. The future of the territory was left in the hands of two newly-formed political parties: the Timorese Democratic Union (UDT, *União Democrática Timorense*), comprising mainly landowners and other economic elites; and the Revolutionary Front for an Independent East Timor (Fretilin, *Frente Revolucionaria de Timor Leste Independente*), consisting of students, academics, and social reformers. For a short while UDT and Fretilin formed a coalition government, but soon the relationship between them deteriorated into civil war. Fretilin prevailed and began charting a course towards the establishment of an independent government, but in late 1975 the Indonesian army invaded, beginning a bitter conflict that would last until 2000. East Timor's dreams of independence would have to wait as it was incorporated into Indonesia as that country's 27th province. Despite the brutality of the invasion, with estimates of as many as 200,000, or more than 10 percent of the population, killed (O'Rourke, 2002; CIA, 2014), Indonesia faced no international condemnation for its actions. The stark reality for the lack of criticism was the invasion satisfied a confluence of self-interest at the national, regional, and international scales.

For Indonesia, the invasion was justified, for as a nascent state having gained independence from the Dutch in 1949, both national identity and separatism were ongoing challenges. During the independence struggle, fighting took place in disparate locations throughout the archipelago, and in many places regional commanders acted virtually independent of the movement's leaders in Jakarta. Because of this, after independence there were several centers of power only loosely controlled by the federal capital. By the end of the 1950s, full-scale rebellion had broken out on the islands of Sumatra and Sulawesi (the Pemesta-PRRI revolt, 1957–1961). Though this insurrection was snuffed out by 1961, the seeds of conflict were planted and regional rebellion would continue to be a concern throughout the post-colonial era, as independence movements smoldered in Aceh and Irian Jaya (Papua).

Indonesia's government also perceived an ideological threat stemming from the potential independence of East Timor. Though Indonesia emerged from colonialism as a democracy, the country's first president, Sukarno (1901–1970) took steps in the late 1950s to curtail democratic processes with the institution of "Guided Democracy," which suspended parliamentary elections. In 1965 a conspiracy attempted to depose Sukarno, whose precarious hold on power had relied on a loose alliance of communists, nationalists, and the military. The confusion surrounding this attempted coup provided an opportunity for Suharto (1921–2008), a middle-level general, to seize power and become Indonesia's second president in 1967.

To Suharto's "New Order" regime (1967–1998), an independent East Timor could become a source of inspiration and support for those opposed to the government's policies of economic development and regional consolidation. Further, Suharto's government prioritized economic development via the exploitation of natural resources, such as timber. While such policies contributed to high rates of economic growth, there were strong criticisms that this development benefited an elite minority with plutocratic ties to the regime, whereas the vast majority of Indonesians were paying significant social, economic, and environmental costs. Moreover, in the wake of the failed coup against Sukarno, Suharto and the military had viciously crushed one of his predecessor's major supporters—the Indonesian Communist Party (PKI, *Partai Komunis Indonesia*). The PKI was banned and the idea of communism in general was denigrated. From this perspective, Fretilin, which had been characterized by many both inside and outside Indonesia as sympathetic to communism, represented an ideological threat to the unquestioned legitimacy of Suharto's economic policies.

For Indonesia, there was no downside to the full-scale invasion and occupation of East Timor in 1975. President Suharto's regime had received strong signals from both the United States and Australia that East Timor's integration into Indonesia would be welcomed and even encouraged. This stance was rooted in broader geopolitical concerns; it was the height of the Cold War and the United States was in the midst of extricating itself from a failed campaign against communism in Vietnam. Moreover, both Laos and Cambodia were governed by anti-Western communist regimes. Thus the possibility of an independent East Timor led by the Communist leaning Fretilin was a major strategic concern for the United States and its allies.

Indeed, East Timor had no geopolitical allies. Indonesia, as a founding member of the Non-Aligned Movement (NAM), an international organization of developing countries which bitterly opposed colonialism, could be confident that its takeover would not be challenged from this quarter. Moreover, the Association of Southeast Asian Nations (ASEAN), a regional cooperation bloc, had a policy of non-intervention and neutrality on matters seen to be "internal affairs." Thus when Indonesia invaded, precipitating another round of regional instability and violent conflict, it was in no one's geopolitical interest to challenge the move.

In short, the gruesome and terrible drama that played out in East Timor from 1975 until 2000 was the result of internal and external political and economic circumstances, not the struggle over natural resources. The exigencies of Cold War geopolitics as well as the obsession of the authoritarian Suharto regime with Indonesian sovereignty conspired to foment conflict and block East Timor's road to self-determination for a quarter of a century.

REFERENCES

Central Intelligence Agency (CIA). (2016). "Timor-Leste." *The World Factbook*. Accessed March 3, 2016, at https://www.cia.gov/library/publications/the-world-factbook/geos/tt.html.

O'Rourke, Kevin. (2002). *Reformasi: The Struggle for Power in Post-Soeharto Indonesia*. Crows Nest, NSW, Australia: Allen & Unwin.

FURTHER READING

Dunn, James. (2003). *East Timor: A Rough Passage to Independence*. Double Bay, NSW, Australia: Longueville Books.

Fernandes, Clinton. (2011). *The Independence of East Timor: Multi-Dimensional Perspectives—Occupation, Resistance, and International Political Activism.* Eastbourne, UK: Sussex Academic Press.

Hill, Helen. (2002). *Stirrings of Nationalism in East Timor: Fretilin 1974–1978: The Origins, Ideologies, and Strategies of a Nationalist Movement.* Sydney, Australia: Otford Press.

38

IS THE RESOURCE OF THE MEKONG RIVER BASIN A POTENTIAL FOR REGIONAL CONFLICT?

OVERVIEW
Jennifer C. Veilleux

The Mekong River basin covers 795,000 square kilometers in Southeast Asia and is home to some 260 million people. A river basin is a geographical designation of an area where any surface water such as springs, rivers, and streams terminate in the river. The surface water in the Mekong comes from tributaries fed by precipitation, especially during monsoon season, and snowmelt from the Tibetan highlands. Cascading from its source in the Tibetan highlands, the river descends 5,000 meters in elevation as it meanders 4,900 kilometers south to empty into the South China Sea. Throughout the basin there are large permanent tributaries and many small seasonal tributaries that contribute to the overall flow of the main Mekong River. The basin spans six countries—Cambodia, China, Myanmar, Laos, Thailand, and Vietnam. The basin contains one of the most bio-diverse regions in the world and, in terms of fish species, the Mekong River is the most biodiverse river in the world. There are more than 1,100 known fish species found in the Mekong. The climate is mostly tropical and subtropical, with the exception of the region where the headwaters are found in Tibet, which is considered alpine.

The river is navigable only in sections as there are many rapids and waterfalls that prevent easy passage for boats.

BACKGROUND

The Mekong River basin is geopolitically divided into the Upper Mekong River basin in China and Myanmar and the Lower Mekong River basin in Cambodia, Laos, Thailand, and Vietnam. Approximately 80 percent of the people in the lower Mekong basin rely on the river for their personal and economic needs. Almost 97 percent of Laos and 86 percent of Cambodia are contained within the basin, which means that the vast majority of people living in these two countries depend on the Mekong River and its associated natural resources. Rapidly growing regional economics and increased consumption patterns on natural resources are changing the face of the basin. The countries of China, Thailand, and Vietnam have significantly developed their portions of the Mekong River basin. Poorer countries such as Laos and Cambodia have development plans for basin resources and are presently putting some of those plans into place.

Large dams and irrigation schemes have been developed on the river in China and on tributaries in Laos, Cambodia, Thailand, and Vietnam. As of 2008, China commissioned five hydropower dams, including large storage capacities, and there are plans to commission at least three more dams by the year 2020. According to those living downstream on the Mekong, it was around 2008 when the flow of the Mekong River became erratic, fish populations decreased, remaining fish populations featured less large-sized fish while some species disappeared altogether, and gold found in the sediments in the riverbanks was reduced. The Mekong River Delta in Vietnam is home to more than 20 million people and provides much of the area's rice crop. The Tonle Sap Lake, a lake that is connected seasonally to the Mekong River, is a major source of freshwater fish in Cambodia. Freshwater fish from the basin accounts for 80 percent of the protein in the Cambodian diet. The river has potential to provide significant hydroelectricity to the region if large dams are constructed to harness the power of the river. Vietnam and Laos mine sediment from the river for building construction. The river is also a major source of food and water for local communities. Local communities rely on river-dependent ecosystems in the forest and the river itself for growing crops and harvesting fish.

Though the water resources are plentiful, resources in the basin (e.g., land, forests, birds, animals, plants, and fish) are under pressure from human activities. Huge swathes of forest have been clear-cut for timber and plantations, mineral resources are being mined in open-pit mining practices, species of wild plants and animals are being harvested for use in medicines and meat, species of fish are being hunted to extinction, and the Mekong dolphin is endangered from human encroachment. Erosion and pollution related to activity such as clear-cutting forest and mining is entering the aquatic and terrestrial systems through runoff and rainfall. Some areas, such as the northeast region of Thailand, are experiencing extended drought. Locals in Laos report changes to the Mekong River flow and levels. Land-use changes, coupled with intensive well-pumping for agriculture, changes in weather patterns due to climate change, and improved regional economies are all factors in local resource changes. The environmental and development challenges in the Mekong River basin are complicated and varied.

The Lower Mekong countries are unified under the Mekong River Commission (MRC) to share development plans and negotiate changes and usage of the river. The recent new regional economic unification, the Association of Southeast Asian Nations (ASEAN), which includes Southeast Asian countries outside of the basin, gives opportunity for continued economic growth and an expanded energy market. The Xayaburi Dam Project in Laos, funded almost entirely by Thailand and with 80-percent energy generation slated for export to Thailand for the next 30 years, is a project that has caused some international controversy. According to the MRC's prior notification requirements, participant countries must submit a proposal six months before the commencement of their domestic development projects to the commission. This allows for any project to be reviewed for downstream impacts and, if necessary, recommendations and mitigations can be requested. The Laos government did in fact submit its project proposal before construction began on Xayaburi. Due to concerns in Vietnam about sediment flows and in Cambodia about fish population impacts, Laos modified the dam's design to incorporate fish passage and sediment traps. This was the first time that the legal process was exercised in the MRC. Legal processes have been put into place so that development does not upset the balance of diplomatic ties between governments in the region, the local cultural diversity in resources use, but also because of the fragile ecosystems in the Mekong River basin.

Due to changes in local economies, development projects are now underway with funding from regional governments. China and Southeast Asia are home to manufacturing of goods that are consumed in the West. The factories need electricity to function and expand. Local populations are growing in China, Vietnam, and Thailand as is the standard of living for those growing populations. Countries of Myanmar, Laos, and Cambodia are among some of the world's least developed countries. The governments in these countries have plans to develop and modernize. Modernization includes use of natural resources to further the goals of progress, but it also means using resources at a much higher rate and wider scale. However, natural resources exploitation changes local environments, leading to unknown and unexpected consequences. Change in the Mekong River basin is inevitable under these conditions, but the governments in countries in the Mekong basin have means to communicate through the MRC, ASEAN, and diplomatic agreements about how they would like to see that change manifest.

FURTHER READING

Osbourne, Milton E. (2000). *Mekong: Turbulent Past, Uncertain Future*, first edition. New York: Grove Press.

Vaidyanathan, Gayathri. (2011). "Dam controversy: remaking the Mekong," *Nature*. Accessed March 3, 2016, http://www.nature.com/news/2011/111019/full/478305a.html.

THE POTENTIAL FOR CONFLICT IN THE MEKONG RIVER BASIN
Aaron Williams and M. Troy Burnett

The Mekong River basin, originating on the Tibetan Plateau, drains 795,000 square kilometers, meandering 4,800 kilometers to its outlet forming the Mekong Delta on the South China Sea. For millennia the river basin and its delta have been the lifeblood of much of South East Asia's population and a vital resource to aspiring regional empires. The nutrient-rich alluvial sediment deposited from

A boat travels along the muddy Mekong River in Phnom Penh, Cambodia. The seventh-longest river in Asia, the Mekong flows for 2,600 miles from the Tibetan Plateau through China's Yunnan Province, Myanmar, Thailand, Laos, Cambodia and Vietnam. (Dreamstime.com)

seasonal monsoon rains and flooding provides fertile soils that when cultivated feeds millions. The basin is also key to making the region a biodiversity hotspot.

Yet, unlike the other major rivers of the world, the Mekong River does not function as a unifying feature (Osbourne, 2000). This is due to the complex rugged physical geography that has acted as a barrier to navigation, population movement, and economic flows. Indeed, even at the end of the 20th century, the Mekong River was considered the last untamed and unexploited river system. In the last 10 years, however, with China as the regional leader, river development and basin modernization have emerged. Hydroelectric dam projects in particular have moved forward at a rapid pace on both the upper Mekong (China) and on the Lower Mekong (Laos, Cambodia, Thailand, Myanmar, and Vietnam). This rapid development, often with minimal evaluation of the social or environmental impacts, is having a profound and arguably destabilizing effect.

The countries of the lower Mekong River, who see themselves at the mercy of their more powerful neighbor, China, have formed the Mekong River Commission (MRC) to address the impacts and mitigate China's strong-armed approach. However, China does not belong to this organization nor does it recognize its authority. Indeed, as development of the river progresses there are no transboundary agreements regulating the flow and use of the Mekong River, leading to an uncoordinated and highly contentious situation (Osbourne, 2000; Sneddon and Fox, 2006).

DAMMING THE MEKONG

Since the 1990s, China has built numerous hydroelectric dams on the upper Mekong, with many large dams completed in the last five years. The cumulative effect is a highly variable river flow—low flow that inhibits navigation and movement of fish stocks, and high flow/flooding that rapidly erodes the river bank causing destruction of agricultural plots and rapid increase in sediment load that can inhibit the movement of migratory spawning fish species and even respiration of fish downstream.

Negotiations between China and the MRC countries downstream to mitigate the effects of the dams on the upper Mekong have been ongoing. Despite these efforts, plans for further hydroelectric dams on the upper Mekong are moving forward. The countries of the lower Mekong have become increasingly frustrated and angry with China's unwillingness to address their concerns.

Plans for numerous dam projects on the lower Mekong River are even more troubling. There are plans for as many as 12 new dams on the lower Mekong River, many of which are already under construction (Grumbine et al., 2015; Vaidyanathan, 2011). These dam projects on the lower Mekong could have catastrophic effects on the biodiversity of the river, agriculture within the Mekong Delta, and, as result, the human population of the Mekong sub-region.

The Mekong in its natural state is considered the second-most biodiverse river in the world, after the Amazon River of South America. The Mekong River contains around 1,100 species of fish, including four of the largest freshwater species in the world (Baran and Myschowoda, 2009; Vaidyanathan, 2011). Of these species that that live within the largest lake and fishery within the Mekong water catchment, Lake Tonal Sap, 60 percent of the fish species are migratory and travel as far as 1,500 kilometers upstream to spawn (Vaidyanathan, 2011). It is estimated that Tonle Sap Lake alone provides 50 percent of the protein for the Cambodian population. Further, upstream from the Lower Mekong Dam projects, there are an estimated 229 species of migratory fish, many of them requiring migration above and below these dam sites to survive as a species. Although there are numerous strategies in the engineering of the dams to allow for fish to travel above and below the dams, previous designs such as fish ladders have failed (Grumbine et al., 2015).

It is estimated that the total economic value of the Mekong fishery in 2004 was between 1.4 and 1.9 billion U.S. dollars annually (Baran and Myschowoda, 2009; Van Zalinge et al., 2004). The potential impact of these dams on fish stalks are astounding and could lead to the collapse of the entire food chain of the lower Mekong that includes the millions of people that depend on the river for livelihood and a crucial food course.

Another serious effect that further dam projects will have on the lower Mekong is the disruption of natural sediment transfer downstream to the delta in Vietnam. Among other impacts, this will dramatically undermine the future viability of agriculture. It is estimated that the dams will block half of the sediment that would naturally reach the delta (Vaidyanathan, 2011). Not only will this reduce soil fertility but it will also sever the flow of materials that sustain the physical structure of the delta itself. This reduction of sediment would be further exacerbated by current anthropogenic effects, such as the destruction of mangroves that hold sediment in place and the global-warming-induced 6mm-average rise in sea level.

The potential for conflict is high—19.4 million people live in an area that will eventually be lost to the sea. For Vietnam in particular, the delta region is the country's primary rice-growing region that supports both the local people as well as being its chief export and major source of income. Doubtless, the country and its people are not going to sit idly by and watch their river and their livelihoods be destroyed by self-serving upstream countries.

CONCLUSION

To avoid conflict, the countries involved need to rely on scientific understanding of the entire basin's hydrological and ecological systems as well as develop a full awareness of the social and economic impacts. While the MRC is a worthy idea, to be an effective institution it will need the full cooperation of China. Presently, China is participating only as a "dialogue partner," and has repeatedly shown an unwillingness to provide the down-river countries with the necessary engineering and hydrologic reports. Again, this unwillingness frustrates the MRC. Though direct, violent confrontation with China is highly unlikely, political tensions and mistrust continue to mount between the neighbors and also within the countries themselves as those most affected increasingly become more dissatisfied with their leaders and with the MRC itself.

REFERENCES

Baran, E., and Myschowoda, C. (2009). "Health of marine ecosystems in South East Asia: dams and fisheries in the Mekong Basin," *Aquatic Ecosystem Health and Management* 12(3), 227–234. Accessed March 3, 2016, at http://www.tandfonline.com/doi/abs/10.1080/14634980903149902.

Grumbine, Edward R., John Dore, and Jianchu Xu. (2012). "Mekong hydropower: drivers of change and challenges," *Frontiers in Ecology and the Environment 5*, 91–98.

Osbourne, Milton E. (2000). *Mekong: Turbulent Past, Uncertain Future*, first edition. New York: Grove Press.

Sneddon, Chris, and Colleen Fox. (2006). "Rethinking transboundary waters: a critical hydropolitics of the Mekong basin," *Political Geography 25*(2), 181–202.

Vaidyanathan, Gayathri. (2011). "Dam controversy: remaking the Mekong," *Nature*. Accessed March 3, 2016, at http://www.nature.com/news/2011/111019/full/478305a.html.

Van Zalinge, N., P. Degen, C. Pongsri, S. Nuov, et al. (eds.). (2004). "The Mekong River System," in *Proceedings of the Second International Symposium on the Management of Large Rivers for Fisheries*, 333–355.

FURTHER READING

Food and Agricultural Organization of the United Nations. (n.d.). Bangkok: FAO Regional Office for Asia and the Pacific. Accessed May 1, 2016, at http://www.fao.org/asiapacific/regional-office/en/.

COOPERATION AND COORDINATION IN THE MEKONG RIVER BASIN
Jennifer C. Veilleux

There are millions of people of various ethnicities and cultural traditions who live and subsist along the Mekong River or one of its many tributaries. These different peoples have a long history of cooperation and peace. Presently, there are at least five governments that rely on the basin's natural resources for national economic development. Though outside observers stress the potential for conflict, the facts and history suggest that the multiethnic peoples of the basin will negotiate and cooperate, as they have for centuries, rather than fight.

The construction of hydropower dams has emerged as the most contentious issue. This development has the potential to irreversibly change the ability for some natural resources uses to continue at the local scale. Upstream dams may also alter economic uses of the river in downstream countries. With all dam projects there are legitimate worries. For this essay, I will focus on the Xayaburi Dam in Laos. I argue that the way it has been managed suggests a positive and hopeful future for basin cooperation and development.

Laos's Xayaburi Dam Project, a large-scale dam with the potential to produce 1,275 megawatts, is under construction on the Mekong River. The dam has been the subject of international attention in the media both within and outside the basin countries. Media attention is commonly focused on perceived negative impacts that changes to the flow of the Mekong River will have on downstream communities and their fishing-based livelihoods, specifically in Cambodia and Vietnam. It is thought that the dam will block passage of nutrient-rich sediment and disrupt fish migration and reproduction patterns. The primary source of protein for the majority of people in Cambodia comes from fish stocks in the Tonle Sap Lake, which is fed by the Mekong River.

The three affected countries have had intricately nuanced diplomatic ties in areas of trade, transport, and political histories, though each are full participants in the Mekong River Commission (MRC). The MRC exists to both gather scientific and development information and to coordinate development. The commission has repeatedly served to bring together appointed members of the basin countries in a dialogue about each country's development plans. While the MRC cannot enforce laws, it can provide advice and suggestions on any development plans and a platform where each country can discuss the compatibility of its national agendas. Each country has focused on different types of economic development according to its national goals and economies.

Though often criticized, the MRC has a respected legal process in place to allow countries to communicate intended development projects; this process is called prior notification. For the Xayaburi Dam, the government of Laos went through the process of prior notification and, when it received commentary on dam construction from Vietnam and Cambodia, readily altered the design of the dam to mitigate the negative impacts. These modifications were for fish passage and sediment transport. Despite strong criticism from abroad about the ecological impacts as the dam project moves forward, there continues to be no official objection from Vietnam or Cambodia.

Although the international community states that fish passage and nutrient movement in sediment will be blocked, there is not enough scientific understanding of what fish exist in the stretch of the river immediately impacted or how much sediment moves through this area. According to local stakeholders, the hydrologic flow of the Mekong has changed significantly in recent years. Local stakeholders claim that fish populations have already significantly altered and sediment is now being mined in Laos. Fish catch are smaller in size than they had been in the past, population numbers have reduced, and some species are completely absent. Locals who pan for gold in river sediment indicated that the amount of gold in the sediment today is much less than it was before. The dam has the potential to exacerbate the situation for fish if it blocks their normal movements for food and reproduction, especially if there is not enough data currently documented about fish population changes. Locals point to changes in local economic policies and more people fishing in the Mekong as well as dam construction in China upstream.

The Xayaburi Dam is the first of several dams planned for the Mekong River in Laos. The project has highlighted need for further communication between stakeholders from Mekong River basin countries and the international community who live there. Since Laos went through the prior notification process, the MRC has found flaws with the process and is in the process of revising how this process works. This bodes well for the organization, as it shows a willingness to evolve and adapt.

Regional governments have not officially been opposed to the Xayaburi Dam. This may be because these other governments have development plans of their own that they can now feel confident about pursuing. The international community calls for careful studies to determine what would be lost due to the dam. Unregulated development of natural resources, it is feared, will change the Mekong landscape and erode the current way of life for tens of thousands of local people. Using natural resources of the Mekong River, the local and national governments contend, is the only way to elevate Laos out of poverty.

Though the ideologies of environmentalists and the national government of Laos are not the same, the dialogue about ongoing development continues. The people who lose the most are the local communities who depend on the river for survival, but these are the same communities that the Laos government is targeting for poverty reduction. Change in the Mekong River basin is inevitable as populations increase, local economies modernize, and demand for electricity increases. The Xayaburi Dam Project is an example of how development, although contentious, can move forward and add to ongoing dialogue about the basin through cooperation and communication. The dam has highlighted areas of concern to international and national agendas where stakeholders can come together to better understand the Mekong River basin system ecology and hydrology, elevate the visibility of fragile communities most impacted, and start to openly discuss development in China as a major impact of change.

39

WILL THE GANGES RIVER BE A SOURCE OF REGIONAL CONFLICT BETWEEN INDIA AND BANGLADESH?

OVERVIEW

Mark Hecht

There is a stark truism: those who live downstream must contend with the actions of those living upstream. The situation is exacerbated when the downstream country is politically and economically less powerful. Such is the case in the Ganges River basin, where the less-developed Bangladesh must contend with the actions of its larger, upstream neighbor India.

The Ganges is the third largest river in the world. The basin contains almost 10 percent of the world's population and the greatest concentration of the world's poor.

However, most geopolitical tensions between the two countries arise not from poverty but from variability in precipitation and river discharge. The Ganges River basin receives some of the highest precipitation volumes in the world during a four-month period from July to October. A seasonally shifting pressure system then reverses wind direction in the winter, bringing desiccating winds off the Tibetan Plateau. Atmospheric extremes give river flow extremes: flooding during the monsoon, drought during the winter. The maximum discharge, as measured at the Hardinge Bridge, which is located in Bangladesh before the Ganges merges with the Brahmaputra and Meghna rivers, often exceeds 70,000 cubic meters per second during monsoon rains, yet once dropped as low as 180 cubic meters per second in the 1997 winter dry season.

The Ganges-Brahmaputra-Meghna tri-river basin has always experienced an extreme decline in flow during winter months, but the 180 cubic meters per second reading on the Ganges in 1997 represented an artificial, and extraordinarily unusual low flow that experts in Bangladesh believed was caused by India's construction of the Farrakka Barrage in 1975.

BACKGROUND

The Farrakka Barrage water diversion project was intended to, and does, divert water flow from the Ganges through a 42-kilometer canal that drains into the Hooghly River. The Farrakka Barrage is capable of diverting as much as 40,000 cubic meters per second with its primary purpose to flush sediment from Kolkata harbor, but also to increase navigation on the Hooghly River. Farrakka Barrage also played an influential role in supplying greater irrigation potential to the West Bengal rice-growing region.

Bangladesh, upon hearing of the original plans in the 1950s, became concerned, and accurately so, that the Barrage would decrease flow in the downstream portion of the Ganges River. The resulting loss of flow, since 1975, has resulted in a decrease of fresh water, incursion of salt water, increased bank erosion, and increasing salinity in the water table throughout southwestern Bangladesh. In the Sunderban wetlands of Bangladesh, at the mouth of the Ganges, salt-tolerant species have been increasing, mangrove forests have been declining and desertification has become apparent in some areas that were normally productive swamps. With most Bangladeshis getting potable water from groundwater sources, increasing salinity has become a severe problem in the country.

Bangladesh was able to negotiate some concessions for minimum water flows between 1977 and 1982 but failed to have political impact until again in 1996 when the Ganges Treaty was signed. The Ganges Treaty set out a 30-year water-sharing time frame although minimum flow rates through Bangladesh during the low season were not included. This lack of minimum flow rates, which should have been legitimized in a treaty that India must abide, left India again with the ability to regulate the Ganges as it pleased. Bangladesh, it seemed, would have to continue suffering the vagaries of India's decision making. The negative effects of Farrakka, and other future diversions, were left unsettled.

Unfortunately, in comparison to India, Bangladesh has little political leverage. A promising policy alternative in other places is the increasing movement to monetize ecosystem service, where downstream users will pay upstream users to take beneficial environmental actions. Upstream actions experienced as downstream benefits can include, for example, maintaining healthy upstream ecosystems that give purified downstream water, maintaining minimum flow levels to downstream users, and decreasing pollution inputs upstream that leads to decreased pollution levels downstream. Ecosystem service payments, while helpful in many cases around the world, are out of reach for Bangladesh. As a poor country, Bangladesh could not offer India enough in payments to override the benefits the Farrakka Barrage provides to India. Ecosystem service payments would also have to overcome the complexities of India's localized water management institutions. Minimal federal oversight in India dilutes central power and leads to slow movement by the India's government on water negotiations with neighboring national governments.

Other than weak political action and a lack of economic negotiating tools, the last line of action in Bangladesh's arsenal, other than acquiescence, is use of direct or proxy violence for political maneuvering and leverage. The northeastern part of India, for example, has long been a geographically and politically isolated region of the country. The region neighbors Bangladesh. How Bangladesh operates in the area directly affects India. The United Liberation Front of Assam (ULFA) has often been a thorn in India's side as it fights an insurgency campaign for independence. Bangladesh has often helped India with counterinsurgency campaigns. Yet, internally, large portions of the Bangladeshi population support the drives and desires of the ULFA and other similar groups. A Bangladesh long ignored by India could easily switch its allegiances. Bangladesh could easily harbor, or at least tacitly ignore, ULFA fighters hiding in its northern provinces. Other insurgent and independence groups of northeastern India could also find themselves safe havens inside Bangladesh's borders. It is a situation India seems to be quietly encouraging by underappreciating its current regional ally. Future policy by Bangladesh's government will be largely based on the actions, or inactions, of the Indian government. If India resolves the "missing water" problem that Bangladesh has experienced since the building of the Farrakka Barrage then the two will likely remain companion allies.

However, the longer India turns a cold ear to Bangladesh, the more it faces the inevitable specter of silently igniting violence on the Ganges.

FURTHER READING

Chellaney, Brahma. (2011). *Water: Asia's New Battleground*. Washington, DC: Georgetown University Press.

Islam, Shafi Noor, and Albrecht Gnauck. (2009). "Threats to the Sundarbans Mangrove Wetlands ecosystem from transboundary water allocation in the Ganges basin: a preliminary analysis," *International Journal of Ecological Economics & Statistics* 13(W09), 64–78.

Kamruzzaman, Mohammad, Simon Beecham, and Gian Maria Zuppi. (2012). "A model for water sharing in the Ganges River basin," *Water and Environment Journal* 26(3), 308–318.

Mirza, M. Monirul Qader (ed.). (2005). *The Ganges Water Diversion: Environmental Effects and Implications*. Water Science and Technology Library Volume 49. Dordrecht, Netherlands, Boston, and London: Kluwer Academic Publishers.

GANGES RIVER AS THE SOURCE OF REGIONAL CONFLICT BETWEEN INDIA AND BANGLADESH
Edward Jackiewicz

One of the longest and most contentious river water conflicts in the world is between India and Bangladesh over the sacred Ganges. The primary issue is over the appropriate allocation and development of the water resources of the Ganges River. These two countries have never come to a concrete treaty to govern the shared water. The Ganges, an international river about 2,510 kilometers long, rises on the southern slope of the Himalayas and moves through India in a southeasterly direction to Bangladesh (Swain, 1993).

The present conflicts between India and Bangladesh over Ganges water dates back to 1951, when Bangladesh formed the eastern province of the federation of Pakistan (Swain, 1993). The Bangladesh economy relies on agriculture as the main source of income, about 70 percent of its GDP is generated from agriculture. To sustain its agriculture sector, reliable water supplies are needed during the dry season for domestic use, industrial purposes, maintaining adequate river depth to permit navigation, avoiding damage to fish, and limiting salt water intrusion (Swain, 1993). For example about 400 million people within the basin are highly dependent on the river for irrigation, domestic uses, fisheries, navigation,

People doing laundry on the banks of the Ganges River in rural Bangladesh. (Shutterstock)

and hydropower (Shmueli, 1999). Unable to fully meet these needs, Bangladesh blames the upstream country, India, as the cause of the problem.

With limited flow of water downstream, all these activities are affected and therefore the Bangladesh people voice their concerns, which are not well received by the Indian people. This has already led to interstate conflicts that need to be addressed. Due to rapid population increase, the demand for clean fresh water also increases, which guarantees that a conflict will erupt between these two nations. The demand for freshwater for irrigation is expected to rise in the near future (Sood and Mathukumalli, 2011). This is because the world is becoming more industrialized and hence the industrial demand for fresh water will increase. India and Bangladesh does not have a good bilateral treaty regarding the sharing of the Ganges water. As demand for water hits the limits of supply, conflicts tend to boil up between India and Bangladesh.

The construction of the Farakka Barrage on the Ganges River near the Bangladesh border has clearly intensified the tension that already existed between these two nations. The dam was built to divert the Ganges River water into the Hooghly River during the dry season (January to June). India built the Farakka Barrage 18 kilometers upstream from the then-East Pakistan (now Bangladesh) border, on the grounds of "preservation and maintenance of Calcutta port by improving the regime and navigability of the Bhagirathi-Hooghly river system" (Swain, 1993). Apart from the dam, there was also the 38-kilometer canal that was built to help in flushing off the silt during the dry season. This reduces water volume in the dry season and lowers the Ganges level causing further concentrations of what is already a high level of pollution caused by human and animal waste, fertilizers, and salts (Sood and Mathukumalli, 2011). However, because the plan to build the facility was unilateral, it faced stiff opposition from the Bangladesh government. The Bangladesh government claimed that the development would cause environmental degradation to the people living on the eastern side of the river. This continues to be a dispute between India and Bangladesh. Because India has an upper hand in the region both politically and economically, Bangladesh's claim was only met with a deaf ear and the project went ahead as planned.

The diversion of water at Farakka led to limited supply of water to the downstream users and this has negative effect on both domestic and industrial uses. This inadequate supply of water worsened during the dry season. Because the Bangladesh economy is agriculture based, a decrease in water supply will jeopardize its economy, leading to catastrophes such as hunger, desertification, and even closure of some its industries. For example, the population of Bangladesh was 157.5 million as of 2008 with a density of 1229.16 persons per square kilometer. The population growth in the region was 1.5 percent in 2001. About 77 percent of the population is rural and agriculture employs 63 percent of the labor force, generating 25 percent of GDP (Sood and Mathukumalli, 2011). With all these interruptions dispute arose between India and Bangladesh over the sharing of the dry season flow at Farakka. Unclear agreement on sharing of Ganges water during the dry season became the center of disputes leading to conflict.

For these regions to prosper economically and co-exist peacefully both India and Bangladesh signed several treaties to facilitate the sharing of Ganges water during the dry season. In 1975, after the completion of Farakka, both India and Bangladesh signed a short-term agreement for 40 days of the dry season (Swain, 1996). The assassination of the pro-Indian president of Bangladesh, Mujibur Rehman, in August 1975 changed the equation between India and Bangladesh (Swain, 1996). With this unexpected event occurring, the agreement was disobeyed by India. In January 1976, India unilaterally began diverting the Ganges dry-season flow at Farakka without any consultation with or concurrence by Bangladesh (Swain, 1996). The dry season is the main cause of conflict between these two nations. In the dry season, the average minimum discharge to Farakka in 1975 was estimated at only 1,557 cubic meters per second. India asks for 40,000 cubic feet per second while Bangladesh needs all 1,557 cubic meters per second if ecological disaster is to be avoided (Swain, 1996).

The deficiencies of the short-term treaty signed in 1975 are an indicator that something has to be done if the economic and political causes of the dispute are to be addressed. Because India has comparative political, military, and trade advantages, and because of its position as the upper riparian state in the dispute, India has an upper hand in controlling the flow of Ganges water. On the other side, Bangladesh is economically, politically, and/or militarily at a disadvantage, which renders it voiceless and without leverage that might encourage India to consider long-term scientific solutions to solve the dispute. The only option for the downriver country is to voice its concerns to the outside world regarding India's unilateral action.

While water diversion at Farakka is considered a success for the Indian government, it has created environmental destruction for Bangladesh. "It has disrupted fishing and navigation, brought unwanted salt deposits into rich farming soil, adversely affected agricultural and industrial production, changed the hydraulic character of the rivers and brought about changes in the ecology of the Delta" (Swain, 1996). These consequences are considered man-made catastrophes. The government of Bangladesh described the situation back in 1976 as a "grave crisis" (Swain, 1996). The Ganges water dispute over Farakka has become an inter-state conflict between India and Bangladesh.

The disputes over Ganges water have also lead to conflict within Bangladesh. Economic disparities within the country result in the poorer people viewing their Hindu fellow citizens as their antagonists, which has resulted in violence between communities. The inability of the country's rulers to improve the deteriorating standards of living has also ignited the discontented masses to wage frequently violent demonstrations and strikes that have brought political instability and chaos to the country—even for the democratically elected government that came to power on an anti-India platform by squarely blaming Mujibur's consent to Farakka withdrawal in 1975 on his daughter-led opposition (Swain, 1993).

The Ganges water-sharing has also created a religious conflict between India and Bangladesh. The Ganges River is considered a religious symbol by Indian Hindus, who perform an annual festival of cleansing. People often arrive at the Ganges River from distant locations for submerging cremation ashes of near and dear ones (National Symbols of India, n.d.). However, the event is environmentally unfriendly because it causes pollution that affects the users downstream. Bangladesh has condemned this act and hence has mistrust against religious Hindus. This has created hostility between Hindus and Muslims.

Agriculture is the backbone of the Bangladesh economy. The reduction in quantity and quality of water due to diversion at Farakka has led to decline in Bangladesh's GDP. Most of the Bangladesh people, therefore, can't support their families and are forced to leave the country in search of better life. This phenomenon has seen high number of environmental refugees in India. For example, out of 52 of the Bangladeshi immigrants whom Ashok Swain was able to locate and interview in India in 1993 and 1994, 43 traced their origin to the affected region in Bangladesh (Swain, 1996). This high number of environmental refugees became a source of conflict in India. This is evidenced by the expression of insecurity among natives as well as immigrants, prompting them to protect their interest one against the other. The large-scale migration of the environmentally displaced Muslim Bangladeshis into "Hindu India" from the late 1970s has culminated in several conflicts in various parts of the country (Swain, 1996). These conflicts have led to deadly fights. The violence between the native Assamese and immigrant Bangladeshis have cost more than 3,000 lives. A few days before the election in 1983, more than 8,000 native Hindu Assamese surrounded a village called Nellie and systematically killed the Bangladeshi Muslim immigrants. The toll of that five-hour rampage was more than 1,700 (Swain, 1996).

Sharing of Ganges water has been a source of disagreement between India and Bangladesh for many decades. Although both nations are trying hard to find a lasting solution, political and economic differences pose risks to any bilateral agreement. Both treaties signed by these nations have been unsuccessful and therefore the Ganges River will continue as a source of regional conflict between India and Bangladesh unless international bodies intervene.

REFERENCES

National Symbols of India. (n.d.). "Ganges River—National River of India." National River. Accessed November 18, 2013, at http://www.indiamapped.com/national-symbols-of-india/national-river/.

Shmueli, Deborah F. (1999). "Water quality in international river basins," *ScienceDirect*. Accessed November 18, 2013, at http://www.sciencedirect.com/science/article/pii/S0962989001061#.

Sood, Aditya, and Bala Krishna Prasad Mathukumalli. (2011). "Managing international river basins: reviewing India–Bangladesh transboundary water issues," *International Journal of River Basin Management 9*(1), 43–52. Accessed March 3, 2016, at https://cgspace.cgiar.org/handle/10568/40465.

Swain, Ashok. (1993). "Conflicts over water: the Ganges water disputes," *Security Dialogue, 24*(4). Accessed March 3, 2016, at http://sdi.sagepub.com/content/24/4/429.

Swain, Ashok. (1996). "Displacing the conflict: Environmental destruction in Bangladesh and ethnic conflict," *Journal of Peace Research, 33*(2), 189–204. Accessed November 18, 2013, at http://www.jstor.org/stable/425436?origin=JSTOR-pdf.

FOR NOW, PEACE AND STABILITY
Mia Bennett

The Ganges is one of the most charismatic rivers in the world. The torrential South Asian river cascades from its icy origins in the Himalayas as it makes its way toward the Bay of Bengal on the Indian Ocean. The Ganges is fed by melt water from pristine snow and glaciers—along with offerings of foods like almonds, coconuts, and sultanas left by devout Hindus (Mallet, 2015). They bathe in the sacred river all along its course, most famously at Varanasi as a purification ritual. The river represents the source of life and death, in the form of deadly floods, for the millions of people living around it in both India and Bangladesh.

Yet while the Ganges symbolically and ecologically unites people up and down the river basin, it also divides. The river cuts across the border between India and Bangladesh before spilling into the low-lying plains of one of the world's most densely populated countries. The reliance of millions of people on the Ganges for irrigation, sanitation, and so much else puts the river in high demand. It thus might appear to be a foregone conclusion that the Ganges would be a source of conflict between India, which controls the river's high ground, and Bangladesh, which is situated precariously at sea level.

Yet in fact, the two countries have achieved a remarkable amount of cooperation over the past two decades. Indeed, the Ganges River is something of an exception when it comes to bilateral management of the rivers straddling India and Bangladesh. Of the 54 rivers that do so, the Ganges is the only one privy to a bilateral agreement (Hanasz, 2014). Relations are much more acrimonious over other rivers, like the Teesta, the flow of which Bangladesh has recently accused India of withholding to the point that it has reduced to a trickle, jeopardizing the welfare of several northern Bangladeshi villages (Roy, 2014).

The 1996 Ganges Water Treaty was not easily reached. It took decades to achieve and did not come about until a pro-India government in Bangladesh gained power. Previously, in 1971, India and Bangladesh were close allies during the Bangladesh Liberation War, in which the country fought for independence from Pakistan—India's longtime rival. Almost as soon as it won independence, however, Bangladesh began wrangling with India for water rights over the Ganges (Anam, 2014). After 25 years of mostly unsuccessful discussions, in 1996, soon after the electoral victory of the Bangladesh Awami League and the ascendance of Prime Minister Sheikh Hasina, who is regarded as holding favorable views towards India, the two countries successfully concluded negotiations on the river. Together, they signed a historic, 30-year treaty that divides the Ganges' water at the Farakka Barrage, a dam near the two countries' mutual border (Jayaram, 2013).

The Farakka Barrage gained new symbolism as a sign of improved mutual relations rather than antagonism. Previously, the dam had stymied the flow of the Ganges into Bangladesh and caused a great deal of tension between the two countries. After unsuccessful talks with Bangladesh regarding its construction in the postwar period, in 1975, India unilaterally decided to build the dam in order to divert water from the Ganges into the Hooghly River, a tributary that flows into the Indian port city of Kolkata. One researcher has argued that with that decision, "the sharing and controlling of the Ganges water became the key source of controversy between the two nations" (Rahman, 2006). Bangladesh blamed India for withholding water at the dam during the dry season and releasing too much during the monsoon season, resulting in the potential for devastating floods. Yet once the treaty was settled, it guaranteed Bangladesh a minimum flow of water of 35,000 cubic feet per second in three alternative 10-day periods between March 1 and May 10, the driest period of each year (Chellaney, 2011). While critics in the opposition Bangladesh Nationalist Party (BNP) accused the ruling Awami League government of having sold the country out (Hossain, 1998), many government officials in India and Bangladesh cheered the treaty.

Sheikh Hasina regained office as prime minister in 2009, again representing the Awami League. Since Bangladesh is a democracy (however fragile), the dominance of a pro-India, pro-Ganges treaty party in office cannot be guaranteed. Were the BNP to regain office around 2026, when the treaty is set to expire, its renewal might be in question. Furthermore, since management of the Ganges involves two countries, domestic politics in India have an impact, too. India's current prime minister, Narendra Modi, represents the Hindu nationalist Bharatiya Janata Party. Bangladesh is over 90 percent Muslim, meaning religious politics could have the potential to enter into the fore and affect bilateral river management. India is also significantly larger in terms of territory and population than Bangladesh (even though it still the world's eighth most populous country), and Indian politicians sometimes lament that they are not able to obtain enough water from the Ganges to meet their country's needs.

With a decade until the treaty runs out, it is too early to make any predictions about whether India and Bangladesh will continue to cooperate on the river's management. Instead, at present, since the treaty has already fixed how the river is shared between the two countries, domestic policies have more of an impact on the river's health. Both countries have prioritized poorly planned irrigation projects instead of sustainable management of the river, and in Bangladesh, rapid population growth and salt-water inundation due in part to climate change and rising sea levels are straining water resources. This means that the amount of water allocated by the treaty is not sufficient to meet increasing demands (Chellaney, 2011).

While India and Bangladesh struggle to implement sensible domestic policies towards the river, more all-encompassing management of the river basin could one day assist their efforts. Bangladesh is eager to involve Nepal in management of the Ganges (Jayaram, 2013), particularly since the country holds the ultimate source of its flow in the glaciated Himalayas. This inclusion would be truly integrated basin management. The potential for trilateral cooperation on the Ganges demonstrates that rather than dividing, mighty rivers in international basins sometimes have the potential to unite.

REFERENCES

Anam, Tahmima. (2014, August 3). "The battle of the Bay of Bengal," *New York Times*. Accessed March 3, 2016, at http://www.nytimes.com/2014/08/04/opinion/the-battle-by-the-bay-of-bengal.html.

Chellaney, Brahma. (2011). *Water: Asia's New Battleground*. Washington, DC: Georgetown University Press, 174.

Hanasz, Paula. (2014, July 28). "Sharing water vs. sharing rivers: the 1996 Ganges Treaty," *Global Water Forum*. Accessed March 3, 2016, at http://www.globalwaterforum.org/2014/07/28/sharing-waters-vs-sharing-rivers-the-1996-ganges-treaty/.

Hossain, Ishtiaq. (1998). "Bangladesh-India relations: the Ganges water-sharing treaty and beyond," *Asian Affairs: An American Review* 25(3), 131–150.

Jayaram, Dhanasree. (2013, December 20). "India-Bangladesh river water sharing: politics over cooperation," *International Policy Digest*. Accessed March 3, 2016, at http://www.internationalpolicydigest.org/2013/12/20/india-bangladesh-river-water-sharing-politics-cooperation/.

Mallet, Victor. (2015, February 13). "The Ganges: holy, deadly river," *The Financial Times*. Accessed March 3, 2016, at http://www.ft.com/cms/s/2/dadfae24-b23e-11e4-b380-00144feab7de.html.

Rahaman, Muhammad M. (2006). "The Ganges water conflict: a comparative analysis of 1977 agreement and 1996 treaty," *Asteriskos, Journal of International & Peace Studies* 1(2), 196.

Roy, Pinaki. (2014, April 17). "Teesta River Runs Dry as India and Bangladesh Fail to Resolve Disputes." The Third Pole: Understanding Asia's Water Crisis. Accessed March 3, 2016, at http://www.thethirdpole.net/2014/04/17/teesta-river-runs-dry-as-india-and-bangladesh-fail-to-resolve-disputes/.

40

HOW HAVE NATURAL RESOURCES CAUSED POLITICAL INSTABILITY IN POST-COMMUNIST CENTRAL ASIA?

OVERVIEW
M. Troy Burnett

Since the collapse of the Soviet Union, Central Asia has become a tangle of unresolved transboundary disputes over natural resources—water, land, minerals, and oil/gas. Along with the general instability following the profound social, political, and territorial changes, resources are unevenly distributed between and within the five post-communist republics—Kazakhstan, Kyrgyzstan, Tajikistan, Turkmenistan, and Uzbekistan. Both resource scarcity and abundance have been drivers of conflict between these newly formed republics. The problems in this region have been further complicated by the continued involvement of China and Russia.

BACKGROUND

As a semi-arid region, water has more often been the driver of competition rather than the focus of conservation and cooperation (Hogan, 2000). While Kyrgyzstan and Tajikistan have surpluses, the down-river nations rarely receive a viable share from the two primary rivers, the Syr Darya and Amu Darya). Further, the population of the region has surged by more than 10 million since 2000, placing further strain on the already fragile arable land, a resource that continues to be depleted by over-use and outdated farming technologies. Global warming and climate change have contributed to more unpredictable and unreliable weather patterns and increased soil desiccation. As economic development lags and political systems and institutions struggle, heightened nationalism, border disputes, and ethno-religious tensions will complicate efforts to address the water crisis.

Many argue that the root of the problem is the archaic and dysfunctional regional resource system implemented by the Soviet Union. Soviet planners prioritized large-scale hydrological engineering schemes in order to transform the traditional subsistence agricultural and pastoral lifestyle and replace it with cotton—a crop that requires a large amount of water. This resulted in the displacement of the traditional system and the people reliant upon it as well as the degradation of the river system, violence in the Ferghana Valley, as Mia Bennett highlights in her essay, and the Aral Sea disaster.[1] Further, the Soviet-backed system collapsed in 1991 leaving both remnants of corruption as well as no viable institutions for transboundary management. As such, inadequate infrastructure, a poor and self-serving water management framework, and outdated irrigation methods remain unresolved. Local leaders, focused on economic ambitions and political rivalries show little cooperation and plenty of suspicion. National level disputes over shared water resources continue to threaten regional security.

Yet, as Natalie Koch argues her essay, water stresses can be a driver of peace. Despite the fear and apprehension, violent conflict is the exception not that norm. The Central Asian states have largely cooperated via a series of evolving multilateral agreements. Furthermore, the new governments in the region's three resource rich states—Kazakhstan, Turkmenistan, and Uzbekistan—have used the wealth garnered from natural resources to solidify their political systems and provide a large degree of political stability.

---

[1] Probably one of the most devastated regions within the former Soviet republics is the Aral Sea—once the world's fourth-largest lake and one of the most fertile wildlife habitats on the planet. Kazakhstan, Uzbekistan, Kyrgyzstan, Tajikistan, and Turkmenistan draw water from the rivers that have fed the lake for centuries, usage that has caused the Aral Sea's water level to drop 45 feet in 30 years. In the early 1960s, the Aral Sea had an area of some 26,000 square miles; by 2004, it had shrunk to about 6,600 square miles. The sea is also heavily polluted because of weapons testing, industrial waste, and fertilizer runoff during the Soviet era. The shrinkage has split the sea into a northern portion—primarily in Kazakhstan—and a southern section in Uzbekistan. While the southern part continues its decline, Kazakhstan's government has constructed dams and a series of dikes to raise the water level in the north. Although it is unlikely the Aral Sea will ever return to its original levels, the northern portion has experienced increased water levels that promise to improve water quality and launch a modest revival of the local fishing industry.

Koch also argues that because the Aral Sea disaster was so dramatic and devastating, it caught the attention of the international community, which rushed to get involved. International organizations made strong efforts to encourage regional actors to develop frameworks for inter-state cooperation regarding the Aral Sea disaster in particular, and water sharing more generally. These included the Interstate Commission for Water Coordination of Central Asia (1992), the International Fund for Saving the Aral Sea (1993), and the Aral Sea Basin Program (1994). In short, despite occasional tensions, the countries of post-communist central Asia have learned to commiserate and cooperate: "The depressing realization that the Aral Sea will never be what it once was will continue to upset the Central Asian people and outside observers, but will not cause an all-out war amongst the nations" (Vajpeyi, 2012).

To complicate matters in the region, oil and gas deposits have been more fully explored and mapped. Turkmenistan is estimated to contain the world's fourth largest reserve of natural gas (17.5 trillion cubic meters). Kazakhstan's crude oil reserves are approximately 30 billion barrels, ranking it 11th in terms of global supply. Though the mere presence of oil does not imply conflict or stability for that matter, again remnants of the Soviet-inspired patrimonial networks are in place. The fear is that regional elites will enrich themselves and their cronies in the authoritarian governments at the expense of broader development. It has been repeatedly shown that repressive political and social systems are able to maintain their brand of tyranny via the proceeds from oil and gas. Further, some of the oil and gas reserves are located in disputed border regions making it unclear who controls the resources.

With the collapse of the Soviet Union, the unclear motives behind the involvement of China and Russia, and the stresses over natural resources, Central Asia is at another historical crossroads—one path leading to stability and prosperity, the other to conflict and violence. As Michal Romanowski noted in a 2014 essay:

> Central Asia is rapidly emerging as the key playing field in the contest to access energy resources and the leverage they offer. The new Great Game is played out once again in the region, only this time it is not over political or territorial influence, but over the vast raw material deposits that are in the possession of the former Soviet Union republics, especially those situated by the Caspian Sea. The Caspian's share of oil and gas global exports is set to rise to 9 and 11 percent, respectively, in the coming 20 years. Much is at stake. (Romanowski, 2014)

REFERENCES

Hogan, Bea. (2000, April 4). "Central Asian States Wrangle over Water." asiaNet Environment, EurasiaNet. Accessed May 1, 2016, at http://www.eurasianet.org/departments/environment/articles/eav040500.shtml.

Romanowski, Michal. (2014, July 3). "Central Asia's energy rush," *The Diplomat*. Accessed March 3, 2016, at http://thediplomat.com/2014/07/central-asias-energy-rush/.

Vajpeyi, Dhirendra K. (ed.). (2012). *Water Resource Conflicts and International Security: A Global Perspective*. Lanham, MD: Lexington Books, 180.

TENSIONS IN POST-COMMUNIST CENTRAL ASIA—THE CASE OF THE FERGHANA VALLEY

Mia Bennett

Central Asia is often described as a crossroads. The Silk Road ran through the steppes connecting Asian and European markets via Central Asian cities like Bukhara, Tashkent, and Almaty. The region's economically and geographically strategic location is one reason why so many empires have sought to control it throughout history, from the Achaemenids to the Mongols to the Russians. More recently, following the global energy transition to oil and gas, interest has grown in Central Asia's sizeable fossil fuel deposits. The Kashagan Field, for instance, lying in Kazakh territory in the Caspian Sea, represents one of the largest oil discoveries

Pumping station delivers water from Kairakkum reservoir to the fields of Tajikistan. (Viktormigr/Dreamstime.com)

of the past 30 years. Yet the project has failed to meet target after target and is now $30 billion over budget (Williams et al., 2014). These types of problems have plagued many oil and gas developments in Central Asia. Corrupt and autocratic leadership, spats between neighboring countries, and a lack of transparency have created a challenging environment for the foreign investment necessary to extract these natural resources.

But the equation could easily be reversed. One could argue that natural resources like oil and gas have themselves caused political instability in the five post-Soviet states in Central Asia—Kazakhstan, Kyrgyzstan, Tajikistan, Turkmenistan, and Uzbekistan. Oil and gas production has led to rentierism in Kazakhstan (Franke et al., 2009), the country that has most intensively developed its fossil fuel reserves, while conflicts over water resources and hydropower have worsened relations between the Central Asian republics. Some countries, like Uzbekistan, are at the mercy of decisions made by the countries like Tajikistan and Kyrgyzstan that sit at higher elevations, and therefore control the water flow.

At a smaller scale, natural resources have also caused political instability in various regions within Central Asia such as the Ferghana Valley. Soviet leader Joseph Stalin decided to split up this valley between the then-Soviet republics of Uzbekistan, Kyrgyzstan, and Tajikistan, and the complicated borders are one reason why territorial conflicts persist to this day. Nestled between the Tien-Shan Mountains to the north and the Gissar-Alai Mountains to the south, the valley is some 190 miles long and 43 miles wide, at its widest point. With its fertile soils and two major rivers running through it, the Ferghana Valley has for centuries attracted people to settle, farm, and establish towns, including Alexander the Great in 329 BCE (Scheffer, 2009). Today, the valley is densely populated, largely consisting of Muslim Uzbeks, Tajiks, Kyrgyz, and Uiyghurs.

Despite this history of diversity, violence has intermittently marred relations between the variety of ethnic and religious groups living within the Ferghana Valley. Scholarly accounts often frame the region as the "mythical epicenter" of a "civilizational clash" (Reeves, 2005). While perhaps overblown, there is some truth to these ethnic clashes. In recent history, the 1990 Osh riots between Kyrgyz and Uzbeks living in the Ferghana Valley resulted in the deaths of hundreds of people. While these riots were not directly over natural resources, conflicts over the Ferghana Valley's limited water resources have sparked small-scale disputes, with reports in 2014 of Tajik mortars that "targeted strategic facilities like a small dam and electricity substation inside Kyrgyzstan" (Trilling, 2014). Pressures on water supplies in the Ferghana Valley are especially intense due to the Soviet introduction of industrial cotton production in the 20th century. Entire villages from the valley's highlands were resettled at lower elevations so that they could help grow and pick cotton (Reeves, 2014). The continued growth of the lowland population has further taxed water resources in the region, contributing again to conflict.

Oil and gas development in the Ferghana Valley has been less prone to violence than hydropower, but that is partly because it has hardly been developed in the first place due to the prevalence of unsettled borders and poor infrastructure. Furthermore, the Ferghana Valley has only a small amount of oil and gas—a total of some 4 billion barrels of discovered and undiscovered recoverable oil, according to a 1994 estimate by the United States Energy Information Administration (USEIA, 1994). Eager to capitalize on this small but promising resource, by 1987, the Soviets had developed 53 oil and gas fields in the valley's basin. After the collapse of the USSR, however, no drilling occurred until 2007 when a new set of investors entered the picture from China rather than Russia (Oil and Gas Journal, 2007). While the amount of oil and gas being developed at present is not enough to affect the world market for fossil fuels, it is enough to make a difference to the three Central Asian republics that have claims to the resources. Most of Kyrgyzstan's proven oil reserves are located in the Ferghana Valley, while some 15 percent of Uzbekistan's are found there (Laruelle and Peyrouse, 2015). Only oil fields lying wholly within any individual country in the Ferghana Valley have yet been explored, perhaps suggesting that foreign corporations wish to avoid operating in areas directly under dispute.

Other problems continue to plague the Ferghana Valley. High unemployment and low salaries, often below subsistence levels, persist. Unresolved border issues strain regional tensions while intermittently closed borders challenge the export of goods across borders, stymieing economic development. Aside from that, road quality in the region is very poor. Islamic militants have operated out of the Ferghana Valley for decades (Charlick-Paley et al., 2003), taking advantage of the treacherous terrain on the mountain slopes. Tajik Islamists made it their base during the 1990s civil war, while in Uzbekistan, Islamism's "epicenter" shifted to the Uzbek portion of the Ferghana Valley in the late 1990s (Salmorbekova and Yemelianova, 2009).

Conflicts over natural resources are therefore just one issue among many in the Ferghana Valley. Hope for a swift resolution of disputes over territory and natural resource use seems futile. In January 2014, Kyrgyzstan's vice prime minister stated that it had not delimited any of its borders with Uzbekistan or Kyrgyzstan in the past seven years (AKI Press, 2014). As long as the three countries fail to improve trilateral relations in the Ferghana Valley, development of the area will falter and its residents will suffer. This is all the more ironic given the valley's lush and fertile nature—perhaps qualities that make it too desirable for its own good.

REFERENCES

AKI Press. (2014, October 10). "Kyrgyzstan Hasn't Delimited Any Border Sections with Uzbekistan, Tajikistan over 7 Years—Vice PM Mamytov." Accessed March 3, 2016, at http://www.akipress.com/news:533409/.

Charlick-Paley, Tanya, Phil Williams, and Olga Oliker. (2003). "The political evolution of Central Asia and South Caucasus: implications for regional security," in Olga Oliker, Thomas S. Szayna, Scott Pace, and Peter A. Wilson (eds.), *Faultlines of Conflict in Central Asia and the South Caucasus: Implications for the U.S. Army.* Santa Monica, CA: RAND Corporation, 7–40.

Franke, Anja, Andrea Gawrich, and Gurban Alakbarov. (2009). "Kazakhstan and Azerbaijan as post-Soviet rentier states: Resource incomes and autocracy as a double 'curse' in post-Soviet regimes," *Europe-Asia Studies* 61(1), 109–140.

Laruelle, Marlene, and Sebastian Peyrouse. (2015). *Globalizing Central Asia: Geopolitics and the Challenges of Economic Development.* London: Routledge, 166.

Oil and Gas Journal (eds.). (2007). "Fergana basin draws seismic surveys, drilling," *Oil and Gas Journal* 105(43). Accessed March 3, 2016, at http://www.ogj.com/articles/print/volume-105/issue-43/exploration-development/Ferghana-basin-draws-seismic-surveys-drilling.html.

Reeves, Madeleine. (2005). "Locating danger: Konfliktologiia and the search for fixity in the Ferghana Valley borderlands," *Central Asian Survey* 24(1), 67–81.

Reeves, Madeleine. (2014). *Border Work: Spatial Lives of the State in Rural Central Asia.* Ithaca, NY: Cornell University Press, 41.

Salmorbekova, Zumrat, and Galina Yemelianova. (2009). "Islam and Islamism in the Ferghana Valley," in Galina M. Yemelianova (ed.), *Radical Islam in the Former Soviet Union.* London: Routledge, 221.

Scheffer, Martin. (2009). *In Post-Communist Worlds: Living and Teaching in Estonia, Lithuania, Ukraine and Uzbekistan.* Bloomington, IN: iUniverse, 161

Trilling, David. (2014, January 13). "Kyrgyzstan-Tajikistan: What's next after border shootout?" EurasiaNet. Accessed March 13, 2016, at http://www.eurasianet.org/node/67934.

U.S. Energy Information Administration (USEIA). (1994). *Oil and Gas Resources of the Fergana Basin (Uzbekistan, Tadzhikistan, and Kyrgyzstan).* Washington, DC: U.S. Department of Energy.

Williams, Selina, Géraldine Amiel, and Justin Scheck. (2014, March 31). "How a giant Kazakh oil project went awry," *Wall Street Journal.* Accessed March 3, 2016 at http://www.wsj.com/articles/SB10001424052702303730804579437492040999738.

A FRAGILE STABILITY IN CENTRAL ASIA
Natalie Koch

Political geographers and political ecologists, as their titles imply, study the political origins of conflicts over natural resources. Post-communist Central Asia provides an ideal context for this type of analysis. Central Asia is a region generally understood to include five countries—Kazakhstan, Kyrgyzstan, Tajikistan,

Turkmenistan, and Uzbekistan—that were once autonomous republics within the Soviet Union (USSR). In 1991, the USSR broke up into 15 new countries, following the borders of the country's 15 constituent republics. During the Soviet era, the region's water and energy resources were centrally managed by decision makers in Moscow and they paid little attention to the republican borders. Quite suddenly and unexpectedly, in 1991, what were once internal borders (like state borders in the United States) became international borders. When this happened, many international observers feared that Central Asia would plunge into political instability and that there would be armed conflict over resources involving not just local political elites but their former masters in Moscow.

Despite the fear and apprehension, this has not happened. Instead, the Central Asian states have largely cooperated via a series of multilateral agreements. Furthermore, the new governments in the region's three resource-rich states—Kazakhstan, Turkmenistan, and Uzbekistan—have used the wealth garnered from natural resources to solidify their authoritarian political systems and provide a large degree of political stability. Contrary to popular opinion, natural resources have not destabilized post Communist Central Asia.

In the early 1990s, many international observes opined that natural resources would cause political instability. Water was the main concern, since Central Asia is a predominantly arid region and water resources were poorly managed during the Soviet era. For example, since the 1950s, Soviet planners had focused on developing Central Asia into a major site for the cultivation of cotton, as well as various other water-intensive crops. These agricultural developments depended on diverting water from the region's two major rivers, the Amu Darya and the Syr Darya. Originating in the Tien Shan and Pamir mountains of Kyrgyzstan and Tajikistan, these rivers fed the Aral Sea, which was once one of the largest lakes in the world (at 68,000 square kilometers). But due to water diversions from the Amu and Syr Darya, the Aral Sea volume shrank by 80 percent from 1960 to 1998. The desiccation of the sea rapidly became a major environmental and health catastrophe, not only for residents in the area once dependent upon the fishing industry, but also for the entire region. Massive dust storms from the now dry seabed spread across Central Asia, carrying with them enormous amounts of pesticides and other small-particulate matter, which have had negative impacts on the health of residents far from the sea.

The Aral Sea disaster caught the attention of the international community and many aid agencies rushed to get involved in mitigating the problems in the 1990s. As part of this effort, international organizations made a strong effort to encourage regional actors to develop frameworks for inter-state cooperation regarding the Aral Sea disaster in particular, and water sharing more generally. These included the Interstate Commission for Water Coordination of Central Asia (1992), the International Fund for Saving the Aral Sea (1993), and the Aral Sea Basin Program

(1994). The young states of Central Asia were heavily dependent on international aid dollars in the early years of independence, due to the sudden loss of revenue transfers from Moscow with the end of the USSR, and were consequently eager to participate in these initiatives. As political geographers and political ecologists would emphasize in this case, conflict over resources is never inevitable, but rather depends on political context. Although local corruption has been a major hurdle to the effective implementation of Aral Sea disaster mitigation efforts, and regional governments sometimes bicker about resource allocations today, the early introduction of international cooperation frameworks appears to have successfully averted any major conflicts and instability related to water resources.

The second trend to consider in the relationship between natural resources and political stability in post-communist Central Asia is how the authoritarian governments of the region's three resource-rich states have used natural resources to solidify their hold on power. Western observers often assume that authoritarian systems are inherently unstable, but the cases of Kazakhstan, Turkmenistan, and Uzbekistan, where nondemocratic political systems have been in place since independence in 1991, challenge this assumption. While their resource-poor neighbors in Kyrgyzstan and Tajikistan have experienced a great deal of political turmoil in the past several decades, these three governments have managed to develop strong states through the wealth afforded by the exploitation of their resources—particularly oil and gas deposits in and around the Caspian Sea (Kazakhstan also has large reserves of uranium and other precious metals). Although the politics and finances are extremely different in each country, the rulers of Kazakhstan, Turkmenistan, and Uzbekistan have used this income to promote political stability (though certainly not justice), through various tactics falling on a spectrum of being more coercive (e.g., heavy surveillance in Uzbekistan and Turkmenistan) to more persuasive (e.g., economic development agendas in Kazakhstan). All three governments also depend on strong "cults of personality" around the country's president, in which this individual is seen as the guarantor of stability. However, as the resource-poor cases of Kyrgyzstan and Tajikistan illustrate, these leaders' ability to provide stability is largely dependent on having access to resource wealth to bring order and a modicum of prosperity to their people.

In seeking to answer the question of whether natural resources have caused political instability in post-communist Central Asia, political geographers and political ecologists have argued that it is necessary to first consider the political context at hand. In the immediate aftermath of the collapse of the USSR in 1991, it was not clear if the political context inherited by the new states of Central Asia would lead to regional instability or not. Over 20 years since their independence, however, the region has proven to be remarkably stable in this respect—due in part to international intervention and the development of new authoritarian polities dependent on resource wealth. These political contexts are always dynamic, however, and it is not yet clear how resilient this stability is, especially as the old generation of Soviet bureaucrats, who are still largely in power, begin to fade out of the picture. It can only be hoped that younger generations are inclined to both cooperation and democracy as they bring their countries into political maturity.

FURTHER READING

Dalby, Simon. (2002). *Environmental Security*. Minneapolis: University of Minnesota Press.
Dalby, Simon. (2009). *Security and Environmental Change*. Malden, MA: Polity Press.
Deudney, Daniel, and Richard A. Matthew. (1999). *Contested Grounds: Security and Conflict in the New Environmental Politics*. Albany: State University of New York Press.
Weinthal, Erika. (2006). *Water Conflict and Cooperation in Central Asia*. United Nations Development Program Occasional Paper. Accessed March 3, 2016, at http://hdr.undp.org/en/content/water-conflict-and-cooperation-central-asia.

Glossary

Afforestation: The deliberate conversion of nonforested to forested land. Technically, afforestation refers to establishing forests on land that historically had no tree cover, while reforestation refers to doing so in previously forested areas. In practice, however, afforestation is often used to imply either term.

Agenda 21: The global plan adopted by 179 national governments at the Earth Summit, a United Nations (UN) conference that took place in Rio de Janeiro, Brazil, from June 3 to 14, 1992. Nations participating at the Earth Summit recognized that the growth of world population and patterns of production and consumption placed growing stress on the planet's capability to support life.

Amazon rainforest: The Amazon rainforest, located in the South American countries of Brazil, Guyana, Venezuela, Colombia, Suriname, French Guiana, Ecuador, Peru, and Bolivia, covers an area roughly the size of the United States. Home to over 60,000 plant species, 1,000 bird species, and more than 300 mammal species, the Amazon rainforest supports a unique and diverse group of creatures.

Amazon River: Latin America's Amazon River, gathering water from both hemispheres, is the second-longest river in the world, generally flowing eastward for 3,900 miles from its sources in the Andes Mountains.

Amu Darya: The source of Afghanistan's 1,600-mile river, the Amu Darya (also known as the Amu River and known to the ancient world as the River Oxus), lies in the confluence of two large headstreams, the Pyandzh and Vaksh, which drain glaciers of the Pamir Mountains on the flank of the Himalayas, the world's highest mountains. The upper course of the Amu Darya (for about 170 miles downstream) is the boundary between Afghanistan and independent Tajikistan. The lower course of the river also forms a boundary: the border between Uzbekistan and Turkmenistan.

Arctic Council: An intergovernmental forum that addresses emerging issues in the circumpolar North. The eight member countries are: Canada, Denmark, Finland, Iceland, Norway, Russia, Sweden, and the United States. The Arctic Council often has to contend with issues of territory, security, and geopolitical as well as resource exploitation and regional economic development.

Arctic Ocean: The smallest of the Earth's oceans at approximately 5.5 million square miles, the Arctic Ocean occupies about 3 percent of the Earth's surface. Nearly all of the Arctic Ocean lies above the Arctic Circle, and the majority of it is covered by ice most of the year. Surrounded by three continents, with limited outlets to other oceans and a coastline more than 28,000 miles long, it is more like an inland sea. The Arctic Ocean's only outlets are to the Atlantic Ocean via the Davis Strait and the Norwegian Sea and to the Pacific Ocean via the Bering Strait.

Association for the Conservation of Amazonian Wildlife (Asociacion para la Conservacion de la Naturaleza Amazonica—ACONA): is a nongovernmental group that focuses on environmental education and community participation in conservation efforts in and around the Amazon rainforest in northern Peru. Amazonian research and the promotion of sustainable development are major goals of the organization.

(The) Association of Southeast Asian Nations (ASEAN): An organization of countries in Southeast Asia, ASEAN's mission is to promote economic development, unrestricted trade, international understanding, and peaceful relationships among its member countries. Its members are Brunei, Cambodia, Indonesia, Laos, Malaysia, Myanmar, the Philippines, Singapore, Thailand, and Vietnam. East Timor (Timor-Leste) and Papua New Guinea hold observer status. ASEAN's headquarters are in Jakarta, Indonesia.

Biome: A concept that allows spatial organization of vegetation and animals at the planetary scale. More specifically, it accounts for the integration of climate-plant-animal relationships over large areas. Biomes are the world's major life communities classified by the predominant vegetation, often the most prevalent feature on the natural landscape. The biome concept implies that plants and animals have adapted to each biome in ways specific to the biome. The "taiga" and the "semi-arid desert" are examples of biomes.

Borneo: The third largest island in the world, it lies at the heart of Southeast Asia. Covering an area of some 750,000 square kilometers, the island is divided politically among the three states of Malaysia, Indonesia, and

Brunei—the Malaysian states of Sabah and Sarawak; the Indonesian states of East, Central, South, and West Kalimantan; and Brunei Darussalam. Borneo is renowned for its important ecological zones, in particular the expanses of tropical rainforest.

(The) Bureau of Land Management (BLM): Established in 1946 to manage much of the public lands of the United States. The BLM was formed by the consolidation of the General Land Office and the Grazing Service and now is responsible for over 260 million acres, most of which are in Alaska and the West. The BLM's responsibilities regarding natural resources include the leasing of mineral rights. The bureau also is responsible for leasing the rights to timber, oil and gas, geothermal energy, and grazing land. In addition the BLM preserves wildlife habitats, endangered species, wild and scenic rivers, and conservation and wilderness areas. It also develops the recreational potential of its land and works to preserve cultural values.

Cap and Trade: Environmental cap and trade describes a system of reducing pollution by mandating a cap on emissions levels and regulating the exchange of emission allowances. This approach to environmental policy seeks to incorporate free-market principles and represents an alternative to direct taxation and emissions limitation.

Carbon sequestration: One of the most popular ideas in the fossil fuels industry for "greening" the environment and reducing carbon emissions released into the atmosphere, carbon sequestration is a largely untested process that remains highly controversial in environmentalist circles. Envisioned as a process that traps carbon dioxide produced by coal- and oil-burning energy plants and stores it underground or in the ocean rather than allowing it to release into the air, carbon sequestration would be extremely expensive and energy consuming itself. Because of its high costs, it has yet to be adopted by any country or multinational corporation as a solution to greenhouse gas pollution.

Carbon taxes: Taxes on those who contribute to climate change by emitting carbon dioxide into the environment, including homes, businesses, and industries that use petroleum products for energy. Carbon taxes are seen as one way of making those who contribute to pollution pay the cost of doing so. Nations around the world now have carbon taxes.

Carrying capacity: Carrying capacity may be generally defined as the level of use of a resource short of that resource's deterioration. How many head of cattle can graze on an area of grassland and not deteriorate the vegetative cover for the following year? What is the maximum yield of a particular agricultural product on a particular farmstead? How heavily can a transportation system be used before its efficiency begins to decline? What is the ideal number of visitors to a national park in a tourist season? What is the maximum tonnage of fish that may be taken from an ocean fishing ground without depleting the resource for the next season?

Chernobyl Disaster: Chernobyl, a nuclear plant in the Ukrainian city of Pripyat, was the scene of a massive nuclear accident on April 26, 1986. The initial response of the Soviet government was inadequate, and early errors were compounded by the government's unwillingness to speak openly about the situation. The incident, which released 100 times the radiation as the Nagasaki bombing and Hiroshima bombing combined, cast international doubt on the effectiveness of Soviet technology and emboldened internal critics of the regime to raise their voices in unprecedented protests. As of 2006, 20 years after the disaster, the number of direct fatalities from the radioactive fallout was estimated by the World Health Organization at 4,000 people.

Chukchi: The Chukchi (also known as Chukots, Chukcha, or Luorovetlan) are an Arctic indigenous people of northeastern Siberian Russia. Some 35,000 Chukchi are concentrated in the Chukotka Autonomous Okrug, but there are also sizable populations in the neighboring Koryak Autonomous Okrug and the Lower Kolyma District of the neighboring Republic of Sakha.

Climate Change: One of the most controversial topics in today's media is the issue of climate change. Scientists, politicians, and environmentalists have been debating the causes and effects of changing climatic patterns for several decades, and recent popular concern about global warming has made the topic of climate change a political, economic, and scientific hot-button issue. While climatic variation is an historical constant (no two years are ever identical in weather), large-scale climate change poses significant challenges for maintaining plant and animal life as we know it on the planet today. Is the climate skewing warmer due to human behaviors, or is climate change merely a natural cyclical process?

Coal: The most chemically complex fossil fuel that is burned for energy purposes. Although it consists mainly of carbon, the chemical structures within coal matrices contain significant concentrations of nitrogen and sulfur, and trace amounts of many other elements, including mercury, lead, and other metals that are toxic to humans. Coal was formed from the fossilization and compression of large swampy areas or peat bogs.

Comparative Advantage: A principal component of the doctrine of free trade, comparative trade was articulated most coherently in *The Principles of Political Economy*, published in 1819 by the economist David Ricardo. Developing ideas on national economic specialization also discussed by Adam Smith in *The Wealth of Nations*, Ricardo argued that a national economy benefits most from international trade by specializing in the production of goods and services in which it enjoys an advantage in efficiency relative to other national economies.

Conflict Diamonds: Diamonds sold or traded to help fund efforts by opposition forces to undermine or overthrow existing, legally recognized governments. Conflict diamonds, sometimes referred to as blood diamonds, have financed wars in such countries as Sierra Leone, Angola, the Democratic Republic of Congo, and Liberia.

Conservation International (CI): A nonprofit organization that works to preserve endangered ecosystems around the world. CI was founded in 1987 and has more than 800 staff members in more than 40 nations. The organization operates in countries throughout South America, Central America, Africa, and Oceania, helping to protect tens of millions of acres of natural habitat.

(The) Convention on Biological Diversity (CBD): Known informally as the Biodiversity Convention, is a multilateral treaty that went into effect in 1993. Presently, there are 196 signatories. The Convention has three main goals: (1) conservation of biological diversity (or biodiversity); (2) sustainable use of its components; and (3) fair and equitable sharing of benefits arising from genetic resources.

The Convention on International Trade in Endangered Species (CITES): An international agreement that controls trade of endangered plants and animals. The goal is to prevent further endangerment or extinction of protected species. After coming into power in 1975, CITES protects endangered species by regulating the trade of more than 5,000 animal species and 28,000 plant species. Although only 21 countries participated in the early days of the convention, as of 2011, 175 countries now agree to abide by the rules set forth and regulate the trade of endangered species both within and outside their borders.

Darfur: Located in western Sudan, is an ethnically diverse region approximately the size of France. It contains three provinces, North, South, and West Darfur. More than 30 distinct ethnic groups live in the region, though these groups are unified by their common religion, Islam, and have a long history of intermarriage.

Deepwater Horizon Oil Spill (2010): After British Petroleum's (BP) *Deepwater Horizon* drilling platform exploded on April 20, 2010, the well released more than 4.9 million barrels (about 205.8 million gallons) of crude oil into the Gulf of Mexico. It was the United States' worst-ever offshore spill and the world's worst-ever accidental oil spill. Located about 50 miles southeast of Venice, Louisiana, the Macondo well spewed petroleum for 87 days before BP successfully stanched the flow.

Defenders of Wildlife: One of the United States' strongest voices in wildlife conservation. The organization is nongovernmental and nonprofit, supported by donations and grants. Wildlife and habitat protection, animal welfare, refuge management, and preservation of biodiversity are Defenders' main concerns. The group was instrumental in the passage of the U.S. Endangered Species Act in 1973 and took an active role in the creation of the Convention on International Trade in Endangered Species.

Deforestation: The human-induced conversion of forested areas to non-forested land. Approximately 13 million hectares of forest per year have been lost to deforestation since the early 1990s, an area approximately the size of Greece. While some of these losses have been compensated for through afforestation and natural forest expansion, net loss of forests is still around 7.3 million hectares. Deforestation poses a significant threat to the climate, as much of the world's carbon is stored in forests. These forests are both sources and sinks of atmospheric CO_2: they absorb carbon through photosynthesis and release carbon when they decompose and burn.

(The) Demographic Transition Model: Defines four progressive stages of demographic development in an attempt to elucidate and analyze the various conditions and factors that influence population growth. The key relationship is the dynamic between death rates and birth rates, and how these are altered by changing socio-economic conditions over time. In particular, the model relates increasing rates of economic advancement and higher levels of urbanization to a general reduction in population growth. The model is based on the experience of economically advanced countries that underwent industrialization during the late 19th and early 20th centuries.

Desertification: The spread of desert due to natural or human causes. The removal of vegetation is the most immediate cause, driven by a combination of factors such as drought, changing climate, tillage for agriculture, overgrazing, deforestation, and pestilence. Mitigation techniques include reforestation, soil fixation, shelter belts, managed grazing, contour trenching, the introduction of soil building and drought tolerant crops, and elaborate hydration schemes.

Earth Summit: The United Nations Conference on Environment and Development, popularly known as the Earth Summit, was held in Rio de Janeiro, Brazil, during June 3–14, 1992. The conference was convened in an attempt to reach an international agreement on how to continue economic development while simultaneously conserving the world's nonrenewable energy resources and overall environment. Attended by delegates from 178 countries, the Earth Summit was the largest international environmental conference ever held. The most important of the binding treaties that were signed was the Framework Convention on Climate Change, which dealt with the problem of global warming by requiring all countries to reduce their emissions of such gases as carbon dioxide.

East Timor: The Democratic Republic of East Timor is one of the world's newest independent nations. Lying 435 miles north of Port Darwin on Australia's northwest coast, East Timor comprises the eastern half of the island of Timor (West Timor remains an Indonesian province), which is part of the Malay archipelago.

Easter Island: The small Pacific island of Rapa Nui, better known as Easter Island, 2,300 miles west of Chile, is the most remote inhabited island in the world. Its nearest neighbor, Pitcairn, is 1,400 miles away. The staggering architectural achievement of the people of Rapa Nui was the creation and especially the transportation and erection of hundreds of *moai* monoliths—stylized giant human heads on torsos—carved in hardened volcanic tufa (rock).

Ecofeminism: Ecological feminism, more commonly known as ecofeminism, is a philosophy and movement resulting from the fusion of feminist and ecological thought. Followers of this movement argue that the exploitation and oppression of women stems directly from the social attitudes used to exploit and pollute the environment.

Ecosystems: Made up of communities of living organisms along with their physical environment. The "system" in the term ecosystem comprises the different interactions, generally referred to as energy and matter flows, between the living and physical environment. Ecosystems are always dynamic; they adapt and evolve to internal and external forces such as water and carbon cycles, as well as changes in food chains.

Ecotourism: The International Ecotourism Society (TIES) defines ecotourism as "responsible travel to natural areas that conserves the environment and improves the well-being of local people." TIES is the oldest and largest organization dedicated to ecotourism around the world.

El Niño: The disruptive global weather pattern known as El Niño is the warm phase of an irregular warm/cold fluctuation of the Pacific Ocean and its atmosphere called the El Niño/Southern Oscillation (ENSO). Eight to 10 months in duration, El Niño is characterized by warmer-than-usual ocean temperatures and weakened trade winds, which together cause anomalies of temperature and precipitation that have consequences for the entire planet. The result is heavy rains, hurricanes, and flooding along the Pacific coast of the Americas and major drought in the South Pacific, many parts of Asia, and in the western part of South America. Many weather irregularities in Africa are also linked to El Niño. The cold phase of the three- to seven-year ENSO cycle is called La Niña and occurs less often than El Niño. The term El Niño (meaning "the little boy" or "the Christ child" in Spanish) was coined by Peruvian fishermen who noted the tendency of the warming trend to begin around the Christmas holiday.

Endangered Species Act (ESA): A set of laws, enacted in 1973, intended "to provide for the conservation of endangered and threatened species of fish, wildlife, and plants, and for other purposes." Regulatory responsibility for the laws in the act is delegated to the U.S. Department of the Interior. One of the most significant mandates in the Endangered Species Act was the creation of the Endangered Species List, for which the Fish and Wildlife Service is responsible for maintaining a catalog of threatened plants and animals. Species on the list receive protection from habitat destruction and are granted a recovery plan. As described in Section 9, it is illegal to carry out commercial trade in endangered species.

Environmental Justice: Is characterized by the disproportionate siting of polluting industries, toxics disposal sites and landfills, energy production facilities, and factories in the environments of poor and/or minority communities. Historically, this has meant that these communities are at greater risk of exposure to environmental hazards, including poor quality air, water, or soils; heavy metals and other toxic substances; unsafe workplace conditions; and carcinogens (cancer-causing compounds). Defining the environment broadly as "where we live, work, and play," the movement seeks redress from the various "environmental" ills that affect poor and minority communities and aims for a more equitable distribution of both environmental risks and benefits.

Environmental Refugee: A person who has been displaced from his or her country of residence because of natural disasters or possible long-run changes in the global environment. In light of ongoing global climate change and global warming, it is expected that more and more persons living in various parts of the world will become environmental refugees in the foreseeable future. The United Nations Environmental Program has defined environmental refugees as "those people who have been forced to leave their traditional habitat, temporarily or permanently, because of a marked environmental disruption (natural and/or triggered by people) that jeopardized their existence and/or seriously affected the quality of their life."

The U.S. Environmental Protection Agency (EPA): An independent executive agency responsible for controlling pollution of the air and water, as well as environmental damage from solid waste, pesticides, radiation, and toxic substances. The EPA was founded in 1970 to coordinate the government's efforts to protect the environment. It brings together efforts in research, monitoring, the setting of standards, and enforcement of regulations, and supports the antipollution activities of state and local governments.

Exclusive Economic Zone (EEZ): The area in which a country has sovereign control over territorial waters. Disputes over the extent of EEZs are a common source of conflict between states over marine waters. Generally, a state's EEZ extends to a distance of 200 nautical miles from its coastal baseline as established by the Third United Nations Convention on the Law of the Sea in 1982. This law defines oceanic jurisdiction for all nations and the United Nations Convention on the Law of the Sea (UNCLOS) exists to attempt to resolve disputes through interpretation of and communication about standards.

Fish and Wildlife Service (FWS): A branch of the U.S. Department of the Interior and is the successor to the Bureau of Fisheries, which was founded in 1871. The agency was given its current name in 1974. The Fish and Wildlife Service is charged with identifying, protecting, conserving, and enhancing fish and wildlife and their habitats, including migratory birds, some marine mammals, endangered species, and inland sports fisheries; and with conducting some fish and wildlife research.

(The) Forest Stewardship Council (FSC): An NGO that promotes sustainable management of the world's forests through a market-based approach in which forests and forest management companies are certified. By late 2013, the FSC had certified more than 180 million acres of forest in 80 countries. The FSC maintains 10 principles leading to a product's certification, including: Obey the law, protect the rights of native peoples, limit waste, preserve species, contribute to the economic well-being of nearby communities, and preserve the forest.

Fossil Fuels: Are extracted from beds of once-living organic matter (primarily plant) that was compressed among and between layers of rock throughout geologic history. The heat and pressure caused by compression in different types of rock layers formed the different types of fossil fuels. The composition of these fuels is primarily made up of carbon, oxygen, and hydrogen, but depending on the fossil fuel type, may contain many other elements and impurities. Hydrocarbons, which are molecules composed of carbon and hydrogen atoms, are a group of important compounds associated with these fuels.

Ganges River Valley: Includes the lands whose rivers drain into the Ganges River. The Ganges is one of the great rivers of the world and is the most important in Indian history. The Ganges Valley includes most of northeastern India and remains one of the most densely populated, as well as religiously important, regions in the subcontinent.

(The) Global Environmental Monitoring System (GEMS): Created by the United Nations to provide scientifically sound data and information on the state and trends of global inland water quality. The United Nations collects and provides this information because it is necessary for the management of the world's freshwater supplies in efforts of protecting the environment. More than 100 countries participate in the GEMS water program.

Global Warming: Global warming refers to an increase in the temperature of Earth's lower atmosphere that many scientists believe is caused by the so-called greenhouse effect. As glass panes allow sunlight into a greenhouse, which then retains the heat, so a layer of carbon dioxide and other gases allows solar radiation into Earth's atmosphere but then traps some of that heat. The main greenhouse gases are carbon dioxide, produced mostly by the burning of fossil fuels and forest fires; methane, a byproduct of both fossil fuels and animal waste; and chlorofluorocarbons, used in aerosols and refrigerants. While natural levels of carbon dioxide create a livable atmosphere, scientists worry that excessive levels of greenhouse gases are creating a dangerous warming effect. Global warming could lead to, among other things, the flooding (or actual disappearance) of some countries as global ice melts and sea levels rise. Crops and wildlife would also be affected.

Globalization: Emerging in the 20th century, globalization has sharply influenced the evolution of world politics and economics. It is generally defined as the growth of systems and activities of economic and commercial production, trade, and services on a global scale of which one state cannot control alone. Globalization has brought greater prosperity to hundreds of millions of people around the world. However, as globalization benefits certain people, it can also lead to greater poverty and exploitation of others.

Greenhouse Effect: The phenomenon in which the release of certain gases, particularly carbon dioxide, forms a layer above the Earth's surface that traps warmth, such as from solar radiation. The effect is like that achieved by a clear plastic cover over a greenhouse, which lets in sunlight but does not allow heat to escape. The production of greenhouse gases has been accelerated by the burning of fossil fuels and the destruction of large tracts of rainforests where these gases are trapped in the soil. Scientists blame these activities for an apparent trend toward global warming.

Greenhouse Gases (GHGs): Chemical compounds that contribute to the greenhouse effect, a process in the atmosphere that causes global warming. Most greenhouse gases are naturally occurring, but certain human activities add to the levels of these gases in the atmosphere. Carbon dioxide (CO_2) is one of the main greenhouse gases. Other greenhouse gases, such as chlorofluorocarbons (CFCs) and halons, are man-made.

Greenpeace: A public interest group founded in 1971 with the goal of raising public awareness about the need to allow the natural environment to sustain itself and for humans to live peaceably. The Greenpeace strategy has been to use "non-violent, creative confrontation to expose global environmental problems, and to force the solutions which are essential to a green and peaceful future." It seeks to end nuclear testing, halt and reverse the destruction of the biosphere, end international trade in toxic wastes, promote arms control and disarmament, promote use of alternative and renewable energy sources, and promote the protection of marine animals and habitat.

Gulf Hypoxia: A condition in which increased nitrogen contributions lead to a reduction of dissolved oxygen in the Gulf of Mexico. The mechanisms that lead to Gulf hypoxia and the feedback loops that in part sustain this condition are complex. Conditions that contribute to Gulf hypoxia are frequently attributed to high levels of nitrogen fertilizer use on agricultural lands in the Mississippi River basin. Organic agricultural methods do not apply these chemicals and thus do not contribute to the runoff of these nitrogen compounds in streams and rivers.

Hutu: The Hutu people, or Bahutu, are concentrated in Central Africa, particularly Rwanda and Burundi. Both countries began as feudal monarchies ruled by the smaller, more aristocratic Tutsi ethnic group, which for many years subjugated the more numerous peasant Hutus. In 1959, a bloody Hutu revolt ousted Rwanda's Tutsi government and led to a huge Tutsi emigration. Successive Hutu governments ruled until 1994, when Hutu forces massacred hundreds of thousands of Tutsi civilians before being defeated by Tutsi rebels. In Burundi, the Tutsi minority maintained its domination until democracy was introduced in the 1990s and the nation elected its first Hutu president. Violent conflict between Hutus and Tutsis continues to destabilize both countries.

Hydraulic Fracturing (Fracking): A process commonly used in connection with horizontal drilling (less commonly used with vertical drilling), is known as hydraulic fracturing or, more colloquially, "fracking" or "hydrofracing." Fracking involves the injection under high pressure of a liquid mixture consisting primarily of water and sand, along with chemicals, into a well site. The force created by the injection process increases the pore size within the reservoir, allowing oil or gas to flow more readily toward the well pipe.

Indigenous: Tribes, nations, or ethnic groups historically inhabiting lands before the advent of colonizing settlers—usually minorities within larger societies, discriminated against in socioeconomic life, at a comparative disadvantage in terms of power and opportunity in their respective states, and linguistically or culturally distinct from the majority. According to language adopted by the United Nations in 1987, the term indigenous refers to peoples experiencing colonialism during the past 500 years.

Intergovernmental Panel on Climate Change (IPCC): Created in 1988 through the joint actions of two United Nations bodies, the World Meteorological Organization (WMO) and the United Nations Environment Programme (UNEP). The IPCC was established in response to a growing realization that the activities of humans were bringing about changes in Earth's climate unprecedented in human history. The mission of the organization is to evaluate scientific data in order to better understand the phenomenon and impacts of climate change, its impacts on global society. IPCC carries out this mission by collecting and analyzing the best information available in peer-reviewed scientific literature and well-documented industrial reports and practices. Based on these analyses, IPCC's experts prepare reports outlining the current status of worldwide climate change. IPCC reports have become standards of excellence and are used by policymakers, scientists, and others involved in decisions about climate change throughout the world.

International Union for Conservation of Nature (IUCN): An independent international association dedicated to ensuring the conservation of nature, the sustainable use of natural resources, and the preservation of biological diversity. Its members include nations, government agencies, and nongovernmental environmental organizations. The IUCN's stated mission is "to influence, encourage and assist societies throughout the world to conserve the integrity and diversity of nature and to ensure that any use of natural resources is equitable and ecologically sustainable."

(The) International Whaling Commission (IWC): Founded in December 1946 in compliance with the International Convention for the Regulation of Whaling. The IWC is devoted to conserving the planet's whale stocks. It promotes research concerning whales and whaling, reviews regulations regarding whaling operations, distributes information regarding ways to increase world whale stocks, and collects and analyzes data on whales and whaling.

Inuit: The Inuit (which means "the people") are a nomadic people who have survived in the harsh far-northern environment of the Arctic by living off the animals they could hunt, both for their food and for many of the materials they needed for clothing, transportation, light, dwellings, weapons, and tools. The Inuit are closely related to the Aleut of the Aleutian Islands and the indigenous peoples of eastern Russia. Ancestors of the Inuit likely originated in Asia and traveled across the Bering Strait to North America.

(The) Inuit Brotherhood (Inuit Ataqatigiit—IA): A socialist party that advocates Greenland's eventual independence from Denmark. The party also contends that citizenship of Greenland should be limited to people with at least one Inuit parent.

Invasive Species: Non-native or non-endemic species in a given area. Invasive species are the second most important threat to biodiversity conservation globally, after habitat loss and fragmentation.

Janjaweed: An informal name for the armed militia that since 2003 have been the principal agents of mass murder, rape, and property destruction in the Darfur region of Sudan. The militia's members hail primarily from a few traditionally nomadic, Arabic-speaking Abbala and Baggara tribes—camel and cattle herders, respectively—and are lighter skinned than most of Darfur's sedentary population.

Jordan River: The Jordan River runs 200 miles from northern Israel to the Dead Sea. The longest and most important watercourse of Palestine, the river rises at the foot of Mount Herman in the three springs near Tel Dan, Banias, and Hasbani. It then descends rapidly to the Huleh Valley, a shallow lake until recent times. From this point the river, now properly called the Jordan, plunges through a gorge to the Sea of Galilee at an elevation of 696 feet below sea level. This rapid drop continues south along the main course of the river on the way to the Dead Sea (called the Salt Sea in ancient times), which lies at the lowest point in the valley, at an elevation of 1,292 feet below sea level. This rapid drop probably explains the river's name (from the Hebrew "to go down").

Kyoto Protocol: In December 1997, members of the United Nations negotiated the Kyoto Protocol, an international treaty on climate change. According to the terms of the Kyoto Protocol, signing parties must reduce their greenhouse gas emissions by a certain percentage below their respective 1990 levels. The treaty made an exception for developing countries, which were excused from reducing their carbon emissions until later agreements. In addition, industrialized nations may swap amounts of pollutions quotas with other states for a price. The gases regulated by the treaty include carbon dioxide, methane, nitrous oxide, hydrofluorocarbons, perfluorocarbons, and sulphur hexafluoride.

Lost Boys: Refers to a group of young boys displaced during the Sudanese Civil War. Beginning in the late 1980s, roughly 26,000 Sudanese boys, mostly from the Dinka and Nuer tribes and predominately Christian, were forced from their villages. Snaking their way through Sudan, hordes of boys ages 5 through approximately 13 gathered in a massive confluence in the hope of finding safety. Many of the boys perished along the way, having succumbed to heat exhaustion, dehydration, starvation, and attacks from lions and other wild animals.

Malthusian Theory: A theory of population growth and its consequences, first articulated by British political economist Thomas Malthus in 1798. Malthus's work set in motion a vigorous debate over how and why human populations increase, and what the consequences of such increases may be. Malthus holds that human populations inevitably exceed the carrying capacity of the land they occupy.

Montreal Protocol: Signed in Montreal on September 16, 1987, the international agreement is mainly directed at efforts to control substances that deplete ozone, notably chlorofluorocarbons (CFCs).

(The) National Center for Atmospheric Research (NCAR): Created in 1960 through the efforts of a number of leading meteorologists looking for a strong, centralized agency that would support and encourage meteorological research. NCAR's mission is four-fold: (1) to study the fundamental problems of the atmosphere on a global level, (2) to bring together the large-scale research facilities needed for such studies, (2) to provide a coordinated and interdisciplinary approach to these problems not possible with individual universities, (4) and to preserve the natural alliance between research and education.

(The) National Coalition for Marine Conservation (NCMC): Founded in 1973 as a non-profit organization for conserving ocean fish and their environment. The organization's primary goals are to combat overfishing and restore depleted fish populations to healthy levels; to promote sustainable use of maritime resources by developing an appropriate balance among commercial, recreational, and ecological values; to eliminate or limit wasteful fishing practices; to improve our understanding of the biological and ecological characteristics of fish; and to preserve water quality and coastal habitats.

Natural Gas: Eighty to 95 percent methane (CH_4), which is a simple fuel containing one carbon atom and four hydrogen atoms. In its natural state in the environment, natural gas deposits may also contain heavier hydrocarbon impurities (e.g., propane or butane), water, carbon dioxide, and hydrogen sulfide. Natural gas is generally transported by pipeline from processing plants to areas of use. Natural gas is the least consumed of all the fossil fuels. It is estimated that the use of natural gas will increase in the future as prices of petroleum rise and the undesirable effects of coal reduce that source's demand.

(The) Natural Resources Defense Council (NRDC): An environmental organization in the United States that is concerned with the wise use of the nation's natural resources. It was started in 1970 by a group of former Yale University Law School classmates who filed lawsuits against the government and industry on environmental matters. It conducts and compiles research on such matters as the urban environment, acid rain, endangered species, energy conservation, forestry, nuclear weapons proliferation, offshore oil development, and hazardous waste. It in turn uses its findings to influence the passage of new legislation and to set legal precedents through lawsuits. NRDC seeks to increase public understanding of the environment and conducts grassroots campaigns in support of its causes.

(The) Nature Conservancy (TNC) is an environmental organization dedicated to protecting endangered flora and fauna in the Americas, Asia Pacific, and Caribbean. Established in 1951, the U.S.-based TNC has chapters in each of the 50 states, as well as more than 25 nations abroad, and oversees more than 1,000 nature preserves in the United States and elsewhere. In addition,

TNC operates about 100 marine conservation projects in several countries and U.S. states. As of 2003, the organization claimed to have protected 117 million acres of land and 5,000 miles of river worldwide. TNC, which boasts more than 1 million members, works in conjunction with government, private groups, and landowners to create and manage land protection programs.

Neocolonialism: The "new colonialism" refers to the economic and political dependency remaining in former colonies despite gaining independence from their colonial rulers. Within 20 years of the end of World War II, the era of colonialism came to an end. The United Kingdom and France, the two leading colonial powers, began to relinquish control of their colonies. Former colonies became newly sovereign states. However, the trade relationships in place during the era of colonialism were, for the most part, retained. The inequitable levels of socioeconomic development that marked colonialism continued to plague the newly independent countries.

Neoliberalism: A world view that states that globalization should be pursued and determined through free markets and is generally skeptical about the dangers of global environmental problems. Neoliberals promote market-based mechanisms to solve environmental problems if and only if environmental problems can be proved to represent an imminent danger to humanity. They insist on conclusive evidence and certainty regarding the dangers of environmental problems before action is taken. Neoliberals argue that unnecessary and burdensome economic regulations designed to solve environmental problems are likely to hurt the global economy.

Nile River Basin Cooperative Framework Agreement: The agreement was formulated by the Nile Basin Initiative (NBI), an organization formed in 1999 by nine countries through which the Nile River flows. The agreement was meant to provide a framework for sharing river resources in a cooperative manner. Presently, there are 10 signatories to the agreement: Egypt, Ethiopia, Kenya, Rwanda, South Sudan, Sudan, Tanzania, Uganda, Burundi, and DR Congo.

Organisation for Economic Co-operation and Development (OECD): A 30-member international organization for coordinating the economic and social policies of its industrialized members. It was founded in 1961 to replace the Organisation for European Economic Co-operation, which was set up under the Marshall Plan. The OECD seeks to achieve a high sustainable economic growth for member nations and maintain financial stability, thereby contributing to international economic development. It also supports nondiscriminatory, multilateral international trade, promotes the social welfare of people in member nations, and seeks to stimulate the economy of developing nations by coordinating the efforts of OECD members.

Organization of Petroleum Exporting Countries (OPEC): Founded in 1960, an organization consisting of nations whose main export income comes from petroleum. OPEC seeks to unify the petroleum policies of these nations, protect the members' mutual interests, and stabilize international oil prices. The group produces more than 40 percent of the world's oil, and it holds nearly 80 percent of worldwide oil reserves. There are now 12 member nations: Algeria, Angola, Indonesia, Iran, Iraq, Kuwait, Libya, Nigeria, Qatar, Saudi Arabia, the United Arab Emirates, and Venezuela.

Ozone: A pure form of oxygen, ozone is a small part of the atmosphere but is crucial to the survival of life on Earth because it acts as a filter to partially protect the planet from ultraviolet rays that radiate from the sun. Ultraviolet radiation causes skin cancer and other ailments, suppresses the human immune system, damages crops, helps in the formation of smog, and helps speed the deterioration of outdoor materials. The natural equilibrium that creates and destroys ozone is undermined by the release of CFCs.

Pastoralism: The practice of raising and husbanding domesticated quadrupedal livestock, typically sheep, goats, cattle, horses, or other animals. Pastoralism may be conducted either on a subsistence level, where stock are kept for the needs of the owner and family, or on a commercial scale, where large numbers of animals are herded on large tracts of land, eventually to be slaughtered and processed for the market.

Petroleum (Oil): Petroleum is composed of a complex mixture of hundreds of different hydrocarbons. Petroleum may also contain impurities, such as sulphur, nitrogen, oxygen, and trace amounts of metals. Because of the complexity of its composition, refining is necessary for getting it into a useable form. There are many useable products that petroleum resources provide. Gasoline, jet fuel, kerosene, and lubricants are a few of the commercial substances extracted from petroleum.

Rachel Carson: Noted biologist and ecology writer whose books played a major role in launching the modern environmental movement. In 1962, her book *Silent Spring* touched off a controversy that led to a fundamental shift in the public's attitudes toward the use of such pesticides as DDT. In *Silent Spring*, Carson managed to correct the prevailing belief that the indiscriminate use of pesticides created no harmful effects on wildlife other than on the insects they were designed to kill. "For the first time in history," she wrote, "every human being is now subjected to contact with dangerous chemicals, from the moment of conception until death."

Rainforests: A contiguous area of woody, broad-leafed native vegetation in an area with a high annual rainfall of at least 100 inches per year. Rainforests may be tropical or subtropical and are habitats for diverse animal and plant life, most of which live under a deep, densely interlacing canopy in which vines and ferns are often present. Rainforests occur in such areas as British Columbia as well as in Latin America, particularly in the Amazon.

(The) Rainforest Action Network (RAN): A nonprofit, volunteer conservation group that works to protect and preserve rainforests all over the world. Its main strategy is to direct citizen action to rally public pressure against corporations, individuals, politicians, and governments whose practices contribute to the destruction of rainforests. RAN mobilizes consumer groups, organizes boycotts, conducts letter-writing campaigns, and creates negative publicity to urge the people and entities responsible for damaging rainforests to change their ways. The group is also involved in protecting the cultures of indigenous peoples who make their homes in rainforests.

Renewable Energy: Energy that is generated by using ongoing natural forces to create electricity and other forms of energy. Some examples of this are utilizing the energy from the sun, wind, water, the Earth's heat, and biological processes. All of these are renewable in that they are easily and often quickly replenishable after they have been used to create energy. Fossil fuels, on the other hand, while theoretically replenishable over decades or centuries, are currently being exploited at rates that are depleting existing supplies more quickly than they can be replenished.

Resource Curse: Developing countries that have such high value natural resources as oil, gold, diamonds, and uranium should be rich from the profits of such resource exploitation, yet exactly the opposite seems to be the case. Instead of economic development and prosperity, such scarce resources as diamonds and other minerals frequently fuel and sustain devastating local conflicts that could not be sustained otherwise. Rebel movements target and occupy the resource area, exploit the resource, and use the proceeds to fund weapons purchases. Activities of opposing sides in such conflicts including amputations, mass executions, rape, and unimaginable atrocities, are designed to force the native residents to leave the area and permit unhindered resource exploitation.

(The) Revolutionary United Front (RUF): A rebel group in Sierra Leone that registered as an official political party in 1999. It waged an 11-year civil war against the government of Sierra Leone that resulted in tens of thousands of deaths and the displacement of more than 2 million people. With the help of the United Nations (UN), the RUF was disbanded and disarmed in 2002.

(The) Rwandan Patriotic Front: Rwanda's dominant political power since July 1994, when the Tutsi rebel group defeated the Rwandan Army and Hutu militia forces in the wake of a genocide against Tutsis. It retained both the presidency and control over the legislature in democratic elections held in 2003.

Sierra Club: An environmental non-governmental organization that was founded in California in 1892 by, among others, John Muir, considered by many to be the father of American environmentalism. The stated purposes of the Sierra Club are to explore and enjoy the wild places on earth, to promote responsible use of the planet's ecosystems and resources, and to educate people in the protection and restoration of the environment.

Silent Spring (1962): A book by Rachel Carson on the impact of industrial chemicals on the ecosystem and human health, with particular emphasis on the effects of DDT on bald eagles. *Silent Spring* sparked a debate about the role of science in society that continues to resonate in contemporary environmentalism.

Slash-and-Burn Agriculture (Swidden): A method of clearing land in preparation for cultivation. It was used by Neolithic Europeans on small plots of land and is used today in logging and other commercial ventures, contributing to the massive destruction of the world's rainforests. The combination of smoke from the burning and the rapid elimination of trees makes this form of clearing a major cause of the increase of carbon dioxide in the Earth's atmosphere, and increases climate change and global warming.

(The) Southern African Development Community (SADC): An organization that promotes economic integration and mutual security and other interests among its member-nations, which are Angola, Botswana, Democratic Republic of Congo, Lesotho, Malawi, Mauritius, Mozambique, Namibia, Seychelles, South Africa, Swaziland, Tanzania, Zambia, and Zimbabwe. The stated goals of the organization are to promote economic cooperation and integration and to encourage growth in Southern Africa while reducing dependence on a South Africa rampant with apartheid.

Sovereignty: A fundamental principle of the modern state system. Sovereignty is the supreme authority for ruling over a state. When one government recognizes the sovereignty of another it not only recognizes that government's right to rule over a designated territory but also that territory's right to exist as an independent nation and its equality with all other sovereign nations in the international community.

Subcomandante Marcos: The acknowledged leader of the Zapatista movement in the southern state of Chiapas, Subcomandante Marcos is one of the most visible figures in Mexico's recent history. His charismatic guerrilla image, complete with mask and pipe, attracted immediate international attention with the beginning of the Zapatista rebellion of 1994. Since that time, although the Zapatistas have faded from public view, Marcos has remained a highly visible figure, and his writings against neoliberalism and in favor of human rights issues (including indigenous rights) have continued to find an audience.

(The) Sudan Liberation Army (SLA): A rebel group operating in Sudan's strife-torn western Darfur region. Following a series of internal power struggles that broke out in late 2005, the group is now divided into numerous factions. Unlike the similarly named Sudan People's Liberation Army, which operates in southern Sudan, the SLA states that its goal is a unified Sudan in which Darfur's people are given political autonomy and economic opportunity. Fighting between the SLA and the Sudanese government–sponsored Janjaweed militias has been ongoing since 2003.

Superfund: A U.S. federal fund to clean up toxic waste. The fund was created by the Comprehensive Environmental Response, Compensation, and Liability Act of 1980 and is administered by the Environmental Protection Agency's Office of Solid Waste and Emergency Response. The money is raised from a tax on the chemical industry.

Sustainable Development: According to the UN's Brundtland Commission (1988), the most accepted definition is "development that meets the needs of the present without compromising the ability of future generations to meet their own needs." Sustainable development is often considered to rest on three fundamental pillars: environmental sustainability, economic sustainability, and sociopolitical sustainability.

Sustainable Forestry: The management of a forest to meet present environmental, economic, and social needs without compromising the needs of the future. Sustainable forestry is both an end and a means to the end, the end being a healthy, sustainable forest ecosystem and the means being the forest management process that yields such a forest. This process integrates soil, air and water quality, wildlife habitat, and aesthetics with the traditional process of forestry that focuses on growing, nurturing, reforesting, and harvesting trees for products.

Tutsi: The Tutsi people, or Watutsi, of Central Africa established the kingdoms of Rwanda and Burundi after migrating south from their original homeland some 400 years ago. For many years, the aristocratic Tutsis ruled members of the more populous Hutu ethnic group as feudal subjects. Rwanda's Tutsi government was overthrown in a bloody 1959 Hutu revolt, and Hutus maintained their dominance there until 1994, when Tutsi rebels defeated Hutu forces who had massacred hundreds of thousands of Tutsi civilians. In Burundi, Tutsis kept their grip on power until the 1990s, when democracy was introduced and a Hutu president was elected.

(The) United Nations Convention on the Law of the Sea (UNCLOS): The Law of the Sea refers to a collective body of jurisprudence that has developed largely over the past three centuries. The fundamental question involved how much territoriality a state could claim over the sea, as an extension of its shoreline. Further, the convention defines the rights and responsibilities of states with respect to their use of the earth's oceans, establishing guidelines for businesses, the environment, and the management of marine natural resources.

United Nations Educational, Scientific, and Cultural Organization (UNESCO): A specialized agency within the United Nations (UN) Economic and Social Council. UNESCO promotes international collaboration in the spreading of knowledge, as well as cultural, educational, and scientific exchanges with the goal of encouraging peace and common welfare. As its name implies, UNESCO focuses on five main fields—education, natural sciences, social and human sciences, culture, and communication and information.

(The) United Nations Environment Programme (UNEP): A United Nations (UN) agency devoted to monitoring the state of the environment on a global level and promoting projects that support sustainable development and environmental conservation. The organization considers the environment an intricate system of complex relationships that extend among all natural and human activities. As human demands on natural resources intensify, the UNEP seeks to promote the sound use of land, water, and marine resources to prevent their degradation.

(The) United Nations Framework Convention on Climate Change (UNFCCC): A nonbinding treaty with 192 members, was the most substantial result of the "Earth Summit" held in Rio de Janeiro in June 1992. Created with the goal of reining in greenhouse gas emissions in an effort to halt global warming, the UNFCCC laid a foundation for creating future updated protocols on international cooperation for reducing human-driven atmospheric pollution. One of the most important elements of the agreement was the creation of an international inventory of greenhouse gas emissions. Member nations are required to submit their countries' data on both emissions and clean up efforts; in turn, nongovernmental regulators give them feedback.

United States Bureau of Reclamation: A part of the U.S. Department of Interior. It has constructed dams, power plants, and canals in the 17 U.S. western states to promote the settlement and economic development of the West. The term "reclamation" refers to transforming areas for farming or residential use. The main task of the Bureau of Reclamation is a balancing act: use scarce water effectively in order to protect local economies while also preserving natural resources and ecosystems.

(The) Wildlife and Environment Society of Southern Africa (WESSA) is a nongovernmental conservation organization dedicated to preserving South Africa's wildlife and natural areas by establishing and maintaining national reserves. The group is involved in environmental education and lobbying and promotes public involvement in nature conservation. Founded in 1926, the Wildlife and Environment Society of Southern Africa is one of the oldest conservation groups in Africa.

World Wildlife Fund (WWF): An international conservation organization that directs its efforts toward conserving and protecting endangered or threatened wildlife and habitats all over the world. With more than 5 million supporters, it bills itself as the world's largest conservation group. Originally a charity called the World Wildlife Fund, the organization changed its name in 1986 to the World Wide Fund for Nature to emphasize that it does not just lobby on behalf of animals, but on behalf of all aspects of nature, including the environment.

(The) Zimbabwe African National Union-Patriotic Front (ZANU-PF): A political group that controlled the federal government of Zimbabwe for two decades—from its creation in 1989 until its leader, Robert Mugabe, was forced to share power with the opposition Movement for Democratic Change (MDC) in 2009. ZANU-PF first formed when the Zimbabwe African National Union (ZANU) was reunited with the Zimbabwe African People's Union (ZAPU). The group adopted a socialist platform that called for the Africanization of state institutions and the establishment of a one-party state.

Volume 1 Bibliography

Abdelhady, Dalia, Karin Aggestam, Dan-Erik Andersson, Olof Beckman, et al. (2015). "The Nile and the Grand Ethiopian Renaissance Dam: is there a meeting point between nationalism and hydrosolidarity?," *Journal of Contemporary Water Research & Education* 155(1), 73–82.

Accenture. (2009). *Multinational Nuclear Power Pulse Survey*, 8–11.

Aditjondro, George. J. (1998). *Is Oil Thicker Than Blood? A Study of Oil Companies' Interests and Western Complicity in Indonesia's Annexation of East Timor*. New York: Nova Science Publishers.

Advanced Research Workshop on Water Resources, NATO. (2009). *The Jordan River and Dead Sea Basin: Cooperation amid Conflict*. Dordrecht, Netherlands: Springer.

Agence France-Presse (AFP). (2015, September 16). "Indonesia moves to stop forest fire pollution as haze grips Singapore," *The Guardian*. Accessed May 1, 2015, at http://www.theguardian.com/environment/2014/sep/16/indonesia-forest-fire-pollution-haze-singapore-palm-oil.

Aggestam, Karin, and Anna Sundell-Elkund. (2014). "Situating water in peacebuilding: revisiting the Middle East peace process," *Water International* 39(1), 10–22.

AKI Press. (2014, October 10). "Kyrgyzstan Hasn't Delimited Any Border Sections with Uzbekistan, Tajikistan over 7 Years—Vice PM Mamytov." Accessed March 3, 2016, at http://www.akipress.com/news:533409/.

Al Jazeera (eds.). (2013, June 11). "Egypt warns Ethiopia over Nile dam." Al Jazeera News: Africa. Accessed March 1, 2016, at http://www.aljazeera.com/news/africa/2013/06/201361144413214749.html.

Al-Khaldi, Salem. (2007). "Education policies in the GCC states." Dubai, UAE: Gulf Research Center.

Alagiri, Priya. (1991). "Give us sovereignty or give us debt: debtor countries' perspective on debt-for-nature swaps," *American Law Review 41*, 485.

Alao, Abiodun. (2007). *Natural Resources and Conflict in Africa: The Tragedy of Endowment*. Rochester, NY: Rochester Press.

Ali, Abdel Gadir Ali, Ibrahim A. Elbadawi, and Atta El-Batahani. (2005). "Sudan's Civil War: why has it prevailed for so long?," in Paul Collier and Nicholas Sambanis (eds.), *Understanding Civil War: Evidence and Analysis. Volume 1: Africa*. Washington, DC: World Bank, 193–220.

Allan, John A. (2002). "Hydro-peace in the Middle East: why no water wars? A case study of the Jordan River basin," *SAIS Review 22*(2), 255–272.

Allan, Tony. (2002). *The Middle East Water Question: Hydropolitics and the Global Economy*. London and New York: I. B. Tauris.

Anam, Tahmima. (2014, August 3). "The battle by the Bay of Bengal," *New York Times*. Accessed March 3, 2016, at http://www.nytimes.com/2014/08/04/opinion/the-battle-by-the-bay-of-bengal.html.

Anderson, Bradley, and Johan Jooste. (2014, May). "Wildlife poaching: Africa's surging trafficking threat," *Africa Security Brief: A Publication of the Africa Center for Strategic Studies 28*, 1–8.

Asante-Duah, D. Kofi, and Imre V. Nagy. (1998). *International Trade in Hazardous Wastes*. Oxford, UK: Taylor & Francis.

Asser, Martin. (2010, September 2). "Obstacles to Arab-Israeli peace: water," *BBC News*. Accessed March 29, 2014, at http://www.bbc.com/news/world-middle-east-11101797.

Australian Government. (n.d.) "Water Trading." National Water Commission. Accessed March 3, 2016, at http://www.nwc.gov.au/www/html/?a=23333.

Bachmann, John. (2007). "Will the circle be unbroken: a history of the U.S. national ambient air quality standards," *Journal of the Air & Waste Management Association 57*, 652–697.

Baena, Benjamin, Amy Bronson, Tobias Jones, and Lindsey Champaigne. (2014). "Applying and assessing free market environmentalism to the Democratic Republic of Congo's coltan resources: challenges and possibilities," *Studies by Undergraduate Researchers at Guelph 7*(1), 5–16.

Bahn, Paul G., and John Flenley. (1992). *Easter Island, Earth Island*. New York: Thames and Hudson.

Baiamonte, Valentina. (2015, February 22). "Environmental crime and instability: the role of criminal networks in the trafficking and illegal dumping of hazardous waste," *Freedom from Fear Magazine 9*. Accessed March 1, 2016, at http://f3magazine.unicri.it/?p=600.

Bannon, Ian, and Paul Collier. (2003). *Natural Resources and Violent Conflict: Options and Actions*. Washington, DC: World Bank Publications.

Baran, E., and Myschowoda, C. (2009). "Health of marine ecosystems in South East Asia: dams and fisheries in the Mekong Basin," *Aquatic Ecosystem Health and Management 12*(3), 227–234. Accessed March 3, 2016, at http://www.tandfonline.com/doi/abs/10.1080/14634980903149902.

Barnett, Jon, and W. Neil Adger. (2007). "Climate change, human security, and violent conflict," *Political Geography 26*, 639–655.

Barta, Patrick. (2007, July 11). "Parched outback: in Australia, a drought spurs a radical remedy," *Wall Street Journal*, A1, A12.

Bavinck, Maarten, Lorenzo Pellegrini, and Erik Mostert. (2014). *Conflicts over Natural Resources in the Global South: Conceptual Approaches*. Leiden, Netherlands, and London: CRC Press/Taylor & Francis.

Bawany, Bilal. (2013, November 1). "The Green Wall of China: enough to keep the Yellow Dragon at Bay?" University of Texas, Agriculture, Major Economies and Climate Change Research Group. Accessed March 3, 2013, at https://sites.utexas.edu/mecc/2013/11/01/the-green-wall-of-china-enough-to-keep-the-yellow-dragon-at-bay/.

BBC. (2014). "Religions: Islam." BBC News: Religion. Accessed March 5, 2015, at http://www.bbc.co.uk/religion/religions/islam/.

BBC. (2014). "Sustainable Fishing: Lamalera Whale-Hunters in Indonesia." BBC: Bitesize. Accessed April 30, 2014, at http://www.bbc.co.uk/learningzone/clips/sustainable-fishing-lamalera-whale-hunters-in-indonesia/11954.html.

BBC News. (1990, October 22). "Aral Sea is 'world's worst disaster,'" *On This Day*. Accessed October 22, 2015, at http://news.bbc.co.uk/onthisday/hi/dates/stories/october/22/newsid_3756000/3756134.stm.

BBC News. (2012, February 22). "South Sudan Expels Chinese Oil Firm Boss." BBC News: Africa. Accessed November 12, 2014, at http://www.bbc.co.uk/news/world-africa-17126340.

BBC News. (2013, June 10). "Egyptian Warning over Ethiopia Nile Dam." BBC News: Africa. Accessed March 3, 2016, at http://www.bbc.com/news/world-africa-22850124.

BBC World News. (2011, July 5). "South Sudan Profile." Accessed April 15, 2014, at http://www.bbc.com/news/world-africa-14069082.

BBC World News. (2015, December 7). "Sudan Profile." Accessed April 15, 2014, at http://www.bbc.com/news/world-africa-14094995.

Bergenas, Johan, and Monica Medina. (2014, January 31). "Break the link between terrorism funding and poaching," *Washington Post*. Accessed March 1, 2016, at https://www.washingtonpost.com/opinions/break-the-link-between-terrorism-funding-and-poaching/2014/01/31/6c03780e-83b5-11e3-bbe5-6a2a3141e3a9_story.html.

Bidlack, Harold W. (1996). "Swords as plowshares: the military's environmental role." PhD dissertation, University of Michigan, Ann Arbor.

Bieri, Franziska. (2010). *From Blood Diamonds to the Kimberley Process: How NGOs Cleaned Up the Global Diamond Industry*. Burlington, VT: Ashgate Publishing Company.

Bigelow, Kathryn (dir.). (2014). *Last Days of Ivory*. Film. Accessed March 1, 2016, at http://www.lastdaysofivory.com/#the-film.

Birmili, Wolfram, Tina Gobel, Andre Sonntag, Ludwig Ries, Ralf Sohmer, et al. (2010). "A case of transatlantic aerosol transport detected at the Schneefernerhaus Observatory (2650 m) on the northern edge of the Alps," *Meteorologische Zeitschrift* 19(6), 591–600.

Biswas, Asit K. (2000). "Scientific assessment of the long-term consequences of war," in Jay E. Autsin and Carl E. Bruch (eds.), *The Environmental Consequences of War*. Cambridge, UK: Cambridge University Press.

Biswas, Asit, K., Eglal Rached, and Cecilia Tortajada (eds.). (2008). *Water as a Human Right for the Middle East and North Africa*. London: Routledge.

Blok, Anders. (2008). "Contesting global norms: politics of identity in Japanese pro-whaling countermobilization," *Global Environmental Politics* 8(2), 39–66.

Bloomberg Businessweek (eds.). (2004, August 16). "How to combat global warming: in the end, the only real solution may be new energy technologies," *Bloomberg Businessweek*, 108.

Bone, Andrew. (2012). "The Kimberly Process Certification Scheme: the primary safeguard for the diamond industry," in Päiva Lujala and Siri Aas Rustad (eds.), *High-Value Natural Resources and Post-Conflict Peacebuilding*. New York: Earthscan, 189–194.

Bonine, Michael E., Abbas Amanat, and Michael Ezekiel Gasper. (2012). *Is There a Middle East?: The Evolution of a Geopolitical Concept*. Stanford, CA: Stanford University Press.

Bosshard, Peter. (2011). "Sustainable Hydropower—Ethiopian Style." International Rivers. Accessed March 20, 2015, at http://www.internationalrivers.org/blogs/227/sustainable-hydropower-%E2%80%93-ethiopian-style.

Braden, Kathleen. E., and Fred M. Shelley. (2014). *Engaging Geopolitics*. New York: Routledge.

Bradsher, Keith. (2008, April 17). "A drought in Australia, a global shortage of rice," *New York Times*. Accessed March 3, 2016, at http://www.nytimes.com/2008/04/17/business/worldbusiness/17warm.html.

Brautigam, Deborah. (2009). "Tanzara: The Tan-Zam Railway," in *The Dragon's Gift the Real Story of China in Africa*. Oxford, UK: Oxford University Press, 40–41.

Brichieri-Colombi, Stephen. (2008). *The World Water Crisis: The Failures of Resource Management*. New York: I. B. Tauris.

Bromwich, Brendan. (2008). "Environmental degradation and conflict in darfur: implications for peace and recovery," *Humanitarian Exchange 39*.

Brown, Lester. (2013, July 10). "The real threat to our future is peak water," *The Guardian*. Accessed March 7, 2016, at http://www.theguardian.com/global-development/2013/jul/06/water-supplies-shrinking-threat-to-food.

Brown, Lester, William U. Chandler, Alan Durning, Christopher Flavin, et al. (1988). *Worldwatch Institute Report—State of the World 1988*. Washington, DC: Worldwatch Institute.

Brown, Marilyn A., and Benjamin K. Sovacool. (2011). *Climate Change and Global Energy Security: Technology and Policy Options*. Cambridge, MA: MIT Press.

Browning, Peter (ed.). (1988). *John Muir in His Own Words: A Book of Quotations*. Lafayette, CA: Great West Books, 65.

Buckley, Brendan M., Kevin J. Anchukaitis, Daniel Penny, Roland Fletcher, et al. (2010). "Climate as a contributing factor in the demise of Angkor, Cambodia," *Proceedings of the National Academy of Sciences* 107(15), 6748–6752.

Bullock, James M., James Aronson, Adrian C. Newton, Richard F. Pywell, and Jose M. Rey-Benayas. (2011). "Restoration of ecosystem services and biodiversity: conflicts and opportunities," *Trends in Ecology & Evolution* 26(10), 541–549.

Burnett, D. Graham. (2012). *The Sounding of the Whale: Science & Cetaceans in the Twentieth Century*. Chicago, IL: The University of Chicago Press.

Büscher, Bram, and Veronica Davidov. (2014). "The ecotourism-extraction nexus," in Bram Büscher and Veronica Davidov (eds.), *The Ecotourism-Extraction Nexus, Political*

Economies and Rural Realities of (Un)Comfortable Bedfellows. Routledge ISS Studies in Rural Livelihoods. London and New York: Routledge, 1–16.

Butzer, Karl W. (2012). "Collapse, environment, and society," *Proceedings of the National Academy of Science 109*(10), 3632–3639. Accessed March 7, 2016, at http://www.pnas.org/content/109/10/3632.abstract.

Buzan, Barry, Ole Wæver, and Jaap De Wilde. (1998). *Security: A New Framework for Analysis*. Boulder, CO: Lynne Rienner Publishers.

Callahan, William A. (2009). *China: The Pessoptimist Nation*. Oxford, UK: Oxford University Press.

Campbell, Greg. (2004). *Blood Diamonds: Tracing the Deadly Path of the World's Most Precious Stones*, revised and expanded edition. New York: Basic Books.

Campbell, Kurt M. (ed.). (2008). *Climatic Cataclysm: The Foreign Policy and National Security Implications of Climate Change*. Washington, DC: Brookings Institution Press.

Carson, Rachel. (1962). *Silent Spring*. New York: Houghton Mifflin.

Catley, Andy, Jeremy Lind, and Ian Scoones. (2013). *Pastoralism and Development in Africa: Dynamic Change at the Margins*. London: Routledge.

Center for Naval Analyses Advisory Board (CNA). (2014). *National Security and the Accelerating Risks of Climate Change*. Washington, DC: CNA Analysis and Solutions, U.S. Department of Defense. Accessed March 1, 2016, at http://www.cna.org/sites/default/files/MAB_2014.pdf.

Central Intelligence Agency. (2016). "Timor-Leste." *The World Factbook*. Accessed March 3, 2016, at https://www.cia.gov/library/publications/the-world-factbook/geos/tt.html.

Charlick-Paley, Tanya, Phil Williams, and Olga Oliker. (2003). "The political evolution of Central Asia and South Caucasus: implications for regional security," in Olga Oliker, Thomas S. Szayna, Scott Pace, and Peter A. Wilson (eds.), *Faultlines of Conflict in Central Asia and the South Caucasus: Implications for the U.S. Army*. Santa Monica, CA: RAND Corporation, 7–40.

Chatty, Dawn. (2014). "Syrian tribes, national politics and the uprising." Accessed February 29, 2016, at dawnchatty.wordpress.com.

Chellaney, Brahma. (2011). *Water: Asia's New Battleground*. Washington, DC: Georgetown University Press.

Chellaney, Brahma. (2011). *Water: Asia's New Battleground*. Washington, DC: Georgetown University Press.

Chenoweth, Jonathan. (2008, August 23). "Water, water everywhere," *New Scientist 199*, 28–32.

China View. (2007, July 15). "Three Gorges Project." Accessed March 3, 2016, at http://news.xinhuanet.com/english/2006-05/13/content_4540727.htm

Chinafolio. (2014). "Hydro-power and Hydro-Hegemony: China's Prolific Dam-Building." Accessed March 1, 2016, at http://www.chinafolio.com/hydro-power-and-hydro-hegemony/.

Chiropolos, Michael L. (1994). "Inupiat subsistence and the bowhead whale: can indigenous hunting cultures coexist with endangered animal species," *Colorado Journal of Environmental Law and Policy 5*, 213.

Clapham, Phil, and Yulia Ivashchenko. (2009). "A whale of a deception," *Marine Fisheries Review 71*(1), 44–52.

Cleary, Paul. (2007). *Shakedown: Australia's Grab for Timor Oil*. Crows Nest, NSW, Australia: Allen & Unwin.

Clifford, Stephanie. (2013, May 28). "Wal-Mart is fined $82 million over mishandling of hazardous wastes," *New York Times*. Accessed March 1, 2016, at http://www.nytimes.com/2013/05/29/business/wal-mart-is-fined-82-million-over-mishandling-of-hazardous-wastes.html?_r=0.

Clout, Michael N., and Peter A. Williams. (2009). *Invasive Species Management: A Handbook of Principles and Techniques*. Oxford and New York: Oxford University Press.

CNA Corporation Military Advisory Board and Study Team. (2007). "National Security and the Threat of Climate Change." Alexandria, VA: CNA Corp.

Cohen, Joel E. (1995). *How Many People Can the Earth Support?* New York and London: Norton.

Collier, Paul. (2007). *The Bottom Billion*. Oxford, UK: Oxford University Press.

Collier, Paul. (2009). *War, Guns, and Votes: Democracy in Dangerous Places*. New York: Harper/HarperCollins Publishers.

Collier, Paul, and Anke Hoeffler. (2004). "Greed and grievance in civil war," *Oxford Economic Papers* 56(4), 563–595.

Collins, Robert O. (2008). *A History of Modern Sudan*. Cambridge, UK: Cambridge University Press.

Connell, Daniel. (2007). *Water Politics in the Murray-Darling Basin*. Annandale, Australia: Federation Press.

Convention on International Trade in Endangered Species of Wild Fauna and Flora (CITES). (2013). "Status of African Elephant Populations and Levels of Illegal Killing and the Illegal Trade in Ivory: A Report to the African Elephant Summit," 7–16. Accessed March 5, 2016, at https://cmsdata.iucn.org/downloads/african_elephant_summit_background_document_2013_en.pdf.

Cooke, Stephanie. (2011, June 8). "Japan says it was unprepared for post-quake nuclear disaster," *Los Angeles Times*. Accessed May 1, 2016, at https://web.archive.org/web/20110608222345/http://www.latimes.com/news/nationworld/world/la-fg-japan-nuclear-report-20110608,0,7481490.story?track=rss.

Coonan, Clifford. (2006, March 17). "The dammed: environmentalists watch and wait for opening of world's largest dam," *The Independent*. Accessed July 8, 2007, at http://www.independent.co.uk/news/world/asia/the-dammed-environmentalists-watch-and-wait-for-opening-of-worlds-largest-dam-5545071.html.

Crutzen, Paul J., and Eugene F. Stoermer. (2000). "The 'Anthropocene,'" *Global Change Newsletter 41*, 17–18.

Crutzen, Paul J. (2002). "Geology of mankind," *Nature 415*, 23.

Dabelko, Geoffrey. (2008). "An uncommon peace: environment, development and the global security agenda," *Environment: Science and Policy for Sustainable Development 50*, 32–45.

Dalby, Simon. (2002). *Environmental Security*. Minneapolis: University of Minnesota Press.

Dalby, Simon. (2009). *Security and Environmental Change*. Malden, MA: Polity Press.

Davenport, Carol. (2014, May 13). "Climate Change Deemed Growing Security Threat by Military Researchers," *New York Times*. Accessed May 22, 2014, at http://www.nytimes.com/2014/05/14/us/politics/climate-change-deemed-growing-security-threat-by-military-researchers.html.

Davies, Jonathan. (2012). *Conservation and Sustainable Development: Linking Practice and Policy in Eastern Africa*. New York: Routledge.

Davison, William, and Ahmed Feteha. (2015, March 24). "Egypt, Sudan edge toward cooperation on Ethiopia's Nile Dam," Bloomberg. Accessed March 7, 2016, at http://www.bloomberg.com/news/articles/2015-03-24/egypt-and-sudan-edge-toward-cooperation-on-ethiopia-s-nile-dam.

De Albuquerque, Catarina. (2011, March 4). Statement of UN Independent Expert on the Human Right to Water and Sanitation at the conclusion of her mission to the United States (February 22 to March 4, 2011). Accessed May 1, 2016, at http://aquadoc.typepad.com/files/un-ie-end-of-mission-statement-mar-4-2011.pdf.

De Stefano, Lucia, Paris Edwards, Lynette de Silva, and Aaron T. Wolf. (2010). "Tracking cooperation and conflict in international basins: historic and recent trends," *Water Policy 12*(6), 871–884.

Del Mar, David Peterson. (2014). *Environmentalism*. London: Routledge.

DeMarban, Alex. (2013, July 18). "Fermented 'stink whale' landed in Barrow, and it's a blessing during tough season," *Alaska Dispatch*. Accessed April 30, 2014, at http://www.alaskadispatch.com/article/20130718/fermented-stink-whale-landed-barrow-and-its-blessing-during-tough-season.

Deng, Francis. (1995). *War of Visions: Conflict of Identities in the Sudan*. Washington, DC: Brookings Institution.

Deudney, Daniel, and Richard A. Matthew. (1999). *Contested Grounds: Security and Conflict in the New Environmental Politics*. Albany: State University of New York Press.

Diamond, J. (2005). *Collapse: How Societies Choose to Fail or Succeed*. New York: Viking.

Diamond, Jared M. (1994). "Ecological collapses of past civilizations," *Proceedings of the American Philosophical Society*, 363–370.

Diamond, Jared M. (2005). *Collapse: How Societies Choose to Fail or Succeed*. New York: Viking.

Diamond, Jared M. (1994). "Ecological collapses of past civilizations," *Proceedings of the American Philosophical Society*.

Diamond, Jared. M. (1994). "Ecological collapses of ancient civilizations: the golden age that never was," *Bulletin of the American Academy of Arts and Sciences*, 37–59.

Dijk, Meine Pieter van. (2009). *The New Presence of China in Africa*. Amsterdam, Netherlands: Amsterdam University Press.

Diop, Ndiame, Daniela Marotta, and Jaime de Melo. (2012). *Natural Resource Abundance, Growth, and Diversification in the Middle East and North Africa: The Effects of Natural Resources and the Role of Policies*. Washington, DC: World Bank Publications.

Dockery, Douglas W., C. Arden Pope III, Xiping Xu, John D. Spengler, et al. (1993). "An association between air pollution and mortality in six U.S. cities," *New England Journal of Medicine 329*, 1753–1759.

Douglas, Leo R., and Kevin Alie. (2014, January 17). "High-value natural resources: linking wildlife conservation to international conflict, insecurity, and development concerns," *Biological Conservation 171*, 270–277.

Draper, Robert. (2009, April). "Australia's dry ruin," *National Geographic*, 34–59.

Dugmore, Andrew J., Thomas H. McGovern, Orri Vésteinsson, Jette Arneborg, et al. (2012). "Cultural adaptation, compounding vulnerabilities and conjunctures in Norse Greenland," *Proceedings of the National Academy of Sciences, 109*(10), 3658–3663.

Dukhovny, Victor. A. (2003). "The Aral Sea basin—rumors, realities, prospects," *Irrigation and Drainage 52*(2), 120.

Dunn, James. (2003). *East Timor: A Rough Passage to Independence*. Double Bay, NSW, Australia: Longueville Books.

Eberstadt, Nicholas. (2010). "The demographic future," *Foreign Affairs* 89(6), 54–64.

The Economist (eds.). (2013, March 16). "The endangered species trade: on the way out," *The Economist*. Accessed January 13, 2015, at http://www.economist.com/blogs/banyan/2013/03/endangered-species-trade.

The Economist (eds.). (2006). "A terrible beauty is born; the Three Gorges Dam," *The Economist* 379(8479), 39.

Ehrlich, Paul R. (1968). *The Population Bomb*. New York: Ballantine Books.

Ehrlich, Paul. (1996). Quoted in Julian Simon, *The Ultimate Resource 2*. Princeton, NJ: Princeton University Press.

Eichstaedt, Peter. (2011). *Consuming the Congo: War and Conflict Minerals in the World's Deadliest Place*. Chicago, IL: Chicago Review Press.

Em-Dat. (2014). The International Disaster Database. Accessed February 29, 2016, at www.emdat.be.

Enough Project. (2011). "Understanding Conflict Minerals Provisions." Accessed March 2, 2016, at http://www.enoughproject.org/special-topics/understanding-conflict-minerals-provisions.

Environmental Protection Agency. (n.d.). "Household Hazardous Waste." Accessed March 5, 2016, at http://www3.epa.gov/epawaste/conserve/materials/hhw.htm.

Erian, Wadid, Amjad Abbashar, and Luna Abo-Swaireh. (2010). *Drought Vulnerability in the Arab Region, Special Case Study: Syria, Ten Years of Scarce Water (2000–2010)*. Geneva, Switzerland: UN International Strategy for Disaster Risk Reduction.

Essick, Kristi. (2001, June 11). "Guns, money and cell phones," *The Industry Standard Magazine*. Accessed March 2, 2016 at http://www.globalissues.org/article/442/guns-money-and-cell-phones.

European Union. (2014). "Syrian Refugees: A Snapshot of the Crisis—in the Middle East and Europe." Accessed February 29, 2016, at syrianrefugees.eu/.

Fabricius, Christo, Eddie Koch, Hector Magome, and Stephen Turner. (2013). *Rights, Resources and Rural Development: Community-Based Natural Resource Management in Southern Africa*. London: Earthscan.

Fairhead, James, Melissa Leach, and Ian Scoones. (2013). *Green Grabbing: A New Appropriation of Nature*. London: Routledge.

Fairlie, Ian, and David Sumner. (2006). *The Other Report on Chernobyl (TORCH)*. The Greens/European Free Alliance in the European Parliament. Accessed May 1, 2016, http://www.greens-efa.eu/the-other-report-on-chernobyl-torch-206.html.

Fatal Transactions and European Coalition on Oil in Sudan. (2008, April). "Sudan: Whose Oil? Sudan's Oil Industry: Facts and Analysis." Accessed November 13, 2014 at https://www.globalpolicy.org/images/pdfs/042008sudanoil.pdf.

Femia, Francesca, Troy Sternberg, and Caitlin E. Werrell. (2014). *Climate Hazards, Security and the Arab Uprisings*. Eastbourne, UK: Sussex Academic Press.

Fernandes, Clinton. (2011). *The Independence of East Timor: Multi-Dimensional Perspectives—Occupation, Resistance, and International Political Activism*. Eastbourne, UK: Sussex Academic Press.

Figuères, Caroline, Cecilia Tortajada, and Johan Rockström (eds.). (2012). *Rethinking Water Management: Innovative Approaches to Contemporary Issues*. New York: Routledge.

Foley, James. A. (2013, November 16). "Deforestation in Brazil up 28 percent on the year," *Nature World News*. Accessed March 4, 2014, at http://www.natureworldnews.com/articles/4942/20131116/deforestation-brazil-up-28-percent-year.htm.

Food and Agriculture Organization of the United Nations. (2015). Ganges-Brahmaputra-Meghna Basin. AQUASTAT. Accessed February 28, 2015, at http://www.fao.org/nr/water/aquastat/basins/gbm/index.stm.

Food and Agricultural Organization of the United Nations. (n.d.). Bangkok: FAO Regional Office for Asia and the Pacific. Accessed May 1, 2016, at http://www.fao.org/asiapacific/regional-office/en/.

Franek, William, and Lou DeRose. (2003). *Principles and Practices of Air Pollution Control: Student Manual*, second edition. Research Triangle Park, NC: Air Pollution Training Institute.

Franke, Anja, Andrea Gawrich, and Gurban Alakbarov. (2009). "Kazakhstan and Azerbaijan as post-Soviet rentier states: resource incomes and autocracy as a double 'curse' in post-Soviet regimes," *Europe-Asia Studies* 61(1), 109–140.

Freeman, Milton M. R., Lyudmila Bogoslovskaya, Richard A. Caulfield, Ingmar Egede, et al. (1998). *Inuit, Whaling, and Sustainability*. Contemporary Native American Communities Volume 1. Walnut Creek, CA: Altamira Press.

French, Howard. (2007, September 7). "The Chinese and Congo take a giant leap of faith," *New York Times*. Accessed May 1, 2016, at http://www.nytimes.com/2007/09/21/world/asia/21iht-letter.1.7595719.html.

Friedland, Elliot. (2014, February 19). "Women's rights under Sharia." Understanding Islamism. *The Clarion Project*. Accessed March 5, 2015, at http://www.clarionproject.org/understanding-islamism/womens-rights-under-sharia.

Friends of the Earth Middle East. (2013, November 12). "Covenant for the Jordan River." Save the Jordan. Accessed February 25, 2014, at http://foeme.org/uploads/13832213651~%5E$%5E~JR_Covenant.pdf

Fujita, Akiko. (2012, January 30). "Japan's population to shrink nearly a third by 2060." ABC News. Accessed February 19, 2014, at http://abcnews.go.com/blogs/headlines/2012/01/japans-population-to-shrink-nearly-a-third-by-2060/.

Gales, Nichoas J., Toshio Kasuya, Phillip Clapham, and Robert L. Brownell. (2005). "Japan's whaling plan under scrutiny," *Nature* 435(7044), 883–884.

Gardner, Gerald T., and Paul C. Stern. (2008, September/October). "The short list: the most effective actions U.S. households can take to curb climate change," *Environment*. Accessed May 7, 2016, at http://www.environmentmagazine.org/archives/back%20issues/september-october%202008/gardner-stern-full.html.

Gasana, J. (2002, September/October). "Remember Rwanda," *Worldwatch Magazine*, 15(5).

Gebreluel, Goitom. (2014). "Ethiopia's Grand Renaissance Dam: ending Africa's oldest geopolitical rivalry?," *The Washington Quarterly* 37(2), 25–37.

Girouard, Étienne. (2008). "China In Africa: Neo-Colonialism or a New Avenue for South-South Cooperation? A Review Oof Perspectives." Canadian Coalition to End Global Poverty.

Gleave, M. B. (1992). "The Dar es Salaam transport corridor: an appraisal," *African Affairs*, 249–267.

Gleick, Peter H. (1993). "Water and conflict: fresh water resources and international security," *International Security* 18(1), 79–112.

Gleick, Peter H. (2015). Pacific Institute Water Conflict Chronology Database. Accessed March 7, 2016, at http://worldwater.org/water-conflict/.

Global Issues. (n.d.). "The Impact of the Debt Crisis on All of Us." Accessed March 4, 2014, at http://www.globalissues.org/article/226/the-impact-of-the-debt-crisis-on-all-of-us.

Global Witness. (2013). "The Kimberley Process." Accessed March 10, 2016, at https://www.globalwitness.org/en/campaigns/conflict-diamonds/kimberley-process/

Gockel, Catherine Kilbane, and Leslie C. Gray. (2011). "Debt-for-nature swaps in action: two case studies in Peru," *Ecology and Society* 16(3), 13.

Godfray, H. Charles, John R. Beddington, Ian R. Crute, Lawrence Haddad, David Lawrence, et al. (2010, February). "Food security: the challenge of feeding 9 billion people," *Science* 327, 813.

Good, David H., and Raphael Reuveny. (2009). "On the collapse of historical civilizations," *American Journal of Agricultural Economics* 91(4), 863–879. Accessed March 7, 2016, at http://ajae.oxfordjournals.org/content/91/4/863.

Gourevitch, Philip. (1998). *We Wish to Inform You That Tomorrow We Will Be Killed with Our Families*. New York: Picador USA.

Grant, J. Andrew. (2013). "Consensus dynamics and global governance frameworks: Insights from the Kimberley Process on conflict diamonds," *Canadian Foreign Policy* 19(3), 323.

Grant, J. Andrew, and Ian Taylor. (2004). "Global governance and conflict diamonds: the Kimberley Process and the quest for clean gems," *The Round Table: The Commonwealth Journal of International Affairs* 93(375), 385–401.

Griffin, Roger D. (2007). *Principles of Air Quality Management*, second edition. Boca Raton, FL: Taylor & Francis.

Grumbine, Edward R., John Dore, and Jianchu Xu. (2012). "Mekong hydropower: drivers of change and challenges," *Frontiers in Ecology and the Environment* 5, 91–98.

Guangqi, Sun. (1992). "Zheng He's expeditions to the western ocean and his navigation technology," *Journal of Navigation* 45(03), 329–343.

Gusev, Sergei V., Andrey V. Zagoroulko, and Alexsey V. Porotov. (1999). "Sea mammal hunters of Chukotka, Bering Strait: recent archaeological results and problems," *World Archaeology* 30(3), 354–369.

Guynup, Sharon. (2014, April 29). "Tigers in traditional Chinese medicine: A universal apothecary," *National Geographic*. Accessed March 1, 2016, at http://voices.nationalgeographic.com/2014/04/29/tigers-in-traditional-chinese-medicine-a-universal-apothecary/.

Hall, Anthony. (2006). "Extractive reserves: building natural assets in the Brazilian Amazon," in James K. Boyce, Sunita Narain, and Elizabeth A. Stanton (eds.), *Reclaiming Nature: Environmental Justice and Ecological Restoration.* London: Anthem.

Hanasz, Paula. (2014, July 28). "Sharing water vs. sharing rivers: the 1996 Ganges Treaty," *Global Water Forum.* Accessed March 3, 2016, at http://www.globalwaterforum.org/2014/07/28/sharing-waters-vs-sharing-rivers-the-1996-ganges-treaty/.

Hannam, Kevin, and Dan Knox. (2010). *Understanding Tourism: A Critical Introduction.* Thousand Oaks, CA: SAGE Publications.

Hardin, Garrett. (1968). "The tragedy of the commons," *Science 162,* 1243–1248.

Harris, Leila. M., and Samer Alatout. (2010). "Negotiating hydro-scales, forging state: comparison of the upper Tigris/Euphrates and the Jordan River basins," *Political Geography 29,* 148–156.

Harris, Stuart. A. (2011). "Mega-hydroelectric power generation on the Yangtze River: the Three Gorges Dam," in Stanley D. Brunn (ed.), *Engineering Earth: The Impacts of Megaengineering Projects,* 1569–1581. New York: Springer.

Hassoun, Nicole. (2012). "The problem of debt-for-nature swaps from a human rights perspective," *Journal of Applied Philosophy 29*(4), 359–377.

Hastie, Jo, and Tania McCrea-Steele. (2014). "Wanted—Dead or Alive: Exposing Online Wildlife Trade." International Fund for Animal Welfare. Accessed March 1, 2016, at http://www.ifaw.org/sites/default/files/IFAW-Wanted-Dead-or-Alive-Exposing-Online-Wildlife-Trade-2014.pdf.

Haufler, Virginia. (2009). "The Kimberley Process Certification scheme: an innovation in global governance and conflict prevention," *Journal of Business Ethics 89*(4).

Hayes, Karen. (2002). *Coltan Mining in the Democratic Republic of Congo: The Implications and Opportunities for the Telecommunications Industry.* Cambridge, UK: Fauna and Flora International.

Heming, Li, Paul Waley, and Phil Rees. (2001). "Reservoir resettlement in China: past experience and the Three Gorges Dam," *The Geographical Journal 167*(3), 195–212.

Heshmati, G. Ali, and Victor R. Squires. (2013). *Combating Desertification in Asia, Africa and the Middle East: Proven Practices.* Dordrecht, Netherlands, and New York: Springer.

Hill, Helen. (2002). *Stirrings of Nationalism in East Timor: Fretilin 1974–1978: The Origins, Ideologies, and Strategies of a Nationalist Movement.* Sydney, Australia: Otford Press.

Hill, Jennifer, and Tim Gale. (2012). *Ecotourism and Environmental Sustainability: Principles and Practice.* Burlington, VT: Ashgate.

Hintjens, Helen M. (1999). "Explaining the 1994 genocide in Rwanda," *The Journal of Modern African Studies 37*(02), 241–286.

Hiponia, Malcolm C., and Enrique G. Oracion. (2009). "Nature and people matter: conservation and ecotourism in Balanan Lake, Negros Oriental," *Philippine Studies: Chinese Filipinos and Citizenship 57*(1), 105–136. Accessed March 7, 2016, http://www.jstor.org/stable/42633990.

Hogan, Bea. (2000, April 4). "Central Asian States Wrangle over Water." asiaNet Environment, EurasiaNet. Accessed May 1, 2016, at http://www.eurasianet.org/departments/environment/articles/eav040500.shtml.

Holden, Andrew. (2008). *Environment and Tourism,* second edition. New York: Routledge.

Homer-Dixon, Thomas F. (1991). "On the threshold: environmental changes as causes of acute conflict," *International Security* 16(2), 76–116.

Hoorn, Carina, and Frank Wesselingh. (2010). *Amazonia: Landscape and Species Evolution. A Look into the Past.* Oxford, UK: Wiley-Blackwell.

Horton, Lynn R. (2009). "Buying up nature: economic and social impacts of Costa Rica's ecotourism boom," *Latin American Perspectives* 36(3), 93–107. Accessed March 1, 2016, at http://www.jstor.org/20684606.

Hossain, Ishtiaq. (1998). "Bangladesh-India relations: the Ganges water-sharing treaty and beyond," *Asian Affairs: An American Review* 25(3), 131–150.

Howard, Brian C. (2014, October 2). "Aral Sea's eastern basin is dry for the first time in 600 years," *National Geographic*. Accessed March 1, 2016, at http://news.nationalgeographic.com/news/2014/10/141001-aral-sea-shrinking-drought-water-environment/.

Hrynik, Tamara J. (1990). "Debt-for-nature swaps: effective but not enforceable," *Case Western University Journal of International Law* 22, 141.

Hsu, Sara. (2014, August 14). "China's model for Africa," *The Diplomat*. Accessed November 12, 2014, at http://thediplomat.com/2014/08/chinas-model-for-africa/.

Hunter, Emily. (2009, May 4). "Whaling: the latest culture war," *This Magazine*. Accessed May 2, 2016, at http://this.org/magazine/2009/05/05/whaling-culture-war/.

Hurd, Ian. (2012). "Almost saving whales: the ambiguity of success at the International Whaling Commission," *Ethics and International Affairs* 26(1), 103–112.

Hutton, Guy, and Laurence Haller. (2004). "Evaluation of the Costs and Benefits of Water and Sanitation Improvements at the Global Level." Water, Sanitation and Health: Protection of the Human Environment. Geneva, Switzerland: World Health Organization. Accessed May 1, 2016, at http://www.who.int/water_sanitation_health/wsh0404.pdf.

Institute for Human Rights and Business. (2009). "Draft: Business, Human Rights and the Right to Water Challenges, Dilemmas and Opportunities." Roundtable Consultative Report, January.

Intergovernmental Panel on Climate Change. (2007). *Climate Change 2007: Synthesis Report*. Geneva, Switzerland: IPCC.

International Atomic Energy Agency. (2008). *Climate Change and Nuclear Power*. Vienna, Austria: IAEA.

International Commission for the Protection of the Danube River. (2009). Danube River Basin District Management Plan. Document Number IC/151. Vienna, Austria: ICPDR Secretariat.

International Court of Justice. (2014, March 31). "Whaling in the Antarctic (Australia v. Japan: New Zealand Intervening)." Reports of Judgments Advisory Opinions and Orders. Accessed April 30, 2014, at http://www.icj-cij.org/docket/files/148/18136.pdf.

International Ecotourism Society. (2009). "What Is Ecotourism?" Accessed February 27, 2016, at https://www.ecotourism.org/what-is-ecotourism.

International Fund for Animal Welfare. (2013, June). "Criminal Nature: The Global Security Implications of the Illegal Wildlife Trade." Accessed March 2, 2016, at https://d2mlnkprj9wd81.cloudfront.net/sites/default/files/ifaw-criminal-nature-2013-low-res_0.pdf.

International Monetary Fund. (2012, March 8). "IMF Executive Board Concludes 2010 Article IV Consultation with the Democratic Republic of Timor-Leste." Public Information Notice (PIN) No. 11/31.

International Rivers. (2012). "Field Visit Report." GERD Project. Accessed March 2, 2016, at http://www.internationalrivers.org/files/attached-files/grandren_ethiopia_2013.pdf.

International Rivers. (2012). "Three Gorges Dam: A Model of the Past." internationalrivers.org.

International Whaling Commission. (1946). "International Convention for the Regulation of Whaling." Accessed March 5, 2016, at http://avalon.law.yale.edu/20th_century/whaling.asp.

International Whaling Commission. (2014). "Aboriginal Subsistence Whaling." Accessed March 2, 2016, at http://iwc.int/aboriginal.

Irivuzumugabe, Eric. (2009). *My Father, Maker of the Trees*. Grand Rapids, MI: Baker Books.

Islam, Shafi Noor, and Albrecht Gnauck. (2009). "Threats to the Sundarbans Mangrove Wetlands ecosystem from transboundary water allocation in the Ganges basin: a preliminary analysis," *International Journal of Ecological Economics & Statistics* 13(W09), 64–78.

Jägerskog, Anders. (2003). *Why States Cooperate over Shared Water: The Water Negotiation in the Jordan River Basin*. Unitruck, Sweden: Linköping University Press.

Japan Nuclear Power. (2002). "Japan's Nuclear Program." Accessed November 30, 2009, at http://www.japannuclear.com/nuclearpower/program/.

Jayaram, Dhanasree. (2013, December 20). "India-Bangladesh river water sharing: politics over cooperation," *International Policy Digest*. Accessed March 3, 2016, at http://www.internationalpolicydigest.org/2013/12/20/india-bangladesh-river-water-sharing-politics-cooperation/.

Johansen, Bruce E. (2009, October). "The carbon footprint of war," *The Progressive*, 27–29.

Johnson, Douglas H. (2003). *The Root Causes of Sudan's Civil Wars*. Volume 5. Bloomington: Indiana University Press.

Johnson, Douglas H. (2003). "The root causes of Sudan's civil wars," *African Security Review* 12(2), 115–115.

Johnson, Douglas H. (2011). *The Root Causes of Sudan's Civil Wars: Peace or Truce*, revised edition. Martlesham, UK: James Currey.

Jones, William C., and Marsha Freeman. (2005). "Three Gorges Dam: the TVA on the Yangtze River," *21st Century: Science and Technology Magazine*. Accessed March 7, 2016, at http://www.21stcenturysciencetech.com/articles/Three_Gorges.html.

Joseph, Suad. (1996). "Gender and citizenship in Middle Eastern states," *Middle East Research and Information Project 26*, Spring. Accessed March 5, 2015, at http://www.merip.org/mer/mer198/gender-citizenship-middle-eastern-states.

Juan, Du. (2012, December 10). "Sinopec drills deep into Africa," *China Daily*. Accessed November 12, 2014, at http://usa.chinadaily.com.cn/epaper/2013-12/10/content_17164264.htm.

Kahn, James R., and Judith A. McDonald. (1995). "Third-world debt and tropical deforestation," *Ecological Economics* 12(2), 107–123.

Kameri-Mbote, Patricia. (2007). *Navigating Peace: Water, Conflict, and Cooperation, Lessons from the Nile River Basin.* Washington, DC: Woodrow Wilson International Center for Scholars.

Kamruzzaman, Mohammad, Simon Beecham, and Gian Maria Zuppi. (2012). "A model for water sharing in the Ganges River basin," *Water and Environment Journal* 26(3), 308–318.

Kaplan, Robert D. (1994). "The coming anarchy," *Atlantic Monthly* 273, 44–76.

Katsukawa, Toshio, Hisao Iwasaki, and Mitsutaku Makino. (2010). "Perspective of Japanese future fisheries II—management and sustainable utilization of fisheries stocks," *Nippon Suisan Gakkaishi (Japanese Edition)* 76(2), 216–48.

Kellogg, Scott T., and Stacy Pettigrew. (2008). *Toolbox for Sustainable City Living: A Do-It-Ourselves Guide.* Brooklyn, NY: South End Press.

Kennedy, Bruce. (2001). "China's Three Gorges Dam." CNN. Accessed March 3, 2016, at http://www.cnn.com/SPECIALS/1999/china.50/asian.superpower/three.gorges.

Kessel, Andrew. (2006). "Debt-for-Nature Swaps: A Critical Approach." Comparative Environment and Development Studies: A Seminar in Cultural and Political Ecology. Accessed March 2, 2016, at http://www.macalester.edu/academics/geography/courses/coursepages/kessel.pdf.

Kidokoro, T., N. Harata, L. P. Subanu, J. Jessen, A. Motte, and E. P. Seltzer (eds.). (2008). *Sustainable City Regions: Space, Place and Governance.* New York: Springer.

Kimberley Process Certification Scheme. (2003). "Core Document." Accessed March 8, 2014, at http://www.kimberleyprocess.com/en/kpcs-core-document.

Kolbert, Elizabeth. (2011, March). "Enter the age of man," *National Geographic* 219, 60–85.

Kontogeorgopoulos, Nick. (2004). "Ecotourism and mass tourism in Southern Thailand: Spatial interdependence, structural connects, and staged authenticity," *Geojournal* 61(1), 1–11.

Kramer, Annika. (2008). "Regional Water Cooperation and Peacebuilding in the Middle East." Initiative for Peacebuilding. Accessed March 7, 2016, at http://nl.ircwash.org/sites/default/files/Kramer-2008-Regional.pdf.

Kreutzmann, Hermann. (2012). *Pastoral Practices in High Asia: Agency of "Development" Affected by Modernisation, Resettlement and Transformation.* Dordrecht, Netherlands, and New York: Springer.

Krupnik, Igor I. (1987). "The bowhead vs. the gray whale in Chukotkan aboriginal whaling," *Arctic* 40(1), 16–32.

Kummer, Katherine. (1995). *International Management of Hazardous Wastes.* Oxford, UK: Oxford University Press.

Kunzig, Robert. (2011, January). "Population 7 billion," *National Geographic* 219, 62.

Laitner, John A. "Skip," Karen Ehrhardt-Martinez, and Vanessa McKinney. (2009). "Examining the Scale of the Behavior Energy Efficiency Conundrum." Paper presented to the 2009 American Council for an Energy-Efficient Economy Summer Study, Washington, D.C.

Land, Graham. (2014, February 3). "The Great Green Wall: reforesting China," *Asian Correspondent.* Accessed March 3, 2016, at http://asiancorrespondent.com/119175/reforesting-china/.

Lappé, Frances Moore, and Rachel Schurman. (1990). *Taking Population Seriously*. San Francisco: The Institute for Food and Development Policy.

Large, Daniel. (2008). "China & the contradictions of 'non-interference' in Sudan," *Review of African Political Economy* 35(115), 93–106.

Laruelle, Marlene, and Sebastian Peyrouse. (2015). *Globalizing Central Asia: Geopolitics and the Challenges of Economic Development*. London: Routledge.

Lawrence, T. E. (1927). *Revolt in the Desert*. New York: George H. Doran and Company.

Le Billon, Philippe. (2005). *Fuelling War: Natural Resources and Armed Conflict*. New York: International Institute for Strategic Studies.

Le Billon, Philippe. (2012). *Wars of Plunder: Conflicts, Profits and the Politics of Resources*. New York: Columbia University Press.

Leung, Denise, and Lihoun Zhou. (2014). "Where are Chinese investments in Africa headed?," *World Resources Institute*. Accessed November 12, 2014, at http://www.wri.org/blog/2014/05/where-are-chinese-investments-africa-headed.

Li, Kaifeng, Cheng Zhu, Li Wu, and Linyan Huang. (2013). "Problems caused by the Three Gorges Dam construction in the Yangtze River basin: a review," *Environmental Reviews* 21(3), 127–35.

Li, Qinbin, Daniel J. Jacob, Isabelle Bey, Paul I. Palmer, et al. (2002). "Transatlantic transport of pollution and its effects on surface ozone in Europe and North America," *Journal of Geophysical Research* 107, D13.

Lillis, Joanna. (2012). "Uzbekistan Leader Warns of Water Wars in Central Asia." EurasiaNet.org. Accessed September 7, 2015, at http://www.eurasianet.org/node/65877.

Little, Douglas. (2008). *American Orientalism: The United States and the Middle East Since 1945*. Chapel Hill, NC: University of North Carolina Press.

Liu, Shumeng. (2014). "Analysis of Electronic Waste Recycling in the United States and Potential Application in China." Masters degree thesis, Earth Engineering Center, Columbia University, New York, NY.

Luoma, Jon R. (2012, January 17). "China's reforestation programs: big success or just an illusion?," *Environment 360: Opinion, Analysis, Reporting and Debate*, Yale University. Accessed March 3, 2016, at http://e360.yale.edu/feature/chinas_reforestation_programs_big_success_or_just_an_illusion/2484/.

Lutke, Elin. (2013, June 14). "Illegal Trafficking of Hazardous Waste from Europe to Somalia." *Prezi*. Accessed February 27, 2015, at https://prezi.com/spwyprjbjuez/illegal-trafficking-of-hazardous-waste-from-europe-to-somalia/.

Machlis, Gary E., and Thor Hanson. (2008, September). "War ecology," *BioScience* 58(8), 729–736.

Macleod, Melissa. (2013, January 5). "Transnational trafficking of hazardous waste from developed to developing nations: policies and recommendations," *Interdisciplinary Journal of Health Sciences* 3(1).

Majeed, Abeer. (2004). *The Impact of Militarism on the Environment: An Overview of Direct and Indirect Effects*. Ottawa, Canada: Physicians for Global Survival.

Malik, Sonia, Rosa M. Cusidó, Mohammad Hossein Mirjalili, Elisabeth Moyano, et al. (2011). "Production of the anticancer drug taxol in Taxus baccata suspension cultures: a review," *Process Biochemistry Process Biochemistry* 46(1), 23–34.

Mallet, Victor. (2015, February 13). "The Ganges: holy, deadly river," *The Financial Times*. Accessed March 3, 2016, at http://www.ft.com/cms/s/2/dadfae24-b23e-11e4-b380-00144feab7de.html.

Malthus, Thomas R. (1798). *An Essay on the Principle of Population*. Public Domain Books: Kindle Edition, 9–10.

Malthus, Thomas. (1798). *An Essay on the Principle of Population*. London: J. Johnson, in St. Paul's Church-Yard, Electronic Scholarly Publishing Project (1998), 44. Accessed March 7, 2016, at http://www.esp.org/books/malthus/population/malthus.pdf.

Marbury, Hugh R. (1995). "Global Environmental Racism," *Vanderbilt Journal of Transnational Law 251*, 293.

Marcus, Gail H. (2008). "Innovative nuclear energy systems and the future of nuclear power," *Progress in Nuclear Energy 50*(2), 92–96.

Marino, Giuseppe. (2010). *La Casta Dell'acqua—Come la Privatizzazione Sta Assetando L'Italia*. Modena, Italy: Nuovi Mondi.

Marshall, Jessica. (2006, February 25). "New Three Gorges Dam threatens vast fishery," *New Scientist*. Accessed July 8, 2007, at http://www.newscientist.com/channel/earth/energy-fuels/mg18925404.800.html.

McClatchy Newspapers, Omaha (eds.). (2011, February 13). "Pentagon budget reflects growth of security needs," *World-Herald*, 2-A.

McConnell, Robert. (2011, April 26). "Remembering the Soviet response to Chernobyl," *The National Review*. Accessed May 1, 2015, at http://www.nationalreview.com/corner/265612/remembering-soviet-response-chornobyl-robert-mcconnell.

McGaw, George. (2010). "Water for life: the challenge posted by un-codified human right to water in international law," *University for Peace Law Review 1*(30), 39–51.

McHaney, Sarah, and Peter Veit. (2009, August 10). "Stopping the Resource Wars in Africa." World Resources Institute, wri.org.

McKee, Jeffrey Kevin. (2003). *Sparing Nature: The Conflict Between Human Population Growth and Earth's Biodiversity*. Piscataway, NJ: Rutgers University Press.

Micklin, Philip. (1988). "Desiccation of the Aral Sea: a water management disaster in the Soviet Union," *Science 241*(4870), 1170–1176.

Micklin, Philip. (2007). "The Aral Sea disaster," *Annual Review of Earth and Planetary Science 35*, 47–72.

Mirza, M. Monirul Qader (ed.). (2005). *The Ganges Water Diversion: Environmental Effects and Implications*. Water Science and Technology Library Volume 49. Dordrecht, Netherlands, Boston, and London: Kluwer Academic Publishers.

Miyazawa, Naori. (2013). *Role of Customary Law and Communities in Natural Resource Management in Post-Conflict East Timor*. London: Routledge.

Moeliono, Moira, Eva Wollenberg, and Godwin Limberg. (2012). *The Decentralization of Forest Governance: Politics, Economics and the Fight for Control of Forests in Indonesian Borneo*. London and Sterling, VA: Earthscan.

Montague, Dena. (2002). "Stolen goods: coltan and conflict in the Democratic Republic of Congo," *Sais Review 22*(1), 103–118.

Montgomery, D. R. (2007). *Dirt: The Erosion of Civilizations*. Berkeley: University of California Press.

Mooney, Harold A., and Richard J. Hobbs. (2000). *Invasive Species in a Changing World*. Washington, DC: Island Press.

Moran, Daniel. (2011). *Climate Change and National Security: A Country-Level Analysis*. Washington, DC: Georgetown University Press.

Moxley, Mitch. (2010, September 23). "China's Great Green Wall grows in climate fight," *The Guardian*. Accessed March 3, 2016, at http://www.theguardian.com/environment/2010/sep/23/china-great-green-wall-climate.

Mulder, Michelle. (2014). *Every Last Drop: Bringing Clean Water Home*. Victoria, BC, Canada: Orca Book Publishers.

Murphy, Deborah. (2005). *Climate Change and Technology*. New York: International Institute for Sustainable Development.

Murphy, Shannon K. (2010). "Clouded diamonds: without binding arbitration and more sophisticated dispute resolution mechanisms, the Kimberley Process will ultimately fail in ending conflicts fueled by blood diamonds," *Pepperdine Dispute Resolution Law Journal* 11, 207–228.

Murray-Darling Basin Authority. (n.d.). "Aboriginal Culture and Heritage." Australian Government. Accessed April 28, 2015, at http://www.mdba.gov.au/about-basin/basin-people/aboriginal-culture-heritage.

Murray-Darling Basin Authority (n.d.). "Irrigated Agriculture in the Basin—Facts and Figures." Australian Government. Accessed April 28, 2015, at http://www.mdba.gov.au/about-basin/irrigated-agriculture-in-the-basin.

Murray-Darling Basin Authority. (n.d.). "Sustainable Rivers Audit: Interpreting the Results." Australian Government. Accessed April 28, 2015, at http://www.mdba.gov.au/what-we-do/mon-eval-reporting/sustainable-rivers-audit/interpreting-the-results.

Murray-Darling Basin Authority. (2014, December 24). "About MDBA." Australian Government. Accessed April 28, 2015, at http://www.mdba.gov.au/about-mdba.

NASA. (2008, June 4). "Drought in Iraq." NASA Earth Observatory. Accessed March 3, 2016, at http://earthobservatory.nasa.gov/NaturalHazards/view.php?id=38914.

Natali, J., Philip Williams, Rachel Wong, and G. M. Kondolf. (2013). "After Three Gorges Dam: what have we learned?," *AGU Fall Meeting Abstracts, vol. 1*, 1155.

National Geographic (eds.). (2015). "Toxic Waste: Man's Poisonous Byproducts." *National Geographic*. Accessed March 5, 2016, at http://environment.nationalgeographic.com/environment/global-warming/toxic-waste-overview/.

National Park Service. (2013). "Where Does Air Pollution Come From?" Accessed February 26, 2016, at http://www.nature.nps.gov/air/AQBasics/sources.cfm.

National Symbols of India. (n.d.). "Ganges River—National River of India." National River. Accessed November 18, 2013, at http://www.indiamapped.com/national-symbols-of-india/national-river/.

Neuman, Scott. (2013). "Have Your Picture Taken with Hong Kong's (Smog-Free) Skyline." *The Two-Way*, National Public Radio. Accessed May 1, 2015, at http://www.npr.org/blogs/thetwo-way/2013/08/29/216802749/have-your-picture-taken-with-hong-kongs-smog-free-skyline.

Nicholls, Neville. (2004). "The changing nature of Australian droughts," *Climatic Change* 63, 323–336.

Nichols, Julie E. (2012). "A Conflict of diamonds: the Kimberley Process and Zimbabwe's Marange diamond fields," *Denver Journal of International Law & Policy* 40(4), 648–685.

Northeast Fisheries Science Center. (2011). "NEFSC Fish FAQ." Accessed March 2, 2016, at http://www.nefsc.noaa.gov/faq/fishfaq9.html.

Nowak, Martin, with Roger Highfield. (2011). *SuperCooperators: Altruism, Evolution, and Why We Need Each Other to Succeed*. New York: Free Press.

O'Rourke, Kevin. (2002). *Reformasi: The Struggle for Power in Post-Soeharto Indonesia*. Crows Nest, NSW, Australia: Allen & Unwin.

Ochola, Washington Odongo, P. C. Sanginga, and Isaac Bekalo. (2011). *Managing Natural Resources for Development in Africa: A Resource Book*. Nairobi: University of Nairobi Press in association with International Development Research Centre, International Institute of Rural Reconstruction, Regional Universities Forum for Capacity Building in Agriculture.

Ogodo, Ochieng. (2003, July 7). "Resolving the conflict calls for a tight balancing act-legislator," *East African Standard Newspaper*, The Standard Limited.

Oil and Gas Journal (eds.). (2007). "Fergana basin draws seismic surveys, drilling," *Oil and Gas Journal* 105(43). Accessed March 3, 2016, at http://www.ogj.com/articles/print/volume-105/issue-43/exploration-development/Ferghana-basin-draws-seismic-surveys-drilling.html.

Okech, Roselyne N. (2010). "Wildlife-community conflicts in conservation areas in Kenya," *African Journal on Conflict Resolution* 10(2), 68.

Okello, Moses Makonjio, and B. E. Wishitemi. (2006). "Principles for the establishment of community wildlife sanctuaries for ecotourism: lessons from Maasai group ranches, Kenya," *African Journal of Business and Economics* 1(1), 90–109.

Okudera, Atsushi, Nozomu Hayashi, and Keiko Yoshioka. (2013, February 1). "Air pollution from China reaches Japan, other parts of Asia," *The Asahi Shibun*. Accessed March 31, 2014, at http://ajw.asahi.com/article/sci_tech/environment/AJ201302010087.

Oregon State University (OSU). (2015). Transboundary Freshwater Dispute Database, College of Earth, Ocean and Atmospherics Sciences. Accessed March 7, 2016, at http://www.transboundarywaters.orst.edu/.

Oreskes, Naomi. (2004). "The scientific consensus on climate change," *Science* 306(5702), 1686–1686.

Orogun, Paul. (2004). "'Blood diamonds' and Africa's armed conflicts in the post–cold war era," *World Affairs* 166(3), 151–161.

Osbourne, Milton E. (2000). *Mekong: Turbulent Past, Uncertain Future*, first edition. New York: Grove Press.

Pachauri, Rajendra K., and Andy Reisinger. (2007). *IPCC Fourth Assessment Report*. Geneva, Switzerland: IPCC.

Paes, W. C. (2005). "'Conflict diamonds' to 'clean diamonds': the development of the Kimberley Process Certification scheme," in Matthias Basedau and Andreas Mehler (eds.), *Resource Politics in Sub-Saharan Africa*. Hamburg, Germany: Institut fur Afrika-Kunde, 305–323.

Page, Susan E., Florian Siegert, John O. Rieley, Hans-Dieter V. Boehm, et al. (2002, November 7). "The amount of carbon released from peat and forest fires in Indonesia during 1997," *Nature* 420, 61–65.

Parry, Martin, Osvaldo Canziani, Jean Palutikof, Paul van der Linden, and Clair Hanson. (2007). *Climate Change 2007: Impacts, Adaptation and Vulnerability: Working Group II Contribution to the Fourth Assessment Report of the Intergovernmental Panel on Climate Change*. Cambridge, UK: Cambridge University Press.

People's Republic of China, Information Office of the State Council. (2013). "China-Africa Economic and Trade Cooperation." White paper. Accessed March 3, 2016, at http://english.gov.cn/archive/white_paper/2014/08/23/content_281474982986536.htm.

Percival, Val, and Thomas Homer-Dixon. (1996, September). "Environmental scarcity and violent conflict: the case of Rwanda," *Journal of Environment and Development* 5(3), 270–291.

Phalen, Robert F. (2007). *The Particulate Air Pollution Controversy: A Case Study and Lessons Learned*. Boston, MA: Kluwer Academic Publishers.

Pigram, John J. (2006). *Australia's Water Resources: From Use to Management*. Clayton, Australia: CSIRO Publishing.

Pincock, Steve. (2007, November 15). "Showdown in a sun-burnt country," *Nature* 450, 336–338.

Polan, Magdalena, Parmeshwar Ramlogan, and Carlos I. Medeiros. (2007). *A Primer on Sovereign Debt Buybacks and Swaps*. Washington, DC: International Monetary Fund.

Policy Research Division of the Department of Foreign Affairs and International Trade Canada. (2008). *The Global Water Crisis: A Question of Governance*. Ottawa, Canada: Foreign Affairs and International Trade.

Pope, C. Arden, Richard T. Burnett, Michael J. Thun, Eugenia E. Calle, et al. (2002). "Lung cancer, cardiopulmonary mortality, and long-term exposure to fine particulate air pollution," *Journal of the American Medical Association* 287(9), 1132–1141.

Porterfield, Andrew, and David Weir. (1989, October 3). "The export of U.S. toxic waste," *The Nation*.

Pottinger, Lori. (2013). "Field Visit Report on the Grand Ethiopian Renaissance Dam." International Rivers. Accessed March 20, 2016, http://www.internationalrivers.org/resources/field-visit-report-on-the-grand-ethiopian-renaissance-dam-7815.

Prendergast, John, and Sasha Lezhnev. (2009, November 10). "From Mine to Mobile Phone: The Conflict Minerals Supply Chain." Enough, the Project to End Genocide and Crimes against Humanity. Accessed March 8, 2016, at http://www.enoughproject.org/publications/mine-mobile-phone.

Prosterman, Roy, and Jeffrey Riedinger. (1987). *Land Reform and Democratic Development*. Baltimore, MD: Johns Hopkins University Press.

Puddington, Arch. (2013). *Freedom in the World 2013: Democratic Breakthroughs in the Balance*. Washington, DC: Freedom House.

Quah, Euston. (2002). "Transboundary pollution in Southeast Asia: the Indonesian fires," *World Development* 30(3), 429–441.

Quiggin, John, Thilak Mallawaarachchi, and Sarah Chambers. (2012). *Water Policy Reform: Lessons in Sustainability from the Murray-Darling Basin*. Cheltenham, UK: John Quiggin.

Quince, Annabelle. (2011, March 30). "The history of nuclear power," Interview, ABC Radio National.

Rahaman, M. M. (ed.). (2012). "Special Issue: Water wars in 21st century along international rivers basins: speculation or reality?," *International Journal of Sustainable Society* 4(1/2).

Rahaman, Muhammad M. (2006). "The Ganges water conflict: a comparative analysis of 1977 agreement and 1996 treaty," *Asteriskos, Journal of International & Peace Studies* 1(2), 196.

Ramutsindela, Maano. (2007). *Transfrontier Conservation in Africa: at the Confluence of Capital, Politics, and Nature*. Cambridge, MA: CAB International.

Reeves, Madeleine. (2005). "Locating danger: Konfliktologiia and the search for fixity in the Ferghana Valley borderlands," *Central Asian Survey* 24(1), 67–81.

Reeves, Madeleine. (2014). *Border Work: Spatial Lives of the State in Rural Central Asia*. Ithaca, NY: Cornell University Press.

Reeves, Randall. (2002). "The origins and character of 'aboriginal subsistence' whaling: a global review," *Mammal Review* 32(2), 71–106. Accessed March 2, 2016, at http://onlinelibrary.wiley.com/doi/10.1046/j.1365-2907.2002.00100.x/full.

Reisner, Marc. (1993). *Cadillac Desert: The American West and Its Disappearing Water*. London: Penguin.

Renner, Michael. (2002). *The Anatomy of Resource Wars*. Volume 162. Washington, DC: Worldwatch Institute.

Resor, James P. (1997). "Debt-for-nature swaps: a decade of experience and new directions for the future," *Unasylva* 1(188), 1–74. Accessed March 2, 2016, at http://www.fao.org/docrep/w3247e/w3247e06.htm#TopOfPage.

Reuters. (2008, June 4). "Hunger, water scarcity displaces thousands of Afghans," *New York Times*. Accessed March 3, 2016, http://www.nytimes.com/reuters/world/international-afghan-displacement.html.

Reuters. (2009, September 14). "China says Three Gorges Dam cost $37 billion." Accessed March 1, 2016, at http://www.reuters.com/article/2009/09/14/idUSPEK84588.

Reuters. (2014, August 7). "China loses appeal of WTO ruling on rare earth exports." Accessed on November 14, 2014, at http://www.reuters.com/article/2014/08/07/china-wto-rareearths-idUSL6N0QD5T820140807.

Reuters. (2013, November 1). "China's Gezhouba to build dams in Argentina worth $4.7 billion." Accessed March 1, 2016, at http://www.reuters.com/article/2013/11/01/us-gezhouba-argentina-idUSBRE9A00KH20131101.

Revkin, Andrew C., and Timothy Williams. (2007, April 15). "Global warming called security threat," *New York Times*. Accessed May 20, 2014, at http://www.nytimes.com/2007/04/15/us/15warm.html.

Reyntjens, Filip. (1996). "Rwanda: genocide and beyond," *Journal of Refugee Studies* 9(3), 240–251.

Richardson, Michael. (2002, December 13). "Indonesian peat fires stoke rise of pollution," *International Herald-Tribune*, 5.

Robertson, Melanie. (2012). *Sustainable Cities: Local Solutions in the Global South*. Ottawa, Canada: Practical Action Publishing.

Rockström, Johan, Will Steffen, Kevin Noone, Asa Persson, et al. (2009). "A safe operating space for humanity," *Nature* 461, 472–475.

Romanowski, Michal. (2014, July 3). "Central Asia's energy rush," *The Diplomat*. Accessed March 3, 2016, at http://thediplomat.com/2014/07/central-asias-energy-rush/.

Rosenthal, Elisabeth. (2008, June 3). "Water is new battleground in drying Spain," *New York Times*, A1, A12.

Ross, Michael. (2002). "Natural Resources and Civil War: An Overview with Some Policy Options." Draft report prepared for conference on The Governance of Natural Resources Revenues, World Bank and Agence Française de Développement, Paris, December 9–10.

Ross, Michael. (2003). "The natural resource cures: How wealth can make you poor," in Ian Bannon and Paul Collier (eds.), *Natural Resources and Violent Conflict*. Washington, DC: World Bank.

Ross, Michael. (2012). *The Oil Curse: How Petroleum Wealth Shapes the Development of Nations*. Princeton, NJ: Princeton University Press.

Ross, Michael L. (2004). "How do natural resources influence civil war? Evidence from thirteen cases," *International Organization 58*(01), 35–67.

Ross, Michael L. (2004). "What do we know about natural resources and civil war?," *Journal of Peace Research 41*(3), 337–356.

Ross, Michael L. (2008). "Oil, Islam, and women," *American Political Science Review 102*(1), 107.

Ross, Michael L. (2009). "Does oil wealth hurt women? A reply to Caraway, Charrad, Kang, and Norris," *Politics & Gender 5*(4), 575.

Rotberg, Robert I. (2009). *China into Africa: Trade, Aid, and Influence*, illustrated edition. Washington, DC: Brookings Institution Press.

Roth, Dik, Rutgerd Boelens, and Margreet Zwarteveen. (2005). *Liquid Relations: Contested Water Rights and Legal Complexity*. Piscataway, NJ: Rutgers University Press.

Roy, Pinaki. (2014, April 17). "Teesta River Runs Dry as India and Bangladesh Fail to Resolve Disputes." The Third Pole: Understanding Asia's Water Crisis. Accessed March 3, 2016, at http://www.thethirdpole.net/2014/04/17/teesta-river-runs-dry-as-india-and-bangladesh-fail-to-resolve-disputes/.

Rushton, Lesley. (2003). "Health hazards and waste management," *British Medical Bulletin, Oxford Journals*. Accessed March 5, 2016, at http://bmb.oxfordjournals.org/content/68/1/183.full.

Ryerson, William N. (2010). "Population, the multiplier of everything else," *The Post Carbon Reader Series: Population 3*. Accessed March 7, 2016, at http://www.postcarbon.org/Reader/PCReader-Ryerson-Population.pdf.

Sakakibara, Chie. (2010). "Kiavallakkikput agviq (into the whaling cycle): cetaceousness and climate change among the Iñupiat of Arctic Alaska," *Annals of the Association of American Geographers 100*(4), 1003–1012.

Sala-i-Martin, Xavier, and Arvind Subramanian. (2003). "Addressing the Natural Resource Curse: An Illustration from Nigeria." Working Paper No. w9804, National Bureau of Economic Research.

Salih, Kamal Osman. (1990). "British policy and the accentuation of inter-ethnic divisions: the case of the Nuba Mountains region of Sudan, 1920–1940," *African Affairs*, 417–436.

Salmorbekova, Zumrat, and Galina M. Yemelianova. (2009). "Islam and Islamism in the Ferghana Valley," in Galina. M. Yemelianova (ed.), *Radical Islam in the Former Soviet Union*. London: Routledge, 221.

Sánchez, Roberto. (1994). "International trade in hazardous wastes: a global problem with uneven consequences for the third world," *The Journal of Environment & Development* 3(1), 139–152.

Santos, Filipe Duarte. (2012). *Humans on Earth: From Origins to Possible Futures*. Volume 1612–3018. New York: Springer.

Savelle, John, and Nobuhiro Kishigami. (2013). "Anthropological research on whaling: prehistoric, historic and current contexts," *Senri Ethnological Studies* 84(1), 1–48.

Scheffer, Martin. (2009). *In Post-Communist Worlds: Living and Teaching in Estonia, Lithuania, Ukraine and Uzbekistan*. Bloomington, IN: iUniverse.

Scheffran, Jürgen. (2012). *Climate Change, Human Security and Violent Conflict: Challenges for Societal Stability*. New York: Springer Verlag.

Schwartz, Glenn M., and John J. Nichols. (2010). *After Collapse: The Regeneration of Complex Societies*. Tucson: University of Arizona Press.

Schwartz, Julia A. (2006). "International nuclear third party liability law: the response to Chernobyl," *International Nuclear Law in the Post-Chernobyl Period*, 41–44. Accessed May 1, 2016, at https://www.oecd-nea.org/law/chernobyl/SCHWARTZ.pdf.

SeaWeb. (2012). "About the 10th International Seafood Summit in Hong Kong." 10th International Seafood Summit. Accessed February 19, 2014, at http://www.seafoodsummit 2012.org/.

Service, Robert F. (2008, February 8). "Solar power: can the upstarts top Silicon?," *Science* 319, 718.

Sethi, Rajat. (2013). *Air Pollution: Sources, Prevention, and Health Effects*. Hauppauge, NY: Nova Science Publishers.

Sethi, S. Prakash. (2011). *Globalization and Self-Regulation: The Crucial Role That Corporate Codes of Conduct Play in Global Business*. New York: Palgrave Macmillan.

Sharife, K., and J. Grobler. (2013, December). "Kimberley's illicit process," *World Policy Journal*, 30(4), 65–77.

Sheikh, Prevaze. A. (2009). "Debt-for-nature initiatives and the Tropical Forest Conservation Act: status and implementation," Congressional Research Service, Library of Congress.

Shiva, Vandana. (1991). *Ecology and the Politics of Survival: Conflicts over Natural Resources in India*. New Delhi, India, and Tokyo, Japan: United Nations University Press.

Shmueli, Deborah F. (1999). "Water quality in international river basins," *ScienceDirect*. Accessed November 18, 2013, at http://www.sciencedirect.com/science/article/pii/S0962989001061#.

Shultz, Jim. (2005, January 28). "The politics of water in Bolivia," *The Nation*. Accessed March 1, 2016, at http://www.thenation.com/article/politics-water-bolivia.

Siebert, Stefan, J. Burke, J. M. Faures, K. Frenken, et al. (2010). "Groundwater use for irrigation—a global inventory," *Hydrology and Earth System Sciences* 14(10), 1863–1880.

Siegel, Matt. (2013, March 4). "Report blames climate change for extremes in Australia," *New York Times*. Accessed March 3, 2016, at http://www.nytimes.com/2013/03/05/world/asia/australian-government-blames-climate-change-for-angry-summer.html.

Sierra Club. (2011). "Accra Declaration on the Right to Water of 2001." Accessed April 18, 2011, at http://www.sierraclub.org/committees/cac/water/human_right/.

Simoes, Alexander. (n.d.). "Country Profile: Zambia." Observatory of Economic Complexity. Accessed November 12, 2014, at http://atlas.media.mit.edu/profile/country/zmb/.

Sims, Jocelyn, and Jesse Romero. (2013, November 22). "Latin American Debt Crisis of 1980s—A Detailed Essay on an Important Event in the History of the Federal Reserve." Federal Reserve History. Accessed March 4, 2014, at http://www.federalreservehistory.org/Events/DetailView/46.

Singh, Jang B., and V. C. Lakhan. (1989). "Business ethics and the international trade in hazardous wastes," *Journal of Business Ethics* 8(11), 889–899.

Smillie, I. (2005). "What lessons from the Kimberley Process Certification Scheme?," in Karen Ballentine and Heiko Nitzschke (eds.), *Profiting from Peace: Managing the Resource Dimensions of Civil War*. Boulder, CO: Lynne Rienner Publishers.

Sneddon, Chris, and Colleen Fox. (2006). "Rethinking transboundary waters: a critical hydropolitics of the Mekong basin," *Political Geography* 25(2), 181–202.

Sood, Aditya, and Bala Krishna Prasad Mathukumalli. (2011). "Managing international river basins: reviewing India–Bangladesh transboundary water issues," *International Journal of River Basin Management* 9(1), 43–52. Accessed March 3, 2016, at https://cgspace.cgiar.org/handle/10568/40465.

Sosland, Jeffrey K. (2007). *Cooperating Rivals: The Riparian Politics of the Jordan River Basin*. Albany: State University of New York Press.

Sovacool, Benjamin K. (2011). *Contesting the Future of Nuclear Power: A Critical Global Assessment of Atomic Energy*. Hackensack, NJ: World Scientific.

Springer, A. M., J. A. Estes, G. B. Van Vliet, T. M. Williams, D. F. Doak, et al. (2003). "Sequential megafaunal collapse in the north Pacific Ocean: an ongoing legacy of industrial whaling?," *Proceedings of the National Academy of Sciences* 100(21), 12223–12228.

Stelley, Santiago. (2013, January 8). "Documenting Asia's Illegal Animal Trade." YouTube video. Accessed March 1, 2016, at https://www.youtube.com/watch?v=PQC3jp1udUg.

Stephens, Sharon (ed.). (1995). *Children and the Politics of Culture*. Princeton, NJ: Princeton University Press.

Stockholm Environment Institute. (2008). "Regional Air Pollution in Developing Countries." Accessed March 30, 2014, at http://www.sei-international.org/rapidc/apina.htm.

Stone, Richard. (2008). "A new great lake—or dead sea?," *Science* 320, 1002–1005.

Strausz, Michael. (2014). "Executives, legislatures, and whales: the birth of Japan's scientific whaling regime," *International Relations of the Asia-Pacific*.

Suliman, Mohamed. (1994). "Civil War in Sudan: the impact of ecological degradation". Zurich, Centre for Security Studies and Conflict Research and Bern, Swiss Peace Foundation, Environment and Conflicts Project.

Sultana, Farhana, and Alex Loftus. (2013). *The Right to Water: Politics, Governance and Social Struggles*. London: Routledge.

Sun, Yun. (2013, April 5). "China's Increasing Interest in Africa: Benign but Hardly Altruistic." The Brookings Institution. Accessed March 30, 2015, at http://www.brookings.edu/blogs/up-front/posts/2013/04/05-china-africa-sun.

Swain, Ashok. (1993). "Conflicts over water: the Ganges water disputes," *Security Dialogue* 24(4). Accessed March 3, 2016, at http://sdi.sagepub.com/content/24/4/429.

Swain, Ashok. (1996). "Displacing the conflict: environmental destruction in Bangladesh and ethnic conflict," *Journal of Peace Research* 33(2), 189–204. Accessed November 18, 2013, at http://www.jstor.org/stable/425436?origin=JSTOR-pdf.

Tainter, J. (1988). *The Collapse of Complex Societies*. Cambridge, UK: Cambridge University Press.

Tearfund. (2007). "Darfur: Relief in a Vulnerable Environment." Accessed March 2, 2016, http://www.tearfund.org/webdocs/website/Campaigning/Policy%20and%20research/Relief%20in%20a%20vulnerable%20envirionment%20final.pdf.

Tearfund, (2007). "Darfur: Water Supply in a Vulnerable Environment." Accessed March 2, 2016, at http://www.unep.org/disastersandconflicts/portals/155/countries/Sudan/pdf/dafur_water/Darfur%20Water%20Resources%20TF.pdf.

Thapa, Bnjesh. (1998). "Debt-for-nature swaps: an overview," *The International Journal of Sustainable Development & World Ecology* 5(4), 249–262.

Thapa, Brijesh. (2000). "The relationship between debt-for-nature swaps and protected area tourism: a plausible strategy for developing countries," *Forest Service Proceedings, 15*.

Thornton, P. K., P. G. Jones, T. Owiyo, R. L. Kruska, et al. (2006). "Mapping Climate Vulnerability and Poverty in Africa." International Livestock Research Institute, Energy and Resources Institute and Africa Centre for Technology Studies. Accessed March 2, 2016, at www.napa-pana.org/extranapa/UserFiles/File/Mapping_Vuln_Africa.pdf.

Tortajada, Cecilia, Doğan Altınbilek, and Asit K. Biswas. (2012). *Impacts of Large Dams: A Global Assessment*. Berlin, Germany: Springer.

Trafford, Abigail. (2014, February 1). "Can China's great, green wall stop its creeping deserts?," *Toronto Star* (republished from the *Washington Post*). Accessed March 3, 2016, at http://www.thestar.com/news/world/2014/02/01/can_chinas_great_green_wall_stop_its_creeping_deserts.html.

Tremblay, William O. (2011). *Barriers to Climate Change Mitigation Technologies and Energy Efficiency*. New York: Nova Science Publishers.

Trilling, David. (2014, January 13). "Kyrgyzstan-Tajikistan: What's next after border shootout?" EurasiaNet. Accessed March 13, 2016, at http://www.eurasianet.org/node/67934.

Tripp, Aili. (2009). "Debate: oil, Islam, and women debate: does oil wealth hurt women?," *Politics & Gender* 5(4), 545–546.

Tripp, Emily. (2012, December 11). "Whale meat being sold illegally in Greenland and Denmark," *Marine Science Today*. Accessed March 2, 2016, at http://marinesciencetoday.com/2012/12/11/whale-meat-being-sold-illegally-in-greenland-and-denmark/.

Tvedt, Terje. (2010). *The River Nile in the Post-Colonial Age: Conflict and Cooperation among the Nile Basin Countries*. London: I. B. Tauris.

Udasin, Sharon. (2013, May 26). "Water flows from Lake Kinneret to Jordan River," *Jerusalem Post*. Accessed February 19, 2014, at http://www.jpost.com/Enviro-Tech/Water-flows-from-Lake-Kinneret-to-Jordan-River-314442.

UN General Assembly. (2010, August 3). "The human right to water and sanitation." Resolution adopted by the General Assembly, 64th session, Agenda item 48 A/RES/64/292. New York: United Nations.

UN Secretary-General's High Level Panel on Threats, Challenges and Change. (2004). *A More Secure World: Our Shared Responsibility—Report of the Secretary-General's High-Level Panel on Threats, Challenges and Change.* New York: United Nations General Assembly.

UN Security Council Group of Experts. (2005). *Report of the Group of Experts Submitted Pursuant to Paragraph 7 of Security Council Resolution 1584 Concerning Cote d'Ivoire.* New York: United Nations.

United Nations. (2010). "The Right to Water." Fact Sheet No. 35, Office of the United Nations High Commissioner for Human Rights. New York, Geneva, Switzerland: United Nations.

United Nations. (2014). "The United Nations World Water Development Report 2014." New York: United Nations.

United Nations Department of Economic and Social Affairs. (2015). "International Decade for Action 'Water for Life' 2005–2015." Accessed October 24, 2015, at http://www.un.org/waterforlifedecade/water_cooperation.shtml.

United Nations Development Programme. (2010). *The Real Wealth of Nations: Pathways to Human Development.* New York: Palgrave Macmillan.

United Nations Development Reports. (2013). "International Human Development Indicators." Accessed March 2, 2016, at http://hdr.undp.org/en/countries.

United Nations Economic Commission for Europe (UNECE). (n.d.). "Environmental Policy: Air: Introduction." Accessed May 1, 2015, at http://www.unece.org/env/lrtap/30anniversary.html.

United Nations Economic Commission for Europe (UNECE). (n.d.). "The Convention: The 1979 Geneva Convention on Long-range Transboundary Pollution." Accessed May 1, 2015, at http://www.unece.org/fr/env/lrtap/lrtap_h1.html.

United Nations Educational, Scientific and Cultural Organization (UNESCO). (2013). "UN Water World Water Day 2013: International Year of Water Cooperation." Accessed March 1, 2016, at http://www.unwater.org/water-cooperation-2013/water-cooperation/facts-and-figures/it/.

United Nations Educational, Scientific and Cultural Organization (UNESCO). (2015). World Water Day infographic. Accessed March 1, 2016, at http://www.unesco.org/new/en/world-water-day.

United Nations Environmental Program. (2004). "Environmental Degradation as a Cause of Conflict in Darfur." Conference proceedings, University for Peace, Khartoum. Accessed March 2, 2016, at http://cms.unige.ch/isdd/IMG/pdf/darfur_unpeace.pdf.

United Nations Environmental Program. (2013). "Elephants in the Dust: The African Elephant Crisis: A Rapid Response Assessment." Accessed March 2, 2016, at http://www.unep.org/pdf/RRAivory_draft7.pdf.

University of California, Berkeley. (2011). "Understanding Sudan: A Teaching and Learning Resource." International and Area Studies. Accessed April 20, 2014, at http://understandingsudan.org/index.html.

Uppsala Conflict Data Program, Uppsala University. (2008). *Conflict Termination Dataset* 2(1), 1946–2007. Accessed March 22, 2016, at http://www.pcr.uu.se/research/ucdp/datasets/ucdp_conflict_termination_dataset/.

U.S. Department of Defense. (2015). "Annual Report on the Military Power of the People's Republic of China." Accessed January 28, 2007, at http://www.defense.gov/Portals/1/Documents/pubs/2015_China_Military_Power_Report.pdf.

U.S. Department of State. (n.d.). "The Montreal Protocol on Substances that Deplete the Ozone Layer." Accessed May 1, 2015, at http://www.state.gov/e/oes/eqt/chemicalpollution/83007.htm.

U.S. Energy Information Administration. (1994). *Oil and Gas Resources of the Fergana Basin (Uzbekistan, Tadzhikistan, and Kyrgyzstan)*. Washington, DC: U.S. Department of Energy.

Uvin, Peter. (1998). *Aiding Violence: The Development Enterprise in Rwanda*. West Hartford, CT: Kumarian Press.

Vaidyanathan, Gayathri. (2011). "Dam controversy: remaking the Mekong," *Nature*. Accessed March 3, 2016, http://www.nature.com/news/2011/111019/full/478305a.html.

Vajpeyi, Dhirendra K. (ed.). (2012). *Water Resource Conflicts and International Security: A Global Perspective*. Lanham, MD: Lexington Books.

Van Zalinge, N., P. Degen, C. Pongsri, S. Nuov, et al. (eds.). (2004). "The Mekong River System," in *Proceedings of the Second International Symposium on the Management of Large Rivers for Fisheries*, 333–355.

Vandenbergh, Michael P., and Anne C. Steinemann. (2007). "The carbon-neutral individual," *New York University Law Review 82*, 1673–1745

Veilleux, Jennifer C. (2013). "The human security dimensions of dam development: the Grand Ethiopian Renaissance Dam," *Global Dialogue 15*(2), 1–15.

VICE. (2014). "An Inside Look at the Exotic Animal Trade: Profiles by VICE." YouTube video. Accessed March 1, 2016, at https://www.youtube.com/watch?v=LSQ8blCdAtA. Elwell, Frank W. (2009). *Macrosociology: The Study of Sociocultural Systems*. Lewiston, NY: Edwin Mellen Press.

Vidas, Davor, and Peter Johan Schei. (2011). *The World Ocean in Globalisation: Climate Change, Sustainable Fisheries, Biodiversity, Shipping, Regional Issues*. Leiden, Netherlands, and Boston: Martinus Nijhoff Publishers.

Vidyanagar, Vallabh (ed.). (2002). "The challenges of integrated river basin management in India: issues in transferring successful river basin management models to the developing world." *Water Policy Briefing*, International Water Management Institute, IWMI-TATA Water Policy Program. Gujarat, India: International Water Management Institute, 1–6.

Vir, Arti K. (1989). "Toxic trade with Africa," *Environment, Science & Technology Journal 23*(1).

Visser, Dana R., and Guillermo A. Mendoza. (1994). "Debt-for-nature swaps in Latin America. [Canje de deuda externa por naturaleza en Latinoamérica]," *Journal of Forestry 92*(6), 14.

Wadhams, Nick. (2007, October 28). "Endangered Gorillas 'Held Hostage' by Rebels in Africa Park," *National Geographic News*. Accessed March 1, 2016, at http://news.nationalgeographic.com/news/2007/05/070523-gorillas-hostage.html.

Wald, Matthew. (2008, March 6). "Turning glare into watts," *New York Times*. Accessed March 1, 2016, at http://www.nytimes.com/2008/03/06/business/06solar.html.

Wall, Geoffrey. (1996). "Change, impacts and opportunities," in Joseph A. Miller and Elizabeth Malek-Zadeh (eds.), *The Ecotourism Equation: Measuring the Impact*. Bulletin Series 99, Yale School of Forestry and Environmental Studies. New Haven, Connecticut, 108–117.

Wall Street Journal (eds.). (2008, May 14). "Drought forces Barcelona to ship in drinking water," *Wall Street Journal*, A13.

Wallis, Annie. (2005). "Data mining: lessons from the Kimberley Process for the United Nations' development of human rights norms for transnational corporations," *Northwestern Journal of International Human Rights* 4(2), 388.

Wang, Guangyu, John L. Innes, Sara W. Wu, Judi Krzyzanowski, Yongyuan Yin, Shuanyou Dai, Xiaoping Zhang, and Sihui Liu. (2012). "National park development in China: conservation or commercialization?" *Ambio* 41(3), 247–261. Accessed March 7, 2016, http://www.jstor.org/stable41510579.

Wang, X. M., C. X. Zhang, E. Hasi, and Z. B. Dong. (2010). "Has the Three Norths Forest Shelterbelt Program solved the desertification and dust storm problems in arid and semiarid China?," *Journal of Arid Environments*, 74(1), 13–22.

Waterbury, John. (1979). *Hydropolitics*. Syracuse, NY: Syracuse University Press.

Wegerich, Kai. (2008). "Hydro-hegemony in the Amu Darya basin," *Water Policy* 10(2), 71–88.

Weinberg, Bill. (1991). *War on the Land: Ecology and Politics in Central America*. London: Zed Books Ltd.

Weinthal, Erika. (2006). "Water Conflict and Cooperation in Central Asia." United Nations Development Program Occasional Paper. Accessed March 3, 2016, at http://hdr.undp.org/en/content/water-conflict-and-cooperation-central-asia.

Weirum, Brian K. (2007, December 29). "Tiger Bone Wine." Big Cat Rescue. Accessed January 14, 2015, at http://bigcatrescue.org/tiger-bone-wine/.

Western Regional Air Partnership. (2010). "Welcome to the WRAP." Accessed March 31, 2014, at http://www.wrapair2.org/.

White, Kathryn, Brendan O'Neill, and Zdravka Tzankova. (2004). "At a Crossroads: Will Aquaculture Fulfill the Promise of a Blue Revolution?" SeaWeb Aquaculture Clearinghouse Report. Accessed February 19, 2014, at http://www.seaweb.org/resources/documents/reports_crossroads.pdf.

White, Mel. (2008, November). "Borneo's moment of truth," *National Geographic*. Accessed March 7, 2016, at http://ngm.nationalgeographic.com/2008/11/borneo/white-text.

Whitfield, Stephen C., Eugene A. Rosa, Amy Dan, and Thomas Dietz. (2009). "The future of nuclear power: value orientations and risk perception," *Risk Analysis* 29(3), 425–437.

Williams, Horace O., and Viktor T. Grante (eds.). (2011). *Illegal Trade in Wildlife*. New York: Nova Science Publishers.

Williams, Selina, Géraldine Amiel, and Justin Scheck. (2014, March 31). "How a giant Kazakh oil project went awry," *Wall Street Journal*. Accessed March 3, 2016 at http://www.wsj.com/articles/SB10001424052702303730804579437492040999738.

Willoughby, John. (2008). "Segmented feminization and the decline of neopatriarchy in GCC countries of the Persian Gulf," *Comparative Studies of South Asia, Africa and the Middle East 28*(1), 184–199.

Winetroub, Andrew H. (2013). "A diamond scheme is forever lost: the Kimberley Process's deteriorating tripartite structure and its consequences for the scheme's survival," *Indiana Journal of Global Legal Studies 1425*, 20.

Wolf, Aaron T. (1998). "Conflict and cooperation along international waterways," *Water Policy 1*(2), 251–265.

Wolf, Aaron T. (2004). *Regional Water Cooperation as Confidence Building: Water Management as a Strategy for Peace*. Berlin, Germany: Adelphi Research.

Wolf, Aaron, Annika Kramer, Alexander Carius, and Geoffrey D. Dabelko. (2006). "Water can be a pathway to peace, not war," *Navigating Peace 1*, 1–6.

Wong, Edward. (2015, January 12). "On a scale of 1 to 500, Beijing's air quality tops 'crazy bad' at 755," *New York Times*. Accessed May 1, 2015, at http://www.nytimes.com/2013/01/13/science/earth/beijing-air-pollution-off-the-charts.html.

Workman, James G. (2010). "Water Challenges and Solutions, H2Ownership: Ancient, Equitable Traditions of Efficient Water Resource Trading in Desert Cultures." Globalwater, Accessed March 1, 2016, at http://globalwater.jhu.edu/magazine/article/h2ownership_ancient_equitable_traditions_of_efficient_water_resource_tradin/.

World Bank. (2013, December 9). "Senior Israeli, Jordanian and Palestinian representatives sign milestone water sharing agreement." Accessed February 19, 2014, at http://www.worldbank.org/en/news/press-release/2013/12/09/senior-israel-jordanian-palestinian-representatives-water-sharing-agreement.

World Bank. (2014, July 10). "World Bank and Kazakhstan Plan Further Improvements in the Northern Aral Sea Area." Accessed March 1, 2016, at http://www.worldbank.org/en/news/press-release/2014/07/10/world-bank-and-kazakhstan-plan-further-improvements-in-northern-aral-sea-area.

World Bank. (2015). "CO_2 Emissions (Metric Tons per Capita)." Accessed April 28, 2015, at http://data.worldbank.org/indicator/EN.ATM.CO2E.PC?order=wbapi_data_value_2010+wbapi_data_value+wbapi_data_value-first&sort=desc.

World Bank. (2015, October 22). "Regional Collaboration for Combating Illegal Wildlife Trade in Bangladesh." Accessed March 1, 2016, at http://www.worldbank.org/en/news/feature/2014/10/14/regional-collaboration-for-combating-illegal-wildlife-trade-in-bangladesh.

World Coal Association. (n.d.). "Coal Statistics." worldcoal.org.

World Diamond Council. (2014). "Diamonds and Their Benefits to Africa Fact Sheet." Accessed May 1, 2016, at http://www.diamondfacts.org/pdfs/media/media_resources/fact_sheets/Diamonds_and_Their_Benefits_to_Africa_Fact_Sheet.pdf.

World Health Organization. (2003). *Emerging Issues in Water and Infectious Disease*. Geneva, Switzerland: World Health Organization.

World Health Organization. (2014, March 25). "7 Million Premature Deaths Annually Linked to Air Pollution." Accessed May 1, 2015, at http://www.who.int/mediacentre/news/releases/2014/air-pollution/en/.

World Nuclear Association. (2002). "Japan's Nuclear Program." world-nuclear.org.

World Wildlife Fund. (n.d.). "Yangtze River." Accessed March 1, 2016, at http://wwf.panda.org/about_our_earth/about_freshwater/freshwater_problems/river_decline/10_rivers_risk/yangtze.

World Wildlife Fund. (2005, June 7). "Borneo: Treasure Island at Risk." Accessed March 3, 2016, at http://wwf.panda.org/wwf_news/?21037%2FReport-Borneo-Treasure-Island-at-Risk.

World Wildlife Fund. (2008, June 11). "Monumental Debt-for-Nature Swap Provides $20 Million to Protect Biodiversity in Madagascar, WWF Announces." Accessed March 2, 2016, at http://www.worldwildlife.org/press-releases/monumental-debt-for-nature-swap-provides-20-million-to-protect-biodiversity-in-madagascar-wwf-announces.

World Wildlife Fund. (2011). "Closing a Deadly Gateway." YouTube video. Accessed March 1, 2016, at https://www.youtube.com/watch?v=uc1XbBvcFqo.

World Wildlife Fund. (2014). "Conservation Finance, Initiatives." Accessed March 4, 2014, at https://worldwildlife.org/initiatives/conservation-finance.

World Wildlife Fund. (2014). "Debt-for-Nature Swaps." Accessed February 24, 2014, at https://worldwildlife.org/initiatives/conservation-finance.

Wright, Pamela A. (1993). "Sustainable ecotourism: balancing economic, environmental and social goals within an ethical framework," *The Journal of Tourism Studies* 4(2), 54–66.

Wroe, Stephen. (2013, May 23). "What killed Australia's megafauna?," *Australian Geographic*. Accessed April 28, 2015, at http://www.australiangeographic.com.au/topics/science-environment/2013/05/opinion-what-killed-australias-megafauna/.

Wyler, Liana Sun, and Pervaze A. Sheikh. (2008). *International Illegal Trade in Wildlife*. New York: Novinka Books.

Yablokov, Alexey V., and Vassily B. Nesterenko. (2009). "1. Chernobyl contamination through time and space," in Alexey V. Yablokov, Vassily B. Nesterenko, Alexey V. Nesterenko (eds.), *Chernobyl: Consequences of the Catastrophe for People and the Environment*. Volume 1181. New York: Annals of the New York Academy of Sciences.

Yanagizawa-Drott, D. (2010). "Propaganda and conflict: theory and evidence from the Rwandan genocide," in *The Ghost of Causation in International Speech Crime Cases*, 267. Draft on file with author.

Yeh, Yun-Hu, Huan-Sheng Tseng, Dong-Taur Su, and Ching-Hsiewn Ou. (2015). "Taiwan and Japan: a complex fisheries relationship," *Marine Policy* 51, 293–301.

Yoshida, Yuki. (2013). "Interethnic conflict in Jonglei state, South Sudan: emerging ethnic hatred between the Lou Nuer and the Murle," *African Journal on Conflict Resolution*, 13(2), 39–57.

Young, Juliette C., Mariella Marzano, Rehema M. White, David I. McCracken, et al. (2010). "The emergence of biodiversity conflicts from biodiversity impacts: characteristics and management strategies," *Biodiversity and Conservation* 19(14), 3973–3990.

Zeitoun, Mark. (2008). *Power and Water in the Middle East: The Hidden Politics of the Palestinian-Israeli Water Conflict*. New York: I. B. Tauris.

Zeitoun, Mark, and Jeroen Warner. (2006). "Hydro-hegemony-a framework for analysis of trans-boundary water conflicts," *Water Policy 8*(5), 435–460.

Zhang, Davd D., Peter Brecke, Harry F. Lee, Yuan-Qing He, and Jane Zhang. (2007). "Global Climate Change, War, and Population Decline in Recent Human History." *Proceedings of the Academy of the National Academy of Sciences, 104*(19), 214–219.

Zhang, Kefei, Will Featherstone, S. F. Bian, and B. Z. Tao. (1996). "Time variations of the Earth's gravity field and crustal deformation due to the establishment of the Three Gorges reservoir," *Journal of Geodesy, 70*(7), 440–449.

Zhao, Shelly. (2011, May). "The China-Angola partnership: a case study of China's oil relations in Africa," *China Briefing*. Accessed March 8, 2016, at http://www.china-briefing.com/news/2011/05/25/the-china-angola-partnership-a-case-study-of-chinas-oil-relationships-with-african-nations.html.

Ziganshima, Diana. (2008). "Rethinking the concept of the human right to water," *Santa Clara Journal of International Law 1*,113–128.

Zonn, Igor S. (2014). "Karakum Canal: artificial river in a desert," in Igor Zonn and Andrey Kostianoy (eds.), *The Turkmen Lake Altyn Asyr and Water Resources in Turkmenistan*. Berlin, Germany: Springer-Verlag, 95–106.

About the Editor and Contributors

M. Troy Burnett is currently an Associate Professor of geography and geography program coordinator at Mount Royal University in Calgary, Alberta. He earned a doctorate in geography in 2005 from UCLA, where he also earned a master's degree in geography in 2000. He has bachelor's degrees in both economics and environmental studies from the University of California, Santa Barbara.

John Agnew is Distinguished Professor of Geography at UCLA. Born in England, he graduated from the University of Exeter (BA, 1970), the University of Liverpool (Cert. Ed., 1971) and Ohio State University (PhD 1976). He specializes in political geography. A recipient of the Guggenheim Fellowship in 2004, he also received the Distinguished Scholarship Award of the Association of American Geographers in 2006, the UCLA Distinguished Teaching Award in 2007, and was president of the Association of American Geographers in 2008–2009.

Besty Baker is an associate professor and senior fellow for oceans and energy at the Institute for Energy and the Environment at Vermont Law School. She previously oversaw the graduate program for international students at Harvard University Law School from 2003 to 2007, before which she spent over a decade in Germany, where she earned her doctorate in law, worked as legal historian at the Heidelberg Academy of Sciences, and was affiliated with the Max Planck Institute for Comparative Public Law and International Law. Baker earned a BA from

Northwestern University, a JD from the University of Michigan, and an LLM and Dr. iur from Christian-Albrechts-Universitat in Kiel, Germany.

Peter Baker manages the Pew Environment Group's efforts to reform fisheries management in New England. He leads a highly skilled team of specialists in a campaign for science-based annual catch limits, strong fisheries monitoring programs, and fishery accountability. His work with elected officials, decision makers, the general public, the media, and the fishing industry has helped him understand the diverse constituencies that rely on New England's fishing heritage. This insight guides his policy work as he moves the organization's conservation goals forward. Peter came to the Pew Charitable Trusts from the Cape Cod Commercial Hook Fishermen's Association, where he served as campaign director. His responsibilities included campaign design and implementation, educating government officials, media relations, and public speaking. Prior to this role, Baker held various positions with the Sierra Club in Asheville, North Carolina, and also served as press secretary for Sam Neill for Congress and campaign manager for Peter Clavelle for Mayor of Burlington, Vermont.

Paul Bartel is a resource economist, specializing in economic and geographic analysis of humanitarian assistance and natural resource management issues. He has more than 25 years of experience working in various locations, from remote parts of Somalia and Morocco to urban centers in Western Africa and the Caribbean. He has an international reputation for establishing innovative approaches to humanitarian and environmental information systems and decision support mechanisms in support of analysis, policy development, and programs. He has advised numerous organizations and agencies, including the United States Agency for International Development (USAID), the U.S. Department of State, the International Agricultural Research Centers, and international organizations.

Mia Bennett is a PhD student in the Department of Geography at UCLA and manager of the Cryopolitics blog. Her research examines the pathways and processes of Arctic natural resource and infrastructure development using methods from political geography and remote sensing, specifically satellite imagery of night lights in the Arctic and Russian Far East. Bennett holds an MPhil in Polar Studies from the University of Cambridge, where she was a Gates Scholar, and has interned at the U.S. Embassy in Oslo, Norway. She speaks French, Swedish, and Russian.

Keith Andrew Bettinger is a lecturer in geography at Leeward Community College in Honolulu, Hawai'i. He received his BA in History from Hendrix College, his MA in International Affairs from George Washington University, and his doctorate from the Department of Geography at the University of Hawai'i in 2014. He was the recipient of the United States-Indonesia Society's (USINDO) Sumitro Fellowship for field research in 2012. He has conducted extensive research in Malaysia and Indonesia and has an active research program on the island of Sumatra investigating political and economic drivers of environmental change. His refereed articles on the politics of environmental issues have appeared in *Indonesia* and *Conservation and Society*.

William T. (Tom) Bogart became president of Maryville College in 2010.

Duane Bratt is chair and associate professor in the Department of Policy Studies at Mount Royal University in Calgary, Alberta. He was educated at the universities of Windsor (BA 1991, MA 1992) and Alberta (PhD 1996). He teaches in the area of international relations and Canadian public policy, with a specialty in the subfield of Canadian foreign policy. His primary research interest is in the area of Canadian nuclear policy.

Eric Brazer Jr. is a policy analyst for the Cape Cod Commercial Hook Fishermen's Association (CCCHFA) in Chatham, Massachusetts. Working closely with the local fishing fleet, Brazer's aim is to reform how commercial fisheries are managed in New England by aligning conservation goals with business objectives, and promoting more-effective policies that support local, traditional fishing communities and the natural resources on which they depend. Brazer also manages two local fishing "harvesting cooperatives" (or sectors) on Cape Cod—the Georges Bank Cod Hook and Fixed Gear Sectors. These Sectors are voluntary, self-governing, independent coalitions of small-boat gillnet and hook fishermen on Cape Cod that work cooperatively to manage an annual allocation of cod. Brazer works directly with the fishermen to foster novel and highly adaptive means of local decision making, self-monitoring, and enforcement that serve as a model for the future of sustainable fisheries in New England. Brazer grew up in a small fishing village in Maine, lobstering and harpooning bluefin tuna with his father. He holds a BA in environmental studies from Brown University and a master of environmental management degree from Duke University.

Rhett A. Butler is founder and president of Mongabay.com, a popular environmental science and conservation news website focused on tropical forest issues. Butler specializes on deforestation, especially trends and economic drivers of forest conversion and degradation. Rhett is also the co-founder of *Tropical Conservation Science*, an academic journal; the director of the Bay Area Tropical Forest Network; and tropical forests advisor to the Skoll Foundation. In 2010 he was a finalist for Climate Change Communicator of the Year Award granted by George

Mason University. In 2011 the U.S. State Department recognized him by invited him to join its official Speakers Program in Indonesia.

Brian Chaffin recently received his PhD in Geography from Oregon State University and holds a BS in Natural Resources and a MS in Environmental Science from the University of Idaho. His dissertation included a case study investigation of the relationship between laws and policies, agencies, communities, and natural resources in the Klamath Basin. While at Oregon State, Chaffin also received training under the internationally recognized Program in Water Conflict Management and Transformation. He has interest and expertise in emerging mechanisms for governing water and associated natural resources in the face of extreme uncertainty such as that posed by a rapidly changing global climate. He is the author of a journal article on "adaptive governance" featured in the journal *Ecology & Society* (2014) and a book chapter on "adaptive management" (Springer, 2014). Chaffin received a National Research Council (NRC) funded postdoctoral fellowship to study adaptive management of urban water resources at the U.S. Environmental Protection Agency's National Risk Management Laboratory in Cincinnati, Ohio, during 2014–2015. In addition to his research on environmental governance and management of natural resources, Brian is interested in ways in which U.S. environmental law can provide flexibility and capacity for local communities to address natural resource conflicts more proactively.

Roman Adrian Cybriwsky, PhD, is professor of geography and urban studies at Temple University, Philadelphia, Pennsylvania. His published works include *Historical Dictionary of Tokyo* (Scarecrow Press, 2011); *Roppongi Crossing: The Demise of a Tokyo Nightclub District and the Reshaping of a Global City* (University of Georgia Press, 2011); *Tokyo: The Shogun's City at the 21st Century* (Academy Press, 1998); and *Capital Cities around the World: An Encyclopedia of Geography, History, and Culture* (ABC-CLIO, 2013). Cybriwsky holds a doctorate in geography from Pennsylvania State University.

Gerardo Del Guercio teaches English in Montreal, Quebec, Canada. He has previously taught at The Royal Military College of Canada (St-Jean) and College Jean De Brébeuf. His research interests lie greatly in 19th- and 20th-century American literature. He received his bachelor's of arts from Concordia University in 2002, his master's of arts from l'université de Montréal in 2004, and his teaching certificate in 2010 from Groupe SLC. Presently he is completing teacher training at CUNY (York College). He is the author of *The Fugitive Slave Law in The Life of Frederick Douglass, an American Slave* and *Harriet Beecher Stowe's Uncle Tom's Cabin: An American Society Transforms Its Culture* (Edwin Mellen) and *Interdisciplinary Poe* (Lehigh University Press). His work has appeared in *College Literature, Southern*

Studies, Early America Review, Journal of the American Studies Association of Texas, Cambridge Scholars Press, and Oxford University Press. Currently, he is working on his first collection of poetry provisionally titled *No Particular Order* (Siglio).

Nathan Eidem is an adjunct lecturer at the University of Nebraska, Kearney. He holds both BS and MS degrees in geography, as well as a doctorate in geography from Oregon State University. His expertise is in water resources planning and management. He has worked as a consultant for the National Geographic Society, United Nations, USAID, and the Mekong River Commission.

Elizabeth Elliot-Meisel is associate professor of history at Creighton University in Omaha, Nebraska, where she has taught since 1993. She teaches courses in United States history since 1867, United States foreign relations, United States Constitutional History, and 20th- and 21st-century Russian/Soviet history. She received her PhD in history from Duke University in 1992, and her dissertation was titled "The Northwest Passage: the Emerging Issues in Canadian-American Relations, 1939–1963."

Bruce Everett is an adjunct associate professor of international business at the Fletcher School at Tufts University. Before joining the Fletcher faculty in 2003, he held a series of management positions at ExxonMobil Corporation from 1980 to 2002 and served in the U.S. Department of Energy from 1974 to 1980. He grew up in the Boston area and holds an AB degree from Princeton University and a PhD from the Fletcher School.

Micah Fisher is working on his PhD in the Geography Department at the University of Hawai'i, at Manoa in Honolulu, Hawai'i, where he received a master's degree in urban and regional planning. He received his BA from University of Richmond in urban practice and policy. Previously, Fisher worked at the USDA Forest Service International Programs office on building bilateral relationships between the United States and Indonesia, coordinating with scientists, practitioners, and policy makers to help develop the Indonesia Climate Change Center. Before that Micah spent four years working at the World Bank Office, Jakarta, on regional development, infrastructure, and resource management issues.

Anabel Ford has distinguished herself as a Mesoamerican archaeologist in the field of settlement and environmental studies of the lowland Maya of Guatemala and Belize. Her landmark study of the settlement patterns between Tikal and Yaxhá in Guatemala has challenged the perceptions of rural and urban divides, demonstrating that preferred locations for farming settlements are equally occupied when near or far from centers. Living in the Maya forest for her dissertation fieldwork and relying on the resources that were native to that place, she gained an appreciation for the local knowledge of and economic value inherent in the jungle. Her current focus at El Pilar, a new tour destination in the Maya world, integrates her growing academic knowledge of the region's ancient occupants and her investment in the living people of region. Over the past 10 years, Ford has spearheaded a unique development that focuses on one cultural and natural resource in two countries. She won the prestigious Rolex Award for Enterprise for her work in spearheading the creation of a bi-national protected area around the major center of El Pilar. The model development of El Pilar is an inclusive management design with government protection, local leadership and community participation, along with academic research input. Now she is part of a consortium of Belizean and Guatemalan archaeologists launching the El Pilar Peace Park Initiative.

Charles Fuller has a PhD in geography from the University of Georgia. He specializes in China and economic geography. His MA in East Asian studies and BA in Chinese are both from Indiana University. Fuller has lived in Asia for more than 15 years, including China (1985–1987; 1993–1995), Taiwan (1975–1982), and Macau (1988–1990). He served in the U.S. Air Force as a Chinese linguist and was stationed in Okinawa (1973–1974) and South Korea (1974–1975). In 2003, he was awarded a Fulbright-Hays Summer Seminar grant and traveled extensively in Nepal and India. Fuller currently teaches geography and Asian history at Triton College in the Chicago area.

Lynn Galvin, BA (history), JD (law), is a board member and past president of the Arizona Council for the Social Studies, a National Consortium for Teaching Asia Master Teacher, curricula writer for the Japanese American Museum's Enduring Communities Project, and a teacher consultant with the Arizona Geographic Alliance. She taught middle and high school social studies, college, and university classes for over 30 years. She is an adjunct faculty member at Arizona State University.

Camille Gaskin-Reyes is a geographer specializing in the field of development policy in Latin America and the Caribbean. She currently serves as adjunct professor in the Department of Geography and Elliott School of International Affairs at George Washington University, where she teaches courses on socioeconomic and spatial inequities in Latin America and development paradigms and practice in Latin America and the Caribbean. From 1983 to 2007, Gaskin-Reyes served in various capacities at the Inter-American Development Bank (IDB), including positions as IDB representative to Panama (1996–1998), deputy manager of regional operations for the Andean and Caribbean region (2004–2005), and manager *ad interim* of the Department of Development Effectiveness and Strategic Planning

(2006–2007). She holds a PhD in Geography and Urban/Regional Planning from the University of Bonn, Germany.

Paul H. Gelles is an associate professor of anthropology at the University of California, Riverside. After receiving his PhD from Harvard University in 1990, he was postdoctoral fellow in the College of Natural Resources at the University of California, Berkeley. His extensive research and publication in the areas of Andean political ecology, ethnography, and the history and cultural politics of irrigation systems include authorship of the book *Water and Power in Highland Peru: The Cultural Politics of Irrigation and Development* (2000). He is also the co-translator of *Andean Lives: Gregorio Condori Mamani and Asunta Quispe Huamán* (1996).

Jeffery Gentry holds the Greg Kunz Chair and heads the Department of Communications at Rogers State University, Claremore, Oklahoma. His research spans political communication, argumentation, and higher-education administration. He also produces public-affairs specials for public television. Before entering departmental administration in 2004 he coached intercollegiate debate for 15 years. Gentry was recognized by the Oklahoma Speech, Theatre, and Communication Association as outstanding college educator in 2006 and outstanding college forensics coach in 1994. He has received two "Top-Paper" awards in Political Communication from the Central States Communication Association. He took a sabbatical recently to conduct research at the University of Canterbury in Christchurch, New Zealand.

Albert C. Hine is a professor in the College of Marine Science at the University of South Florida. He was also associate dean for nine years. He specializes in geological oceanography particularly the depositional systems associated with the continental margins from the coastline to the base of slope. He is particularly interested in how climate and sea level fluctuations have affected the seafloor beneath the coastal ocean surrounding the continents. He has used geophysical acoustic research instruments to image the seafloor and to examine the strata beneath the seafloor. He has taught regional geology courses that include the origin and development of the Gulf of Mexico, Florida/Bahamas Platform, Caribbean Sea, and the western Atlantic Ocean He has published over 140 peer-reviewed scientific articles, obtained about $12 million in federal scientific awards, served on nearly 100 graduate student committees, and sailed as co-chief scientist on more than 70 research cruise totaling more than 800 days at sea in a number of the Earth's oceans during his 36 years since receiving his PhD. Hine was a Distinguished Lecturer for the Joint Oceanographic Institutions (now Consortium of Ocean Leadership in Washington, D.C.). He was the 2009 recipient of the prestigious Francis P. Shepard Medal for sustained, outstanding contributions in marine geology.

Christopher Hrynkow, PhD, is an assistant professor in the Department of Religion and Culture at St. Thomas More College, University of Saskatchewan, where he also contributes to the minor in Social Justice and the Common Good. Previously, amongst other assignments, Hrynkow taught Conflict Resolution Studies at Menno Simons College, University of Winnipeg and Peace and Conflict Transformation Studies at the Canadian Mennonite University. He earned his doctorate in Peace and Conflict Studies at the Arthur V. Mauro Centre for Peace and Justice, St. Paul's College, University of Manitoba.

Peter Jacques received his PhD in political science in 2003 from Northern Arizona University, the same year that his book with Zachary Smith, *Ocean Politics and Policy: A Reference Handbook* (with ABC-CLIO) was published. He currently teaches sustainability and global environmental politics at the University of Central Florida in the Department of Political Science. He has since published *Globalization and the World Ocean* with AltaMira/Rowman and Littlefield and published articles in *Global Environmental Politics*, *The Social Science Journal*, *Peace Review*, *Review of Policy Research*, among other academic journals. He is currently working with the Climate Impacts on Top Oceanic Predators (CLIOTOP), an international long-term research project aimed at understanding the dual pressures of human fishing and climate change on top ocean species. He is working to understand the way in which human institutions can be sustainable in the face of complex and sudden catastrophic changes and the vulnerabilities that societies that come with this challenge. In another research area, Jacques has worked with Riley Dunlap and UCF graduate student Mark Freeman to understand and quantify the "environmental skepticism" movement, a project from the U.S. Conservative Movement that denies the authenticity of environmental problems.

Bruce E. Johansen is a professor of communication and Native American studies, University of Nebraska at Omaha. He has been teaching and writing in the School of Communication at UNO since 1982. He had authored 33 books as of 2010. Johansen's first academic specialty was the influence of Native American political systems on United States political and legal institutions; his best-known books in this area are *Forgotten Founders* and *Exemplar of Liberty*. Johansen has described the present-day debate over this issue in *Debating Democracy* and *Native American Political Systems and the Evolution of Democracy: An Annotated Bibliography*. He also writes as a journalist in several national forums, including the *Washington Post* and *The Progressive*, with letters to the editor in *The Atlantic*, *New York Times*, *National Geographic*, *Wall Street Journal*, et al. Johansen also writes frequently about environmental subjects, including *Indigenous Peoples and Environmental Issues*, a 200,000-word encyclopedia of indigenous peoples' struggles with corporations with a worldwide scope.

Kelly Kay is a doctoral candidate in Geography at Clark University in Worcester, Massachusetts. She has also received a BA degree in Environmental Studies from Lewis and Clark College in Portland, Oregon. The author has published work on the influence of the European Union on environmental governance in Croatia, and is currently working on her dissertation, which looks at the relationship between conservation land-trust groups and environmental policy in the United States.

Elizabeth J. Leppman received her PhD in geography from the University of Georgia in 1997. Her BA in history is from Vermont's Middlebury College, and her MA in geography is from York University, Toronto. She lived and taught English in China from 1993 to 1995 and has taught geography at universities in Pennsylvania, Georgia, Ohio, Minnesota, and Kentucky. Leppman is the author of *Changing Rice Bowl* (2005) and served for three and a half years as editor of *Journal of Geography*. She currently teaches geography at Eastern Kentucky University and works as a writer and editor in Lexington.

Margaret Lowman is research professor of physical and mathematical sciences at North Carolina State University and director of the Nature Research Center at the North Carolina Museum of Natural Sciences. Lowman pioneered the science of canopy ecology and for 30 years has designed hot-air balloons and walkways for treetop exploration to solve mysteries in the world's forests, especially the links between insect pests and ecosystem health. Educated in the United States, Scotland, and Australia, Lowman addresses environmental policy solutions using science education as a tool, drawing upon a lifetime of research and conservation. She has received numerous conservation education awards and authored more than 100 peer-reviewed publications. Her first book, *Life in the Treetops*, received a cover review in *The New York Times Sunday Book Review*. Its sequel, *It's a Jungle Up There*, co-authored with her two sons, advocates for a family conservation ethic. Reflecting her love for linking kids to nature, Lowman's personal mantra is "no child left indoors."

Max Lu is an associate professor in the Department of Geography at Kansas State University. He earned his BA and MA degrees in China and his PhD from Indiana University in Bloomington, Indiana. His research mainly concerns population migration, geography of health, and regional economic development. He has published peer-reviewed articles in such journals as *Environment and Planning A*, *Population and Environment*, *Growth and Change*, *The Geographical Review*, *International Journal of Population Geography*, *Global Environmental Change*, and *Geografiska Annaler*. In addition to teaching and research, he co-chairs the College Board's Advanced Placement Human Geography Development Committee and serves as the associate editor of *The Geographical Review*.

Jason MacLeod received his BA from the University of Washington graduating magna cum laude and Phi Beta Kappa. He received his first law degree (JD) from the Seattle University School of Law and his second (LLM) from University of California, Berkeley, School of Law. Jason also earned a Masters in Science Degree from the University of Oxford in *Nature, Society, and Environmental Policy*. He is currently the Associate Editor for the Berkeley Journal of International Law.

Dan L. McNally earned his PhD in environmental engineering at Michigan Technological University and is an associate professor in the Department of Science and Technology at Bryant University in Smithfield, Rhode Island.

Barbara McNicol has taught as an assistant professor at Mount Allison University in New Brunswick, Canada, and as an instructor at the University of Calgary, Canada. She is currently an associate professor of geography in the Earth and Environmental Sciences Department at Mount Royal University in Calgary.

Coralie Noël has been the deputy director of the International Office for Water since 2007. She graduated from two French high-level engineering high schools, the Institut National Agronomique Paris-Grignon (INA P-G) in agronomics and life sciences, and the École Nationale du Génie Rural des Eaux et Forêts (ENGREF) in water management, and received a PhD in environmental law from Paris Sorbonne University. She was responsible for European water policy at the French Ministry of Environment from 2000 to 2003, served as head of the European Affairs Department and adviser to the prefect of the Picardy Region from 2003 to 2005, and worked as an adviser to the minister of health in 2005 and to the minister of work and employment on industrial, environmental, and health risks from 2005 to 2007.

Joseph Oppong is an associate professor of geography at the University of North Texas. He has a PhD from the University of Alberta, Edmonton, Canada, and a BA from the University of Ghana.

Joel Palka is associate professor of anthropology and Latin American and Latino studies at the University of Illinois, Chicago. Palka's research specialties are Maya archaeology and ethnohistory, Maya art and hieroglyphic writing, and colonialism and culture change. His publications include *Unconquered Lacandon Maya: Ethnohistory and Archaeology of Indigenous Culture Change*, articles in Latin American Antiquity and Ancient Mesoamerica, and several book chapters. He currently directs an archaeological and historical research project examining colonial period Maya cultural transformations in the forests of Chiapas, Mexico, and Peten, Guatemala.

Joyce A. Quinn retired from California State University, Fresno, as professor emerita after 21 years of teaching a variety of courses in physical geography and mapping techniques. She earned a master's degree from the University of Colorado and a PhD from Arizona State University, both in geography, specializing in the effect of climate and soils on the distribution of plants. She has traveled extensively throughout North America, Latin America, Europe, northern and southern Africa, Uzbekistan, Nepal, China, Southeast Asia, Micronesia, and elsewhere. She is a member of the Cactus and Succulent Society of America and the California Invasive Plant Council and is the author of two volumes of *Greenwood Guides to Biomes of the World* (2009) and co-author of *Encyclopedia of Invasive Species: From Africanized Honey Bees to Zebra Mussels* (2011).

Donald Rallis was until 2013 an associate professor of geography at the University of Mary Washington in Fredericksburg, Virginia. He received his BA and BSc (Hons) degrees at the University of the Witwatersrand in Johannesburg, South Africa, his MA from the University of Miami, and his PhD from Penn State University. In 2014, Rallis was appointed professor at the American University of Phnom Penh, where he teaches courses on geography and world history. He is an avid traveler who tries wherever possible to visit the places he talks about in his regional geography classes, and uses his travels as a basis for writing about geography on his web site and blog.

John Rumpler is senior attorney with Environment America, a federation of state-based, citizen-supported environmental advocacy organizations in 29 states. Since 2003, Rumpler has coordinated the organization's work on fracking and clean water—including state-level campaigns from California to New York. He has co-authored numerous research reports, most recently, "Fracking by the Numbers: Key Impacts of Dirty Drilling at the State and National Level." He has also testified before the U.S. Congress regarding enforcement of the nation's clean water laws. Prior to his position at Environment America, Rumpler practiced public interest and environmental law, representing community organizations in land use, zoning, and permitting matters. He holds a JD from the Northeastern University School of Law.

Larry Simpson earned his doctorate from West Virginia University and now teaches at High Point University in North Carolina. He offers courses on the history of Africa, the Middle East, Russia, and Western Civilization. He is adviser for the College Republicans.

Zachary Smith is Regents' Professor of Political Science at Northern Arizona University. He received his BA from California State University, Fullerton and his

MA and PhD from the University of California, Santa Barbara. A consultant both nationally and internationally on natural resource and environmental matters, he is the author or editor of 20 books and many articles on environmental and natural resource policy topics. He currently teaches environmental and natural resource policy and administration in the public policy PhD program at Northern Arizona University.

Benjamin K. Sovacool is an assistant professor at the Lee Kuan Yew School of Public Policy at the National University of Singapore. He is also a research fellow in the Energy Governance Program at the Centre on Asia and Globalization.

Leeann Sullivan is a recent graduate of Boston University and the publishing assistant for the Frederick S. Pardee Center for the Study of the Longer-Range Future. She was awarded a MA in international relations and environmental policy in May of 2014, and was the sole recipient of the department award for excellence. Her work on transboundary river governance evolved during her time as a graduate summer fellow with the Pardee Center where she researched community-level water management in the Okavango, and through her MA thesis, which compared water governance institutions in developing and industrialized regions. She received her BA in political science and area studies from Ohio Northern University in 2010.

Grenetta Thomassey is policy director at Tip of the Mitt Watershed Council in Petoskey, Michigan, and holds a PhD in public policy. As an advocate for the Great Lakes and inland water resources of northern Michigan, she operates at the local, state, and federal levels. Thomassey has taught political science at the University of Minnesota-Duluth and at Northern Arizona University. Her research is focused on federalism and interest groups in the freshwater policy arena. She is the primary author of ABC-CLIO's *Freshwater Issues: A Reference Handbook* and is currently researching a new book on collaborative public-private partnerships involving freshwater resource restoration efforts.

Jacqueline Vaughn is professor of political science at Northern Arizona University, where she specializes in public policy and administration. Professor Vaughn holds a PhD from the University of California, Berkeley, where she also attended the Graduate School of Public Policy. She taught previously at the University of Redlands and at Southern Oregon University. Professor Vaughn has a broad spectrum of nonacademic experience in both the public and private sectors. Her environmental background stems from her work with the South Coast Air Quality Management District in southern California, and with Southern California Edison, where she served as a policy analyst. Professor Vaughn's previously published environmental work include *Green Backlash: The History and Politics of Environmental Opposition in the U.S.*; *Environmental Activism: A Reference Handbook*; *George W. Bush's Healthy Forests: Reframing the Environmental Debate*; and *Environmental Politics: Domestic and Global Dimensions*, now in its fifth edition.

Jennifer Veilleux is a water geographer and lead researcher for Aaron Wolf's Transboundary Freshwater Dispute Database at Oregon State University. Jennifer also works as water advisor for The Nile Project, a music-based organization with a mission to build bridges between identity, culture, and sustainable resource use. She received her PhD in geography from Oregon State University, her MS and BS in environmental science from the University of New Haven in Connecticut, and her AA in Liberal Arts from Naugatuck Valley Community College in Connecticut. Jennifer has field research experience in internationally shared water resources issues of the Nile River basin, Mekong River basin, and Lake Ohrid watershed. She formerly worked as a geospatial analyst on environmental security issues for the U.S. government, as an environmental consultant for United Nations Development Programme, and as a political economy consultant for the World Bank. Veilleux is co-author of 2012 paper: "Case Studies on Water Security: Analysis of System Complexity and the Role of Institutions," 2014 book chapter: "The Relationship Between Freshwater Resources, Socio-Cultural Dynamics, and Geopolitical Stability," as well as sole author of the 2013 paper "The Human Security Dimensions of Dam Development: The Grand Ethiopian Renaissance Dam," She maintains "The Way of Water" blog on water resources issues, primarily concerned with water development in the Nile and Mekong river basins.

Riley Walters is a research assistant for The Heritage Foundation's Japan Fellows Program in their Asian Studies Center. He received his BA from George Mason University in economics with a minor in Japanese studies. He also served as a research associate for the Competitive Enterprise Institute.

Susan L. Woodward received her PhD in geography—with a specialization in biogeography—from the University of California at Los Angeles in 1976. Her doctoral research included three years along the Lower Colorado River studying feral burros, considered by some then and now to be an invasive species. When her work began, the burro (along with the feral horse) had just been placed under the jurisdiction of the U.S. Bureau of Land Management (BLM), which had a federal mandate to manage this living symbol of the Old West. The results of her field work provided the BLM with some of its earliest baseline data on burro population biology and ecology. Woodward taught biogeography, physical geography, and human ecology for 22 years at Radford University in Virginia before retiring in 2006. She is the author of *Biomes of Earth* (2003), served as general editor and author of three volumes for *Greenwood Guides to Biomes of the World* (2009), and is co-author of *Encyclopedia of Invasive Species: From Africanized Honey Bees to Zebra Mussels* (2011).

Barry Zellen is the author of *Arctic Doom, Arctic Boom: The Geopolitics of Climate Change in the Arctic* (2009) as well as *Breaking the Ice: From Land Claims to Tribal Sovereignty in the Arctic* (2008) and *On Thin Ice: The Inuit, the State, and the Challenge of Arctic Sovereignty*. He directs the Arctic Security Project at the Naval Postgraduate School, and also serves as managing editor of *The Culture and Conflict Review*. Zellen lived in Canada's Northwest Territories and the Yukon from 1988 to 2000, working in the field of indigenous media and language preservation. He writes frequently on Arctic issues for numerous publications.